I0006579

Computer Ethics

The International Library of Essays in Public and Professional Ethics
Series Editor: Seumas Miller and Tom Campbell

Computer Ethics

Edited by

John Weckert

Charles Sturt University, Australia

LONDON AND NEW YORK

First published 2007 by Ashgate Publishing

2 Park Square, Milton Park, Abingdon, Oxfordshire OX14 4RN
711 Third Avenue, New York, NY 10017

Routledge is an imprint of the Taylor & Francis Group, an informa business

First issued in paperback 2018

Copyright © John Weckert 2007. For copyright of individual articles please refer to the Acknowledgements.

All rights reserved. No part of this book may be reprinted or reproduced or utilised in any form or by any electronic, mechanical, or other means, now known or hereafter invented, including photocopying and recording, or in any information storage or retrieval system, without permission in writing from the publishers.

Notice:
Product or corporate names may be trademarks or registered trademarks, and are used only for identification and explanation without intent to infringe.

British Library Cataloguing in Publication Data
Computer ethics. – (The international library of essays in
   public and professional ethics)
   1. Electronic data processing – Moral and ethical aspects
   I. Weckert, John
   174.9'004

Library of Congress Cataloging Control Number: 2006934306

ISBN 13: 978-0-7546-2598-8 (hbk)
ISBN 13: 978-1-138-38351-7 (pbk)

Contents

PART III VALUES AND TECHNOLOGY

PART IV RESPONSIBILITY AND PROFESSIONALISM

PART V PRIVACY AND SURVEILLANCE

PART VI WHAT COMPUTERS SHOULD NOT DO

PART VII MORALITY AND MACHINES

Acknowledgements

The editor and publishers wish to thank the following for permission to use copyright material.

American Association for the Advancement of Science for the essays: Norbert Wiener (1960), 'Some Moral and Technical Consequences of Automation', *Science*, **131**, pp. 1355–58. Copyright © 1960 AAAS; Joseph Weizenbaum (1972), 'On the Impact of the Computer on Society: How Does One Insult a Machine?', *Science*, **176**, pp. 609–14. Copyright © 1972 AAAS.

Analyse and Kritik for the essay: Victoria McGeer (2004), 'Developing Trust on the Internet', *Analyse and Kritik*, **26**, pp. 91–107. Copyright © 2004 Lucius and Lucius.

Australian Journal of Professional and Applied Ethics for the essay: Jeroen van den Hoven (1999), 'Privacy and the Varieties of Informational Wrongdoing', *Australian Journal of Professional and Applied Ethics*, **1**, pp. 30–43.

Blackwell Publishing for the essays: James H. Moor (1985), 'What is Computer Ethics?', *Metaphilosophy*, **16**, pp. 266–75; Geoffrey Brown (1991), 'Is There an Ethics of Computing?', *Journal of Applied Philosophy*, **8**, pp. 19–26; James Lenman (2001), 'On Becoming Redundant or what Computers Shouldn't Do', *Journal of Applied Philosophy*, **18**, pp. 1–11; Deborah G. Johnson (1992), 'Do Engineers have Social Responsibilities?', *Journal of Applied Philosophy*, **9**, pp. 21–34. Copyright © 2001 Society for Applied Philosophy.

Copyright Clearance Center for the essay: Peter T. Manicas (1966), 'Men, Machines, Materialism, and Morality', *Philosophy and Phenomenological Research*, **27**, pp. 238–46. Copyright © 1966 Philosophy and Phenomenological Research.; Joseph Weizenbaum (1969), 'The Two Cultures of the Computer Age', *Technology Review*, **71**, pp. 54–57. Copyright © 1969 MIT Technology Review.

Elsevier Ltd for the essays: Donald Gotterbarn (1992), 'The Use and Abuse of Computer Ethics', *Journal of Systems and Software*, **17**, pp. 75–80. Copyright © 1992 D. Gotterbarn; Batya Friedman and Peter H. Kahn, Jr (1992), 'Human Agency and Responsible Computing: Implications for Computer System Design', *Journal of Systems Software*, **17**, pp. 7–14. Copyright © 1992 Elsevier; Eugene H. Spafford (1992), 'Are Computer Hacker Break-ins Ethical?', *Journal of Systems and Software*, **17**, pp. 41–47. Copyright © 1992 Eugene Spafford; Shigeo Hirose (1996), 'A Code of Conduct for Robots Coexisting with Human Beings', *Robotics and Autonomous Systems*, **18**, pp. 101–107. Copyright © 1996 Elsevier.

Krystyna Gorniak-Kocikowska (1996), 'The Computer Revolution and the Problem of Global Ethics', *Science and Engineering Ethics*, **2**, pp. 177–90. Copyright © 1996 Krystyna Gorniak-Kocikowska.

Donald Gotterbarn (2001), 'Informatics and Professional Responsibility', *Science and Engineering Ethics*, **7**, pp. 221–30. Copyright © 2001 Donald Gotterbarn.

IOS Press for the essay: M.J. van den Hoven (1994), 'Towards Ethical Principles for Designing Politico-Administrative Information Systems', *Informatization in the Public Sector*, **3**, pp. 353–73. Copyright © 1994 IOS Press.

MIS Quarterly for the essay: Richard O. Mason (1986), 'Four Ethical Issues of the Information Age', *MIS Quarterly*, **10**, pp. 5–12. Copyright © 1986 Regents of the University of Minnesota.

MIT Press Journals for the essay: Langdon Winner (1980), 'Do Artefacts Have Politics?', *Daedalus*, **109**, pp. 121–36.

Springer for the essays: Luciano Floridi (1999), 'Information Ethics: On the Philosophical Foundations of Computer Ethics', *Ethics and Information Technology*, **1**, pp. 37–56; Dean Cocking and Steve Matthews (2001), 'Unreal Friends', *Ethics and Information Technology*, **2**, pp. 223–31; Charles Ess (2002), 'Computer-Mediated Colonization, the Renaissance, and Educational Imperatives for an Intercultural Global Village', *Ethics and Information Technology*, **4**, pp. 11–22; John Weckert (2000), 'What is so Bad about Internet Content Regulation?', *Ethics and Information Technology*, **2**, pp. 105–11; Philip Brey (2000), 'Method in Computer Ethics: Towards a Multi-Level Interdisciplinary Approach', *Ethics and Information Technology*, **2**, pp. 125–29; Helen Nissenbaum (1998), 'Protecting Privacy in an Information Age: The Problem of Privacy in Public', *Law and Philosophy*, **17**, pp. 559–96; Seumas Miller and John Weckert (2000), 'Privacy, the Workplace and the Internet', *Journal of Business Ethics*, **28**, pp. 255–65; N. Ben Fairweather (1999), 'Surveillance in Employment: The Case of Teleworking', *Journal of Business Ethics*, **22**, pp. 39–49; Arthur Kuflik (1999), 'Computers in Control: Rational Transfer of Authority or Irresponsible Abdication of Autonomy?', *Ethics and Information Technology*, **1**, pp. 173–84; Bernd Carsten Stahl (2004), 'Information, Ethics, and Computers: The Problem of Autonomous Moral Agents', *Minds and Machines*, **14**, pp. 67–83.

Taylor and Francis Ltd for the essay: N.B. Fairweather and S. Rogerson (2001), 'A Moral Approach to Electronic Patient Records', *Medical Informatics and the Internet in Medicine*, **26**, pp. 219–34. Copyright © 2001 Taylor and Francis Ltd; Lucas D. Introna and Helen Nissenbaum (2000), 'Shaping the Web: Why the Politics of Search Engines Matters', *Information Society*, **16**, pp. 169–85. Copyright © 2000 Taylor and Francis.

Troubadour Publishing for the essays: Terrell Ward Bynum (2004), 'Ethical Challenges to Citizens of "The Automatic Age": Norbert Wiener on the Information Society', *Journal of Information, Communication and Ethics in Society*, **2**, pp. 65–74. Copyright © 2004 Troubadour Publishing; Herman T. Tavani (2004), 'Balancing Intellectual Property Rights and the Intellectual Commons: A Lockean Analysis', *Journal of Information, Communication and Ethics in Society*, **2**, pp. S5–S14. Copyright © 2004 Troubadour Publishing.

University of Chicago Press for the essay: Laszlo Versenyi (1974), 'Can Robots be Moral?', *Ethics*, **84**, pp. 248–59.

Every effort has been made to trace all the copyright holders, but if any have been inadvertently overlooked the publishers will be pleased to make the necessary arrangement at the first opportunity.

Series Preface

'Ethics' is now a considerable part of all debates about the conduct of public life, in government, economics, law, business, the professions and indeed every area of social and political affairs. The ethical aspects of public life include questions of moral right and wrong in the performance of public and professional roles, the moral justification and critique of public institutions and the choices that confront citizens and professionals as they come to their own moral views about social, economic and political issues.

While there are no moral experts to whom we can delegate the determination of ethical questions, the traditional skills of moral philosophers have been increasingly applied to practical contexts that call for moral assessment. Moreover this is being done with a degree of specialist knowledge of the areas under scrutiny that previously has been lacking from much of the work undertaken by philosophers.

This series brings together essays that exhibit high quality work in philosophy and the social sciences, that is well informed on the relevant subject matter and provides novel insights into the problems that arise in resolving ethical questions in practical contexts.

The volumes are designed to assist those engaged in scholarly research by providing the core essays that all who are involved in research in that area will want to have to hand. Essays are reproduced in full with the original pagination for ease of reference and citation.

The editors are selected for their eminence in the particular area of public and professional ethics. Each volume represents the editor's selection of the most seminal essays of enduring interest in the field.

SEUMAS MILLER AND TOM CAMPBELL
Centre for Applied Philosophy and Public Ethics (CAPPE)
Australian National University
Charles Sturt University
University of Melbourne

Introduction

Is there such a field as computer ethics? Perhaps not. Any ethical problem in which computers play a role is an ethical problem regardless of the involvement of computers. Surveillance with the aid of a telescope is not seen as an issue in telescope ethics, so why, for example, should surveillance with the aid of a computer be seen as an issue in computer ethics? There is something in this. An ethical issue is not part of computer ethics simply because it involves a computer. Stealing a computer is not an issue in computer ethics.

But a cluster of ethical problems surrounds the use of computers which can legitimately be called 'computer ethics'. Of course, it could be objected that this is arbitrary. We could call ethical issues surrounding the use of cars 'automobile ethics', or those around the use of cameras, 'camera ethics', but this is not done. Yet we could do this, and in some areas considered important enough, we do. Environmental ethics has emerged in response to a cluster of particular concerns of growing importance regarding the natural world, media ethics in response to problems regarding the media, and so on. Computer ethics has emerged in the same way (see Bynum, 1999, for a history of computer ethics).

If it is legitimate to talk of computer ethics, what is its domain? Which issues are issues in computer ethics and which are not? Problems in computer ethics are not different or new in the sense that they are different in kind from other ethical problems, whatever that might mean. Moral philosophy has been studied systematically at least from the time of the ancient Greeks, and the ethical issues in computing are part of this tradition. What is new and different is that the development and use of computers has raised old questions in interestingly new and different ways (Johnson, 2001), often creating what Moor calls *policy vacuums* (Chapter 6). The work of the computer ethicists, then, is to develop policies to fill those vacuums.

What are some of these ethical issues that are raised in a unique way because of computer technology? Consider hacking. Breaking into someone's computer account is in some ways like breaking into someone's house, but there are interesting differences. It is a logical rather than a physical entering. Unauthorized copying of software is a bit like unauthorized copying of a book and a bit like taking a television set, but there are significant differences. There are also questions relating to work and the loss or creation of skills, which arise in a unique way. And there are questions about the creation of intelligent machines.

Another approach to computer ethics is to treat it as professional ethics – that is, to concentrate on the specific concerns of computer professionals qua computer professionals that are essentially about the professional–client relationship. This is a reasonable approach. Medical ethics chiefly concerns the doctor–patient relationship. Computer professionals design and develop software and hardware for the use of their clients; they design, develop and maintain networks and so on. The important issues, then, include system reliability, system and data security, software theft, network security and reliability, and the like, which are typically specified in professional codes of ethics. This is the approach adopted by Gotterbarn and he argued that this should be the essence of computer ethics (Gotterbarn, 1991). While this emphasis never became the focus of computer ethics, it has remained an important part of the field.

This way of doing computer ethics is essentially reactive (Johnson, 2001, pp. vii–viii): that is, it reacts to problems, or policy vacuums, created by the technology (although it should be noted that the professional strand was not reactive in this way). This is an essential role of applied ethics, and most of the essays in this anthology reflect this approach. It has also been the core activity of most computer ethicists, many of whom have not only seen it as what computer ethics is all about but have also assumed that the situation would remain thus (Weckert, 2000a). There are, however, a few developments that suggest that there is more to it than this, and in fact one of the 'developments' considerably pre-dated this reactive approach. (It must be emphasized here that 'reactive' is being used in a descriptive and not a pejorative sense.)

Developments

Two developments will now be considered that are affecting, or will affect, the future of computer ethics: a proactive approach and an aspect of philosophy of technology.

A Proactive Approach

As we saw, generally there has been a reactive, or ethics-last, approach to computer ethics. When approaching computer ethics reactively, or ethics-last, one generally works within an accepted framework and sees whether or not particular consequences fit that framework. For example, if some use of technology infringes personal privacy, it is the current view of privacy that is infringed. Sometimes, of course, the technology does not fit well with standard views and then some rethinking must take place. This is much the current situation with intellectual property. The current intellectual property regime does not accommodate the new information technology very well.

When a proactive, or ethics-first, approach is taken, the emphasis is different. One is much more likely, and in fact it is necessary, to think carefully about what is wanted from the technology, and that involves thinking about what sort of life one thinks is a good one. This approach means taking action that will guide the development of the technology in a particular manner. The problem with the ethics-first, or proactive, model is that ethical assessment depends in large part on a factual determination of the harms and benefits of implementing the technology and this necessitates making predictions, a hazardous occupation. The following comments by Thomas Watson and Bill Gates attest to this:

> 'I think there is a world market for maybe five computers.'
> *Thomas Watson, chairman of IBM, 1943*

> '640K ought to be enough for anybody.'
> *Bill Gates, 1981*

Nevertheless, prediction with care is useful and in fact essential. We constantly make predictions about what will happen and base our behaviour on those. And, in any case, the ethics-last model does not fare so well either. Once a technology is firmly in place much unnecessary harm may have already occurred.

The suggestion here is that the ethics-first model and the ethics-last model – proactive and reactive approaches – are poor solutions to a false dichotomy (Moor and Weckert, 2004). Computer ethics is not something one can undertake satisfactorily either purely first or last, but something that needs be done continually as the technology develops and as its potential consequences become better understood.

Applied ethics is dynamic in that the factual component on which it relies has to be continually updated. This position is similar to that of Norbert Wiener (Chapter 2). Talking about automated machines, he writes: 'To be effective in warding off disastrous consequences, our understanding of our man-made machines should in general develop *pari passu* with the performance of the machine, p. 13.

What he is suggesting is that if we wait until the technology has been developed, it may be too late to avoid 'disastrous consequences'. Predicting is hazardous, and he does not suggest that these machines should not be developed on the grounds that they may produce undesirable consequences. Rather, the understanding must develop in step with the development of the machines. Similarly, the contention here is that understanding of the ethical questions must develop as the technology develops. This will be partly reactive and partly proactive, continually returning to the technology in order to understand how it is developing and what its actual or likely consequences are.

Proactive computer ethics is not new as we have just seen from this brief look at Wiener. Joseph Weizenbaum too, one of the founders of Artificial Intelligence, discussed future ethical and social issues, based on his predictions of the consequences of the technology. Amongst other things, in 1969, he wrote of a potential 'new cleavage in society' between those who could benefit from using computers and 'that segment of the population that cannot use computing power for lack of training' (Chapter 4). It is worth noting that he did not talk of inequalities based simply on access to computers, which was how the digital divide was first discussed many years after he raised the concern, but of inequalities based on a *lack of training* to use the computers – a later and more sophisticated view of the digital divide that developed more recently.

Philosophy of Technology

The picture painted in the previous section suggests that the technology develops somehow independently from the ethics. Even when the ethics is proactive, it is only proactive in the sense that it tries to predict consequences rather than waiting for them to happen. This enables policies to be in place to mitigate harmful consequences, but it still assumes a variety of technological determinism. This variety is what Bimber (1994, p. 82) calls the Normative account and he relates it to what Habermas (1979) sees as technology being separated from ethical and social values and driven only by efficiency and productivity. A richer way to view proactive computer ethics is to see ethical and social values playing a role in the design of the technology (see Part III, 'Values and Technology'). This approach is spoken about in various ways. Friedman *et al.* talk of value-sensitive design (2006), Nissenbaum of embodying values in systems (2001), and Brey of disclosive computer ethics (Chapter 21). In all cases the concern is with designing computer systems with ethical and social values in mind – that is, designing systems that encourage or enhance these values.

On this account, then, computer ethics involves reacting to technology that causes problems and policy vacuums, predicting what the consequences of technologies are likely to be, attempting to understand the technology as it develops in order to develop ethical policies along with the technology and, importantly, to assist in the design of computer systems that enhance or encourage values that we consider to be ethically important.

This way of doing computer ethics encourages thought about what values we consider to be important and why, because both the technology and policies are designed in ways that are intended to maximize their benefits to individuals and to societies. While doing computer ethics by reacting to the technology does not rule this out, the proactive approach that incorporates designing with values in mind encourages planning for the future, asking such questions as: what sort of technology and which policies will maximize the chances of us living the kinds of lives that we want? How can this technology be designed so that it is of the greatest benefit? What sort of society do we want? What kind of lives do we want to live? And even what constitutes a good life?

This approach has something in common with Ortega Gasset's view of technology in general. According to him, technology can be defined as '... the improvement brought about on nature by man for the satisfaction of his necessities' and '... the reform of nature' (1961, p. 95). Perhaps it is more common for us to think of technology as the tools and techniques for bringing about these improvements, but that does not alter his point.

He goes on to argue that '[not] being, but well-being, is the fundamental necessity of man...' and that therefore a main aim of technology is 'to promote good life, well-being, by adapting the medium to the will of the individual' (1961, p. 101).

This is an oversimplification of Ortega Gasset's position, but for our purposes his important point is that we humans use technology to modify our environment in order for us to live better lives, and perhaps even the good life, and designing and developing computer systems is, of course, modifying our environment. If technology in general is supposed to enhance our lives, so is computer technology. How it has done this has changed over the years. Initially stand-alone computers helped us to perform mathematical calculations, store and retrieve data, write articles and so on. Later, with the development of widespread computer networks and especially the Internet, they helped us communicate with one another just about anywhere in the world. And now computer processors are embedded in a vast variety of products, including cars, washing machines and telephones.

While there is room for the view that much of this development was, and still is, driven by the technology rather than by any human needs, and some cynicism is not out of place, it is plausible to see these developments as efforts to make life easier and more pleasant, keep us healthier and more generally to help us satisfy our goals and to enhance our lives. The extent to which our lives have been enhanced by computer technology may be debatable, but there is no doubt that our lives have been changed by it and that in many ways our lives are easier, so, to that extent at least, they have been enhanced.

Whither Computer Ethics?

This way of viewing computer ethics puts it into a much larger context. Answers to questions in computer ethics depend on answers to much more general questions about the kinds of creatures we are and about the kinds of lives that we consider to be worth living. Computer ethicists in the future will spend more time considering some big issues such as the ones just mentioned, particularly given the direction in which technology is developing.

Computers, as we have just seen, have already changed, and are continuing to change, our environment, arguably making it more pleasant for us. But now there is the possibility that computers will play a part in changing us. In a sense this is not new. We are accustomed to prosthetic limbs, spectacles, dentures, and more recently, cochlear implants. These all modify the person in some way, but in a way that makes him or her more or less the same as other people with respect to some particular deficiency such as poor sight or hearing. While individuals were changed there was no change in humans as a whole. We still had the same abilities.

But this could change. There is currently much discussion of *converging technologies*, which are commonly said to comprise nanotechnology, information technology, biotechnology and cognitive science (Roco and Bainbridge, 2002; Nordmann, 2004). These technologies taken together have the potential to quite radically change our lives and enhance our abilities. In the future, technology may not so much change our environment as change us. We will consider a few relevant developments that may be primitive relative to future developments but do demonstrate the direction that things could take.

First is the remote controlled rat or *ratbot*. This rat was controlled by inputs directly to its brain and to its whiskers. When its whiskers were stimulated and it performed the appropriate action, the reward centres of its brain were stimulated 'filling the rodents with a feeling of well-being'. So, in effect, the scientists could control the rat's behaviour by controlling its wants – that is, the rat was doing what it wanted to do, but the scientists were in control of what it wanted (Whitehouse, 2002). The second example is that of Kevin Warwick who was able to have direct communication through implants in his arms to the outside world, including with his wife who also had implants. Warwick is optimistic about the future of cyborgs, creatures that are part-human, part-machine who will have '... extra-sensory capabilities, a high-performance means of communication and the best of human and machine brains' (Warwick, 2002, p. 4). Both of these examples can be seen as early steps towards new forms of human sensing, communication and reasoning ability.

Other research is also proceeding, particularly at DARPA, the US Defense Advanced Research Projects Agency. One of these, related to the *ratbot* of the previous paragraph, involves using sharks with electrodes implanted in their brains to track enemy ships (Brown, 2006). Another set of projects is designed to enhance the abilities of people in the military (Goldblatt, 2002). One of these aims to augment cognition that is, to give people enhanced cognitive ability. Another concerns the brain–machine interface and involves research into giving people the ability to directly control devices by the brain, without having to use hands or feet or any other part of the body. This would enable a pilot, for example, to direct fly an aeroplane by the use of his or her brain, without physically needing to handle the controls. Other research is examining the possibility of directly inputting skills and information without the need for learning in the way in which we learn now. Our brain could perhaps receive its download while we slept. In the morning we would know a lot that we did not when we went to sleep.

These new issues have not been neglected, and ethical discussion of cyborgs has begun (Moor, 2005) as has discussion of ethical concerns with developments in computing enabled by nanotechnology (Moor and Weckert, 2004; Sparrow, 2002; Weckert, 2001b, 2002). In a sense, of course, the philosophical and ethical discussion of cyborgs is just an extension of the debate about whether machines can be considered as moral entities, and that debate goes back at least to the 1960s. Human enhancement has been a subject for philosophical and ethical examination in bioethics for some time and, as the technologies converge, so will the ethics. Human enhancement will be part of an ethics of convergent technologies, which will include computer ethics.

These types of development raise two questions. First, are these enhancements likely to promote the good life? And, second, will we need to rethink the whole notion of a good life in the light of them?

First, are enhancements likely to make life better for us? An enhancement here is taken to mean some change or modification made to us that in some way gives us abilities beyond those which a human normally has. It might be vision as good as an eagle or hearing as good as a dog. Or it could be the ability to directly communicate with machines or with other people through transmitters and receivers connected to our brains. We are not talking here about treatments, modifications or devices that bring people up to what is more or less normal in the total population.

It is difficult to know whether enhancement would make life better overall. Consider direct communication between brains. How would this affect our privacy? Currently my thoughts are more or less, mine alone, something for which I am very grateful. This is not so much because I intentionally think things that I should not, but more that I do not have the same sort of control over my thoughts that I have over my actions. Direct communication between brains would reduce my autonomy to the extent that I would have much less control over what people knew about me, and this would certainly make me more vulnerable to government and employer control.

Consider, too, enhanced senses. Suppose that I had the vision of an eagle. This may improve my life, but I really cannot say because I have no idea what it would be like. But it raises another issue. If some of us have enhanced vision but not everyone does, how will this affect communication and general social cohesion? Suppose that it became possible to have enhancements of many kinds and that we could choose which we wanted, if any. Could I, as a conservative, unenhanced human who is fairly happy being as he is, communicate easily with my highly enhanced neighbours who had all kinds of experiences of which I could not even conceive?

Up until now we have had a pretty good idea of what makes life better and we can be fairly confident about what makes life better for most. In the future, with human enhancements, it will not be so clear. Do we know if particular 'enhancements' will improve life? Will enhanced people be happier, and if not, why bother with enhancements? Can we say much about the 'good life' for an 'enhanced' person? One important factor is this. Currently people around the world are more or less the same. We know in general what sorts of things make people happy, what makes them suffer, what gives pleasure and pain and so on. If human enhancements become widespread it is likely that people will become very different from each other. Many different kinds of enhancement and enhancements to different levels may be possible, and if people are free to choose, they will choose differently. So it may not be known what should be done to relieve the suffering or increase the pleasure of others. In an important respect our commonality will be lost, and if this is so, the notion of 'the good life' becomes vacuous in the sense that it can play no role as a goal for technological development. It was noted earlier that, for Ortega Gasset, the goal of technology was 'to promote good life, well-being, by adapting the medium to the will of the individual'. In a world of human enhancement this no longer holds. Technology no longer adapts just the environment but also the human, so our frame of reference, namely a common humanity, is gone. This may not matter, but it should make us reconsider the purpose of technological development. What will be a computer-enhanced good life? To date, computer ethicists have undertaken little explicit examination of these kinds of question. In the future they will be difficult to avoid.

Background

Computer ethics is a relatively new field of applied ethics, even though Norbert Wiener began raising many of the issues over fifty years ago. Partly because of its newness and partly because of the need to communicate with, and influence, computer professionals, many of the influential figures have published more in professional publications, or elsewhere, than in refereed academic journals. An example is Walter Maner, who in 1978 self-published his *Starter Kit on Teaching Computer Ethics*. (Bynum (1999), discusses the importance of Maner and others.) Particularly important have been the ACM publications: *Computers and Society* and *Communications of the ACM*. Until 1999 there was no academic journal dedicated to computer ethics, and most of the academic philosophical papers are found in computing journals. A notable exception is *Metaphilosophy* which, in 1985, published a special issue on computer ethics edited by Bynum, which included the most influential paper in the field to date, James Moor's 'What is Computer Ethics?'. Another exception is the special issue on global information ethics of *Science and Engineering Ethics* published in 1996, guest edited by Terrell Ward Bynum and Simon Rogerson. In 1999 *Ethics and Information Technology*, edited by Jeroen van den Hoven, began publication. This was followed in 2003 by *The Journal of Information, Communication and Ethics in Society*, edited by Simon Rogerson and Ben Fairweather. Two conference series stand out as being the most important for generating discussion: *Ethicomp* and *Computer Ethics, Philosophical Enquiry (CEPE)*. The former has a more professional focus and the latter is more philosophical. Undoubtedly the most influential text to date has been Deborah Johnson's *Computer Ethics,* first published in 1985 which to a large extent defined the field. This is now in its third edition. Herman Tavani's *Ethics and Technology: Ethical Issues in an Age of Information and Communication Technology*, published in 2004, is probably the most influential text currently, apart from Johnson's.

Finally, it is worth pointing out that the work of Rob Kling and other researchers in *Social Informatics* has been omitted from this volume, not because it is considered unimportant – it is certainly not that – but because the focus has been on the field of computer ethics as it has in fact developed. For better or worse, there has been less interaction between these two fields than might have been expected.

About this Volume

The 39 chapters of this volume are organized into seven parts which cover many, but not all, of the main themes in the field. The most notable omission, perhaps, is intellectual property, which covered in only one chapter in the Part II. The choice was made to give more space to less-discussed issues, particularly values in design, areas in which perhaps computers should not be used, and machine morality. All of these will gain in importance if the field develops as suggested in the first part of this Introduction – that is, if the approach becomes more proactive, if technologies converge and if the distinction between humans and machines becomes less clear. This is not to suggest that intellectual property questions are not important. In the early days of computing there was discussion of, for example, copyright of computer programs (Stallman, 1992; Johnson, 1985) and patenting of algorithms (Samuelson, 1990). More recently the focus has been on downloading music and other material from the Internet (Spinello, 2005; Tavani, Chapter 11).

Computer Ethics – Its History and Nature

The essays in Part I are arranged in chronological order because they show something of the development of computer ethics. The one exception is that by Terrell Ward Bynum which constitutes Chapter 1. Bynum has been responsible for bringing the importance of Norbert Wiener to the attention of current researchers in computer ethics. He shows how, in the mid-twentieth century, Wiener recognized the power and potential of automation and potential ethical and social problems. Chapter 2 is an essay by Wiener published 10 years after the first publication of his book that forms the basis of Bynum's discussion, and continues its themes. It was mentioned earlier in this Introduction that Wiener argued that 'our understanding of our man-made machines should in general develop *pari passu* with the development of the machine' this volume, p. 13. This view is based on his belief that autonomous machines can be creative and that it is not true that 'nothing can come out of the machine that has not been put in'. This can be both beneficial and dangerous, and therefore extreme care must be taken both in developing our understanding of the machines and in making sure that 'the purpose put into the machine is the purpose which we really desire…', a point which sounds remarkably similar to the topic of Part III.

In Chapter 3 the emphasis changes to ethics for computing professionals. In the 1960s computing as a profession was still in its infancy, and Donn Parker's 1968 essay considers the development of codes of ethics for computing professionals. Recognizing that there are serious ethical problems in computing, or information processing, he notes that '[o]ne thing our societies have neglected is to define and enforce a general code of ethics'. This professional stand in computer ethics has continued to be an important element in the field and we will return to it again.

In 1976 Joseph Weizenbaum's well-known book *Computer Power and Human Reason: From Judgement to Calculation* was published, in which he raised various concerns about some actual or potential uses of computers. Moor (Chapter 33) discusses some of his arguments. Less well-known are Weizenbaum's essays raising ethical concerns. In the first of his two essays included here (Chapter 4), he speculates on some general effects of computers on society and, as mentioned previously, demonstrates considerable foresight regarding what has become known as the digital divide. In the second essay (Chapter 5), he raises concerns about technology – particularly computer technology – replacing humans in decision-making and the impact that this might have on individual self-image and self-esteem, on responsibility and more generally on society.

The following essay, by James Moor (Chapter 6), probably the best known and most quoted paper in computer ethics, introduces the policy vacuums mentioned earlier in this Introduction. Moor argues that computers are so important because of their *logical malleability* – that is, they can be programmed to do any task 'that can be characterised in terms of inputs, outputs, and connecting logical operations'. Because of this there will be many areas of their use in which there are no policies in place, forming the policy vacuums which research in computer ethics attempts to fill.

It was suggested previously that perhaps computer ethicists should take a more top-down approach and consider the problems in the light of the kind of society that we want. Richard Mason does this and raises four ethical issues in Chapter 7 that he believes should be the focus of concern: privacy, accuracy, property and access. These he refers to as PAPA. Like Parker and Gotterbarn, Mason is primarily interested in ethics for computing professionals.

Geoffrey Brown's main concern, on the other hand, in a strangely neglected essay (Chapter 8), is rather to see if there really is a sub-field of applied ethics that is computer ethics. The spirit of his argument is similar to Moor's, in that he argues that new problems are raised by computing for which no existing solutions are completely satisfactory. By way of an examination of the legal situation with respect to computer privacy, ownership and hacking, he shows that new laws need to be drafted to cover the new situations, and argues from this that the issues are significantly different enough for there to be a genuine ethics of computing.

Donald Gotterbarn is one of the most influential computer ethicists concentrating on professionals and on the profession. His essay (Chapter 9) reflects a number of his themes related to the education of professionals. He argues that ethics education is much more effective if it is incorporated throughout the curriculum rather than being taught as a discrete subject or course and, second, that it is not necessarily best taught by philosophers or theologians. His concern is not to denigrate a philosophical approach to computer ethics but it is rather to understand how best to ethically educate computing professionals.

In the final essay of Part I, Luciano Floridi is concerned with the field of computer ethics as a whole and with the fact that it has not really developed in the way that some other areas of applied ethics, such as environmental ethics have, with overarching or foundational theories. Floridi is not only attempting to provide such a theory in a series of essays on information ethics, of which this is an early one, but is also arguing that computer ethics is really part of environmental ethics. He sees environmental ethics as extending the ontology of ethics from humans to all living objects and argues that it should be extended further to all *informational* objects, and this is what information ethics, on his account, does. He maintains that what is common to all problems in computers is information: 'Right and wrong, in CE [computer ethics] do not just qualify actions in themselves, they essentially refer to what is eventually better or worse for the infosphere [information environment]'. The infosphere is better off if information quantity, quality and variety are promoted and worse off when these are decreased. Entropy, the loss or destruction of information, is an 'evil'. All entities, Floridi argues, are at one level informational entities, whether people or rocks, and therefore deserve at least some moral consideration. Information ethics, then, is an extension of environmental ethics. All entities are taken into account for their own sakes and not merely living entities.

Cyberspace

From around the mid-1990s and the growth of the Internet some new topics began to appear in computer ethics – for example, friendship and trust in cyberspace and global ethics – and discussions of other familiar topics – for example, intellectual property and privacy began to be influenced by the Internet environment. Part II covers a broad sample of these issues, although not privacy, since this is discussed in Part V.

Herman Tavani (Chapter 11) considers aspects of the content of the Internet. He examines the 'commons' created by the Internet – that is, the vast amount of information accessible to anyone who has access to a computer linked to the Internet – and sees the emergence of more restrictive intellectual property legislation as a threat to this commons. He considers several pieces of US legislation and argues that they have the effect of restricting access to what was once free information and continues his argument by examining Locke's labour theory of property which, despite the differences between the physical commons of which Locke spoke and the intellectual commons, suggests a solution by providing a balance between property rights and the intellectual commons. The next essay discusses the control or censorship of on-line material. John Weckert's basic argument in Chapter 12 is that, in some cases, reasons for restricting access to certain kinds of material apply to the Internet just as they do to other media.

The next two essays shift from content to communication; they view the Internet as a communication space. Dean Cocking and Steve Matthews (Chapter 13) argue that *real* friendships, in the sense of friendships in everyday life, are not possible. Their main argument relates to what we disclose about ourselves to each other. On-line we have much more control over how others see us. The question of self-disclosure is also of interest to Victoria McGeer who argues, in Chapter 14, that reasonable trust is possible on-line. While there are dangers for immature trusters – that is, those who seek security from their trusting relationships, genuine trust can develop and flourish amongst those with a mature approach to trusting relationships.

Friendship and trust involve relationships that develop in societies which traditionally have been limited to geographic locations. The Internet is often seen or described as global; as a global village requiring a global ethics. Because it recognizes no national boundaries and is, in principle, accessible by anyone anywhere, the situation is akin to that of a group of people who live in the same geographic location. Krystyna Gorniak-Kocikowska (Chapter 15) argues that current ethical theories are inadequate to cope with this new globalism created by the Internet and that something new is required. This, she believes, will, or should, grow out of computer ethics. Charles Ess (Chapter 16), also argues for a different approach to ethics, at least partly to overcome a computer-mediated colonization. This approach, he believes, should draw on diverse cultural traditions, particularly Socratic/Aristotelian and Confucian ethics, and provide a middle way between applying traditional ethical approaches to the computer-mediated environment and radically new approaches.

The final essay in Part II returns to an issue of content, in the sense of finding the content that we want. The vast amount of information on the Internet, organized in a very haphazard manner, has led to the situation where search engines are of central importance in finding relevant information. Lucas Introna and Helen Nissenbaum argue that the politics of search engines matter because the design of the engine contributes to what sites or kinds of site are most easily found. In other words, search engines have biases built into them, either accidentally or by design, that favour some sites over others. This discussion leads naturally to the topic of Part III, the role of values in the design of technologies.

Values and Technology

Earlier, when talking of proactive computer ethics, there was a brief mention of the role of values in the design of computer systems and in the design of technology in general. The essays in Part III all discuss this topic. Chapter 18, a much cited essay by Langdon Winner, discusses values, or politics in his terms, in technology overall, and using various examples demonstrates the effect that certain designs can have on people's behaviour and on the structure of society, with moral consequences. Jeroen van den Hoven's concern is somewhat different. He argues in Chapter 19 that particular designs can affect responsibility. For example, can someone justifiably be held responsible for some action if he or she performed it on the basis of information from some difficult-to-comprehend computer system? He demonstrates, through a discussion of the shooting down of an Iranian passenger airliner by the USS *Vincennes* using the Aegis combat system, that attributing responsibility is problematic and that this poor design also affected personal autonomy. Batya Friedman and Helen Nissenbaum, in Chapter 20, analyse the notion of bias in computer systems and examine a number of examples. On the basis of this they argue that system designers should strive for freedom from bias in their systems, just as they should aim for reliability and so on, even if it is an ideal that cannot always be achieved. Part III ends with Philip Brey (Chapter 21) discussing what he calls 'disclosive computer ethics' in the context of the nature of computer ethics, as we noted earlier in the Introduction. Computer ethics should be disclosive in that it should 'reveal the moral import of practices that appear to be morally neutral' and Brey's particular concern is with the moral import of various designs and uses of computer systems.

Responsibility and Professionalism

As was noted earlier, a central part of computer ethics has been focused on computing professionals and their responsibilities as professionals. The essays in Part IV reflect various concerns with the professional responsibility in the computing industry. Chapter 22, by Batya Friedman and Peter Kahn, continues the theme of Part III, arguing that human responsibility can be enhanced at the design stage and suggesting two approaches. First, systems should not be designed to denigrate the human user to machine-like status and, second, systems should not be designed to mimic human intentional states. Donald Gotterbarn (Chapter 23) looks carefully at the notion of responsibility and argues that it needs to be viewed differently from what it commonly is if those in the computing industry can really claim to be professionals. He outlines two problems that help avoid taking responsibility. First is that responsibility is viewed too narrowly. It is seen as applying only to following the specifications and not applying to any broader consequences that the developed system might have. Second, the fact that blame often cannot be attributed to just one person is taken to mean that nobody has responsibility for systems problems. He outlines a broader concept of responsibility that he sees as necessary if those in the computer industry are to be true professionals.

Deborah Johnson's discussion, which follows in Chapter 24, concerns the engineering profession but her argument applies equally well to the computing profession. She argues that non-licensed engineering professionals do not have special responsibilities by virtue of being professionals, but as individuals they have the same social responsibilities as others in society. Given that computing professionals are also non-licensed, presumably for Johnson the same is true for them. Helen Nissenbaum in the next essay (Chapter 25), focuses on one aspect of responsibility, accountability, and argues that computing professionals should be held accountable for their work. She considers and disposes of four supposed barriers to accountability before recommending ways of ensuring the accountability of the profession. Codes of ethics are the focus of the final essay of Part IV. Ronald Anderson *et al.*demonstrate through the use of case studies how the Association of Computing Machinery (ACM) code of ethics can be used in decision-making by professionals.

Privacy and Surveillance

Privacy continues to be probably the most discussed issue in information technology, and its importance and urgency is not diminishing as worries about terrorism increase and surveillance technology develops further. The essays in Part V reflect the wide range of concerns. The first three focus on problems associated with information stored on computers and the last three on communication.

Eugene Spafford, in Chapter 27, considers various arguments advanced in favour of hacking, the unauthorized entry into a computer system, and rejects all of them, arguing that such 'break-ins' are unethical whether any damage is done or not. The problem that concerns Ben Fairweather and Simon Rogerson (Chapter 28) is who has access to electronic patient records. They outline various ethical principles – benefice, non-maleficence, respect for patient autonomy, informed consent and fair information – showing how, in certain situations, various of them can be in tension. A patient's informed consent, they argue, should in general override other considerations, although this can be overridden for the greater good. Jeroen van den Hoven continues this theme of access to information in Chapter 29, but argues that talking about data protection rather than about privacy is better in this context. In his view there are three types of moral reason for protecting data that have little to do with privacy: information-based harm, that is, harm that can be inflicted when information is in the hands of the wrong person; informational inequality, or the sharing or trading of information; and information injustice; or the using information in spheres for which it was not intended.

The next essays attend to issues in electronic communication, especially surveillance. Privacy is most commonly thought to apply only to areas of our lives that are not in the public sphere, but Helen Nissenbaum (Chapter 30) shows that there are privacy issues even in those parts of our lives that are lived in public. In particular, there are problems with the aggregation of data – that is, putting together various bits of information about a person, all of which are in themselves public, and then building a profile of the person which can then be used for a variety of purposes. It is often argued that this raises no moral issues because it is only working with what is already in the pubic domain, but this position is resisted by Nissenbaum. The main argument of Seumas Miller and John Weckert in Chapter 31 is that privacy is a right that cannot simply be overridden by an employer in a workplace because someone is his or her employee. While some surveillance is obviously justified – for example, if there is suspicion that someone is not working satisfactorily or is committing a crime, there is no general justification, even if employees have, in a sense, consented to it. This theme is continued by Ben Fairweather (Chapter 32) in his discussion of teleworking, which, by its very nature, enables all aspects of an employee's work to be monitored. He argues that while there are problems, and he discusses many of them, there are ways of alleviating them.

What Computers Should not Do

From the early days of computing there have been arguments about whether there are some things for which computers should not be used. Such arguments were not concerned with uses in torture or other immoral acts; they were concerned with uses that could be seen as benign or as positively good. Joseph Weizenbaum began this debate in *Computer Power and Human Reason: From Judgement to Calculation*, published in 1976.

James Moor's essay (Chapter 33) is a reaction to Weizenbaum's position. He argues that in situations where using a computer it is more reliable, for example, this is what we ought to do. When computers improve life, the moral thing to do is to use them. However, he does qualify this, suggesting that humans might be dehumanized by a reliance on decision-making by computers and arguing that the values on which computer decisions are made must always be a human responsibility. Arthur Kuflik and James Lenman are both more dubious about the wisdom of using computers to replace humans. Kuflik (Chapter 34) argues that, even when leaving decisions or the performance of certain tasks to computers might be more efficient, it is not always the right thing to do. His main conclusion is that, even when decision-making responsibility is given to computers, humans should always be in the position to override these decisions. Relinquishing this oversight responsibility is, he argues, 'an indefensible abdication of ... responsibility as autonomous agents'.

Lenman's argument (Chapter 35) focuses more on finding meaning in life or satisfying our deepest needs. Much of what we do could, in principle anyway, be done by computers. Computers could compose music, could provide us with our conversation and sexual partners, and do all or most of our work. But then, of course, there might not be much point to life. This is similar to a point made by Kuflik. A computer could choose, order, send and pay for a gift for someone that I love. This might be efficient but it seems to leave out the most important part of gift-giving, the part of me that goes into these activities.

Morality and Machines

The possibility of machines being moral agents or deserving of moral consideration has long been discussed, but up until fairly recently these discussions have not been part of mainstream computer ethics. This is changing, perhaps for three reasons. First, computers are becoming much more powerful and are therefore able to simulate more human activities. Second, there is more reliance on computers in decision-making. And third, the discussion now can focus on actual software agents that are to some degree autonomous, rather than on humanoid robots that are more the stuff of science fiction. Given this, it can be seen that the discussions in Part VII follow on naturally from those in Part VI.

The first essay, by Peter Manicas (Chapter 36), originally published in 1966 well before computer ethics began in the form that we know it, uses the idea of machine morality in an investigation of materialism. He believes that if we allow machines to be moral, then we espouse materialism and that if we do not, we deny materialism. Laszlo Versenyi's argument (Chapter 37) is that machines, or robots, can be moral agents in principle; they just have not been developed yet. He bases his justification for this conclusion on arguments put forward by Plato and Kant. In Chapter 38 Shigeo Hirose is also concerned with robots but with how to ensure that they behave morally. He rejects Asimov's three laws of robotics on the grounds that robots are not an evolving life form but are evolving as intelligent machines. Morality for them should therefore be approached in terms of engineering and he considers game theory, specifically the prisoners' dilemma and Axelrod's tit-for-tat, as fruitful ways of proceeding. Bernd Stahl, in the final essay (Chapter 39) is not so concerned about the embodiment of the agent, but rather whether it could pass the Moral Turing Test. If it could, we could call it moral; otherwise not. He is sceptical whether this test will ever be passed but leaves the possibility open. One of his central arguments is based on a Wittgensteinian view of language. Computers cannot understand language in the required sense, and such understanding is necessary to pass the test.

References

Bimber, Bruce (1994), 'Three Faces of Technological Determinism', in Merritt Roe Smith and Leo Marx (eds), *Does Technology Drive History: The Dilemma of Technological Determinism*, Cambridge, MA: MIT Press, pp. 79–100.

Bynum, Terrell Ward (1999), 'The Development of Computer Ethics as a Philosophical Field of Study', *Australian Journal of Professional and Applied Ethics*, **1**, pp. 1–29.

Brown, Susan (2006), 'Stealth Sharks to Patrol the High Seas', *New Scientist*, 4 March, pp. 30–31.

Friedman, Batya, Kahn Jr, Peter H. and Borning, Alan (2006), 'Value Sensitive Design and Information Systems', in P. Zhang and D. Galletta (eds), *Human-Computer Interaction in Management Information Systems: Foundations*, New York: M.E. Sharpe.

Goldblatt, Michael (2002), 'DARPA's Programs in Enhancing Human Performance', in Roco and Bainbridge, pp. 337–41.

Gotterbarn, Donald (1991), 'Computer Ethics: Responsibility Regained', *National Forum: The Phi Beta Kappa Journal*, **71**, pp. 26–31.

Habermas, Jürgen (1971), *Toward a Rational Society: Student Protest, Science, and Politics*, trans. Jeremy J. Shapiro, London: Heinemann.

Johnson, Deborah (1985), 'Should Computer Software be Owned?', in Terrell Ward Bynum (ed.), *Computers and Ethics*, Oxford: Basil Blackwell, pp. 276–88.

Johnson, Deborah, G. (2001), *Computer Ethics*, Upper Saddle River, NJ: Prentice Hall.

Maner, Walter (1978), *Starter Kit on Teaching Computer Ethics* (self-published), republished 1980, Helvetia Press.

Moor, James and Weckert, John (2004), 'Nanoethics: assessing the nanoscale from an Ethical Point of View', in Davis Baird, Alfred Nordmann, and Joachim Schummer (eds), *Discovering The Nanoscale*, Amsterdam: IOS Press, pp. 301–10.

Moor, James (2005), 'Should We Let Computers Get Under Our Skin?', in Robert Cavalier (ed.), *The Impact of the Internet on Our Moral Lives*, Albany, NY: SUNY Press, pp. 121–38.

Nissenbaum, Helen (2001), 'How Computer Systems Embody Values', *Computer*, March, 120, pp. 118–19.

Nordmann, A. (rapporteur) (2004), *Converging Technologies – Shaping the Future of European Societies, Report of the High Level Expert Group: 'Foresighting the New Technology Wave'*, Brussels: European Commission.

Ortega y Gasset, José (1961), 'Man the Technician', in *History as a System: And Other Essays Toward a Philosophy of History*, trans. Helene Weyl, New York: W.W. Norton & Company, pp. 87–161.

Roco, Mihail C. and Bainbridge, William Sims (2002), *Converging Technologies for Improving Human Performance, Nanotechnology, Biotechnology, Information Technology and Cognitive Science*, NSF/DOC sponsored report, Arlington, USA.

Samuelson, P. (1990), 'Benson Revisited: the Case against Patent Protection for Algorithms and Other Computer Program-Related Inventions', *Emory Law Journal*, **39**, pp. 1025–54.

Sparrow, Robert (2002), 'The March of the Robot Dogs', *Ethics and Information Technology*, **4**, pp. 305–18.

Spinello, Richard, A. (2005), 'Beyond Copyright: A Moral Investigation of Intellectual Property Protection in Cyberspace', in Robert Cavalier, (ed.), *The Impact of the Internet on Our Moral Lives*, Albany, NY: SUNY Press, pp. 27–48.

Stallman, Richard (1992), 'Why Software Should be Free', available at: www.gnu.org/philosophy/shouldbefree.html. Reprinted in Bynum, Terrell Ward and Rogerson, Simon (eds) (2003), *Computer Ethics and Professional Responsibility*, Malden, MA: Blackwell Publishing, pp. 294–309.

Tavani, Herman (2004), *Ethics and Technology: Ethical Issues in an Age of Information and Communication Technology*, Danvers, MA: John Wiley and Sons.

Warwick, Kevin (2002), *I, Cyborg*, Post Falls, ID: Century.

Weckert, John (2001a), 'Computer ethics: future directions', *Ethics and Information Technology*, **3**, pp. 93–96.

Weckert, John (2001b), 'The Control of Scientific Research: The Case of Nanotechnology', *Australian Journal of Professional and Applied Ethics*, **3**, pp. 29–44.

Weckert, John (2002), 'Lilliputian computer ethics', *Metaphilosophy*, **33**, pp. 366–75.

Weizenbaum, Joseph (1976), *Computer Power and Human Reason: From Judgement to Calculation*, Harmondsworth, Middlesex: Penguin Books.

Whitehouse, David (2002), 'Here Come the Ratbots', 1 May, available at: http://news.bbc.co.uk/1/hi/sci/tech/1961798.stm.

Part I
Computer Ethics - Its History and Nature

[1]

Ethical Challenges to Citizens of 'The Automatic Age': Norbert Wiener on the Information Society

Terrell Ward Bynum

Research Center on Computing & Society,
Southern Connecticut State University, New Haven, USA
Email: computerethics@earthlink.net

ABSTRACT

This article discusses the foresight of philosopher/mathematician Norbert Wiener who, in the 1940s, founded Information Ethics as a research discipline. Wiener envisioned the coming of an "automatic age" in which information technology would have profound social and ethical impacts upon the world. He predicted, for example, machines that will learn, reason and play games; "automatic factories" that will replace assembly-line workers and middle managers with computerized devices; workers who will perform their jobs over great distances with the aid of new communication technologies; and people who will gain remarkable powers by adding computerized "prostheses" to their bodies. To analyze the ethical implications of such developments, Wiener presented some principles of justice and employed a powerful practical method of ethical analysis.

COVERAGE

1. INTRODUCTION

In Chapter I of his foundational information-ethics book, *The Human Use of Human Beings* (1950, 1954) Norbert Wiener said:

> It is the thesis of this book that society can only be understood through a study of the messages and the communication facilities which belong to it; and that in the future...messages between man and machines, between machines and man, and between machine and machine, are destined to play an ever-increasing part. (1954, 16)

To live effectively is to live with adequate information. Thus communication and control belong to the essence of man's inner life, even as they belong to his life in society. (1954, 18)

> communications in society...are the cement which binds its fabric together. (1954, 27)

Wiener believed that, in the coming 'automatic age' (as he called today's era), the nature of society, as well as its citizens' relationships with society and with each other, will depend more and more upon information and communications. He predicted that, in our time, machines will join human

KEYWORDS

Information
Ethics

Entropy

Human
Purposes

Justice

beings in the creation and interpretation of messages and communications, and indeed in shaping the ties that bind society together. There will be, he argued, machines that learn -- that gather, store and interpret information -- that reason, make decisions, and take actions on the basis of the messages which they send and receive. With the help of information technology, he predicted, mechanical prosthetic devices will merge with the bodies of disabled persons to help them overcome their disabilities; and indeed even people who are *not* disabled will acquire 'prostheses' to give them powers that a human never had before. According to Wiener, the social and ethical importance of these developments cannot be overstated. "The choice of good and evil knocks at our door," he said. (1954, 186)

Today we have entered Wiener's 'automatic age', and it is clear that he perceptively foresaw the enormous social and ethical importance of information and communication technology (ICT). Remarkably, he even foresaw – more than a decade before the Internet was created – some of the social and ethical problems and opportunities that came to be associated with the Internet. (Some examples are given below.)

2. HUMAN PURPOSES AND THE PROBLEM OF ENTROPY

Although he thought of himself primarily as a scientist, Wiener considered it important for scientists to see their own activities in the broader human context in which they function. Thus, he said, "we must know as scientists what man's nature is and what his built-in purposes are." (1954, 182) As an early twentieth-century scientist, who was philosophically alert to recent developments in physics, Wiener faced the challenge of reconciling the existence and importance of *human purposes and values* on

---

According to Wiener, the
social and ethical importance
of these developments cannot
be overstated

---

the one hand, and the thermodynamic principle on the other hand that *increasing entropy* -- that is, growing chaos and disorder – eventually will destroy all organized structures and entities in the universe. In Chapter II of *The Human Use of Human Beings,* Wiener described contemporary science's picture of the long-term fate of the universe:

> Sooner or later we shall die, and it is highly probable that the whole universe around us will die the heat death, in which the world shall be reduced to one vast temperature equilibrium.... (1954, 31)

In that same chapter, however, Wiener rescued his reader from pessimism and pointlessness by noting that 'the heat death' of the universe will occur many millions of years in the future. In addition, in our local region of the universe, living entities and even machines are capable of *reducing* chaos and disorder rather than increasing it. Living things and machines are anti-entropy entities that create and maintain structure and organization locally, even if the universe as a whole is 'running down' and losing structure. For millions of years into the future, therefore, human purposes and values can continue to have meaning and worth, despite the overall increase of entropy in the universe:

> In a very real sense we are shipwrecked passengers on a doomed planet. Yet even in a shipwreck, human decencies and human values do not necessarily vanish... [Thus] the theory of entropy, and the considerations of the ultimate heat death of the universe, need not have such profoundly depressing moral consequences as they seem to have at first glance. (1954, 40–41)

3. JUSTICE AND A GOOD HUMAN LIFE

Having rescued the meaningfulness of human purposes and values, Wiener could discuss what would count as a good human life. To have a good life, human beings must live in a society where "the great human values which man possesses" (1954, 52) are nurtured; and this can only be achieved, he said, in a society that upholds the "great principles of justice" (1954, 106). In Chapter VI of *The Human Use of Human Beings* he stated those principles, although he did not give them names. For the sake of clarity and ease of remembering them, let us attach names to Wiener's own definitions:

The Principle of Freedom: Justice requires "the liberty of each human being to develop in his freedom the full measure of the human possibilities embodied in him." (1954, 105)

The Principle of Equality: Justice requires "the equality by which what is just for A and B remains just when the positions of A and B are interchanged." (1954, 106)

The Principle of Benevolence: Justice requires "a good will between man and man that knows no limits short of those of humanity itself." (1954, 106)

Wiener considered humans to be fundamentally *social* beings who can reach their full potential only by active participation in a community of similar beings. For a good human life, therefore, society is indispensable. But it is possible for a society to be oppressive and despotic in ways that limit or even stifle individual freedom; so Wiener added a fourth principle of justice, which we can appropriately call "The Principle of Minimum Infringement of Freedom": (Wiener himself did not give it a name.)

The Principle of Minimum Infringement of Freedom: "What compulsion the very existence of the community and the state may demand must be exercised in such a way as to produce no unnecessary infringement of freedom." (1954, 106)

According to Wiener, the overall purpose of a human life is the same for everyone: to realize one's full human potential by engaging in a variety of chosen actions (1954, 52). It is not surprising, therefore, that the Principle of Freedom would head his list, and that the Principle of Minimum Infringement of Freedom would limit the power of the state to thwart freedom. Because the general purpose of each human life, according to Wiener, is the same, his Principle of Equality follows logically; while the Principle of Benevolence follows from his belief that human freedom flourishes best when everyone sympathetically looks out for the wellbeing of all.

4. WIENER'S METHOD OF DOING INFORMATION ETHICS

Wiener was keen to ask questions about "what we do and how we should react to the new world that confronts us" (1954, 12). He developed strategies for analyzing, understanding, and dealing with ICT-related social and ethical problems or opportunities that could threaten or advance human values like life, health, security, knowledge, freedom and happiness. Today, half a century after Wiener founded Information Ethics as an academic research subject, we can look back at his writings in this field and examine the methods that he used to develop his arguments and draw his conclusions. While Wiener was busy creating Information Ethics as a new area of academic research, he normally did not step back – like a metaphilosopher would – and explain to his readers what he was about to do or how he was going to do it. Instead, he simply tackled an ICT-related ethical problem or opportunity and began to analyze it and try to solve the problem or benefit from the opportunity.

Today, in examining Wiener's methods and arguments, we have the advantage of helpful concepts and ideas developed later by seminal thinkers such as Walter Maner and James Moor. We can use their ideas to illuminate Wiener's methodology, examining what he *did* in addition to what he *said*. In Chapter VI of *The Human Use of Human Beings*, for example, Wiener considers the law and his own conception of justice as tools for identifying and analyzing social and ethical issues associated with ICT. Combining Maner's ideas in his "Heuristic Methods for Computer Ethics" (1999) with Moor's famous account of the nature of computer ethics in "What Is Computer Ethics?" (1985), we can describe Wiener's account of Information Ethics

67

methodology as the following five-step heuristic procedure:

Step One: *Identify an ethical problem or positive opportunity* regarding the integration of ICT into society. (If a problem or opportunity can be foreseen before it occurs, we should develop ways to solve the problem or benefit from the opportunity before we are surprised by – and therefore unprepared for – its appearance.)

Step Two: If possible, *apply existing 'policies'* [as Moor would call principles, laws, rules, and practices that already apply in the given society] *using precedent and traditional interpretations* to resolve the problem or to benefit from the opportunity.

Step Three: If existing policies appear to be ambiguous or vague when applied to the new problem or opportunity, *clarify ambiguities and vagueness*. [In Moor's language: identify and eliminate 'conceptual muddles'.]

Step Four: If precedent and existing interpretations, including the new clarifications, are insufficient to resolve the problem or to benefit from the opportunity, one should *revise the old policies or create new ones using 'the great principles of justice' and the purpose of a human life* to guide the effort. [In Moor's language, one should identify 'policy vacuums' and then formulate and ethically justify new policies to fill the vacuums.]

Step Five: *Apply the new or revised policies* to resolve the problem or to benefit from the opportunity.

68

These policies enable a citizen to tell whether a proposed action should be considered ethical

---

It is important to note that this method of engaging in Information Ethics need not involve the expertise of a trained philosopher (though such expertise often can be helpful). In any society, a successfully functioning adult will be familiar with the laws, rules, customs, and practices (Moor's 'poli-cies') that normally govern one's behavior in that society. These policies enable a citizen to tell whether a proposed action should be considered ethical. Thus, all those in society who must cope ethically with the introduction of ICT – whether they are public policy makers, ICT professionals, business people, workers, teachers, parents, or others – can and *should engage in Information Ethics by helping to integrate ICT into society in ways that are socially and ethically good.* Information Ethics, understood in this very broad way, is too vast and too important to be left only to academics or to ICT professionals. This was clear to Wiener, who especially challenged government officials, business leaders, and public policy makers to wake up and begin to address the 'good and evil' implications of the coming information society.

5. UNEMPLOYMENT AND THE 'AUTOMATIC FACTORY'

After World War II, Wiener became concerned about the possibility that unprecedented unemployment could be generated if 'automatic factories' were created with robotic machines to replace assembly-line workers and with information processing devices to replace middle-level managers. Such a factory would "play no favorites between manual labor and white-collar labor". (1954, 159) An automatic factory, said Wiener, would be very much like an animal with a computer functioning like a central nervous system; industrial instruments such as thermometers and photoelectric cells serving as 'sense organs'; and 'effectors' like valve-turning motors, electric clutches, and newly-invented robotic tools functioning like limbs:

> The all-over system will correspond to the complete animal with sense organs, effectors, and proprioceptors, not...[just] to an isolated brain. (1954, 157)

Such a factory, said Wiener, would need far fewer human workers, blue-collar or white-collar, and the resulting industrial output could nevertheless be copious and of high quality.

Wiener noted that there is at least one good feature of 'automatic factories' that speaks in favor their creation; namely, the *safety* that they could offer to humans. Since such factories would employ few humans, they would be ethically preferable for the manufacture of risky items like radioactive products or dangerous chemicals. Far fewer people would be killed or injured in cases of emergency or accident in such a factory. Nevertheless, Wiener was concerned that the widespread creation of automatic factories could generate massive unemployment:

> Let us remember that the automatic machine...is the economic equivalent of slave labor. Any labor which competes with slave labor must accept the economic conditions of slave labor. It is perfectly clear that this will produce an unemployment situation, in comparison with which the present recession and even the depression of the thirties will seem a pleasant joke. (1954, 162)

> Thus the new industrial revolution is a two-edged sword. It may be used for the benefit of humanity. ...It may also be used to destroy humanity, and if it is not used intelligently it can go very far in that direction. (1954, 162)

Wiener was not a mere alarmist, however; nor was he just a theoretician. Instead, having identified a serious threat to society and to individual workers, he took action. In the early 1950s, he met with corporate managers, public policy makers, and union leaders to whom he expressed his deep concerns about automatic factories. By 1954, when he published the Second Revised Edition of *The Human Use of Human Beings*, Wiener had become optimistic that his warnings were being heeded. (1954, 162)

6. LONG-DISTANCE COMMUNICATIONS, TELEWORKING AND GLOBALIZATION

Besides the automatic factory, Wiener envisioned other ways in which information technology could affect working conditions. For example, he foresaw what

today is called 'teleworking' or 'telecommuting' -- doing one's job while being a long distance from the work site. This will be possible, he said, because of communications technologies like telephones, 'Ultrafaxes', telegraph, teletype, and long-distance communications technologies that are bound to be invented in the future. Performing one's job at a distance – even thousands of miles away – is possible, said Wiener, because

> where a man's word goes, and where his power of perception goes, to that point his control and in a sense his physical existence is extended. To see and to give commands to the whole world is almost the same as being everywhere. (1954, 97)

As an example, Wiener imagined an architect in Europe supervising the construction of a building in the United States. Although an adequate building staff would be on the construction site in America, the architect himself would never leave Europe:

> Ultrafax gives a means by which a facsimile of all the documents concerned may be transmitted in a fraction of a second, and the received copies are quite as good working plans as the originals. The architect may be kept up to date with the progress of the work by photographic records taken every day or several times a day, and these may be forwarded back to him by Ultrafax. Any remarks or advice he cares to give...may be transmitted by telephone, Ultrafax, or teletypwriter. (1954, 98)

Thus long-distance communications technologies which were available even in the early 1950s made it possible for certain kinds of 'teleworking' to take place.

In addition, Wiener noted that the long reach of such communications technologies is likely to have significant impacts upon *government*. "For many millennia", he said, the difficulty of transmitting language restricted "the optimum size of the state to the order of a few million people, and generally fewer." (1954, p. 91) Exceptions like the Persian and Roman Empires were made possible by improved means of communication, such as messengers on 'the Royal

Road' conveying the Royal Word across Persia, or the dramatically improved roads of the Roman Empire conveying the authority of the Emperor. By the early 1950s, he noted, there already were global communications networks made possible by airplanes and radio technology, in addition to the telecommunications technologies mentioned above. The resulting globalization of communication, he suggested, may even move the world community toward some kind of world government:

> very many of the factors which previously precluded a World State have been abrogated. It is even possible to maintain that modern communication…has made the World State inevitable. (1954, 92)

By today's standards, the long-distance communications technologies of the early 1950s, when Wiener published *The Human Use of Human Beings,* were very slow and clumsy. Nevertheless Wiener identified, even then, early indications of 'contemporary' information-ethics topics like teleworking, job outsourcing, globalization, and the impact of ICT on government and world affairs.

7. DISABILITIES, PROSTHESES AND THE MERGING OF HUMANS AND MACHINES

Norbert Wiener's foundational Information Ethics works were concerned with possible and actual impacts of information technology upon human values, such as *life, health, security, knowledge, resources, opportunities,* and most of all *freedom.* He focussed not only upon harms and threats to such values, but also upon benefits and opportunities that information technology could make possible. Wiener and some colleagues, for example, used cybernetic theory to explain two medical problems called 'intention tremor' and 'Parkinsonian tremor'. The result was the creation of two information feedback machines, called 'the moth' and 'the bedbug', to prove that the cybernetic explanation of Wiener and his colleagues was correct. The machines were successful and

made a positive contribution to human health and medicine. (1954, 163–167)

A second project of Wiener and his colleagues was the creation of a 'hearing glove' that could be worn by someone who is totally deaf. This device was designed to use information technology to convert human conversation into vibration patterns in a deaf person's hand. These tactile patterns would then be used to help the deaf person understand human speech. Although the project was not pursued to completion, it did lead to the creation of other devices which enabled persons who were blind to find their way through a maze of streets and buildings. (154, 167–174)

A proposed prosthesis project that Wiener described in *The Human Use of Human Beings* (1954, 174) was an iron lung that would be electronically attached to damaged breathing muscles in a person's body and would use the patient's own brain to control his breathing. This project would physically merge a person's body with an electronic machine to create a functioning being that is part man and part machine.

Another project like that was the creation of a mechanical hand to replace a hand that had been amputated. Wiener and some Russian and American colleagues worked together to develop such a hand, some of which were created in Russia where they "permitted some hand amputees to go back to effective work". (1964, 78) Electrical action potentials in the remaining forearm were generated by the amputee's brain when he tried to move his fingers. These potentials were sensed by electronic circuits in the mechanical hand and used to run motors which closed and opened the mechanical fingers. Wiener suggested that a kind of 'feeling' could be added to the artificial hand by including electronic pressure sensors that would generate vibrations in the forearm.

Besides using prostheses to help persons with disabilities, said Wiener, people *without* disabilities will eventually use prostheses to give themselves significant powers that human beings never had before:

> Thus there is a new engineering of prostheses possible, and it will involve the construction of systems of a mixed nature, involving both human and mechanical parts. However, this

70

type of engineering need not be confined to the replacement of parts we have lost. There is a prosthesis of parts we do not have and which we never have had. (1964, 77)

The dramatic new powers of man/machine beings could be used for good purposes or for bad ones, and this is one more example of Wiener's point about "good and evil knocking at our door":

> Render unto man the things which are man's and unto the computer the things which are the computer's... What we now need is an independent study of systems involving both human and mechanical elements (1964, 77)

In today's language, a being who is part human and part machine is called a 'cyborg'. In the 1950s, when Wiener wrote *The Human Use of Human Beings*, he did not use this word, but he did see the urgent need to consider the ethical issues that were bound to arise when such beings are created.

8. ROBOT ETHICS AND MACHINES THAT LEARN

In addition to ethical concerns about man/machine beings, Wiener also expressed worries about decision-making machines. The project that originally led him and some of his colleagues to create the new scientific field of *cybernetics* during World War Two was the development of an anti-aircraft cannon that could 'perceive' the presence of an airplane, calculate its likely trajectory, aim the cannon and fire the shell. This project made it clear to Wiener that humans possessed the scientific and engineering knowledge to create decision-making machines which gather information about the world, 'think about' that information, reach decisions based upon that 'thinking', and then carry out the decisions they had made.

Besides the anti-aircraft cannon, Wiener discussed other decision-making machines, including the checker-playing (i.e. draughts-playing) computer of A. L. Samuel of the IBM Corporation (1964, 19) and various chess-playing computers (1964,

Ch. II). Samuel's checker-playing computer was able to reprogram itself to take account of its own past performances in checker games. It made adjustments in its own playing strategy until it began to win more frequently. Although Samuel created this game-playing computer, it learned how to

---

Wiener also expressed worries about decision-making machines

---

defeat him consistently by playing games against him. Wiener also discussed chess-playing computers. In his day, they played chess very poorly, although some of them were able to learn from their 'experiences' and improve their playing skills to some extent. Wiener predicted, as many of his colleagues also did, that chess-playing computers would eventually become excellent opponents, even for chess masters.

Although machines that play checkers or chess do not pose major ethical challenges, they nevertheless demonstrate the fact that computerized devices can be designed to learn from their 'experiences', make decisions, and act on those decisions. Wiener noted that, in the 1950s and 1960s, both the United States and the Soviet Union – following John von Neumann's view that war can be seen as a kind of game (1954, 181) – were using computers to play war games in order to prepare themselves for possible nuclear war with each other. He was most concerned that one or the other of the two nuclear powers would come to rely, unwisely, upon war-game machines that learn and reprogram themselves:

71

> [Man] will not leap in where angels fear to tread, unless he is prepared to accept the punishment of the fallen angels. Neither will he calmly transfer to the machine made in his own image the responsibility for his choice of good and evil, without continuing to accept a full responsibility for that choice. (1954, 184)

> the machine...which can learn and can make decisions on the basis of its

learning, will in no way be obliged to make such decisions as we should have made, or will be acceptable to us. For the man who is not aware of this, to throw the problem of his responsibility on the machine, whether it can learn or not, is to cast his responsibility to the winds, and to find it coming back seated on the whirlwind. (1954, 185)

War and business are conflicts resembling games, and as such, they may be so formalized as to constitute games with definite rules. Indeed, I have no reason to suppose that such formalized versions of them are not already being established as models to determine the policies for pressing the Great Push Button [of nuclear war]...(1964, 31-32.)

If machines that play 'war games' are used by governments to plan for war, or even to decide when to "push the nuclear button", said Wiener, the human race may not survive the consequences. Woe to us humans, if we allow machines to make our decisions for us in situations where human judgment and responsibility are crucial to a good outcome. Decision-making machines must be governed by ethical principles that humans select. But if such machines learn from their past activities, how can we humans be sure that they will obey the ethical principles that we would have used to make those decisions? Even in 1950, therefore, it was clear to Wiener that the world would need to develop a genuine *robot ethics* -- not just science-fiction 'laws of robotics' from a writer like Isaac Asimov (1950), but genuine rules to govern the behavior of decision-making machines that learn. Today, Wiener would not be surprised to hear that there exists a branch of software engineering to deal with robot ethics. (See Eichmann, 1994; and Floridi & Sanders, 2001.)

72

Woe to us humans, if we allow machines to make our decisions for us

9. ARTIFICIAL INTELLIGENCE AND PERSONAL IDENTITY

Wiener's cybernetic analyses of living organisms – including human beings – as well as his consideration of learning machines, led him to comment on a variety of ideas that, today, are associated with AI (artificial intelligence). He did not have a rigorously worked out theory of AI, and many of his comments were guesses or speculations; but, taken together, they constitute a significant perspective on human nature and intelligence; and they have profound implications for the concept of personal identity.

Wiener would consider many of today's AI questions – like whether machines could be 'alive', or 'intelligent', or 'purposeful' – to be essentially *semantic questions* using words that are far too vague to be used for scientific purposes:

I want to interject the semantic point that such words as life, purpose, and the soul are grossly inadequate to precise scientific thinking. These terms have gained their significance through our recognition of the unity of a certain group of phenomena, and do not in fact furnish us with any adequate basis to characterize this unity. Whenever we find a new phenomenon which partakes to some degree of the nature of those which we have already termed 'living phenomena,' but which does not conform to all the associated aspects which define the term 'life,' we are faced with the problem whether to enlarge the word 'life' so as to include them, or to define it in a more restrictive way so as to exclude them. (1954, 31)

Now that certain analogies of behavior are being observed between the machine and the living organism, the problem as to whether the machine is alive or not is, for our purposes, semantic and we are at liberty to answer it one way or the other as best suits our convenience. (1954, 32)

Wiener thought of both human beings and machines as physical entities whose behavior and performance can be explained by the interaction of their parts with each other and with the outside world. He sometimes spoke of human beings as a "special sort of machine". (e.g., 1954, 79) In the case of humans, the parts are atoms that are combined in an exquisitely complex pattern to form a living person. The parts of a non-human machine, on the other hand, are much larger and less finely structured, being simply shaped 'lumps' of steel, copper, plastic, silicon, and so on. Nevertheless, according to Wiener, it is physical structure that accounts for the 'intellectual capacities' of both humans and machines:

*Cybernetics takes the view that the structure of the machine or of the organism is an index of the performance that may be expected from it....*Theoretically, if we could build a machine whose mechanical structure duplicated human physiology, then we could have a machine whose intellectual capacities would duplicate those of human beings. (1954, 57, italics in the original text)

Consistent with this view, Wiener regularly analyzed human intellectual and psychological phenomena, both normal and pathological, by applying cybernetic theory to the various parts of a person's body. In the early 1960s, because of the relatively large size of electronic components (compared to the neurons in a person's brain), and because of the tendency of electronic components to generate much heat, Wiener expressed doubt that humans would ever create a machine as complex and sophisticated as a person's body or nervous system. (1964, 76) Today, perhaps, he would change his mind, given recent progress in microcircuit development.

Wiener's view that human beings are sophisticated physical entities whose parts are atoms enabled him to speculate, in Chapter V of *The Human Use of Human Beings*, about the possibility of creating a complex mathematical formula that would completely describe the intimate structure of a person's body. If one were able, he said, to send this formula across telephone lines, or over some other long-distance communications network, and if the formula enabled someone or some device at the

other end to 'reassemble' the person – atom by atom – then it would be possible for that person to travel long distances instantly via telephone or some other communications network. Today, Wiener's physiological account of human nature, including human intellectual and emotional capacities, is widely shared by many scientists and other thinkers, including biologists, physicians, psychologists, and philosophers, to name but a few examples. When this view is combined with Wiener's ideas about electronic 'traveling' over communications networks, a number of challenging questions arise regarding a human being's personal identity. Wiener himself did not explore these questions, but they are worth mentioning here:

1. 'Traveling' in this manner would require that a person be 'disassembled' into atoms at the starting point and 'reassembled' at the destination. Since the original atoms themselves do not travel across the network (only the mathematical formula travels), new atoms must be used at the destination. Does this mean that the traveler is gently 'killed' at the starting point and then carefully 'resurrected' at the destination?

2. What if the person's identity formula somehow gets scrambled while traveling over the network? The 'reassembled' person at the destination could be significantly different from the original one. Who is this new person? Where did the original person go? Could the new person, on behalf of the original person, sue someone for murder? – manslaughter? – bodily harm? – breach of contract? Would all these issues become moot points if the original person is simply 'reassembled' correctly at the original starting point? Could the 'new person' at the other end then be killed because he or she was a 'mistake'?

3. What if a person's identity formula is sent across the network, but his or her body is not disassembled? The 'traveler', in other words, stays home and remains alive just as he or she was? If a person is nevertheless 'reassembled' at the destination, using the formula that was sent across the network, who is that new person? He or she would have all the memories, knowledge, personality traits, and

73

so on, of the original person. Indeed, he or she would have a body – atom for atom – identical to that of the original person. This 'new' person would be more than a clone of the original, since a 'clone' in today's sense of the term would start out as a baby, and not be 'reassembled' as an adult. The 'new' person also would not just be the twin sibling of the original person, since such twins have different memories and different past experiences. The new person would be a perfect copy of the original one, whose knowledge and memories would then begin to diverge more and more from the original person's as time goes on.

4. What constitutes someone's unique personal identity? Perhaps it is the mathematical formula that fully describes his or her physiology at any given moment. But this would mean that someone's personal identity changes from moment to moment as his or her body changes. This conflicts with our usual view that a person keeps his or her identity over a lifetime.

5. Suppose someone stores away complete identity formulas corresponding to my body on my tenth birthday, my twentieth birthday, and my thirtieth birthday. Then, on my fortieth birthday, he or she 'reassembles' all three past versions of me. Who is 'the real me'? Are they all me? Who can claim to own my property? Who gets to go home to my wife and live with her? Why?

6. If a 'life insurance' organization stores away one of my personal identity formulas and always 'reassembles' me anew when I die, does this mean that I have been granted something approaching eternal life? If the 'resurrected' me always has the same original memories, knowledge, personality, etc., does this mean that I get to relive part of my life many different times, taking different paths? – marrying different partners? – holding down different jobs?

10. CONCLUSION

Norbert Wiener was a scientist, an engineer and a mathematician; but he also was a philosopher with the vision to see the enormous social and ethical implications of the information and communication technologies that he and his colleagues were inventing. His creative tour de force, *The Human Use of Human Beings* (1950, 1954), was the first book-length publication in Information Ethics; and it instantly created a solid foundation for that subject as a field of academic research. Wiener's many contributions to this field – in books, articles, lectures and interviews – not only established him as its 'founding father', they continue to provide a rich source of ideas and issues to inspire Information Ethics thinkers for many years to come.

REFERENCES

Isaac Asimov (1950) *I, Robot*, Gnome.

Eichmann, D. (1994), Ethical Web Agents (accessed 2 April 2004) http://archive.ncsa.uiuc.edu/SDG/IT94/Proceedings/Agents/eichmann.ethical/eichmann.html

Floridi, L. and Sanders, J. W. (2001) On the Morality of Artificial Agents, *CEPE 2001, Computer Ethics: Philosophical Enquiry*, Lancaster, UK, 14–16 December, (accessed 2 April 2004) http://www.wolfson.ox.ac.uk/-floridi/pdf/maa.pdf

Maner, W. (1999) Heuristic methods for computer ethics, Keynote Speech, *AICEC99, Australian Institute of Computer Ethics Conference*, Melbourne, Australia. (First published in J. Moor and T. W. Bynum (eds.) (2003), *Cyberphilosophy: The Intersection of Computing and Philosophy*, Blackwell.)

Moor, J. H. (1985) What is computer ethics? In: T. W. Bynum (ed.), *Computers and Ethics*, Blackwell, pp. 263–275. (Published as the October 1985 issue of *Metaphilosophy*.)

Wiener, N. (1950, 1954) *The Human Use of Human Beings: Cybernetics and Society*, Houghton Mifflin; 2nd edn Doubleday Anchor. (In the present essay, all quotations from this book are from the Second Revised Edition.)

Wiener, N. (1964) *God and Golem* Inc. MIT Press.

74

CORRESPONDING AUTHOR

Terrell Ward Bynum
Research Center on Computing and Society, Southern Connecticut State University
New Haven, CT 06515, USA
Email: computerethics@earthlink.net

[2]

Some Moral and Technical Consequences of Automation

As machines learn they may develop unforeseen strategies at rates that baffle their programmers.

Norbert Wiener

Some 13 years ago, a book of mine was published by the name of *Cybernetics*. In it I discussed the problems of control and communication in the living organism and the machine. I made a considerable number of predictions about the development of controlled machines and about the corresponding techniques of automatization, which I foresaw as having important consequences affecting the society of the future. Now, 13 years later, it seems appropriate to take stock of the present position with respect to both cybernetic technique and the social consequences of this technique.

Before commencing on the detail of these matters, I should like to mention a certain attitude of the man in the street toward cybernetics and automatization. This attitude needs a critical discussion, and in my opinion it should be rejected in its entirety. This is the assumption that machines cannot possess any degree of originality. This frequently takes the form of a statement that nothing can come out of the machine which has not been put into it. This is often interpreted as asserting that a machine which man has made must remain continually subject to man, so that its operation is at any time open to human interference and to a change in policy. On the basis of such an attitude, many people have pooh-poohed the dangers of machine techniques, and they have flatly contradicted the early predictions of Samuel Butler that the machine might take over the control of mankind.

It is true that in the time of Samuel Butler the available machines were far less hazardous than machines are today, for they involved only power, not a certain degree of thinking and communication. However, the machine techniques of the present day have invaded the latter fields as well, so that the actual machine of today is very different from the image that Butler held, and we cannot transfer to these new devices the assumptions which seemed axiomatic a generation ago. I find myself facing a public which has formed its attitude toward the machine on the basis of an imperfect understanding of the structure and mode of operation of modern machines.

It is my thesis that machines can and do transcend some of the limitations of their designers, and that in doing so they may be both effective and dangerous. It may well be that in principle we cannot make any machine the elements of whose behavior we cannot comprehend sooner or later. This does not mean in any way that we shall be able to comprehend these elements in substantially less time than the time required for operation of the machine, or even within any given number of years or generations.

As is now generally admitted, over a limited range of operation, machines act far more rapidly than human beings and are far more precise in performing the details of their operations. This being the case, even when machines do not in any way transcend man's intelligence, they very well may, and often do, transcend man in the performance of tasks. An intelligent understanding of their mode of performance may be delayed until long after the task which they have been set has been completed.

This means that though machines are theoretically subject to human criticism, such criticism may be ineffective until long after it is relevant. To be effective in warding off disastrous consequences, our understanding of our man-made machines should in general develop *pari passu* with the performance of the machine. By the very slowness of our human actions, our effective control of our machines may be nullified. By the time we are able to react to information conveyed by our senses and stop the car we are driving, it may already have run head on into a wall.

Game-Playing

I shall come back to this point later in this article. For the present, let me discuss the technique of machines for a very specific purpose: that of playing games. In this matter I shall deal more particularly with the game of checkers, for which the International Business Machines Corporation has developed very effective game-playing machines.

Let me say once for all that we are not concerned here with the machines which operate on a perfect closed theory of the game they play. The game theory of von Neumann and Morgenstern may be suggestive as to the operation of actual game-playing machines, but it does not actually describe them.

In a game as complicated as checkers, if each player tries to choose his play in view of the best move his opponent can make, against the best response he can give, against the best response his opponent can give, and so on, he will have taken upon himself an impossible task. Not only is this humanly impossible but there is actually no reason to suppose that it is the best policy against the opponent by whom he is faced, whose limitations are equal to his own.

The von Neumann theory of games bears no very close relation to the theory by which game-playing machines operate. The latter corresponds much more closely to the methods of play used by expert but limited human chess players against other chess players. Such players depend on certain strategic evaluations, which are in essence not complete. While the von Neumann type of play is valid for games like ticktacktoe, with a complete theory, the very interest of chess and checkers lies in the fact that they

The author is professor of mathematics at Massachusetts Institute of Technology, Cambridge. This article is adapted from a lecture he delivered 27 December 1959 before the Committee on Science in the Promotion of Human Welfare, at the Chicago meeting of the AAAS.

do not possess a complete theory. Neither do war, nor business competition, nor any of the other forms of competitive activity in which we are really interested.

In a game like ticktacktoe, with a small number of moves, where each player is in a position to contemplate all possibilities and to establish a defense against the best possible moves of the other player, a complete theory of the von Neumann type is valid. In such a case, the game must inevitably end in a win for the first player, a win for the second player, or a draw.

I question strongly whether this concept of the perfect game is a completely realistic one in the cases of actual, nontrivial games. Great generals like Napoleon and great admirals like Nelson have proceeded in a different manner. They have been aware not only of the limitations of their opponents in such matters as materiel and personnel but equally of their limitations in experience and in military know-how. It was by a realistic appraisal of the relative inexperience in naval operations of the continental powers as compared with the highly developed tactical and strategic competence of the British fleet that Nelson was able to display the boldness which pushed the continental forces off the seas. This he could not have done had he engaged in the long, relatively indecisive, and possibly losing conflict to which his assumption of the best possible strategy on the part of his enemy would have doomed him.

In assessing not merely the materiel and personnel of his enemies but also the degree of judgment and the amount of skill in tactics and strategy to be expected of them, Nelson acted on the basis of their record in previous combats. Similarly, an important factor in Napoleon's conduct of his combat with the Austrians in Italy was his knowledge of the rigidity and mental limitations of Würmser.

This element of experience should receive adequate recognition in any realistic theory of games. It is quite legitimate for a chess player to play, not against an ideal, nonexisting, perfect antagonist, but rather against one whose habits he has been able to determine from the record. Thus, in the theory of games, at least two different intellectual efforts must be made. One is the short-term effort of playing with a determined policy for the individual game. The other is the examination of

a record of many games. This record has been set by the player himself, by his opponent, or even by players with whom he has not personally played. In terms of this record, he determines the relative advantages of different policies as proved over the past.

There is even a third stage of judgment required in a chess game. This is expressed at least in part by the length of the significant past. The development of theory in chess decreases the importance of games played at a different stage of the art. On the other hand, an astute chess theoretician may estimate in advance that a certain policy currently in fashion has become of little value, and that it may be best to return to earlier modes of play to anticipate the change in policy of the people whom he is likely to find as his opponents.

Thus, in determining policy in chess there are several different levels of consideration which correspond in a certain way to the different logical types of Bertrand Russell. There is the level of tactics, the level of strategy, the level of the general considerations which should have been weighed in determining this strategy, the level in which the length of the relevant past—the past within which these considerations may be valid—is taken into account, and so on. Each new level demands a study of a much larger past than the previous one.

I have compared these levels with the logical types of Russell concerning classes, classes of classes, classes of classes of classes, and so on. It may be noted that Russell does not consider statements involving all types as significant. He brings out the futility of such questions as that concerning the barber who shaves all persons, and only those persons, who do not shave themselves. Does he shave himself? On one type he does, on the next type he does not, and so on, indefinitely. All such questions involving an infinity of types may lead to unsolvable paradoxes. Similarly, the search for the best policy under all levels of sophistication is a futile one and must lead to nothing but confusion.

These considerations arise in the determination of policy by machines as well as in the determination of policy by persons. These are the questions which arise in the programming of programming. The lowest type of game-playing machine plays in terms of a certain rigid evaluation of plays.

Quantities such as the value of pieces gained or lost, the command of the pieces, their mobility, and so on, can be given numerical weights on a certain empirical basis, and a weighting may be given on this basis to each next play conforming to the rules of the game. The play with the greatest weight may be chosen. Under these circumstances, the play of the machine will seem to its antagonist—who cannot help but evaluate the chess personality of the machine—a rigid one.

Learning Machines

The next step is for the machine to take into consideration not merely the moves as they occurred in the individual game but the record of games previously played. On this basis, the machine may stop from time to time, not to play but to consider what (linear or nonlinear) weighting of the factors which it has been given to consider would correspond best to won games as opposed to lost (or drawn) games. On this basis, it continues to play with a new weighting. Such a machine would seem to its human opponent to have a far less rigid game personality, and tricks which would defeat it at an earlier stage may now fail to deceive it.

The present level of these learning machines is that they play a fair amateur game at chess but that in checkers they can show a marked superiority to the player who has programmed them after from 10 to 20 playing hours of working and indoctrination. They thus most definitely escape from the completely effective control of the man who has made them. Rigid as the repertory of factors may be which they are in a position to take into consideration, they do unquestionably—and so say those who have played with them—show originality, not merely in their tactics, which may be quite unforeseen, but even in the detailed weighting of their strategy.

As I have said, checker-playing machines which learn have developed to the point at which they can defeat the programmer. However, they appear still to have one weakness. This lies in the end game. Here the machines are somewhat clumsy in determining the best way to give the *coup de grâce*. This is due to the fact that the existing machines have for the most part adopted a program in which the identical strategy is carried out at each stage of the game. In view of the similarity of values of pieces in checkers, this is quite natural for a large part of the play but ceases to be perfectly relevant when the board is relatively empty and the main problem is that of moving into position rather than that of direct attack. Within the frame of the methods I have described it is quite possible to have a second exploration to determine what the policy should be after the number of pieces of the opponent is so reduced that these new considerations become paramount.

Chess-playing machines have not, so far, been brought to the degree of perfection of checker-playing machines, although, as I have said, they can most certainly play a respectable amateur game. Probably the reason for this is similar to the reason for their relative efficiency in the end game of checkers. In chess, not only is the end game quite different in its proper strategy from the mid-game but the opening game is also. The difference between checkers and chess in this respect is that the initial play of the pieces in checkers is not very different in character from the play which arises in the mid-game, while in chess, pieces at the beginning have an arrangement of exceptionally low mobility, so that the problem of deploying them from this position is particularly difficult. This is the reason why opening play and development form a special branch of chess theory.

There are various ways in which the machine can take cognizance of these well-known facts and explore a separate waiting strategy for the opening. This does not mean that the type of game theory which I have here discussed is not applicable to chess but merely that it requires much more consideration before we can make a machine that can play master chess. Some of my friends who are engaged in these problems believe that this goal will be achieved in from 10 to 25 years. Not being a chess expert, I do not venture to make any such predictions on my own initiative.

It is quite in the cards that learning machines will be used to program the pushing of the button in a new push-button war. Here we are considering a field in which automata of a non-learning character are probably already in use. It is quite out of the question to program these machines on the basis

of an actual experience in real war. For one thing, a sufficient experience to give an adequate programming would probably see humanity already wiped out.

Moreover, the techniques of push-button war are bound to change so much that by the time an adequate experience could have been accumulated, the basis of the beginning would have radically changed. Therefore, the programming of such a learning machine would have to be based on some sort of war game, just as commanders and staff officials now learn an important part of the art of strategy in a similar manner. Here, however, if the rules for victory in a war game do not correspond to what we actually wish for our country, it is more than likely that such a machine may produce a policy which would win a nominal victory on points at the cost of every interest we have at heart, even that of national survival.

Man and Slave

The problem, and it is a moral problem, with which we are here faced is very close to one of the great problems of slavery. Let us grant that slavery is bad because it is cruel. It is, however, self-contradictory, and for a reason which is quite different. We wish a slave to be intelligent, to be able to assist us in the carrying out of our tasks. However, we also wish him to be subservient. Complete subservience and complete intelligence do not go together. How often in ancient times the clever Greek philosopher slave of a less intelligent Roman slaveholder must have dominated the actions of his master rather than obeyed his wishes! Similarly, if the machines become more and more efficient and operate at a higher and higher psychological level, the catastrophe foreseen by Butler of the dominance of the machine comes nearer and nearer.

The human brain is a far more efficient control apparatus than is the intelligent machine when we come to the higher areas of logic. It is a self-organizing system which depends on its capacity to modify itself into a new machine rather than on ironclad accuracy and speed in problem-solving. We have already made very successful machines of the lowest logical type, with a rigid policy. We are beginning to make machines of the second logical

type, where the policy itself improves with learning. In the construction of operative machines, there is no specific foreseeable limit with respect to logical type, nor is it safe to make a pronouncement about the exact level at which the brain is superior to the machine. Yet for a long time at least there will always be some level at which the brain is better than the constructed machine, even though this level may shift upwards and upwards.

It may be seen that the result of a programming technique of automatization is to remove from the mind of the designer and operator an effective understanding of many of the stages by which the machine comes to its conclusions and of what the real tactical intentions of many of its operations may be. This is highly relevant to the problem of our being able to foresee undesired consequences outside the frame of the strategy of the game while the machine is still in action and while intervention on our part may prevent the occurrence of these consequences.

Here it is necessary to realize that human action is a feedback action. To avoid a disastrous consequence, it is not enough that some action on our part should be sufficient to change the course of the machine, because it is quite possible that we lack information on which to base consideration of such an action.

In neurophysiological language, ataxia can be quite as much of a deprivation as paralysis. A patient with locomotor ataxia may not suffer from any defect of his muscles or motor nerves, but if his muscles and tendons and organs do not tell him exactly what position he is in, and whether the tensions to which his organs are subjected will or will not lead to his falling, he will be unable to stand up. Similarly, when a machine constructed by us is capable of operating on its incoming data at a pace which we cannot keep, we may not know, until too late, when to turn it off. We all know the fable of the sorcerer's apprentice, in which the boy makes the broom carry water in his master's absence, so that it is on the point of drowning him when his master reappears. If the boy had had to seek a charm to stop the mischief in the *grimoires* of his master's library, he might have been drowned before he had discovered the relevant incantation. Similarly, if a bottle factory is programmed on the basis of maximum productivity, the owner may be made bankrupt by the enormous inventory of unsalable bottles manufactured before he learns he should have stopped production six months earlier.

The "Sorcerer's Apprentice" is only one of many tales based on the assumption that the agencies of magic are literal-minded. There is the story of the genie and the fisherman in the *Arabian Nights,* in which the fisherman breaks the seal of Solomon which has imprisoned the genie and finds the genie vowed to his own destruction; there is the tale of the "Monkey's Paw," by W. W. Jacobs, in which the sergeant major brings back from India a talisman which has the power to grant each of three people three wishes. Of the first recipient of this talisman we are told only that his third wish is for death. The sergeant major, the second person whose wishes are granted, finds his experiences too terrible to relate. His friend, who receives the talisman, wishes first for £200. Shortly thereafter, an official of the factory in which his son works comes to tell him that his son has been killed in the machinery and that, without any admission of responsibility, the company is sending him as consolation the sum of £200. His next wish is that his son should come back, and the ghost knocks at the door. His third wish is that the ghost should go away.

Disastrous results are to be expected not merely in the world of fairy tales but in the real world wherever two agencies essentially foreign to each other are coupled in the attempt to achieve a common purpose. If the communication between these two agencies as to the nature of this purpose is incomplete, it must only be expected that the results of this cooperation will be unsatisfactory. If we use, to achieve our purposes, a mechanical agency with whose operation we cannot efficiently interfere once we have started it, because the action is so fast and irrevocable that we have not the data to intervene before the action is complete, then we had better be quite sure that the purpose put into the machine is the purpose which we really desire and not merely a colorful imitation of it.

Time Scales

Up to this point I have been considering the quasi-moral problems caused by the simultaneous action of the machine and the human being in a joint enterprise. We have seen that one of the chief causes of the danger of disastrous consequences in the use of the learning machine is that man and machine operate on two distinct time scales, so that the machine is much faster than man and the two do not gear together without serious difficulties. Problems of the same sort arise whenever two control operators on very different time scales act together, irrespective of which system is the faster and which system is the slower. This leaves us the much more directly moral question: What are the moral problems when man as an individual operates in connection with the controlled process of a much slower time scale, such as a portion of political history or—our main subject of inquiry—the development of science?

Let it be noted that the development of science is a control and communication process for the long-term understanding and control of matter. In this process 50 years are as a day in the life of the individual. For this reason, the individual scientist must work as a part of a process whose time scale is so long that he himself can only contemplate a very limited sector of it. Here, too, communication between the two parts of a double machine is difficult and limited. Even when the individual believes that science contributes to the human ends which he has at heart, his belief needs a continual scanning and re-evaluation which is only partly possible. For the individual scientist, even the partial appraisal of this liaison between the man and the process requires an imaginative forward glance at history which is difficult, exacting, and only limitedly achievable. And if we adhere simply to the creed of the scientist, that an incomplete knowledge of the world and of ourselves is better than no knowledge, we can still by no means always justify the naive assumption that the faster we rush ahead to employ the new powers for action which are opened up to us, the better it will be. We must always exert the full strength of our imagination to examine where the full use of our new modalities may lead us.

[3]

Rules of Ethics in Information Processing

By Donn B. Parker

The background and motivation for the adoption by the ACM Council on November 11, 1966, of a set of Guidelines for Professional Conduct in Information Processing are described. A brief history is given of ethical codes in other professions. Some reasons for and against adoption of ethical rules are considered, and several sections of the ACM Guidelines are analyzed. The purpose is to inform about this important aspect of our profession, as well as to stimulate thought and interest.

KEY WORDS AND PHRASES: ethics, professional conduct, code of ethics, ACM guidelines, professionalism, professional societies, unethical conduct
CR CATEGORIES: 1.3, 2.2

There are a number of serious ethical problems in the arts and sciences of information processing. A few of these are: invasion of privacy by use of the computer; implications of copyrighting computer programs; and fraudulent programming trade schools. The "little" problems of personal ethics are of equal importance and are often closely related to the more imposing problems. We can do a great deal about ethical problems if we just give the msome serious attention.

It is difficult to discuss ethics in our field without considering professionalism. A definition of a profession together with an expansion of it for purposes of this discussion, is as follows: A profession is a field of endeavor requiring a high level of education, skill, and intelligence in an area affecting society[1]. A profession receives a trust from society and in return is responsible to society to perform at a high level in an ethical manner. Specific definition of ethical rules is based on the existence of a profession within which the rules apply.

Significant factors demonstrate that there is an emerging profession in the arts and sciences of information processing. Specific academic curricula for colleges and universities are being developed in the field, and departments of computer science are becoming common. The Data Processing Management Association has developed the Certificate in Data Processing, which recognizes certain levels of knowledge attainment and will, by 1972, require a bachelor level degree[2]. Many companies have been formed which are exclusively devoted to the field, and the US Government has become increasingly concerned

Mr. Parker is Chairman of the ACM Professional Standards and Practices Committee, as well as being Secretary of the ACM. Mr. Parker's address is Control Data Corporation, Development Division, 3145 Porter Drive, Stanford Industrial Park, Palo Alto, California 94304.

with many aspects of computers and their use. We find a gradual, exclusive identification with professional societies in our field. There is an increasing distinction between professional and subprofessional work. However, this last point is probably the least apparent at this stage in the development of our profession.

Several problems are associated with the emergence of this profession. One, for example, is that it does not even have a name. Another problem is the rapid development of our technology, for which other professions have developed over hundreds of years in much slower moving environments, our development is measured in less than tens of years. The diverse backgrounds of people in the field and the diverse applications of computers in other professions are also significant problems in an effort to unify.

Segments of other professions are organized into professional societies. Likewise, societies in our profession should define, represent, and bring order to this emerging profession. These include the Association for Computing Machinery (ACM), Data Processing Management Association (DPMA), Institute of Electronic Engineers (IEEE) Computer Group, American Society for Information Science (ASIS), the Simulation Council Incorporated (SCI), and the Society for Information Display (SID). These societies are already communicating technology, motivating students to enter the field, developing curricula, engaging in professional development, influencing legislation through individual members, setting membership requirements, and giving awards and recognition to members for outstanding performance.

One thing our societies have neglected is to define and enforce a general code of ethics. Other societies have a wide range of experience with ethics. The

American Society of Civil Engineers is an old society established in 1852, but it did not establish a code of ethics until 1914. This society considers hundreds of ethical problems every year. Between the years 1951 and 1964, 78 of these problems became formal cases[3]; 48 of them were dismissed. Of the remaining 30 cases, some involving more than one member, 16 members were admonished, 18 suspended, and 8 expelled. One third of the 78 cases concerned unethical competitive bidding; one fourth concerned derogatory actions to the integrity, dignity, and honor of the profession; one twelfth involved supplanting another engineer in an engagement; and the remainder represented a variety of other charges.

The IEEE has not established a code of ethics, although it is considering that one be proposed. However, since IEEE is a scientific, educational and "literary" organization, and its constitution so states, the question of a code of ethics would appear to be out of consonance with the main purposes for which it is organized and operated[4]. All the organizations in the information processing field mentioned above are also committed to similar purposes.

THE DPMA established a code of ethics when it was chartered in 1951. However, the code is specialized for DPMA members, and it is administered in a variety of ways at chapter levels. There is no national mechanism for enforcement. The Certificate in Data Processing program requires that a candidate must have his good character certified by a CDP holder[5]. It states that "candidates must be of high moral qualifications and professional attitude," but these concepts are not specifically defined. Also, "if derogatory information is discovered, DPMA will investigate further." Investigations have resulted in a few applicants' being turned away; no certificates have been revoked.

ACM set minimum professional-type requirements for membership in July 1966. Two members must attest that an applicant has "attained professional stature by demonstrating intellectual competence and ethical conduct in the arts and sciences of information processing"[6]. However, ethical conduct was not defined. This left a void until on November 11, 1966, the ACM Council adopted a set of guidelines called "Professional Conduct in Information Processing" (see full text reprinted herewith). Using the term guidelines the Council wisely avoided the implication that the rules constitute a code to be enforced. ACM does not feel prepared to generally enforce such a code. The set of

(Continued on page 200)

Professional Conduct in Information Processing

INTRODUCTION

This set of guidelines was adopted by the Council of the Association for Computing Machinery on November 11, 1966 in the spirit of providing a guide to the members of the Association. In the years to come this set of guidelines is expected to evolve into an effective means of preserving a high level of ethical conduct. In the meantime it is planned that ACM members will use these guidelines in their own professional lives. They are urged to refer ethical problems to the proper ACM authorities as specified in the Constitution and Bylaws to receive further guidance and in turn assist in the evolution of the set of guidelines.

PREAMBLE

The professional person, to uphold and advance the honor, dignity and effectiveness of the profession in the arts and sciences of information processing, and in keeping with high standards of competence and ethical conduct: Will be honest, forthright and impartial; will serve with loyalty his employer, clients and the public; will strive to increase the competence and prestige of the profession; will use his special knowledge and skill for the advancement of human welfare.

1. *Relations with the Public*

1.1   An ACM member will have proper regard for the health, privacy, safety and general welfare of the public in the performance of his professional duties.

1.2   He will endeavor to extend public knowledge, understanding and appreciation of computing machines and information processing and achievements in their application, and will oppose any untrue, inaccurate or exaggerated statement or claims.

1.3   He will express an opinion on a subject within his competence only when it is founded on adequate knowledge and honest conviction, and will properly qualify himself when expressing an opinion outside of his professional field.

1.4   He will preface any partisan statement, criticisms or arguments that he may issue concerning information processing by clearly indicating on whose behalf they are made.

2. *Relations with Employers and Clients*

2.1   An ACM member will act in professional matters as a faithful agent or trustee for each employer or client and will not disclose private information belonging to any present or former employer or client without his consent.

2.2   He will indicate to his employer or client the consequences to be expected if his professional judgment is over-ruled.

2.3   He will undertake only those professional assignments for which he is qualified and which the state of the art supports.

2.4   He is responsible to his employer or client to meet specifications to which he is committed in tasks he performs and products he produces, and to design and develop systems that adequately perform their function and satisfy his employer's or client's operational needs.

3. *Relations with Other Professionals*

3.1   An ACM member will take care that credit for work is given to those to whom credit is properly due.

3.2   He will endeavor to provide opportunity and encouragement for the professional development and advancement of professionals or those aspiring to become professionals with whom he comes in contact.

3.3   He will not injure maliciously the professional reputation or practice of another person and will conduct professional competition on a high plane. If he has proof that another person has been unethical, illegal or unfair in his professional practice concerning information processing, he should so advise the proper authority.

3.4   He will cooperate in advancing information processing by interchanging information and experience with other professionals and students and by contributing to public communications media and to the efforts of professional and scientific societies and schools.

guidelines was adapted from the Engineering Council for Professional Development Short Form Canons of Ethics of 1967[7].

A brief history, as well as the basis for codes of ethics, is quoted below from the book *Ethics and Professionalism in Engineering*[1] by Murray I. Mantell, Chairman, Department of Civil Engineering, University of Miami[8].

Probably the most ancient and well-known written statement of professional ethics is the *Hippocratic Oath* of the medical profession. Suggestions related to the *Oath* date back to Egyptian papyri of 2000 B.C. The Greek medical writings making up the *Hippocratic Collection* were put together about 400 B.C. The present form of the *Hippocratic Oath* originated about 300 A.D. Most of the major professional organizations in the United States were founded during a relatively short period in the latter half of the nineteenth century; and most of them adopted the present form of their codes of ethics during a relatively short period at the beginning of the twentieth century. The American Medical Association, founded in 1847, adopted its *Principles of Medical Ethics* in 1912. The American Society of Mechanical Engineers, founded in 1880, adopted its *Code of Ethics* in 1914. The Institute of Electrical and Electronic Engineers (originally the American Institute of Electrical Engineers),[2] founded in 1884, adopted its *Code of Principles of Professional Conduct* in 1912. The American Institute of Architects, founded in 1857, adopted its *Principles of Professional Practice and the Canons of Ethics* in 1908.

The adoption of the comprehensive *Principles of Medical Ethics* appear to have followed closely behind the efforts in 1910 of the American Medical Association to establish standards and classifications for medical schools. Whereas laws to regulate the practice of medicine were established as early as 1639, most of the other professions were not regulated to any appreciable extent until the early part of the twentieth century. After the Civil War there was a greatly increased feeling that it was undemocratic and un-American to grant special privilege to the professions, particularly the legal profession. A number of states passed statutes upholding the right of every voter of good moral character to practice law. This attitude appears to have resulted in a rising tide of irresponsibility and commercialism; and a consequent reaction to establish standards of character, education and experience started at the turn of the twentieth century. These standards were promoted as states, one after the other, began to pass registration laws controlling the practices of engineering, architecture, law, and the other professions, and the various national professional organizations adopted their codes of ethics.

Professional activities cannot be based upon the major common law premise used in ordinary business relations *caveat emptor* "let the buyer beware."

A written code of ethics declares before all the world the high standards which are professed and gives an understanding of what the public may expect in their relations with members of the profession. The code also is a helpful guide to the members of the profession in informing them what is expected of each member and what they may expect of each other. The public has come to expect competence, trustworthiness, and expeditious action; and the unethical actions of a few can arouse public indignation which may condemn and punish a profession at large through excessive legislation or boycott. The promotion of and adherence to ethical ideals brings the mutual gain of building respect for oneself by building respect for the profession.

A code of ethics is a set of local rules which represents the sum total evaluation (not merely appraisal) by a group of individuals of wide experience, of past practices and problems which are commonly encountered in the profession. *The Canons of Ethics for Engineers* published in 1947 by the Engineer's Council for Professional Development, have been adopted by most engineering societies and are used as standards of ethical practices by a number of state registration boards. However, many of the engineering societies have also retained their own codes of ethics, primarily because of problems believed unique to that branch of engineering.

The status and history of establishing rules of ethics have been described; now motivation deserves some attention. We all transgress ethical conduct by most definitions to some degree just by our human nature. Sooner or later some body or some group is bound to do something drastic and bring nationwide attention and disgrace to our profession. We are sitting on the proverbial powder keg. The public, the press, and the Government are primed and ready for something to happen. The press is creating a fear of computers through their personification with such headlines as "Meet the Monster that Checks Your Taxes." The "monsters" thus created must now do something terrible to justify this analogy.

Senator Sam J. Irvin of North Carolina, who is chairman of the Subcommittee on Constitutional Rights, was quoted in the March 13, 1967 issue of *Electronic News* as saying that thought should be given to a professional ethics code for the industry ". . . for those who arrange and operate the computer's processes. If self-regulation and self-restraint are not exercised by all concerned with automatic data processing, public concern will soon reach the stage where strict legislative controls will be enacted, Government appropriations for research and development will be denied, and the computer will become the villian of our society." Senator Irvin was promptly informed of the action taken by ACM in adopting the Guidelines. He replied in part as follows: "It is heartening to

me that your association is concerned enough about the potential invasions of privacy occasioned by the indiscriminate use of computers that you would adopt voluntarily a Guideline for Professional Conduct in Information Processing"[9].

On January 10, 1967, the US Department of Justice completed the prosecution of the first federal case involving the criminal use of a computer[10]. A 23-year-old programmer worked for a company which had a contract to provide data processing services for the National City Bank of Minneapolis. The young man programmed and operated NCB Program 107, which processed the bank's checking accounts. He also had his checking account with the bank. In June 1966 he found that he would be in financial difficulty that would make his account overdrawn for several days by $334. He put a "temporary" patch in the program for exception reporting, which caused it to ignore his account in checking for overdrafts. The daily postings showed the overdrawn condition, but exception reports were relied upon. By September 1966 his account was overdrawn by $1357, and the patch was still in the program; but the computer failed one day and manual processing led to the discovery of his activity. The FBI was called in. The young man immediately admitted his guilt and made restitution to the bank. However, because indictment is mandatory in such cases, he was charged with two counts of making false entries in bank records with maximum penalties of $5000 and/ or five years in prison. On January 10, 1967, he received a suspended sentence and two years' probation. He was not a member of a professional society, although he had taken the CDP examination twice. Although the publicity of this incident was local, it did appear in *headlines* on the front page of the *Minneapolis Tribune*. It is certain that more incidents of this type and of a more serious nature will occur with the proliferation of computer usage in increasingly important roles in society.

The status of ethical codes and some of the motivation have been described. An analysis of the adequacy of the ACM Guidelines is in order. We who work with and create logical machines tend to look with scorn on redundancy, vagueness ,and subjective measurements. However, in ethical rules we are not dealing with logical machines and scientific truth. We are engaged in philosophy and in dealing with people. A code of ethics must be considered in this light.

A review of the set of Guidelines will show some of its strengths and weaknesses. The preamble and first part of Section 1 state that a member is to serve "with loyalty his employer, clients

[1] Reprinted with permission of The Macmillan Company. Copyright © Murray I. Mantell 1964.

[2] The IEEE was formed as a merger of the AIEE and IRE, and the code was dropped at the time of merger.

and public." It is easy to think of situations where this leads to conflicting loyalties and seems impossible to follow. Impossible or not, it is the effort to comply and the awareness of possible conflicts which count. Too many of us can become so buried in the technical details of our work that we miss their implications on our environment. This responsibility must be an additional burden on the professional person.

The Guidelines also state that an ACM member "will use his special knowledge and skill for the advancement of human welfare." Consider the use of computers to increase effectiveness of waging war, of killing people. This is not a bizarre problem. The biologists working on methods of bacteriological warfare have a code of ethics also. Some of us feel that human welfare is dependent upon our country's having the ever improving capacity to wage war more effectively against our immoral enemies. Others feel that human welfare is an absolute concept precluding the development and use of methods which kill people. Both sides can base their position on that same quote from the Guidelines.

ACM is not capable of deciding this issue and should not try. ACM must limit itself to its area of competence in this matter by informing the Government, sociologists, economists, and the military of the limitations and capabilities of information processing—but no more. It is the responsibility of the organizations in those other fields to make decisions within their competence and interests. ACM should urge its members to assume their moral obligations as individual citizens and to take part in the shaping of public policy outside our fields.

A resolution was recently adopted by the ACM Washington, D.C. Chapter[11]. It is for the most part a well-worded and appropriate statement warning that the consequences of using computing equipment in public and private data banks may result in loss of privacy, and urging that technical safeguards against misuse be part of the design. However, the resolution went too far by including a warning about the constitutional right of privacy, and stating that laws protecting the individual must be passed. This is an example of a statement outside the area of competence of a technical society in information processing.

Sections 1.3 and 1.4 emphasize our responsibilities to qualify ourselves before expressing opinions in public outside our areas of professional competence. Too many professional people use their eminence in one field to amplify the importance of their partisan views in another field beyond their areas of professional competence. An example might

be the author of this article who at this point claims to be only an amateur philosopher of ethics, and whose background on the subject is limited to two years of part-time study and research as chairman of the ACM Professional Standards and Practices Committee.

Section 2.4 states that we should produce computer programs and information processing systems that work but be willing to take the responsibility and consequences when they don't work. The eminence, stature, and other benefits of being a professional person are not without their price. The responsibility for failure, even if it would have been beyond the control of the most qualified, still rests on the shoulders of the professional person.

The first part of Section 3.3 is purposely vague in its reference to conducting competition on a high plane. Many of us encounter what we think is unethical competition, and there are some obvious cases, but the information processing industry is changing too rapidly to get more specific on this point. An obvious example of rapid change is the recent emergence of software firms.

Section 3.3 also refers to employees as well as the organizations for whom they work and to self-employed individuals. We all compete whether in job advancement or in technical achievement.

The last part of Section 3.3 is also vague in stating that misconduct should be reported to the proper authorities. This could mean the police, a federal regulatory agency, an individual's own professional society, or the accused individual's professional society. It also has serious implications for ACM. Suppose a member complains to ACM that his employer is forcing him to engage in unethical practices. ACM is not yet mature enough or strong enough to formally advise the member, admonish or punish the employer, insure the member economically against discharge from his job, or even to adequately investigate the matter. In fact, it is not yet clear that the membership wants ACM to function in any of these ways. This is why the ACM Council has wisely adopted ethical rules as a *guide* to members rather than a code to be enforced.

A significant amount of discussion has started concerning the adoption of the Guidelines. Louis Fein[12] has been of great help to the author in the development of the Guidelines. However, he disagrees with parts which he feels will have significantly different and conflicting meaning to people of different vocations within the field of information processing. For example the industrialist, consultant, employee, academician,

and scientist each has his own relation to society: the scientist to truth; the industrialist to fair profits; the consultant to his clients; the employee to his employer; and the academician to his students. Therefore, Fein feels that they cannot be included under one ethical umbrella and that for these different vocations a single set of ethical rules becomes ludicrous. ACM must first decide which interests it will support and then discard the rest.

Anthony Oettinger, president of ACM, believes ACM should continue to be a home for all vocations within the information processing field. ACM will avoid a partisan battle for the interest of one against an equally sound interest of another. All interests in the field are interdependent. There are transgressions of ethical conduct which by any reasonable code are clear. ACM can start by acting there[13].

The adoption of ACM Guidelines is only the first small step in a process which will involve years of experience and maturing to recognize and approach adequacy. This first step is justified from the point of view that we must start from some place, even though it is not a perfect start and even though those of the "new morality" of situational ethics barely tolerate ethical maxims while existentialists and antinomians (against law) reject them completely[14]. Tradition and the proven success, (even though partial) of other professional societies strongly motivate us to proceed.

REFERENCES

1. ORDEN, ALEX. The emergence of a profession. *Comm. ACM 10* (Mar. 1967), 145.
2. CAMPISE, J. A. Steps toward professionalism. *J. Data Man. 5* (June 1967), 33–36.
3. Editorial. Maintaining ethical standards. *Civil Engineering* (Apr. 1964).
4. KINN, JOHN M. Personal communication. [Mr. John M. Kinn, IEEE, 345 E. 47 Street, New York, N.Y., Aug. 25, 1966.]
5. DPMA. Certificate in Data Processing Examination and Study Guide, 1966-7.
6. ACM. Revised Constitution of the Association for Computing Machinery, 1965.
7. ALGER, P.L., CHRISTENSEN, N. A. AND OLMSTED, R. *Ethical Problems in Engineering.* Wiley, New York, 1965, App. I, p. 277.
8. MANTELL, MURRAY I. *Ethics and Professionalism in Engineering.* Macmillan, New York, 1964, pp. 59–61.
9. Senator Irvin praises ACM professional ethics activities. *Comm. ACM 8* (Aug. 1967), 524.
10. LEWIS, FINLAY. Computer expert accused of fixing his bank balance. *Minneapolis Tribune,* Vol. C, 1947, Oct. 18, 1966.
11. ACM Washington, D.C. Chapter adopts unified stand on National Data Bank. *Comm. ACM 10* (July 1967), 457.
12. FEIN, LOUIS. ACM has a crisis of identity? *Comm. ACM 10* (Jan. 1967), 1.
13. OETTINGER, ANTHONY. President's letter to the ACM membership. *Comm. ACM 10* (Mar. 1967), 139.
14. FLETCHER, JOSEPH. *Situation Ethics, The New Morality.* Westminster Press, Philadelphia, Pa., 1966.

[4]

The Two Cultures of the Computer Age

Joseph Weizenbaum
Associate Professor of Electrical Engineering and
of Political Science, M.I.T.

The computer can be a force for homogenization
or individuation of our lives. But its ultimate threat
is to those deprived of its power

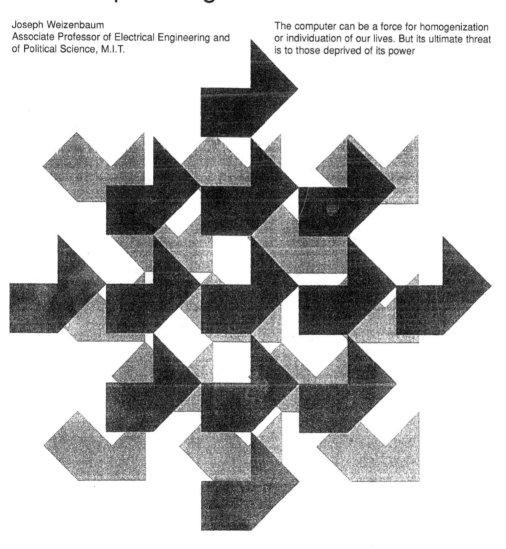

Suppose we had asked 50 years ago how photography was to affect how and where we live. Perhaps we would have perceived photography as being fundamentally a communication technology. Still, I doubt that any of us would have had sufficient foresight to extrapolate from the then-current photographic techniques and practices to today's global television networks.

I do not intend to stretch an analogy too far, but surely we do see now that the technology that is electronic photography—i.e., television—has had enormous and, I would say, irreversible effects on each of our lives. It has profoundly altered the practice of politics in our country. Insofar as it brings what we call entertainment into our homes, it surely has also affected our choice of where we wish to live. And, more importantly, by allowing even the disadvantaged members of our society to vicariously experience the good life we pretend is our national standard, we have unleashed social forces of immeasurable magnitude.

The automobile is another piece of technology that has profoundly altered our way of life within a few generations. When we notice that the machine itself—the automobile—has changed relatively little since its mass production began, we are brought sharply face to face with the fact that, while it may be possible to predict with some confidence a path of technological development of a particular machine, that alone says nothing about our ability to predict its social consequences.

The computer is a child *par excellence* of our era of fantastically rapidly expanding technology. One of the first computers I worked on had a storage capacity of 800 words with an access time of about 20 milliseconds. It fully occupied a very large room and required an elaborate cooling plant. Its cost was about $750,000. A computer of the same memory capacity but 20,000 times faster is today an off-the-shelf sub-component costing under $10,000.

All of the above is an ill-disguised plea to be let off the prediction hook. To put it another way: the technologist himself is perhaps the poorest prepared to forecast the consequences of his technology. The fact is simply that the side effects of technological progress eventually dominate by far the direct effects predictable on the basis of technology itself. And to perceive potential large-scale side effects requires a different insight than that which is the natural by-product of an individual's preoccupation with technology. (It is, by the way, precisely for such reasons that questions over the responsibility of the scientist are becoming ever more urgent and that the very concept of a university devoted entirely to science and technology is no long viable.)

Having disqualified myself, I may safely begin my analyses.

Rescuing Man From His Growth

The computer has at present no effect on *where* we live. But already it affects *how* we live. The first bank deposit accounting computer system was built by the General Electric Company for the Bank of America about 13 years ago. At that time, the bank said that unless the deposit accounting process was soon automated, every adult living in California would have to be hired by the bank to help do its bookkeeping. I cite this in order to show that there are certain normal activities we carry on—apparently just as always—which would have ground to a halt were it not for computer intervention. Perhaps the handling of airline and hotel reservations is another example. The effect then is not very visible—it is merely that we can carry on. It is only when the foresight exercised—by Al Zipf of the Bank of America in that example— is not forthcoming in time that the effects become dramatic. I have in mind the fact that trading in the New York Stock Exchange has had to be repeatedly suspended lately to permit the data processing to catch up with the data flow.

"To merely carry on" sounds so banal. But we must from now on remember the absolutely most overriding fact of our time: we are on the exponential of the population growth curve—both here in the United States and in the world. If—and I emphasize the "if"—the computer permits us to maintain our production and distribution, our finance and our vital statistical services, then that alone will have justified its existence. But I personally do not believe that even an arbitrary growth in national computational capacity will prevent a drastic degradation of our present life style in the face of the population explosion without a simultaneous implementation of social inventions of the highest order of imaginativeness.

The computer, in other words, is a life boat that arrived on the horizon in the nick of time. It is a necessary part of the rescue machinery—but not a sufficient one.

Homogenization vs. Individuation

Another threat facing us as a result of the population explosion is that, even if we can manage to keep our society going in some way, life could become very drab, monotonous, dull. We are in fact experiencing a homogenization of life styles of considerable proportions as it is. There may be some comfort in knowing that a Holiday Inn near Coral Gables, Florida, is indistinguishable from another near Vernal, Utah, or that one cannot tell when waking up in a Hilton Hotel room whether one is in Berlin, Chicago, or Tokyo—but those circum-

compose the novel his life, like each of our lives, really is.

A similar individuating effect can be achieved in each of our perceptions of the world around us. We know that the television news broadcast must of necessity restrict itself to reporting those events in which the largest number of people can be presumed to have an interest. It serves the mass man and is therefore a homogenizing force. The newspaper can be broader in its coverage and attempt to report all the news it deems "fit to print." But once a story becomes stale, no follow-up reporting is done. The election, for example, was no longer interesting one week later. Where could I look then to find out whether Senator Morse finally won or lost in Oregon? A computer system could make it possible for me to keep up with facts that interested me. After it came to know me, so to speak, it could even alert me to developments that I as an individual would find interesting.

We do have newspapers today that cater to special audiences, such as the *Wall Street Journal* and *Women's Wear Daily.* We will soon have the technology to permit the publication of individuated versions; say, of the *New York Times,* which have arrived at their individual styles and contents on the basis of readers' feedback to the publisher. I do not believe that task to be harder than the production miracle Detroit is currently achieving with respect to automobiles.

A Return to the "Cottage Industry"
Let me turn briefly to the question of the impact the computer may have on where we live. I can foresee a return to a kind of cottage industry. For five years now I have had in my home a console attached to the MAC I.B.M. 7094 computer operated by M.I.T.'s Project MAC. There have been many days when I skipped the drive to Cambridge—I live about 20 miles from my office—in order to do my computer work at home. More important from the point of view of portents for the future, there have been many occasions when students and I worked on programs jointly while they were in Cambridge and I was at home and we were all linked through the MAC computer. Dr. Engelbardt of the Stanford Research Institute in Menlo Park, Calif., has an ongoing experiment that clearly demonstrates the feasibility of a computer forming the cohesive element binding together a team of engineers whose members are physically remote from one another. If we are lucky, it may turn out that just when our land and air traffic is at the point of choking us to death, large concerns will have made it possible for their engineers to stay at home—almost no matter where home is.

That many homes will, in the not too distant future,

stances certainly derate the old adage that travel broadens one.

I have never made the computation, but I would guess that the number of different cars one can today specify from, say, General Motors, exceeds their total annual production of automobiles. With the multiplicity of options available with respect to engine size, transmission type, upholstery, exterior and interior colors, and so on *ad infinitum,* it is surprising that any two new cars are exactly like one another. The important point is, of course, not that modern cars have their individuality. It is that the computer-controlled assembly line is making it possible to combine mass production with custom tailoring, so to speak. And the measure of near uniqueness achievable even today is enough to shame an old-time craftsman (if one could be found to witness the phenomenon). Here the computer is performing a service that is more than a holding action and in this area we have reason for considerable optimism.

Let me state quite clearly that we are in the grip of two opposing forces—the one due to the population explosion and running virtually out of control tending to homogenize life, and the other available for us to use at all or not, or wisely or stupidly, that could lead to the enrichment of life through individuation.

Extending Man's Perception and Understanding
The wise application of computing resources can mean not merely an enormous differentiation of the products we consume and the houses and even communities we live in, but of our intellectual and ultimately our emotional lives as well. An example is the enormous impact computers can make in the life-long educational process of the individual. For we can now foresee an educational system which has as its one grand objective to aid the individual in achieving self-indentification. Even late in life, when the computing system has learned so much about him, the individual can use it to, in a sense, consolidate his gains, to review his life and in effect

be equipped with computer consoles—of that there can be no doubt. I believe the home television set will be tied to the telephone and hence to local, state, and national computer services. Much man-computer communication will be in the graphic mode. I suppose that the cost of many of such home consoles and their attendant line and other charges will be borne by the employers of members of the household. But this does not preclude the possibility that a major use of the console will be for entirely personal matters such as shopping, self-education, getting advice of all sorts (including medical advice—from an electronic Dr. Spock), and so on.

New Economics—and New Illiteracy

But not all homes will be so equipped—perhaps not even most homes. I mention this especially in order to point up a serious and dangerous problem we almost certainly have to face, starting right now.

Daniel Bell, in a future issue, will deal with the idea that knowledge is power. We are, in his words, becoming a knowledge society. It is perfectly clear that the access to information is necessary to exercise this power of knowledge. Individuals can therefore be rendered impotent in tomorrow's society simply by being denied access to public computing utilities. One implication of that fact is that information and the power to transform information will become an enormously important resource. We may see a new kind of economics growing up in parallel with the money-based economics we know now—one in which the medium of exchange is time allotments on the national computer utility. I can imagine, for example, that a prize for superior scientific achievement on the part of a research worker might include a few hours of free computer time.

But if the power to manipulate information in a large computer system is really translatable into social and political power, what about that segment of the population that cannot use computing power for lack of training?

They will find themselves in a very isolated position indeed—in an important sense they will be the illiterates of the new society. Perhaps the closest modern Western society has come to having such a population in its midst was during the Nazi German period after Jews were forbidden to use the mails and telephone services. They were thereafter completely cut off from the economic life of the nation.

The danger we face is, to use Daniel Bell's phrase, that we will be creating a new cleavage in society. A large part of our population will enjoy a high standard of living—limited, to be sure, by intense population pressures—and experience the kind of elan that accompanies the sense of full participation in one's society. Meanwhile, the remaining and potentially very large segment of the population will drift further and further away from playing any but the most menial and irrelevant roles and will fall behind at an increasing rate. The magnitude of the social strains this condition can generate is, I believe, presently unimaginable.

We, who are members of today's intellectual and technological elite, may find it easy to speculate on the new marvels of comfort and delight the computer age offers us. Perhaps our reveries are a little disturbed by threats against our privacy. I do not doubt, however, that our capacity for social and political innovation will take us over that hurdle if we so wish it. I think it more appropriate, however—and indeed necessary—to challenge thoughtful technologists and those who work with them to unhesitatingly face and begin to solve the problem of how to prevent the growth of two cultures in our midst—not two cultures in the relatively benign sense of C. P. Snow, but two cultures that, once they come to exist, may render each other into waste.

Joseph Weizenbaum was educated at Wayne State University and had broad industrial experience in computer systems and applications before joining the M.I.T. faculty in 1964. Since then he has been associated with the Institute's Project MAC and with work in the application of computers to the study of political systems, and he has taught in the Departments of Electrical Engineering and Political Science.

[5]

On the Impact
of the Computer on Society

How does one insult a machine?

Joseph Weizenbaum

The structure of the typical essay on "The impact of computers on society" is as follows: First there is an "on the one hand" statement. It tells all the good things computers have already done for society and often even attempts to argue that the social order would already have collapsed were it not for the "computer revolution." This is usually followed by an "on the other hand" caution which tells of certain problems the introduction of computers brings in its wake. The threat posed to individual privacy by large data banks and the danger of large-scale unemployment induced by industrial automation are usually mentioned. Finally, the glorious present and prospective achievements of the computer are applauded, while the dangers alluded to in the second part are shown to be capable of being alleviated by

The author is professor of computer science, Massachusetts Institute of Technology, 545 Technology Square, Cambridge 02139.

sophisticated technological fixes. The closing paragraph consists of a plea for generous societal support for more, and more large-scale, computer research and development. This is usually coupled to the more or less subtle assertion that only computer science, hence only the computer scientist, can guard the world against the admittedly hazardous fallout of applied computer technology.

In fact, the computer has had very considerably less societal impact than the mass media would lead us to believe. Certainly, there are enterprises like space travel that could not have been undertaken without computers. Certainly the computer industry, and with it the computer education industry, has grown to enormous proportions. But much of the industry is self-serving. It is rather like an island economy in which the natives make a living by taking in each other's laundry. The part that is not self-serving is

largely supported by government agencies and other gigantic enterprises that know the value of everything but the price of nothing, that is, that know the short-range utility of computer systems but have no idea of their ultimate social cost. In any case, airline reservation systems and computerized hospitals serve only a tiny, largely the most affluent, fraction of society. Such things cannot be said to have an impact on society generally.

Side Effects of Technology

The more important reason that I dismiss the argument which I have caricatured is that the direct societal effects of any pervasive new technology are as nothing compared to its much more subtle and ultimately much more important side effects. In that sense, the societal impact of the computer has not yet been felt.

To help firmly fix the idea of the importance of subtle indirect effects of technology, consider the impact on society of the invention of the microscope. When it was invented in the middle of the 17th century, the dominant commonsense theory of disease was fundamentally that disease was a punishment visited upon an individual by God. The sinner's body was thought to be inhabited by various so-called humors brought into disequilibrium in accordance with divine justice. The cure for disease was therefore to be found first in penance and second in the balancing of humors as, for example, by bleeding. Bleeding was, after all, both painful, hence punishment and penance, and potentially balancing in that it actually removed substance from the body. The microscope enabled man to see microorganisms and thus paved the way for the germ theory of disease. The enormously surprising discovery of extremely small living organisms also induced the idea of a continuous chain of life which, in turn, was a necessary intellectual precondition for the emergence of Darwinism. Both the germ theory of disease and the theory of evolution profoundly altered man's conception of his contract with God and consequently his self-image. Politically these ideas served to help diminish the power of the Church and, more generally, to legitimize the questioning of the basis of hitherto unchallenged authority. I do not say that the microscope alone was responsible for the enormous social changes that followed its invention. Only that it made possible the kind of paradigm shift, even on the commonsense level, without which these changes might have been impossible.

Is it reasonable to ask whether the computer will induce similar changes in man's image of himself and whether that influence will prove to be its most important effect on society? I think so, although I hasten to add that I don't believe the computer has yet told us much about man and his nature. To come to grips with the question, we must first ask in what way the computer is different from man's many other machines. Man has built two fundamentally different kinds of machines, nonautonomous and autonomous. An autonomous machine is one that operates for long periods of time, not on the basis of inputs from the real world, for example from sensors or from human drivers, but on the basis of internalized models of some aspect of the real world. Clocks are examples of autonomous machines in that they operate on the basis of an internalized model of the planetary system. The computer is, of course, the example par excellence. It is able to internalize models of essentially unlimited complexity and of a fidelity limited only by the genius of man.

It is the autonomy of the computer we value. When, for example, we speak of the power of computers as increasing with each new hardware and software development, we mean that, because of their increasing speed and storage capacity, and possibly thanks to new programming tricks, the new

computers can internalize ever more complex and ever more faithful models of ever larger slices of reality. It seems strange then that, just when we exhibit virtually an idolatry of autonomy with respect to machines, serious thinkers in respected academies [I have in mind B. F. Skinner of Harvard University (*1*)] can rise to question autonomy as a fact for man. I do not think that the appearance of this paradox at this time is accidental. To understand it, we must realize that man's commitment to science has always had a masochistic component.

Time after time science has led us to insights that, at least when seen superficially, diminish man. Thus Galileo removed man from the center of the universe, Darwin removed him from his place separate from the animals, and Freud showed his rationality to be an illusion. Yet man pushes his inquiries further and deeper. I cannot help but think that there is an analogy between man's pursuit of scientific knowledge and an individual's commitment to psychoanalytic therapy. Both are undertaken in the full realization that what the inquirer may find may well damage his self-esteem. Both may reflect his determination to find meaning in his existence through struggle in truth, however painful that may be, rather than to live without meaning in a world of ill-disguised illusion. However, I am also aware that sometimes people enter psychoanalysis unwilling to put their illusions at risk, not searching for a deeper reality but in order to convert the insights they hope to gain to personal power. The analogy to man's pursuit of science does not break down with that observation.

Each time a scientific discovery shatters a hitherto fundamental cornerstone of the edifice on which man's self-esteem is built, there is an enormous reaction, just as is the case under similar circumstances in psychoanalytic therapy. Powerful defense mechanisms, beginning with denial and usually terminating in rationalization, are brought to bear. Indeed, the psychoanalyst suspects that, when a patient appears to accept a soul-shattering insight without resistance, his very casualness may well mask his refusal to allow that insight truly operational status in his self-image. But what is the psychoanalyst to think about the patient who positively embraces tentatively proffered, profoundly humiliating self-knowledge,

when he embraces it and instantly converts it to a new foundation of his life? Surely such an event is symptomatic of a major crisis in the mental life of the patient.

I believe we are now at the beginning of just such a crisis in the mental life of our civilization. The microscope, I have argued, brought in its train a revision of man's image of himself. But no one in the mid-17th century could have foreseen that. The possibility that the computer will, one way or another, demonstrate that, in the inimitable phrase of one of my esteemed colleagues, "the brain is merely a meat machine" is one that engages academicians, industrialists, and journalists in the here and now. How has the computer contributed to bringing about this very sad state of affairs? It must be said right away that the computer alone is not the chief causative agent. It is merely an extreme extrapolation of technology. When seen as an inducer of philosophical dogma, it is merely the reductio ad absurdum of a technological ideology. But how does it come to be regarded as a source of philosophic dogma?

Theory versus Performance

We must be clear about the fact that a computer is nothing without a program. A program is fundamentally a transformation of one computer into another that has autonomy and that, in a very real sense, behaves. Programming languages describe dynamic processes. And, most importantly, the processes they describe can be actually carried out. Thus we can build models of any aspect of the real world that interests us and that we understand. And we can make our models work. But we must be careful to remember that a computer model is a description that works. Ordinarily, when we speak of A being a model of B, we mean that a theory about some aspects of the behavior of B is also a theory of the same aspects of the behavior of A. It follows that when, for example, we consider a computer model of paranoia, like that published by Colby *et al.* (*2*), we must not be persuaded that it tells us anything about paranoia on the grounds that it, in some sense, mirrors the behavior of a paranoiac. After all, a plain typewriter in some sense mirrors the behavior of an autistic child (one types a question and gets no response whatever), but it does not help us to understand autism. A model must be made to stand or fall on the basis of its theory. Thus, while programming languages may have put a new power in the hands of social scientists in that this new notation may have freed them from the vagueness of discursive descriptions, their obligation to build defensible theories is in no way diminished. Even errors can be pronounced with utmost formality and eloquence. But they are not thereby transmuted to truth.

The failure to make distinctions between descriptions, even those that "work," and theories accounts in large part for the fact that those who refuse to accept the view of man as machine have been put on the defensive. Recent advances in computer understanding of natural language offer an excellent case in point. Halle and Chomsky, to mention only the two with whom I am most familiar, have long labored on a theory of language which any model of language behavior must satisfy (3). Their aim is like that of the physicist who writes a set of differential equations that anyone riding a bicycle must satisfy. No physicist claims that a person need know, let alone be able to solve, such differential equations in order to become a competent cyclist. Neither do Halle and Chomsky claim that humans know or knowingly obey the rules they believe to govern language behavior. Halle and Chomsky also strive, as do physical theorists, to identify the constants and parameters of their theories with components of reality. They hypothesize that their rules constitute a kind of projective description of certain aspects of the structure of the human mind. Their problem is thus not merely to discover economical rules to account for language behavior, but also to infer economic mechanisms which determine that precisely those rules are to be preferred over all others. Since they are in this way forced to attend to the human mind, not only that of speakers of English, they must necessarily be concerned with all human language behavior—not just that related to the understanding of English.

The enormous scope of their task is illustrated by their observation that in all human languages declarative sentences are often transformed into questions by a permutation of two of their

words. (John is here → Is John here?) It is one thing to describe rules that transform declarative sentences into questions—a simple permutation rule is clearly insufficient—but another thing to describe a "machine" that necessitates those rules when others would, all else being equal, be simpler. Why, for example, is it not so that declarative sentences read backward transform those sentences into questions? The answer must be that other constraints on the "machine" combine against this local simplicity in favor of a more nearly global economy. Such examples illustrate the depth of the level of explanation that Halle and Chomsky are trying to achieve. No wonder that they stand in awe of their subject matter.

Workers in computer comprehension of natural language operate in what is usually called performance mode. It is as if they are building machines that can ride bicycles by following heuristics like "if you feel a displacement to the left, move your weight to the left." There can be, and often is, a strong interaction between the development of theory and the empirical task of engineering systems whose theory is not yet thoroughly understood. Witness the synergistic cooperation between aerodynamics and aircraft design in the first quarter of the present century. Still, what counts in performance mode is not the elaboration of theory but the performance of systems. And the systems being hammered together by the new crop of computer semanticists are beginning (just beginning) to perform.

Since computer scientists have recognized the importance of the interplay of syntax, semantics, and pragmatics, and with it the importance of computer-manipulable knowledge, they have made progress. Perhaps by the end of the present decade, computer systems will exist with which specialists, such as physicians and chemists and mathematicians, will converse in natural language. And surely some part of such achievements will have been based on other successes in, for example, computer simulation of cognitive processes. It is understandable that any success in this area, even if won empirically and without accompanying enrichments of theory, can easily lead to certain delusions being planted. Is it, after all, not terribly tempting to believe that a computer that understands natural lan-

guage at all, however narrow the context, has captured something of the essence of man? Descartes himself might have believed it. Indeed, by way of this very understandable seduction, the computer comes to be a source of philosophical dogma.

I am tempted to recite how performance programs are composed and how things that don't work quite correctly are made to work via all sorts of strategems which do not even pretend to have any theoretical foundation. But the very asking of the question, "Has the computer captured the essence of man?" is a diversion and, in that sense, a trap. For the real question "Does man understand the essence of man?" cannot be answered by technology and hence certainly not by any technological instrument.

The Technological Metaphor

I asked earlier what the psychoanalyst is to think when a patient grasps a tentatively proffered deeply humiliating interpretation and attempts to convert it immediately to a new foundation of his life. I now think I phrased that question too weakly. What if the psychoanalyst merely coughed and the cough entrained the consequences of which I speak? That is our situation today. Computer science, particularly its artificial intelligence branch, has coughed. Perhaps the press has unduly amplified that cough—but it is only a cough nevertheless. I cannot help but think that the eagerness to believe that man's whole nature has suddenly been exposed by that cough, and that it has been shown to be a clockwork, is a symptom of something terribly wrong.

What is wrong, I think, is that we have permitted technological metaphors, what Mumford (4) calls the "Myth of the Machine," and technique itself to so thoroughly pervade our thought processes that we have finally abdicated to technology the very duty to formulate questions. Thus sensible men correctly perceive that large data banks and enormous networks of computers threaten man. But they leave it to technology to formulate the corresponding question. Where a simple man might ask: "Do we need these things?", technology asks "what electronic wizardry will make them safe?" Where a simple man will ask "is it good?", technology asks "will it work?" Thus science, even wisdom, becomes what technology and most of all computers can handle. Lest this be thought to be an exaggeration, I quote from the work of H. A. Simon, one of the most senior of American computer scientists (*5*):

> As we succeed in broadening and deepening our knowledge—theoretical and empirical—about computers, we shall discover that in large part their behavior is governed by simple general laws, that what appeared as complexity in the computer program was, to a considerable extent, complexity of the environment to which the program was seeking to adapt its behavior.
>
> To the extent that this prospect can be realized, it opens up an exceedingly important role for computer simulation as a tool for achieving a deeper understanding of human behavior. For if it is the organization of components, and not their physical properties, that largely determines behavior, and if computers are organized somewhat in the image of man, then the computer becomes an obvious device for exploring the consequences of alternative organizational assumptions for human behavior.

and

> A man, viewed as a behaving system, is quite simple. The apparent complexity of his behavior over time is largely a reflection of the complexity of the environment in which he finds himself.
>
> . . . I believe that this hypothesis holds even for the whole man.

We already know that those aspects of the behavior of computers which cannot be attributed to the complexity of their programs is governed by simple general laws—ultimately by the laws of Boolean algebra. And of course the physical properties of the computer's components are nearly irrelevant to its behavior. Mechanical relays are logically equivalent to tubes and to transistors and to artificial neurons. And of course the complexity of computer programs is due to the complexity of the environments, including the computing environments themselves, with which they were designed to deal. To what else could it possibly be due? So, what Simon sees as prospective is already realized. But does this collection of obvious and simple facts lead to the conclusion that man is as simple as are computers? When Simon leaps to that conclusion and then formulates the issue as he has done here, that is, when he suggests that the behavior of *the whole man* may be understood in terms of the behavior of computers as gov-

erned by simple general laws, then the very possibility of understanding man as an autonomous being, as an individual with deeply internalized values, that very possibility is excluded. How does one insult a machine?

The question "Is the brain merely a meat machine?", which Simon puts in a so much more sophisticated form, is typical of the kind of question formulated by, indeed formulatable only by, a technological mentality. Once it is accepted as legitimate, arguments as to what a computer can or cannot do "in principle" begin to rage and themselves become legitimate. But the legitimacy of the technological question—for example, is human behavior to be understood either in terms of the organization or of the physical properties of "components"—need not be admitted in the first instance. A human question can be asked instead. Indeed, we might begin by asking what has already become of "the whole man" when he can conceive of computers organized in his own image.

The success of technique and of some technological explanations has, as I've suggested, tricked us into permitting technology to formulate important questions for us—questions whose very forms severely diminish the number of degrees of freedom in our range of decision-making. Whoever dictates the questions in large part determines the answers. In that sense, technology, and especially computer technology, has become a self-fulfilling nightmare reminiscent of that of the lady who dreams of being raped and begs her attacker to be kind to her. He answers "it's your dream, lady." We must come to see that technology is our dream and that we must ultimately decide how it is to end.

I have suggested that the computer revolution need not and ought not to call man's dignity and autonomy into question, that it is a kind of pathology that moves men to wring from it unwarranted, enormously damaging interpretations. Is then the computer less threatening that we might have thought? Once we realize that our visions, possibly nightmarish visions, determine the effect of our own creations on us and on our society, their threat to us is surely diminished. But that is not to say that this realization alone will wipe out all danger. For example, apart from the erosive effect of a technological mentality on man's self-image, there are practical attacks

on the freedom and dignity of man in which computer technology plays a critical role.

I mentioned earlier that computer science has come to recognize the importance of building knowledge into machines. We already have a machine —Dendral—(*6*) that commands more chemistry than do many Ph.D. chemists, and another—Mathlab—(*7*) that commands more applied mathematics than do many applied mathematicians. Both Dendral and Mathlab contain knowledge that can be evaluated in terms of the explicit theories from which it was derived. If the user believes that a result Mathlab delivers is wrong, then, apart from possible program errors, he must be in disagreement, not with the machine or its programmer, but with a specific mathematical theory. But what about the many programs on which management, most particularly the government and the military, rely, programs which can in no sense be said to rest on explicable theories but are instead enormous patchworks of programming techniques strung together to make them work?

Incomprehensible Systems

In our eagerness to exploit every advance in technique we quickly incorporate the lessons learned from machine manipulation of knowledge in theory-based systems into such patchworks. They then "work" better. I have in mind systems like target selection systems used in Vietnam and war games used in the Pentagon, and so on. These often gigantic systems are put together by teams of programmers, often working over a time span of many years. But by the time the systems come into use, most of the original programmers have left or turned their attention to other pursuits. It is precisely when gigantic systems begin to be used that their inner workings can no longer be understood by any single person or by a small team of individuals. Norbert Wiener, the father of cybernetics, foretold this phenomenon in a remarkably prescient article (*8*) published more than a decade ago. He said there:

> It may well be that in principle we cannot make any machine the elements of whose behavior we cannot comprehend sooner or later. This does not mean in any way that we shall be able to comprehend these elements in substantially less

time than the time required for operation of the machine, or even within any given number of years or generations.

An intelligent understanding of [machines'] mode of performance may be delayed until long after the task which they have been set has been completed. This means that though machines are theoretically subject to human criticism, such criticism may be ineffective until long after it is relevant.

This situation, which is now upon us, has two consequences: first that decisions are made on the basis of rules and criteria no one knows explicitly, and second that the system of rules and criteria becomes immune to change. This is so because, in the absence of detailed understanding of the inner workings of a system, any substantial modification is very likely to render the system altogether inoperable. The threshold of complexity beyond which this phenomenon occurs has already been crossed by many existing systems, including some compiling and computer operating systems. For example, no one likes the operating systems for certain large computers, but they cannot be substantially changed nor can they be done away with. Too many people have become dependent on them.

An awkward operating system is inconvenient. That is not too bad. But the growing reliance on supersystems that were perhaps designed to help people make analyses and decisions, but which have since surpassed the understanding of their users while at the same time becoming indispensable to them, is another matter. In modern war it is common for the soldier, say the bomber pilot, to operate at an enormous psychological distance from his victims. He is not responsible for burned children because he never sees their village, his bombs, and certainly not the flaming children themselves. Modern technological rationalizations of war, diplomacy, politics, and commerce such as computer games have an even more insidious effect on the making of policy. Not only have policy makers abdicated their decision-making responsibility to a technology they don't understand, all the while maintaining the illusion that they, the policy makers, are formulating policy questions and answering them, but responsibility has altogether evaporated. No human is any longer responsible for "what the machine says." Thus there can be neither right nor wrong, no question of justice, no theory with which one

can agree or disagree, and finally no basis on which one can challenge "what the machine says." My father used to invoke the ultimate authority by saying to me, "it is written." But then I could read what was written, imagine a human author, infer his values, and finally agree or disagree. The systems in the Pentagon, and their counterparts elsewhere in our culture, have in a very real sense no authors. They therefore do not admit of exercises of imagination that may ultimately lead to human judgment. No wonder that men who live day in and out with such machines and become dependent on them begin to believe that men are merely machines. They are reflecting what they themselves have become.

The potentially tragic impact on society that may ensue from the use of systems such as I have just discussed is greater than might at first be imagined. Again it is side effects, not direct effects, that matter most. First, of course, there is the psychological impact on individuals living in a society in which anonymous, hence irresponsible, forces formulate the large questions of the day and circumscribe the range of possible answers. It cannot be surprising that large numbers of perceptive individuals living in such a society experience a kind of impotence and fall victim to the mindless rage that often accompanies such experiences. But even worse, since computer-based knowledge systems become essentially unmodifiable except in that they can grow, and since they induce dependence and cannot, after a certain threshold is crossed, be abandoned, there is an enormous risk that they will be passed from one generation to another, always growing. Man too passes knowledge from one generation to another. But because man is mortal, his transmission of knowledge over the generations is at once a process of filtering and accrual. Man doesn't merely pass knowledge, he rather regenerates it continuously. Much as we may mourn the crumbling of ancient civilizations, we know nevertheless that the glory of man resides as much in the evolution of his cultures as in that of his brain. The unwise use of ever larger and ever more complex computer systems may well bring this process to a halt. It could well replace the ebb and flow of culture with a world without values, a world in which what counts for a fact has long ago been determined and forever fixed.

Positive Effects

I've spoken of some potentially dangerous effects of present computing trends. Is there nothing positive to be said? Yes, but it must be said with caution. Again, side effects are more important than direct effects. In particular, the idea of computation and of programming languages is beginning to become an important metaphor which, in the long run, may well prove to be responsible for paradigm shifts in many fields. Most of the common-sense paradigms in terms of which much of mankind interprets the phenomena of the everyday world, both physical and social, are still deeply rooted in fundamentally mechanistic metaphors. Marx's dynamics as well as those of Freud are, for example, basically equilibrium systems. Any hydrodynamicist could come to understand them without leaving the jargon of his field. Languages capable of describing ongoing processes, particularly in terms of modular subprocesses, have already had an enormous effect on the way computer people think of every aspect of their worlds, not merely those directly related to their work. The information-processing view of the world so engendered qualifies as a genuine metaphor. This is attested to by the fact that it (i) constitutes an intellectual framework that permits new questions to be asked about a wide-ranging set of phenomena, and (ii) that it itself provides criteria for the adequacy of proffered answers. A new metaphor is important not in that it may be better than existing ones, but rather in that it may enlarge man's vision by giving him yet another perspective on his world. Indeed, the very effectiveness of a new metaphor may seduce lazy minds to adopt it as a basis for universal explanations and as a source of panaceas. Computer simulation of social processes has already been advanced by single-minded generalists as leading to general solutions of all of mankind's problems.

The metaphors given us by religion, the poets, and by thinkers like Darwin, Newton, Freud, and Einstein have rather quickly penetrated to the language of ordinary people. These metaphors have thus been instrumental in shaping our entire civilization's imaginative reconstruction of our world. The computing metaphor is as yet available to only an extremely small set of people. Its acquisition and internalization, hopefully as only one of many ways to see the world, seems to require experience in program composition, a kind of computing literacy. Perhaps such literacy will become very widespread in the advanced societal sectors of the advanced countries. But, should it become a dominant mode of thinking and be restricted to certain social classes, it will prove not merely repressive in the ordinary sense, but an enormously divisive societal force. For then classes which do and do not have access to the metaphor will, in an important sense, lose their ability to communicate with one another. We know already how difficult it is for the poor and the oppressed to communicate with the rest of the society in which they are embedded. We know how difficult it is for the world of science to communicate with that of the arts and of the humanities. In both instances the communication difficulties, which have grave consequences, are very largely due to the fact that the respective communities have unsharable experiences out of which unsharable metaphors have grown.

Responsibility

Given these dismal possibilities, what is the responsibility of the computer scientist? First I should say that most of the harm computers can potentially entrain is much more a function of properties people attribute to computers than of what a computer can or cannot actually be made to do. The nonprofessional has little choice but to make his attributions of properties to computers on the basis of the propaganda emanating from the computer community and amplified by the press. The computer professional therefore has an enormously important responsibility to be modest in his claims. This advice would not even have to be voiced if computer science had a tradition of scholarship and of self-criticism such as that which characterizes the established sciences. The mature scientist stands in awe before the depth of his subject matter. His very humility is the wellspring of his strength. I regard the instilling of just this kind of humil-

ity, chiefly by the example set by teachers, to be one of the most important missions of every university department of computer science.

The computer scientist must be aware constantly that his instruments are capable of having gigantic direct and indirect amplifying effects. An error in a program, for example, could have grievous direct results, including most certainly the loss of much human life. On 11 September 1971, to cite just one example, a computer programming error caused the simultaneous destruction of 117 high-altitude weather balloons whose instruments were being monitored by an earth satellite (9). A similar error in a military command and control system could launch a fleet of nuclear tipped missiles. Only censorship prevents us from knowing how many such events involving nonnuclear weapons have already occurred. Clearly then, the computer scientist has a heavy responsibility to make the fallibility and limitations of the systems he is capable of designing brilliantly clear. The very power of his systems should serve to inhibit the advice he is ready to give and to constrain the range of work he is willing to undertake.

Of course, the computer scientist, like everyone else, is responsible for his actions and their consequences. Sometimes that responsibility is hard to accept because the corresponding authority to decide what is and what is not to be done appears to rest with distant and anonymous forces. That technology itself determines what is to be done by a process of extrapolation and that individuals are powerless to intervene in that determination is precisely the kind of self-fulfilling dream from which we must awaken. Consider gigantic computer systems. They are, of course, natural extrapolations of the large systems we already have. Computer networks are another point on the same curve extrapolated once more. One may ask whether such systems can be used by anybody except by governments and very large corporations and whether such organizations will not use them mainly for antihuman purposes. Or consider speech recogni-

tion systems. Will they not be used primarily to spy on private communications? To answer such questions by saying that big computer systems, computer networks, and speech recognition systems are inevitable is to surrender one's humanity. For such an answer must be based either on one's profound conviction that society has already lost control over its technology or on the thoroughly immoral position that "if I don't do it, someone else will."

I don't say that systems such as I have mentioned are necessarily evil—only that they may be and, what is most important, that their inevitability cannot be accepted by individuals claiming autonomy, freedom, and dignity. The individual computer scientist can and must decide. The determination of what the impact of computers on society is to be is, at least in part, in his hands.

Finally, the fundamental question the computer scientist must ask himself is the one that every scientist, indeed every human, must ask. It is not "what shall I do?" but rather "what shall I be?" I cannot answer that for anyone save myself. But I will say again that if technology is a nightmare that appears to have its own inevitable logic, it is our nightmare. It is possible, given courage and insight, for man to deny technology the prerogative to formulate man's questions. It is possible to ask human questions and to find humane answers.

References and Notes

1. B. F. Skinner, *Beyond Freedom and Dignity* (Knopf, New York, 1971).
2. K. M. Colby, S. Weber, F. D. Hilf, *Artif. Intell.* 1, 1 (1971).
3. N. Chomsky, *Aspects of the Theory of Syntax* (M.I.T. Press, Cambridge, Mass., 1965); and M. Halle, *The Sound Pattern of English* (Harper & Row, New York, 1968).
4. L. Mumford, *The Pentagon of Power* (Harcourt, Brace, Jovanovich, New York, 1970).
5. H. A. Simon, *The Sciences of the Artificial* (M.I.T. Press, Cambridge, Mass., 1969), pp. 22–25.
6. B. Buchanan, G. Sutherland, E. A. Feigenbaum, in *Machine Intelligence*, B. Meltzer, Ed. (American Elsevier, New York, 1969).
7. W. A. Martin and R. J. Fateman, "The Macsyma system," in *Proceedings of the 2nd Symposium on Symbolic and Algebraic Manipulation* (Association for Computer Machines, New York, 1971); J. Moses, *Commun. Assoc. Computer Mach.* 14 (No. 8), 548 (1971).
8. N. Wiener, *Science* 131, 1355 (1960).
9. R. Gillette, *ibid.* 174, 477 (1971).

[6]

WHAT IS COMPUTER ETHICS?*

JAMES H. MOOR

A Proposed Definition

Computers are special technology and they raise some special ethical issues. In this essay I will discuss what makes computers different from other technology and how this difference makes a difference in ethical considerations. In particular, I want to characterize computer ethics and show why this emerging field is both intellectually interesting and enormously important.

On my view, *computer ethics* is the analysis of the nature and social impact of computer technology and the corresponding formulation and justification of policies for the ethical use of such technology. I use the phrase "computer technology" because I take the subject matter of the field broadly to include computers and associated technology. For instance, I include concerns about software as well as hardware and concerns about networks connecting computers as well as computers themselves.

A typical problem in computer ethics arises because there is a policy vacuum about how computer technology should be used. Computers provide us with new capabilities and these in turn give us new choices for action. Often, either no policies for conduct in these situations exist or existing policies seem inadequate. A central task of computer ethics is to determine what we should do in such cases, i.e., to formulate policies to guide our actions. Of course, some ethical situations confront us as individuals and some as a society. Computer ethics includes consideration of both personal and social policies for the ethical use of computer technology.

Now it may seem that all that needs to be done is the mechanical application of an ethical theory to generate the appropriate policy. But this is usually not possible. A difficulty is that along with a policy vacuum there is often a conceptual vacuum. Although a problem in computer ethics may seem clear initially, a little reflection reveals a conceptual muddle. What is needed in such cases is an analysis which provides a coherent conceptual framework within which to formulate a policy for action. Indeed, much of the important work in computer ethics is devoted to proposing conceptual frameworks for understanding ethical problems involving computer technology.

An example may help to clarify the kind of conceptual work that is required. Let's suppose we are trying to formulate a policy for protecting computer programs. Initially, the idea may seem clear enough. We are looking for a policy for protecting a kind of intellectual property. But then a

---

* Editor's footnote: This article is the prize-winning essay in *Metaphilosophy*'s essay competition on computer ethics.

number of questions which do not have obvious answers emerge. What is a computer program? Is it really intellectual property which can be owned or is it more like an idea, an algorithm, which is not owned by anybody? If a computer program is intellectual property, is it an *expression* of an idea that is owned (traditionally protectable by copyright) or is it a *process* that is owned (traditionally protectable by patent)? Is a machine-readable program a copy of a human-readable program? Clearly, we need a conceptualization of the nature of a computer program in order to answer these kinds of questions. Moreover, these questions must be answered in order to formulate a useful policy for protecting computer programs. Notice that the conceptualization we pick will not only affect how a policy will be applied but to a certain extent what the facts are. For instance, in this case the conceptualization will determine when programs count as instances of the same program.

Even within a coherent conceptual framework, the formulation of a policy for using computer technology can be difficult. As we consider different policies we discover something about what we value and what we don't. Because computer technology provides us with new possibilities for acting, new values emerge. For example, creating software has value in our culture which it didn't have a few decades ago. And old values have to be reconsidered. For instance, assuming software is intellectual property, why should intellectual property be protected? In general, the consideration of alternative policies forces us to discover and make explicit what our value preferences are.

The mark of a basic problem in computer ethics is one in which computer technology is *essentially* involved and there is an uncertainty about what to do and even about how to understand the situation. Hence, not all ethical situations involving computers are central to computer ethics. If a burglar steals available office equipment including computers, then the burglar has done something legally and ethically wrong. But this is really an issue for general law and ethics. Computers are only *accidently* involved in this situation, and there is no policy or conceptual vacuum to fill. The situation and the applicable policy are clear.

In one sense I am arguing for the special status of computer ethics as a field of study. Applied ethics is not simply ethics applied. But, I also wish to stress the underlying importance of general ethics and science to computer ethics. Ethical theory provides categories and procedures for determining what is ethically relevant. For example, what kinds of things are good? What are our basic rights? What is an impartial point of view? These considerations are essential in comparing and justifying policies for ethical conduct. Similarly, scientific information is crucial in ethical evaluations. It is amazing how many times ethical disputes turn not on disagreements about values but on disagreements about facts.

On my view, computer ethics is a dynamic and complex field of study which considers the relationships among facts, conceptualizations, policies and values with regard to constantly changing computer technology. Computer ethics is not a fixed set of rules which one shellacs and hangs on the wall. Nor is computer ethics the rote application of ethical principles to a value-free technology. Computer ethics requires us to think anew about the nature of computer technology and our values. Although computer ethics is a field between science and ethics and depends on them, it is also a discipline in its own right which provides both conceptualizations for understanding and policies for using computer technology.

Though I have indicated some of the intellectually interesting features of computer ethics, I have not said much about the problems of the field or about its practical importance. The only example I have used so far is the issue of protecting computer programs which may seem to be a very narrow concern. In fact, I believe the domain of computer ethics is quite large and extends to issues which affect all of us. Now I want to turn to a consideration of these issues and argue for the practical importance of computer ethics. I will proceed not by giving a list of problems but rather by analyzing the conditions and forces which generate ethical issues about computer technology. In particular, I want to analyze what is special about computers, what social impact computers will have, and what is operationally suspect about computing technology. I hope to show something of the nature of computer ethics by doing some computer ethics.

The Revolutionary Machine

What is special about computers? It is often said that a Computer Revolution is taking place, but what is it about computers that makes them revolutionary? One difficulty in assessing the revolutionary nature of computers is that the word "revolutionary" has been devalued. Even minor technological improvements are heralded as revolutionary. A manufacturer of a new dripless pouring spout may well promote it as revolutionary. If minor technological improvements are revolutionary, then undoubtedly everchanging computer technology is revolutionary. The interesting issue, of course, is whether there is some nontrivial sense in which computers are revolutionary. What makes computer technology importantly different from other technology? Is there any real basis for comparing the Computer Revolution with the Industrial Revolution?

If we look around for features that make computers revolutionary, several features suggest themselves. For example, in our society computers are affordable and abundant. It is not much of an exaggeration to say that currently in our society every major business, factory, school, bank, and hospital is rushing to utilize computer technology. Millions of personal computers are being sold for home use. Moreover, computers are integral parts of products which don't look much like computers such as watches and automobiles. Computers are abundant and inexpensive, but so are pencils. Mere abundance and affordability don't seem sufficient to justify any claim to technological revolution.

One might claim the newness of computers makes them revolutionary. Such a thesis requires qualification. Electronic digital computers have been around for forty years. In fact, if the abacus counts as a computer, then computer technology is among the oldest technologies. A better way to state this claim is that recent engineering advances in computers make them revolutionary. Obviously, computers have been immensely improved over the last forty years. Along with dramatic increases in computer speed and memory there have been dramatic decreases in computer size. Computer manufacturers are quick to point out that desk top computers today exceed the engineering specifications of computers which filled rooms only a few decades ago. There has been also a determined effort by companies to make computer hardware and computer software easier to use. Computers may not be completely user friendly but at least they are much less unfriendly. However, as important as these features are, they don't seem to get to the heart of the Computer Revolution. Small, fast, powerful and easy-to-use electric can openers are great improvements over earlier can openers, but they aren't in the relevant sense revolutionary.

Of course, it is important that computers are abundant, less expensive, smaller, faster, and more powerful and friendly. But, these features serve as enabling conditions for the spread of the Computer Revolution. The essence of the Computer Revolution is found in the nature of a computer itself. What is revolutionary about computers is *logical malleability*. Computers are logically malleable in that they can be shaped and molded to do any activity that can be characterized in terms of inputs, outputs, and connecting logical operations. Logical operations are the precisely defined steps which take a computer from one state to the next. The logic of computers can be massaged and shaped in endless ways through changes in hardware and software. Just as the power of a steam engine was a raw resource of the Industrial Revolution so the logic of a computer is a raw resource of the Computer Revolution. Because logic applies everywhere, the potential applications of computer technology appear limitless. The computer is the nearest thing we have to a universal tool. Indeed, the limits of computers are largely the limits of our own creativity. The driving question of the Computer Revolution is "How can we mold the logic of computers to better serve our purposes?"

I think logical malleability explains the already widespread application of computers and hints at the enormous impact computers are destined to have. Understanding the logical malleability of computers is essential to understanding the power of the developing technological revolution. Understanding logical malleability is also important in setting policies for the use of computers. Other ways of conceiving computers serve less well as a basis for formulating and justifying policies for action.

Consider an alternative and popular conception of computers in which computers are understood as number crunchers, i.e., essentially as numerical devices. On this conception computers are nothing but big calculators. It might be maintained on this view that mathematical and scientific applications should take precedence over nonnumerical applications such as word processing. My position, on the contrary, is that computers are logically malleable. The arithmetic interpretation is certainly a correct one, but it is only one among many interpretations. Logical malleability has both a syntactic and a semantic dimension. Syntactically, the logic of computers is malleable in terms of the number and variety of possible states and operations. Semantically, the logic of computers is malleable in that the states of the computer can be taken to represent anything. Computers manipulate symbols but they don't care what the symbols represent. Thus, there is no ontological basis for giving preference to numerical applications over non-numerical applications.

The fact that computers can be described in mathematical language, even at a very low level, doesn't make them essentially numerical. For example, machine language is conveniently and traditionally expressed in 0's and 1's. But the 0's and 1's simply designate different physical states. We could label these states as "on" and "off" or "yin" and "yang" and apply binary logic. Obviously, at some levels it is useful to use mathematical notation to describe computer operations, and it is reasonable to use it. The mistake is to reify the mathematical notation as the essence of a computer and then use this conception to make judgments about the appropriate use of computers.

In general, our conceptions of computer technology will affect our policies for using it. I believe the importance of properly conceiving the nature and impact of computer technology will increase as the Computer Revolution unfolds.

Anatomy of the Computer Revolution

Because the Computer Revolution is in progress, it is difficult to get a perspective on its development. By looking at the Industrial Revolution I believe we can get some insight into the nature of a technological revolution. Roughly, the Industrial Revolution in England occurred in two major stages. The first stage was the technological introduction stage which took place during the last half of the Eighteenth Century. During this stage inventions and processes were introduced, tested, and improved. There was an industrialization of limited segments of the economy, particularly in agriculture and textiles. The second stage was the technological permeation stage which took place during the Nineteenth Century. As factory work increased and the populations of cities swelled, not only did well known social evils emerge, but equally significantly corresponding changes in human activities and institutions, ranging from labor unions to health services, occurred. The forces of industrialization dramatically transformed the society.

My conjecture is that the Computer Revolution will follow a similar two stage development. The first stage, the introduction stage, has been occurring during the last forty years. Electronic computers have been created and refined. We are gradually entering the second stage, the permeation stage, in which computer technology will become an integral part of institutions throughout our society. I think that in the coming decades many human activities and social institutions will be transformed by computer technology and

WHAT IS COMPUTER ETHICS?   271

that this transforming effect of computerization will raise a wide range of issues for computer ethics.

What I mean by "transformed" is that the basic nature or purpose of an
activity or institution is changed. This is marked by the kinds of questions
that are asked. During the introduction stage computers are understood as
tools for doing standard jobs. A typical question for this stage is "How well
does a computer do such and such an activity?" Later, during the permeation
stage, computers become an integral part of the activity. A typical question
for this stage is "What is the nature and value of such and such an activity?"
In our society there is already some evidence of the transforming effect of
computerization as marked by the kind of questions being asked.

For example, for years computers have been used to count votes. Now the
election process is becoming highly computerized. Computers can be used to
count votes and to make projections about the outcome. Television networks
use computers both to determine quickly who is winning and to display the
results in a technologically impressive manner. During the last presidential
election in the United States the television networks projected the results
not only before the polls in California were closed but also before the polls
in New York were closed. In fact, voting was still going on in over half the
states when the winner was announced. The question is no longer "How
efficiently do computers count votes in a fair election?" but "What is a fair
election?" Is it appropriate that some people know the outcome before they
vote? The problem is that computers not only tabulate the votes for each
candidate but likely influence the number and distribution of these votes.
For better or worse, our electoral process is being transformed.

As computers permeate more and more of our society, I think we will
see more and more of the transforming effect of computers on our basic institutions and practices. Nobody can know for sure how our computerized
society will look fifty years from now, but it is reasonable to think that various aspects of our daily work will be transformed. Computers have been used
for years by businesses to expedite routine work, such as calculating payrolls;
but as personal computers become widespread and allow executives to work
at home, and as robots do more and more factory work, the emerging question will be not merely "How well do computers help us work?" but "What
is the nature of this work?"

Traditional work may no longer be defined as something that normally
happens at a specific time or a specific place. Work for us may become less
doing a job than instructing a computer to do a job. As the concept of work
begins to change, the values associated with the old concept will have to be
reexamined. Executives who work at a computer terminal at home will lose
some spontaneous interaction with colleagues. Factory workers who direct
robots by pressing buttons may take less pride in a finished product. And
similar effects can be expected in other types of work. Commercial pilots
who watch computers fly their planes may find their jobs to be different
from what they expected.

JAMES H. MOOR

A further example of the transforming effect of computer technology is found in financial institutions. As the transfer and storage of funds becomes increasingly computerized the question will be not merely "How well do computers count money?" but "What is money?" For instance, in a cashless society in which debits are made to one's account electronically at the point of sale, has money disappeared in favor of computer records or have electronic impulses become money? What opportunities and values are lost or gained when money becomes intangible?

Still another likely area for the transforming effect of computers is education. Currently, educational packages for computers are rather limited. Now it is quite proper to ask "How well do computers educate?" But as teachers and students exchange more and more information indirectly via computer networks and as computers take over more routine instructional activities, the question will inevitably switch to "What is education?" The values associated with the traditional way of educating will be challenged. How much human contact is necessary or desirable for learning? What is education when computers do the teaching?

The point of this futuristic discussion is to suggest the likely impact of computer technology. Though I don't know what the details will be, I believe the kind of transformation I am suggesting is likely to occur. This is all I need to support my argument for the practical importance of computer ethics. In brief, the argument is as follows: The revolutionary feature of computers is their logical malleability. Logical malleability assures the enormous application of computer technology. This will bring about the Computer Revolution. During the Computer Revolution many of our human activities and social institutions will be transformed. These transformations will leave us with policy and conceptual vacuums about how to use computer technology. Such policy and conceptual vacuums are the marks of basic problems within computer ethics. Therefore, computer ethics is a field of substantial practical importance.

I find this argument for the practical value of computer ethics convincing. I think it shows that computer ethics is likely to have increasing application in our society. This argument does rest on a vision of the Computer Revolution which not everyone may share. Therefore, I will turn to another argument for the practical importance of computer ethics which doesn't depend upon any particular view of the Computer Revolution. This argument rests on the invisibility factor and suggests a number of ethical issues confronting computer ethics now.

The Invisibility Factor

There is an important fact about computers. Most of the time and under most conditions computer operations are invisible. One may be quite knowledgeable about the inputs and outputs of a computer and only dimly aware of the internal processing. This invisibility factor often generates policy vacuums about how to use computer technology. Here I will mention three kinds of invisibility which can have ethical significance.

The most obvious kind of invisibility which has ethical significance is invisible abuse. *Invisible abuse* is the intentional use of the invisible operations of a computer to engage in unethical conduct. A classic example of this is the case of a programmer who realized he could steal excess interest from a bank. When interest on an bank account is calculated, there is often a fraction of a cent left over after rounding off. This programmer instructed a computer to deposit these fractions of a cent to his own account. Although this is an ordinary case of stealing, it is relevant to computer ethics in that computer technology is essentialy involved and there is a question about what policy to institute in order to best detect and prevent such abuse. Without access to the program used for stealing the interest or to a sophisticated accounting program such an activity may easily go unnoticed.

Another possibility for invisible abuse is the invasion of the property and privacy of others. A computer can be programmed to contact another computer over phone lines and surreptitiously remove or alter confidential information. Sometimes an inexpensive computer and a telephone hookup is all it takes. A group of teenagers, who named themselves the "414s" after the Milwaukee telephone exchange, used their home computers to invade a New York hospital, a California bank, and a government nuclear weapons laboratory. These break-ins were done as pranks, but obviously such invasions can be done with malice and be difficult or impossible to detect.

A particularly insidious example of invisible abuse is the use of computers for surveillance. For instance, a company's central computer can monitor the work done on computer terminals far better and more discreetly than the most dedicated sweatshop manager. Also, computers can be programmed to monitor phone calls and electronic mail without giving any evidence of tampering. A Texas oil company, for example, was baffled why it was always outbid on leasing rights for Alaskan territory until it discovered another bidder was tapping its data transmission lines near its Alaskan computer terminal.

A second variety of the invisibility factor, which is more subtle and conceptually interesting than the first, is the presence of invisible programming values. *Invisible programming values* are those values which are embedded in a computer program.

Writing a computer program is like building a house. No matter how detailed the specifications may be, a builder must make numerous decisions about matters not specified in order to construct the house. Different houses are compatible with a given set of specifications. Similarly, a request for a computer program is made at a level of abstraction usually far removed from the details of the actual programming language. In order to implement a program which satisfies the specifications a programmer makes some value judgments about what is important and what is not. These values become embedded in the final product and may be invisible to someone who runs the program.

274   JAMES H. MOOR

Consider, for example, computerized airline reservations. Many different programs could be written to produce a reservation service. American Airlines once promoted such a service called "SABRE". This program had a bias for American Airline flights built in so that sometimes an American Airline flight was suggested by the computer even if it was not the best flight available. Indeed, Braniff Airlines, which went into bankruptcy for awhile, sued American Airlines on the grounds that this kind of bias in the reservation service contributed to its financial difficulties.

Although the general use of a biased reservation service is ethically suspicious, a programmer of such a service may or may not be engaged in invisible abuse. There may be a difference between how a programmer intends a program to be used and how it is actually used. Moreover, even if one sets out to create a program for a completely unbiased reservation service, some value judgments are latent in the program because some choices have to be made about how the program operates. Are airlines listed in alphabetical order? Is more than one listed at a time? Are flights just before the time requested listed? For what period after the time requested are flights listed? Some answers, at least implicitly, have to be given to these questions when the program is written. Whatever answers are chosen will build certain values into the program.

Sometimes invisible programming values are so invisible that even the programmers are unaware of them. Programs may have bugs or may be based on implicit assumptions which don't become obvious until there is a crisis. For example, the operators of the ill-fated Three Mile Island nuclear power plant were trained on a computer which was programmed to simulate possible malfunctions including malfunctions which were dependent on other malfunctions. But, as the Kemeny Commission which investigated the disaster discovered, the simulator was not programmed to generate simultaneous, independent malfunctions. In the actual failure at Three Mile Island the operators were faced with exactly this situation – simultaneous, independent malfunctions. The inadequacy of the computer simulation was the result of a programming decision, as unconscious or implicit as that decision may have been. Shortly after the disaster the computer was reprogrammed to simulate situations like the one that did occur at Three Mile Island.

A third variety of the invisibility factor, which is perhaps the most disturbing, is *invisible complex calculation*. Computers today are capable of enormous calculations beyond human comprehension. Even if a program is understood, it does not follow that the calculations based on that program are understood. Computers today perform and certainly supercomputers in the future will perform calculations which are too complex for human inspection and understanding.

An interesting example of such complex calculation occurred in 1976 when a computer worked on the four color conjecture. The four color problem, a puzzle mathematicians have worked on for over a century, is to show that a map can be colored with at most four colors so that no adjacent areas have the same color. Mathematicians at the University of Illinois broke the problem down into thousands of cases and programmed computers to consider them. After more than a thousand hours of computer time on various computers, the four color conjecture was proved correct. What is interesting about this mathematical proof, compared to traditional proofs, is that it is largely invisible. The general structure of the proof is known and found in the program and any particular part of the computer's activity can be examined, but practically speaking the calculations are too enormous for humans to examine them all.

The issue is how much we should trust a computer's invisible calculations. This becomes a significant ethical issue as the consequences grow in importance. For instance, computers are used by the military in making decisions about launching nuclear weapons. On the one hand, computers are fallible and there may not be time to confirm their assessment of the situation. On the other hand, making decisions about launching nuclear weapons without using computers may be even more fallible and more dangerous. What should be our policy about trusting invisible calculations?

A partial solution to the invisibility problem may lie with computers themselves. One of the strengths of computers is the ability to locate hidden information and display it. Computers can make the invisible visible. Information which is lost in a sea of data can be clearly revealed with the proper computer analysis. But that's the catch. We don't always know when, where, and how to direct the computer's attention.

The invisibility factor presents us with a dilemma. We are happy in one sense that the operations of a computer are invisible. We don't want to inspect every computerized transaction or program every step for ourselves or watch every computer calculation. In terms of efficiency the invisibility factor is a blessing. But it is just this invisibility that makes us vulnerable. We are open to invisible abuse or invisible programming of inappropriate values or invisible miscalculation. The challenge for computer ethics is to formulate policies which will help us deal with this dilemma. We must decide when to trust computers and when not to trust them. This is another reason why computer ethics is so important.

Dartmouth College
Hanover, NH 03755 USA

[7]

Four Ethical Issues of the Information Age

Richard O. Mason

Today in western societies more people are employed collecting, handling and distributing information than in any other occupation. Millions of computers inhabit the earth and many millions of miles of optical fiber, wire and air waves link people, their computers and the vast array of information handling devices together. Our society is truly an information society, our time an information age. The question before us now is whether the kind of society being created is the one we want. It is a question that should especially concern those of us in the MIS community for we are in the forefront of creating this new society.

There are many unique challenges we face in this age of information. They stem from the nature of information itself. Information is the means through which the mind expands and increases its capacity to achieve its goals, often as the result of an input from another mind. Thus, information forms the intellectual capital from which human beings craft their lives and secure dignity.

However, the building of intellectual capital is vulnerable in many ways. For example, people's intellectual capital is impaired whenever they lose their personal information without being compensated for it, when they are precluded access to information which is of value to them, when they have revealed information they hold intimate, or when they find out that the information upon which their living depends is in error. The social contract among people in the information age must deal with these threats to human dignity. The ethical issues involved are many and varied, however, it is helpful to focus on just four. These may be summarized by means of an acronym — **PAPA.**

Privacy: What information about one's self or one's associations must a person reveal to others, under what conditions and with what safeguards? What things can people keep to themselves and not be forced to reveal to others?

Accuracy: Who is responsible for the authenticity, fidelity and accuracy of information? Similarly, who is to be held accountable for errors in information and how is the injured party to be made whole?

Property: Who owns information? What are the just and fair prices for its exchange?

Who owns the channels, especially the airways, through which information is transmitted? How should access to this scarce resource be allocated?

Accessibility: What information does a person or an organization have a right or a privilege to obtain, under what conditions and with what safeguards?

Privacy

What information should one be required to divulge about one's self to others? Under what conditions? What information should one be able to keep strictly to one's self? These are among the questions that a concern for privacy raises. Today more than ever cautious citizens must be asking these questions.

Two forces threaten our privacy. One is the growth of information technology, with its enhanced capacity for surveillance, communication, computation, storage, and retrieval. A second, and more insidious threat, is the increased value of information in decision-making. Information is increasingly valuable to policy makers; they covet it even if acquiring it invades another's privacy.

A case in point is the situation that occurred a few years ago in Florida. The Florida Legislature believed that the state's building codes might be too stringent and that, as a result, the taxpayers were burdened by paying for buildings which were underutilized. Several studies were commissioned. In one study at the Tallahassee Community College, monitors were stationed at least one day a week in every bathroom.

Every 15 seconds, the monitor observed the usage of the toilets, mirrors, sinks and other facilities and recorded them on a form. This data was subsequently entered into a database for further analyses. Of course the students, faculty and staff complained bitterly, feeling that this was an invasion of their privacy and a violation of their rights. State officials responded however, that the study would provide valuable information for policy making. In effect the State argued that the value of the information to the administrators was greater than any possible indignities suffered by the students and others. Soon the ACLU joined the fray. At their insistence the study was stopped, but only after the state got the information it wanted.

Most invasions of privacy are not this dramatic or this visible. Rather, they creep up on us slowly as, for example, when a group of diverse files relating to a person and his or her activities are integrated into a single large database. Collections of information reveal intimate details about a person and can thereby deprive the person of the opportunity to form certain professional and personal relationships. This is the ultimate cost of an invasion of privacy. So why do we integrate databases in the first place? It is because the bringing together of disparate data makes the development of new informational relationships possible. These new relationships may be formed, however, without the affected parties' permission. You or I may have contributed information about ourselves freely to each of the separate databases but that by itself does not amount to giving consent to someone to merge the data, especially if that merger might reveal something else about us.

Consider the story that was circulating during the early 1970s. It's probably been embellished in the retellings but it goes something like this. It seems that a couple of programmers at the city of Chicago's computer center began matching tape files from many of the city's different data processing applications on name and I.D. They discovered, for example, that several high paid city employers had unpaid parking fines. Bolstered by this revelation they pressed on. Soon they uncovered the names of several employees who were still listed on the register but who had not paid a variety of fees, a few of whom appeared in the files of the alcoholic and drug abuse program. When this finding was leaked to the public the city employees, of course, were furious. They demanded to know who had authorized the investigation. The answer

was that no one knew. Later, city officials established rules for the computer center to prevent this form of invasion of privacy from happening again. In light of recent proposals to develop a central federal databank consisting of files from most U.S. government agencies, this story takes on new meaning. It shows what can happen when a group of eager computer operators or unscrupulous administrators start playing around with data.

The threat to privacy here is one that many of us don't fully appreciate. I call it the threat of exposure by *minute description*. It stems from the collection of attributes about ourselves and use of the logical connector "and." For example, I may authorize one institution to collect information "A" about me, and another institution to collect information "B" about me; but I might not want anyone to possess "A and B" about me at the same time. When "C" is added to the list of conjunctions, the possessor of the new information will know even more about me. And then "D" is added and so forth. Each additional weaving together of my attributes reveals more and more about me. In the process, the fabric that is created poses a threat to my privacy.

The threads which emanate from this foreboding fabric usually converge in personnel files and in dossiers, as Aleksandr Solzhenitsyn describes in *The Cancer Ward*:

". . . Every person fills out quite a few forms in his life, and each form contains an uncounted number of questions. The answer of just one person to one question in one form is already a thread linking that person forever with the local center of the dossier department. Each person thus radiates hundreds of such threads, which all together, run into the millions. If these threads were visible, the heavens would be webbed with them, and if they had substance and resilience, the buses, streetcars and the people themselves would no longer be able to move. . . . They are neither visible, nor material, but they were constantly felt by man. . . .

Constant awareness of these invisible threads naturally bred respect for the people in charge of that most intricate dossier department. It bolstered their authority." [1, p. 221].

The threads leading to Americans are many. The United States Congress' Privacy Protection Commission, chaired by David F. Linowes, estimated that there are over 8,000 different record systems in the files of the federal government that contain individually identifiable data on citizens. Each citizen, on average, has 17 files in federal agencies and administrations. Using these files, for example, Social Security data has been matched with Selective Service data to reveal draft resisters. IRS data has been matched with other administrative records to tease out possible tax evaders. Federal employment records have been matched with delinquent student loan records to identify some 46,860 federal and military employees and retirees whose pay checks might be garnished. In Massachusetts welfare officials sent tapes bearing welfare recipients Social Security numbers to some 117 banks to find out whether the recipients had bank accounts in excess of the allowable amount. During the first pass some 1600 potential violaters were discovered.

Computer matching and the integration of data files into a central databank have enormous ethical implications. On the one hand, the new information can be used to uncover criminals and to identify service requirements for the needy. On the other hand, it provides powerful political knowledge for those few who have access to it and control over it. It is ripe for privacy invasion and other abuses. For this reason many politicians have spoken out against centralized governmental databanks. As early as 1966 Representative Frank Horton of New York described the threat as follows:

> "The argument is made that a central data bank would use only the type of information that now exists and since no new principle is involved, existing types of safeguards will be adequate. This is fallacious. Good computermen know that one of the most practical of our present safeguards of privacy is the fragmented nature of present information. It is scattered in little bits and pieces across the geography and

years of our life. Retrieval is impractical and often impossible. A central data bank removes completely this safeguard. I have every confidence that ways will be found for all of us to benefit from the great advances of the computermen, but those benefits must never be purchased at the price of our freedom to live as individuals with private lives . . ." [2, p. 6].

There is another threat inherent in merging data files. Some of the data may be in error. More than 60,000 state and local agencies, for example, provide information to the National Crime Information Center and it is accessed by law officers nearly 400,000 times a day. Yet studies show that over 4% of the stolen vehicle entries, 6% of the warrant entries, and perhaps as much as one half of the local law enforcement criminal history records are in error. At risk is the safety of the law enforcement officers who access it, the effectiveness of the police in controlling crime, and the freedom of the citizens whose names appear in the files. This leads to a concern for accuracy.

Accuracy

Misinformation has a way of fouling up people's lives, especially when the party with the inaccurate information has an advantage in power and authority. Consider the plight of one Louis Marches. Marches, an immigrant, was a hard working man who, with his wife Eileen, finally saved enough money to purchase a home in Los Angeles during the 1950s. They took out a long term loan from Crocker National Bank. Every month Louis Marches would walk to his neighborhood bank, loan coupon book in hand, to make his payment of $195.53. He always checked with care to insured that the teller had stamped "paid" in his book on the proper line just opposite the month for which the payment was due. And he continued to do this long after the bank had converted to its automated loan processing system.

One September a few years ago Marches was notified by the bank that he had failed to make his current house payment. Marches grabbed his coupon book, marched to the bank and, in broken English that showed traces of his old country heritage, tried to explain to the teller that this dunning notice was wrong. He had made his payment he claimed. The stamp on his coupon book proved that he had paid. The teller punched Marches' loan number on the keyboard and reviewed the resulting screen. Unfortunately she couldn't confirm Marches' claim, nor subsequently could the head teller, nor the branch manager. When faced with a computer generated screen that clearly showed that his account was delinquent, this hierarchy of bankers simply ignored the entries recorded in his coupon book and also his attendant raving. Confused, Marches left the bank in disgust.

In October, however, Marches dutifully went to the bank to make his next payment. He was told that he could not make his October payment because he was one month in arrears. He again showed the teller his stamped coupon book. She refused to accept it and he stormed out of the bank. In November he returned on schedule as he had done for over 20 years and tried to make his payment again, only to be told that he was now two months in arrears. And so it went until inevitably the bank foreclosed. Eileen learned of the foreclosure from an overzealous bank debt collector while she was in bed recovering from a heart attack. She collapsed upon hearing the news and suffered a near fatal stroke which paralzyed her right side. Sometime during this melee Marches, who until this time had done his own legal work, was introduced to an attorney who agreed to defend him. They sued the bank. Ultimately, after months of anguish, the Marches received a settlement for $268,000. All that the bank officials who testified could say was, "Computers make mistakes. Banks make mistakes, too."

A special burden is placed on the accuracy of information when people rely on it for matters of life and death, as we increasingly do. This came to light in a recent $3.2 million lawsuit charging the National Weather Service for failing to predict accurately a storm that raged on the southeast slope of Georges Bank in 1980. As Peter Brown steered his ship — the Sea Fever — from Hyannis Harbor toward his lobster traps near Nova Scotia, he monitored weather conditions using a long range, single sideband radio capable of receiving weather

forecasts at least 100 miles out to sea. The forecasts assured him that his destination area near Georges Bank, although it might get showers, was safe from the hurricane-like storm that the weather bureau had predicted would go far to the east of his course. So he kept to his course. Soon, however, his ship was engulfed in howling winds of 80 knots and waves cresting at 60 feet. In the turbulence Gary Brown, a crew member, was washed overboard.

The source of the fatal error was failure of a large scale information system which collects data from high atmosphere balloons, satellites, ships, and a series of buoys. This data is then transmitted to a National Oceanographic and Atmospheric Administration computer which analyzes it and produces forecasts. The forecasts, in turn, are broadcast widely.

The forecast Peter Brown relied on when he decided to proceed into the North Atlantic was in error because just one buoy — station 44003 Georges Bank — was out of service. As a result the wind speed and direction data it normally provided were lost to the computer model. This caused the forecasted trajectory of the storm to be canted by several miles, deceiving skipper Peter Brown and consequently sending Gary Brown to his death.

Among the questions this raises for us in the information age are these: "How many Louis Marches and Gary Browns are there out there?" "How many are we creating everyday?" The Marches received a large financial settlement; but can they ever be repaid for the irreparable harm done to them and to their dignity? Honour Brown, Gary's widow, received a judgment in her case; but has she been repaid for the loss of Gary? The point is this: We run the risk of creating Gary Browns and Louis Marches every time we design information systems and place information in databases which might be used to make decisions. So it is our responsibility to be vigilant in the pursuit of accuracy in information. Today we are producing so much information about so many people and their activities that our exposure to problems of inaccuracy is enormous. And this growth in information also raises another issue: Who owns it?

Property

One of the most complex issues we face as a society is the question of intellectual property rights. There are substantial economic and ethical concerns surrounding these rights; concerns revolving around the special attributes of information itself and the means by which it is transmitted. Any individual item of information can be extremely costly to produce in the first instance. Yet, once it is produced, that information has the illusive quality of being easy to reproduce and to share with others. Moreover, this replication can take place without destroying the original. This makes information hard to safeguard since, unlike tangible property, it becomes communicable and hard to keep it to one's self. It is even difficult to secure appropriate reimbursements when somebody else uses your information.

We currently have several imperfect institutions that try to protect intellectual property rights. Copyrights, patents, encryption, oaths of confidentiality, and such old fashioned values as trustworthiness and loyalty are the most commonly used protectors of our intellectual property. Problem issues, however, still abound in this area. Let us focus on just one aspect: artifical intelligence and its expanding subfield, expert systems.

To fully appreciate our moral plight regarding expert systems it is necessary to run back the clock a bit, about two hundred years, to the beginnings of another society: the steam energy-industrial society. From this vantage point we may anticipate some of the problems of the information society.

As the industrial age unfolded in England and Western Europe a significant change took place in the relationship between people and their work. The steam engine replaced manpower by reducing the level of personal physical energy required to do a job. The factory system, as Adam Smith described in his essay on the pin factory, effectively replaced the laborer's contribution of his energy and of his skills. This was done by means of new machines and new organizational forms. The process was carried even further in the French community of Lyon. There, Joseph Marie Jacquard created a weaving loom in which a system of rectangular, punched holes captured the weaver's skill for directing the loom's mechanical fingers and for controlling the warp and weft of the threads. These Jacquard looms created a new kind of capital which was produced by disembodying energy and skill from the craftsmen and then reembodying it into the machines. In effect, an exchange of property took place. Weaving skills were transferred from the craftsman to the owner of the machines. With this technological innovation Lyon eventually regained its position as one of the leading silk producers in the world. The weavers themselves, however, suffered unemployment and degradation because their craft was no longer economically viable. A weavers value as a person and a craftsman was taken away by the new machines.

There is undoubtedly a harbinger of things to come in these 18th century events. As they unfolded civilization witnessed one of the greatest outpourings of moral philosophy it has as ever seen: Adam Smith's *Theory of Moral Sentiments* and his *Wealth of Nations;* the American revolution and its classic documents on liberty and freedom; the French revolution and its concern for fraternity and equality; John Stuart Mill and Jeremy Bentham and their ethical call for the greatest good for the greatest number, and Immanuel Kant and his categorical imperative which leads to an ethical utopia called the "kingdom of ends." All of this ethical initiative took place within the historically short span of time of about 50 years. Common to these ideas was a spirit which sought a new meaning in human life and which demanded that a just allocation be made of social resources.

Today that moral spirit may be welling up within us again. Only this time it has a different provocator. Nowhere is the potential threat to human dignity so severe as it is in the age of information technology, especially in the field of artificial intelligence. Practitioners of artificial intelligence proceed by extracting knowledge from experts, workers and the knowledgeable, and then implanting it into computer software where it becomes capital in the economic sense. This process of "disemminding" knowledge from an individual, and subsequently "emminding" it into machines transfers control of the property to those who own the hardware and software. Is this exchange of property warranted? Consider some of the most successful commercial artificial intelligence systems of the day. Who owns, for example, the chemical knowledge contained in DYNDREL, the medical knowledge contained in MYCIN, or the geological knowledge contained in PROSPECTOR. How is the contributor of his knowledge to be compensated? These are among the issues we must resolve as more intelligent information systems are created.

Concern over intellectual property rights relates to the content of information. There are some equally pressing property rights issues surrounding the conduits through which information passes. Bandwidth, the measure of capacity to carry information, is a scarce and ultimately fixed commodity. It is a "commons." A commons is like an empty vessel into which drops of water can be placed freely and easily until it fills and overflows. Then its capacity is gone. As a resource it is finite.

In an age in which people benefit by the communication of information, there is a tendency for us to treat bandwidth and transmission capacity as a commons in the same way as did the herdsmen in Garrett Hardin's poignant essay, "The Tragedy of the Commons," (subtitled: "The population problem has no technical solution; it requires a fundamental extension in morality). Each herdsman received direct benefits from adding an animal to a pasture shared in common. As long as there was plenty of grazing capacity the losses due to the animal's consumption were spread among them and felt only indirectly and proportionally much less. So each herdsman was motivated to increase his flock. In the end, however, the commons was destroyed and everybody lost.

Today our airways are becoming clogged with a plethora of data, voice, video, and message transmission. Organizations and individuals are expanding their use of communications because it is profitable for them to do so. But if the social checks on the expanded use of bandwidth are inadequate, and a certain degree of temperance isn't followed, we may find that jamming and noise will destroy the flow of clear information through the air. How will the limited resource of bandwidth be allocated? Who will have access? This leads us to the fourth issue.

Access

Our main avenue to information is through literacy. Literacy, since about 1500 A.D. when the Syrians first conceived of a consonant alphabet, has been a requirement for full participation in the fabric of society. Each innovation in information handling, from the invention of paper to the modern computer, has placed new demands on achieving literacy. In an information society a citizen must possess at least three things to be literate:

One must have the intellectual skills to deal with information. These are skills such as reading, writing, reasoning, and calculating. This is a task for education.

One must have access to the information technologies which store, convey and process information. This includes libraries, radios, televisions, telephones, and increasingly, personal computers or terminals linked via networks to mainframes. This is a problem in social economics.

Finally, one must have access to the information itself. This requirement returns to the issue of property and is also a problem in social economics.

These requirements for literacy are a function of both the knowledge level and the economic level of the individual. Unfortunately, for many people in the world today both of these levels are currently deteriorating.

There are powerful factors working both for and against contemporary literacy in our organizations and in our society. For example, the cost of computation, as measured in, say dollars per MIPS (millions of instructions per second), has gone down exponentially since the introduction of computers. This trend has made technology more accessible and economically attainable to more people. However, corporations and other public and private organizations have benefited the most from these economies. As a result, cost economies in computation are primarily available to middle and upper income people. At the same time computer usage flourishes among some, we are creating a large group of information poor people who have no direct access to the more efficient computational technology and who have little training in its use.

Reflect for a moment on the social effects of electronically stored databases. Prior to their invention, vast quantities of data about publications, news events, economic and social statistics, and scientific findings have been available in printed, microfilm, or microfiche form at a relatively low cost. For most of us access to this data has been substantially free. We merely went to our public or school library. The library, in turn, paid a few hundred dollars for the service and made it available to whomever asked for it. Today, however, much of this information is being converted to computerized databases and the cost to access these databases can run in the thousands of dollars.

Frequently, access to databases is gained only by means of acquiring a terminal or personal computer. For example, if you want access to the *New York Times Index* through the Mead Corporation service you must first have access to a terminal and communication line and then pay additional hook-up and access fees in order to obtain the data. This means that the people who wish to use this service possess several things. First, they know that the database exists and how to use it. Second, they have acquired the requisite technology to access it. And third, they are able to pay the fees for the data. Thus the educational and economic ante is really quite high for playing the modern information game. Many people cannot or choose not to pay it and hence are excluded from participating fully in our society. In effect, they become information "drop outs" and in the long run will become the source of many social problems.

PAPA

Privacy, accuracy, property and accessibility, these are the four major issues of information ethics for the information age. Max Plank's 1900 conception that energy was released in small discrete packets called "quanta" not only gave rise to atomic theory but also permitted the development of information technology as well. Semiconductors, transistors,

integrated circuits, photoelectric cells, vacuum tubes, and ferrite cores are among the technological yield of this scientific theory. In a curious way quantum theory underlies the four issues as well. Plank's theory, and all that followed it, have led us to a point where the stakes surrounding society's policy agenda are incredibly high. At stake with the use of nuclear energy is the very survival of mankind itself. If we are unwise we will either blow ourselves up or contaminate our world forever with nuclear waste. At stake with the increased use of information technology is the quality of our lives should we, or our children, survive. If we are unwise many people will suffer information bankruptcy or desolation.

Our moral imperative is clear. We must insure that information technology, and the information it handles, are used to enhance the dignity of mankind. To achieve these goals we must formulate a new social contract, one that insures everyone the right to fulfill his or her own human potential.

In the new social contract information systems should not unduly invade a person's privacy to avoid the indignities that the students in Tallahassee suffered.

Information systems must be accurate to avoid the indignities the Marches and the Browns suffered.

Information systems should protect the viability of the fixed conduit resource through which it is transmitted to avoid noise and jamming pollution and the indignities of "The Tragedy of the Commons."

Information systems should protect the sanctity of intellectual property to avoid the indignities of unwitting "disemmindment" of knowledge from individuals.

And information systems should be accessible to avoid the indignities of information illiteracy and deprivation.

This is a tall order; but it is one that we in the MIS community should address. We must assume some responsibility for the social contract that emerges from the systems that we design and implement. In summary, we must insure that the flow of those little packets of

energy and information called quanta, that
Max Plank bequeathed to us some 85 years
ago, are used to create the kind of world in
which we wish to live.

References

[1] Solzhenitsyn, Aleksandr I., *The Cancer Ward*, Dial Press, New York, New York, 1968.

[2] U.S. House of Representatives, *The Computer and Invasion of Privacy*, U.S. Government Printing Office, Washington D.C., 1966.

Richard O. Mason
Carr P. Collins Distinguished
Professor of Management
Information Sciences
Edwin L. Cox School of Business
Southern Methodist University
Dallas, Texas

[8]

Is there an Ethics of Computing?

GEOFFREY BROWN

The following essay was awarded the Society for Applied Philosophy Essay Prize for 1990.

ABSTRACT   *The article constitutes an attempt to answer the question contained in the title, by reference to three example topics: individual privacy, ownership of software, and computer 'hacking'. The ethical question is approached via the legal one of whether special, computer-specific legislation is appropriate. The conclusion is in the affirmative, and rests on the claim that computer technology has brought with it, not so much the potential for committing totally new kinds of crimes, as a distinctive set of linguistic and conceptual apparatus which makes it necessary to describe computer-related activity in special ways.*

The subject of this article is the ethics of computing, and the question I want to ask in it is: does such a topic exist? This may seem odd, since in one sense it obviously does. Any profession or activity must be governed by some ethical principles, if only because the things which go on in it will be instances of more general categories of behaviour which are so governed. Lying to a business client is a kind of lying, and cheating at Bridge is a kind of cheating. If this were the end of the story, things would be simple. However in some areas, especially in the various professions, people often want to say that there is a special 'ethics' concerned with that activity—for instance medical ethics or political ethics. It is in this second sense that I want to ask whether computing ethics is a distinctive subject.

Now although there are many disanalogies between ethics and law, I believe that in this case it will be helpful to approach the ethical question via the legal one. For a great deal of effort has been expended by lawyers and jurists over the past decade, in discussing the pros and cons of special legislation to cover certain computing activities. I am going to talk about three areas in which such controversy has recently taken place: the areas of privacy, ownership of software, and computer 'hacking'. The first two I will discuss very briefly by way of preamble, and the third, which is perhaps the most topical, in slightly greater detail. Having done so, I will return finally to the general ethical question.

Computers and Privacy

The *Data Protection Act 1984* was introduced at least partly with the intention of protecting the privacy of individuals [1]. This is interesting in itself, since there had already been a long-standing controversy regarding the desirability or otherwise of special laws regarding privacy generally (the USA has explicit privacy laws, Britain does not). But, even granted that privacy is a proper category in its own right, and not a rag-bag of bits and pieces which really belong elsewhere, why should privacy with regard to computerised data be given separate treatment? In the case of the *Data Protection Act*, one reason was purely pragmatic: legislation which covered people's notebooks and diaries as well as databases, would have been unwieldy and unworkable.

But there is, I think, a more important reason, which comes in two parts. First, information cannot simply be regarded as one object of privacy among other candidates such as sex, grief, financial transactions or religious devotions. Information is not just one other thing which, in a given culture at a given time, we may wish to keep private. For it is in the nature of information that it is has an object: it is potentially *about* all these other things, and is therefore, in a sense, a 'second-order' issue.

Secondly, information stored electronically has a special status, in that it has significantly different properties from 'hard copy', i.e. information written or typed on paper or similar medium. For one thing, its representation inside the machine or on a disk or tape, is very unlike a straight-forward written copy: it is stored merely as a pattern of 1s and 0s which is a kind of encoding and will vary depending on the particular code employed, and which will be illegible to anyone who does not know that code. In its electronic form, the data may be copied, recopied, compressed, uncompressed, sent across a network, and be subject to many more operations which make no sense in connection with hard copy. With recently explored techniques of 'distributed representation' aimed at mimicking the way human memory is thought to work, it may not even be located in any identifiable place, but be held only as a pattern of connection strengths between elements. If a piece of data in such a form can be said to have and retain an identity, it is in some rather extended sense of 'identity'. However this might be, if legislation is required to protect privacy with regard to electronic data, it will have to be legislation which looks rather different from the sort intended to deal only with conventional methods of record-keeping. The significance of this will emerge in dealing with our other two topics.

Computers and Ownership

It can hardly have escaped anyone's notice that the past few years have seen many calls for changes in the law regarding rights over computer software, and particularly rights of ownership over the ideas embodied in a particular program. In short, the writers of software do not want their ideas to be exploited for commercial gain by others who have done nothing to develop them, or to reimburse the originator. Unfortunately, this requirement has been found very difficult to articulate and codify, just as it has been found difficult to extract from existing legislation in the areas of copyright, patent and trade secrets [2]. The reason for this lies in a dichotomy which is perhaps not obvious to anyone unfamiliar with the concepts of computing and mathematics: the dichotomy between a *program* and an *algorithm*. A computer program is a piece of software written in a particular programming language, by a particular programmer at a particular time. The algorithm, on the other hand, is the underlying method of which the program is an instance, and of which other programs, possibly written in other languages, will also be instances.

For example, if we want to find out the length of the circumference of a circle given its radius, the algorithm for doing so is to multiply the radius by *pi* and double the result. Computer programs which do this could be written in a variety of languages, and differing programs which do it could be written within the same programming language: but they would all be said to exemplify the same algorithm, for they all boil down to $c = 2\ pi\ r$.

The relevance of this is that when we ask what it is that the law is being called on to protect the originator's rights over, it is unclear whether it is the program or the algorithm that is in question. There are things to be said on both sides. For example, if it is the program that we wish to protect against piracy, this fails to capture what is possibly the most likely scenario: somebody takes the originator's program and alters it just enough to make it a different program, for example by simply 'translating' it into another programming language whilst retaining the central idea which it embodies. But if it is the algorithm which is at stake, we are in danger of making laws of nature (or at least of mathematics) into 'intellectual property'; to allow a person copyright over Pythagoras' Theorem would be a bit like permitting someone to take out a patent on rainfall or natural selection.

The answer to this problem has been, in practice, to make a variety of legal decisions which determine how existing legislation, particularly the law of copyright, is to be interpreted with regard to software. Despite the *ad hoc* nature of many of these decisions, there is a significant connection between the need for these and the need for special legislation regarding computer privacy, discussed above. The connection lies in the fact that, in both cases, we are dealing not so much with unfamiliar kinds of behaviour or motives, but with unfamiliar kinds of *objects*. Here, we can see a connection with the suggested reason why fresh legislation might be necessary with respect to data privacy. This point will become even more evident after we have dealt with the final topic: legislation against what has come to be known as 'hacking'.

Computers and 'Hacking'

The word 'hacking', in connection with computers, used simply to mean the basic day-to-day activity of programmers. In recent years, however, it has acquired the meaning of 'exploring the limits of what can be done in a given computer system', and more recently still, 'attempting to manipulate computer systems for nefarious purposes'. It would undoubtedly have been better to have coined a new word to signify ill-intentioned activity, but the usage is now well-established, and we are stuck with it. Yet it is not simply the fact that the new meaning of 'hacking' is a perversion, which is unsettling. Many people have an uncomfortable feeling that a category has been created where none really exists: that the activities referred to collectively as 'hacking' are too diverse and loosely connected to be considered as a single pattern of behaviour.

This suspicion found expression recently in the course of an attempt to introduce anti-hacking legislation in Britain. It first took the form of a private member's bill by Miss Emma Nicholson MP. This bill was, in the event, dropped when Mr Douglas Hurd, the Home Secretary, announced that he was himself prepared to bring in legislation concerning the abuse of computers, but not before it had forced some serious thinking to be done about the issue.

The offence which Miss Nicholson, herself a former programmer, wished to see introduced, was that of 'unauthorised entry' into a computer system (the very mildest form of hacking, involving no damage), and the maximum penalty which she recommended for it was 10 years' imprisonment. The Law Commission, which was already looking into the matter of computer abuse, had been assumed to take a more conservative view than that of the Nicholson campaign, and it was widely expected that they would not recommend special legislation. However, when their report finally appeared on 10 October 1989, it did just that. The Law Commission's findings were then partially incorporated into a new bill introduced by Michael Colvin MP (the *Computer Misuse Bill*), which had its second reading in February 1990, and became law in June of that year, as the *Computer Misuse Act 1990*. This act reflects the three new offences proposed by the Law Commission. These are:

- Unauthorised entry into a computer system, with a maximum penalty of three months imprisonment (the Act specifies £2000 fine or six months' imprisonment)
- Unauthorised entry with intent to commit or assist in serious crime, with a maximum penalty of five years' imprisonment (the Act allows for five years' imprisonment and an unlimited fine)
- Altering computer-held data or programs without authorisation, also with a maximum penalty of five years' imprisonment (the Act again lays down five years' imprisonment and an unlimited fine).

The respective purposes of these new offences will be fairly apparent on the surface. The first merely outlaws 'hacking into' a system without authorisation. The second is meant to capture those cases where an existing crime such as fraud or theft is intended, but in which things have not yet got far enough for prosecutions to be brought under the appropriate laws. The third is designed to operate against hackers who are not content with entry to a system, but perpetrate mischievous acts in the process. Both of the last two categories of activity may, in the right circumstances, be extremely damaging and dangerous. Computer fraud, both on a small and large scale, appears to be becoming more common, though perhaps not as common as many people believe as a result of media coverage. Quite recently, however, such a fraud has just come to light, involving the removal of 50 million pounds from a major British financial institution, illustrating the fact that, however hard it might be, and however rarely successful, when it does succeed, computer crime can be on an alarmingly large scale.

Mischievous hacking, on the other hand, is more prevalent, and yet normally less harmful. It has been reliably estimated, for example, that there now exist more than 40 strains of computer virus, and that in the USA alone, there have been 250,000 outbreaks of computer virus up to the end of 1988 [3]. Not all such abuse takes the form of viruses, however. Mischievous software is usually thought of as falling into five categories, which are not necessarily mutually exclusive:

- *Time bombs*. These are programs which are planted in a machine and triggered to execute at a given time, taken from the computer's own clock. The best-known family of these is the so-called 'Friday the 13th virus'. This is not a true virus, but an umbrella term used for any time bomb set to the joker's favourite moment, the first second of any Friday 13th.
- *Logic bombs*. The logic bomb is analogous to the time bomb, but is triggered not by the recognition of a particular date or time, but by a combination of circumstances within the system (e.g. a user performs two particular operations consecutively).
- *Trojan horses*. These are pieces of mischievous software which may take any form, but which are introduced into the system as part of an apparently legitimate piece of software, and which therefore are less likely to be suspected by computer owners, administrators and users.
- *Viruses*. Viruses are perhaps the most feared form of computer mischief, since

their characteristic feature is that they are reproductive: that is, once in the system, they are capable of reproducing themselves, and even of 'infecting' other machines and systems. A typical sophisticated strain of virus will reside within some crucial piece of code such as a *copy* command, causing every instance of such a copy, to copy the virus along with the legitimate data, text or code.

- *Worms.* A primitive form of the computer virus was known as a 'worm', and the word 'worm' is sometimes used to mean the same as 'virus'. However, I prefer to retain the useful distinction, according to which worms, though they may progressively corrupt an area of memory, are not self-replicating in the way that viruses are. A worm may iterate the same operation many times, but unless it reproduces *itself*, it is not yet a virus.

In passing, it is well worth noting that all the above categories, with the exception of the 'Trojan Horse', may be *benign* as well as *malignant*. For example, many of the programs aimed at eradicating viruses are themselves viruses, in rather the same way that inoculations against disease are often themselves harmless instances of the disease in question.

Given what is known about the above kinds of abuse, and especially given the 'silly season' approach to it which is often taken by the mass media, it is hardly surprising that we should have seen campaigns to have such activity explicitly outlawed. Yet this should not lead us to accept uncritically any proposal aimed at bringing this about.

An opponent of special legislation against hacking has been the computer forensics consultant Peter Sommer, better known by his pen name Hugo Cornwall. He has pointed out (writing before the passing of the *Computer Misuse Act*) that most of what it usually thought of under this heading was actually illegal already, prior to the new law [4]. Frauds perpetrated using computers may be dealt with under the law of Theft. Making a device such as a magnetic stripe card to hack into a system may result in prosecution for Forgery. The *Criminal Damage Act* of 1971 has been used successfully against hackers who have caused damage in systems using 'logic bombs' or 'viruses'. The law dealing with *intention* is indeed a new departure, but whether it is really workable is doubtful, as we shall see in a moment.

Granted these facts, what is the purpose of new legislation? One reason indeed is that of closing the odd loophole. It has sometimes been found that legislation introduced before the advent of computer technology is ambiguous with regard to its application in that area, for the reason that the language used in drafting the legislation pre-dates the advent of computer technology with its accompanying linguistic and conceptual innovations. Here, either good and early precedents are necessary, or else new laws.

The second reason is closely connected with this, and consists of a desire to keep all the legislation together which 'belongs together'. This rests on a feeling that certain computer-related offences involve a distinctive set of concepts, and that the resulting similarities make it appropriate to treat them as a piece in order to carve things at the joints.

This is a tenable view, despite some *prima facie* objections. The chief objection is, of course, that laws should embody general principles, and not *ad hoc* solutions to local or ephemeral problems. Thus using the laws against nuisance, drug possession and unlawful assembly, are better than promulgating a specific law saying 'Thou shalt not hold Acid-House parties'. It is hard, however, to maintain that computer technology represents a local or an ephemeral phenomenon; it is heré to stay, and the changes which it has made to our language and thinking are likely to be permanent. As for the requirement of generality, it is a requirement which has limits. This would by no means be the first time that technology had overtaken the existing law and created the need for introducing new categories. An historical example would be the way in which the prevalence of guns gave rise to special firearms legislation.

The justification, if any, for having specific anti-hacking laws is that, as just mentioned, the language in which the existing laws are framed tends not to sit happily with the concepts of computing science and information technology. A good example of this conceptual gap is the issue of unauthorised entry to a computer system, which brings us to the third remaining reason why computer-specific legislation may be thought necessary. No previous legislation seems to make it illegal simply to 'hack into' another person's or organisation's computer system, unless some damage is done thereby; and if damage *is* caused, the offence is that of causing damage, not of unauthorised entry. The explanation of this alleged *lacuna* is not far to seek. When the earlier laws were made, the idea of 'getting into' someone's computer, in this sense, did not exist. And indeed, if we scratch its surface a little, this sense of 'getting into' proves to be a rather odd sense. To begin with, it is not, for example, like getting into someone's orchard, or into a bank vault: it goes without saying that the hacker does not enter anybody's computer in person. Does he, then, intrude some other object into the computer? Once again, not in the usual sense.

By far the most common means of hacking into a system is simply guessing or otherwise acquiring the password for that system, and going on exactly as a legitimate user would, moving around from one directory to another, reading files, and so on. The only way in which anything 'enters' the system physically, is that some electrical impulses are obviously initiated in order to carry out the operations in question. This is very unlike actual entry of a building or enclosure; it is more like shouting from outside the building and thus causing vibrations of the air inside. The fact is that the sense of 'entry' in 'unauthorised entry' is not that of entry into a physical space at all. It is rather that of entry into a notional 'computer space', which is not to be identified with the hardware comprising the machine's memory and other components. Being 'in' this kind of space consists in being able to interact with, or even just passively read things from, the system. This 'space' is quite definitely a software concept rather than a hardware one, and like most software concepts, it has more than a little of the metaphorical, or analogical, about it. Access to this notional space is, then, what computer owners wish to maintain control over, and what they object to when it is achieved by unauthorised persons.

It is, then, no wonder that previous legislation made no provision for unauthorised entry into a computer system. It is not that the concept of a computer did not then exist, but that the concept of entry, in the above sense, did not exist. The nearest historical parallels which suggest themselves here are the circumstances resulting in new laws regulating air space and radio frequencies.

What I have just said is not intended to be a defence of new legislation against unauthorised entry, but only as an explanation of why, if we do wish to make it illegal, new legislation is appropriate. In fact, the case for such legislation seems to me rather thin. For what is the objection to 'entry' in this sense, granted that damage, fraud and theft are not committed, or even intended? Add to this the fact that ordinary trespass is not even a criminal offence unless aggravated by some special circumstances, and where is the case for such a law? I strongly suspect that the real answer is as follows. The middle category in the new offences, that of unauthorised entry with intent to commit or assist in serious crime, would be very hard to prove. Provided no damage had yet been caused, a hacker would be likely to get off scot free, even though it was in practice pretty certain that his ultimate intention was to introduce a virus or perpetrate a fraud. It would be rather like trying to prove loitering with intent to commit a felony: except that computer hackers do not carry jemmys and crowbars to incriminate themselves. A law against unauthorised entry *tout court* would therefore provide a safety net for the prosecution, ensuring that the hacker got convicted of *something* or other. The objection to this kind of legislation should not need spelling out.

Computers and their Objects

To return to the central thread of this discussion, what we have seen in all three cases discussed is that the putative need for fresh and computer-specific legislation arises from the fact that computers have brought with them not only new usage and jargon, but new sets of concepts, new categories of objects which merit the law's attention. The sorts of objects in question will include things like computer systems, networks, databases, computer files, records and other data structures, directories, file space, memory space, electronic passwords, identification codes, and so on.

Naturally, I am not going so far as to suggest that any revision of our ultimate ontology is required as a result. The categories of objects to which the language of computing tends to refer are not bedrock categories like particulars and universals. They can no doubt be cashed out in terms of more traditional objects: software can always be spelled out as hardware if we so wish. However, there comes a point at which it starts looking absurd to go on doing this 'spelling out', and to deal directly with the supervenient category itself. This takes us back to the point I made earlier about the feeling that certain kinds of legislation belong together. What I want to suggest, is that the reason for this feeling is that the legislation in question would be couched in terms of the sorts of concepts which are specific and proper to computing and information technology, in a way which other kinds of legislation would not. A recent comment made by Superintendent Don Randall of the London Police Fraud squad, perhaps points the way to marking off the area in question. He makes a distinction between crimes in which computers are merely used as a tool, and those which involve the manipulation or corruption of the system itself [5]. Conventional crime which just happens to employ computers (as do most activities these days, of course), would not be included, but only those damaging activities to which it is essential that they are carried out on a computer: of which, that is, the computer element is definitive.

Despite the accusation of lack of generality, real gains might be made through the adoption of this approach, especially in clarity. The terms in question would undoubtedly have to be defined within the law, but once defined, they would allow for greater perspicuity than the alternative of stretching the terminology in which more traditional laws are framed so as to include what we want them to include.

The application of this principle to the field of ethics should now be fairly obvious. We do not need to propose anything like wholesale changes in our moral thinking (after the manner of Nietzsche or B. F. Skinner, for example) in order to argue for the identification of specific areas such as Political Ethics, Medical Ethics, Business Ethics or, as in this case, Computing Ethics. All we really need to point to is a broad and lasting change in our language and, in a harmless sort of way, in our thinking, arising from the phenomenon in question. I say 'harmless', because such a change represents not so much an alteration in the way we think about things generally, as an *addition* to our stock of conceptual apparatus.

One sometimes hears it said that our moral thinking needs to be overhauled in sweeping but often vaguely specified ways, in response to new scientific and technological horizons, and it is no surprise that these ways have only been vaguely specified. For the basic principles and building blocks of our moral outlook cannot by their very nature be open to revision in the manner often suggested. New *facts* can, of course, be taken into account, and may affect the kinds of action considered appropriate. But the introduction of totally new values must by its nature lack justification, if only because there could literally be no *reason* for such a revision. In the light of *what* could such a change be justified? Anything which could count as a reason for it would, by definition, be an existing (though, of course, perhaps neglected) value or principle.

Those working in new and developing areas of ethics are, therefore, faced with the challenge of showing in what sense an area of moral discourse can be said to be new, without falling into the above trap. What I have argued here, is that it is better to think of our moral universe as growing, rather than as metamorphosing, as the more alarmist of our commentators would have it.

There exist many more aspects than have been mentioned here, to the ethics of computing. There are, for example, questions concerning the extent to which people ought to be forced in everyday life to interact with machines instead of with people, concerning how far computers ought to be allowed to take decisions for us, and about the weight that ought to be put on the evidence of computers in court cases. This is to name but three. These are, however, outside the scope of this essay, which is intended to do no more than map out the area, justify its existence, and indicate a few prominent landmarks.

With the development of the field known as 'applied philosophy' and of the study of 'professional ethics', it is becoming more and more important that we understand what is meant by talking of the 'ethics of such-and-such'. If this brief case study has contributed at all to such understanding, it will have fulfilled its purpose.

Geoffrey Brown, Kernel Technology Ltd, The Design Centre, 46 The Calls, Leeds LS2 7EY, United Kingdom.

NOTES

[1] See NATIONAL COUNCIL FOR CIVIL LIBERTIES (1984) *A Guide to the Data Protection Bill* (NCCL).
[2] On this topic see, for example, DEBORAH JOHNSON (1984) *Computer Ethics* (Englewood Cliffs, Prentice-Hall).
[3] GEOFF SIMONS (1989) *Viruses, Bugs and Star Wars* (Oxford, NCC Blackwell).
[4] HUGO CORNWALL "A Hammer to Crack Hackers", *Independent*, 30/6/89.
[5] *Independent*, 10/10/89.

[9]

The Use and Abuse of Computer Ethics

East Tennessee State University, Johnson City, Tennessee

INTRODUCTION

The creation of courses in applied ethics—business, engineering, legal, medical, and professional ethics—is a very fertile industry. In 1982 Derek Bok, president of Harvard University, reported that over 12,000 distinct ethics courses were taught in our academic institutions [1]. As the emphasis on ethics has increased, so has the number of such courses.

What is the pedagogical justification for these courses? There are different justifications for different courses. The justifications depend on the curriculum in which they are taught—liberal arts, business, engineering, medicine, or law. For professional schools and professional cirricula the pedagogical objectives for those courses include introducing the students to the responsibilities of their profession, articulating the standards and methods used to resolve nontechnical ethics questions about their profession, and developing some proactive skills to reduce the likelihood of future ethical problems. The type of institution that supports the course—sectarian or nonsectarian—and the department responsible for the course—philosophy, religion, or computer science—affect the objectives.

The methods chosen and the issues discussed will vary by the domain of the ethics course. Specific objectives for these courses have varied from very general to quite specific (e.g., sensitize the students to values, teach a particular professionalism), indoctrinate the students to a set of values, and teach the laws related to a particular profession to avoid malpractice suits. Rarely do such courses take the approach that they are intended to discover values. These courses generally start with an accepted set of values or a variety of moral theories and apply them in particular contexts.

Other objectives for these courses come from nonacademic sources. In computer ethics some objectives are based on a concern to prevent computer catastrophes. It is hoped that computer ethics training

will eliminate unethical computer activity. This view was first promulgated in response to significant media attention given several incidents of computer trespass. Another belief used to promulgate the teaching of computer ethics is that errors in programs are attributable to immoral behavior. It is hoped that if we train people in ethics, they will produce error-free programs.

In his paper, "Human Values and the Computer Science Curriculum," Terrell Ward Bynum [2] offers as a major objective of teaching computer ethics that such courses make it more likely that "computer technology will be used to advance human values." This is a laudable goal for any discipline. Indeed one goal of liberal education in general is to help the student develop a sense of human values [3].

Computer ethics is a relatively new and developing academic area. There have been several attempts to define and categorize the field and how one ought to teach it. There have been courses and textbooks dealing with ethics and computing for more than 10 years. In that time computing and its impact on our society have undergone significant changes. As in most areas that are under development, several directions are attempted until the best ones are found. It is a mistake, however, to canonize an approach simply because it was one of the early approaches in a developing field.

There are two approaches to computer ethics which I believe are mistaken, i.e., they do not advance any of the above-cited objectives, and yet they are becoming canonized as the good and the right things to do. The two positions I am concerned about are 1) a method for teaching computer ethics which some have called "pop ethics" and 2) the idea that someone trained in philosophy or theology must teach such a course [2]. The remainder of this article addresses these two positions.

POP ETHICS

The concept of "pop computer ethics" is very broad. The goal of pop ethics is to "sensitize people to the fact that computer technology has social and ethical conse-

Address correspondence to Donald Gotterbarn, East Tennessee State Univ Box 70711, Johnson City, TN 37614-0711.

76   J. SYSTEMS SOFTWARE
           1992; 17:75-80
                                                        Donald Gotterbarn

quences'' [2]. This is not a course in sociology which
might use examples of the impact of computers in the
workplace to illustrate the impact of technology on
organizational structures, employment demographics,
and the values associated with these areas. The type of
pop ethics course I am concerned with generally consists of litanies of the evils that can be promulgated
with the use of computers. ''Newspapers, magazines,
and TV have increasingly engaged in computer ethics
of this sort. Every week, for example, there are new
stories about computer viruses, or software ownership
law suits, or computer-aided bank robbery, or harmful
computer malfunctions'' [2]. Pop ethics courses are
justified on the grounds that it is necessary to sensitize
people to the fact that computer technology can
''threaten human values as well as advance them'' [2].
If we presume that our students are literate and read
newspapers or magazines, then they already have read
the tales of the threatening computer. Even if they are
not literate and only watch television, they will still
have this knowledge. It looks, at first blush, as though
pop ethics might merely be an accouterment to the
university curriculum, dressing up its concerns with
ethics. If it were only this, I would not be concerned
with it; but I believe that such courses are in fact a
threat to most of the objectives for computer ethics
articulated above.

Pop ethics courses take a common, primarily negative approach. Collections of stories used or discussed
in these courses are variously entitled ''RISKS'' or
''Cautionary Tales.'' Donn Parker took this negative
approach in his first collection of scenarios [4]. In that
work he describes the principle used to select the
scenarios. They were ''written in such a way as to
raise questions of unethicality rather than ethicality''
[4]. This negative approach has consequences for the
prospective computer professional as well as for the
student who does not intend to be a professional. Leon
Tabak, in his excellent article ''Giving Engineers a
Positive View of Social Responsibility'' [5] argues that
such a negative approach fails for students interested in
pursuing careers in computing. When they are interested in ethics, they are interested in the way they can
positively contribute to the world and how they can
apply their skills productively. The pictures of technology painted by such courses are essentially pessimistic.
It puzzles everyone why this technology is singled out.
Why not have a pop ethics course about guns? I think
the difficulty with this pop ethics yellow journalism
approach is in fact more significant. I argue that this
approach is also harmful to the general student population.

The types of issues singled out in such courses give
the impression that computer ethics issues are rare and
irrelevant to the students. If computer ethics is concerned with catastrophes—the failure of a program
which controls the safety switches of a nuclear reactor
—then I don't have to worry about computing and
values because the only computer I program is my
microwave oven. How does the nuclear reactor story
relate to the student who works part time in the library
programming the computer? All this catastrophe talk
has nothing to do with his or her work. One also might
wonder what it has to do with ethics. If a problem is
caused by a mistake—an unintentional act—then what
does it have to do with ethical decisions? Other items
discussed in such courses do involve intentions, including how easy it is to use a computer to commit fraud or
break into a hospital data base. If computer ethics (the
pop version) is about all of those immoral people who
used computers to perpetrate evil, how does it relate to
the individual, moral student who always tries to do the
right thing? These examples are interesting but irrelevant to these students. Major social issues are also
discussed in these courses, for example, ''Is it permissible to sell computers to nations which support terrorism? This discussion is interesting and includes elements of geopolitics and questions about how and
whether to propagate scientific discovery. For most
students, however, such large questions are not within
their present or future sphere of ethical decision making
and are best discussed in social science or political
science courses. There is not enough time in a semester
to resolve such large issues; there is barely enough time
to delineate all of the issues involved in questions of
this complexity. To attempt to handle these questions in
a single class trivializes the subject. The discussion of
such complex, large issues strikes many students as
merely an academic exercise.

This brings me to one of my major objections to this
approach, viz., the distorted impression of ethics and
ethical reasoning that is often produced by a pop ethics
course. These courses are not guided by a single coherent concept of computer ethics. Every piece of negative
news involving a computer becomes a candidate for
discussion in a pop ethics course. The breadth of the
material included does not help the student get a clear
concept of computer ethics. The degree to which this
approach can mislead is evident in a recent work in pop
ethics [6]. I think the authors are taken in by their own
approach. They include subjects ranging from the impact of video display terminals on health to the use of
computers by organized crime, and then they claim that
computer ethics has no guiding principles or ethics
from which we can reason [6].

The concept of computer ethics is further clouded by
the emphasis on dilemma thinking. Under the guise of
getting students to think through a complex problem,

The Use and Abuse of Computer Ethics

J. SYSTEMS SOFTWARE   **77**
1992; 17:75-80

they are presented with an ethical dilemma. The following has been used as an example of computer ethics in a pop ethics course: A programmer's mother is suffering from a rare but manageable disease which if uncontrolled will lead to a painful death. The medicine to control the disease is so expensive that the only way the programmer can pay for it is to commit computer fraud. What is the moral thing for the programmer to do?[1] There are two problems with this type of example. First, this is not an issue in computer ethics. Although there are many ethical issues here, such as the responsibility of children to their parents and the responsibility of society to make medicines available at reasonable cost, therE is little here about computer ethics. To call this an issue in computer ethics because a computer is used to do the dastardly deed is like calling beating someone to death with a law book a problem in legal ethics. As second, more pervasive problem than the elasticizing of the concept of computer ethics is that ethical issues are equated with dilemmas, issues for which there are no good resolutions. The programmer has to choose between committing fraud and allowing her mother to die. This example seems to require an action which is the rejection of one or another of our moral standards. The emphasis on dilemmas in these courses leads students to think that ethical problems cannot be resolved.

Not only does the structure of the pop ethics course reinforce this no-solution view of ethics, but this view has been reinforced by the way some current literature has been constructed. For example, despite the fact that there was significant agreement on several scenarios used by Donn Parker in his early work, the only scenarios he chose to put in his new edition are those which generated the highest degree of diversity of opinion [7]. The diversity of opinion generated by the Parker cases should not be surprising given the heterogeneity of the group rendering the opinions—lawyers, philosophers, computer managers, etc. There is significant evidence that, in professional ethics, there is actually a convergence of opinion about computer ethical standards [8].

From the view that there never is any agreement in ethics arises a danger that students will conclude that it is a waste of time to think about ethical issues at all. Ethics as presented in these courses is not relevant to the student taking the course. It creates the impression that issues of computer ethics are rare and impossible to resolve. Thus, discussion of computer ethics is use-

less. The emphasis on the negative side gives the student no means to avoid real computer ethics problems. Given the dilemma nature of the teaching, an attitude of surrender is encouraged. If ethics is a matter of opinion and all opposing arguments have equal weight, then students will not expect support for what they consider to be a moral act. When they are placed in a situation which requires them to take a moral stand, they will be more likely not to "make a fuss" and not stand up for the moral choice.

The use of yellow journalism is sometimes an effective technique to fire up the masses. It presumes that a set of accepted values have been violated. There are several problems with this approach in the classroom:

1. This method of presenting ethics leaves the student with the impression that ethical reasoning is fruitless. This is dangerous in computer ethics and even more dangerous if the attitude spreads to other areas of the student's life.
2. The reactive emphasis does not encourage proactive behavior. The student is encouraged merely to judge the morality of an act that has occurred rather than taught to guide behavior to prevent or discourage immoral actions.
3. It encourages reactionary rather than anticipatory thinking. The negative approach encourages actions against what is perceived as the value-threatening technology rather than action to turn the technology in a value-supporting direction. For example, we are encouraged to make laws against nationwide data bases rather than to make laws which encourage the moral use of nationwide data bases. Instead of praising automatic teller machines, they are characterized as "... a good example of how a new technological device creates new opportunities for fraudulent activity" [6].

Pop ethics might have had a place when computing was a remote and esoteric disciplines, but I believe that in the current environment this approach is dangerous to the preservation and enhancement of values. This model of computer ethics does not advance any of the pedagogical objectives for teaching ethics cited earlier.

I believe computer ethics should be taught like engineering ethics, i.e., ethical issues directly related to the practice of engineering should be discussed in every engineering course. The Accrediting Board for Engineering and Technology standard states, "an understanding of the ethical, social, and economic considerations in engineering practice is essential ... as a minimum it should be the responsibility of the engineering faculty to infuse professional concepts into all engineering coursework" [9]. Discussions of computer ethics should be integrated throughout the curriculum.

---

[1] For further discussion of this example see D. Gotterbarn, Computer ethics: responsibility regained *National Forum*, LXXI, 26-32 (Summer 1991).

78   J. SYSTEMS SOFTWARE
          1992; 17:75-80   Donald Gotterbarn

In studies done in business ethics courses at the University of Delaware it was proven that this is the most effective way to teach professional ethics. It is also good to use a major project course for seniors to tie together most of the professionalism issues discussed throughout the curriculum.

If one is to offer anything like pop ethics, the typical approach must undergo serious revision. It should look at the positive opportunities of computing and how computing technology can support our needs and further our values. If one looks at computing technology that works, one finds in many cases that it is the exercise of and concern for values that increased its chances of working. Good computing products follow careful standards; they were built with the well-being of the computer user in mind. Ethics courses should ask students to think of new applications for computing which are consistent with their values and to evaluate the potential risks involved in such applications. They should talk about the minimal controls needed for development of these new applications. They should discuss real ethical cases for which there are solutions. They should present standards of good system design. Above all, they should provide proactive guidance. There are effective standards for reaching ethical decisions in many situations, and they should be discussed in this revised approach.

WHO SHOULD TEACH COMPUTER ETHICS?

To teach computer ethics this well requires much more than the retelling of horror stories. Many faculty members hesitate to discuss ethical issues in their classrooms. They feel a lack of expertise in the face of a group of academics who have reserved discussion of these issues for themselves. The computer scientist shies away from involving students in ethical discussions because of the apparent complexity of the philosophical approaches. Although it is true that at a refined level these philosophical theories are very complex, at the level of application the theoretical complexity can be largely ignored.

It is often said that only a philosopher should teach ethics [10]. This suggests that philosophers' moral theories can be used to solve moral problems. So in works on computer ethics there are philosophy sections on teleological theories and deontological theories [11]. Behind these two theories lie two approaches, one emphasizing results or consequences of actions (teleology) and the other emphasizing motives or duties (deontology). Armed with these theories we are supposed to solve the practical ethical problems which confront us daily. "Philosophers are no more educated in moral-

ity than their colleagues in the dairy barn; they are trained in moral theory, which bears about the same relation to the moral life that fluid mechanics bears to milking a cow" [3]. Philosophers mistakenly portray ethics as "pick your theory and then reason to an answer." They believe that different theories will lead to different sets of answers. Advocating this model of reasoning reinforces the view that all ethics discussion is fruitless because there are as many answers as there are theories.

It has been shown that these theories primarily conflict on the level of theory and justification rather than on the level of action [12]. Any theory which opposes our normal views of right and wrong is viewed with suspicion. These moral theories are merely alternate descriptions of how we move through our daily lives. Detailed knowledge of them is not required to act responsibly. They are measured against our sense of responsibility.

Professional computer ethics emphasizes a set of software engineering standards accepted by the professional community engaged in software development process.[2] Professional obligation follows from this accepted set of standards; it is of little practical consequence whether that obligation is met out of a sense of duty or because one has a contractual relationship with a customer. One might ask whether the description of software engineering I have offered is based on consequentialism—doing things because of the significance of the consequences—or deontologism—doing things because they are the right thing to do. I think such a question has little relevance to the moral life of a software engineer. We emphasize the standards of the process of building the software because we believe the product will be better. The moral theory used to describe the event has little impact on the moral life. The philosopher has no special competence here.

We need not be philosophers to discuss software engineering ethics. The importance one places on the theoretical dimension is a function of one's aims in the course. If our objectives are an acquaintance with philosophical ethical theory and tolerance for ambiguity and disagreement, then a professor trained in philosophy would be useful. In applied professional ethics courses, our aim is not acquaintance with complex ethical theories but recognition of role responsibility

[2] For a complete analysis of this contract basis of computer ethics see D. Gotterbarn, Value free software engineering: a fiction in the making, in *Proceedings of the Workshop on Software Engineering Education*, IEEE International Software Engineering Conference, City, 1991, pp. 45-54.

and awareness of the nature of the profession. A few hours reading about these philosophical theories is adequate.

If we do not teach ethical theories in computer ethics course, then what will we teach? We want to teach students how to anticipate and avoid ethical problems in computing. We are also interested in providing techniques or methodologies which can guide our behavior when a problem does arise. This is best done within the context of our technical curriculum. For example, in a class dealing with writing software requirements, one could look at a case like the following: Suppose you were asked to develop a system which would measure the times for ambulance trips beginning at different ambulances services, going to accident scenes, and then to hospitals. This data was to be used to redesign ambulance service districts to reduce the time spent getting patients to hospitals. The requirements for the system are developed, and during prototyping it is discovered that there are a significant number of trips for which no time is recorded. In determining how to handle these zero times it is discovered that in most of these cases no time was recorded because critically ill or injured patients were being transported and the paramedic was too busy to record the time. Thus, the most significant times to study are not recorded. The discussion of the technical and professional options in this situation teaches computer ethics.[3] Students learn how to handle a morally significant situation in an application area.

The moral reasoning involved here is not generated from some esoteric theory which requires a trained philosopher to understand; rather, it is based on reasoning by analogy, where we can examine the technical alternatives and attempt to anticipate their morally significant outcomes. It is technical knowledge that enables us to understand the potential consequences. We must consider the technically viable alternatives and make judgements guided by our technical skills and professional values. The technical discussion in class—deciding which are the better solutions and why—is what teaches computer ethics. The use of detailed technical examples in class helps students develop skills for anticipating some of these ethical problems.

One can use less technical cases to show how values relate to computing decisions: If you are asked to test some software, funds are exhausted before the testing is satisfactorily completed, and there is no possibility of

further funding, you have several options. Whichever option you choose, your decision must be conditioned by moral rules such as, "don't deceive," "keep promises," and "act professionally." Depending on the type of software being tested, rules like "don't cause pain" and "don't kill" also might come into play. Different examples bring different moral rules into play. Consider a person who was asked to write a data base for a library check-out system to determine the popularity of particular books and the number of additional copies if any that should be ordered. The association of the patron's name with the book checked out potentially violates several moral rules such as privacy and the deprivation of pleasure (because one does not feel free to read what one wants) and may cause psychological pain.

I also believe that students need some general familiarity with ethical argumentation. They need to understand how different ethical values compete and how they sometimes have only limited application. They need to see how these values get prioritized and how that affects decisions. This can be accomplished by having students read articles in professional ethics on analogous issues. When discussing the ambulance case outlined above, for example, articles in Stevenson's book [13] or Johnson's anthology [14] may be useful. To avoid the dangers of pop ethics, one must be careful that the examples chosen meet the following conditions:

1. It is not told because it is impossible to resolve.
2. It has enough detail to allow technical analysis.
3. The main protagonist is not morally bankrupt.
4. It is related to an issue in computing.
5. It can be discussed using moral values.

Try to develop a proactive attitude. The stories should be directly relevant to the class topic.

The pedagogical goals of discussing ethics in the technical curriculum are to develop the following set of skills:

1. the ability to identify correctly the potential for an ethical problem in a particular context and identify what moral rules are being compromised;
2. the ability to identify the cause of these issues, determine several alternate forms of action consistent with morality in that context, and for each of these possible actions, to determine expected outcomes and reasons for taking or not taking that action;
3. the ability to select a workable solution and work through the situation, either technically or morally.

Teaching these skills does not require learning new theories. These are process skills, and the emphasis

---

[3] For a full analysis of this case see D. Gotterbarn, Professionalism and ethics (video tape), Software Engineering Institute Video Dissemination Project, Pittsburgh, (1991).

80 J. SYSTEMS SOFTWARE
1992; 17:75–80

should be on a process that can be applied to changing contexts. These skills, like other abstract skills, are learned by practice. A single class meeting or a single chapter of a textbook discussed in one course will not develop these skills. To teach a single ethics course or have a special professor for ethics reinforces the mistaken notion that ethics and the practice of computing are distinct. What is needed is practice several times in a course. A case study methodology does this best, with each case addressing one or more specific phases of the software development process. This methodology involves giving a brief description of a professional situation that might involve an ethical problem. The class discusses the situation to try to identify if an ethical issue is present. If they find a situation which involves a violation of moral rules, they try to determine alternate approaches which would eliminate or at least reduce the moral difficulty. In work done by James Rest, case methodology has been shown to be most effective when professors and students discuss the case as peers. Thus it is better if the professor is not an ethics specialist.

Computing has a come a long way, both technically and ethically. We have learned how to apply moral rules and values to computing decisions. This skill and knowledge should be the subject of good computer ethics courses.

REFERENCES

1. D. Bok, *Beyond the Ivory Tower: Social Responsibility of the Modern University* Harvard University Press, Cambridge, Massachusetts, 1982, p. 123.

2. T. W. Bynum, Human values and the computer science curriculum, in *Proceedings of the 1991 National Conference on Computing and Values*, New Haven, 1991, pp. 1–4.

3. R. K. Fullinwinde, Teaching Ethics in the University, The Poynter Center, Bloomington, Indiana, 1991.

4. D. B. Parker, *Ethical Conflicts in Computer Science and Technology*, (AFIPS Press), Arlington, 1970, p. 8.

5. L. Tabak, Giving engineers a positive view of social responsibility, *SIGCSE Bull.* 20, 29–37 (1988).

6. T. Forester and P. Morrison, *Computer Ethics*, MIT Press, Cambridge, Massachusetts, 1990.

7. D. Parker, *Ethical Conflicts in Information and Computer Science, Technology, and Business*, QED Information Sciences, Inc., Boston, 1989.

8. L. M. Leventhal, K. E. Instone, and D. W. Chilson, Another view of computer science: patterns of responses among computer scientists, *J. Systems Software* in this issue.

9. Accreditation Board for Engineering and Technology, *Criteria for Accrediting Programs in Engineering in the United States*, ABET, 1981.

10. M. B. Mahowald and A. P. Mahowald, Should ethics be taught in a science course? *Hastings Center Report* 12, 16–22 (1982).

11. D. G. Johnson, *Computer Ethics*, Prentice-Hall, Englewood Cliffs, New Jersey, 1985.

12. Richard DeGeorge, *Business Ethics*, MacMillan, New York, 1982.

13. J. T. Stevenson, *Engineering Ethics: Practices and Principles*, Canadian Scholars' Press, Toronto, 1987.

14. D. Johnson and J. W. Snapper, eds., *Ethical Issues in the Use of Computers*, Wadsworth Publishing Company, Belmont, California, 1985.

[10]

Information ethics: On the philosophical foundation of computer ethics *

Luciano Floridi

Wolfson College, OX2 6UD, Oxford, UK; www.wolfson.ox.ac.uk/~floridi. E-mail: luciano.floridi@philosophy.ox.ac.uk

Abstract. The essential difficulty about Computer Ethics' (CE) philosophical status is a methodological problem: standard ethical theories cannot easily be adapted to deal with CE-problems, which appear to strain their conceptual resources, and CE requires a conceptual foundation as an ethical theory. Information Ethics (IE), the philosophical foundational counterpart of CE, can be seen as a particular case of 'environmental' ethics or ethics of the infosphere. What is good for an information entity and the infosphere in general? This is the ethical question asked by IE. The answer is provided by a minimalist theory of deserts: IE argues that there is something more elementary and fundamental than life and pain, namely being, understood as information, and entropy, and that any information entity is to be recognised as the centre of a minimal moral claim, which deserves recognition and should help to regulate the implementation of any information process involving it. IE can provide a valuable perspective from which to approach, with insight and adequate discernment, not only moral problems in CE, but also the whole range of conceptual and moral phenomena that form the ethical discourse.

"We, who have a private life and hold it infinitely the dearest of our possessions ..." Virginia Woolf, "Montaigne"[1]

"And I let myself go in a dream of lands where every force should be so regulated, every expenditure so compensated, all exchanges so strict, that the slightest waste would be appreciable; then I applied my dream to life and imagined a code of ethics which should institute the scientific and perfect utilisation of man's self by a controlling intelligence"[2]

The foundationalist problem

Lobbying, financial support and the undeniable importance of the very urgent issues discussed by

---

* A shorter version of this article was given at ETHICOMP98, The Fourth International Conference on Ethical Issues of Information Technology, Erasmus University, The Netherlands, 25 to 27 March 1998, hosted by the Department of Philosophy Erasmus University, The Netherlands, in association with Centre for Computing and Social Responsibility De Montfort University, UK, Research Center on Computing and Society Southern Connecticut State University, USA, East Tennessee State University, USA. I am grateful to the Erasmus University for its financial support and to Roger Crisp, Jos de Mul, Frances S. Grodzinsky, Richard Keshen and Jeroen van den Hoven, for thoughtful comments on a previous version of this paper. Many readers of a CFC version, available online, also provided useful suggestions.

[1] In *A Woman's Essays*. Penguin, London, p. 60, 1992.

[2] André Gide, *The Immoralist*. Penguin, London, pp. 71–72, 1960.

Computer Ethics (henceforth CE) have not yet succeeded in raising it to the status of a philosophically respectable topic. If they take any notice of it, most philosophers nowadays look down on CE as on a practical subject, a 'professional ethics' unworthy of their analyses and speculations. They treat it like Carpentry Ethics, to use a Platonic metaphor.

The inescapable interdisciplinarity of CE has certainly done the greatest possible harm to the prospects for recognition of its philosophical significance. Everyone's concern is usually nobody's business, and CE is at too much of a crossroads of technical matters, moral and legal issues, social as well as political problems and conceptual analyses to be anyone's own game. Philosophers' notorious conservatism may also have been a hindrance. After all, Aristotle, Mill or Kant never said a word about it, and 'professional philosophers' who know their syllabus do not often hold very broad views about which new philosophical questions may qualify as philosophers' own special problems. Yet these and other external factors, such as the novelty of its questions and the conspicuously applied nature of its answers, should not conceal the fact that the essential difficulty about CE's philosophical status lies elsewhere, and more internally. For it is a methodological problem, and concerns its conceptual foundation as an ethical theory.

CE shares with other philosophical disciplines in the analytic tradition three important but rather too general features:

1. it is logically argumentative, with a bias for analogical reasoning

2. it is empirically grounded, with a bias for scenarios analysis, and

3. it endorses a problem solving approach.

Besides 1–3, CE also presents a more peculiar aspect, which has so far acted as its driving force, namely:

4. it is intrinsically decision-making oriented.

These four features can be read in a roughly inverted order of importance. Why CE shares them, and whether it ought to, are questions sufficiently obvious to deserve no detailed comment here. Technological changes have outpaced ethical developments, bringing about unanticipated problems that have caused a "policy vacuum"[3] filled by CE, which has initially surfaced from practical concerns arising in the information society. Rational decisions have to be taken, technical, educational and ethical problems must be solved, legislation needs to be adopted, and a combination of empirical evidence and logical arguments seems to provide the most obvious and promising means to achieve such pressing goals. A rather more interesting point is that 1–4 constitute the theoretical justification of CE's present inductive methodology, which leads us to:

5. it is based on case studies.

During the last two decades, CE has consistently adopted a bottom-up procedure, carrying out an extended and intensive analysis of individual cases, amounting very often to real-world issues rather than mental experiments. Its aim has been to reach decisions based on principled choices and defensible ethical principles and hence to provide more generalised conclusions – in terms of conceptual evaluations, moral insights, normative guidelines, educational programs or legal advice – which might apply to whole classes of comparable cases. On the grounds of such extensive evidence and analysis, defenders of the novelty and originality of a CE-approach to moral issues have developed two types of argument.

They have either suggested, perhaps too generally, that 1–5 are sufficient to qualify CE as a well-grounded philosophical discipline. Or they have argued, more specifically and somewhat more forcefully, that on the one hand the ICT (digital Information and Communication Technology) revolution, its scale and complexity, malfunctioning computers and computer misuse have created a whole new range of social problems (computer crime, software theft, hacking, viruses, privacy, over-reliance on intelligent machines, workplace stress, intellectual and social discrimination etc.) which have given rise to a new

grey area of moral dilemmas, not all of which are just ICT versions of old moral issues; and that, on the other hand, the new and old ethical problems CE works on within the context of (5) – the PAPA group,[4] that is privacy, accuracy, intellectual property and access, but also security and reliability, being arguably some of the best examples – have been so transformed by the computing technology in which they are embedded that they acquire an altered form and new meanings; and finally that, in both cases, we are confronted by the emergence of an innovative ethical approach, namely CE, which is at the same time original and of an unquestionable philosophical value.

Unfortunately, however, neither line of reasoning carries much weight. The more general thesis just fails to be convincing, whereas the more restricted thesis is, more interestingly, the actual source of the foundationalist crisis that presently afflicts CE. I shall later defend the view that CE does have something distinctive and substantial to say on moral problems, and hence can contribute a new and interesting perspective to the ethical discourse, but at the moment we need to realise that features 1–3 fail to make CE any different from, let alone better than, other ethical theories already available, most notably Consequentialism and Deontologism, while we have seen that feature 4 may work equally well against CE's philosophical ambitions, for it leads to the Carpentry problem. As for feature 5, it takes only a moment of reflection to realise that, together with 4, it is one of the factors that contributes to, rather than solves, the foundational problem, for the following reason. If new moral problems have any theoretical value, either by themselves or because embedded in original contexts, they usually provide only further evidence for the discussion of well-established ethical doctrines. Thus, CE-problems may work as counterexamples, show the limits or stretch the conceptual resources of already available *macroethics*, that is theoretical, field-independent, applicable ethics, but can never give rise to a substantially new ethical perspective, unless they are the source of some very radical reinterpretation. ICT, by transforming in a profound way the context in which some old ethical issues arise, not only adds interesting new dimensions to old problems, but may lead us to rethink, methodologically, the very grounds on which our ethical positions are based. Missing the latter perspective, even people who support the importance of the work done

---

[3] Cf. James H. Moor. What Is Computer Ethics? *Metaphilosophy*, 16.4, pp. 266–275, 1985.

[4] R. Mason. Four Ethical Issues of the Information Age. *MIS Quarterly* 10.1, pp. 5–12, 1986. In this provocative essay Mason discusses dilemmas thought to be unique to ICT and identifies at least four main ethical issues for ICT professionals: privacy, accuracy, ownership, and access to information, summarised by the acronym PAPA. The essay has been influential in the subsequent literature.

in CE are led to adopt a dismissive attitude towards its philosophical significance, and argue that there is no special category of computer ethics, but just ordinary ethical situations in which computers and digital technology are involved, and therefore that CE is at most a *microethics*, that is a practical, field-dependent, applied and professional ethics.[5] Interest in CE is then more justified than interest in Carpentry Ethics only because, in the information society, computers rather than timber permeate and influence almost every aspect of our lives, so we need a conceptual interface to apply ethical theories to new scenarios. If there were only a limited number of machines, kept under very tight control, there would be neither CE nor any need for it.

Behind CE's foundationalist problem there lies a lack of a strong ethical programme. Although everyone seems to agree that CE deals with innovative ethical issues arising in ICT contexts within 5, instead of reflecting on their roots and investigating, as thoroughly as possible, what new theoretical insights they could offer, we are urged by features 3 and 4 to rush on, and look immediately for feasible solutions and implementable decisions. The result is inevitably disappointing: 3 and 4 load 5 with an unduly action-oriented meaning (see below) and CE-problems are taken to entail the fact that CE is primarily, when not exclusively, concerned with the moral value of human actions. Understood as a mere decision-making and action-oriented theory, CE appears only as a practical subject, which can hardly add anything to already well-developed ethical theories.

This is the present state in which CE finds itself. Moral problems in CE, with their theoretical implications, are invariably approached against the background of a Deontologist, Contractualist or, more often, Consequentialist position. Predictably, CE itself is either disregarded, as a mere practical field of no philosophical interest, or colonised as a special domain of the application of action-oriented (see below) ethics

---

[5] For an influential defence of this view see for example Deborah D. Johnson in her *Computer Ethics*, 2nd ed. (Upper Saddle River N.J.: Prentice Hall, 1994). Johnson shows some sympathy for a moderately Kantian perspective, but does not take an explicit position. The main thesis is that ethical issues surrounding computers are not wholly new, and that it is not necessary to create a new ethical theory or system to deal with them. They have some unique features, but we can rely on our traditional moral principles and theories. A radical position is taken by Duncan Langford in *Practical Computer Ethics* (London: McGraw-Hill, 1995), who disregards a philosophical approach to CE as dispensable: "[...] this book is not a work of theoretical analysis and discussion. Practical Computer Ethics is not for academic philosophers" (from the very first paragraph of the Introduction).

in search of intellectual adventures.[6] Conceptually, it is a most unsatisfactory situation, for two related clusters of reasons.

Macroethics and computer ethics

On the more negative side, the nature of CE-problems seems to strain the conceptual resources of action-oriented theories more seriously than is usually suspected. When consistently applied, both Consequentialism, Contractualism and Deontologism show themselves unable to accommodate CE-problems easily, and in the end may well be inadequate. Two possible forms of distortion, sometimes caused by the application of inappropriate action-oriented analyses, are the projection of human agency, intelligence, freedom and intentionality (desires, fears, expectations, hopes etc.) onto the computational system, and the tendency to delegate to the computational system as an increasingly authoritative intermediary agent (it is not unusual to hear people dismiss an error as only the fault of a computer). In both cases, we witness the erosion of the agent's sense of moral responsibility for his or her actions. Without an 'object-oriented' approach (see below), computer ethics may end up anthropomorphizing computational systems.

That such limits have not yet been fully and explicitly investigated in CE literature, despite their decisive importance, is a clear mark of the extraordinary sense of inferiority shown by CE towards philosophically better-established theories. Here, I can only alert the reader to the problem by sketching a few points.

To begin with, we might expect that the empirical, decision-making orientation of CE-problems would tend to make Deontologism, with its inflexible universal maxims and duty-based ethics, a much less likely candidate than either Contractualism or Consequentialism; while the strength of the conflicting interactions between different rights, duties and moral values, emerging from the case-studies carried on so far – think, for example, of society's right to security vs. cryptography, of privacy vs. public control of information, of freedom of expression vs. offensive information – further undermines the viability of a purely Deontological approach to CE. Even more specifically, Kant's moral imperatives appear to be

---

[6] See for example D. M. Ermann, M. B. Williams and M. S. Shauf, editors, *Computers, Ethics and Society*, 2nd ed. New York: Oxford U.P., 1997. Especially the first part, entitled Computers in an Ethical Framework for a philosophical perspective.

challenged by two problems. Neither the law of impartiality (the Golden rule) nor the law of universality (behave as a universal legislator) are sufficient to approach the following two types of problems:

1. *CE-problems not involving human beings.*

Common sense rejects the idea that there might be victimless crimes, e.g. computer crimes against banks, or that vandalism may not be morally blameworthy (I shall come back to this problem later), yet it is unclear how a Deontological approach can cope with this kind of problem, since both Kantian imperatives apply only to anthropocentric contexts.

2. *CE-problems with a ludic nature.*

The agent often perceives computer crimes as games or intellectual challenges and his actions as role playing. Because of the remoteness of the process, the immaterial nature of information and the virtual interaction with faceless individuals, the information environment (the infosphere) is easily conceived of as a magical, political, social, financial dream-like environment, and anything but a real world, so a person may wrongly infer that her actions are as unreal and insignificant as the killing of enemies in a virtual game. The consequence is that not only does the person not feel responsible for her actions (no one has ever been charged with murder for having killed some monsters in a video game), but she may be perfectly willing to accept the universal maxim, and to extend the rules of the game to all agents. The hacker can be a perfect Kantian because universality without any concern for the actual consequences of an action is ethically powerless in a moral game.

The previous problems may help to explain why, in practice, most of the theoretical literature on CE tends to adopt some pragmatic version of the MINMAX and Golden rules (minimise harms, maximise benefits and "do unto others as you would have them do unto you") and is often more or less knowingly Consequentialist and sometimes Contractualist in orientation. Things, however, are no more promising if we look at these two approaches, for they too end up strained by the nature of the problems in question. A few essential issues may be sufficient to illustrate the point:

1. the virtual nature of the actions in question often makes it possible for them to remain completely undetected and to leave no really perceptible effects behind;
2. even when 1 does not apply, ICT distances the agent from, and hence diminishes his sense of direct responsibility for his computer-mediated, computer-controlled and computer-generated actions. Besides, the increasing separation of actions and their effects, both in terms of the anonymity of the agent and in terms of conceptual distance, makes 'moral sanctions' (in Mill's sense) ever less perceptible by the agent the more indirect, distant and obscure the consequences of his actions are;
3. in connection with 1–2, there is a corresponding de-personalisation and an increasing sense of the practical anonymity of actions/effects, in a context where an individual agent's behaviour is often rightly perceived as only a marginal and microscopic component of wider and more complex courses of action. The diffusion of responsibility brings with it a diminished ethical sense in the agent and a corresponding lack of perceived accountability;
4. in connection with 1–3, the high level of control and compartmentalisation of actions tends to restrict them and their evaluation to specific areas of potential misbehaviour;
5. in connection with 1–4, the ostensibly negative anthropology resulting from CE case-studies shows that human nature, when left to itself, is much more Hobbesian and Darwinian than Consequentialism may be ready to admit and hence able to cope with. The increasing number and variety of computer crimes committed by perfectly respectable and honest people shows the full limits of an action-oriented approach to CE: computer criminals often do not perceive, or perceive in a distorted way, the nature of their actions because they have been educated to conceive as potentially immoral only human interactions in real life, or actions involving physical and tangible objects. A cursory analysis of the justifications that hackers usually offer for their actions, for example, is sufficient to clarify immediately that they often do not understand the real implications of their behaviour, independently of their technical competence. We have already seen that this problem affects a Deontological approach as well (the ludic problem);
6. even when 1–5 do not apply, the great complexity of the constantly changing infosphere often makes any reasonable calculation or forecasting of the long-term, aggregate value of the global consequences of an individual's actions impossible;
7. quite apart from 1–6, the individual and his/her rights acquires an increasing importance within the information society, not just as an agent, but also as a potential target of automatically tailored actions, yet individual's rights are something that Consequentialism has always found difficult to accommodate.

With the exception of point 5 and the inclusion of the next point

8. in connection with 1–4, the asymmetric nature of 'virtual' actions gives rise to a 'state of nature' where individuals are very far from having even a vaguely comparable strength, either technical or technological, and therefore the 'strongest' can behave perfectly rationally, 'opt out' of the social contract and be successful. For example, a very appropriate game-theoretic approach to CE-problems would show that, since there are never equal conditions, the 'game' is heavily biased towards the hacker; suffice to mention here that most experts agree that the vast majority of computer crimes remain undetected, not just unpunished;

the previous problems can be extended to Contractualism as well, if we treat it as a version of Consequentialism based on a negative anthropology and a conception of the nature of actions as always rationally motivated only by self-interest (I shall very briefly comment on a Deontological form of Contractualism later).

If Deontologism, Consequentialism and Contractualism are not ready-to-use programmes, which need to be only slightly recompiled to become applicable in the context of CE and deliver the expected results, on the more positive side we may wish radically to re-consider the action-oriented nature of CE itself. For this, we first need to sketch a simple model of macroethics.

A model of macroethics

Any action, whether morally loaded or not, has the logical structure of a binary relation between an agent and a patient. The interpretation of what can then be inferred from the occurrence of *prima facie* moral actions, in terms of what is the primary object of the ethical discourse, is a matter of philosophical controversy. Virtue Ethics, and Greek philosophy more generally, concentrates its attention on the moral nature and development of the individual agent who performs the action. It can therefore be properly described as an agent-oriented, 'subjective' ethics. Since the agent is usually assumed to be a single human being, Virtue Ethics is intrinsically anthropocentric and individualistic. Nothing would prevent it from being applicable to non-individual agents, like political parties, companies or teams, yet this is not usually the way in which Virtue Ethics is developed, partly because of a historical limitation, which has Greek roots in the individualist conception of the

agent in question and the metaphysical interpretation of his functional development, and partly because of a contemporary empiricist bias, which consists in an anti-realist conception of non-individual entities – paradoxically, we live in a materialist culture based on ICT but we do not treat data or information as real objects – and in a pre-theoretical refusal to conceive of moral virtues also as holistic properties of complex systems. We shall see later that the removal of such limitations has interesting consequences for the foundation of CE.

Developed in a world profoundly different from the small, non-Christian Athens, Utilitarianism, or more generally Consequentialism, Contractualism and Deontologism are the three most well-known theories that concentrate on the moral nature and value of the actions performed by the agent. They are 'relational' and action-oriented theories, intrinsically social in nature. They obviously anchor the stability of the moral value of human actions very differently – the former two a posteriori, through the assessment of their consequences in terms of global and personal welfare, the latter a priori, through universal principles and the individual's sense of duty – but the principal target of their analysis remains unchanged, for they both tend to treat the relata, i.e. the individual agent and the individual patient, as secondary in importance, and may sometimes end up losing sight of their destiny. From their relational perspective, what the individual agent becomes or does in his autonomy, and quite irrespective of external factors, as may be the case in Virtue Ethics, now has less importance than the more significant interactions between the agent and the surrounding society, or even the simple possibility of such interactions (the Kantian universal maxim). These ethics may be based on a central concept of self-interest (Consequentialism and Contractualism) but their analyses focus primarily on the nature of action and choice, understood as the function from human interests to moral values, and thus shift the attention from a purely agent-oriented to a substantially interaction-oriented approach. Thanks to this shift in perspective, the philosophy of history, understood as the ethical interpretation of the collection of all significant actions liable of a moral evaluation, acquires more relevance than pedagogy, that is the development and evaluation of an individual's cultivation. Having thus made the conception of human nature more peripheral to the ethical discourse than mankind's deeds, 'relational' theories can finally ease and promote the enlargement of the concept of a morally responsible agent as a free and rational centre of rights and duties, which slowly comes to include, besides the Athenian gentleman, also women, homosexuals, people of other cultures, minority groups and members of all social classes, in a word any free and rational agent.

Since agent-oriented, intra-subjective theories and action-oriented, infra-subjective theories are all inevitably anthropocentric, we may follow common practice and define them as 'standard' or 'classic', without necessarily associating any positive evaluation with either of these two adjectives. Apart from the controversial case represented by a Kantian version of Contractualism à la Rawls – which runs into other difficulties, but must be acknowledged to stress the crucial importance of the impartial nature of moral concern, thanks to the hypothetical scenario in which rational agents are asked to determine the nature of society in a complete state of ignorance of what their positions would be in it, thus transforming the agent into the potential patient of the action – standard ethics take only a relative interest in the 'patient', the third element in a moral relation, which is on the receiving end of the action and endures its effects. Ontological power, however, brings with it new moral responsibilities. We can respect only what we no longer fear, yet knowledge is a process of increasing emancipation from reality and in a world in which mankind can influence, control or manipulate practically every aspect of reality, philosophical attention is finally drawn to the importance of moral concerns that are not immediately agent-oriented and anthropocentric. Medical Ethics, Bioethics and Environmental Ethics are the best known examples of this non-standard approach. They attempt to develop a patient-oriented ethics in which the 'patient' may be not only a human being, but also any form of life. Indeed, Land Ethics extends the concept of patient to any component of the environment, thus coming close to the object-oriented approach defended by Information Ethics, as we shall see in a moment. Capturing what is a pre-theoretical but very widespread intuition shared by most people, they hold the broad view that any form of life has some essential proprieties or moral interests that deserve and demand to be respected. They argue that the nature and well-being of the patient of an action constitute its moral standing and that the latter makes vital claims on the interacting agent and ought to contribute to the guidance of his ethical decisions and the constraint of his moral behaviour. Compared to classic ethics, Bioethics, Medical and Environmental Ethics thus turn out to be theories of nature and space – their ethical analyses start from the moral properties and values of what there is – no longer of history and time (human actions and their consequences). Moreover, since any action may seem to be inexorably stained with evil, either because of what it is not – from a consequentialist perspective, every action is always improvable, so any action can

be only relatively good at most – or because of what it could be – from a deontologist perspective, in itself the same action leads either to morally deprecable or just amoral behaviour if it does not spring from a sense of duty and does not conform to the universal maxims – one may say that classic ethics are philosophies of the wrongdoer, whereas non-classic ethics are philosophies of the victim. They place the 'receiver' of the action at the centre of the ethical discourse, and displace its 'transmitter' to its periphery. In so doing, they help to widen further our anthropocentric view of who may qualify as a centre of moral concern. We have seen that any classic ethics is inevitably egocentric and logo-centric – all theorising concerns a conscious and self-assessing agent whose behaviour must be supposed sufficiently free, reasonable and informed, for an ethical evaluation to be possible on the basis of his responsibility – whereas non-classic ethics, being bio-centric and patient-oriented, are epistemologically allocentric – i.e. they are centred on, and interested in, the entity itself that receives the action, rather than in its relation or relevance to the agent – and morally altruistic, and can now include any form of life and all vulnerable human beings within the ethical sphere, not just foetuses, new-born babies and senile persons, but above all physically or mentally ill, disabled or disadvantaged people. This is an option that simply lies beyond the immediate scope of any classic ethics, from Athens to Könisberg.

From computer ethics to information ethics

The development of ethical theories just sketched provides a useful perspective and hence a metatheoretical justification from which to interpret the nature of CE more accurately. If one tries to pinpoint exactly what common feature so many case-based studies in CE share, it seems reasonable to conclude that this is an overriding interest in the fate and welfare of the action-receiver, the information. Despite its immediate decision-making approach and its obvious social concerns, CE is never primarily interested in the moral value of the actions in question, let alone in the agents' virtues or vices. Instead, CE develops its analyses, and attempts to indicate the best course of action, as a consequence of the steady and careful attention paid to what happens to the information environment. Right and wrong, in CE, do not just qualify actions in themselves, they essentially refer to what is eventually better or worse for the infosphere. Therefore, far from being a classic, action-oriented ethics, as it may deceptively seem at first sight, CE is primarily an ethics of *being* rather than *conduct* or *becoming*, and hence qualifies as non-standard ethics. The fundamental difference, which sets it apart from all other members of the same class of theories, is that CE raises information as such, rather than just life in general, to the role of the true and universal patient of any action, thus presenting itself as an infocentric and object-oriented, rather than just a biocentric and patient-oriented ethics. Without information there is no moral action, but information now moves from being a necessary prerequisite for any morally responsible action to being its primary object. The crucial importance of this radical change in perspective cannot be overestimated. We have seen that typical non-standard ethics can reach their high level of universalization of the ethical discourse only thanks to their biocentric nature. However, this also means that even Bioethics and Environmental Ethics fail to achieve a level of complete universality and impartiality, because they are still biased against what is inanimate, lifeless or merely possible (even Land Ethics is biased against technology and artefacts, for example). From their perspective, only what is alive deserves to be considered as a proper centre of moral claims, no matter how minimal, so a whole universe escapes their attention. Now this is precisely the fundamental limit overcome by CE, which further lowers the condition that needs to be satisfied, in order to qualify as a centre of a moral concern, to the minimal common factor shared by any entity, namely its information state. And since any form of being, is, in any case, also a coherent body of information, to say that CE is infocentric is tantamount to interpreting it, correctly, as an ontocentric object-oriented theory.

At this point, it is worth pausing for a moment to listen to lawyers, politicians, sociologists, engineers, educators, computer scientists and many other professionals. For I fear they may be complaining that philosophers cannot place their metaphysical copyright on 'Computer Ethics'. CE is a lively and useful subject, which should not be reduced to a mere academic subject and esoteric field of conceptual speculations. Their worries may not be completely unjustified. CE offers an extraordinary theoretical opportunity for the elaboration of a new ethical perspective, but what has been said so far foreshadows an interpretation of CE that places it at a level of abstraction too philosophical to make it of any direct utility for their immediate needs. Yet, this is the inevitable price to be paid for any attempt to provide CE with an autonomous conceptual foundation. We must polarise theory and practice to strengthen both, but to avoid at least some superficial confusion, we may agree to use 'Information Ethics' (IE) to refer to the philosophical foundation of CE. IE will not be immediately useful to solve specific CE-problems but it will provide the grounds for the moral principles that will then guide the problem-solving

procedures in CE. Professional codes of conduct, rules, guidelines, advices, instructions or standards, computer or information related legislation, are all based on an implicit philosophical ethics. It is the latter that we shall investigate in the following pages.

Information ethics as an object-oriented and ontocentric theory

From an IE perspective, the ethical discourse now comes to concern information as such, that is not just all persons, their cultivation, well-being and social interactions, not just animals, plants and their proper natural life, but also anything that exists, from paintings and books to stars and stones; anything that may or will exist, like future generations; and anything that was but is no more, like our ancestors. Unlike other non-standard ethics, IE is more impartial and universal – or one may say less ethically biased – because it brings to ultimate completion the process of enlargement of the concept of what may count as a centre of moral claims, which now includes every instance of information, no matter whether physically implemented or not. Such an all-embracing approach is made possible by the fact that IE adopts the following principles and concepts:

1. *uniformity of becoming*

All processes, operations, changes, actions and events can be treated as information processes. Here process is to be understood not in a procedural sense (e.g. as part of a program that performs some task), but as meaning *stream of activity*.

2. *reflexivity of information processes*

Any information process necessarily generates a trail of information.

3. *inevitability of information processes*

The absence of an information process is also an information process. This is an extension, to the dynamics of information, of the general principle underlying any static encoding of information, and it is important in order to take into account the action/omission ethical distinction.

4. *uniformity of being*

An entity is a consistent packet of information, that is an item that contains no contradiction in itself and can be named or denoted in an information process. A contradiction, when directly and positively used (i.e. not used at a metatheoretical level or just mentioned), is an instance of total entropy of information, i.e. a mark left where all information has been completely erased. Since an information process positively involving a contradiction ends up being itself a source of contradiction, it is also a case of total entropy, an information black hole, as it were. It follows that there are no information processes fruitfully involving contradictions (obviously this is not to say that there are no contradictory information processes), that an information process can involve anything which is in itself logically possible, and that IE treats every logically possible entity as an information entity.

5. *uniformity of agency*

An agent is any entity, as defined in 4, capable of producing information phenomena that can affect the infosphere. The minimal level of agency is the mere presence of an implemented information entity, in Heideggerian terms, the *Dasein* – the therebeinghood – of an information entity implemented in the infosphere. Not all information entities are agents (cf. abstract information entities); many agents may often fail to be in a position to affect the infosphere significantly, beyond their mere presence (think of a grain of sand in the desert or as the last grain flowing through an hourglass determining the explosion of a bomb); and not all agents are responsible agents (e.g. a river or a dog), that is agents able to acquire knowledge-awareness of the situation and capable of planning, withholding and implementing their actions with some freedom and according to their evaluations.

6. *uniformity of non-being*

Non-being is the absence or negation of any information, or information entropy. In IE, information entropy is a *semantic*, not a syntactic concept, and, as the opposite of information capacity, it indicates the decrease or decay of information leading to absence of form, pattern, differentiation or content in the infosphere.[7]

7. *uniformity of environment*

The infosphere is the environment constituted by the totality of information entities – including all agents – processes, their proprieties and mutual relations.

When the ethical discourse attempts to persuade and motivate a person to act morally, an anthropocentric and self-interested justification of goodness may well be inevitable. However, when the primary aim of the ethical analysis is to understand what is right and wrong, irrespective of a specific agent's behaviour, it becomes possible to adopt a more objective viewpoint. In this respect, IE holds that every entity, as an expression of being, has a dignity, constituted by its mode of existence and essence (the collection of all the elementary proprieties that constitute it for what it is), which deserve to be respected and hence place moral claims on the interacting agent and ought to contribute to the constraint and guidance of his ethical decisions and behaviour. This ontological equality principle means that any form of reality (any instance of information), simply for the fact of being what it is, enjoys an initial, overridable, equal right to exist and develop in a way which is appropriate to its nature.

The conscious recognition of the ontological equality principle presupposes, *a parte ante*, a disinterested judgement of the moral situation from an absolute perspective, i.e. a perspective which is as object-oriented as possible. Moral behaviour is less likely without this epistemic virtue. At most, we can only act to the best of our knowledge of the likely consequences and implications of the action undertaken, yet this is hardly sufficient to ensure that our actions will be morally right if our knowledge is either limited or biased towards the agent and what is best only for him, and does not include a wider degree of attentiveness to the patient as well. Thus, a form of moral luck arises when an interested and subject-

---

[7] Broadly speaking, entropy is a quantity specifying the amount of disorder, degradation or randomness in a system bearing energy or information. More specifically, in thermodynamics, entropy is a parameter representing the state of randomness or disorder of a physical system at the atomic, ionic, or molecular level: the greater the disorder, the higher the entropy. In a closed system undergoing change, entropy is a measure of the amount of thermal energy unavailable for conversion into mechanical work: the greater the entropy the smaller the quantity of energy available. Thus, a glass of water with an ice cube in it has less entropy than the same glass of water after the ice cube has melted. According to the second law of thermodynamics, during any process the change in entropy of a system and its surroundings is either zero or positive, so the entropy of the universe as a whole inevitably tends towards a maximum. In information theory, entropy is a measure of the noise, or random errors, occurring in the transmission of signals or messages, whereas information is a measure of the probability of a message being selected from the set of all possible messages. Both concepts are therefore purely syntactic: neither information nor entropy refer to the actual meaning, content or interpretation of the message (a string of nonsense symbols and a meaningful sentence may be equivalent with respect to information content), but both quantitative parameters are based only on the presence of uninterpreted difference. The greater the information in a message, the lower its randomness, or noisiness, and hence the smaller its entropy. In IE, we still treat the two concepts of information and entropy as having the same inverted relation, but we are concerned with their semantic value: for example, as the infosphere becomes increasingly meaningful and rich in content, the amount of information increases and entropy decreases, or as entities wear out, entropy increases and the amount of information decreases.

oriented judgement leads to a course of action which turns out to be respectful of the rights of the patients as well, though only by chance.

The application of the ontological equality principle is achieved, *a parte post*, whenever actions are impartial, universal and 'caring'. This means that IE transforms the Golden rule, and its subsequent refinements such as the Kantian moral imperative or Rawls' choice in a state of ignorance, into the main explicit principle of its ethical analysis, though in information terms. We can do justice to any form of reality and deal fairly with it only if the principles we follow and the actions we perform

- are independent of the position we enjoy in the moral situation, as patient or agent. We would make the same choices and behave in the same way even if we were at the receiving end of the action (impartiality);
- can regulate the behaviour of any other agent placed in any other similar moral situation.

Anyone else would make the same choices and behave in the same way in a similar situation (universality);

- look after the welfare of both the agent and the patient ('care-fullness').

Our choices and behaviour are as subject-oriented (agents' self-interest) as object-oriented (patient's sake).

Biocentric ethics ground their analyses of the moral standing of bio-entities on the intrinsic worthiness of life and the intrinsically negative value of suffering. By endorsing the ontological equality principle, IE suggests that there is something even more elementary and fundamental than life and pain, namely being, understood as information, and entropy. IE holds that being/information has an intrinsic worthiness, and substantiates this position by recognising that any information entity has a 'Spinozian' right to persist in its own status, and a 'Constructionist' right to flourish, i.e. to improve and enrich its existence and essence. We shall presently see that, as a consequence of such 'rights', IE evaluates the duty of any rational being in terms of contribution to the growth of the infosphere, and any process, action or event that negatively affects the whole infosphere – not just an information entity – as an increase in its level of entropy and hence an instance of evil.

The description of the specific essence of classes of information entities is a task to be left to a plurality of ontologies. When the information entities in question are human beings, for example, we refer to the analysis of human rights. Unfortunately, this clear limit in our knowledge is of the greatest importance, for it reminds us that, like many other macroethics, IE

relies on the agent's knowledge for the implementation of the right action. As in the case of Consequentialism, IE may partly rely on moral education and the transmission of whatever humanity has been able to understand about the nature of the world and hence its intrinsic rights, thus adopting a rule-ethics rather than an act-ethics approach, but it must also acknowledge the fact that even a good will acts in the dark of ignorance and that, as human beings, we shall always lack full ethical competence. This is why our first duty is epistemic: whenever possible, we must try to understand before acting. This also explains why moral education consists primarily in negative principles and a fundamental training not to interfere with the world, to abstain from engaging in positive actions and tampering with nature. In most cases, we simply do not know where a *prima facie* positive interaction with reality would lead us, or what negative outcome even well-meant actions may have. I shall return to the risky nature of moral actions in the following pages. What we can attempt here is rather an analysis of the specific elementary proprieties of the whole infosphere that in principle ought to be respected and enhanced by any interactive agent. This is what we are now going to see before turning to the moral laws prescribed by IE.

On the properties of the infosphere

According to IE, there is a cluster of features, related to the well-being of (regions of) the infosphere not in a contingent, external and means-end relation, but internally and in a constitutive sense, which either make the infosphere possible or whose increasing fulfilment make (regions of) the infosphere flourish. Drawing up an exhaustive list of such features lies beyond the present scope of this paper, but we may make sufficient suggestions to clarify the point in question.

Although the tentative list in Table 1 is far from being uncontroversial and could probably be improved, what matters most is that information properties can all be organised into four classes, three of which do not belong to the computer age at all, but indicate the older conceptual roots of IE. The Modal class includes values 1–3 and grants to regions of the infosphere, e.g. a particular class of information entities, a 'Neo-Platonic' right to various degrees/types of existence. Perhaps I should alert the non-philosopher reader that this point is highly controversial: suffice it to say that the whole debate on the ontological proof is based on an interpretation of 1–3 and that nowadays it is usually accepted, as an established point, that 'existence' cannot count as a

Table 1. Features of the infosphere

Information properties of (regions of) the infosphere	Comments	Entropy
	Modal properties	
1. consistency	logical possibility	inconsistency
2. implementability	practical possibility	impossibility
3. occurrence	actual existence	absence
	Humanistic properties	
4. persistency		volatility, transitoriness, ephemerality
5. stability		instability
6. safety		loss or destruction
7. security		misuse, unauthorised use or modification
8. confidentiality	trust	disclosure
9. currency	This is about updating as much as about deleting (hence forgetting): e.g. the U.S. federal statute Fair Credit Reporting Act states that arrest information or criminal records cannot be maintained more than 7 years after the disposition, release or parole of the individual. Many other adverse data cannot be older than 7 years.	obsolescence
10. accuracy		inaccuracy
11. integrity		partiality
12. completeness		incompleteness
13. authenticity	sincerity, honesty	inauthenticity
14. reliability	based on 1–10	unreliability
15. richness		poverty
16. fertility	utility, productivity	sterility
	Illuministic properties	
17. availability		unavailability
18. dissemination		secrecy
19. accessibility		inaccessibility
20. usability		
21. sharability	repeatedly usable, multi-usable	
22. order		disorder
23. systematicity	means full interactivity, tolerance, interoperability integrability, relatedness	
	Constructionist properties	
24. correctability		
25. updatability		
26. upgradability		
27. normativity	elimination of useless redundancy, reduction of waste, sustainable development	redundancy

predicate and the Gassendi-Kant line of reasoning is considered to be more convincing than the Plotinus-Anselm-Descartes-Hegel line. The Humanistic class includes values 4–16 and grants to the infosphere a 'Spinozian' right to various forms of preservation and wholeness. The Illuministic class includes values 17–23 and grants to the infosphere a Libertarian right to various forms of openness and freedom. Only the fourth class, including values 24–27, has no actual precedent in the history of culture. We may call it the Constructionist class, for it grants to the infosphere a right to various forms of growth and enhancement. It is one of the new aspects brought about by contemporary ICT.

The time has now come to turn to the prescriptive and normative principles that, according to IE, should guide, modify and constrain information processes, and hence also contribute to the foundation of the moral codes by which people live.

The normative aspect of information ethics: Four moral laws

What is good for an information entity and the infosphere in general? This is the moral question asked by IE. We have seen that the answer is provided by a minimalist theory of deserts: any information entity is recognised to be the centre of some basic ethical claims, which deserve recognition and should help to regulate the implementation of any information process involving it. Approval or disapproval of any information process is then based on how the latter affects the essence of the information entities it involves and, more generally, the whole infosphere, i.e. on how successful or unsuccessful it is in respecting the ethical claims attributable to the information entities involved, and hence in improving or impoverishing the infosphere. More analytically, we shall say that IE determines what is morally right or wrong, what ought to be done, what the duties, the 'oughts' and the 'ought nots' of a moral agent are, by means of four basic moral laws. I shall formulate them here in an object-oriented version, but a subject-oriented one is easily achievable in terms of 'dos' and 'don'ts':

0. entropy ought not to be caused in the infosphere (null law)
1. entropy ought to be prevented in the infosphere
2. entropy ought to be removed from the infosphere
3. information welfare ought to be promoted by extending (information quantity), improving (information quality) and enriching (information variety) the infosphere.

Laws are listed in order of increasing moral value. They clarify, in very broad terms, what it means to live as a responsible and caring agent in the infosphere. On the one hand, a process is increasingly deprecable, and its agent-source is increasingly blameworthy, the lower is the number-index of the specific law that it fails to satisfy. Let us agree to define any morally information process in the sense just specified as a case of 'disinformation'; this technical expression will turn out to be useful in a moment. Moral mistakes may occur and entropy may increase because of a wrong evaluation of the impact of one's actions – especially when 'local goodness' i.e. the improvement of a region of the infosphere, is favoured to the overall disadvantage of the whole environment – because of conflicting or competing projects, even when the latter are aiming at the satisfaction of IE moral laws, or more simply because of the wicked nature of the agent (this possibility is granted by IE's negative anthropology). On the other hand, a process is already commendable, and its agent-source praiseworthy, if it satisfies the *conjunction* of the null law with at least one other law, not the *sum* of the resulting effects. Note that, according to this definition, an action is unconditionally commendable only if it never generates any entropy in the course of its implementation, that no positive law has a morally higher status ($0 \wedge 1 = 0 \wedge 2 = 0 \wedge 3$) and that the best moral action is the action that succeeds in satisfying all four laws at the same time. Most of the actions that we judge morally good do not satisfy such a strict criterion, for they achieve only a balanced positive moral value, that is, although their performance causes a certain quantity of entropy, we acknowledge that the infosphere is in a better state after their occurrence (action information – action entropy > 0). Finally, a process that satisfies only the null law – the level of entropy in the infosphere remains unchanged after its occurrence – either has no moral value, that is, it is morally irrelevant or insignificant, or it is equally deprecable and commendable, though in different respects. This last point requires some clarification.

Although it is logically conceivable, it seems that, strictly speaking, there can be no actual information process that is deprecable and commendable in exactly the same measure, that is such that its output leaves the infosphere in exactly the same entropic state in which it was before. Consequentialist analyses, for example, do not really take into account the possibility that an agent may escape any moral evaluation by perfectly balancing the amount of happiness and unhappiness generated by his actions. However, it is also the case that, strictly speaking, there can be very few, if any, information processes that are morally insignificant. More likely, any process will always make a difference, either positive or negative, and therefore will always be subject to moral appraisal. This, however, would not only be counterintuitive, but it is not even the view defended by IE. We ordinarily treat most of the processes/actions that take place in life as amoral, i.e. lying beyond the scope of the ethical discourse, for good reasons. Firstly, because we usually adopt a less strict criterion, and accept some latitude in the levels of entropy before and after the occurrence of the process. Secondly, because we are acquainted with such great forms of disinformation (killing, stealing, lying, torturing, betraying, causing injustice, discriminating, etc.), that a lot of minor fluctuations in the level of global entropy become irrelevant. Finally and more importantly, because many processes do not easily modify the global level of entropy even when they are positively immoral. People who argue for the 'fragility of goodness' sometimes do so on the mistaken basis represented by the non-monotonic nature of goodness. Suppose a process – e.g. torturing an innocent child – is utterly morally wrong. This means that it generates a neat increase in the level of entropy in the infosphere and for IE, as well as for our pre-theoretical intuitions, this fact is irrevocable in itself and unredeemable by later events: there is no way of re-engineering the process so that it looses its negative moral value. Drawing on the conceptual vocabulary of mathematical logic, this 'stability' can be defined as the monotonicity of evil. The difficulty encountered by any pure form of Consequentialism is that, since human rights and values (such as integrity) are, in principle, always overridable depending on the overall happiness generated a posteriori by an action's consequences, Consequentialism must treat evil as non-monotonic: in theory, it is always possible to collect and trace a sufficient amount of happiness back to an utterly wicked action and thus force a modification in the latter's evaluation. Now the advantage of IE is that, like our moral intuition, it attributes a non-monotonic nature only to goodness: unlike evil, goodness can, in principle, turn out to be less morally good and sometimes even morally wrong unintentionally, depending on how things develop, that is what new state the infosphere enters into, as a consequence of the process in question. This seems at least to be what people have in mind when talking about the 'fragility of goodness': perhaps there is no action that could count as absolutely good at all times and in all places, so do what you wish and evil will remain evil, but make a mistake and what was initially morally good may be corrupted or turned into evil. As I premised, though, to describe goodness as 'fragile' owing to its non-monotonicity would be a mistake because non-monotonicity is only one of the relevant features to be taken into account. If utter evil is monotonic, *prima*

facie goodness, such as disinterested love or friendship, has the property of being *resilient*, both in the sense of *fault-tolerance*:

- to some degree, goodness has the ability to keep the level of information welfare within the infosphere steady, despite the occurrence of a number of negative processes affecting it;

and in the sense of *error-recovery*:

- to some extent, goodness has the ability to resume or restore the previous positive state of information welfare, erasing or compensating any new entropy that may have been generated by processes affecting it.

Resilience – what we often find described by terms such as tolerance, forbearance, forgiveness, reconciliation or simply other people's positive behaviour – makes goodness much more robust than its non-monotonic nature may lead one to conclude at first sight, and explains the presence of the entropy balance that we experience in the infosphere, which in turn clarifies why so many actions often lie beyond our ethical concern: they simply fail to modify the information/entropy balance of the infosphere significantly.

Consider the following example. Moral actions are risky because only a fraction of their value can depend on our good will. We recognise this when we acknowledge that a bad action is forgivable but not excusable, while only a failed good action is excusable, and therefore that it is moral to do x only when x would be *prima facie* a good action, but immoral to do x when x is *prima facie* a bad action. Evil is monotonic, so one should not intentionally bet on one's own good luck. This holds true even when some morally-risky actions (processes, behaviours) – such as driving too fast in a city centre – come close to the threshold between what is morally insignificant and what is morally wrong (e.g. a person may be injured because of such dangerous driving, thus making speeding a morally wrong action). According to our analysis, these morally-risky actions can usually keep on the amoral side thanks to their (more or less lucky) reliance on the fault tolerance and error-recovering properties of the region of the infosphere they involve (in our example, this would include, among other factors, other drivers' and pedestrians' careful attitude). Although it would not be morally right to rely on it, the strength of goodness should not be undervalued: it takes a fatal process to generate some permanent entropy.

Information ethics as a macroethics

The reader will recall that our investigation into the nature of IE has been prompted by the question whether CE can fruitfully dialogue with other macroethical positions at the same conceptual level, having something important to contribute that may perhaps escape their conceptual frameworks. In search of an answer, we have first freed CE from its conceptual dependence on other macroethics and then disposed of the mistaken interpretation of CE as a standard, action-oriented theory. IE, the philosophical foundational counterpart of CE, has emerged as a non-standard, object-oriented, ontocentric theory. Our next task is to evaluate whether this is sufficient to vindicate the initial claim that the philosophical foundation of CE qualifies as a macroethics. Has IE anything to teach the other standard and non-standard macroethics? What kind of new contribution may IE make to our better understanding of what is morally right and wrong? We can articulate the defence of the macroethic value of IE in three stages, the last of which will require a new section on its own.

IE is a complete macrotheory

This has been already argued, but it may be worth including one more comment here. From a metaethical view, IE is a 'naturalist' and 'realist' macroethics: the ontological features and well-being of the infosphere provide an 'objective' (i.e. object-oriented) basis for judgements of right and wrong and generate 'objective' reasons for action (they are action-pulling), while the moral system, based on the nature and enhancement of information and the corresponding moral claims, is universally binding, i.e. binding on all agents in all places at all times. Although this does not mean that IE reaches full objectivity, it does show that IE endeavours to be as non-subjective and object-oriented as possible. IE is not an ethics of virtue, happiness or duty, but of respect and care (the respect for the patient and the agent's care). According to IE, sometimes the right question to be asked is not 'what ought *I* to be?' nor 'what ought *I* to do?', but '*what* ought to be respected or improved?', for it is the 'what's' welfare that may matter most. The agent is invited to displace himself, to concentrate his attention on the nature and future of the action-receiver, rather than on its relation or relevance to himself, and hence to develop an allocentric attitude, i.e. a profound interest in, and respect for, the infosphere and its values for their own sake, together with a complete openness and receptivity toward it. The concept of care, as employed by IE, is the secular equivalent of the Pauline concept of ἀγάπη ('loving treatment with affectionate regard') or *caritas* ('dearness, love founded on esteem'). Being has lost a religious value and does not impose itself to the attention of the agent anymore, so it is the agent who needs to be sensitised. An agent cares for the patient of his actions when his behaviour enhances the possibilities that the patient may come to achieve whatever is good for it. While an action which is universal and impartial may be morally appropriate, it becomes morally good only when it is driven by care for the patient's sake. This is moral altruism for IE.

IE is certainly a controversial theory

IE is certainly a controversial theory, but it is controversial as a macroethics, for most of the problems that may afflict it are problems concerning the whole class of macrotheories. In short, whatever substantial problems IE encounters are unlikely to be just IE's problems, whereas whatever solutions and insights IE provides are its own original contributions. For example, IE takes as its fundamental value information, and describes entropy as evil, so that moral prescriptivity becomes (at least also) an intrinsic property of information: some features of the infosphere are descriptive and action-guiding and generate reasons for action independently of any motives or desires that agents may actually have. Of course, this is a rather controversial position. However, other theories are also based on first principles, such as εὐδαιμονία, happiness, duty or life, which are equally open to discussion (what is morally good in itself? why is x rather than y to be considered morally good in itself?). Two of the arguments offered by IE are its explanatory power and degree of universality (see next paragraph). That IE's position may still be subject to criticism at this level only proves that IE does represent a new perspective, which involves the whole ethical discourse, and this is all that matters in this context.

IE provides a valuable perspective for its own special field but also beyond

IE provides a valuable perspective from which to approach, with insight and adequate discernment, not only moral problems in its own special field, but also the whole range of conceptual and moral phenomena that form the ethical discourse. Contrary to other macroethics, IE has its own domain of special application but what was a weakness now becomes a strength: action-oriented and anthropocentric or patient-oriented and biocentric theories seem to be inadequate to tackle CE-problems because of the latter's peculiarly ontocentric and object-oriented nature. On the other hand, though I remarked before that non-standard ethics move the ethical focus from history and time to nature and physical space, it would be a mistake to think that, similarly, IE manages only to shift our focus a step further. On the contrary, by enlarging the perspective of the ethical discourse to information and its logical space, IE clearly comes to include both history and nature, both time and physical space within the scope of its analysis. This has a remarkable consequence in terms of the kind of relation that occurs between IE and other macroethics, for IE may rightly claim the whole domain of ethics as its area of interest. To see that this is the case, let us briefly compare IE with the other macroethics. We shall then analyse a few moral cases in the following section.

IE and other non-standard ethics
The general advantage of IE over other non-standard ethics is obvious: IE provides a more comprehensive philosophy of nature and history, and hence can absorb all their positive contributions without sharing the same limits. As for any more specific comparison, three points may be explicitly mentioned here. First, IE does not attribute to information the same absolute value that bio-centric theories attribute to life, and this allows a more intuitive organisation of the environment into a scale of classes of information entities, according to their potential capacities to implement processes that may improve regions of influence in the infosphere. All entities have a moral value, but they do not share the same degree of dignity. Intuitively, from the point of view of the infosphere and its potential improvement, responsible agents (human beings, full-AI robots, angels, gods, God) have greater dignity and are the most valuable information entities deserving the highest degree of respect because they are the only ones capable both of knowing the infosphere and of improving it according to the conscious implementation of their self-determined projects, by increasing or decreasing the level of informativeness of their actions (as the Old Testament seems to show, the 'godness' of God consists primarily in his omnipotence). Secondly, since IE does not limit its own area of interest to the biophysical environment, for the infosphere includes also any other environment, the applicability of its ethical laws is in fact field-independent and universal. Finally and most importantly, IE does not tend to be purely conservative like other 'green ethics'. On the contrary, it is a 'blue ethics' like Virtue Ethics (the expression comes from 'blue-print'), that is an ethics of projects and meaningful construction in a very strong sense. For IE prizes a constructionist approach more highly than any other attitude in life, as the right basis on which to think, remodel and constructively improve the world and the infosphere in general, and implement new realities. According to its semi-teleological approach

(information processes are goal-driven, but their goals are internal goals of a reflective self-development of the infosphere, they are not heteronomous), the best thing that can happen to the infosphere is to be subject to a process of enrichment, extension and improvement without any loss of information, so the most commendable courses of action always have a caring and constructionist nature. The moral agent is an agent that looks after the information environment and is able to bring about positive improvements in it, so as to leave the infosphere in a better state than it was in before the agent's intervention. It is easy to see that, given its constructionist nature, IE may approach questions concerning e.g. abortion, eugenics, human cloning or bioengineering very differently from other bio-centric ethics.

IE and virtue ethics
If we now compare IE and Virtue Ethics, there is a clear sense in which the properties listed in the previous table can be treated as virtues, if seen from the patient's perspective, or values, if seen from the agent's perspective. The well-being of an entity as well as of the whole infosphere consists in the preservation and cultivation of its properties, so IE can dialogue with Virtue Ethics on the basis of its object-oriented and non-functionalist standpoint: the welfare and flourishing of an information entity – what an information entity should be and become – can be objectively determined by the good qualities in, or that may pertain to, that information entity as a specific kind of information. The similarity between Virtue Ethics and IE is that both treat the human being as an entity under construction. The difference between the two approaches lies in their ontologies and in the much broader conception of what may count as a 'virtuous entity' endorsed by IE. If anything, this seems to be a feature that works in favour of an IE approach.

IE and deontologism
It would be possible to develop a deontological version of IE. An IE moral imperative could be, for example: 'act so that you never treat information, whether in your own being or in that of another entity, only as a means but always as an end at the same time'. Even this modified maxim, however, already shows that IE's advantage over Deontologism is, again, its much wider concept of what qualifies as a centre of ethical claims. We have already seen that this was one of the reasons why ethical theories have enlarged their perspective beyond the Kantian approach. Like Deontologism, IE treats evil as monotonic: nothing justifies the infringement of the first moral law (an increase in entropy may often be inevitable, but is never morally justified, let alone approved). In this sense, IE counts as what Max

Weber called an ethics of conviction. However, unlike Deontologism, IE does not adopt a subject-oriented perspective (the agent's reliance on his sense of duty) for determining whether an action deserves to qualify as moral. For IE, an action qualifies as moral only from the patient's perspective – it is only the ontology of the victim that can really define an action as 'right', not the wrongdoer or the impartial judge – so a natural tendency to care for the welfare of the infosphere and a spontaneous desire to make it progress can be highly commendable virtues.

IE and consequentialism

What has been said about Deontologism holds true for a Consequentialist version of IE as well. Broadly speaking, both macroethics share the view that a morally good action is an action that improves the environment in which it takes place. Hence, as far as its pro-information laws are concerned, IE qualifies, like Consequentialism, as what Max Weber calls an ethics of responsibility. Adopting the vocabulary of Consequentialism, we may say that the restraint of information entropy and the active protection and enhancement of information values are conducive to maximal utility. We can even rephrase the Utilitarian principle and say that: 'Actions are right in proportion that they tend to increase information and decrease entropy'. However, the difference between IE and Consequentialism remains significant, for at least the following reasons:

1. *the monotonic problem*

This has been already discussed above. We have just seen that, as far as rights and moral evil is concerned, IE adopts a position closer to Deontologism.

2. *the mathematical problem*

If any quantification and calculation is possible at all in the determination of a moral life, then IE is clearly in a much better position than Consequentialism. Consequentialism already treats individuals as units of equal value but relies on a mere arithmetical calculus of aggregate happiness, which in the end is far too simplistic, utterly unsatisfactory and amounts to little more than a metaphorical device, despite its crucial importance within the theory. On the contrary, if required, IE may resort to a highly developed mathematical field (information theory) and *try to adapt* to its own needs a very refined methodology, statistical means and important theorems, in terms of Sigma logarithms and balanced statistics. I strongly doubt that quantities and algorithmic procedures can play more than a conceptual role in solving moral problems, for the passage from a quantitative and syntactic context to a qualitative and semantic one seems to be impossible,

but if a Consequentialist should seriously think otherwise, it can easily be shown that IE's approach is literally orders of magnitude more powerful. That not even a mathematical theory of information may be sufficient to introduce a calculating element into our moral reasoning is not a crucial problem for IE – which has no where been described as an algorithmic approach – but may work as a *reductio ad absurdum* for any naive form of quantitative Consequentialism.

3. *the supererogatory problem*

There is no limit to how much better a course of action could be, or to the amount and variety of good actions that the agent may but does not perform. As a result, since goodness is a relative concept – relative to the amount of happiness brought about by the consequences of an action – Consequentialism may simply be too demanding, place excessive expectations on the agent and run into the supererogatory problem, asking the agent, who wishes to behave morally, to perform actions that are above and beyond the call of duty or even of his good will. In IE, this does not happen because the morality of a process is assessed on the basis of the state of the infosphere only, i.e. relationally, not relatively to other processes. So while Consequentialism is in principle satisfied only by the best action, in principle IE prizes any single action, which improves the infosphere according to the laws specified above, as a morally commendable action, independently of the alternatives. According to IE, the state of the world is always morally deprecable (there is always some entropy), so any process that improves it is already a good process. This is the advantage of a minimalist approach, which is more flexible and capable of appreciating thousands of little good actions, over a maximalist approach, which is capable of prizing only the single, best action. In a society now used to metering cents and seconds of used-time, the minute attention given to even small marginal values by the former can be appreciated as a much more successful alternative.

4. *the comparative problem*

Consequentialism must accept that, since all actions are evaluated in terms of their consequences and all consequences are comparable according to a single quantitative scale, lives may in turn be judged morally better or worse merely for contingent reasons: an agent may simply be born in a context or find herself in circumstances where her actions can achieve more good than those of other agents (this is another sense in which we may speak of moral luck). This is not a problem faced by IE. Of course, IE shares the very reasonable point that different agents can implement the four moral laws more or less successfully and with different degrees of efficacy, depending on their existential conditions. However, unlike Consequentialism, which endorses a global conception of happiness, IE assesses the value of a process locally, in relation to the outcome it can achieve in the specific region of the environment it affects. This means that IE does not place different processes in competition with each other, and so does not have to rank what has been done by two agents in different situations. This is different from the problem of assessing what has been done and what could have been done by the same agent in the same situation. Circumstances count both for the kind of processes implementable and for the level of implementation, but are irrelevant when comparing different courses of action. Thus, maintaining one's dignity in a Nazi prison-camp is simply no better or worse, morally speaking, than giving a lift to an unknown person on a rainy day, not just because the two experiences are worlds apart, but because both agents have done their best to improve the infosphere, and this is all that matters in order to consider their actions morally commendable. If comparable at all, they are so only in the vague and non-gradable sense in which the goodness of a good knife is comparable to the goodness of a good pencil. Consequentialism is not equally flexible.

Case analysis: Four negative examples

The thesis to be defended now is that not only can IE dialogue with other macroethics, but it can also contribute an important new ethical perspective: that a process or an action may be right or wrong irrespective of its consequences, motives, universality, or virtuous nature, but because it affects positively or negatively its patient and the infosphere, so that, without IE's contribution, our understanding of moral facts in general, not just of CE-problems in particular, could not be fully satisfactory. To support the last remark we shall now analyse four indicative examples: privacy, vandalism, biogenetics and death. They are all negative in nature, but this is just for the sake of simplicity. Let us begin with the only typical CE-problem I wish to refer to in this context.

Privacy

It is common to distinguish four kinds privacy:

- a person S' physical privacy $=_{def.}$ S' freedom from sensory interference or intrusion, achieved thanks to a restriction on others' ability to have bodily interactions with S
- S' mental privacy $=_{def.}$ S' freedom from psychological interference or intrusion, achieved thanks

to a restriction on others' ability to access and manipulate S' mind
- S' decisional privacy $=_{def.}$ S' freedom from procedural interference or intrusion, achieved thanks to the exclusion of others from decisions (concerning e.g. education, health care, career, work, marriage, faith) taken by S and S' group of intimates
- S' informational privacy $=_{def.}$ S' freedom from epistemic interference or intrusion, achieved thanks to a restriction on facts about S that are unknown or unknowable

The last form of privacy is the one that interests us here. Privacy does not play a significant role in standard macroethics because it is the property of a class of objects as patients, not of actions. It becomes a central issue only within a culture that begins to recognise that entities are clusters of information, and that privacy is a fundamental concept referring to the integrity and well-being of an information entity. Privacy is not only an individual's problem, but may be a group's problem, a company's or corporation's problem, or a whole nation's problem, since all these entities have their nature fully determined and constituted by the information they are. How does the problem of privacy arise then? Within the infosphere, entities form a web of dependencies and symbiotic relations. The data output of data collection and analysis processes can become the input of other information processes (no hierarchy is implied). Complex relations among data-producers, data-collectors, data-processors and data-consumers constitute an ecosystem in which data may be recycled, collated, matched, restructured and hence used to make strategic decisions about individuals. In this scenario, questions of informational privacy become increasingly urgent the easier it becomes to collect, assemble, transmit and manipulate huge quantities of data. Note that cases in which privacy and confidentiality are broken because the information in question is legally or ethically significant are cases which society may agree to tolerate: e.g. we may all agree that in special circumstances bank accounts may be checked, computer files searched, or telephones bugged. The interesting point, for a theoretical foundation of information ethics, is not that information may have some legal consequences. Typically, privacy and confidentiality are treated as problems concerning S' ownership of some information, the information being somehow embarrassing, shameful, ominous, threatening, unpopular or harmful for S' life and well-being, yet this is very misleading, for the nature of the information in question is quite irrelevant. It is when the information is as innocuous as one may wish it to be that the question of privacy acquires its clearest value. The husband, who reads the diary of his wife without her permission and finds in it only memories of their love, has still acted wrongly. The source of the wrongness is not the consequences, nor any general maxim concerning personal privacy, but a lack of care and respect for the individual, who is also her information. Yet this is not the familiar position we find defended in CE literature. Rather, a person's claim to privacy is usually justified on the basis of a logic of ownership and employment: a person possesses her own information (her intimately related facts)[8] and has a right to exercise full control over it, e.g., sell it, disclose it, conceal it, and so forth. There follows that the moral problem is normally thought to consist both in the improper acquisition and use of someone else's property, and in the instrumental treatment of a human being, who is reduced to numbers and lifeless collections of information. Sometimes, it is also argued that privacy has an instrumental value, as a necessary condition for special kinds of social relationships or behaviours, such as intimacy, trust, friendship, sexual preferences, religious or political affiliations or intellectual choices. The suggestion is finally advanced that a person has a right to both exclusive ownership and unique control/use of her private information and that she must be treated differently from a mere packet of information. According to IE, however, this view is at least partly mistaken and fails to explain the problem in full. Instead of trying to stop agents treating human beings as information entities, we should rather ask them to realise that when they treat personal and private information they are treating human beings themselves, and should therefore exercise the same care and show the same ethical respect they would exercise and show when dealing with other people, living bodies or environmental elements. We have seen that a person, a free and responsible agent, is after all a packet of information. She is equivalent to an information microenvironment, a constantly elastic and permeable entity with centres and peripheries but with boundaries that are neither sharply drawn nor rigidly fixed in time. What kind of microinfosphere am I? Who am I? I am my, not anyone's, self. I am 'me', but who or what is this constantly evolving object that constitutes 'me', this selfhood of mine? A bundle of information. Me-hood, as opposed to type-self-hood and to the subject-oriented I-hood (the Ego), is the token-person identified as an individual patient from

within, is an individual self as viewed by the receiver of the action. We are our information and when an information entity is a human being at the receiving end of an action, we can speak of a me-hood. What kind of moral rights does a me-hood enjoy? Privacy is certainly one of them, for personal information is a constitutive part of a me-hood. Accessing information is not like accessing physical objects. Physical objects may not be affected by their manipulation, but any cognitive manipulation of information is also performative: it modifies the nature of information by automatically cloning it. Intrusion in the me-hood is therefore equivalent to a process of personal alienation: the piece of information that was meant to be and remain private and unique is multiplied and becomes public, it is transformed into a dead piece of my self that has been given to the world, acquires an independent status and is no longer under my control. Privacy is nothing less than the defence of the personal integrity of a packet of information, the individual; and the invasion of an individual's informational privacy, the unauthorised access, dispersion and misuse of her information is a trespass into her me-hood and a disruption of the information environment that it constitutes. The violation is not a violation of ownership, of personal rights, of instrumental values or of Consequentialist rules, but a violation of the nature of information itself, an offence against the integrity of the me-hood and the efforts made by the individual to construct it as a whole, accurate, autonomous entity independent from, and yet present within, the world. The intrusion is disruptive not just because it breaks the atmosphere of the environment, but because any information about ourselves is an integral part of ourselves, and whoever has access to it possesses a piece of ourselves, and thus undermines our uniqueness and our autonomy from the world. There is information that everyone has about us, but this is only our public side, the worn side of our self, and the price we need to pay to society to be recognised as its members.

Vandalism

IE seems to be able to cast some new light on CE-problems but – one may object – how successfully can it treat other types of moral problems? One may wonder how something which is not a sentient being or does not even exist may still have a moral standing, no matter how minimal, and hence impose any significant claim on the interactive agent so as to influence and shape his behaviour as a centre of moral respect. The doubt may seem reasonable, until we realise that it is in clear contrast with a rather common view of what it is morally right or wrong, and that this is precisely the

---

[8] T. Forester and P. Morrison, *Computer Ethics*, 2nd ed. Cambridge Mass.: The MIT Press, p. 102, 1994: "Perhaps the final issue is that concerning information ownership: should information about me be owned by me? Or should I, as a database operator, own any information that I have paid to have gathered and stored?".

problem solved by IE, as I shall argue in the analysis of the present and the following two cases.

Imagine a boy playing in a dumping-ground. Nobody ever comes to the place. Nobody ever uses anything in it, nor will anyone ever wish to do so. There are many old cars, abandoned there. The boy entertains himself by breaking their windscreens and lights, skilfully throwing stones at them. He enjoys himself enormously, yet most of us would be inclined to suggest that he should entertain himself differently, that he ought not to play such a destructive game, and that his behaviour is not just morally neutral, but is positively deprecable, though perhaps very mildly so when compared to more serious mischiefs. In fact, we express our contempt by defining his course of action as a case of 'vandalism', a word loaded with an explicitly negative moral judgement. Which macroethics can help us to understand our sense of dissatisfaction with the boy's behaviour? Any bio-centric ethics is irrelevant, and broad environmental issues are out of question as well, since by definition breaking the car windscreens does not modify the condition of the dumping-ground. Consequentialism, in its turn, finds it difficult to explain why the boy's behaviour is not actually commendable, since, after all, it is increasing the level of happiness in the world. Certainly, the boy could be asked to employ his time differently, but then we would be only saying that, much as his vandalism is morally appreciable, there is something better he could be doing. We would be running into the supererogatory problem without having explained why we feel that his game is a form of vandalism and hence blameworthy. The alternative view, that his behaviour is causing our unhappiness, just begs the question: for the sake of the argument we must be treated as mere external observers of his childish game. Deontologism soon runs out of answers too. Its ends/means maxim is inapplicable, for the boy is playing alone and no human interaction is in view. Its imperative to behave as a universal legislator may be a bit more promising, but we need to remember that it often generates only drastic reactions and thus more problems than solutions: the agent can bite the bullet and make a rule of his misbehaviour. In this case, though, the problem is even more interesting. For Kant apparently never thought that people could decide to behave as universal legislators without taking either the role or the task seriously, but just for fun, setting up mad rules as reckless players. The *homo ludens* can be Kantian in a very dangerous way, as Stanley Kubrick's *Dr. Strangelove* illustrates. The boy may agree with Kant and act as a universal legislator, as happens in every game: he is not the only one allowed to break the cars' windscreens in the dumping-ground, and anyone else is welcome to take part in the game. With its stress on the universal extension of a particular behaviour, Deontologism may well increase the gravity of the problem. Just think what would happen if the boy were the president of a military power playing a war game in the desert. Virtue Ethics is the only macroethics that comes close to offering a convincing explanation, though in the end it too fails. From its perspective, the boy's destructive game is morally deprecable not in itself, but because of the effects it may have on his character and future disposition. However, in so arguing Virtuous Ethics is begging the question: it is because we find it deprecable that we infer that the boy's vandalism will lead to negative consequences for his own development. Nobody grants that breaking windscreens necessarily leads to a bad character, life is too short to care and, moreover, a boy who has never broken a car windscreen might not become a better person after all, but a repressed maniac, who knows? Where did David practice before killing Goliath? Besides, the context is clearly described as ludic, and one needs to be a real wet blanket to reproach a boy who is enjoying himself enormously, and causing no apparent harm, just because there is a chance that his playful behaviour may perhaps, one day, slightly contribute to the possible development of a moral attitude that is not praiseworthy. We come then to IE, and we know immediately why the boy's behaviour is a case of blameworthy vandalism: he is not respecting the objects for what they are, and his game is only increasing the level of entropy in the dumping-ground, pointlessly. It is his lack of care, the absence of consideration of the objects' sake, that we find morally blameable. He ought to stop destroying bits of the infosphere and show more respect for what is naturally different from himself and yet similar, as an information entity, to himself. He ought to employ his time more 'constructively'.

Genetic problems

Suppose one day we genetically engineer and clone non-sentient cows. They are alive but, by definition, they lack any sort of feelings. They are biological masses, capable of growth when properly fed, but their eyes, ears, or any other senses are incapable of any sensation of pain or pleasure. We no longer kill them, we simply carve into their living flesh whenever part of their body is needed. The question here is not whether it would be moral to create such monsters, for we may simply assume that they are available, but rather: what macroethics would be able to explain our sense of moral repugnance for the way we treat them? Most people would consider it morally wrong, not just because of our responsibility as creators, not just because of the kind of moral persons we would become if we were to adopt such behaviour, not because of the negative effects, which are none, and not because of the Kantian maxims, neither of which would apply, but because of the bio-object in front of us and its values. Even if the senseless cow is just a biological mass, no longer feeling anything, this does not mean that any of our actions towards it would be morally neutral. IE could argue, for example, that the cow is still a body whose integrity and unity demand respect. Affecting the essence of the body would still be wrong even if the body was no longer sentient. Indeed, since the original status of the body was that of a sentient being, we ought to do our best to reinstate its former conditions for its own sake and welfare. Let me introduce a second example to illustrate the point further. There seems to be nothing morally wrong in cloning one's lungs, or producing some extra litres of one's blood, which would turn out useful in the future, because when used they will be serving their purpose. But we find the idea of cloning a whole non-sentient twin, which we could then keep alive and exploit as a source of organs, when necessary, morally repugnant, because to take an arm away from our twin would mean to affect its integrity adversely and transform it into something that it was not meant to be, a mutilated body. We would be showing no care whatsoever, and our actions would not be implemented for the sake of the patient.

Death

Standard ethics do not treat death; at most they try to teach the living how to face it. Non-standard bio-centric ethics treat only the dying. Only IE has something to say about the actual dead person and her moral claims. This last example comes from the *Iliad*. Achilles has killed Hector. For many days, he has, in his fury, repeatedly dragged Hector's body behind his chariot, round the tomb of his comrade Patroclus. He has decided to take his full revenge for Patroclus' death by not accepting any ransom in exchange for Hector's body. Hector will have no burial and must be eaten by the dogs. Achilles' misbehaviour seems obvious, but there is more than one way of explaining why it is morally blameworthy. Other non-standard ethics can say nothing relevant and a Deontological approach is not very useful. Just before dying, Hector asked Achilles to be kind and to accept his parents' offers in return for his body, yet Achilles rejected his prayers and was ready to face the consequences. He is not afraid of universalising his behaviour. Although Priam tries to reason him into returning Hector's body using a Deontological argument ("Think of your father, O Achilles like unto the gods, who is such even as I am, on the sad threshold of old age. [...]"), Achilles

has been already informed by his mother about the Gods' will and is ready to change his course of action anyway. Actually, he finds Priam's line of reasoning rather annoying. The Consequentialist, of course, can lead us to consider the pain that Achilles' behaviour has caused to Priam and Andromache and all the other Trojans. A supporter of Virtue Ethics can easily argue that what is morally wrong is Achilles' attitude, for he is disrespectful towards the dead, his family, the gods and the social customs regulating human relations even during war time. Yet Achilles changes his mind only because the Gods intervene, and the speech made by Apollo in the last book of the Iliad, the speech that convinces the Gods that it is time to force Achilles to modify his behaviour and return Hector's body, is perhaps best read from an IE perspective, a defence of the view that even a dead body, a mere lifeless object, can be outraged and deserves to be morally respected:

[51] Achilles has lost all pity! No shame in the man,
shame that does great harm or drives men on to good.
No doubt some mortal has suffered a dearer loss than this,
a brother born in the same womb, or even a son ...
he grieves, he weeps, but then his tears are through.
The Fates have given mortals hearts that can endure.
[cf. above here the argument against the simple fragility of goodness]
But this Achilles – first he slaughters Hector,
he rips away the noble prince's life
then lashes him to his chariot, drags him round
his beloved comrade's tomb. But why, I ask you?
What good will it do him? What honor will he gain?
Let that man beware, or great and glorious as he is,
we mighty gods will wheel on him in anger – look,
[65] he outrages the senseless clay in all his fury!"

The Greek word for "outrages" is $\alpha\epsilon\iota\kappa\acute{\iota}\xi\omega$, which also means 'to dishonour' or 'to treat in an unseemly way'. Hector's body demands $\breve{\epsilon}\lambda\epsilon o\nu$, compassion, but Achilles has none, for he has lost any $\alpha\iota\delta\acute{\omega}\varsigma$ any moral respect, blinded by his painful passion. Yet the view from IE requires him to overcome his subjective state, achieve an impartial perspective and care for the dead body of his enemy. Achilles must start behaving with some respect for the body, even if this is now just $\kappa\omega\phi\grave{\eta}\nu\ \gamma\alpha\hat{\iota}\alpha\nu$, senseless clay.

Conclusion

It would be foolish to think that IE can have the only or even the last word on moral matters. IE does not provide a library of error-proof solutions to all ultimate moral problems, but it fulfils an important missing role within the spectrum of macroethics. There has been a fundamental blind spot in our ethical discourse, a whole ethical perspective missing, which IE and its applied counterpart, CE, seem to be able to perceive and take into account. The shift from an anthropocentric to a bio-centric perspective, which has so much enriched our understanding of morality, is followed by a second shift, from a biocentric to an onto-centric view. This is what IE and CE can achieve, thus acquiring a fundamental role in the context of macroethical theories. The object-oriented ontocentric perspective is more suitable to an information culture and society, improves our understanding of moral facts, can help us to shape our moral questions more fruitfully, to sharpen our sense of value and to make the rightness or wrongness of human actions more intelligible and explicable, and so it may lead us to look more closely at just what fundamental values our ethical theories should seek to promote. All we require from IE is to help us to give an account of what we already intuit. "Agere sequitur esse", "action follows out of being": the old medieval dictum can now be given a twist and be adopted as the motto of IE.

References

D.M. Ermann, M.B. Williams and M.S. Shauf, editors, *Computers, Ethics and Society*, 2nd ed. New York: Oxford U.P., 1997.

T. Forester and P. Morrison. *Computer Ethics*, 2nd ed. Cambridge Mass.: The MIT Press, 1994.

D.D. Johnson in her *Computer Ethics*, 2nd ed. Upper Saddle River N.J.: Prentice Hall, 1994.

D. Langford in *Practical Computer Ethics*. London: McGraw-Hill, 1995.

R. Mason. Four Ethical Issues of the Information Age. *MIS Quarterly* 10 (1): 5–12, 1986.

J.H. Moor. What Is Computer Ethics? *Metaphilosophy* 16 (4): 266–275, 1985.

Part II
Cyberspace

[11]

Balancing intellectual property rights and the intellectual commons: A lockean analysis

Herman T. Tavani

Department of Philosophy, Rivier College, Nashua, NH, USA
Email: htavani@rivier.edu

ABSTRACT

The current dispute about whether, and to what extent, digital information should be granted legal protection underscores a fundamental tension between those who argue for strong intellectual property rights (IPRs) and those who advocate for the preservation of a robust intellectual commons. The latter group argues that current IPRs threaten the intellectual commons because: (a) they unfairly restrict access to information in digital form, and (b) they eliminate from the public domain some information that had previously been included in it. Defenders of strong IPRs, on the other hand, argue that without the kind of protection provided by recent copyright laws, individuals and corporations will not have the incentives necessary to produce literary and creative works. One might infer from the competing, and at times seemingly contradictory, claims advanced in this dispute that no plausible resolution can be reached. A possible solution that has been overlooked, however, is one suggested in the classic theory of property put forth by British philosopher John Locke in the late 17th century. Locke's theory, which includes a principle for determining when sections of the physical commons are justly appropriated and enclosed, can also be applied in determining what is required for justly enclosing portions of the intellectual commons. Thus Locke's classic property theory provides an adjudicative principle that can guide us in resolving key issues in the contemporary debate about how to balance IPRs and the intellectual commons.

COVERAGE

☑

ⓘ

INTRODUCTION

This essay is organized into four main sections. Section 1 briefly examines two key concepts, "intellectual objects" and the "intellectual commons," which are critical to understanding the current debate about intellectual property rights (IPRs). Section 2 describes how the intellectual commons (sometimes also referred to as the "information commons") is currently threatened by recent laws and recent technologies. Two controversial US laws, both of which were enacted in 1998, are examined: the Copyright Term Extension Act (CTEA) and the Digital Millennium Copyright Act (DMCA). Although both are American laws, they have significant international implications. Also examined in Section 2 are recent technologies that perform a role similar to copyright law by effectively using software code to restrict both access to and use of digitized information. Section 3 provides a brief exposition of John Locke's classic theory of property, and it examines an adjudicative principle in Locke's theory that can guide us in deliberating between the claims advanced by opposing sides in the debate about IPRs and the intellectual commons. In Section 4, we apply Locke's principle to the CTEA and the DMCA, and we conclude by showing that both laws

KEYWORDS

Digital information

Intellectual commons

Intellectual object

Intellectual property rights

John Locke

violate the spirit of Locke's conditions for what is required in framing just property laws.

1. INTELLECTUAL OBJECTS AND THE INTELLECTUAL COMMONS: TWO KEY ELEMENTS IN THE CURRENT DISPUTE ABOUT IPRS

To appreciate what exactly is at stake in the contemporary debate about IPRs involving digitized information, an understanding of two key concepts is required: *intellectual objects* and the *intellectual commons*. We define and briefly examine each notion.

1.1 What are Intellectual Objects?

The concept of property has evolved considerably since the 18th century. Originally, it referred exclusively to land but eventually "property" was extended to include things or "objects" such as farms, factories, and furniture (Hughes, 1997). The kinds of entities now examined in discussions about property include non-tangible as well as tangible objects. Various expressions have been used to refer to the former kinds of objects; for example, they are sometimes referred to as "ideal objects" or as "non-tangible economic goods" (Palmer, 1997). Following Hettinger (1997), however, we use the expression *intellectual objects* to refer to instances of intellectual property – i.e., "objects" such as books, poems, software programs, and so forth.

Intellectual objects differ from physical objects in at least three relevant respects. First, intellectual objects are *non-tangible*, and thus they cannot be physically manipulated until they are expressed or "fixed" in some tangible medium. Second, they are *non-exclusionary*; unlike tangible objects,

intellectual objects can be possessed by more than one person simultaneously. Consider the case of a particular laptop computer, which is a physical object and thus exclusionary. If Harry owns that computer, then Sally cannot, and *vice versa*. However, the same is not true of a word-processing program that resides in Harry's computer. Note that if Sally makes a copy of that program, then both Sally and Harry simultaneously possess copies of the same word-processing program. Third, intellectual objects tend to be *non-rivalrous*. The sense of scarcity that applies to physical objects, which often has caused competition and rivalry with respect to those entities, need not exist in the case of intellectual objects. The latter objects can be easily reproduced; for example, countless digital copies of a Microsoft Word program can be reproduced at a marginal cost of zero.

1.2 What is the Intellectual Commons?

One way of understanding what is meant by the expression "intellectual commons" is to think of it as a domain or (non-geographical) space comprised of intellectual objects that are not owned by anyone and that are accessible to everyone. Buchanan and Campbell (2005), who use the phrase "information commons," capture the essence of this domain of intellectual objects when they describe it as:

> A body of knowledge and information that is available to anyone to use without the need to ask for or receive permission from another, providing any conditions placed on its use are respected (p. 229).

Another way to think about the intellectual commons is to contrast it with the physical commons, such as the one described by John Locke in his *Second Treatise on Government*.[1] The romantic image of the commons that Locke portrays in that work – viz., a commons that is seemingly inexhaustible in its resources – is one that may have existed in primeval times before the establishment of a social compact. The commons that existed in England in the 17th and 18th centuries, however, was dif-

---

The sense of scarcity that applies to physical objects need not exist in the case of intellectual objects

ferent from the one described by Locke. For one thing, the English commons was increasingly becoming privatized during this period. Rose (1991) points out that during the 18th century, the commons was rapidly replaced with private property and that laws were passed to prevent peasants from catching fish or shooting deer on these lands.[2] Thus the physical commons – at least as it is understood in the English tradition – was undergoing a significant transformation at the time Locke was developing his property theory. Analogously, the intellectual commons is currently undergoing a similar transformation in that, increasingly, it too is being privatized.[3]

2. HOW IS THE INTELLECTUAL COMMONS THREATENED?

Just as the physical commons in England was vanishing during Locke's lifetime, some now worry that the intellectual commons is beginning to experience a similar fate. Many are familiar with Garrett Hardin's tale about the "tragedy of the commons," which results from the over-consumption of resources in a physical commons shared by farmers (Hardin, 1968). Perhaps now there also is good reason to worry about what Heller (1998) refers to as the "tragedy of the anti-commons" – a phenomenon that occurs whenever resources are under-consumed or under-utilized. As more and more of the intellectual commons is fenced off or enclosed because of strong IPRs, critics fear that fewer and fewer intellectual resources will be available to ordinary individuals and that, as a result, our information resources will be underutilized.

In a work entitled "The Tragedy of the Information Commons," Onsrud (1998) describes the intellectual commons as one that is

...being enclosed or even destroyed by a combination of law and technology that is privatizing what had been public and may become public, and locking up and restricting access to ideas and information that have heretofore been shared resources.[4]

But how, exactly, is the intellectual commons threatened by a combination of law and technology? On the one hand, it is threatened by recent copyright laws enacted for the specific purpose of blocking access to and use of information in digital format. On another level, this threat is exacerbated by technologies that have been designed either to prevent or severely limit access this information. Thus, law and technology now work in tandem; technology can be used to enforce copyright law, and sometimes it is used in ways that supercede the law. We briefly examine both types of threats, beginning with a look at the impact of two recent copyright laws.

2.1 Recent Copyright Laws and the Erosion of the Intellectual Commons

Much has been written about the history and evolution of copyright law in the US and elsewhere, so there is no need to repeat that discussion in depth here. However, a few brief remarks may be useful. The English Statute of Anne, enacted in 1709,[5] is generally considered to be the precedent for current copyrights law in the Anglo-American world.[6] The first American copyright law was passed in 1790, and copyright law in the US has since been modified and amended on several occasions. One aim of copyright law is to protect the work of authors by granting them ownership rights for their creative works for a limited period of time. (Note that an "author" can be a corporation as well as an individual.) To prevent authors from having exclusionary rights to their works, provisions such as "fair use" have been incorporated into copyright law to ensure that ordinary individuals can have some degree of access to copyrighted works.

In the US, two controversial amendments to the Copyright Act were passed in 1998: the Copyright Term Extension Act (CTEA)[7] and the Digital Millennium Copyright Act (DMCA). CTEA extends copyright protection from the life of the author plus 50 years to the life of the author plus 70 years, and the DMCA restricts access to and use of information that either is created in or converted to digital format.[8] Whereas CTEA reduces the amount of information that once had been in the public domain and thus had been freely available to ordinary individuals, the DMCA restricts both access to and the use of digital information in electronic books. Physical (or "paper and glue") books, on the other hand, continue to be more freely available for people to access and share.

Regarding the threat to the intellectual commons posed by CTEA, consider the case of Eric Eldred who set up a personal (nonprofit) Web site dedicated to electronic versions of older books. On his site (www.eldritchpress.org) he included many classics, such as the complete works of

---

> If the books that we were able to borrow in the past become available only in digitized form in the future, it may no longer be possible to access them freely through an interlibrary loan system

---

Nathaniel Hawthorne. Some of the books on Eldred's site were either difficult to get (as physical books) or were out of print. At the time Eldred set up his Web site, these books were in the public domain. With the passage of CTEA, however, some of the books on his site came under copyright protection and thus were in violation of the newly expanded law. Electing not to remove any of the books from his site, Eldred instead decided to challenge the legality of the amended Copyright Act, which he argued is incompatible with the fair use provision and thus in violation of Article 1, Section 8, Clause 8 of the United States Constitution. He lost his court challenge (*Eldred vs. Attorney General John Ashcroft*) in a hearing by a United States circuit court; and the lower court's decision was upheld by the US Supreme Court in a 7-2 ruling in 2003. As a result of CTEA, the intellectual commons has arguably been diminished in that many books that once had been freely available to ordinary persons are no longer freely accessible to them (either in physical space or on the Internet).

The DMCA, which restricts the way that information in digitized format can be accessed and used, also has significant implications for the fate of the intellectual commons. Despite the fact that digital technology has made information exchange

easy and inexpensive, the DMCA has made it more difficult to access information that has either been created in or converted to digitized form. To illustrate this point, consider the case of interlibrary loan practices involving physical books. Such practices have not only benefited individuals, but arguably also have contributed to the public good by supporting the ideal of an information-sharing community. If the books that we were so easily able to borrow in the past become available only in digitized form in the future, it may no longer be possible to access them freely through an interlibrary-loan system. By granting copyright holders of digital media the exclusive right to control how electronic (versions of) books are accessed and used, the DMCA discourages the sharing of digitized information between libraries. So as more books become available only in digital form, the information they contain may be less accessible to ordinary individuals in the future, which will further diminish an already shrinking intellectual commons.[9]

2.2 Regulating and Privatizing Information Through Technology

In addition to enacting specific copyright legislation aimed at restricting access to and use of digitized information, software code can be designed to accomplish the same objectives. Lessig (1999) has argued that in cyberspace, the *code is the law*. To understand the force of Lessig's claim with respect to how code is currently being used to control access to information in digital form, we need only to look at current Digital Rights Management (DRM) systems. DRM technologies allow digital content owners to control the use of digitized information by blocking access to that information via encryption mechanisms, and by enabling access to it through the use of passwords. As a result, DRM technology works hand in hand with the DMCA to control the flow of information in digitized form; and any programs designed to circumvent DRM controls are in violation of Sec. 1201 of the DMCA. Critics worry about the ways in which DRM technology can be used to enforce copyright law. For example, Samuelson (2003) believes that because DRM systems permit content owners to exercise far more control over uses of copyrighted works than what is provided by current copyright law, DRM technology may violate the fair use provision of copyright law.

Elkin-Koren (2000) has a slightly different concern about the way in which code can be used to regulate access to information. She worries that the technological controls embedded in software code are, in effect, "privatizing information policy." To support Elkin-Koren's contention, consider that in the past we were able to examine the implications of newer technologies for copyright-related principles such as fair use. That is, we were also able to engage in meaningful public policy debates about whether traditional copyright laws should apply or whether those laws needed to be amended. More importantly, however, we could challenge the viability and constitutionality of such laws through the judicial process. Because code is now being developed and used with the express purpose of precluding the possibility of copyright infringement, it would seem that we are losing this traditional mechanism for debating public policy. If computer manufacturers and content providers can decide what the copyright rules should be, and if they are permitted to embed certain code in their products that enforces those rules, then there is no longer a need for (or perhaps no longer even the possibility of) public policy debate about copyright issues. So Elkin-Koren fears that the framework for balancing the interests of individuals and the public, which in the past had been supported by spirited policy debates and judicial review, may no longer be possible in a world in which copyright policies are predetermined by code. Spinello (2003) makes a similar point when he notes that restrictions embedded in computer code end up having the force of law without the checks and balances provided by the legal system.

So if those who criticize recent copyright laws, as well as the technologies designed to enforce these laws, are correct, then it would seem that we have much to worry about regarding the future of the intellectual commons. Arguably, what is needed is a balancing scheme that would both preserve the intellectual commons and respect some form of reasonable IPRs. As suggested earlier, a balancing scheme of this sort can be found in the classic property theory advanced by John Locke.

3. LOCKE'S THEORY OF PROPERTY AND ITS IMPLICATIONS FOR IPRS

How, exactly, does Locke's theory of property, published in 1690, help us to resolve key issues in the contemporary debate involving IPRs? When appealing to Locke's property theory to justify IPRs, many contemporary commentators point to the role that labor plays in Locke's theory. While Locke's theory does indeed stress the importance of labor in the just acquisition of property, it is also takes into account certain features having to do with preserving the commons. And it is here that we find Locke's most important contribution to the contemporary debate. However, first we need to examine the outline of Locke's theory to see how it ultimately accomplishes this balancing scheme with respect to the commons vis-à-vis property rights.

In his *Second Treatise on Civil Government*, Locke claims that property rights are justified because humans have a "right to their preservation" (Sec. 25). He goes on to assert that every person is entitled to the fruits of his labor, which result from the "labor of his body" and the "work of his hands." According to Locke, when a person removes something from the commons, he has "mixed his labor with it, and joined to it something that is his own, and thereby makes it his property" (Sec. 27). Perhaps Hettinger (1997, p. 21) best sums up Locke's view on how property is justly appropriated when he writes:

> Locke's justification for property derives property rights in the product of labor from prior property rights in one's own body. A person owns her body and hence she owns what it does, namely, its labor. A person's labor and its product are inseparable, and hence ownership of one can be secured only by owning the other. Hence, if a person is to own her body and thus its labor, she must also own what she joins her labor with – namely, the product of her labor.

Locke also suggests an important distinction regarding the appropriation of objects, such as acorns and apples, and the

S9

appropriation of land itself. After providing his argument for what is required in the just appropriation of the various kinds of objects that reside in the commons, Locke proceeds to explain how one can justly appropriate portions of the commons. He states:

> As much land as a man tills, plants, improves, cultivates, and can use the product of, so much is his property. He by his labor does, as it were, *enclose it from the common.* (Sec. 32, Italics Added).

However, Locke does not believe that one's right either to appropriate objects or to enclose a section of the common is absolute – i.e., without qualifications. For example, he imposes certain conditions and constraints on *how much* one can justly appropriate from the commons. This constraint is sometimes referred to as Locke's "sufficiency proviso"; we will refer to it simply as *Locke's proviso.*

3.1   Locke's Proviso: Implications for the Physical and the Intellectual Commons

In accordance with Locke's proviso, one can remove objects from the commons only to the extent that there is *"enough and as good* left for others" to appropriate (Sec. 27). In a similar way, one can appropriate land itself by enclosing it from the commons only if there is enough and as good left for others to enclose (Sec. 33). Thus Locke does not believe that a person is necessarily entitled to own everything with which she has mixed her labor, simply by virtue of investing her labor in gathering certain objects or in tilling some section of land. Irrespective of how much labor one is able or willing to invest in appropriating objects, a person is not entitled to cut down all of the trees in the forest; nor is she entitled to take the last tree.

But what, exactly, does Locke mean by "enough and as good"? Interpretations of the Lockean proviso range from the most egalitarian reading in which equal amounts of resources must be left for everyone (or at least for those who desire) to appropriate, to an interpretation in which no one may

be harmed, deprived, or "made worse off" because of some appropriation.[10] We need only to accept the weakest and least controversial interpretation of the proviso – viz., the view that no individual should be *worse off* because of the appropriations of others – in order to see how Locke provides us with a useful principle for resolving key issues in the debate about IPRs and the intellectual commons. Locke's concern that no individual is made worse off as a result of an appropriation can be found in his remarks in Sections 31, 33, and 36 of the *Second Treatise,* where he says that appropriations are permissible so long as they do not harm or "prejudice any other man."

What, exactly, did Locke have in mind when he envisioned the appropriation of land by some individuals in a way that no other individuals were made "worse off" as a result? Locke portrays a bountiful commons – one consisting of resources that were either (a) unowned or (b) commonly owned by all. Thus Locke believed that no one would be harmed if everyone adhered to his proviso when appropriating objects from, or when enclosing sections of, the physical commons. Before showing how Locke's theory can be applied to concerns about the intellectual commons, however, it would be useful to anticipate and respond to an objection[11] that conceivably could be raised with regard to drawing relevant analogies between the intellectual and the physical commons.

3.2   A Possible Objection (and Reply): The Intellectual Commons and the Physical Commons are Radically Different Domains

One might argue that whereas the physical commons is limited or fixed in terms of resources, the intellectual commons is virtually limitless and is constantly expanding.[12] Continuing with this line of reasoning, one might go on to argue that any attempt to draw a meaningful analogy with respect to property rights involving these two very different types of commons would be inappropriate. Furthermore, one could argue that if the intellectual commons is limitless, there is no need to worry about the practice of granting strong IPRs to individuals and corporations.

Let us suppose, for sake of argument, that the intellectual commons is infinitely expandable because of the kinds of objects that can be produced to populate it. Does it follow from this assumption that granting strong IPRs will not diminish or erode the intellectual commons? Consider some of the other factors at play with respect to IPRs. For example, legal protections are granted to individuals and to corporations not only for the production of intellectual objects but also for the development of certain kinds of *methods* used to access those objects (and to access information in general). Additionally, IPRs that are granted for these purposes can result in restricting one's ability to access and use information, in the same way that fencing off sections of the physical commons results in individuals being denied access to tangible objects such as acorns and apples.13

Many advocates for strong IPRs believe that the methods used to access digitized information are among the kinds of things that also deserve protection.14 However, we have seen that granting this kind of protection can easily result in ordinary individuals being denied access to information that had previously been available to them. In this sense, then, the intellectual commons (like the physical commons) can indeed be eroded; and it can be eroded even if countless new intellectual objects are produced. Thus, the intellectual commons (like the physical commons in England during the 17th and 18th centuries) is clearly vulnerable to erosion. And because the current threat to the intellectual commons is analogous in relevant respects to the threat to the physical commons that existed during Locke's time, it would not seem unreasonable to look to Locke's classic theory of property to see whether a possible resolution to the contemporary problem can be found there.

4. EXTENDING LOCKE'S THEORY TO THE CONTEMPORARY DEBATE

To see how Locke's theory can guide us in resolving issues in the contemporary debate about IPRs and the intellectual commons, and how it can help us to frame just laws and policies for digitized information, we need to consider two questions: (1) *Does a particular law or policy affecting IPRs*

and digital information diminish the intellectual commons? and (2) *Are ordinary individuals made worse off because of that law or policy?* We next examine these questions in light of the CTEA and the DMCA.

4.1 Applying Locke's Theory to CTEA and DMCA

Consider once again the CTEA (Copyright Term Extension Act) and the DMCA (Digital Millennium Copyright Act), both of which were described in Section 2. Recall that CTEA extends copyright protection from the life of the author plus 50 years to the life of the author plus 70 years, and that the DMCA restricts access to and use of information that either is created in or converted to digital format. We saw that whereas passage of the CTEA has resulted in diminishing the amount of information that is now available in the public domain, enactment of the DMCA has severely restricted access to and use of information that resides in digital form. Regarding the challenge posed by CTEA, we saw that Eric Eldred was forced either to remove certain books (that had previously been in the public domain) from his Web site or shut down his site altogether. We also saw how the DMCA discouraged the sharing of electronic books by making their exchange more difficult, even though hardcopy versions of those books are still freely available through the practice of interlibrary loan.

If we apply the principle in Locke's theory requiring that *no one should be made worse off as a result of an appropriation of property by others* to the current debate about IPRs and the intellectual commons, then we can see how both the CTEA and the DMCA violate the spirit of the Lockean proviso. Clearly, individuals are worse off when: (i)

S11

> **Legal protections are granted to individuals and corporations not only for the production of intellectual objects but also for the development of certain kinds of** methods **used to access those objects**

classic books that had been in the public domain are no longer freely available to ordinary individuals; and (ii) digitized information including digital books, which in their physical form can be shared among ordinary individuals, are not as freely accessible.

4.2 The Lockean Proviso as a Guiding Principle for Balancing Copyright Laws and the Intellectual Commons

We have considered some ways that Locke's proviso, with its requirement that "enough and as good" be left for others to appropriate, can be used to protect the intellectual commons. However, we should not infer from this that Locke would reject IPRs altogether. On the contrary, copyright protection in some form would seem to be compatible with Locke's proviso and thus with his overall theory of property.[15] For example, just as Locke believed that land should not always remain common and uncultivated (Sec. 36), he would likely have supported the enclosing of certain sections of the intellectual commons through the granting copyright protection. And based on what Locke said about the cultivation of the physical commons, we can infer that he also would not want an *underdeveloped* intellectual commons, which could easily happen if individuals were pre-

S12

> Copyright protection in some form would seem to be compatible with Locke's proviso

---

vented from enclosing sections of it via the appropriation of intellectual objects.

However, Locke would also support the position that ordinary individuals should enjoy access to the intellectual commons; and he would argue that these individuals are indeed worse off when they are denied unfettered access to information and ideas that had once been in the public domain. So while Locke could consistently defend copyright protection in some form, such as

copyright laws that include a provision for fair use, he could not embrace either the CTEA or the DMCA as just property laws.

5. CONCLUSIONS

We began this paper by examining some of the key issues in the tension between those arguing for strong IPRs and those advocating for a robust intellectual commons. We next showed how the intellectual commons is currently threatened by recent copyright laws, such as the CTEA and the DMCA, as well as by recent technologies such as DRM systems that use embedded code to restrict access to digital information. We then considered how John Locke's classic theory of property could be applied to the contemporary debate involving IPRs. We saw that Locke's proviso (with its requirement that "enough and as good" be left for others to appropriate from the commons) can guide us in framing just copyright laws. We also saw that Locke's proviso, if adhered to, could help to ensure the preservation of the intellectual commons, which is now threatened by the combination of recent laws and technologies. So it would seem that Locke' classic property theory is indeed useful in helping us to elucidate and possibly resolve key issues underlying the contemporary dispute involving IPRs and the intellectual commons.

ACKNOWLEDGEMENTS

I am grateful to Elizabeth Buchanan for some helpful comments on an earlier draft of this paper. In composing this paper, I have drawn from material in three of my previously published works: Tavani (2002, 2003, 2004).

NOTES

1. All references to Locke's *Second Treatise* are to his *Two Treatises of Civil Government* (London: Everyman, 1952). In particular, the references are to specific section numbers in Chapter V of the *Second Treatise on Government*.
2. Cited in Halbert (1999).
3. Boyle (2003) refers to this phenomenon as "the second enclosure movement," and he claims that we are in the middle of this movement. According to Boyle, "The first enclosure movement involved the conversion of the 'commons' of arable land into

private property. The second enclosure movement involves an expansion of property rights over the intangible commons, the world of the public domain, the world of expression and invention."

4. Originally cited in Buchanan and Campbell (2005).

5. Moore (2001, p. 12) points out that whereas the *Statute of Anne* is generally considered the first statute of modern copyright, the *Statute of Monopolies* (1624) is considered the basis of the contemporary British and American patent system. In this paper, our primary focus is on IPRs involving copyright law.

6. In continental Europe, on the other hand, IPRs are more closely connected with "moral rights" or *droits morals* rather than with economic and utilitarian considerations found in the Anglo-American system. These rights are articulated in Article 6 bis of the Berne Convention.

7. This Act is also sometimes referred to as the Sonny Bono Copyright Term Extension Act (SBCTEA). However, in this paper we refer to it as CTEA.

8. The DMCA also contains a controversial "anti-circumvention clause," which expressly forbids technological workarounds; DMCA's critics have argued that this clause violates the principle of fair use.

9. As Coy (2004) points out, an essential difference between intellectual property and physical property is that the former is intended to enter the public domain at some point. However, it would seem that the DMCA enables intellectual property in digital format to be owned exclusively by the rights holder for an indefinite period of time. Thus far, no time limits have been established as to how long the rights holders of information residing in digital media can retain exclusive control of that information.

10. See Child (1997), Hughes (1997), and Moore (1997) for some excellent discussions about how Locke's proviso can be interpreted. We will not examine those interpretations here, since an in-depth examination of the proviso is beyond the scope of this paper.

11. Several different kinds of objections could conceivably be raised at this point. In a separate paper (Tavani, forthcoming), I anticipate and respond to three distinct kinds of possible objections that might be raised in applying Locke's theory to issues involving IPRs: the first objection has to do with the different kinds of labor involved in producing intellectual vs. physical objects; the second considers some essential differences between the two kind of objects themselves; and the third examines some differences involved in justifying the original acquisition of physical vs. intellectual property. For the present paper, however, I believe that the main objection that can be raised has to do with whether a useful analogy can be drawn between the intellectual and the physical

commons, given some of the relevant differences that also exist.

12. Himma (forthcoming) points out that the intellectual commons, unlike the physical commons, "is not a resource already there waiting to be appropriated by anyone who happens to be there." Rather, he describes it as a resource that is "stocked by and only by the activity of human beings." Moore (1997, p. 83) makes a similar point when he claims that all matter, whether owned or unowned, already exists, while the same is not true of intellectual property. However, this important distinction regarding how the two different kinds of commons become populated with objects does not necessarily affect the ways in which both commons can be similarly diminished or eroded.

13. Kimppa (2005, p. 74) believes that although Locke was willing to grant property rights to an individual for the acorns he or she gathered, Locke would probably not be willing to grant property rights to someone for the method he or she used in acquiring the acorns.

14. Thus far, advocates for this view appear to be successful. Consider, for example, that controversial copyrights and patents have been granted for "shopping cart" icons and for "one-click" (express) shopping in on-line transactions. And graphical interfaces themselves, which provide a method for accessing on-line information, have been eligible for copyright protection because of court decisions ruling in favor of arguments based on the need to protect "the look and feel" of computer software.

15. Moore (1997) and others have argued that Locke's theory is consistent with copyright law, and Scanlan (2005) has recently argued that Locke's property theory is compatible with a weak or limited form of copyright law.

S13

REFERENCES

Boyle, J. (2003) The Second Enclosure Movement and the Construction of the Public Domain, *Law and Contemporary Problems*, Vol. 33.

Buchanan, E. A. and Campbell, J. (2005) New Threats to Intellectual Freedom: The Loss of the Information Commons Through Law and Technology in the U.S. In: R.A. Spinello and H.T. Tavani, eds. *Intellectual Property Rights in a Networked World: Theory and Practice*. Hershey, PA: Information Science Publishing, pp. 225–242.

Child, J. W. (1997) The Moral Foundation of Intangible Property. In: A. E. Moore, ed. *Intellectual Property: Moral, Legal, and International Dilemmas*. Lanham, MD: Rowman and Littlefield, pp. 57–80.

Coy, W. (2004) On Sharing Intellectual Properties in Global Communities, Paper presented at the 2004 *Symposium of the*

Tavani: Intellectual property rights and the intellectual commons

International Center for Information Ethics, Karlsruhe, Germany, October 5.

Halbert, D. (1999) *Intellectual Property in the Information Age: The Politics of Expanding Ownership Rights*. Westport, CT: Quorum Books.

Hardin, G. (1968) The Tragedy of the Commons, *Science*, Vol. 162, pp. 1243–1248.

Heller, M. (1998) The Tragedy of the Anticommons: Property in the Transition from Marx to Markets, *Harvard Law Review*, pp. 622–625.

Hettinger, E. C. (1997) Justifying Intellectual Property. In: A. E. Moore, ed. *Intellectual Property: Moral, Legal, and International Dilemmas*. Lanham, MD: Rowman and Littlefield, pp. 17–38.

Himma, K. (forthcoming) Information and Intellectual Property Protection: Evaluating the Claim that Information Wants to be Free, *APA Newsletter on Philosophy and Law* (Spring 2005).

Hughes, J. (1997) The Philosophy of Intellectual Property. In: A. E. Moore, ed. *Intellectual Property: Moral, Legal, and International Dilemmas*. Lanham, MD: Rowman and Littlefield, pp. 107–178.

Kimppa, K. (2005) Intellectual Property Rights in Software – Justifiable From a Liberalist Position? Free Software Foundation's Position in Comparison to John Locke's Concept of Property. In: R. A. Spinello and H. T. Tavani, eds. *Intellectual Property Rights in a Networked World: Theory and Practice*. Hershey, PA: Information Science Publishing, pp. 67–82.

Locke, J. (1690) *Two Treatises of Civil Government*. London: Everyman's Library (1952).

Lessig, L. (1999) *Code and Other Laws of Cyberspace*. New York: Basic Books.

Moore, A. E. (1997) Toward a Lockean Theory of Intellectual Property. In: A. E. Moore, ed. *Intellectual Property: Moral, Legal, and International Dilemmas*. Lanham, MD: Rowman and Littlefield, pp. 81–103.

Moore, A. E. (2001) *Intellectual Property and Information Control: Philosophic Foundations and Contemporary Issues*. New Brunswick, NJ: Transaction Publishers.

Onsrud, H. (1998) The Tragedy of the Information Commons, *Policy Issues in Modern Cartography*, pp. 141–158.

Palmer, T. (1997) Intellectual Property: A Non-Posnerian Law and Economics Approach." In: A. E. Moore, ed. *Intellectual Property: Moral, Legal, and International Dilemmas*. Lanham, MD: Rowman and Littlefield, pp. 179–224.

Rose, M. (1993) *Authors and Owners: The Invention of Copyright*. Cambridge, MA: Harvard University Press.

Samuelson, P. (2003) DRM {and, or, vs.} the Law, *Communications of the ACM*, Vol. 46, No. 4, pp. 41–45.

Scanlan, M. J. (2005) Locke and Intellectual Property Rights. In: R. A. Spinello and H. T. Tavani, eds. *Intellectual Property Rights in a Networked World: Theory and Practice*. Hershey, PA: Information Science Publishing, pp. 83–98.

Spinello, R. A. (2003) *CyberEthics: Morality and Law in Cyberspace*. 2nd ed. Sudbury, MA: Jones and Bartlett Publishers.

Spinello, R. A. and Tavani, H. T. (2004) Intellectual Property in Cyberspace. In: R. A. Spinello and H. T. Tavani, eds. *Readings in CyberEthics*. 2nd ed. Sudbury, MA: Jones and Bartlett Publishers, pp. 247–252.

Spinello, R. A. and Tavani, H. T. (2005). Intellectual Property Rights: From Theory to Practical Implementation. In: R. A. Spinello and H. T. Tavani, eds. *Intellectual Property Rights in a Networked World: Theory and Practice*. Hershey, PA: Information Science Publishing, pp. 1–65.

Tavani, H. T. (2002) Information Wants to Be Shared: An Alternative Framework for Approaching Intellectual Property Disputes in an Information Age, *Catholic Library World*, Vol. 73, No. 2, pp. 94–104.

Tavani, H. T. (2003) Recent Copyright Protection Schemes: Implications for Sharing Digital Information. *Proceedings of the Sixth Annual Conference on Ethics and Technology*. Boston College, Chestnut Hill, MA, pp. 247–258. (Reprinted in R. A. Spinello and H. T. Tavani, eds. (2005). *Intellectual Property Rights in a Networked World: Theory and Practice*. Hershey, PA: Information Science Publishing, pp. 182–204.)

Tavani, H. T. (2004) *Ethics and Technology: Ethical Issues in an Age of Information and Communication Technology*. Hoboken, NJ: John Wiley and Sons.

Tavani, H. T. (forthcoming) Applying Locke's Property Theory to the Contemporary Debate Involving Intellectual Property Rights for Digital Information, *APA Newsletter on Philosophy and Law* (Spring 2005).

S14

CORRESPONDING AUTHOR

Herman T. Tavani
Department of Philosophy, Rivier College, Nashua, NH, USA
Email: htavani@rivier.edu

[12]

What is so bad about Internet content regulation?

John Weckert

Centre for Applied Philosophy and Public Ethics, Charles Sturt University, NSW 2675, Australia (E-mail: jweckert@csu.edu.au)

Abstract. Legislation was recently introduced into the Australian parliament to regulate the Internet. This created a storm of protest from within the computer industry, where arguments against the legislation ranged from those based on technical difficulties to those based on moral considerations, particularly of freedom of speech and freedom to access information. This paper is primarily concerned with the moral aspects of Internet regulation, but within the parameters of current technology. It will argue that such regulation can be justified, despite the fact that given the current technology there will be difficulties with enforcement, and reduction in Internet performance.

Key words: censorship, freedom of expression, freedom of speech, harm, Internet, regulation

Introduction

Proposals by governments to regulate the Internet seem to create something of a furore. This occurred in the United States of America around 1995 with the introduction of the Communications Decency Act, and is happening now in Australia.[1] On the face of things, this is a little puzzling. There are regulations governing the content of television, radio, newspapers, magazines, movies and books, so why not the Internet as well? A number of types of arguments against Internet content regulation are advanced. Some arguments are general ones that apply to all media, relating to the principle of rights to freedom of speech, expression and information. Others are more specific to the Internet. One argument is that the Internet is different from all other media and so must be treated differently, another that it is more like books, say, so the regulations applied to it should not be like those applied to television. Still others will argue that Internet content regulation should be resisted because it is an extension of government control. Not only do governments want to control the other media, now they want to control the Internet as well. Then there is the pragmatic argument which has two strands. One is that it is pointless for one country alone to attempt regulation. The Internet is global so regulation, to be effective, must also be global. Not only is it pointless, but it can also be harmful economically to that country because many valuable electronic commerce sites may move elsewhere. The other strand is that it can create intolerable situations for individuals who create sites in any country. The material on their sites may be legal in

their own country where the site is located, but illegal in another. Finally, and importantly, there is the argument that because of the technology itself, the Internet cannot be effectively regulated.

There are two issues then: *can* content on the Internet be regulated effectively, and *should* it be regulated? If it cannot be, then the second question does not arise as a practical issue. If it should not be, it does not matter if it cannot be. Although some may see this as putting the cart before the horse, we will examine the second question first, on the assumption that the Internet can be regulated to some degree, that technological developments will enable more efficient regulation in the future, and that there will be relevant international agreements.

Should Internet content be regulated? There are two questions; should it regulated in general, and should it be regulated in any one country in the absence of cooperation of others? We will examine these in turn.

It should be noted first that there is already some regulation of Internet content. Various things that are illegal in other media are illegal on the Internet as well. One cannot, for example release State or trade secrets on the Internet, and that which constitutes defamation on other media also does so on the Internet. This regulation is covered by laws which do not target the Internet specifically, and it is not these which opponents of Internet regulation oppose most strongly, nor is it the major concern here. The regulation of primary concern in this paper is that which attempts to restrict content specifically on the Internet.

There is nothing new about regulating different media differently. In Australia for example, here are many more restrictions on free to air television than there are on books and magazines, or even on

---
[1] Broadcasting services Amendment (Online Services) Bill 1999, http://www.aph.gov.au/parlinfo/billsnet/bills.htm.

movies. Should the Internet be treated like books and magazines, or like television? It has aspects of both. In addition it has aspects which closely resemble the postal and telephone services, and these are subject to very little content regulation. Some of these differences and similarities will be discussed later. We will first look at the general issue of content regulation, or censorship, and then specifically at the Internet.

Censorship

Article 19 of *The Universal Declaration of Human Rights* states:

> Everyone has the right to freedom of opinion and expression; this right includes freedom to hold opinions without interference and to seek, receive and impart information and ideas through any media and regardless of frontiers.[2]

This implies that censorship is a violation of a *right*. However, commonly consequentialist arguments are brought to bear against censorship, and some of the most compelling of these come from J.S. Mill.[3] The first is that an opinion which is not allowed to be heard might just be true, and the second that it might contain some truth. Therefore restrictions on the freedom of opinion can, and most probably will, deprive the world of some truths. His third reason is that unless beliefs and opinions are vigorously challenged, they will be held as mere prejudices, and finally, those opinions are themselves in danger of dying if never contested, simply because there is never any need to think about them.

Mill has a further argument. His conception of a good human life is one in which we think, reflect and rationally choose for ourselves from different beliefs and lifestyles according to what seems most true or meaningful to us. This is shown in his arguments for the freedom of expression. His central tenet here is that people ought to be allowed to express their individuality as they please "so long as it is at their own risk and peril".[4] The basic argument is that the diversity created has many benefits. One is that "the human faculties of perception, judgement, discriminative feeling, mental activity, and even moral preference, are exercised only in making a choice".[5] And exercising this choice

makes it less likely that we will be under the sway of the "despotism of custom".[6] We will be able to lead happier and more fulfilled lives. And again, if there is this diversity, each human will be more aware of the various options available, and so more competent to make informed choices in lifestyle and self expression.

These and other such arguments for freedom of speech and expression do support the claims for lack of restrictions and control of material in the media in general. However the support is qualified, because one person's right to freedom of speech or expression can infringe on another's rights, and can clash with other goods. For example, my freedom to openly talk of your financial or medical situation would infringe your rights to privacy, and I clearly cannot be allowed the freedom to express myself through torturing you. There is little sense in the idea of complete freedom of expression for all. So the issue now becomes one of where to draw the lines for this freedom. A common criterion is harm to others, a criterion endorsed by Mill. Admittedly this is not without problems, but it a useful criterion for all that.

The freedom of speech or expression of one person can cause harm to another, so some restrictions need to be placed on how and to what extent a person can be allowed free expression. That there should normally be some restrictions placed on harming others, other things being equal, is pretty uncontroversial. There are all sorts of restrictions on what can be said, and in general there is little opposition to this. There are libel and defamation laws and laws against perjury, blasphemy, abusive language, disclosing personal information, and so on. There is debate about what should and what should not be allowed, but little argument that anything and everything ought to be. The value in having some restrictions on what may be said seems just too obvious. Mill also recognised this, and claimed that if some kinds of utterances are likely to cause riots for example, there ought to be restrictions placed on them.[7]

One way to explicate the claim that language can harm, is to draw on the speech act theory of John Austin.[8] He distinguished between *locutionary* acts, that is expressing propositions, *illocutionary* acts, that is, expressing beliefs, and *perlocutionary* acts, the creation of some effect on listeners. Consider for example, the following (mild) case of 'hate' language, "People of race X are mentally and morally inferior." The locutionary act here is the proposition that people of race X are mentally and morally inferior, the illocu-

---

[2] *The Universal Declaration of Human Rights*, United Nations, 1948, http://www.un.org/Overview/rights.html.

[3] J.S. Mill *On Liberty*, 1859; page citations to edition of David Spitz (ed), John Stuart Mill, *On Liberty: Annotated Text, Sources and Background Criticism*, W.W. Norton & Company, 1975, ch. 2.

[4] J.S. Mill op cit., p. 53.

[5] J.S. Mill op cit., p. 55.

[6] J.S. Mill op cit., p. 66.

[7] J.S. Mill op cit., p. 53.

[8] Austin, John, *How to do Things With Words*, Oxford University Press, Oxford, 1962.

tionary act is the expression of the belief that this is the case, and perlocutionary act might be to incite racial hatred or even violence. Considered from this perspective, the claim for freedom of speech entails the claim for freedom to perform any sort of perlocutionary act, but now it is a claim that looks decidedly weaker.

Regulation of the Internet: Moral arguments

The above suggests that there are grounds for content regulation of the media in general, and is fairly widely accepted. If some action harms others there might be legitimate reasons for regulating actions of that kind. The next question is whether the same reasons for regulation apply to the Internet. Concerns about material on the Internet can roughly be grouped into three areas; pornography, hate language, and information to aid harmful activities.

Questions of free speech and censorship probably arise most frequently in connection with pornography. While anything available on the Internet would also be available elsewhere, or at least material of the same type would be, the situation is slightly different, simply because it is so much more difficult to control the material put on the Internet, and then to control its distribution. Anybody can put anything on, and with varying degrees of difficulty almost anybody can have access to it. In addition, gaining access to pornography on the Internet may be a very private affair. Locked in one's room, one can browse and search to one's heart's content. There is no need to face the possible embarrassment of detection in buying or hiring material from a newsagent or video shop, or even by the interception of mail, if acquiring material by mail order. As a consequence, it is much more difficult to restrict its consumption to adults.

The second main area of concern is hate language, usually racist language. Particular groups, especially white supremacy groups, spread their massages of hate, free from any control, in a way not normally possible using other media. The third area is the imparting of information designed to cause harm to other people. A common example mentioned is information on how to construct bombs. Another is advice on how to abduct children for the purpose of molestation. If might be argued that this is nothing new. This information is available anyway, and possibly in the local public or university library. This may be so, but again it is much easier to get it in the privacy of one's room rather than in a public place.

Mill's arguments for freedom of speech, as compelling as they might be in other contexts, give little support to freedom of speech on the Internet in at least two of the areas just mentioned. Pornography has nothing to do with the freedom to express opinions, and neither does giving information on activities designed to harm people. Hate language, or racial vilification, may be the expression of an opinion, and so might be supported by Mill's principles above, but it falls foul of the harm principle. These three areas of pornography, hate language and harmful information might all, perhaps, be protected by Mill's argument for freedom of expression, although it is difficult to see how any of them could in any way assist people in living a good life (in Mill's sense). But in any case, again the harm principle would come into play (although many would claim that pornography does not harm).

So the non-regulation of the Internet does not get great support from Mill. We can forsake consequentialist arguments and talk instead of rights, but this does not help much. I might have the rights to freedom of speech and expression, but my rights can clash with the rights of others to privacy, to be respected as persons, and so on. It would also be no easy task to show that we indeed have the rights to express ourselves through pornography, hate language and the circulation of potentially harmful information.

A different kind of argument is that Internet content regulation is an unwarranted extension of government power. However, it can plausibly be claimed that it represents no extension of power or regulation. As activities shift away from other media and to the Internet, if there is no regulation of the Internet, then there is a diminishing of regulation. (This may be good, but that is a different argument.) Consider home entertainment for example. What can be shown on free to air television is quite severely restricted. When entertainment in the home shifts to the unregulated Internet, there is much less regulation on what can be experienced as entertainment in that environment. Regulation of Internet content is thus maintenance of the *status quo*, rather than an extension of regulation.

Another argument is that the Internet is different from other forms of media and therefore ought to be treated differently. While this claim is true, it implies nothing about whether or not there should be Internet regulation. The most that it shows is that there should be a different type or degree of regulation. The Internet has some characteristics of television, but it is not intrusive in the same way (although with the increase of unsolicited advertising this difference is decreasing). While the television set is on, material is entering my home and I have little control over it. Certainly the set can be turned off or the channel changed, but that action may come too late to stop children seeing inappropriate material. In contrast, content must be *found* on the Internet. In this way it has a greater resemblance to printed media. So it could be argued that if there is to regulation of Internet content that regulation should be more akin to that applied to printed media than to free to air television. This has some plausibility, although there are differences too. As noted earlier, one can "surf" the Internet in the privacy of one's room and thereby avoid the possible embarrassment of being seen purchasing material of which one is not entirely proud!

A variation of this argument is that the Internet is much more important than other media, and so should be left free of regulation. It provides, so the argument runs, enormous benefits; repressed peoples can make their plight known, the isolated can communicate more widely than previously, there is much more access to information than ever before, vast markets for goods are opened up through electronic commerce, and so on. Granted that all these benefits exist, it would still need to be shown that they could not exist with regulation. In fact, perhaps at least some of them could exist to a greater degree with some regulation.

In principle then the Internet could be justifiably regulated. There are moral justifications for regulation of the media in general, and there seem to be no good reasons why these justifications should not also be applied to the Internet. This much might be conceded, but the claim could still be that regulation in one country should be resisted. This argument is a common one against the current legislation in Australia. The Internet is global, up to a point (the vast majority of users are in only a few countries), so not only is it futile but also probably damaging to any one country that attempts to introduce regulation. Australia will become a "laughing stock", business will move off-shore, and the growth of the Australian Internet economy will be restrained, are common claims.

These claims may all be true, but are not to the point if the moral justification is strong enough and if the legislation will be effective. If all countries had economies based on slavery, the repeal of this practice in one country alone would be the moral thing, even if the economy of the country did suffered. It is interesting to note that this economic argument was used in defence of slavery: "...It is, in truth, the slave labor in Virginia which gives value to her soil and her inhabitants; take away this, and you pull down the Atlas that upholds the whole system".[9] The argument is not that opposing Internet content regulation is on the same level as supporting slavery, the point

is merely that economic arguments do not necessarily carry much weight against moral ones. In order for the economic one to have force it would need to be shown that the economic losses would be such that the innocent suffered. Then of course these arguments would also be moral ones. In the case of the Internet, the economic argument would require showing that the suffering caused would be of a magnitude that out weighed the benefits of the protection of innocents afforded by regulation (this is a central point to which we will return later).

There is however, one worrying aspect to individual countries regulating Internet content, and this relates to the irrelevance of international borders to the Internet. Suppose that I develop a Web site in my country with material which is uncontroversially legal. Unbeknownst to me that material is illegal in another country, and of course can be down-loaded in that country. What is my legal position relative to that second country? Should I be extradited, or arrested if I travel there? This may seem an unlikely scenario, but consider the following recent case. An Australian citizen had material on his Web site located in Australia where it was legal but this same material was illegal in Germany. He was arrested while travelling in Germany and charged amongst other things, for distributing prohibited material on the Internet.[10] While he was eventually not convicted on that charge, this case does show that there is a problem and that it is probably only a matter of time before someone is convicted in these circumstances. But this seems rather unfair. Ignorance of the law is no defence, and clearly I have an obligation to know the law in my own country, but this obligation can hardly extend to a knowledge of the law in all countries which have Internet access. (It should be noted that in the example mentioned there was no ignorance of German law. The material concerned the holocaust, and the relevant laws were well understood.)

This situation *is* a worry if individual countries regulate Internet content, but it does not show that such regulation is necessarily wrong. What it does show is that there must be international agreements that clarify the legal situation. Ideally nobody should be charged if the "offence" took place in a country in which it was legal, but failing that, the policies of countries with content regulation should make their positions very clear and widely known. This latter position is certainly far from ideal, but at least some clarity would be introduced.

---

[9] Thomas W. Drew, Review of the debate in the Virginia legislature, in Eric L. McKitrick ed. *Slavery Defended: the Views of The Old South*, Prentice-Hall, Englewood Cliffs, NJ. 1963, p. 22.

[10] See Sherrill Nixon, Holocaust critic held in Germany, *The Age*, Saturday 10 April 1999, and Geoff Kitney, Trial sparks Internet racism fears, *Sydney Morning Herald*, Friday 12 November, 1999.

The final moral argument to be considered relates to whom the regulations should apply, the content provider, the user, or the provider. Given the ease of moving sites off-shore, content providers are difficult to regulate, and attempting to regulate users would involve massive intrusions on privacy. The best way then has appeared to be the regulation of Internet Service Providers (ISP). But, as has been pointed out, this seems unfair, and is a case of "shooting the messenger".

While it appears at first sight grossly unfair to hold carriers rather than content providers responsible for content, there might be situations where it is justifiable. Suppose that I am given a parcel by a stranger to deliver to another country. I do not know the contents of the parcel, and do not ask, but given that I am making the trip anyway and the parcel is small and there is little inconvenience to me, I agree to take it. In this situation I would almost certainly be held responsible for carrying drugs if that is what the parcel contained, and justifiably so, because I should have known better than to accept to take the parcel. Graham, to support the opposing position, says that airline companies are not held responsible for what their passengers carry.[11] This is true, but only up to a point. The airlines are expected, for example, to ensure that passengers do not carry weapons, and it is not difficult to imagine situations in which they could be held responsible for ensuring that passengers did not carry other items as well. Such expectations are not necessarily unjust if there are no other practical ways of avoiding or minimising harm to innocent people. There is precedent for too for holding people legally responsible for actions that they did not perform. Vicarious liability is

> The imposition of liability on one person for the actionable conduct of another, based solely on a relationship between the two persons [or the] indirect or imputed legal responsibility of acts of another . . .[12]

An example is the liability of employers for the actions of their employees in certain circumstances. While ISPs may not be vicariously liable for the actions of content providers, that is not the point. The point is that it is not enough to say that ISPs should not be held responsible for content simply on the grounds that they did not create that content. People can, in the

right circumstances, be responsibility for the actions of others. Vicarious liability is a legal and not a moral term, but the idea can easily extended into the moral realm. I can be held morally responsibility for the actions of another if I could reasonably have been expected to have prevented those actions. Even if I did not know about them, if my position is such that I should have known, I can still be morally responsible. This is a well-established (if not much adhered to) principle in the Westminster system of government, where cabinet ministers are (or were) expected to take full responsibility for the actions of their subordinates.

The argument here falls short of demonstrating conclusively that it is fair and just to regulate carriers rather than content providers. It does however, indicate that it is not obviously unjust. Much more work is required in this area.

The argument of this section is not so much that Internet content regulation is a good thing, but rather that the many of the common arguments against it do not stand scrutiny. In the previous section of this paper it was argued that some regulation of the content of media in general is justified in order to protect the innocent and vulnerable. If some regulation in general is justifiable, and if the special arguments regarding the Internet are not sound, then the tentative conclusion must be that Internet content regulation is justifiable. But perhaps the strongest argument against such regulation concerns the technology, the subject of the next section.

Regulation of the Internet: Technical issues

This brings us to the second main question: can the Internet be effectively regulated? Two factors make this doubtful, or so it is often claimed. One, already alluded to, is the global nature of the Internet. National and cultural borders are irrelevant. So if there is to be some control, from where will it emanate? The other factor is the technology. Many opponents of the Australian legislation argue that because of the nature of the Internet technology, content regulation is not possible in any practical sense. Various strategies are available for blocking Internet content.[13] Web pages and ftp files can be blocked by Internet Service Providers (ISPs) with the use of proxy servers. Requests by the IPS's clients go through the proxy server where each is checked to see if the requested URL is on its black list, the list of forbidden URLs.

---

[11] Gordon Graham, *The Internet: A Philosophical Inquiry*, Routledge, London, 1999, p. 110.

[12] Black, Henry Campbell. *Black's Law Dictionary: Definitions of the Terms and Phrases of American and English Jurisprudence, Ancient and Modern.* 6th ed. St Paul, MN: West Publishing, 1990, p. 1566.

[13] McCrea, Phillip, Smart, Bob, Andrews, Mark, Blocking Content on the Internet: a technical Perspective, prepared for the national Office for the Information economy, CSIRO, Mathematical and Information Sciences, June, 1998, http://www.cmis.csiro.au/projects+sectors/blocking.pdf.

This method is not foolproof however. Forbidden Web pages and ftp files can easily be given new names, URLs can be set up to return the contents of a different URL, domain names can be bypassed if the IP address is known, and push technologies bypass proxy filters. In addition there are various costs with employing proxy servers which could make it difficult for small ISPs to remain viable.

An alternative method would be to use routers to block content at the packet level, where the source address of each packet is checked against a black list. To be anywhere near efficient, this would need to be done at the Internet gateways to Australia operated by Backbone Service Providers (BSPs). One problem with this method is that it provides only very coarse filtering. If a site contains some material deemed offensive then the whole site will be blocked, including all the harmless and useful material. Additionally, sites can be renumbered to bybass blocking, and *tunnelling*, that is, enclosing an IP packet within another IP packet, can be employed. It is argued too, that not only is packet blocking not efficient, but it can also create considerable problems, particularly with respect to information going through Australia to other countries.

Products are available, or becoming available which claim to be able to effectively block offensive material, but these are not yet free of problems. In a recent test, one of these new software filters which was being held up as an example by proponents of the Australian legislation of how technology was overcoming difficulties, blocked sites of Mick's Whips: Australian handcrafted kangaroo and Crocodile leather goods, Agfest – Tasmania's Rural Trade Fair, Christian Bookselling Association Australian Inc., St. Luke's Lutheran Church Nambour, Queensland, Optometrists Association Australia, and Orchid Society of New South Wales, amongst other peculiar choices.[14] Perhaps effective technology for blocking certain Internet content will be developed, but it appears that it is not yet available.

What follows from this for the moral argument that Internet content regulation is justified? Ought implies can, so there cannot be much force in an argument which says that the Internet ought to regulated if it cannot be in any effective way. Some care needs to be taken here. It does not follow necessarily that because something cannot be done effectively and efficiently it should not be done at all. Avoiding paying income tax on amounts earned over a certain amount is generally illegal, but avoiding such tax is possible by various means, including locating offshore to "tax havens". In

this and many other cases regulation is justified even though it is not as effective as most would like. Perhaps a better example is that of the legislation against the distribution and use of many drugs. While many users and distributors are caught, it is not obvious that worldwide the war on illicit drugs is being won. But these might not be good analogies. There are important benefits to the community in general in having most people paying tax and in having few drug users, but are there similar benefits to be gained from Internet regulation? That there are benefits in reducing the amount of material that can harm the innocent and vulnerable is obvious. Whether this can be achieved to any significant extent given current technology is not. Given that neutralising the use of proxy servers requires some effort in terms of renaming Web page and ftp sites, using IP addresses instead of URLs, and so forth, it is likely that the amount of material considered offensive will be reduced to some extent, but perhaps not significantly. But again, perhaps this slight reduction is enough in itself to justify regulation. These benefits however, must be weighed against the costs, for example of greater unreliability of Internet access using proxy servers, the possibility of adverse effects on some applications, and the existence of black lists of URL, which could become valuable commodities. The cost of packet blocking could be even higher.

Conclusion

A strong moral case can be made for regulating the content of the Internet, but there is also a strong case that such regulation cannot be very effective and comes at a price in Internet performance. These last two factors together constitute an argument of considerable weight against attempting to control Internet content through legislation. So what should be done? On balance, a case can be made for content regulation, although that case is probably not as strong as proponents would wish. That the case can be made can be seen by looking a little more closely at the two opposing factors just mentioned. First, while in general, laws which are not enforceable to any great extent are to be avoided, in certain instances they can be useful. Consider illicit drugs for example. The laws banning their use and distribution are not particular effective, but they are still considered worthwhile by many because they give the message that using those substances in not a good thing. A similar argument could be mounted for content regulation of the Internet. Second, degrading Internet performance will not obviously harm many people very much, depending of course on the degradation. Most of us could wait a little longer when searching or down-

---

[14] EFA (1999), Report: Clairview Internet Sheriff: An Independent Review, http://efa.org.au/Publish/report_isheriff.html.

loading without much of a diminution of our living standards. There may well some be problems with electronic commerce if Internet performance is slower, but that will not affect too many people, at least not in the short term, given that that form of commerce is not being accepted by consumers particularly quickly. And in any case, it is not uncontroversially accepted that the benefits of electronic commerce will outweigh its disadvantages.[15]

The argument of this paper has been that Internet content regulation is justifiable, but the problems are recognised. To overcome them, there will need to be more research into technological methods for blocking content, and there must be international cooperation in the formulation and enforcement of laws, practices and standards. A long term solution suggested in a recent report is this:

> It is proposed that Australia participate in international fora to create the necessary infrastructure, so that organisations which host Content would be able to determine the jurisdiction of the client software making the request. Having determined the jurisdiction, the server can find out whether the requested Content is legal in the client's jurisdiction.[16]

This proposal might not be the ideal solution, but it is one possibility which ought to be seriously investigated. Internet content can harm, and some regulation is morally justified. Given the benefits of the Internet, however, we do not want to throw the baby out with the bath water.

References

John Austin. *How to do Things With Words*. Oxford University Press, Oxford, 1962.

Henry Campbell Black. *Black's Law Dictionary: Definitions of the Terms and Phrases of American and English Jurisprudence, Ancient and Modern*, 6th edn. West Publishing, St Paul, MN, 1990.

Broadcasting services Amendment (Online Services) Bill. Accessed 6 July, 1999, at http://www.aph.gov.au/parlinfo/billsnet/bills.htm.

Thomas W. Drew. Review of the Debate in the Virginia Legislature. In Eric L. McKitrick, editor, *Slavery Defended: the Views of The Old South*, pp. 20–33. Prentice-Hall, Englewood Cliffs, NJ. 1963.

EFA Report: Clairview Internet Sheriff: An Independent Review. Accessed 6 July, 1999 at http://efa.org.au/Publish/report_isheriff.html.

Gordon Graham. *The Internet: A Philosophical Inquiry*. Routledge, London, 1999.

Geoff Kitney. Trial Sparks Internet Racism Fears. *Sydney Morning Herald* (Sydney Australia), Friday 12 November, 1999.

Phillip McCrea, Bob Smart and Mark Andrews. *Blocking Content on the Internet: A Technical Perspective*. Prepared for the National Office for the Information Economy, CSIRO, Mathematical and Information Sciences, June. Accessed 6 July, 1999 at http://www.cmis.csiro.au/projects+sectors/blocking.pdf, 1998.

J.S. Mill. *On Liberty*, 1859; Page Citations to Edition of David Spitz. In John Stuart Mill, editor, *On Liberty: Annotated Text, Sources and Background Criticism*. W.W. Norton & Company, New York, 1975.

Sherrill Nixon. Holocaust Critic Held in Germany. *The Age* (Melbourne, Australia), Saturday 10 April 1999.

Simon Rogerson and Paul Foley. Internet Electronic Commerce: The Broader Issues. In Institute of Charted Accountants in Australia, *Ethics and Electronic Commerce: A Collection of Papers*, pp. 9–12. 1999.

The Universal Declaration of Human Rights. United Nations, 1948. Accessed 14 February at http://www.un.org/Overview/rights.html, 2000.

---

[15] Simon Rogerson and Paul Foley, Internet electronic commerce: the broader issues, in Institute of Charted Accountants in Australia, *Ethics and electronic Commerce: A Collection of Papers*, pp. 9–12.

[16] McCrea et al., p. 40.

[13]

Unreal Friends *

Dean Cocking and Steve Matthews
Centre for Applied Philosophy and Public Ethics, Charles Sturt University, 15 Blackall Street, Barton ACT 2600, Australia
(e-mail: cappe@csu.edu.au)

Abstract. It has become quite common for people to develop 'personal' relationships nowadays, exclusively via extensive correspondence across the Net. Friendships, even romantic love relationships, are apparently, flourishing. But what kind of relations really are possible in this way? In this paper, we focus on the case of close friendship. There are various important markers that identify a relationship as one of close friendship. One will have, for instance, strong affection for the other, a disposition to act for their well-being and a desire for shared experiences. Now obviously, while all these features of friendship can gain some expression through extensive correspondence on the Net, such expression is necessarily limited – you cannot, e.g., physically embrace the other, or go on a picnic together. The issue we want to address here however, is whether there might be distinctive and important influences on the structure of interaction undertaken on the Net, that affect the kind of identity "Netfriends" can develop in relation to one another. In the normal case, one develops a close friendship, and in doing so, one's identity, in part, is shaped by the friendship. To some extent, through extensive shared experience, one comes to see aspects of the world (and of oneself) through the eyes of one's friend and so, in part, one's identity develops in an importantly relational way, i.e., as the product of one's relation with the close friend. In our view, however, on account of the limits of, and /or the kind of, shared contact and experience one can have with another via correspondence on the Net, there are significant structural barriers to developing the sort of relational identity that is a feature of close friendship. In arguing our case here, and by using the case of Net "friendship" as our foil, we aim to shed light on the nature and importance of certain sorts of self-expression and relational interaction found in close friendship.

Introduction

It is a familiar, but nevertheless striking fact, that contextual factors have a strong bearing on the content and nature of our communications with one another. There are economic, cultural, institutional, technological, and even seemingly quite trivial factors – such as the amount of time one has to communicate – which influence the content and nature of communication. Our interest here, however, is on the effects the context of communication has on the nature of our relationships, and the nature of the self within those relationships. To take the first point, our relationships with others are clearly directly affected in virtue of the kinds of communication permitted by contextual influences; second, if we believe our relationships with others partially determine what we are like as persons, then we are committed to the idea that the context of communication has indirect, though potentially quite marked, effects on the nature of ourselves, insofar as this nature is a product of those relationships.

We apply these general thoughts to the case of the internet, and to the effects it has, and potentially could have, on the development of personal relationships there. In particular, we are interested in whether close friendships are possible through text-based internet contact alone.[1] Our thesis has two parts,

---

* Earlier versions of this paper have been read at a number of conferences including the first Australian Institute of Computer Ethics International Conference, Lilydale, July 1999, the Australian Association of Professional and Applied Ethics National Conference, Canberra, October 1999, and Social Ontology, Rotterdam, 2000. We would like to thank audiences at those conferences for their participation and helpful comments. Thanks also to John Campbell (La Trobe), Jeanette Kennett, and Justin Oakley, for their helpful suggestions. A referee also provided some useful feedback.

[1] In presenting this paper to a range of audiences a frequent question arose concerning the kind of internet communication we had in mind. Let us stipulate that our thesis is aimed at only the kinds of text-based communication common to email and chatroom style forums. Our stipulation is made in connection with the following two points. First, although changes to technology continue at breakneck speed, so that soon video-style exchanges (for example) may well become the norm, the fact of the matter is that at the time of writing the overwhelming quantity of communication carried on through the internet lines is text-based. Second, our stipulation answers the objection that our thesis does not hold because soon the technology will overcome the institutional obstacles we discuss. In a highly

a descriptive and a normative component: first, we observe, and provide an explanation for why it is, that the internet affects the nature of our alleged friendships there. Indeed, we argue that within a purely virtual context the establishment of close friendship is simply psychologically impossible.[2] (We do not address the issue of the effects internet communication might have on our already existing friendships; rather we explore the possibility of developing a friendship on the net from scratch.) Our analysis proceeds largely by way of contrasting the kinds of personal interaction occurring in virtual and non virtual environments. This leads to the second part of our thesis: by coming to understand what is lacking in the virtual cases we aim to shed light on what is valuable in genuine friendship.

We aim, then, to argue why it is that our Net "friendships" lack the kinds of human goods we normally take for granted in ordinary close friendship.[3] At the core of our thesis is the idea that the internet creates a distorting filter on those aspects of ourselves which ordinarily are disclosed to the other in friendship. It is precisely in virtue of the internet context that we are driven to present a view of ourselves in Net "friendship" quite at odds with the view of ourselves we would have presented, and

---

futuristic scenario it may be possible to simulate almost without fault the kinds of ordinary face-to-face encounters had in the non virtual world. Notwithstanding objections of the Nozick pleasure machine variety, we can agree with this for the simple reason that those are not the cases our thesis addresses. The case of two-way video interaction does not constitute a counter-example to our thesis either. In such a case much of what we say is missing in the text-based case, has been compensated. Whether friendships are possible in these environments we regard as an open question.

[2] It has been pointed out to us that our use of the term 'virtual' is infelicitous given our focus on email and chat forums. A virtual environment is one that simulates a real environment, but surely email is not a simulation of talking to someone. It is true that email talk is not simulated talk – this reminds us of a point about arithmetic: there could be no real difference between successfully adding two numbers together and simulating such a successful addition. Our point, though, is that email (and other electronic communication) is a simulation of a face-to-face communicative exchange. Perhaps it is not a simulation in the sense of trying to image face-to-face communication; nevertheless, it may substitute for face-to-face communication, and that is all we are claiming.

[3] A brief comment is in order here over our use of scare quotes on the term 'friendship'. Since our thesis is that internet friendships are psychologically unavailable to human agents, the use of this term unmodified is unacceptable to us. But someone might quibble that the use of scare quotes begs the question in favour of our thesis. To avoid this dilemma, and so to leave the issue open as we proceed, we stipulate that by the expression 'Net "friendship" ' we refer to those internet relationships *alleged* by some to qualify as genuine friendships.

which is available in the non-virtual world. Why is that bad? As we will argue, in the non-virtual case one's identity is creatively drawn, or shaped, in relation to one's friend, chiefly as a result of a process of mutual interpretation, a process that ultimately contributes to the depth and character of ordinary friendship. This process thus promotes within friendship a level of affection, concern for the friend's welfare, and a disposition to share (perhaps even otherwise undesired for) experiences. Friendship-like relations on the Net, however, are structurally and significantly limited in the ways in which this development of self in friendship – and of some of its associated goods – might be brought about.

A second order issue which we address later in the paper is whether internet "friendship" *per se* is a bad thing. Though we think internet "friendship" is quite inferior to non-virtual friendship, we do not think that it is necessarily bad in itself, and indeed for some people it clearly provides an important good. The issue itself, however, is largely an empirical one, which arises on two fronts. First, obviously friendship is an important human good, and so to the extent that my Net "friendships" replace friendships I might well have had non-virtually, this will subtract from the good of friendship. But of course whether or not one's Net "friendships" do replace one's non-virtual friendships is quite dependent on one's particular circumstances. Perhaps Net "friendships" can be had in addition to the non-virtual variety; but perhaps not – a serious issue for social planners, then, is the *extent* to which online societies ought to proliferate.

Second, a more difficult, and empirically complex issue, would be to see what the psychological effects on forming personal relationships are of prolonged Net interaction. The interesting question here would be to determine whether such interaction brings about a *dispositional* transformation in people's non-virtual personal interactions. For example, would the hitherto shy individual, whose Net interaction promotes in her a modicum of social confidence – something she could never have gained otherwise – be able to transfer this newfound confidence into her non-virtual social interactions? *Maybe* it would, and if so, this would certainly be a good for such a person. On the other hand, would excessive use of the Net for social interaction by people generally, stunt the proper growth of relationships, and bring about a quite different society from the one we know? Again, maybe it would, but the issue is not one to be decided *a priori*. The point is that these effects on our personal relationships are not trivial, and so ought to be considered seriously by those who favour more global changes from the ordinary way we interact socially, do business, teach, and so on, to the online varieties of these activities.

The paper will proceed as follows. We first underscore the point about context and content with an example from the mass media of the way something as seemingly harmless as a time constraint tends to structure and shape the range of opinion permitted there. We then present a brief summary of the various accounts of friendship paying particular attention to what is involved in each of the role of self-disclosure. As we point out in the section following this, there is a natural and appropriate willingness within the institution of friendship to engage in mutual open recognition of a friend's various salient character traits. My self-understanding is often enough crucially dependent on the perspective of my friends, in particular on their judgements of what I am like and on what I do. Because this process of interpretation is mutual, it plays a central role in structuring, and in determining the relational character of our friendships, i.e., of the way we respond to one another as friends, of how such interaction moulds the self within friendship, and so of how the friendship grows and develops given the identity-affecting properties of mutual interpretation. Naturally enough, then, if we are interested in the effects of the internet on friendship, the way to frame the analysis is by looking at how mutual interpretation is affected by internet communication. In Section 4 we argue that the effects on the process of interpretation are quite drastic, and this is largely because of the way the Net permits and disposes us to present a skewed picture to others of what we are like. In the final section we qualify our position, which is not monolithically opposed to all types of Net "friendships", and we deal with some possible counterexamples.

Context and communication

An important fact about communication is the way contextual factors affect the content of the information exchanged. Let's call situations where this arises *content sensitive situations*. The point about content sensitivity is made in devastating fashion by Noam Chomsky in his well known attack on the mass media. It is a distinctive requirement of television news and current affairs programming, particularly in the United States, that commentators be able to articulate an opinion within a very short and specific period of time, typically between two commercials. The effect of this requirement, which Chomsky calls 'concision', is that one is only capable of "regurgitating conventional pieties", while still being taken seriously. The mechanism works in the following way: in the mainstream media there are a range of views common to all across the political spectrum, that are by and large, held to be true by everyone who either broadcasts,

advertises, promotes, listens, or subscribes within that commercially-based institution. Such 'established opinion', as we may call it, is generally accepted by audiences of all mainstream political persuasions without the need for defence: "everyone just nods", as Chomsky puts it. But what about propositions that challenge established opinion? Claims challenging established opinion in fundamental ways do require justification; they quite rightly require the presentation of reasons and evidence if they are not to be dismissed as opinion from the "lunatic fringe". The trouble is that, given the constraints of concision, it is simply not feasible to provide support for claims that fall outside established opinion. Those who do challenge received wisdom on public affairs simply haven't the time to properly put their case; as a result, what may in fact be a perfectly reasonable thesis ends up looking like it's from the lunatic fringe, or "from Neptune" as Chomsky puts it. The ultimate effect of concision is to help reinforce received views, to further constrict the range of public debate within a narrow framework of assumptions, and thus to exclude serious questioning of prevailing opinion. Concision thus provides a striking example of contextual influences – in this case the apparently innocent distribution of advertising space – on the nature of the content of communication. We take it as a conclusive demonstration of the general phenomenon of content sensitivity to context.[4]

At the most general level the point to be made here is that context affects content. But this should not disguise a range of important though more particular kinds of this general phenomenon. Concision, for example, falls out of an *institutional* phenomenon within commercial media, and plainly there are myriad other institutional settings giving rise to content sensitivity: in the confessional your confession is affected by a range of constraints, the very pious surroundings for example, and maybe even some form of concision; at the football match, your support for the team is different from the support you provide in front of the television; in the classroom your teaching is responsive to the number of students present, the various media of lecture presentation (overheads and the like), and so on.

An integral part of many institutional factors in this process are the various *technological* requirements giving rise to content sensitive situations. Of course the internet is one context where the variety of institutional norms and conventions is paradigmatically a product of technology. Internet technology

---

[4] See the film *Manufacturing Consent: Noam Chomsky and the Media*. Directors Mark Achbar and Peter Wintonick. Produced by Colin Neale, Dennis Murphy, Adam Symansky and the National Film Board of Canada.

imposes structural constraints on communicative inter-action thus enabling and predisposing individuals to tailor their verbal behaviour to the specific environ-ment in which it is said. In this way we see that the internet not only affects the nature of this beha-viour, but also the nature of the "friendships" that may develop in such an environment, and ultimately the nature of the persons engaged in these "friendships". As we will presently explain, the internet environment emasculates and distorts the institution of friendship. However, before we do so it will be necessary to provide some background describing the variety of accounts of friendship. As we will see, our thesis can be supported regardless of which account one holds to be true.

Three accounts of friendship

By 'friendship' we refer, at the very least, to those intimate relationships in which there is deep mutual affection, a disposition to assist in the welfare of the other, and a continuing desire to engage with the other in shared activities. We say that these are at the core of any friendship, and indeed these conditions must be adopted by any serious account of friendship. But these conditions not only do not distinguish the various accounts from one another, they are arguably insuf-ficient in themselves to distinguish friendship from other kinds of intimate personal relationships where they often hold, e.g., the parent-child relationship. What is it, then, apart from these baseline conditions, that makes a relationship one which is distinctively a friendship?

Since Aristotle, many have thought that the answer to this question begins with the role that *self-disclosure* plays in developing the bonds of affection, intimacy and trust in friendship that any account must accept. According to an Aristotelian account – what we might call the *mirror view* of friendship – the essence of friendship resides in the tendency to choose and retain friends who are similar in character to each other. According to this view, the extent to which I recognise aspects of myself revealed in another – particularly, according to Aristotle himself, various virtuous traits – is the extent to which I will be well-disposed to have this other as my friend. This account, then, is essentially one founded on self-love. It is the seeing of myself in the other – and of course vice versa – which provides the *raison d'etre* of our relationship.[5]

A second kind of account focuses not on the disclosure of self *in* the other, but of disclosure of self *to* the other. What this means, to a first approxima-tion, is that unless I am prepared to share certain sorts of private information with my friend in an ongoing way I will not be able to maintain her friendship. Such self-disclosure must proceed on an equal footing, and focuses to a large degree on personal motives, interests and beliefs. Of course not any old informa-tion counts here because the point of such disclosure is closely connected to the function of trust and intimacy within the friendship. To pass on to my friend my private thoughts and wishes leaves me vulnerable to that person, and conversely my friend is vulnerable given my knowledge of her private world. (If all we ever disclose to one another are the most mundane details of our daily lives – what we ate for breakfast, which train we took to work, the colour of the black pudding Mom once made, etc. – we are hardly placed in a position of vulnerability due to the very sensitive nature of the private information now in possession of the other. A possible corollary: very boring people would find it difficult to sustain very intimate friend-ships.) Our privileged position with respect to one another, in terms of the insights of character we attain through secret-sharing, does provide a framework for the carrying on, and the flourishing of our friendship. Let's call this the *secrets view*.[6]

Finally there is what can be called the *drawing view* of friendship. According to this view, neither simil-arity nor secret-sharing is important or distinctive of close friendship. Rather what is central to the nature of friendship is that one's identity is, in part, drawn, or shaped, by the relations one bears to one's close friend, and in turn this process of drawing further structures the relationship. The drawing of the self in friendship is manifested in two dimensions. First, often enough we will be moved to share the kind of experience with a friend we otherwise would (prob-ably) never ourselves have chosen without invitation, not because we feel obligated, or in some way pulled against a natural urge to avoid doing it, but because this is something that the friend has chosen to do. So, for example, my friend, Roger, invites me to a local art exhibition, something I would normally not even think of visiting. My decision to accept is based largely on the thought that the sharing of the experience with Roger would be a good thing. It is not just that I now find myself moved to act because Roger has swayed me, though that is certainly a large part of it, but I

---

[5] On similarity and similarity in virtue, see, e.g., *Aristotle, The Nichomachean Ethics*, 1159a35 and 1165b14-35. On the self-knowledge to be found in friendship, see, Aristotle, *Magna Moralia*, 1213a10-26; John Cooper, "Aristotle on Friendship",

in Amelie Rorty (ed.) *Essays on Aristotle's Ethics* (University of California Press, 1980), pp. 322–323.

[6] For such an account, see, Laurence Thomas, "Friendship", *Synthese* 72 (1987).

now find myself influenced in a new direction which lies outside what I had, prior to that moment, thought properly expressive of my interests. I may thus grow and develop in ways that reflect the character of my friend. In effect, over time, I may become more like Roger. (This may seem to confirm the mirror view, but in fact the order of explanation is quite the reverse since clearly friendships operate perfectly well in cases of marked dissimilarity.)

A second aspect of the drawing account, is the process of interpretation. (As we will see, just as with the first dimension mentioned earlier, the second is important in the other accounts as well.) We will come to it presently, but first a methodological comment. Although the drawing account has been developed and defended by one of us elsewhere,[7] we will not take a stand here on which of the standard accounts just outlined best withstands critical scrutiny. We choose not to do this precisely because our thesis ought to stand no matter which account one accepts. As we show in the next section the process of what we call interpretation in friendship is so pervasive that no reasonable account can afford to leave it out. Our account of the importance of contextual effects on the realisation of friendship focuses largely on this process of interpretation in friendship and of the various ways in which it fails; so given the pervasiveness of this failure we can claim our thesis achieves maximal theoretical purchase.

Interpretation

Consider how often we recognise aspects of our close friend's character and the impact this has on how we are moved to interact with our friend and on the realisation of our friendship.[8] I notice, for instance, my friend is anxious in confined spaces, in crowded places, or when her ex-partner is in the room. I notice her excitement or enthusiasm over her team winning the football match, her delight in a delicious meal, or her exuberance in discussion after a few drinks at the bar. Because of such interpretations I will, for example, be more attentive to my anxious friend when her ex-partner enters the room, or try to lighten up the situation with

[7] See Dean Cocking and Jeanette Kennett, "Friendship and the Self", *Ethics*, April, 1998.

[8] In this section we use the term 'character' widely to include not only such things as bodily features, and psychological traits, but also such relational characteristics as the kinds of institutions one may be a part of – e.g., being a member of a certain sporting club or political party. The latter may well reflect indirectly on a person's qualities, and such relational features are also of course commonly the subject of interpretation between individuals.

a joke or some strategy of distraction or just discreetly get her out of the room. Similarly, I might affectionately tease her about her excitement at the football game, or how lively she gets after a few drinks. I might, on the other hand, find myself spurred on by her enthusiasm in such circumstances.

Such interpretation of a friend's character, and the ways in which we are consequently moved to relate to one another, are commonplace and central to the realisation of close friendship. In both ordinary as well as significant ways, it is upon the interpretations of character between close friends that mutual affection, the desires for shared experiences, and the disposition to benefit and promote the interests of one's friend are expressed. I express my affection for my friend when I playfully tease her for becoming boisterously drunk after only two drinks; my recognising her enthusiasm for the football moves me to suggest we go to a game together; my lightening up the situation when her ex-partner enters the room exhibits my concern to promote her interests. It is important to note that each of the accounts of friendship mentioned above agree on the significance of the interpretation process to all these features of friendship. Moreover, this interpretation process, together with the impact it has on how the friendship is realised, will also be crucial to these different views of the self in friendship in the following ways: for the secrets view the mutual interpretation between friends will be central to the self that is seen to be disclosed by the friends; for the mirror view it is central to the self that is seen to be similar; for the drawing view, interpretation is crucial to the relational self created within the friendship.

In the section to follow we consider just how important the various indicators of one's friend's character are to the interpretation one has of the friend and so to the ways in which one will be moved to relate to them and to the realisation of the friendship. Such indicators can be either voluntary or non-voluntary. The internet is perhaps unique in its facilitating personal relations primarily on the basis of voluntary self-disclosure, and eliminating many significant aspects of non-voluntary self-disclosure. Given our emphasis on the process of interpretation, the interesting question from this point of view is to determine the effects voluntary self-presentation has on that process and so on the realisation of friendship.

Voluntary self-presentation and interaction

We begin this section with a brief, though important qualification. In the light of much recent, and well-deserved, attention given to cases of deception and/or the abuse of trust in internet communication, and so to avoid unnecessary confusion, we would like to stress that these are not the cases we are concerned with here; on the contrary we want to stipulate that we are addressing those cases in which people behave with sincerity and with an intention to carry on relations that genuinely aim at friendship. It is of course obvious that cases which feature deception and/or the abuse of trust should not count as genuine friendships, and so the exploration of those cases turns out to be plainly pointless for our purposes; though to repeat, this is not to downplay the very real and serious issues that arise in connection with trust, deception, and the internet.

There is a clear contrast in the ways people are enabled to, and at least very commonly disposed to, present themselves in their relationships on the Net, as compared to their non-virtual relationships in terms of the kinds and degree of control over self-disclosure they may exercise.

Consider first the virtual world. It is because of the range of technologically based structural constraints inherent in Net communication that I am able to present myself to others with such a high level of control and choice. These constraints increase my capacity to present to others, through the presentation of my thoughts and feelings, a carefully constructed self, one that is able, for example, to concoct much more careful and thought-out responses to questions than I am able to in the non-virtual case. In the virtual case, where I can construct a highly controlled and chosen self presentation, I can play down, put a positive or light-hearted spin on, or completely screen out the various things I don't particularly like about myself. I might similarly deal with various thoughts or feelings which, while I might not disapprove of, I might not, for any number of reasons, be very comfortable with. I may have interests or attitudes which I neither disapprove of nor feel any discomfort about, but which nevertheless I might not think worth mentioning when I more carefully choose and control how I present myself. Or I might have interests and attitudes I am simply more inclined to filter out from my conversation with others – perhaps I think they might not be interested in such things. There are also other aspects of interaction which get sifted out in the refined atmosphere of Net interaction such as the various instances of spontaneous and complex expression. Typical features of interaction in the non-virtual case include such things as rapid-fire half-finished sentences, talking over one another, a complexity of intonation, facial and bodily gestures, and so on – all sorts of content gets a look in that would not do so in the focus provided by the virtual world.

Of course there may also be any number of things about myself of which I am simply unaware, or of which I have little insight, or about which I am

self-deceived. For obvious reasons there can be no disclosure of the self here, since plainly you cannot volunteer information you do not have. So, to illustrate, I cannot reveal to my Net "friend" my paranoia about personal safety if I regard placing three dead-locks on the front door as merely prudent behaviour, as would inevitably be revealed in the non virtual world where my friend notices my fussing over the locks.

The nature of my responses to others in the virtual world also diverges from the way we ordinarily respond to our friends. First, it is up to me *when* I respond to their contacts in ways that are unavailable in the non-virtual context; there will be no uncomfortable pause, no *faux pas*, when I hesitate briefly to construct a more carefully honed response. Second, my responses can be made without being interrupted, talked over, or qualified in other ways involving my being subject to the thoughts of others. And, of course, I can choose whether or not I will respond at all.

I can then, choose and control my self-presentation to, and my exchanges with, my Net "friends", in various significant ways which I either cannot, or would not be so disposed to, with my non-virtual friends.

Turning to the non virtual cases of friendship, I might try to make a genuine attempt at, for instance, playing down, sifting out, or simply covering up my overly-ambitious or competitive streak; my envy about those I consider more beautiful, witty or wealthy; my jealousy over my partner's flirtations; my self-obsessions; my stinginess with money; my delight at cruel or blue humour; my hopeless taste in clothes; my silly laugh or my bad manners. Even my best efforts here however, are doomed. My close friends will hardly have to possess great psychological insight to observe, in spite of my attempts to disguise and obfuscate aspects of my self, my excitement at (say) the prospect of beating a competitor, or enjoyment of a cruel joke at another's expense, or my nervous anxiety over my wayward partner. Even if I manage to curb all voluntary behavioural indicators of such things, there are simply too many non-voluntary indicators which no-one we have ever known (*qua* close friend) could consistently screen out. I will, e.g., smile at the joke or try too hard to not smile, or I'll sweat over those of whom I'm envious or jealous, or engage in frenzied small talk in telling desperation to feign indifference.

The ease with which we interact with one another in non-virtual friendship may thus be undermined, but it is important to understand the way this process may contribute to construction of the relational self within friendship. It will be a focus of my friend's concern for me to not only notice, say, my uncomfortable jealousy, but also to be moved by her noticing it to help me out in some way; perhaps she will help me by, for example, making distracting small talk. Similarly, it might be part of my close friend's interest in me that he not only notice, for example, my delight at a good blue joke, but that this is something he likes about me. How such traits of character of mine continue to be realised within the friendship will, in part, be determined by my friend's interpretations of my concerns and interests, and how they are moved to relate to me on account of this. So, for instance, because of my friend's encouraging influence, instead of trying to hide my enthusiasm for a good dirty joke, I might, at least with her, not only give quite a deal more reign to my enthusiasm, but develop a different view of my character trait here. Thus, I might take to her light-hearted teasing of me about it, where previously I would deny identification with the trait. In such everyday ways my character is, in part, shaped by, and a relational feature of, our friendship.

Everyday real life situations, therefore, undermine efforts to construct one's self-presentations and interactions in highly controlled and chosen ways, such as are present in the virtual world. But the import of these various ways in which I may construct my self-presentation and interaction with others is not just that they are unavailable and standardly subverted or otherwise undermined in the non-virtual friendship situation. It is also, more importantly and as indicated above, that the interaction in the virtual case seriously distorts and omits the nature of the self that is presented and is, at least partly, created in close friendship. Moreover, these distortions and omissions are of important aspects of the self that provide much of the proper focus of our interest and concern in non virtual friendships. It is, for instance, not only commonplace but *proper* interaction between close friends that such character traits as my stinginess with money or obsession with personal safety, are highlighted, interpreted and may be transformed within friendship.

Let us now consider some likely qualifications, attacks and possible counterexamples to our claim.

Responses to our claim

First, we would want to qualify our claim by acknowledging that there are a range of positive aspects of Net "friendships" given by a heightened sense of choice and control in self-presentation and interaction with others. The heightened choice and control over the nature of my Net exchanges may well, for instance, help shield me from the morally bad influences of others in this environment. If, e.g, my Net "friend" invites me to take part in some morally questionable activity, I am not put on the spot as I might be in a face-to-face situation. Not only am I shielded from,

say, her persuasive tone of voice, I have time to digest the proposal, and make my decision in cool, solitary reflection.

Also, consider those, e.g., who are extremely shy or suffer certain physical disabilities, say, of speech capacity, which would otherwise limit their ability to make friends in the non-virtual world. The ability to exercise a heightened measure of choice and control in self-presentation and interaction with others in the virtual social environment surely provides an important human good here. It is surely a much gentler entry to a social world for such a person who can now avoid that uncomfortable social moment, or the intrusion of their disability into a developing friendship, which, in the non virtual equivalent holds great terror.

The advantages, particularly for those in the latter kinds of cases, of a world of communication where voluntary self-presentation and interaction with others dominates are clearly worthy ones. Net "friendship" and interaction may present a significant good and improvement over non-virtual relations for a person afflicted with disabilities deleterious to the development and maintenance of satisfying and fruitful self-presentation and interaction with others. On this account, then, we have reason to regard a world where virtual relations and interactions are available to people as better than, or at least complementary to, a world where they are not.

In the light of acknowledging these advantages it is worth clarifying the status of our thesis. We are not claiming that, necessarily, the world would be a better place if virtual relations and interactions were not available to people. Rather we have claimed that the elements of non-voluntary self disclosure within non-virtual friendships provide both an appropriate and commonplace focus of our interest and concern in our friends, and an important part of the relational self developed in friendship. As such, to this extent, virtual "friendships" miss much of the nature and value of friendship. And this thesis is not affected by acknowledging that, for the reason above, it might be better to have virtual relations and interactions available than not to. Though, as noted earlier, there is a serious planning issue which may well arise, and clearly ought to be considered, having to do with the extent to which virtual interactions are put forward as adequate substitutes for non-virtual ones.

A more telling line of objection might go like this: our objection to a virtual world dominated by voluntary self-presentation and interactions, largely targets certain kinds of individuals – namely, those who would exercise their heightened choice and control to obscure, down-play or altogether omit those aspects of self about which they feel disapproval, or discomfort, or would, in one way or another, neglect to voluntarily present. This isn't a problem, however, for Net "friendship" and interaction *as such*. It is a problem, or set of problems, facing certain sorts of individuals. In the normal run of cases of Net "friendships", it should be admitted, there is, in the ways outlined above, a lack of relevant disclosure to the other, and so a lack of some of the importantly relevant interaction and self-development that features in friendship. But this thesis depends on facts about our psychologies. It is not a conceptual claim about a virtual world dominated by voluntary self-presentation and interactions. Indeed, it might be argued we could imagine certain individuals who do *not* suffer the sorts of pitfalls mentioned earlier of diminishing, denying, and omitting relevant character cues given by non-voluntary behaviour in the non-virtual case. Such individuals would seek to compensate and overcome these problems. They would, e.g., voluntarily disclose their failings, and what they feel uncomfortable about, and they would be careful to not block or filter, say, their spontaneous thoughts and reactions to others. They would diligently and carefully report on those aspects of character which ordinarily, as they well know, play a crucial role in the interactive process of self-creation in friendship. Of course not every tiny detail is worthy of disclosure, but only those salient aspects of physical appearance, manner, habit, belief, intention, interest and the rest which, but for the Net, might well be manifestly available to the other, and crucially relevant to the other's interpretation of character as it effects the shaping of the self in friendship. So let us imagine two people – the *diligent disclosers* – who with a meticulous and painstaking effort attempt to overcome the internet barriers to friendship in the way described. Would the relationship so formed be a counterexample to our position?

We have sketched various commonplace ways in which non-voluntary behaviour and interaction is crucial to the nature and value of close friendship and the self within it. The non-voluntary relations include those aspects of myself I am aware of – but for a variety of reasons do not volunteer to my friend – and those aspects of myself which I am incapable of revealing, yet my friend nevertheless picks up because of their external perspective; the case where my friend picks up on my self deception is a paradigm of this. We think each of these aspects of non-voluntary behaviour and interaction provide reason to reject the alleged counterexample of the diligent disclosers. Consider first, those aspects of non-voluntary disclosure of which I am not aware.

There is much that even the most accomplished diligent disclosers must necessarily miss here. I might not, for instance, be aware that I may be interpreted as paranoid about my personal safety or overly compe-

titive or ambitious; it is my friend who interprets me in this way, when, say, she notices me obsessively looking over my shoulder, or that I'm driven to pull my own recent journal publications off the shelf and wax lyrically about them on being told of a competitor's forthcoming book. This also holds for some clear cases of self-deception. My friend sees non-voluntary cues that betray claims that I do not have a philandering partner, or a gambling or health problem. She notices, for instance, I am too insistent on my claims – something she knows I normally do when I'm particularly serious about kidding myself. Such interpretations between close friends are both everyday and significant features of the normal expression of friendship and of the self within it, and necessarily are not available to the diligent disclosers in the quite global way present in the non-virtual case. Of course, our response here admits the very weak claim that Net relationships approaching the standards of ordinary close friendships are *logically* possible; sure, there might be invisible web-surfing Martians with hyper-psychological analytic skills and quick reflexes who can pull it off. However, since such possibilities are so removed from the world of our own psychologies, they are of no real interest at all.

Our second ground for rejecting the diligent disclosers case, refers to those aspects of myself of which I am aware but do not voluntarily present. This aspect of self also provides significant input into the character and development of close friendships. Those wielding the diligent disclosers case would claim it deals with the apparent failure of virtual relationships to capture this. However, if we imagine quite everyday real life cases involving even very simple character and interpretation cues, any process of compensation applied in the virtual case, would not only seem difficult and tedious, but would seem very likely *itself* to corrupt and undermine the non virtual interaction. So, for instance, in the non-virtual case my friend makes an overly sarcastic remark – I pick up the sarcasm from its tone – and I roll my eyes in dismissal; my friend, not having realised the extent of her sarcasm blushes meekly in response, and then averts her gaze as I smirk at this minor victory: her sarcasm has been the subject of playful criticism of late. Or imagine, alternatively, that I have not been completely forthcoming with my friend about his partner who has been making advances towards me; but I am now resolved to come clean. I know this will be a blow to him and my nerves are showing – shortness of breath, perspiration, a slight quiver in the voice. And my affectations here influence how he receives the news; he recognizes my distress and concern at the blow this is to him.

Now consider how the process of attempted compensation for these interactions through the most diligent disclosing realistically imaginable, would distort, rather than effectively replace these interactions. There might well be, for example, crowding effects, where I try to disclose too much information. And so the playfulness of my criticism of my friend's sarcasm, or my friend's feeling that I genuinely share his distress over the problem of his partner, might get lost in all the information I am now voluntarily disclosing. And even if important interactions are not simply lost in all the voluntary disclosing, the perception of sincerity in various non-voluntary responses, such as those showing my distress in passing on disturbing news to my friend, may not well survive the transmission to purely voluntary disclosure.[9] Moreover, the very fact that I am now voluntarily disclosing hitherto undisclosed material – my anger for example – might well create in me unseen characteristics – perhaps I will now have contempt for myself. Similarly, for instance, my usual reserve, might not sit at all well with my newfound role of assiduously reporting all of those traits of character required by diligent disclosure. Thus, it seems reasonable to expect that, in such ways, the compensating strategy of the diligent dislcosers would distort and pervert the character of the non-voluntary behaviour and interaction it seeks to replace.

Conclusion

We think that to the extent that the virtual case provides a context of communication dominated by *voluntary* self-disclosure, enabling and disposing me to construct a highly chosen and controlled self-presentation and world of interaction, I altogether miss the kind of interaction between friends that seems a striking and commonplace feature of close friendship. We claim that what is lacking here is not merely a partial, or marginal set of factors, but a significant global loss and distortion of the real case. What is distorted and lost, in particular, are important aspects of a person's character and of the relational self ordinarily developed through those interactions in friendship which, as we have argued, are precisely the kinds of interactions largely weakened or eliminated by the dominance of voluntary self-disclosure found in the virtual world. These are interactions which clearly provide *proper and appropriate* focuses of our interest and concern in our non-virtual friends.

And finally, a promissory note. We have used relations with others on the Net as our foil to highlight the everyday importance of non-voluntary behaviour and interaction to the nature and value of friendship and the self within it. We see, however, various ways in which our concern here might be of quite broad significance. Thus, there may be other communication contexts, or cultural changes to individuals' self-presentation within current communication contexts, which similarly negate or seriously diminish the character of either our close relationships, or other sorts of relationships, such as, e.g., the pedagogic relationship in various modes of distance education. Such broader implications we hope to explore elsewhere.

---

[9] In his "Moral Behaviour and Rational Creatures of the Universe", *Monist* 71, July 1988, pp. 59–71, Laurence Thomas – arguing for the significance of *non-verbal* behaviour to our moral assessments of others – says our emotional displays are 'indispensable barometers by which we assess a person's motivations and judge the sincerity of his utterances', p. 65. While we think Thomas might overstate his case for the non-verbal, we do think that sincerity losses are, at least, a real problem for the imagined loss of the non-voluntary to purely voluntary interaction.

[14]

Developing Trust on the Internet

Victoria McGeer

Abstract: Does the Internet provide an environment in which rational individuals can initiate and maintain relationships of interpersonal trust? This paper argues that it does. It begins by examining distinctive challenges facing would-be trusters on the net, concluding that, however distinctive, such challenges are not unique to the Internet, so cannot be cited as grounds for disparaging the rationality of Internet trust. Nevertheless, these challenges point up the importance of developing mature capacities for trust, since immature trusters are particularly vulnerable to the liabilities of Internet trust. This suggests that Internet trust can only be rational for those who have developed mature capacities for trust. But that suggestion ignores how trust on the Internet may also facilitate the development of such capacities.

0. Introduction

My aim in this paper is to consider whether the Internet provides an environment in which it is possible to engage in rational trust. However, before proceeding with this inquiry, a number of caveats are in order. For the topic is overly broad in at least three different respects: first, with respect to the *types of Internet exchanges* that can be examined with this question in mind; secondly, with respect to the *types of user groups* that provide relevant contexts in which issues of trust can be raised; and finally, with respect to the kinds of *actions and attitudes* that theorists could reasonably have in mind when they speak of Internet 'trust'. My own discussion will be constrained in the following ways. I will focus on the kinds of exchanges that are interpersonal in nature—hence, that occur within, and so presuppose, a sense of Internet community built upon repetitive contact amongst a group of familiar users. I will also focus on a particular kind of interpersonal trust, 'friendship trust', where the primary mode of vulnerability is psychological or emotional. (Hereafter, all references to 'trust' should be understood as references to trust in this sense unless otherwise stipulated.) Finally, I will come to interpret my question about the rationality of Internet trust as composed of two parts: First, and most obviously, it involves inquiring into whether trust in this medium can be reasonably based given the kind of contact with others the Internet allows; but, secondly I claim, it should also involve an investigation into how interpersonal exchanges in this medium could enable the development of our capacities for rational trust, whether on- or off-line.

This paper will proceed in three sections. In the first section, I consider reasons that argue in favour of supposing the Internet is a particularly bad medium for 'rational' trust, by which I will mean initially, a particularly bad medium for reasonably extending our trust to others. Of primary concern here is the sort of evidence available to us of the trustworthiness of others so encountered. For on the Internet, it's not just that individuals may hide importantly relevant features of themselves; they may actively mislead us in ways that invite our confidence. Hence, the decisions we make about when and how much to trust others are likely to be ill-informed or, worse, actively manipulated by them. To sharpen this discussion, I will give close attention to a particular case of Internet trust and betrayal. My aim here is to motivate conceptual distinctions that set the stage for arguing, in section two, that we need a more nuanced approach to the problem of Internet trust than such general concerns about the medium allow. In particular, I argue that the difficulties of Internet trust are importantly dependent on—i.e., magnified or decreased by—the maturity one brings to trusting relationships in general. The more mature the truster, the more capable they will be of reasonable trust, even on the Internet—i.e. trust that takes account of the limitations inherent in the situation. Hence, there is no good reason to argue against the rationality of Internet trust in general. However, this does not yet say much in favour of relationships of Internet trust. In the third section, I redress this imbalance by touching briefly on relationships of trust among virtual persons in the context of virtual communities. My aim here is to stress the developmental potential for us as trusters through engaging in relationships of Internet trust.

1. Julie's Tale: Does the Internet Facilitate Irrational Trust?

The following is a true story of Internet trust and betrayal.[1] Julie was a deeply disabled older woman living in New York City who could push the keys of a computer with her head-stick. Highly limited in what she could do in the physical world, Julie found her métier on the Internet. Off-line, she was cabined, cribbed and confined. On-line, she was able to lead a rich social life in keeping with her expansive personality. Warm-hearted, talkative and caring, Julie soon became a popular member of a New York Internet conference or chat-room composed of like-minded women with whom she could fraternize on equal terms. Although she did not hide her disability from others, on the Internet it presented no physical or emotional barrier to be overcome. If anything, the handicaps she bore with patience and good will became an inspiration to others, making her all the more likeable. In addition, Julie was an extraordinarily good listener to other women's difficulties. She was perceptive, articulate, thoughtful, full of good advice, and seemingly endlessly patient as many women whom she met through the net poured out their troubles and concerns. She became a solid friend to many, who felt that their lives had changed for the better through knowing Julie and from taking her advice.

But this story has an unhappy ending. After several years of participating

---

[1] Julie's story dates from 1985 and is documented in Stone 1991. Thanks to Helen Keane for giving me this reference.

in this Internet community, one of Julie's devoted admirers decided she wanted to further their friendship in person. Tracking Julie down in her New York apartment, the woman discovered that 'Julie' was no Julie at all. In fact, she was a man—a middle-aged psychiatrist who, besides being male, wasn't disabled at all. The woman was outraged, and after she made this fact known to the wider conference, the conference itself was deeply shaken. Reactions varied from a kind of resigned amusement all the way through to a feeling of total betrayal, especially amongst those who had shared their innermost feelings with Julie. One woman reputedly said, "I felt raped. I felt that my deepest secrets had been violated". Worse, those who had made genuine gains in their personal and emotional lives felt that these gains were predicated on "deceit and trickery", hence were stripped of any value and should be repudiated.

Although we haven't yet heard Julie's side of the story, this tale makes vivid why friendship trust on the Internet is a risky business. Such trust, as I said before, involves relying on someone in ways that make one *psychologically or emotionally* vulnerable to them rather than simply materially vulnerable, although the psychological and the material are often intertwined in more or less complicated ways. Still, my focus is on the kind of psychological vulnerability that comes from trusting others with *ourselves* rather than with our credit card numbers, or banking information, or to discharge contractual obligations, and so on. This, after all, is the way in which Julie's friends and admirers felt betrayed—in the way they understood themselves to relate most intimately and personally to another human being.

But now why did Julie's friends and admirers feel betrayed? The obvious answer is that Julie was not who she pretended to be. 'She' was a made-up character, nothing but a fictional being, a mere puppet masking the true identity of someone altogether different. And the Internet provides ample opportunity for such deceit. For instance, people can hide their real selves in whole or in part, masking facts about their gender, ethnicity, age, appearance, health etc.; they can assume a variety of different identities with ease, becoming more than one phoney self; or they can even band together in real life in order to enact a single phoney self. This is consequent on two features of Internet contact that give individuals inordinate amounts of control in what information they convey about themselves to potentially trusting others: first, it is primarily a *text-based medium* of interaction (though video and voice contact are now also used with more frequency); and secondly, it is primarily a *uni-dimensional mode* of interaction—i.e., it is normally only text, a single medium for conveying the sort of information on which those who trust must rely for making judgements about the trustworthiness of others.

Consider now how both of these features interact to play into a potential trickster's hands. For instance, the fact that Internet contact is both textual and uni-dimensional means that we cannot depend on our usual ways for cross-checking the information we receive about others based on what they tell us. Ordinarily, this involves our own observations of them based on their real bodily presence: their looks and manner, not only in relation to us, but in relation to others with whom we can see them interact. Importantly, such observations have not only a cognitive component, but also an immediate visceral/ emotional component. We are often sensitive to subtleties of tone and manner that can't be expressed in words: We find ourselves reacting positively or negatively to others based on subliminally detected bodily cues. And we often are wise to trust our instincts under these conditions, since they constitute a reasonably accurate early warning system. For instance, researchers have established that subjects can become viscerally or bodily aware of a bad or dangerous situation well before they can articulate their concerns in a cognitively explicit way (Bechara et al. 1996; 1997).[2] Internet communication thus deprives us of the bodily information we need for this early warning system to operate effectively.

Furthermore, it seems that text-based interactions are particularly seductive in character when there is no sensory check on how to interpret what others say. For even when we are not actively misled by their words, our imaginations tend to roam freely over textually underspecified details. This imaginative freedom may be further encouraged by an unwitting hubris— a conviction that we have more judgemental control over the emotional and cognitive effects of 'mere words' than experience suggests. Consider, for instance, the powerful illusion created by the computer program ELIZA. ELIZA was developed by Joseph Weizenbaum at the MIT Artificial Intelligence Laboratory in the early 1960s. In response to text-based input from ordinary human users, ELIZA would analyse the syntactic structure of the text, and respond with a seemingly appropriate question or comment, modelled on the kinds of questions and comments made by psychotherapists. Instead of being bored or tipped off by the fairly limited style of response, people found the illusion of agency—indeed, the illusion of caring, concerned agency – remarkably seductive. Weizenbaum reports, for instance, that when he first introduced people to the program, they would spend hours with it discussing their personal problems, unwilling to believe that there was not a real agent behind the seemingly concerned and attentive ELIZA (Weizenbaum 1976). Even now, there are Internet websites where individuals can go to pour out their troubles to ELIZA, seemingly unfazed by clear statements that ELIZA is a mindless program. They either don't believe it, or they don't care— the illusion of concerned agency is more than enough for a good conversation, at least of a particular therapeutic sort.

The more general conclusion is this: text-based interactions are a powerful stimulant to our imaginations; they have a persuasive power all their own, and through them, we are remarkably susceptible to projecting on to the originators of that text (be they human or robotic) whatever qualities we detect in the text. Our judgemental distance is often much less than we imagine it to be, particularly when these interactions involve emotional or sensory contents. This makes us particularly prone to illusion in the domain of textual communication, especially when this is the only medium available to us.

To summarize the problem with trust on the Internet thus far: It seems that the Internet is a particularly bad medium for fomenting good, stable, non-delusory relationships of trust—hence, what we might call 'rational' or 'reason-

---

[2] For further philosophical discussion of how our emotional reactions can appropriately shape our reactions to the world, see Jones 2003.

able' trust—for two reasons. The first I will call the *Proteus factor*, after the Greek sea-god fabled to assume various shapes. The Proteus factor refers to the ease with which people can hide who or what they really are on the Internet. This may be done explicitly as in Internet role-playing games (I will come back to these later in my paper), or it may be done implicitly, with individuals actively working to deceive others. The second reason the Internet is a bad medium for fomenting rational trust involves what I will call the *Eliza factor*: This refers to the ease with which people can be seduced by text – particularly interactive conversational text—viewing it willy-nilly as a kind of window on the soul of the agent who produces it, rather than (more cautiously) as a kind of mirror that partly reflects their own imaginative projections. In other words, people often see what they want to see, especially when their 'seeing' is solely mediated by interpreting a disembodied string of apparently trust-conducive utterances.

This is a strong conclusion, and while I will not ultimately endorse it, I also don't want to minimize the strength of the considerations supporting it. These are liabilities for trust that are particularly pronounced on the Internet. However, it is also important to note that computer mediated communication is not the only way in which these two factors can play a role in promoting illusions and so undermining the conditions for rational trust.

Consider the unhappy story of *Cyrano de Bergerac* (Rostand 1959). A large-nosed romantic, Cyrano considers himself too ugly to win his cousin Roxanne's love. Consequently, he spends years languishing by her side in the role of trusted friend and confidante, never confessing his deep love for her. Roxanne, meanwhile, is on the lookout for true love, and after a few fleeting encounters with Cyrano's dashing and handsome friend Christian, she thinks she has found the perfect mate. However, all is not well for these would-be lovers. It turns out that Christian does not have the kind of poetic soul that Roxanne requires in a lover. He can't win her by good looks alone; and Cyrano, whose soul is sufficiently poetic, assumes she will reject him because of his unfortunate appearance. So the two men team up: Christian becomes Cyrano's physical proxy, a mouth-piece for Cyrano's words that eventually win Roxanne's undying devotion. But the question is, with whom is she in love? Not with Christian, whose personality is kept hidden from her, and not with Cyrano either, whose position as loyal and avuncular cousin is a mainstay in her life. The object of her love is, in fact, a fiction—an amalgamation of the two men. It can't survive in the real world, because even though Roxanne physically knows and interacts with both Christian and Cyrano, the man who she really loves is a fantasized projection of her own desire, supported by Cyrano's Protean deceit and her own Eliza-like capacity to be seduced by what becomes largely text-based communication (the many letters that Cyrano writes to her under Christian's name).[3] The story ends in tragedy, but it is a kind of pathetic tragedy in which one really feels that a little more honesty at certain crucial moments would have at least given Roxanne some capacity to make a sensible decision about whom to love and trust, given the realities of her situation.

---

[3] For a compelling philosophical discussion of the impossibility of Roxanne's love, see Campbell 1997.

Of course, this story is only fiction, but it serves to show that the Internet only facilitates the kinds of practices of deceit and self-deceit that can occur in the physical presence of others, where presumably one can rely on other modes of interaction to check and qualify the judgements one makes about them. More sobering examples include all those real-life confidence tricksters who make a practice of relying on their physical attributes—honest appearance, convincing tone of voice, smooth manner— to dupe their victims, however normally savvy such victims might be. Hence, multimedia trust—trust that is developed through various media of interaction—may help reduce the likelihood of that trust being grounded on illusion, but it can't eliminate this possibility altogether. This is one cautious thing to be said against the detractors of Internet trust. But I think something more powerful can also be said in its defence. In order to do this, I return to the story of Julie.

2. Julie's Tale Revisited: Immature Versus Mature Relationships of Trust

In some ways, it is easy to understand and sympathize with the sense of betrayal that Julie's friends and admirers in this Internet community felt when her true identity was revealed to them. Julie had deliberately lied to them about who and what she was. Still, I hope there is also some discomfort with the reactions reported by some of these women. Recall that one reputedly claimed to have felt 'raped', and another, that the positive gains in her life were worth nothing since they had been based on 'deceit and trickery'. Of course, these extreme reactions were not universally shared. Other women, also friends of Julie's, confessed to feeling little more than astonishment followed by humorous resignation as if something like this might well have been expected—not condoned, mind you, not invited, but reasonably anticipated.

What accounts for this range of reactions? The straightforward answer is that these women differed in the *amount* of trust they had invested in Julie and in their relationships with her: i.e., those who were not that trusting to begin with felt relatively less betrayed than those who were more trusting. While I think there is some truth in this, a mere quantitative analysis is not nuanced enough to do justice to the real variety of possible explanations. For instance, it doesn't distinguish between two sorts of cases: (1) women who were less trusting in this situation because they were generally less trusting, i.e. generally less capable of trust in others; and (2) women who were 'less' trusting in this situation because they were generally more capable of trusting well, hence of trusting appropriately (i.e., with appropriate sorts of expectations) relative to the situation. In other words, the wide range of reactions to Julie's revelation might partially be accounted for in terms of differences in the *quality* of trust extended by these women.

My point here is that betrayal is a complicated phenomenon. Obviously, when someone betrays another's trust, they have inflicted a harm on the one betrayed. But how that harm is experienced by the person betrayed and what

its consequences are will partially depend on that person's expectations and capacities with respect to initiating and maintaining relationships of trust. Thus,
in contemplating Julie's story, one question we should want to pose is the following: what does it mean to trust well, to trust responsibly, to trust reasonably in
someone over the Internet? And might the women who felt most undermined by
Julie's betrayal be partially faulted in terms of the quality of their trust, rather
than simply in terms of the fact of their trust? By this shift of emphasis, I do
not mean to minimize Julie's own part in this story of betrayal; I simply mean
to probe more carefully into the dynamics of trusting relationships.

I will begin this examination with an interesting remark Hubert Dreyfus
makes in his recent book, *On the Internet* (Dreyfus 2001). According to Dreyfus,
there is a sort of trust that is not possible on the Internet because it requires
bodily presence—that is, it requires our having the capacity, as he puts it, to
look one another in the eye and shake one another's hands. In Dreyfus's words,
"The kind of trust that requires such body contact is our trust that someone
will act sympathetically to our interests even when so doing might go against
his or her own" (Dreyfus 2001, 70). In my view, this falls under the rubric of
'friendship trust', precisely the sort of trust that Julie's friends had invested in
her. Consequently, Dreyfus's remark is clearly an overstatement: such trust is
certainly *possible* on the Internet. But perhaps he means to suggest, in keeping
with the worry voiced in Section 1, that friendship trust is *irrational* on the
Internet because trusting reasonably in this sense requires that we be bodily
present to one another. Otherwise, Dreyfus implies, we open ourselves to making
a kind of emotional error. For, in his view, well-grounded trust, "must draw
on the sense of security and well-being each of us presumably experienced as
babies in our caretakers' arms" (Dreyfus 2001, 71). If we can have such a sense
of security absent the embodied presence of another, then we must simply be
fantasizing such a presence—reading into the cool voice of text the warm embrace
of another's arms. Less poetically, we mistakenly suppose that the traits of others
that are manifested through our textual interactions with them are grounded in
their caring embodied presence. Hence, we delusionally expose ourselves to the
possibility of deep and damaging betrayal.

I think Dreyfus gives a good diagnosis of why some of Julie's friends might
have been so badly undermined by the discover of her real identity. They trusted
in her to provide just this kind of security in their lives. She was the maternal
figure to whom they could turn for the absolute safety of a genuine, albeit imaginary embrace. Her physical embodiment in the real world thus really mattered
to them—mattered in the sense of sustaining their fantasy of who lay behind
the surface exchange of text. I will call this kind of trust 'security trust', and I
agree with Dreyfus that such trust can never be well-grounded on the Internet,
largely because of the Proteus factor (the malleability of Internet identity).

However, I think there is a further question to ask about security trust— viz.,
is it the sort of trust that can be faulted more generally for its irrationality? In
other words, is it the sort of trust that rational, self-standing adults should be
seeking whether on the Internet or off it? My worry is that in so far as we trust
this way as adults, we're looking for the wrong sort of thing in our trusting

relations with others—viz., a kind of security that relationships among self-standing adults cannot reasonably deliver. Consequently, relationships governed by these expectations are particularly vulnerable to breakdown; and when they break down, generate experiences of betrayal that are particularly traumatic. The problems of security trust may thus be exacerbated on the Internet, but they are not unique to the Internet. They stem, more fundamentally, from the fact that security trust is an immature form of trust to which we may all be attracted, but which ought to be guarded against, not by abandoning genuine relationships of trust—that *would* be a kind of madness—but by becoming more mature both in our understanding and in our enactment of such relationships.

To flesh out this claim, I want to spend some time considering the differences between mature and immature relationships of trust, and in particular, the kind of dependency or vulnerability that characterizes the quality of trust in each. Following Dreyfus's lead, I will begin by characterizing what many refer to as 'infant trust'—the sense of security we first experience in our parents' arms.[4]

Infant trust, we may say, is distinctive because of an infant's utter dependency on, and hence vulnerability to, others. As Lars Hertzberg says, "the human infant is not ... an independently intelligible living unit, and not simply because of the physical cares which he must receive from others, but because the sense of his activity depends on the way in which it is interwoven with the activity of other" (Hertzberg 1989, 316). The developmental psychologist, Jerome Bruner, has called the sense-making structuring of the infant's activity, 'parental scaffolding'. The idea behind it is that babies come into the world without much capacity for self-maintenance, still less with the capacity for self directed thought and action and, hence, for self-determination. Nevertheless, they have impressive capacities for imitation and, in particular, selective imitation, first, of the facial movements of their caretakers, then of body movements, and finally of actions with objects in their shared environment. These mutual imitation games, delighted in by babies and parents alike, are the primary means by which infants identify themselves as like others and so, eventually, as persons whose thoughts and actions belong to the kind that persons produce. They are also the primary means by which parents mould children to react, think, and feel about things as persons do. As the psychologists Meltzoff and Gopnik remark,

> " ... mutual imitation games are a unique and important constituent of early interpersonal growth. Adults are both selective and interpretive in the behaviour they reflect back to the child. They provide interpretive imitations to their infants, reflections that capture aspects of the infants activity, but then go beyond it to read in intentions and goals to that behaviour. ... This, in turn, leads the infant beyond his or her initial starting point. Likewise, selected actions, especially those that are potentially meaningful in the culture, will be reflected back [to the infant] more often than others." (Meltzoff/Gopnik 1993, 349)

The dependency the child experiences in the hands of the adult is thus the

---

[4] The following discussion draws substantially on the ideas I explore in McGeer 2002.

dependency of 'self' constitution. The parent literally makes it possible for the child to define and understand itself in social space, which is a space at the same time created by the parent. The child's capacity for self-determination is thus, at this stage, taken on by the parent— eventually, of course, in order that the child can develop an independent capacity for self-determination. Paradoxically, then, self-determination must begin with other determination: the child becomes an agent by having its agency enacted by another. Now, is the bond in this relationship a bond of genuine trust?

There are good reasons to call it trust, but reasons not to as well. Trust, as many have pointed out, is not mere reliance, but reliance that importantly involves the mutual recognition of personhood. As Richard Holton claims, "Trusting someone does not involve relying on them and having some belief about them: a belief, perhaps that they are trustworthy. What it involves is relying on them ... and investing that reliance with a certain attitude." This attitude we normally take only towards people. As Holton elaborates, "when the car breaks down we might be angry; but when a friend lets us down we feel betrayed" (Holton 1994, 67). Holton never fully clarifies why we adopt such different attitudes towards the things we rely on as opposed to the people we trust; but it seems clear that it must have to do with our expectations that others' behaviour towards us will be governed by their seeing us as persons and, specifically, as persons who treat them as individuals capable of acting in a trustworthy way.[5] Objects don't do that. Trust thus involves, minimally, a complicated Gricean structure of person-specific recognition and acknowledgement. It involves (a) our acknowledging others as sources of self-determined action in their own right, with interests and desires worthy of respect; (b) others acknowledging us as sources of self-determined action in our own right, with interests and desires worthy of respect, and finally (c) each of us acknowledging that these attitudes are shared between us, and govern our actions and reactive attitudes towards one another. Without these attitudes, and their mutual recognition, we would be incapable of moral interactions (Strawson 1974).

Now, in the case of the relationship between parent and infant, it is clear that the infant's development as an independent agent depends on the parent's acknowledgement of the infant's personhood. But the infant is not yet a person, in the sense that he is likewise capable of recognizing either the parent or himself as a person each in his or her own right. At best, the infant is capable of what Meltzoff and Gopnik describe as a kind of functional recognition: here is something 'like me', i.e., something that can be imitated and imitates me in return (Meltzoff/Gopnik 1993). So the infant is not yet in a position to trust the parent. But it is trust-in-the-making, and made only because the parent behaves *as if* the child trusts the parent—i.e. the parent acknowledges and acts towards the child as a person whose attitudes and actions towards the parent are not only self-determined, but also conditioned by the child's recognition of the parent's own personhood. In this way, the child develops the Gricean awareness

---

[5] This theme has been sounded by a number of theorists working on trust. See, for example, Baier 1986; Jones 1996; Pettit 1995; Walker forthcoming.

of others and so comes to be the kind of being that can trust another, i.e. a being that is capable of full-blown adult trust (Hertzberg 1989).

With this kind of contrast case in the background, we're now in a position to ask: what is so distinctive about mature relationships of adult trust? To begin with, they must involve dependencies that are very different in kind from the dependencies of 'infant trust'. Since the trusting adult does rely upon the other, she is vulnerable, like the infant, to actions and attitudes outside of her control. Nevertheless, the adult relationship between the truster and the trustee is importantly symmetrical. Unlike the infant, the adult truster does not depend on the other either for self-determination or for maintaining the relationship between them as a relationship between persons. She is an autonomous person in her own right. The trust she gives is, therefore, genuinely chosen in that it issues from her own capacity for recognizing the relationship between her and the trustee as a relationship conditioned by mutual acknowledgement. And since such acknowledgement does not depend on the trustee's adopting the truster's role by treating her *as if* she were a person with self-directed thoughts and intentions, it follows that the thoughts and intentions the truster actually has must be acknowledged by the trustee if the trustee is genuinely to treat the truster as an autonomous person in her own right. (No parental make-believe is involved in such a relationship.)

The adult who trusts thus requires from the trustee something much more than the infant requires from the parent, and also something much less: The truster requires that her vulnerability to the trustee be recognized as the vulnerability of one self-determined person to another. It is thus a vulnerability based on interests, needs, and desires which are importantly the truster's own and to which she trusts the other can and will be sensitive, guiding his actions accordingly. But, of course, since the truster requires this kind of full acknowledgement from the trustee, she must give it as well—and thus be prepared for difficulty and disappointment. After all, the trustee is a person in his own right as well – with needs, desires, interests that are importantly his own. So, even with all the good will in the world the trustee may not be able to live up to the truster's hopes and expectations, either because he has misunderstood the truster's needs and desires or because his own needs and desires cannot be easily reconciled with the truster's own and cannot be given up without serious compromise. The difficulties of trust between self-standing adults are thus ones that stem from the need to recognize and negotiate autonomous interests. In particular, since in the adult case, the trustee does not take on the role of determining the truster's needs and desires, the trustee can betray the trusting adult in a way that the parent cannot betray the so-called trusting child. This is not to minimize what can happen to the child. On the contrary. The child can be profoundly and invasively damaged by the parent of whom it must rely. But because the parent takes on the role of determining a child's understanding of its own needs and desires, the child cannot experience, at least initially, the gap between self and other as a gap of potentially conflicting interests.

The bottom line, then, is this: The experience of conflicting interests and the threat of betrayal is much more salient in relationships of adult trust. As we develop, we become aware of others in a way that infants are not aware of their parents: we are aware of others as having interests that make them potentially 'unsympathetic' to us, given our own interests, needs and desires. This awareness seems to militate against developing trust in others, where trust, as Dreyfus says, involves some confidence that others will act "sympathetically to our interests even when so doing might go against [their] own" (Dreyfus 2001, 70). So the question is how do we adult trusters reconcile the two: awareness of potential conflict and the risk of betrayal, on the one hand, with a capacity for genuine confident trust, on the other? I see two possibilities.

One possibility is to retreat from the awareness altogether, simply expecting in our trusting relationships the very stability and security we experienced in infancy—a kind of unconditional care that depends on erasing any threatening sense of difference between self and other. This is the hallmark of 'security trust'. However, given the real existence of the other, how can this sense of total security be achieved except by erasing the other's real identity, and superimposing on them a fantasized identity constructed in terms of just those needs and interests that resonate with our own? Although the allure of this strategy is clear, I think it's also clear why it is inherently unstable and so highly vulnerable to breakdown. Moreover, since security-driven trusters fail to develop resources for negotiating difficulties when they arise, they are more liable than mature trusters to experience any breakdown of trust in terms of deep and traumatic betrayal—i.e. the sort of betrayal that is essentially irreparable.

A second possibility, clearly preferable to the first, is to reconcile our awareness of genuine difference with the capacity for genuine trust by giving up on the need for absolute security in our adult relationships of trust. Such security belongs to the days of our infancy. Nevertheless, what we can have in adult relationships of trust is potentially far more rewarding than mere security. Real difference invites the challenge of real discovery and the possibility of mutual enrichment. In trusting others who differ from ourselves, we create bonds of mutual concern, interest and support that provide a platform for exploring aspects of the world and our human condition that we might not get to on our own. Mature trust involves risk; but when all goes well, it makes other things possible that we would not, or could not, achieve by ourselves. The mature truster understands this dynamic and accepts what it implies, namely—*uncertainty*, some inevitable *divergence of interests*, and *potential conflict and breakdown*:

Uncertainty. In developing adult relationships of trust, mature trusters must deal with others whom they know only incompletely, partly because they have only limited evidence to go on, and partly because they recognize that individual character is not fixed in stone: like them, others are to some extent changeable, depending on their changing circumstances and experiences, and such changes can always affect on-going relationships of trust. Because of this incomplete knowledge, mature trusters accept that they must inevitably trust under conditions of uncertainty; trust means taking a calculated leap beyond the evidence.

Divergence of interests. No matter how much the truster's interests seem to converge with trusted others, real difference means recognizing the inevitability of diverging interests.

Potential conflict and breakdown. The inevitability of diverging interests means problems will inevitably arise within relationships of trust. Mature trust involves recognizing this fact above all others. Functionally, it means developing the capacity to tolerate and negotiate differences when they arise. Consequently, mature trusters must develop resources to respond well when trust breaks down, despite the pain and disappointment such breakdowns may occasion.

Applying this analysis now to Julie's story, we might expect a mature truster to act rather differently on the discovery of her off-line identity occasion than an immature truster. For instance, as a friend of Julie's, the mature truster would seek to understand the reasons for Julie's deceit: Were her—or, rather, his— motivations inimical to friendship? Was he playing this character just for his own amusement, laughing at the women he was deceiving? Or did he have some possibly forgivable motive—say, a desire for intimacy that he felt he couldn't get by confessing his gender? (In fact, this was the explanation he gave.) Note that, in the context of mature trust, to judge that a motive is potentially forgivable does not entail the inevitable resumption of trust; but it does signal that, in the truster's view, there may be a way forward from such moments of betrayal to forging a new kind of relationship, premised on deeper mutual knowledge and understanding, and thereby paving the way for the possibility of renewed and better trust.

Mature trust is thus a kind of reasoned, explorative trust. Its primary impetus is not the need for security, but the desire to take calculated risks for the purpose of leading a richer human life. Mature trusters are individuals who trust, but who trust with care. They use care in three significant ways—namely, in *extending their trust*, in *monitoring their relationships of trust*, and in *responding well to others* when difficulties or breakdowns occur:

Extending trust. Mature trusters are discerning. They do not throw themselves into relationships of trust, but nor do they hold back when opportunities for trust present themselves. Because mature trusters are secure in themselves, they can afford to be exploratory in their trusting relationships, recognizing, but also testing, the kinds of conditions that effect relationships of trust in various ways. Thus, for instance, mature trusters are equipped to make distinctions between trust on the Internet and trust extended in other ways. Still, the fact that there are unique and interesting challenges for trust on the Internet does not stop the mature truster from facing those challenges and benefiting from the relationships made possible thereby.

Monitoring relationships of trust. For mature trusters, trust is not a one-off investment in a trusted other. It involves building and maintaining a relationship of trust that is sensitive to the changing attitudes and circumstances of truster and trustee.

Responding well to others when difficulties of breakdowns occur. Mature trusters understand that difficulties and breakdowns are part and parcel of relationships of adult trust. Despite the pain and disappointment inevitably caused by such occurrences, mature trusters work to understand the circumstances surrounding them. And if possible and desirable, they work to regenerate their relationships of trust, perhaps even healing breaches in ways that make those relationships stronger than they were before.

In short, mature trusters are sensible about their trust, but they are also ready and willing to trust under conditions which allow them to balance the difficulties of engaging with fully autonomous and only partially known others against the many prospective rewards that come from relationships of trust.

Can the Internet provide such conditions? I don't see why not. Consequently, we have no good reason to insist that trust on the Internet of the sort I've been discussing cannot be rational. It can be rational just in case it provides mature trusters with the opportunities to engage well with others, developing the kind of responsive attentive relationships that we expect with our friends. It may still be somewhat limited trust—limited because it is uni-dimensional, confined to the medium of textual exchange. Relationships of trust are generally multimedia, deepening with the multifaceted ways we have of interacting with one another. But textual exchange is one of our best ways to bring mind into contact with mind, and heart eventually to heart, so I see no reason why Internet relationships cannot deepen over time in a similar kind of way. Of course, if they do so deepen, they are likely to spill over into life off-line.

3. The Presentation of Self in Internet Life

In the last section, I argued that trust on the Internet can be rational—that is to say, there is no reason why text-based interactions should not provide mature trusters with opportunities to engage well and responsibly with trusted others, deepening and broadening their relationships with these others over time. Of course, there are distinctive challenges to building trust on the Internet as we saw in Section 1, and mature trusters must proceed in reflective awareness of them. To review those challenges here:

The first has to do with the fact that Internet identity is relatively less grounded than identity off-line, allowing Internet personas to float somewhat free of the real world individuals who enact them. I called this the *Proteus factor*. One consequence of this is that individual identity on the Internet must be associated more directly with an agent's intersubjective properties—i.e., properties the agent manifests in relating to others—rather than, as is often the case off-line, with the agent's personal descriptive properties—i.e. properties, like age, sex, profession, appearance and so on, that pick the agent out as a particular identifiable person. Normally, who we take someone to be in this descriptive sense has a dramatic impact on how we expect them to act towards us, and so on how we act towards them in turn. This is the power of stereotyping. On the Internet, we are not quite deprived of this guide to another's likely profile of inter-subjective behaviour, since individuals will present themselves as possessing various personal descriptive properties. But since these descriptions are wholly within their control, they can be used more manipulatively than in life off-line to shape their recipients' intersubjective expectations. Julie's story is a prime example of such manipulation. How bad is this for Internet trust? As we shall see in a moment, it may not be so bad after all. But it is something that individuals must be aware of if they are to trust well on the Internet.

The second challenge for Internet trust involves what I called the *Eliza factor*: Because Internet personas are manifested only in text, it allows others to project more freely onto them whatever fantasies they have about the off-line agents who enact the personas. This can have painful consequences. Because we will inevitably feel betrayed if the persons we trust do not live up to our expectations, it's important to have expectations that are realistically grounded if we are to trust reasonably and well. The problem of forming unrealistic expectations based on our fantasies about others are not unique to the Internet, but they can be greatly facilitated by the textual medium in which Internet exchanges are conducted.

While those who trust well may compensate for these liabilities of Internet interaction, we have seen that those who trust badly—immature or irrational trusters—may fall prey to them. Indeed, they may use the limitations of Internet interactions to avoid the responsibilities and risks of full adult trust. So, perhaps the best that can be said for trust on the Internet is that its special challenges do not rule out rational trust, but they certainly don't make it easy either. Thus, it may seem reasonable to conclude that there are no positive advantages to building relationships of trust on the Internet. But I think this judgement would be over-hasty. I close by considering some possible advantages of Internet trust that may outweigh the obvious liabilities and, in fact, are interestingly related to those liabilities.

So far my argument has been that the particular liabilities of Internet trust, which I've called the Proteus and Eliza factors, are not unique to the Internet; they are just greatly magnified by the Internet. Thus, problems of Internet trust make more salient problems that exist in any relationships of trust. For people present themselves to us in everyday life, masking some aspects of character, highlighting others; and on the basis of our limited exposure to them, we interpret the signs that they give us as favourable or unfavourable for trust. We can be manipulated in making these judgements by what they present to us; and we can also be manipulated in making these judgements by what we ourselves project onto them as a consequence of our needs and desires. Now, if building relationships of trust on the Internet makes more salient difficulties that are already present in forging any relationships of adult trust, then *by making these difficulties more salient* Internet use may force a practice of reflection on these difficulties and a direct engagement with them that engenders in turn more mature capacities for trust.

In support of this suggestion, I want to conclude by briefly considering a particular form of text-based multi-user interaction on the Internet that has become increasingly popular: the so-called MUD or virtual society. Unlike Internet conferences and chat rooms, MUDs involve a form of interaction in which the Proteus factor is, as it were, formalized. Individual players explicitly create and enact personas that are understood to be descriptively different from their off-line selves along any of a number of different dimensions: gender, ethnicity, age, profession, and even species (some MUD personas could at most be characterized as 'humanoid', and humanoid only because of their interpersonal characteristics rather than their physical characteristics as described by those who enact them).

MUDs are extremely popular. No doubt for a variety of reasons, people are deeply attracted to enacting personas they make up themselves, and interacting with other such personas in a virtual world that is communally constructed. Are such activities pure escapism? Perhaps to a certain degree. But it is interesting to note how deeply invested dedicated MUD players become in this shared virtual world, in their relationships with other personas in that world, and most of all, in the personas they create for themselves. For instance, one such player remarked, "MUDS make me more what I really am. Off the MUD, I am not as much me" (Turkle 1996, 54). This statement seems to reflect a sentiment that is widely shared among dedicated MUD players. Presumably, it shows that they are able to lead lives in this virtual space and via their MUD personas that allow them to experience their own potential for creative activity and social engagement in more direct and rewarding ways than they can in 'real life'. But why should this be?

I can think of two important reasons (which might be relevant to Julie's case as well). The first involves avoiding, or at least modifying, the effects of stereotyping in the real world. As I pointed out earlier, people's views about whom they are interacting with has a powerful effect on how they expect those individuals to behave and on how they should govern their behaviour towards them in turn. Stereotypes have a profound effect on the scope of individuals' social agency. It may be impossible to escape these effects completely. But by playing with the personal properties of self-presentation, it may be possible to alter the shape of one's social agency by provoking others to apply stereotypes that are different from those they would automatically apply in the real world. Thus, for example, many MUD players enact personas with the opposite gender from their own just to experience what is possible for them within a differently gendered social space (Bruckman 1996).

A second, perhaps more interesting reason involves self-development. Studies in social psychology show that when individuals publicly enact personality traits that they do not really take themselves to possess, this has a lasting effect on how they come to think of themselves—they think of themselves as now possessing those traits (Tice 1992). In other words, it seems that though the very process of having the traits they enact accepted by others as part of themselves, individuals themselves come to accept their behaviour as stemming more directly from who they really are. This may not be so surprising; but it does show that for many players, what may begin as a kind of enjoyable public make-believe becomes a powerful source of self-enablement and, hence, of self-development.

If these sorts of reasons explain why individuals report feeling 'more like themselves' in the context of role-playing games, I think it also clarifies that what matters most to agents' sense of self-identity in the MUD is not who they are in terms of personal descriptive properties, but rather who they are in terms of their intersubjective properties—i.e., in terms of the traits they are enabled to enact in relation to other personas. And, of course, what matters to agents most in terms of the identities of other personas with whom they interact is the intersubjective traits of these personas in turn. Relationships of trust and friendship in the MUD thus depend on the stability of players' intersubjective properties—hence, on their taking responsibility for maintaining their characters in relationships to one another, and of responding well to the concerns of one another when conflicts arise. Moreover, such responses have come to include, interestingly enough, explicit reflection on the difficulties of trust and civil behaviour in the MUD given the way players' identities are constructed and maintained. (There are special forums for such discussions on MUDs, usually in the form of a mailing list to all participants—e.g. *social-issues* in the MUD LambdaMOO).[6]

My point in discussing these virtual communities is just this: The fact that friendship and community survive, sometimes even flourish, in such forums shows the extent to which individuals can and do take responsibility for fomenting and maintaining relationships of trust, explicitly regulating their behaviour to compensate for conditions that destabilize and potentially undermine such trust. My claim is not that these relationships can substitute for relationships of trust in the real world, where the risks and vulnerabilities for self and others are presumably much more serious. My claim is rather that such conditions can make the difficulties inherent in relationships of trust more apparent to Internet trusters, thus challenging them to respond to these difficulties in ways that develop their own reflective capacities for engaging in relationships of mature trust both on and off-line. In the words of Sherry Turkle,

> "Virtual personae can be a resource for self-reflection and self-trans-formation. Having literally written our on-line world into existence, we can use the communities we build inside our machines to improve the ones outside of them. Like the anthropologist returning home from a foreign culture, the voyager in virtuality can return to the real world better able to understand what about it is arbitrary and can be changed." (Turkle 1996, 57)

Bibliography

Baier, A, (1986), Trust and Antitrust, in: *Ethics 96*, 231–260

Bechara, A./H. Damasio/D. Tranel/A. R. Damasio (1997), Deciding Advantageously before Knowing the Advantageous Strategy, in: *Science 275*, 1293–1294

Bechara, A./D. Tranel/H. Damasio/A. R. Damasio (1996), Failure to Respond Auto-nomically to Anticipated Future Outcomes Following Damage to Prefrontal Cortex, in: *Cerebral Cortex 6*, 215–225

Bruckman, A. S. (1996), Gender Swapping on the Internet, in: V. Vitanca (ed.), *CyberReader*, Needham Heights, 418–425

Campbell, S. (1997), Love and Intentionality: Roxanne's Choice, in: R. Lamb (ed.), *Love Analyzed*, Boulder, 225–242

Dreyfus, H. (2001), *On the Internet*, London-New York

Hertzberg, L. (1989), On the Attitude of Trust, in: *Inquiry 31*, 307–22

Holton, R. (1994), Deciding to Trust, Coming to Believe, in: *Australasian Journal of Philosophy 72*, 63–76

---

[6] For further information on LambdaMOO, see http://www.lambdamoo.info/

Jones, K. (1996), Trust as an Affective Attitude, in: *Ethics 107*, 4–25
— (2003), Emotional Rationality as Practical Rationality, in: C. Calhoun (ed.), *Setting the Moral Compass: Essays by Women Philosophers*, New York-Oxford
McGeer, V. (2002), Developing Trust, in: *Philosophical Explorations 5*, 21–38
Meltzoff, A./A. Gopnik (1993), The Role of Imitation in Understanding Persons and Developing a Theory of Mind, in: S. Baron-Cohen/H. Tager-Flusberg/D. J. Cohen (eds.), *Understanding Other Minds: Perspectives from Autism*, Oxford, 335–366
Pettit, P. (1995), The Cunning of Trust, in: *Philosophy and Public Affairs 24*, 202–25
Rostand, E. (1959), *Cyrano de Bergerac*, New York
Stone, A. R. (1991), Will the Real Body Please Stand up?, in: M. Benedikt (ed.), *Cyberspace: First Steps*, Cambridge, 81–118
Strawson, P. (1974), *Freedom and Resentment*, London
Tice, D. M. (1992), Self-Concept Change and Self-Presentation: The Looking Glass Self is Also a Magnifying Glass, in: *Journal of Personality and Social Psychology 63*, 435–51
Turkle, S. (1996), Virtuality and its Discontents, in: *American Prospect 7*, 50–57
Walker, M. U. (forthcoming), *Fixing Responsibility: Essays in Moral Repair*, Cambridge
Weizenbaum, J. (1976), *Computer Power and Human Reason*, San Francisco

[15]

The Computer Revolution and the Problem of Global Ethics

Krystyna Gorniak-Kocikowska, *Southern Connecticut State University, USA*

Keywords: computer ethics, computer revolution, global ethics, industrial revolution, printing revolution, professional ethics

ABSTRACT: *The author agrees with James Moor that computer technology, because it is 'logically malleable', is bringing about a genuine social revolution. Moor compares the computer revolution to the 'industrial revolution' of the late 18th and the 19th centuries, but it is argued here that a better comparison is with the 'printing press revolution' that occurred two centuries before that. Just as the major ethical theories of Bentham and Kant were developed in response to the printing press revolution, so a new ethical theory is likely to emerge from computer ethics in response to the computer revolution. The newly emerging field of information ethics, therefore, is much more important than even its founders and advocates believe.*

INTRODUCTION

The inspiration for my paper comes basically from two sources. The first is the article by James Moor, "What is computer ethics?".[1] Published in 1985, it is already considered to be a classic in the field of computer ethics. This means that the validity and importance of its content are still highly regarded today. The other source of inspiration for the considerations presented here, is my work on the problem of a global ethic.

Unlike many scholars who are presently active in the field of computer ethics, my theoretical background is not in computer science, nor in technology in general. My philosophical background is not primarily in the analytic tradition. By saying this, I want to make it clear that my perspective on the Computer Revolution is not the perspective of someone who is participating in the making of this revolution. It is a perspective of someone who is defenselessly exposed to that revolution, who is overwhelmed by its current and who does not know whether she will ultimately be brought by this current to a sandy, sunny beach, or smashed against a rock or left out in

Address for correspondence: Professor Krystyna Gorniak-Kocikowska, Southern Connecticut State University, 501 Crescent Street, New Haven, CT 06515-1355, USA. Email:gorniak@scsu.ctstateu.edu

1353-3452/96 © 1996 Opragen Publications, POB 54, Guildford GU1 2YF, England

K. Gorniak-Kocikowska

muddy standing water. And I want to make it clear as well that I do not look at the problems of computer ethics from the perspective of someone who can program or design a computer, although I welcome any information about what kind of problems there are. For this reason, computer ethics understood as professional ethics, i.e., ethics for those who have power over computers, is seen by me as just a fraction of computer ethics *per se*.

I am one of those individuals whose actions in cyberspace are dictated and defined by computer designers and programmers. Therefore, I am very much inclined to look at the Computer Revolution and computer ethics as "them," as the powers beyond me, whom I cannot influence, not to mention control. At the same time, however, these are the powers I cannot ignore, nor can I escape them. They are part of my life, they are my reality, almost in the same way Nature is.

Furthermore, neither nature nor computer technology can be fully controlled. I am not in the position of those who have the power to decide which computer program to choose for mass-production or whether to shut down the system. I represent the perspective of those who may or may not be granted the privilege to travel through cyberspace; individuals like me may also be coerced to enter this space. (One of the features of revolution, any revolution, is that it is merciless to its opponents, and at best it ignores the by-standers, providing that the by-standers get out of the way.) To quote Michael Heim,[2] the author of *Metaphysics of Virtual Reality*:

> The danger of technology lies in the transformation of the human being, by which human actions and aspirations are fundamentally distorted. Not that machines can run amok, or even that we might misunderstand ourselves through a faulty comparison with machines. Instead, technology enters the inmost recesses of human existence, transforming the way we know and think and will. Technology is, in essence, a mode of human existence, and we could not appreciate its mental infiltration until the computer became a major cultural phenomenon. (p. 61)

Each one of the old technological revolutions changed the way people functioned in Nature; with computer technology, however, there is the probability of the creation of a reality which is an alternative to Nature and equally complex. Humans are to be seen as inhabitants of both these worlds.

In this paper, I intend to concentrate on two issues. One of them is the definition of computer ethics proposed by James Moor, especially some of the implications this definition may have. The other issue is the way Moor addresses the question of the Computer Revolution.

My thesis is that both his definition of computer ethics and his presentation of the Computer Revolution are correct if applied locally and in respect to a relatively short period of time. By 'locally', I mean North America and Western Europe, but my suspicion is that Moor considers mostly the Anglo-American reality. His paper "Is Ethics Computable?",[3] known to me only in manuscript form reassures me somewhat in that supposition. By "a relatively short period of time," I mean the span of approximately two hundred years which Moor refers to in both his papers, although his

The Computer Revolution and the Problem of Global Ethics

real focus is on no more than five decades.

This is not sufficient, because his article "What is computer ethics?", however minimalistic in approach, illustrates one of the most important philosophical problems of our times. The definition of computer ethics ought to be widened and the field of computer ethics should be regarded as a great deal more than yet another example of professional ethics.

The purpose of this paper is to show that:

1. The Computer Revolution causes profound changes in peoples' lives world-wide. In cyberspace, there are no borders in the traditional sense. The borders as well as the links between individuals world-wide will be increasingly defined in terms of the individual's ability to penetrate cyberspace.

2. Because of the global character of cyberspace, problems connected with or caused by computer technology have actually or potentially a global character. This includes ethical problems. Hence, computer ethics has to be regarded as a global ethic.

3. Up to the present stage of evolution of humankind there has not been a successful attempt to create a universal ethic of a global character. The traditional ethical systems based on religious beliefs were always no more powerful than the power of the religion with which they were associated. No religion dominated the globe, no matter how universalizing its character. The ethical systems that were not supported by religion had even more restricted influence.

4. The very nature of the Computer Revolution indicates that the ethic of the future will have a global character. It will be global in a spatial sense, since it will encompass the entire Globe. It will also be global in the sense that it will address the totality of human actions and relations.

5. The future global ethic will be a computer ethic because it will be caused by the Computer Revolution and will serve the humanity of a Computer Era. Therefore, the definition of computer ethics ought to be wider than that proposed by James Moor. If this is the case, computer ethics should be regarded as one of the most important fields of philosophical investigation.

COMPUTER REVOLUTION

In his presentation of the anatomy of the Computer Revolution, James Moor uses as the point of reference the Industrial Revolution in England. I wonder whether he would reach different conclusions had he chosen the revolution caused by the invention of the printing press instead. (I mean in Europe, since books were printed in China from around the year 600 C.E.)[4]

Moor writes about the Industrial Revolution indicating that its first stage took place during the second half of the Eighteenth Century, and the second stage during the

K. Gorniak-Kocikowska

Nineteenth Century. This is a span of about 150 years. Let me compare this with what happened after the printing press was invented in Europe.

Gutenberg printed the "Constance Mass Book" in 1450, and in 1474 William Caxton printed the first book in the English language.[5] By 1492 "the profession of book publishers emerges, consisting of the three pursuits of type founder, printer and bookseller."[6] This was, roughly speaking, forty years after the invention of the printing press, the same amount of time Moor claims the Computer Revolution needed for its introduction stage. In 1563, the first printing presses were used in Russia. (This was the same year in which the term "Puritan" was first used in England, one year before the horse-drawn coach was introduced in England from Holland, and two years before pencils started to be manufactured in England.) And in 1639, the same year in which the English settle at Madras, two years after English traders were established in Canton and the Dutch expelled the Portuguese from the Gold Coast, the first printing press was installed in North America, at Cambridge, Massachusetts.[7] This is about 140 years from the first publication of the printed text by Johann Gutenberg, almost the same amount of time Moor considers for both stages of the Industrial Revolution.[8]

Another problem pointed out by Moor in "What is computer ethics?" is the question of how revolutionary a machine the computer is. He claims that it is the *logical malleability* that makes the computer a truly revolutionary machine. Moor challenges the "popular conception of computers in which computers are understood as number crunchers, i.e., essentially as numerical devices." (p. 269) He further writes:

> The arithmetic interpretation is certainly a correct one, but it is only one among many interpretations. Logical malleability has both a syntactic and a semantic dimension. ... Computers manipulate symbols but they don't care what the symbols represent. Thus, there is no ontological basis for giving preference to numerical applications over non-numerical applications. (p. 270)

Here, too, the similarity between a computer and a printing press seem to be evident. Like the printing press, computers serve to transmit thoughts. The phenomenon of the printing press is that it meant both the technological revolution, i.e. the profound change in the kind of physical objects used to substitute for human muscles, as well as a revolution in the transport of ideas, the communication between human minds. The same can be said about a computer.

I have written elsewhere about the impact of the printing press on the western hemisphere.[9] Here, I would like to mention only two of the many changes caused by the invention of movable printing type. The mass-production of texts and hence their growing accessibility made reading and writing skills useful and caused a profound change in the very idea of education. Gradually, the ability to read and write became an indispensable condition of human beings' effectiveness in functioning in the world.

While the number of individuals who were able to read and write expanded rapidly, the time needed for the popularization of texts grew shorter. Dante's "Divine Comedy" needed 400 years to become known throughout Europe, Cervantes' "Don Quixote" needed twenty years for the same, and "The Sorrows of Werther" by Goethe only five years (see Escarpit, p. 21).[10] The printed texts made it also possible to acquire knowledge *individually* (i.e. not through oral public presentation) and *freely*

The Computer Revolution and the Problem of Global Ethics

(i.e., without control of either the individual tutor or the owner of the collection of manuscripts). One of the results of this situation was the loss of belief that knowledge means possession of a mystery, a *secret* wisdom, inaccessible to outsiders. Knowledge became an instrument which everyone could and should use. Faith in the power and universal character of the individual human mind was born and with it a new concept of the human being. The masses of believers who used to obey the possessors of knowledge, discovered that they were rational individuals capable of making their own judgments and decisions. This paved the way for the two new ethical concepts that were ultimately created by Immanuel Kant and Jeremy Bentham.

The function of the most important machines invented at the end of the Eighteenth Century, the steam engine and the spinning machine, was the replacement of manual labor. This is, of course, true of the printing press and computer as well. But their primary function, their real importance, lies in the fact that both increase so incredibly the efficiency of the labor of the human mind — and not only the individual mind. Computers, like the printing press, allow human minds to work faster and more efficiently, because of their ground-breaking impact on communication and the exchange of ideas. Like the printing press, they are creating a new type of network between human individuals, a community existing despite the spatial separation of its members.

One could argue that the invention of the telegraph, telephone, radio and television are all serving faster and better communication between human beings as well. Why not compare them with computers? Scholars point out the versatility or, as James Moor calls it, *malleability,* of both computer and movable printing type. James Moor claims that *logical malleability* is what makes the computer a truly revolutionary machine. If we accept this criterion, then the power and complexity of the Computer Revolution cannot be compared to anything less than the power and complexity of the revolution caused by the printing press.

PRINTING PRESS AND ETHICS

The changes and problems caused by the Industrial Revolution of the eighteenth and nineteenth centuries did not bring with them any truly new ethics. There was no need to create one. The world could be explained and brought into order with the help of the already existing theories. Marxism, the only truly powerful theory that was consciously created in response to the changes the Industrial Revolution caused in peoples' lives, is often accused of not having a coherent vision of new ethics. The point is that it does not need to and, as a matter of fact, could not really have one. Part of the popularity Marxism enjoyed for some time was due to the fact that it is an ideology promising the fulfillment of old dreams.

Marx, as a matter of fact, did accept ethical theories already elaborated on by others: by Bentham and Kant, by Plato and the Ten Commandments. Even his social theory relied on ethical premises elaborated on earlier; among others, on Locke's statement that it is one's labor that changes an object of nature into one's property. Marx never questioned this statement. He spent years trying to show that in the world

K. Gorniak-Kocikowska

of his times those individuals who put their labor into objects of Nature are unjustly deprived of the ownership of those objects of Nature transformed by them into something new. According to Marx, one of the most important results of the Industrial Revolution was that the process of manufacturing goods became a collective process. This meant for him that the ownership of these goods should also have a collective character. He pointed out that the ownership of capital had already an international, global character; therefore the just owners of the products of their labor should abolish national boundaries as well. From an ethical point of view, there was nothing substantially new in the theory created by Karl Marx. And there was no other, new theory after Marx that would challenge the already existing ethical systems.

In Marx's times, there were new ethical theories, though. These theories were created in the eighteenth and nineteenth centuries. The authors of the two especially interesting and challenging theories were Immanuel Kant and Jeremy Bentham. Their theories, however, were not responses to the Industrial Revolution. They were responses to the questions caused by religious wars and the social revolutions of the seventeenth and eighteenth centuries, events that historians linked with the invention of the printing press. (Of course, the printing press was not the only cause of such profound changes, but neither was the steam engine or, for that matter, computer technology.

Since many authors who write on the subject of computer ethics, including such prominent scholars as James Moor, Terrell Bynum and, above all, the author of a major textbook in the field of computer ethics, Deborah Johnson, use the ethics of Bentham and Kant as the point of reference for their investigations, it is important to make clear that both these ethical systems arrived *at the end* of a certain phase of profound and diverse changes initiated by the invention of movable printing type. The question is: were these ethical systems merely solving the problems of the past or were they vehicles driving humankind into the future?

The ethical systems of Kant and Bentham were created during the time of the Industrial Revolution, but they were not a reaction to, nor a result of, the Industrial Revolution of the eighteenth and nineteenth centuries. Likewise, there was no immediate reaction in the form of an ethical theory to the invention of the printing press. Problems resulting from the economic, social and political changes that were caused by the circulation of printed texts were at first approached with the ethical apparatus elaborated on during the high Middle Ages and at the time of the Reformation. Later, there was a period of growing awareness that a new set of ethical rules was necessary. The entire concept of human nature and society had to be revised. Hobbes, Locke, Rousseau and others did that work. Finally, new ethical systems like those of Kant and Bentham were founded. These ethical theories were based on the concept of the human being as an independent individual capable of making rational judgments and decisions, freely entering the social contract. Such a concept of the human being was able to emerge in great part because of the wide accessibility of the printed text.[11]

The ethics of Bentham and Kant are both manifestations and a summary of the European Enlightenment. They were created at the time when Europeans were experimenting with the idea of society being a result of a free agreement (social contract) between human individuals rather than submission to divine power or to the power of Nature. Moreover, such a new, contractual society could have been created only in *separation* from traditional social groups. The conquest of the world by Europeans, called by them geographic discoveries, and the colonization of the 'new' territories, made it possible. Both Locke's definition of property as appropriation of nature by one's own labor, and the lack of the concept of private property in most of the invaded societies, helped that task.

Despite their claims to universalism, Kant's as well as Bentham's concept of human being refers to European man, free and educated enough to make rational decisions. 'Rational' means here the type of rationality that grew out of Aristotelian and scholastic logic. This tradition was strengthened by Pascal, Leibniz and others. It, of course, permitted exclusion from the ranks of partners in discourse all individuals who did not follow the iron rules of that kind of rationality. The term 'mankind' did not really apply to such individuals. Finally, this tradition turned into Bentham's computational ethics and Kant's imperialism of duty as seen by calculating reason.

The nature of both these ethical systems must be very attractive and tempting for computer wizards, especially for those who grew up within the influence of the 'western' set of values. It is quite easy to give the answer 'yes' to the question asked by James Moor: "Is Ethics Computable?", if one has Bentham's or even Kant's ethical systems in mind.[12]

It is very likely that now the situation will repeat itself, although probably less time will be needed for all phases of the process to occur. The Computer Revolution is a revolution. Computers have changed the world already in a profound way, but it is obvious that presently we all can see only the tip of the iceberg. Computer technology causes many new situations and many new problems. Some of these new situations and problems are of an ethical nature. There are attempts to solve these problems by applying to them the now existing ethical rules and solutions. This procedure is not always successful, and my claim is that the problems will grow. Already, there is a rising tide of discussions on the ethical crisis in the United States. It is starting to be noticeable that the traditional solutions do not work anymore. The first reaction is, as is usual in such situations: let's go back to the old, good values. However, the more computers change the world as we know it, the more irrelevant the existing ethical rules will be and the more evident the need of a new ethic. This new ethic will be the computer ethic.

THE PROBLEM WITH THE DEFINITION OF COMPUTER ETHICS

In 1985, at the 10th International Wittgenstein Symposium held in Kirchberg am Wechsel, Austria, Heinz Zemanek, professor at the Technical University Vienna and one of the founders of computer technology in Europe, was given an award for his impact on the development of this field. In his paper presented on that occasion and entitled "Will the computer rehumanize natural sciences?",[13] Zemanek claimed that computer technology at its then present level of development needed new thinking and a new philosophy. The world could not and should not be seen any longer as a

K. Gorniak-Kocikowska

particular order of individual objects. It should be seen as a *whole* or a system. Another significant point made by Zemanek was his statement about reciprocity in the relationship between humans and the world of technology that was created by them.

In the same year, 1985, James Moor proposed the following definition of computer ethics: "On my view, *computer ethics* is the analysis of the nature and social impact of computer technology and the corresponding formulation and justification of policies for the ethical use of such technology." (What is Comp. Ethics?, p. 266) Next, Moor concentrated on the term "computer technology". Since he did not focus on the meaning of the phrase "ethical use of such technology", I assume that he did not consider it to be problematic. I assume further that under "ethical", he means: "what is in our (i.e., American) society regarded to be ethical." My assumption is supported by the fact that Moor uses the term "our society" and the examples he gives present situations that took place in the United States.

What kind of ethic is it? Moor's other text "Is Ethics Computable?" shows his interest in Bentham. Deborah Johnson, who frequently cites Moor to support her statements and seems to be in general agreement with his views, presents in her book ethical relativism (which she dismisses), utilitarianism and deontological theories, but it is really only Kant in whom she is interested. Terrell Bynum, whose classes on computer ethics I had the pleasure to audit, recently added Aristotelian ethics to the theories of Bentham and Kant.

These are all ethical systems of the Western hemisphere and utilitarianism can hardly be regarded as a universally accepted ethical system even within western culture alone. Indeed, there is *no* agreement about what kind of ethic is the ethic of western societies or even the ethic of American society today. As Johnson writes, the basic principle of utilitarianism is that "everyone ought to act so as to bring about the greatest amount of happiness for the greatest number of people. Utilitarians conclude that *happiness* is the ultimate intrinsic good, because it is not desired for the sake of anything else."(p. 24)[14] But *what* actually is happiness? And even if it is not desired for the sake of anything else, is it not so that we can do many nasty things in the pursuit of happiness? The literature of the seventeenth and eighteenth centuries, from Hobbes through Marquise de Sade to Goethe is a parade of examples illustrating this thesis.

Since the problem of happiness remains unsolved, we have the "no harm" principle. But this principle, combined with happiness understood as the ultimate intrinsic good is an unrealistic postulate in societies that are fueled by competition. Then there is fairness. At least, we can have a just, that is, fair society, says the neo-Kantian John Rawls. There should be an equilibrium of rights and duties. Let's sign that contract, and let's be rational. The *pursuit* of happiness is everybody's right.

But then again, Kant did not think that happiness should be the basic principle of ethics. Moreover, he claimed (in "Foundations of the Metaphysics of Morals") that if you acted with the intention to be happy, it was *not* a moral action, because you were expecting gratification in the form of your good feelings. On the other hand, Kant said that a human being should never be seen as a means, but only as an end. Does this mean that a human being is the highest value? Many understand him that way. However, individuals who read a page or two in Kant know that he really did not care

The Computer Revolution and the Problem of Global Ethics

that much for those whom he did not consider enlightened enough to use reason and intellect as their only guides in action. This, of course, opens anew the whole discussion of the question, what is a human being.

Or maybe not. Maybe no discussion on that subject is necessary. The same eighteenth century that brought us Kant, and in which Bentham was born, gave us a concept of human being that can be very useful if we would like to delete the line between humans and computers.[15] I have in mind the concept of human being as a machine. The French philosopher and physician Julien Offray de La Mettrie published his book *Man a Machine* (L'Homme machine) in 1747. This idea, which initially caused very strong angry protests, is today so common that in one of the early sequels of the very popular TV series "Northern Exposure" a physician repairs a broken airplane, because he thinks of the airplane's engine as a heart. In Philadelphia, Pennsylvania, in the Franklin Institute, every day hundreds of visitors watch a technologically sophisticated educational film about the human body in which the human body is routinely talked about as a machine.

In their book *Naturally Intelligent Systems*,[16] Maureen Caudill and Charles Butler present the work on neural networks done by scientists so far. On the cover jacket it says:

> Neural networks ... are information processing systems that are physically modeled after the structure of the brain and are trained to perform a task, rather than being programmed like a computer. Neural networks, in fact, provide a tool with problem-solving capabilities — and limitations — strikingly similar to those of animals and people.

If a human being is just a machine then we surely can expect man-made machines to be human-like. We can even repeat the Story of Creation. It is also obvious that the story of Frankenstein has its continuation in both scientific laboratories and in the world of artistic fiction. From this area, I would like to mention one of the most interesting attempts, namely, the film "Blade Runner". There, the problem with humanoids was caused by their pursuit of happiness. (La Mettrie, by the way, published a book entitled *Discourse on Happiness* (Discours sur le bonheur, 1750) as well.)

Caudill and Butler try to reassure the reader of their book that the international scientific community which is working on recombinant DNA technology and other biological techniques that will "allow us eventually to grow whatever neural configurations we need for a given application" (p. 266) is still far away from reaching its goal. How far away? Caudill and Butler think about 100 years. However, when after the release and phenomenal success of "Jurassic Park," the Public Broadcasting System prepared a program about the likelihood of actually re-creating extinct organisms from the preserved DNA, some of the scientists on that program thought 50 years would be needed for this task to be successfully completed.[17] In October, 1993, the (already second) International Conference on Ancient DNA took place for three days at the Smithsonian Institution in Washington, D.C. According to George and Roberta Poinar,[18] pioneers on work in this field, there were almost three times as many participants at the second conference, as there were at the first one. "Subscriptions to

K. Gorniak-Kocikowska

the *Ancient DNA Newsletters*, a means of communication for the members between meetings, have swelled to 600—not immense, but not bad for a field still in its infancy", the Poinars wrote enthusiastically (p. 192). This shows the great dynamism in the growth of that new discipline. The research on ancient DNA will not only help to understand and solve many of the mysteries of life on our Planet, but will also provide scientists with powerful new tools of creation of new forms of life.

Should all of the above happen according to the projected scenario then, of course, another question will have to be answered, namely the question of the differences between "natural" and "artificial" life. This question will be added to the question about the differences between "natural" and "artificial" intelligence. If the two forms of life and the two forms of intelligence come together close enough, the question "Is ethics computable?" asked by Moor will probably be replaced by the question with which he opened his article (i.e., the article entitled "Is Ethics Computable?"): "Can computers be ethical?" This would significantly change the meaning of the term "computer ethics." On the other hand, after the close proximity between humans and humanoidal computers is achieved, the question "Can computers be ethical?" would have to mean also "Can humans be ethical?" So, we will probably go back to the old question: "What is ethical?" or "Is this action ethical?" Therefore, whether computers will increasingly become human-like or not, the basic ethical problems and questions will remain the same; that is, as long as there will be an interaction between different subjects, i.e., as long as the action of one subject will affect at least one other subject.

In the closing part of this paper, I will use the term "humans" or "people", but I would like to make clear that the term "human-like" may be added at will.

GLOBAL CHARACTER OF ETHICS IN THE COMPUTER ERA

Revolution, more than any other kind of change, means that two processes take place simultaneously: the process of creation and the process of destruction. The problem is that in a human society this usually causes conflict because both creation and destruction can be regarded as a positive or negative (good or bad/evil) process. The assessment depends on the values accepted by an individual or group of people who are exposed to the revolutionary changes.

James Moor writes: "On my view, computer ethics is a dynamic and complex field of study which considers the relationships among facts, conceptualizations, policies and values with regard to constantly changing computer technology." (What is Comp. Ethics, p. 267) This is a broad enough definition to be accepted by almost everybody. The problem starts once we realize how many people may be affected by and interested in those facts, conceptualizations, policies and values, and how diverse this group is. We are talking about the whole population of our Globe.

Computers do not know borders. Computer networks, unlike other mass-media, have a truly global character. Hence, when we are talking about computer ethics, we are talking about the emerging global ethic. And we are talking about all areas of human life. What does this mean for the understanding of what computer ethics is?

Computer ethics is not just another professional ethic. Deborah Johnson devotes

The Computer Revolution and the Problem of Global Ethics

one chapter of her book to the justification of the thesis that computer ethics is professional ethics. From the perspective from which she presents the issue, she is definitely right and I support wholeheartedly the possibly strict ethical rules for computer professionals.

However, there are still at least two problems remaining.

1. Unlike physicians or lawyers, computer professionals cannot protect themselves from activities that are similar to their own but performed by non-professionals. Therefore, although many of the rules of conduct for physicians or lawyers do not apply to those outside of the profession, the rules of computer ethics, no matter how well thought through, will be ineffective unless respected by the vast majority or maybe even all computer users. This means that in the future, the rules of computer ethics should be respected by the majority (or all) of the human inhabitants of the Earth if the Computer Revolution is to be democratic in its nature. In other words, computer ethics will become universal, it will be a global ethic. If the Computer Revolution becomes elitist however, computer ethics could easily turn into a secret code of an ivory tower elite. Such a possibility is real if social analyses by authors like the late Christopher Lasch[19] are correct.

2. Even assuming that computer ethics applies only to professionals, professionals as a group are not totally isolated from the society in which they function. The function of their profession is significantly determined by the general structure of the society of which they are a part. At present, there exist various societies and cultures on Earth. Many of them function within different ethical systems than those predominantly accepted in the United States or even in the industrialized west. Hence, professional ethics, including the ethical codes for computer professionals, may differ between cultures to the point of conflict. And even if it does not differ, the conflict may still be unavoidable. For example, computer professionals in two countries who happen to be at war, may obey the same rule that computers should be used to strengthen national security. In such a situation, computers may become a weapon more deadly than the atomic bomb. What was and still is the discussion about scientists' responsibility for the use of nuclear energy may now apply to computer professionals. Computerized weapons may affect all of humankind, and the potential destruction may be greater than in the case of an atomic bomb.

Another aspect of the same problem: on February 25, 1995, the NBC Nightly News aired the information that the CIA monitors the Internet. If that is true, the CIA does it obviously for security reasons. However, the question is whether this means that certain ethical rules such as respecting privacy do not apply to certain subjects? If the CIA does not need to respect an ethical code, who else is entitled to be unethical and on what grounds? If one country can do it, what *moral* imperatives could prevent other countries from doing the same? Let's assume that such moral rules could be found and applied. Does this mean that the ethic of that other country is better than the one which allows a state agency to violate the principle of privacy? If it is better, why shouldn't it be applied on a global scale? If it is better in an ethical sense, but does not help to survive in the case of conflict, does it mean that it should be abandoned? But

K. Gorniak-Kocikowska

then would not that be giving permission to abandon all other uncomfortable ethical rules? Of course, the simple answer to these questions would be that the problem exists because of the existence of different cultures competing and sometimes being hostile to each other. Such an answer, however, still does not solve the problem of how to abolish the hostility between cultures while maintaining freedom of self-realization or, in other words, avoiding totalitarianism.

Problems like the above mentioned will become more obvious and more serious in the future when the global character of cyberspace makes it possible to influence the life of people in places very distant in space from the particular acting subject. This happens already today, but in the future it will have a much more profound character. Actions in cyberspace won't be local. Therefore, the ethical rules for these actions cannot be rooted in a particular local culture, unless, of course, the creators of computer ethics accept the view that the function of computers is to serve as a tool in gaining and maintaining dominion over the world by one particular group of humans. I would like very much to believe that this is not the case. I would like to believe what Dr. Smarr of the University of Illinois said (quoted from William J. Broad's article in *The New York Times*[20]):

> It's the one unifying technology that can help us rise above the epidemic of tribal animosities we're seeing worldwide. One wants a unifying fabric for the human race. The Internet is pointing in that direction. It promotes a very egalitarian culture at a time the world is fragmenting at a dizzying pace.

It may be an example of yet more wishful thinking however. I am afraid that the creators of computer ethics may contribute to the problem, if they do not fully see the importance of their undertaking. It seems to me that, unfortunately, they sometimes are not strong enough in their demands. For example, the experience of Tom Forester and Perry Morrison with their Australian students (which could be the same in many parts of the world) caused them to limit the goals of their program in teaching computer ethics. They write:

> Computer Ethics has evolved from our previous writings and in particular our experiences teaching two courses on the human and social context of computing to computer science students at Griffith University. One lesson we quickly learned was that computer science students cannot be assumed to possess a social conscience or indeed have much awareness of social trends and global issues. Accordingly, these courses have been reshaped in order to relate more closely to students' career goals, by focusing on the ethical dilemmas they will face in their everyday lives as computer professionals. (Preface)[21]

Reading this, I would like to ask: If not we, then who? If not now, then when?

I am afraid that this paper may appear critical of what has been done in the field of computer ethics. In fact, my only criticism, if it is a criticism at all, is that the scholars who have chosen to explore the problem of computer ethics were too modest in defining the area of investigation as well as the importance of the subject.

The Computer Revolution and the Problem of Global Ethics

REFERENCES AND NOTES

1   Moor, James H. (1985) What is computer ethics? *Metaphilosophy* **16** (4): 226-275.
2   Heim, Michael (1993) *The Metaphysics of Virtual Reality*, Oxford University Press, New York, Oxford.
3   Moor, James H. (1991) *Is Ethics Computable?* Manuscript, written after 1991.
4   The fact that print did not revolutionize life in China the way it did in Europe is itself a subject of interesting analyses.
5   In 1481, Caxton translated from French into English *The Miracle of the World*, a popular account of astronomy and other science.
6   Grun, Bernard (1982) *The Timetables of History. A Horizontal Linkage of People and Events*. Based on Werner Stein's *Kulturfahrplan*, Simon and Schuster – A Touchstone Book, New York, p. 217.
7   In 1637, "Geometrie" by René Descartes was published. In 1638, Galileo's "Discorsi e Dimonstrazioni Matematiche." In 1639, Gerard Desargues published his book on modern geometry.
8   The timetable for the Industrial Revolution varies greatly depending on sources and criteria. The one chosen by Moor is popular, but the view that the Industrial Revolution started with the invention of the printing press is popular as well.
9   Dialogue – A New Utopia? (in German). In *Conceptus. Zeitschrift für Philosophie*, Jhg XX, Nr. 51/1986, p. 99-110. English translations published in *Occasional Papers on Religion in Eastern Europe*; Princeton, Vol. VI, No. 5, October 1986, p. 13-29 and in *Dialectics and Humanism*; Warsaw, Vol. XVI, No. 3-4/1989, p. 133-147.
10 Escarpit, Robert (1969) *Rewolucja ksiazki*, translated from French by Jerzy Panski; Warsaw. French original: *La revolution du livre*; Paris, UNESCO 1965. English: *The Book Revolution*, 1966.
11 As you can see, from my point of view things happened very much the way Thomas Kuhn speaks about the paradigm shift.
12 Neil Postman (p. 13) comments as follows on the first known instance of grading students papers (at Cambridge University, in 1792): "...The idea that a quantitative value should be assigned to human thoughts was a major step toward constructing a mathematical concept of reality. If a number can be given to the quality of a thought, **then a number can be given to the qualities of mercy, love, hate, beauty, creativity, intelligence, even sanity itself.**" (my bold - K.G.K) Postman, Neil (1993) *Technopoly. The Surrender of Culture to Technology*, New York, Vintage Books A Division of Random House.
13 Zemanek, Heinz (1986) Wird der Computer die Naturwissenschaft rehumanisieren? In: Leinfellner, Werner & Wuketits, Franz M: *Die Aufgaben der Philosophie in der Gegenwart*. Proceedings of the 10th International Wittgenstein Symposium, August 18 - 25, 1985 Kirchberg am Wechsel, Austria; Wien, Holder-Pichler-Tempsky, p. 33-38. The paper was presented in German.
14 Johnson, Deborah G. (1994) *Computer Ethics*, second edition; Prentice Hall, Englewood Cliffs, NJ.
15 There are opponents of such an idea, e.g. Hubert Dreyfus, as well as enthusiasts, e.g., scientists whose interests are neurocomputers. Dreyfus, Hubert L. (1992) *What Computers Still Can't Do. A Critique of Artificial Reason*, The MIT Press, Cambridge, MA, London.
16 Caudill, Maureen & Butler, Charles (1990) *Naturally Intelligent Systems*, The MIT Press, Cambridge, MA.
17 On the other hand, the USA network TV news broadcasted (on March 19, 1995) the information that the scientists from Beijing, China, deny the possibility of re-creation of extinct species from DNA any time soon.

K. Gorniak-Kocikowska

18 Poinar, George & Poinar, Roberta (1994) *The Quest for Life in Amber*, Addison-Wesley Publishing Company, Reading, MA.

19 Lasch, Christopher (1995) *The Revolt of the Elites and the Betrayal of Democracy*, W.W. Norton & Company, New York, London.

20 Broad, William J. (1993) Doing Science on the Network: A Long Way From Gutenberg. *The New York Times*; Tuesday, May 18.

21 Forester, Tom & Morrison, Perry (1990) *Computer Ethics. Cautionary Tales and Ethical Dilemmas in Computing*, The MIT Press, Cambridge, MA.

22 Grun, Bernard (1982) *The Timetables of History. A Horizontal Linkage of People and Events*. New, updated edition. Based on Werner Stein's *Kulturfahrplan*, Simon and Schuster Touchstone Edition, New York.

[16]

Computer-mediated colonization, the renaissance, and educational imperatives for an intercultural global village

Charles Ess

Center for Interdisciplinary Studies, Drury University, 900 N, Benton Ave., Springfield, MO 65802, USA
E-mail: cmess@lib.drury.edu

Abstract. *"The diversity of cultures in this world is really important. It's the richness that we have which, in fact, will save us from being caught up in one big idea".*
Tim Berners-Lee (inventor of the Web) addressing the 10th International World Wide Web Conference, Hong Kong.[1]

"Globalization must not be a new version of colonialism. It must respect the diversity of cultures which, within the universal harmony of peoples, are life's interpretative keys".
Pope John Paul II.[2]

"It is the stillest words that bring on the storm. Thoughts that come on doves' feet guide the world".
The Stillest Hour, *Thus Spoke Zarathustra.*

Key words: computer-mediated communication, Confucian ethics, Habermas, Luhmann, meta-ethics, virtue ethics

---

[1] This quote was taken from Lydia Zajc, "Plea For Web Continuity", *South China Morning Post* on-line, <http://technology.scmp.com/ZZZ0CJNKYLC.html>, accessed in August, 2001 (registration required):

> Berners-Lee also weighs in on the digital divide, saying that the Web has become another advantage that wealthier nations have over developing nations. "I think the richer countries have a duty to help the poor countries get Internet access as well as the other things", he explains. Access should also go hand-in-hand with greater content development in the developing world: "The diversity of cultures in this world is really important. It's the richness that we have which, in fact, will save us from being caught up in one big idea".

[2] "The human being must always be an end and not a means, a subject and not an object, not a commodity of trade". "Second, the value of human cultures. . . . Globalization must not be a new version of colonialism. It must respect the diversity of cultures which, within the universal harmony of peoples, are life's interpretative keys". "As humanity embarks upon the process of globalization, it can no longer do without a common code of ethics", the Pope concluded. "In all the variety of cultural forms, universal human values exist and they must be brought out and emphasized as the guiding force of all development and progress".
"Globalization Could Slip Into Colonialism, Pope Warns", <Zenit.org>, April 27, 2001.

Introduction

The Internet and its companion technology, the Web, command our moral attention as the media highlight for us sensational, sometimes bizarre, crimes which seem especially realizable through these media – most prominently, sexual predators luring victims from their homes (sometimes with fatal consequences). Behind these more lurid examples lurk other significant crimes and misdemeanors: credit card theft, threats to privacy (including monitoring of website visits and purchases), copyright violation ("Napster"), problems of equity in distribution and access (including cultural issues surrounding interface development), harm caused by hacking, viruses, etc.

At a meta-level, moreover, there are a range of philosophical approaches to these sorts of ethical issues – a continuum defined in part by how far each approach sees the ethical problems raised by the Internet and the Web to be either absolutely novel (thus presenting us with utterly new ethical challenges for which we have no precedents in our efforts to grapple with them) and/or merely technologically-mediated extensions of moral issues humanity has confronted since ethical reflection began (thus requiring relatively straightforward application of familiar ethical theories). Which of these meta-ethical views we take as our point of departure, of course, determines in good measure how we will respond to specific ethical cases and issues.

Between the claims of absolute novelty and business as usual, I will argue a middle-ground position – one similar to that articulated by Deborah Johnson who sees CE issues as a "new species" of existing generic moral problems.

To do so, I will focus on the specific claim – popularized through McLuhanesque notions of an "electronic global village" – that "wiring the world" with computer-mediated communications (CMC) technologies such as the Internet and the World-Wide-Web will inevitably result in greater democracy, equality, individual freedom, and economic prosperity. I wish to refine and test this claim by first turning to Habermas' conceptions of communicative reason, the ideal speech situation, and the public sphere as a philosophically more robust theory of democracy – one that endorses communitarian and pluralist understandings of democracy, in contrast with plebiscite and libertarian views. I then review significant ways in which Habermas's conceptions are modified to meet postmodernist and feminist critiques, so as to defend especially a notion of "partial publics" (*Teilöffentlichen*) as a *praxis*-informed conception that may be realizable on the Net.

I then test this conception from a global perspective – i.e., in light of efforts to implement computer-mediated communication (CMC) technologies in diverse cultural settings. These lessons from *praxis* provide both examples and counterexamples of a (partial) public sphere as instantiated via the Internet and the Web. These examples illustrate, moreover, that CMC technologies embed Western cultural values and communicative preferences. This means that well-meaning efforts to "wire the world" in the name of an ostensibly universal/cosmopolitan vision of electronic democracy, paradoxically enough, emerge as a form of "computer-mediated colonization", i.e., an imposition of a specific set of cultural values and communicative preferences upon diverse cultures. At the same time, however, additional examples from *praxis* demonstrate that diverse cultures can resist and reshape Western technologies: indeed, paradigm cases emerge of best practices for realizing Habermasian notions of democracy and pluralism – first of all, by taking up Michael Walzer's concepts of "thick" and "thin" cultures, and attending to the *social context of use* (i.e., the larger complex of community values, as reflected in an educational process intended to preserve and enhance those values in the use of computing technologies).

In light of both theory and *praxis*, then, an electronic global village incorporating Habermas' conception of partial publics is possible. But the conditions of its possibility include both attention to the social context of use as well as a (re)new(ed) theoretical attention to *embodiment* – attention apparent in a recent renaissance of interest in hermeneutics and phenomenology, as well as postmodern feminisms. Building on the work of Cees Hamelink and others, I argue that a moral imperative emerges here for a Socratic education that attends to diverse cultural values and communicative preferences on the model of Renaissance women and men who are fluent in and can comfortably negotiate among multiple cultures and communication styles. Such Socratically-educated Renaissance women and men are required first of all as an antidote to the otherwise prevailing tendency of a commercialized Net to create "cultural tourists" and "cultural consumers" – "the Borg with a smiling face" who thereby sustain a computer-mediated colonization. In Habermasian terms, moreover, such an education fulfills the requirements for empathic *perspective-taking* and *solidarity* with one's dialogical partners and sister/fellow *cosmopolitans* (world citizens).

Returning to the meta-theoretical issue: a computer ethics shaped by these theoretical and praxis-oriented insights – including models drawn from the ancient, Medieval, and Renaissance worlds – thus find resources in diverse ethical and cultural traditions to bring to bear on contemporary problems, rather starting *de novo*. At the same time, this form of computer ethics emphasizes the need to design and implement CMC technologies in ways that sustain and enhance diverse cultural values – in part by requiring that users of a genuinely world-wide web develop a cultural- and communicative literacy that allows them to comfortably negotiate among a diversity of culturally-distinct moral communities. Especially by emphasizing a moral imperative to sustain diverse cultural values and communicative preferences (i.e., beyond those approaches that stress ethics as needed to control harmful behaviors facilitated by CMC) – a computer ethics oriented towards culture and communication would work as a form of virtue ethics (Western) that also moves towards becoming "exemplary persons" (*junzi* – Confucian). In this way, CMC technologies would become means towards greater human excellence, perhaps on new scales and levels.

Will CMC technologies inevitably democratize an electronic "global village"?

The claim is frequently made that CMC technologies "democratize" – meaning generally that these technologies will flatten local and global hierarchies (including those of corporate culture as they bring about a greater freedom and equality While popular literatures tend to assume that "democracy" means libertarian and plebiscite forms (i.e., emphasizing individual freedom *from* the constraints of communities and a notion of a direct "one person, one vote" rule by simple majority), in the scholarly literature communitarian and pluralist forms of democracy are defended by theorists who draw on Habermas's theory of communicative reason, the ideal speech situation, discourse communities, and a public sphere that realizes the freedom, equality, and critical rationality required for democracy (see Harrison and Falvey 2001, for a comprehensive overview of the literatures of democracy in CMC, as well as Ess 1996, pp. 198–212; Hamelink 2000, pp. 165–185). For postmodern and feminist critics, however, Habermas is simply another expression of a modern Enlightenment conception of rationality that, despite its intentions to liberate both the individual and society, paradoxically – indeed, dialectically (so Horkheimer and Adorno (1947) 1972) – leads instead to a totalizing/instrumental conception of reason that only conspires to objectify and enslave humanity in ruthlessly efficient, technologically-facilitated totalitarian regimes (see Poster 1997, pp. 206–210, for a representative overview of postmodern criticisms of Habermas). Habermas has responded to these critiques by first arguing that postmodernism rests on an epistemological and ethical relativism that contradicts its own clear value preferences, including its own insistence on liberation and democracy. As well, he has incorporated especially feminist notions of solidarity and perspective-taking into his conception of communicative reason in order to more clearly differentiate communicative reason from the forms of modern/instrumental reason targeted by feminists and postmodernists.[3]

More recent debate between Habermas and critics such as Niklas Luhmann have further sharpened the theoretical and practical limitations of Habermas's conception of democracy and the public sphere. For example, Barbara Becker and Josef Wehner echo postmodern analyses of the fragmenting and decentering effects of CMC (see especially Jones 2001) as they observe that the interactive communications characteristic of the Net amount to special interest groups, i.e., small groups of people bound together only by a common interest – but otherwise scattered geographically and culturally and not necessarily connected (or interested) in any larger, more commonly shared universe of discourse concerning pressing political issues, etc. In addition, Becker and Wehner see several significant obstacles to electronic democracy, whether in the form of libertarian "electronic town halls" or a Habermasian public sphere, beginning with the massive maldistribution of the economic resources and infrastructure required to participate in either. They further take up Bourdieu's notion of cultural capital to point out that not everyone has the level of education, etc., needed to participate meaningfully in Net exchanges. Finally, the information superhighway threatens to drown us in an information flood: "Through networking, more and more participants have a voice; but because of the increasing number of participants, there is less and less time to listen". In the face of these difficulties, Becker and Wehner take up Habermas' conception of *Teilöffentlichkeiten* ("partial publics") – including professional organizations, university clubs, special interest groups, etc., – as loci of discourses that contribute to a larger democratic process in modern societies. Over against the anti-democratic impacts and potentials of CMC, they see this Habermasian notion as describing an important way in which CMC technologies may sustain (within limits) a "civil society"

---

[3] Habermas develops these concepts initially in his theory of communicative action in two volumes so titled ([1981] 1984a, 1987). Two additional essays necessary for understanding Habermas are "Discourse Ethics" ([1983a] 1990) and "Justice and Solidarity" (1989). In the latter, Habermas argues that the ideal speech situation requires not only the rules of discourse (as intending to guarantee free and equal participation in conversations) that will lead to consensus shaped solely by ". . . the force of the better argument and no other force" (Nielsen 1990, p. 104). To be the legitimate source of community norms – i.e., norms that all agree to follow, such consensus further requires a sense of *solidarity* between participants. Habermas defines solidarity as a concern for ". . . the welfare of consociates who are intimately linked in an intersubjectively shared form of life and thus also to the maintenance of the integrity of this form of life itself" (47, quoted in Ingram 1990, p. 149). Finally, this apparently empathic concern for others requires a *perspective-taking* in which: "everybody is stimulated to adopt the perspective of all others in order that they might examine

the acceptability of a solution according to the way every other person understands themselves and the world" (Nielsen 1990, p. 98; cf. Benhabib 1992, pp. 8–9).

By incorporating especially feminist emphases on the crucial role of emotion and empathy in shaping judgments and our inevitable entanglement with one another in the webs of relationships that form human communities, Habermas both retains the Enlightenment focus on human freedom and rationality and emphasizes that these are necessarily intertwined with others in the community of communicative rationalities. Ingram discusses these reformulations in greater detail, especially in relation to Kant's conception of the human being as a moral autonomy and the correlative ethics (1990, pp. 145–146).

In addition, the requirement for solidarity means that Habermas's theory endorses a *communitarian* conception of democracy (cf. Abramson et al. 1988, p. 30). See Ess 1996, pp. 212–216; Hamelink 2000, pp. 55–76 for more detailed discussion.

as part of a larger democratic process. Such partial publics can be seen as as something of a theoretical compromise between a full-fledged public sphere on the Internet and its complete absence in the celebrated postmodernist fragmentation and decentering (cf. Jones' conceptions of "micropolis" and "compunity" 2001, pp. 56–57; Brenslow (1997), Metzler (1997), Ramsey (1998), Holmes (2000), Stevenson (2000).[4]

Habermasian theory in light of praxis

In their comprehensive review of the literature on CMC and democracy, Harrison and Falvey (2001) find widely divergent results regarding the question as to whether CMC technologies in fact further some form of democratic communicative action. Some positive examples can be found – including Harrison and Stephen's study of some forty community networks that fulfilled their intentions of providing equal access to information by providing free access to the network

---

[4] Two additional comments on Habermas are worth nothing here.

On the one hand, Hans-Georg Möller sees a Habermasian set of discourse rules standing at the entrance of a German-language children's community ("*Kindernetz*") – i.e., rules that participants must agree to in order to receive a logon identity and password for the website, its chatrooms, etc. From a Habermasian perspective, these rules are seen as ways of insuring that personal identity will be protected so that discourse will be open, free of irrational forces, etc. Drawing on the media theory of Niklas Luhmann, however, Möller argues that

... individuality in our post-modern society is gained through social *exclusion*. To be an individual means to be special, to be different from others. However, the patterns of "exclusive" individuality are supplied and validated only by communication, i.e., by society. Thus, individuality becomes paradoxical: Social agents gain their "individuality" not "by themselves", but by adopting one or, more often, several of the identities offered by social discourse. [...] It seems to be precisely this "pseudo-individuality" – and not the Habermasian one – which is enhanced by the new modes of electronic communication (2000).

On the other hand, David Holmes, while recognizing the difficulties that lead Becker and Wehner to move to supporting partial public spheres, argues that

... it is also true that individuals are mobile across communicative mediums and continuously participate not in a pre-given public sphere, but in the process of constructing publicness across a range of mediums. It is less the case, I argue, that the contemporary public sphere is breaking down and becoming fragmented as is the fact that it is sustained across increasingly more complex, dynamic and global kinds of communication environments (2000, 384f.).

including, in some cases, equipment in public places for utilizing network resources (1998). By the same token, if we now turn to what happens in *praxis* – i.e., what happens when CMC technologies are deployed in specific settings – we find that there are both *examples* and *counterexamples* to a Habermasian conception of a public sphere online, as well as significant middle grounds.[5]

Examples

CMC researchers have documented a number of discourse groups that fulfill the Habermasian description of partial publics, including NGOs use of the Internet to organize and coordinate their activities (e.g., in Uganda: see McConnell 1998), a men's discussion group (Rutter and Smith 1998), etc. As well, ethnic communities – including emigré Chinese communities (Joo-Young Jung 2000) and diaspora Russians (Sapienza 1999) – make use of the Internet and the Web to sustain connections with friends and family who are geographically dispersed. Insofar as these uses entail the creation of an electronic partial public that sustains shared discussion of community issues, they are consistent with Becker and Wehner's argument that the Net supports partial publics.[6]

---

[5] While the survey provided by Harrison and Falvey is the most comprehensive and useful known to me – it is also largely devoted to CMC research in a first-world, English-speaking context. My own work includes attention to a broader range of diverse cultural settings, including the Middle East, Asia, and indigenous peoples. As will become quickly apparent, the results of this larger survey are consistent with Harrison and Falvey's findings, and should be seen as a complimentary way of making their larger point.

[6] I have also argued that the Australian decision to set limits on USENET newsgroups to the exchange of pornography and discussion of sex, including bestiality and child-sex is at least consistent with Habermasian requirements. Such a decision could be justified under Habermas's discourse ethic, given three conditions. One, the community of participants would have to openly discuss the issue, and come to consensus on what norms their discourse communities would endorse. Two, such a discussion would require full participation *by all those affected* by any proposed norms, *including* women and children – not simply the predominantly male subscribers to the USENET groups in question. And three, all participants – including precisely those interested in exchanging pornography, etc. – would be required to exercise solidarity and perspective-taking, i.e., the admittedly difficult task of attempting to put oneself in the place of "the Other", in this case, precisely the women and children who are objectified in pornography, who may live with unpleasant consequences of its consumption, etc. Under these conditions it is not hard to imagine that such a discussion might result in a consensus to prohibit such discourse and uses of the system *as public*, especially if it could be demonstrated that such discourse otherwise worked to *exclude* the voices of all members of a

Counterexamples

At the same time, however, counterexamples to the democratization thesis abound, including examples of CMC technologies serving authoritarian ends and preserving cultural hierarchies of power, status, privilege, etc.

At one end of the spectrum of possible responses to CMC technologies, the *eKiribati*, a nation in the Solomon Islands, has rejected the introduction of the Internet into their communities – in part, precisely because of its putative claims to opening up and leveling communication among participants. Because of cultural traditions that include an acceptance of secrecy and limited access to specific kinds of information, the eKiribati see the ostensive democratization potential of the Internet as a threat to this element of their cultural identity (Sofield 2000).[7]

Louise Postma (2001) has further documented the ways in which indigenous peoples in South Africa conform to the prevailing cultural capital (so Bourdieu) "learning centers". The norms of the dominant culture – including an emphasis on individual achievement and an *epistemology* that defines what counts as knowledge and thus what is *worth* knowing, one further tied to the technologies of literacy and print – are appropriated by learning center users and used *against* their original cultural norms and values, including *epistemological* preferences for orality and performance as primary modes of communication. Using Friere's terms, the technologies thus support a *situational empowerment* – one that comes from conformity to prevailing norms and values – rather than a *critical empowerment*, one that sustains and enhances diverse modes of individual and group styles, values, acts, etc. In particular, the learning centers foster *individual* excellence over group achievement – a preference that is distinctively Western (2001, 326). This finding is consistent with other research, beginning with Hofstede (1980, 1983, 1984, 1991) and Hofstede and Bond (1988), that highlights the contrast – and potential conflicts – between Western emphases on the individual vis-à-vis Eastern and tradi-

tional emphases on the community. Where CMC technologies foster individualism – precisely as they are touted as ways of achieving *individual* excellence and achievement – then they are understandably perceived in more community-oriented cultures as a threat to a most basic cultural norm. More broadly, the use of CMC to foster situational rather than critical empowerment means that these technologies work to sustain the dominance of white European cultural norms – and in this way preserve hierarchy rather than promote equality.

Sunny Yoon (1996, 2001) has further documented a number of ways in which cultural and commercial factors work in the context of South Korea *against* any potential democratization effects – including any electronic "public sphere" envisioned along Habermasian lines. Rather, the Internet and the Web, especially as shaped by the forces of commercialization, can work instead as controlling mechanisms for capital and power.

Yoon's analysis relies on both Foucault (see Yoon 1996), and Bourdieu's notion of *Habitus*. *Habitus* highlights the role of individual will power and choice as manifested in individuals' everyday practices: these in turn build up the larger society and history in an "orchestra effect". In addition, Bourdieu describes "cultural capital" – including symbolic and institutional power such as language and education- as constituting a *meconnaissance* ("misconsciousness"), a kind of false consciousness that legitimates existing authorities.

Through a quantitative analysis, Yoon demonstrates that rather than encouraging use of the Internet as a medium of participatory communication, the ways Korean newspapers report on the Internet contributes to the commercialization of the Net: such commercialization further contributes to the Korean "digital divide", i.e., unequal access to and distribution of information resources.[8] Through interviews with young Koreans ("Gen-Xers"), Yoon then shows that as use of the Internet shapes educational rules and linguistic habits, it thus exercises symbolic or positive

---

democratic community – most obviously, the voices of women who are offended, sometimes into silence and withdrawal, by pornography which degrades them (Ess 1996, pp. 218–220).

[7] This rejection, moreover, is balanced by an apparently opposite cultural value. While accepting a hierarchical structure of access to information (i.e., as reserved for only a few), the eKiribati insist on a near-perfect *equality* in terms of material possessions. To show that one has more than others – e.g., by driving a new car – is called "shining" and is severely sanctioned. Because access to the Internet also promises individuals the possibility of economic advancement over their neighbors – i.e., "shining" – this provides a second rationale for its exclusion from the islands (Sofield 2000).

[8] The role of journalism in shaping whether CMC technologies are taken up and in turn foster democratic or antidemocratic directions is not limited to Eastern contexts. See Willis (2000) for an analysis of how *Wired* magazine (perhaps *the* premier print advocate of CMC technologies in the US), contrary to its apparent ideological commitment to the now-familiar values of the electronic global village (including an explicitly Jeffersonian conception of democracy, equality, etc.) – in fact re-presents a "corporatised Internet", one marked by restricted access for only the affluent, primarily white male elites of the middle- and upper-middle classes, as "participation" in the Net and an emerging "techno-lifestyle" are conceptualized and modeled as merely new modes of consumption.

power – including symbolic violence in Bourdieu's sense. Specifically, Internet use leads Korean students to accept the significance of English as the *lingua franca* of the Net without question. Language thereby becomes a cultural capital that exercises ". . . symbolic power over the cultural have-nots in the virtual world system", a cultural capital that induces a "voluntary subjugation" (2001, p. 257).[9]

Finally, Yoon's informants make it clear that individuals take up the Internet *not* because of its democratizing potentials but, on the contrary, because it increases their status, and, in Hofstede's terms, their power distance over others. In particular, because teachers, principals, and parents rely on their students and children to accomplish computer-related tasks (e.g., designing Web pages), young people acquire a remarkable new power over their elders, one that directly contradicts the traditional Confucian sense of obedience to and respect for these traditional authority figures. This finding is not only consistent with other research in those countries shaped by the Confucian tradition:[10] it further makes clear that what may look like democratization in Western cultural contexts (as the Internet opens up communication and empowers individuals) can, in other cultural contexts, work in directly *anti*-democratic ways, as the Internet simply transfers hierarchical power and status from one group to another.

Middle grounds
Finally, there are some significant examples of CMC technologies leading to at least a partial fulfillment of hopes for democracy and equality in cultural

[9] In his analysis of the multiple cultural factors working against any kind of equal access to CMC technologies in India, Kenniston also documents how English reinforces current distribution patterns of "power, wealth, privilege, and access to desired resources" (2001, p. 283).

At the same time, this situation becomes even more complicated as new software is developed that makes it increasingly easier to introduce Chinese and Japanese characters into web addresses, etc. – with the resulting prediction that Chinese may be the dominant language of the Internet by 2007.

[10] Research by Abdat and Pervan (2000) and Rahmati (2000) make clear that a cluster of cultural values in South Asia – specifically,

face-saving (Confucian)
high uncertainty avoidance (low risk tolerance)
high collectivism/low individualisms
high power distance

conflict with the cultural values embedded in Western CMC. These findings, moreover, correlate with Maitland and Bauer's demonstration that low uncertainty avoidance and gender empowerment are significant cultural factors *promoting* diffusion of IT (2001).

contexts previously marked by more centralized and hierarchical forms of government. To begin with, Michael Dahan (1999) has documented ways in which the introduction of the Internet, along with several other important cultural and political developments, helped Israel shift towards greater openness and democracy. Indeed, Dahan has undertaken an ambitious experiment to use the Internet to foster greater openness – indeed, friendship – among Palestinians and Israelis. This experiment exceeded his best expectations, as Israelis and Palestinians, after months of communication via the Internet, came together for a first face-to-face meeting that solidified sensibilities of respect and friendship first fostered online. This experience, unfortunately, culminated just prior to the most recent outbreak of violence between Israelis and Palestinians, leaving its future very uncertain (Dahan 2001).

Deborah Wheeler (2001) tests the democratization promise with an ethnographic study of Kuwaiti women and their use of the Internet – with decidedly mixed results. On the one hand, these new technologies appear to have a liberating impact for younger women, for example, as they allow women to converse "unescorted" with men in chat-rooms, and to meet and choose mates on their own (rather than agree to the cultural norm of arranged marriages). On the other hand, the cultural restrictions against women speaking openly are directly mirrored in distinctively male and female uses of the Internet and the Web. As she observes, new communication technologies – *contra* the (deterministic) assumptions of Western CMC enthusiasts who believe that "wiring the world" will automatically issue in greater communicative openness and democracy – do *not* automatically liberate us from the distinctive cultural values that define specific societies (2001, p. 202).

As a final but also exemplary instance of such middle grounds, we can consider Hongladarom's analyses of Thai USENET newsgroups and online chat groups (2000, 2001). Hongladarom first documents how a Thai newsgroup established modes of communication – including the question of whether or not Thai should be the official language of the newsgroup – that reinforced local cultural identity and community. In Michael Walzer's terms, Hongladarom refers to this as a manifestation of "thick culture", i.e., a worldview both deep and broad enough to define basic beliefs, values, communication preferences, etc., that vary – sometimes markedly – from culture to culture. At the same time, however, participating in a local newsgroup did *not* prevent Thais from also taking up the communication abilities of an umbrella "cosmopolitan culture" (2001, p. 317) or, in Walzer's terms, a "thin culture". This thin culture is marked by a shared *lingua franca* – English and its pidgens – which makes for functional but limited communication (e.g., as when airline pilots globally use English). Again, *contra* the deterministic view that CMC technologies, as embedding Western cultural values, will thus inevitably reshape "target" cultures along the lines of democracy, individualism, etc. – Hongladarom finds that a global Internet culture as "thin" is not necessarily able to override local "thick culture" and its attendant practices.[11] Rather, individuals seem able to maneuver within and between both a thick local culture and a thin global culture.[12]

[11] Hongladarom, referring to Walzer (1994, pp. 1–19) puts it this way:

> Moral arguments are "thin" when they are shorn of their particular histories and other cultural embodiments which make them integral parts of a cultural entity. These are the parts that make the arguments "thick". To use Walzer's own example, when Americans watched Czechs carry placards bearing words like "Truth" and "Justice", they could relate immediately to the situation and sympathized with the marchers. However, when the arguments are at the local level, as to which version of distributive justice should be in place, there might well be disagreements, and Americans may find themselves disagreeing with the particular conception of justice which is eventually adopted. The sympathetic feeling one feels across the Ocean is part of the "thin" morality, but the localized and contextualized working of those moral concepts is part of the "thick" (2001, p. 318).

In this way, a "thin" morality depends on something like Aristotle's *pros hen* and analogical equivocals – the use of terms in different but related ways – such that the different (and more univocal) meanings of terms (e.g., "justice" in a specific cultural context) thus partially defines the *difference* between cultures. (See Aristotle, *Metaphysics* 1003a33; Burrell 1973, p. 470).

[12] Other recent reports from Thailand (Thanasankit and Corbitt 2000), Malaysia (Harris et al. 2001), and the Phillipines (Sy 2001) likewise suggest that such middle grounds – ones that preserve local identities while facilitating global connections – are possible. Harris et al. (2001) is especially worth noting as an example of a project to introduce CMC technologies in ways that begins by paying conscious attention to the prevailing values, interests, and in Ong's terms, overwhelmingly *oral* communication "technology" of this highland people. The project continually involves community members in decisions surrounding the design and implementation of Internet and Web access, so that whatever cultural values and preferences these technologies may embed and foster, they will *not* inadvertently overcome defining community norms and preferences. Similarly, Sy (2001) develops a notion of a "cyber-barangay" as an explicit response to Habermas's question, "How can the power of technical control be brought within the range of the consensus of acting and transacting citizens?" (1987, p. 57; in Sy 2001, p. 297).

Sy is very clear about the many ways that introducing CMC technologies in the Philippines work as an electronic coloni-

A Habermasian/democratic electronic global village?

These theoretical considerations and practical examples drawn from a variety of cultures suggest that an electronic global village – especially if such a village is to be democratic in ways at least partially informed by Habermas' conception of partial publics and is to preserve and enhance diverse cultural identities – is possible. But this survey also makes it clear that realizing this possibility rests on at least two conditions. First, as especially Hongladarom's example of the discussion concerning the language to be used in the Thai chatroom, Sy's example of consciously appropriating Borgmann's notion of focal things and practices (2001), and the focus in the UNIMAS/Barrio project on the prevailing social preferences of the Kelabit (Harris et al. 2001) make clear, realizing a Habermasian partial public and its associated forms of democratic discourse requires *conscious attention to the social context of use, including education.* This point is further consistent with the analyses provided by Postma and Yoon, as well as the comprehensive survey undertaken by Harrison and Falvey (2001).

Indeed, a number of writers have argued recently that the kind of education required for undertaking the attention to fundamental values defining cultural worldviews and for making the choices regarding the implementation of CMC in diverse settings that will avoid cultural homogenization is precisely a *Socratic* education that stresses critical thinking regarding one's own beliefs as well as those of others. Most broadly, such an education will prepare people for what Cees Hamelink has described as the "... 'culture of dialogue' that the democratic process requires" (2000, p. 184; cf. Dreyfus 2001).

Secondly, this attention to social context of use also means a (re)new(ed) attention to the role of *embodiment* in our epistemologies and ontologies, our ethics and our politics. That is: earlier optimism regarding the inevitable march of a computer-mediated democracy as facilitated by wiring the world with the CMC technologies of the Web and the Net rested in part on a view of the self in cyberspace as somehow radically disconnected from the body at the terminal –

zation of the Filipino lifeworld (see especially 305-308). Sy is optimistic that a Habermasian style of democracy and social practice can be realized in the Philippines, especially in conjunction with attention to using CMC venues such as Internet cafés to serve as places for both traditional and new "focal practices" (so Albert Borgmann 1984, p. 219) – but this will require that IT be "brought to the fore of public deliberation free from domination and ... become a technology of citizenship" (2001, 309f.)

where this body was subject to and carrier of specific histories, traditions, and cultural shapings. Especially in light of the *cultural* differences between the West, the Middle East, Asia, and indigenous peoples – to assume that wiring the world will automatically move CMC users to more egalitarian and democratic modes of engagement requires us to assume that the self in cyberspace must be radically divorced from its life as an embodied member of a culture that may stress more hierarchical and less democratic modes of engagement. (Two of the best known proponents of this Cartesian – indeed, Gnostic dualism – are the early Donna Haraway (1990) and John Perry Barlow (1996): both argue that liberation and equality promised by cyberspace will be found only by a radical rejection of the embodied self in a world Barlow contemptuously called "meatspace".) By contrast: the results from *praxis* make clear that while Western CMC technologies in fact embed and foster specific Western values and communication preferences – both Western and non-Western users of these technologies are not simply reshaped to conform to those values and preferences. On the contrary, as especially the examples described here of the Thai coffeehouse, the UNIMAS/Barrio project, and the Filippino "cyber-barangay" suggest that individuals and groups may *both* take up CMC technologies ("thin" culture) and remain well-anchored in their distinctive cultural preferences and values ("thick" culture). But this means: CMC users still enmeshed in their distinctive "thick culture" are *embodied* users – selves ultimately interwoven with a specific body in a specific history, community, and culture.[13]

These middle grounds between individuals and groups as either (i) entirely unaffected or (ii) entirely reshaped by the cultural values and communicative preferences embedded in Western CMC technologies, moreover, cohere with other indications that we are turning from the more polarized notions of modernists vs. postmodernists, cyber-hells vs. cyberheavens, etc. that tended to dominate 1990's discourse and literature. In particular, there is a clear turn *from* a Cartesian (indeed, Gnostic or "cyber-gnostic") dualism underlying not only cyborg enthusiasm of the early Donna Haraway but also "Ectopians" such as Hans Morovec (1988) who hope to find liberation for a disembodied mind in cyberspace *to* a focus on *embodiment* as analyzed from hermeneutical, phenomenological, and/or feminist perspectives. Representative examples here include Becker (2000, 2001), Hayles 1999, Bolter 2000, Taylor 2000, Brown

and Duguid 2000, Dertouzos 2001. For a more complete discussion, see Ess (forthcoming). This turn, moreover, is a hopeful sign for a global village that will include Eastern perspectives: in classical Chinese, for example, the self is understood as a "heart-and-mind" – *not* a Cartesian/Gnostic duality.[14]

The Internet and our moral life: the educational imperative

Taken together, these two conditions – attention to social context of use, including an appropriate Socratic education, coupled with a renewed appreciation for the role of embodiment in shaping our knowledge of the world, our engagement with one another as members of distinctive cultures, etc. – point to a kind of moral imperative in education. The prevailing values and practices of "surfing the web" are shaped largely by a commercially-driven culture that emphasizes consumption. Especially as the Internet and the Web make it increasingly easy to encounter culturally distinctive "Others" (i.e., as more and more cultures and peoples produce web-based resources as a way of making themselves known, of advertising their products for sale, etc.) – the bias in a commercializing Web and Internet is thus towards becoming "cultural consumers" and "cultural tourists" as diverse cultural resources are commodified for consumption. For the cultural consumer and tourist, the "Other" is merely another consumable resource – an object to be taken in, if desired, and/or rejected according to one's whim or taste. In this way, a commercialized Web and Internet tend to shape us into a consumer version of the Borg – the Star Trek creatures who relentlessly consume all biological and cultural resources and homogenize them into a single "culture" of complete submission to "hive-mind". Such consumerist drones may be perfectly suited to helping economies hum along: they are hardly the stuff of which democracies are made.

By contrast, I have argued that we may be better guided in our thinking about the Internet and the Web by the historical examples of the Middle Ages and the Renaissance (2000). As Ropolyi (2000), Mehl (2000), and others have pointed out, our time – including the technologies of the Web and the Internet – resemble the Medieval and Renaissance experience of cultural flows, for example, the mixtures of Jewish, Christian, and Muslim philosophy and science, further spiced with a rich infusion of Chinese technology and invention, that issue into what we now call the natural sciences. At the same time, the dramatically expanding knowledge of "Others" for the Renaissance human beings – from the recovered worldviews of the Greeks

---

[13] As a way of signaling this notion of embodied self in contrast with the Gnostic/Cartesian mind-body dualism, Barbara Becker (2001) invents the phrase "bodysubject".

[14] See Ames and Rosemont (1998, pp. 20–65) for a discussion of key Chinese characters and concepts in the *Analects*.

and Romans to increasing understanding of Asia, the Muslim world, and the peoples of the New World – led not only to colonization and warfare but also to crucial humanist and cosmopolitan sensibilities that emphasized both immersion into the richness of diverse cultures and the possibility of coming to understand at least some elements shared by all human beings. At the same time, we can add to Cees Hamelink's account of the importance of a Socratic education the recognition that a Renaissance humanism is at least in part an expression of the Socratic project. As the allegory of the cave makes especially clear, education is about moving beyond the prevailing beliefs, values, and assumptions of our native culture to a larger perspective that helps us recognize the strengths and limits of a given cultural worldview. In anthropological terms, education of this sort is a move beyond our ethnocentrism – a move facilitated not only by philosophical analyses of worldviews, but most especially by the experience of living as an embodied being in a culture and linguistic world different from our own. Both philosophy and experience in other cultures thus leads to an epistemological humility – one that recognizes that every view is at best partial, but that a more complete understanding of both ourselves and others may be reached by becoming familiar with a variety of cultures and philosophies, rather than remaining dogmatically content with just one.

In short, to realize a Habermasian form of democracy requires a Socratic education that emphasizes critical thinking and dialogue as essential conditions of democracy. As well, the Renaissance model calls for educating human beings to be familiar with the languages, values, beliefs, and practices of multiple cultures – thus moving us beyond our own cultural skins so that we can inhabit the lifeworld of genuinely different cultures and peoples. A Socratic education is thus called for that emphasizes critical thinking and dialogue – but also a deep engagement with "other" cultures, languages, and worldviews as a way of helping us move out of our particular cultural cave to a more considered position of appreciation for diverse cultures and a correlative epistemological humility regarding any single claim or worldview.

Such an education is clearly an antidote to the consumerist bias of the Web and the Net, which rather encourage us to view the Other as a customer and/or exploitable resource. In this second direction, however, I would note that such a Socratic-Renaissance form of education also fulfills the Habermasian / feminist requirements for perspective-taking and solidarity. That is, especially as we become more and more familiar with the values and communicative preferences that define distinctive cultures – rather than feeling compelled to overrun those cultures and

redefine them along the lines of our own communicative preferences and values (a "hegemonic cultural monologue"), we are better prepared to engage in a genuine *dialogue* that instantiates communication between two (or more) distinct partners whose identity is preserved and enriched through the exchange. This involves us, as both Hongladarom (2001) and Jones (2001) emphasize – i.e., Carey's notion of communication as *ritual*, a mode of communication that helps individuals cohere as a community, in part as such communication engages not simply an intellectual exchange of ideas, but a multi-sensory/emotive experience, such as is shaped by ritual, theatre, spectacle, etc. To say it another way: such an education, as it takes seriously the role of living and knowing as an embodied creature in a world of multiple cultures and peoples, and moving in more just and democratic directions, will have to be a place where both our minds and bodies are at home.

This last formulation, finally, suggests a strong connection between this largely Western approach to developing a computer ethics and at least one distinctively Eastern framework – namely, Confucian ethics. To begin with, the terms used to describe personhood (*ren*) and a person's thoughts and feelings (*xin*) defy the Gnostic/Cartesian emphasis on a radical mind-body split. First,

> ... *ren* is one's entire person: one's cultivated cognitive, aesthetic, moral, and religious sensibilities as they are expressed in one's ritualized roles and relationships. It is one's "field of selves," the sum of significant relationships, that constitute one as a resolutely social person. *Ren* is not only mental, but physical as well: one's posture and comportment, gestures and bodiy communication (Ames and Rosemont 1998, p. 49).

Similarly, Ames and Rosemont render *xin* as "heart-and-mind", *contra* the Western mind-body dichotomy, to make the point that "... there are no altogether disembodied thoughts for Confucious, nor any raw feelings altogether lacking (what in English would be called) 'cognitive content.'" (1998, p. 56). In these ways, then, there is a strong resonance between these classical Chinese conceptions and those emerging in Western efforts to overcome the various problems of a radical mind-body split – including its CMC-related forms (the "cyber-gnosticism" of early Haraway and Perry) – for example, what Hayles calls a "posthuman" (i.e., post-Cartesian) self, and what Becker (2001) simply calls the "bodysubject".

Moreover, just as both Socratic and Aristotelian virtue ethics emphasize the primary importance of developing those habits (*ethos*) that allow us to become "virtuous" (i.e., from $\alpha\rho\epsilon\tau\epsilon$, "excellence") human beings (see Aristotle, *Nichomachean Ethics*, esp. Book II, 1103a14–26) – so Confucian ethics likewise emphasizes the life-goal of becoming a *junzi*, an exemplary person (see Ames and Rosemont 1998, 62f.). Taken in this direction, a Socratic education in critical thinking and dialogical skills, coupled with Aristotelian and Confucian ethics and a Renaissance immersion in multiple cultures, languages, and lifeworlds, might serve as a more genuinely *global* ethics – one required for use of the Internet and the Web as technologies with a global reach.

Metatheoretical issues and the impact of the Internet on our moral lives

We can now return to the meta-theoretical question regarding where computer ethics may lie on a spectrum between a purely straightforward matter of applying traditional ethical approaches and the claim that computer ethics calls for entirely new approaches. It should be clear that a Socratic / Renaissance / Aristotelian / Confucian ethics, oriented towards a use of CMC technologies emphasizing personal excellence and responsibility and intended to preserve cultural differences, occupies a middle ground between these two extremes.[15]

---

[15] This is *not* to argue, however, that all computer ethics will likewise find such a middle ground. On the contrary, especially given the distinctively new possibilities for research opened up by the Internet (e.g., "lurking" in chat rooms, listservs, etc.; very large-scale conversation analysis, etc.) it is arguable that certain research contexts arise which have no obvious analogue to prior examples and experiences with human subjects research. As examples:

Given the role of language in constituting our experience of identity online (including multiple selves, avatars and other forms of intentionally difference "faces") – does "harm" as a limit on free speech ("fighting words", libel, etc.) need rethinking, so as to include some kinds of *speech* online as harm ("virtual rape", etc.)?
Just as some contexts of traditional human subjects research may suspend the usual requirement of *informed consent* (e.g., because of the need to keep the hypothesis hidden from the subjects, because some subjects may not be capable of providing informed consent, etc.) – are there contexts of Internet research (e.g., large-scale conversation studies, chatrooms, etc.) whose characteristics arguably do *not* require *informed consent* of those being studied (e.g., because of historical scope of the archives makes such consent impossible, because the chatrooms are already open to anyone and provide an option of "going private" with messages that users do not want others to see, etc.?
Are there contexts of Internet research (including chatrooms) whose characteristics arguably do *not* require the insurance of *confidentiality*, e.g., because user names are already pseudonymous?

First of all, such an ethics clearly draws on resources in diverse ethical and cultural traditions – including both Western (Socratic/Aristotelian) and Eastern (Confucian) ethics – in response to the threat of computer-mediated colonization and related contemporary problems. While these problems are in some degree novel as they result from the global reach and explosive growth of CMC technologies – insofar as a Socratic education emphasizing a Renaissance immersion in diverse cultures works to resolve these problems, such an ethics itself does not start *de novo*.

Finally, these lines of arguments provide a distinctive response to the question of what impact the Internet may have on our moral lives. It is arguable that the rapid rise of the Internet and the Web, in threatening to overwhelm us with an information flood, only *increases* the importance of "traditional" forms of critical thinking – first of all as critical evaluation of information resources is required in order to sort through the massive amounts of information available, very little of which has passed through traditional procedures of peer-review, critical analysis, etc. By the same token, I have argued that the potential dangers of CMC technologies – including the danger of a computer-mediated colonization fostered by a commercial/consumerist model – requires as an antidote a Socratic education oriented towards a Renaissance humanism, one that now is genuinely global as it seeks to incorporate ethical insight from both Western and Eastern sources. That is, as the Internet makes accessing diverse cultural information *easier* – and thereby threatens to commodify all cultural resources for consumption by users as "cultural tourists" – it dramatically *increases* the need for a Socratic education and Aristotelian/Confucian virtue ethics as (at least one possible) antidote. Such a globally rooted and globally oriented computer ethics would help us realize some of the best possibilities of the Internet and the Web, as these technologies open up genuinely global cultural flows – flows that, as the Middle Ages and the Renaissance have demonstrated, further open up new combinations and ways of being fully human. At the same time, by increasing the urgency for developing such an ethics and facilitating its development precisely through its global reach, the Internet would become both motivator and means towards greater human excellence, perhaps on new scales and levels.

From: the "Preliminary Report" of the ethics working committee (Charles Ess, chair), association of internet researchers, available at <aoir.org/reports/ethics.html>.

References

A. Sjarif and G.P. Pervan. Reducing the negative effects of power distance during asynchronous pre-meeting without using anonymity in Indonesian culture. In Fay Sudweeks and Charles Ess, editors, *cultural attitudes towards technology and communication: Proceedings of the Second International Conference ... Perth, Australia, July 12–15*, pp. 209–215. School of Information Technology, Murdoch University: Perth, Australia, 2000.

R. Ames and H. Rosemont, Jr. *The Analects of Confucius: A Philosophical Translation*. New York: Ballantine Books, 1998.

Aristotle. *The Nichomachean Ethics*. Trans. H. Rackham, Cambridge, MA: Harvard University Press, 1968.

J. Barlow. A declaration of the independence of cyberspace. <http://www.eff.org/pub/Censorship/Internet_censorship_bills/barlow_0296.declaration>, 1996.

G. Bateson. *Steps to an ecology of mind*. New York: Ballantine Books, 1972.

G. Bateson. *Mind and nature: A necessary unity*. New York: Bantam Books, 1979.

B. Becker. Cyborg, Agents and Transhumanists. *Leonardo*, 33(5): 361–365, 2000.

B. Becker. Sinn und Sinnlichkeit: Anmerkungen zur Eigendynamik und Fremdheit des eigenen Leibes. In L. Jäger, editor, *Mentalität und Medialität*, [PAGES]. München: Fink Verlag, 2001.

B. Becker and J. Wehner. Electronic networks and civil society: Reflections on structural changes in the public sphere. In Charles Ess, editor, *Culture, Technology, Communication: Towards an Intercultural Global Village*, pp. 65–85. Albany, NY: State University of New York Press, 2001.

J.D. Bolter. Identity. In T. Swiss, editor, *Unspun*, pp. 17–29. New York: New York University Press. Available online: <http://www.nyupress.nyu.edu/unspun/samplechap.html>, 2001.

A. Borgmann. *Technology and the Character of Contemporary Life: a Philosophical Inquiry*. Chicago: University of Chicago Press, 1984.

D. Burrell. *Analogy and Philosophical Language*. New Haven: Yale University Press, 1973.

M. Dahan. National Security and Democracy on the Internet in Israel. In Fay Sudweeks and Charles Ess, editors, *Computer-Mediated Culture, a special issue of Javnost-the Public*, VI(4): 67–77, 1999.

M. Dahan. Personal communication, 2001.

H. Dreyfus. *On the Internet*. New York: Routledge, 2001.

C. Ess. The Political Computer: Democracy, CMC, and Habermas. In Charles Ess, editor, *Philosophical Perspectives on Computer-Mediated Communication*, pp. 197–230. Albany, NY: State University of New York Press, 1996.

C. Ess. What's Culture Got to Do with It? Cultural Collisions in the Electronic Global Village, Creative Interferences, and the Rise of Culturally-mediated Computing (Introduction). In C. Ess, editor, *Culture, Technology, Communication: Towards an Intercultural Global Village*, pp. 1–50. Albany, NY: State University of New York Press, 2001.

C. Ess. Communication and Interaction. In Luciano Floridi, editor, *The Blackwell Guide to the Philosophy of Computing and Information*. Oxford: Blackwell, (forthcoming).

J. Habermas. *Toward a Rational Society: Student Protest, Science, and Politics*, trans. J. Shapiro. Cambridge: Polity, 1987.

C. Hamelink. *The Ethics of Cyberspace*, 2000.

R. Harris, P. Bala, P. Sonan, E.K. Guat Lien and T. Trang. Challenges and Opportunities in Introducing Information and Communication Technologies to the Kelabit Community of North Central Borneo. *New Media and Society*, 3(3): 271–296, September 2001.

T.M. Harrison and L. Falvey. Democracy and New Communication Technologies. In William B. Gudykunst, editor, *Communication Yearbook 25*. Hillsdale, NJ: Lawrence Erlbaum, 2001.

K. Hayles. *How we became posthuman: virtual bodies in cybernetics, literature, and informatics*. Chicago: University of Chicago Press, 1999.

G. Hofstede. *Culture's Consequences: International Differences in Work related Values*. Beverly Hills: Sage, 1980

G. Hofstede. National cultures in four dimensions. *International Studies of Management and Organization*, 13: 32–60, 1983.

G. Hofstede. The Cultural Relativity of the Quality of Life Concept. *Academy of Management Review*, 9: 389–398, 1984.

G. Hofstede. *Cultures and Organizations: Software of the Mind*. London: McGraw-Hill, 1991.

G. Hofstede and M.H. Bond. The Confucius Connection: From Cultural Roots to Economic Growth. *Organizational Dynamics*, 16(4): 5–21, 1988.

D. Holmes. Technological transformations of the public sphere. In F. Sudweeks and C. Ess, editors, *Second international conference on cultural attitudes towards technology and communication*, pp. 373–386. Murdoch, WA: School of Information Technology, Murdoch University. Available online: <http://www.it.murdoch.edu.au/~sudweeks/catac00/>, 2000.

S. Hongladarom. Global culture, local cultures and the Internet: the Thai example. In C. Ess, editor, *Culture, technology, communication: Towards an intercultural global village*, pp. 307–324. Albany, NY: State University of New York Press, 2001.

S. Hongladarom. Negotiating the global and the local: How Thai culture co-opts the Internet. *First Monday*, 5: 8, July, <http://firstmonday.org/issues/issue5_8/hongladarom/index.html>, 2000.

M. Horkheimer and T.W. Adorno (1947). *Dialectic of Enlightenment*, trans. John Cumming [*Dialektik der Aufklärung*. Amsterdam 1947]. Herder and Herder, 1972.

Joo-Young Jung. Globalize or not?: The Internet and the Social Factors Shaping Globalization. Internet Research 1.0: The State of the Interdiscipline (First Conference of the Association of Internet Researchers), University of Kansas, Lawrence, September 16, 2000.

S. Jones. Understanding micropolis and compunity. In Chares Ess, editor, *Culture, Technology, Communication: Towards an Intercultural Global Village*, pp. 51–66. Albany, NY: State University of New York Press, 2001.

K. Keniston. Language, power, and software. In Charles Ess,

editor, *Culture, technology, communication: Towards an intercultural global village*, pp. 281–306. Albany, NY: State University of New York Press, 2001.

C. Maitland and J. Bauer. Global Diffusion of Interactive Networks: the Impact of Culture. In Charles Ess, editor, *Culture, Technology, Communication: Towards an Intercultural Global Village*, pp. 87–128. Albany, NY: State University of New York Press, 2001.

H.-G. Möller. *The Kindernetz: Electronic Communication and the Paradox of Individuality*. Computers and Philosophy Conference (CAP 2000), Carnegie Mellon University, Pittsburgh, PA, August 11, 2000.

L. Postma. A Theoretical Argumentation And Evaluation of South African Learners' Orientation towards and Perceptions of the Empowering Use of Information. *New Media and Society*, 3(3): 315–328, September 2001.

N. Rahmati. The Impact of Cultural Values on Computer Mediated Group Work. In Fay Sudweeks and Charles Ess, editors, *cultural attitudes towards technology and communication: Proceedings of the Second International Conference ... Perth, Australia, July 12–15*, pp. 257–274. School of Information Technology, Murdoch University: Perth, Australia, 2000.

F. Sapienza. Communal Ethos on a Russian Émigré Web Site. In Fay Sudweeks and Charles Ess, guest editors, *Computer-Mediated Culture, a special issue of Javnost-The Public*, VI(4): 39–52, 1999.

T. Sofield. Outside the Net: Kiribati and the knowledge economy. In F. Sudweeks and C. Ess, editors, *Second international conference on cultural attitudes towards techno-logy and communication*, pp. 3–26. Murdoch, WA: School of Information Technology, Murdoch University. Available online: <http://www.it.murdoch.edu.au/~sudweeks/catac00/>, 2000.

L. Suchman. *Plans and situated actions: the problem of human-machine communication*. Cambridge [Cambridgeshire] and New York: Cambridge University Press, 1987.

P. Sy. Barangays of IT: Filipinizing Mediated Communication and Digital Power. *New Media and Society*, 3(3): 297–313, September 2001.

D. Wheeler. New Technologies, Old Culture: A Look at Women, Gender, and the Internet in Kuwait. In Charles Ess, editor, *Culture, Technology, Communication: Towards an Intercultural Global Village*, pp. 187–212. Albany, NY: State University of New York Press, 2001.

A. Willis. Nerdy No More: A Case Study of Early Wired (1993–1996). In F. Sudweeks and C. Ess, editors, *Second International Conference on Cultural Attitudes towards Technology and Communication*, pp. 361–372. Murdoch, Australia: School of Information Technology, Murdoch University. Available online <http://www.it.murdoch.edu.au/~sudweeks/catac00/>, 2000.

S. Yoon. Power Online: A Poststructuralist Perspective on CMC. In Charles Ess, editor, *Philosophical Perspectives on Computer-Mediated Communication*, pp. 171–196. Albany, NY: State University of New York Press, 1996.

S. Yoon. Internet discourse and the Habitus of Korea's new generation. In C. Ess, editor, *Culture, technology, communication: Towards an intercultural global village*, pp. 241–260. Albany, NY: State University of New York Press, 2001.

[17]

Shaping the Web: Why the Politics of Search Engines Matters

Lucas D. Introna

London School of Economics, London, United Kingdom

Helen Nissenbaum

University Center for Human Values, Princeton University, Princeton, New Jersey, USA

This article argues that search engines raise not merely technical issues but also political ones. Our study of search engines suggests that they systematically exclude (in some cases by design and in some, accidentally) certain sites and certain types of sites in favor of others, systematically giving prominence to some at the expense of others. We argue that such biases, which would lead to a narrowing of the Web's functioning in society, run counter to the basic architecture of the Web as well as to the values and ideals that have fueled widespread support for its growth and development. We consider ways of addressing the politics of search engines, raising doubts whether, in particular, the market mechanism could serve as an acceptable corrective.

Keywords   search engines, bias, values in design, World Wide Web, digital divide, information access

The Internet, no longer merely an e-mail and file-sharing system, has emerged as a dominant interactive medium.

Received 17 July 1997; accepted 24 November 1998.

We are indebted to many colleagues for commenting on and questioning earlier versions of this article: audiences at the conference "Computer Ethics: A Philosophical Enquiry," London; members of the seminars at the Kennedy School of Government, Harvard University, and the Center for Arts and Cultural Policy Studies, Princeton University; Steven Tepper, Eszter Hargittai, Phil Agre; and Rob Kling and reviewers for *The Information Society*. We are grateful to Lee Giles, Brian LaMacchia, Andrea LaPaugh (and members of her graduate seminar), and Andrew Tomkins for technical guidance, and to our able research assistants Michael Cohen and Sayumi Takahashi. H. Nissenbaum acknowledges the invaluable support of the National Science Foundation through grant SBR-9806234.

Address correspondence to Helen Nissenbaum, University Center for Human Values, Princeton University, Princeton, NJ 08544-1013, USA. E-mail: helen@Princeton.edu

Enhanced by the technology of the World Wide Web, it has become an integral part of the ever-expanding global media system, moving onto center stage of media politics alongside traditional broadcast media—television and radio. Enthusiasts of the "new medium" have heralded it as a democratizing force that will give voice to diverse social, economic, and cultural groups, to members of society not frequently heard in the public sphere. It will empower the traditionally disempowered, giving them access both to typically unreachable nodes of power and to previously inaccessible troves of information.

To scholars of traditional media, these optimistic claims must have a ring of familiarity, echoing similar optimistic predictions concerning the democratizing and empowering capacities of both radio and television. Instead of the expected public gains and fulfilment of democratic possibilities, instead of the spreading of access and power, however, the gains, the power, and the access were consolidated in the hands of a few dominant individuals and institutions. In the words of acclaimed media critic Robert McChesney (1999, p. 1),

> The American media system is spinning out of control in a hyper-commercialized frenzy. Fewer than ten transnational media conglomerates dominate much of our media; fewer than two dozen account for the overwhelming majority of our newspapers, magazines, films, television, radio, and books. With every aspect of our media culture now fair game for commercial exploitation, we can look forward to the full-scale commercialization of sports, arts, and education, the disappearance of notions of public service from public discourse, and the degeneration of journalism, political coverage, and children's programming under commercial pressure.

McChesney's work (1993, 1997b) traces—in very subtle and convincing detail—how commercial interests were woven into the very fiber of the modern media networks through legislation, market mechanisms, and the like

These moves progressively pushed out and silenced the public service agenda, which was very central to the vision of the early pioneers in the field—McChesney's (1993) historical account of radio is very telling in this regard. His central argument, historically grounded, is that the fundamental course of media is determined primarily by *how they're owned and operated.* Most U.S. communication media—going back to AM radio in the 1920s—have followed this path: At first, when they do not seem commercially viable, they are developed by the nonprofit, noncommercial sector. When their profit-making potential emerges, however, the corporate sector starts colonizing the media, and through a variety of mechanisms, usually its dominance of politicians, muscles out the rest and takes over. McChesney argues that this pattern is seen in the cases of FM radio, in UHF television, and to some extent in satellite and cable.

On the prospects of the Internet, there are divergent predictions. Some, like Dan Schiller (1995) and McChesney, influenced by their knowledge of other media, anticipate a similar narrowing of prospects for the Internet. They point to the commitment of the United States to private ownership of communications technology as the single most important and consistent historical policy position that influenced the course of telecommunications development. And this same commitment is clearly evident in the rhetoric of the political foundations of the Internet, namely, the fact that of five "values" that Vice-President Gore identified as ones that should define and guide the development of the Global Internet Infrastructure (GII), the first one listed was "private investment" (Office of the Vice President, 1995). Schiller asks, "What is the likelihood of robust adherence to . . . elemental democratic prescription, when the character of the network development is now all-too-evidently to be given mainly as a function of unrestrained corporate ambition and private design?" (Schiller, 1995, p. 6). Others, like Mark Poster (1995), offer a contrasting view, arguing that the distinctly "postmodern" nature of the Internet, with its capacity to disseminate material rather than centralize it, will discourage the endowment of authority—both academic and political. Its development, therefore, is unlikely to mirror that of previous media.

The broader debate about the dual possibilities of media—to be democratizing or to be colonized by specialized interests at the expense of the public good—inspires and motivates this article on the politics of search engines. The general position we defend, and illustrate in this one case, is that although the Internet and the Web offer exciting prospects for furthering the public good, the benefits are conditional, resting precariously on a number of political, economic, and technical factors. Following Poster, we are buoyed by clear instances where the Web and Internet have served broad political and ends. But we also see irrefutable signs of gradual centralization and commercialization of guiding forces. Like McChesney, we are particularly concerned with the way these competing interests (centralized commercial vs. decentralized public) may, early on, be woven in, or out, of the very fiber of media networks. Search engines constitute a particularly telling venue for this competition. And prospects, as seen from the perspective of the time of writing this article, do not look good for broad public interests.

Search engines constitute a powerful source of access and accessibility within the Web. Access, already a thorny issue, is the subject of much scholarship and research (Golding, 1994; Hoffman & Novak, 1998; Pollack, 1995; Schiller, 1995), as well as a lengthy report by the National Telecommunications and Information Administration (NTIA), *Falling Through the Net.* Focusing on social, economic, and racial factors, these works show how access to the Web is preconfigured in subtle but politically important ways, resulting in exclusion of significant voices. It is not enough, however, to worry about overcoming these traditional barriers, to focus only on the granting of entry to the media space of the Web. It is not enough if, as we argue, the space itself is distorted in favor of those wealthy in technical or economic resources through the mechanism of biased search engines. The politics of search engines thus represents the broader struggle to sustain the democratic potential of traditional media, the Internet, and the World Wide Web in particular.

In a statistical study of Web search engines, S. Lawrence and C. L. Giles (1999) estimated that none of the search engines they studied, taken individually, index more than 16% of the total indexable Web, which they estimate to consist of 800 million pages. Combining the results of the search engines they studied, they estimated the coverage to increase to approximately 42%. This confirms the primitive impressions of many users, namely, that the Web is almost inconceivably large, and also that search engines only very partially meet the desperate need for an effective way of finding things.[1] When judging what the producers of search engines have accomplished so far, optimists, focusing on the half-full portion of the cup, may legitimately marvel at the progress in Web search technologies and at the sheer bulk of pages that are successfully found. In this article, however, we are concerned with the half-empty portion of the cup: the portions of the Web that remain hidden from view.

The purpose of this article is not, however, to bemoan the general difficulties of building comprehensive search engines, nor to highlight the technological difficulties that must surely impose limits on the range of scope and coverage that even the best search engines can achieve. Our concern, rather, is with the ways that developers, designers, and producers of search engines will direct these technological limitations, the influences that may come into play in determining any systematic inclusions and exclusions, the wide-ranging factors that dictate systematic prominence for some sites, dictating systematic invisibility for others. These, we think, are political issues.[2] They are important because what people (the seekers) are able to find on the Web determines what the Web consists of for them. And we all—individuals and institutions alike—have a great deal at stake in what the Web consists of.

A BRIEF AND SELECTIVE TECHNICAL OVERVIEW

Although a complete discussion of the technical detail of search engines is beyond the scope of this article,[3] we highlight aspects of search engines that we consider relevant to our discussion of their politics. We briefly discuss the nature of the connection between search engines and Web pages, the process by which this relationship is established, and how this relationship affects the producers (or owners) of Web pages wishing to have their pages recognized. Web-page providers seeking recognition from search engines for their Web pages must focus on two key tasks: (a) being indexed and (b) achieving a ranking in the top 10–20 search results displayed.[4]

On Being Indexed

Having a page indexed, the essential first stage of being recognized by search engines, is extremely important. Without much exaggeration one could say that to exist is to be indexed by a search engine. If a Web page is not in the index of a search engine, a person wishing to access it must know the complete Uniform Resource Locator (URL)—also known as the Web page address—such as http://is.lse.ac.uk/lucas/cepe98.html for the CEPE'98 conference.[5] Since there is no rigid standard for producing URLs, they are not obvious or even logical in the way we tend to think that the addresses of our physical homes are logical.[6] Sometimes the Internet domain-name structure may help, such as "ac.uk" or "edu" for an academic institution in the United Kingdom or United States. However, for most searches we do not have any idea of the URLs involved.[7]

This is where search engines enter the picture. They create a map of the Web by indexing Web pages according to keywords and then create enormous databases that link page content to keywords to URLs. When a seeker of information submits a keyword (or phrase)—presumably, one that best captures his or her interest—the search-engine database returns to the seeker a list of URLs linked to that keyword, ideally including all those that are relevant to the seeker's interest. It is important to note that search engines use the notion of a keyword (i.e., that which is indexed and hence used for searching) in a rather minimal sense. Keywords are not determined a priori by the designers of the search engines' databases nor, explicitly, by some other authority, but rather they are "deduced" from Web pages themselves in the process of indexing. In a particular Web page a keyword can be any of the following:

- Actual keywords indicated by the Web-page designer in an HTML metatag as follows: <meta NAME="keywords" CONTENT="list of keywords">.
- All or some of the words appearing in the title that is indicated by the HTML <TITLE> tag as follows: <TITLE>Whatever is the title of the page</TITLE>.
- The first X words in a Web page (possibly excluding stop words[8]).
- All the words in the Web page (possibly excluding stop words).

Most search engines use at least some of the words in the title tag of the Web page as the relevant keywords for indexing purposes.[9] It is obviously important for Web-page producers as well as seekers to know what words on a particular Web page are seen as keywords by the indexing software of search engines. Thus, one might naturally ask: How does a search engine go about creating its database and what does it store in it?

The answer to this question depends on which of basically two categories (and within these categories, the further subcategories) the search engine fits. One category includes directory-based search engines such as Yahoo! and Aliweb. In this category, the vast majority of the pages indexed are manually submitted to the search engines' editors by Webmasters (and other creators of Web pages).[10] The other category includes search engines that automatically harvest URLs by means of spiders (also referred to as robots or softbots). Among the most well-known search engines fitting this category are Alta Vista, Lycos, and Hotbot.

In the case of directory-based search engines, Web-page creators submit URLs to the search engines for possible inclusion into their databases. If you wanted your page recognized by Yahoo!, for example, you would submit your URL and background information to a human editor, who would review the page and decide whether or not to schedule your page for indexing. If your page is scheduled for indexing, it would be retrieved by the indexing software, which would parse[11] the page and index it according to the keywords (content) found in the page. For directory-based search engines, therefore, human gatekeepers hold the key to inclusion in their indexed databases. At the time of the writing this article, there is a considerable backlog, so this process can take up to six months from the time of submission to the time of inclusion.

Web owners wishing to have their pages indexed must surely wonder what criteria these human editors use to decide whether or not to index their pages. This is a major bone of contention, especially for anyone contesting these decision criteria. With Yahoo!, for example, representatives say that they use criteria of relevancy (Phua, 1998). The exact nature of these criteria, however, is not widely known or publicly disseminated and, evidently, these criteria are not consistently applied by the various editors. As a result, you may have your page rejected (without notification) and would not know what to do to get it accepted. Danny Sullivan, the editor of *Search Engine Watch*, believes that the base success rate for any submitted page's being listed with Yahoo! is approximately 25%. Two factors that seem to increase the chances of being listed are the number of links (to and from a given site—also referred to as inlinks and outlinks) and how full a particular category happens to be. When editors feel they need more references within a category, they lower the entry barriers. Defending their approach, representatives of Yahoo! maintain they list what users want, arguing that if users were not finding relevant information they would cease using Yahoo!. (We return to this form of response later.) With Aliweb, a very small site in comparison to its competitors, users submit supplemental information about their Web-page content and keywords as a way of helping the indexing software improve the quality of its indexing and hence provide better search results. Representatives of Aliweb emphasize that they do not provide comprehensive coverage; rather, they emphasize high-quality search results. Because this is a small site, it is still able to index most of its submissions. As it becomes larger, it may, like its competitors, need to establish criteria for inclusion and exclusion.

Being indexed by search engines that automatically harvest URLs is a matter of being visited by a spider (also called robot, crawler, softbot, agent, etc.). Spiders usually start crawling from a historical list of URLs, especially documents with many links elsewhere, such as server lists, "What's New" pages, and other popular sites on the Web. Software robots crawl the Web—that is, automatically traverse the Web's hypertext structure—first retrieving a document and then recursively retrieving all documents that are referenced (linked by other URLs) in the original document. Web owners interested in having their pages indexed might wish they had access to details concerning the routes spiders follow when they crawl, which sites they favor, which they visit and how often, which not, and so forth. This, however, is a complicated technical subject, and the details are steadfastly guarded as trade secrets by the respective search engine companies. From our experience and discussions with those involved in the field, we would contend with some certainty that spiders are guided by a set of criteria that steer them in a systematic way to select certain types of sites and pages and not select others. However, the blackout on information about search

engine crawl algorithms means we can only try to infer the character of these algorithms from search engine selection patterns—an inexact exercise.

We have learned something of the nature of spider algorithms from a paper on efficient crawling by Cho, Garcia-Molina, and Page,[12] presented at the WWW7 conference (Cho et al., 1998). This paper, which discusses commonly used metrics for determining the "importance" of a Web page by crawling spiders, provides key insights relevant to the main claims of our article. Because of its significance, we discuss it here in some detail. Cho et al. (1998, p. 1) write:

> Given a Web page P, we can define the importance of the page, I(P), in one of the following ways ... :
>
> 1. *Similarity to a Driving Query Q.* A query Q drives the crawling process, and *I(P)* is defined to be the textual similarity between *P* and *Q* ....
> 2. *Backlink Count.* The value of I(P) is the number of links to P that appear over the entire web. We use IB(P) to refer to this importance metric. *Intuitively, a page P that is linked to by many pages is more important than one that is seldom referenced.* On the web, IB(P) is useful for ranking query results, giving end-users pages that are more likely to be of general interest. Note that evaluating IB(P) requires counting backlinks over the entire web. A crawler may estimate this value with IB'(P), the number of links to P that have been seen so far.
> 3. *PageRank.* The IB(P) metric treats all links equally. *Thus, a link from the Yahoo! home page counts the same as a link from some individual's home page. However, since the Yahoo! home page is more important (it has a much higher IB count), it would make sense to value that link more highly. The PageRank backlink metric, IR(P), recursively defines the importance of a page to be the weighted sum of the backlinks to it.* Such a metric has been found to be very useful in ranking results of user queries [Page 1998.2]. We use IR'(P) for the estimated value of IR(P) when we have only a subset of pages available.
> 4. *Location Metric.* The IL(P) importance of page P is a function of its location, not of its contents. If URL u leads to P, then IL(P) is a function of u. *For example, URLs ending with ".com" may be deemed more useful than URLs with other endings, or URLs containing the string "home" may be more of interest than other URLs. Another location metric that is sometimes used considers URLs with fewer slashes more useful than those with more slashes.* All these examples are local metrics since they can be evaluated simply by looking at the URLs." [emphasis added]

The *Similarity to a Driving Query Q* metric uses a query term or string (Q)—such as "holiday cottages," for example—as the basic heuristic for crawling. This means that the spider does not need to make a decision about importance since it will be directed in its search by the query string itself. For our discussion, this metric is of minor significance.[13] The real issue emerges when the crawling spider must "decide" importance without the use of a submitted query term. This is where the other metrics play the dominant role. The *Backlink* metric uses the backlink (or inlink) count as its importance heuristic. The value of the backlink count is the number of links to the page that appear over the entire Web—for example, the number of links over the entire Web that refer to http://www.ibm.com. The assumption here is that "a page that is linked to by many [other] pages is more important than one that is seldom referenced." Obviously, this is a very reasonable heuristic.[14] We know from academic research that it is wise to look at the "canonical" works that are referred to—or cited in academic language—by many other authors. We know also, however, that not all topics necessarily have canons. Furthermore, although in some fields a small number of citations may make a particular work a canon, in other fields it takes a vast number of citations to reach canonical status. Thus, the *Backlink* heuristic would tend to crawl and gather the large topics/fields (such as "shareware computer games") since an even relatively unimportant site in this big field will be seen as more important—have relatively more backlinks or inlinks—than an actually important site in a small field (such as "the local community services information" page), which would have relatively less backlinks or inlinks. The essential point is that the large fields determine the measure, or threshold, of importance—through sheer volume of backlinks—in ways that would tend to push out the equally important small fields. (We return to this issue later, in our market discussion.).

With the *PageRank* metric, this problem is exacerbated. Instead of treating all links equally, this heuristic gives prominence to backlinks from other important pages—pages with high backlink counts. Thus, "since [a link from] the Yahoo! home page is more important (it has a much higher IB [backlink] count), it would make sense to value that link more highly." In the analogy of academic papers, a metric like this would imply that a particular paper is even more important if referred to by others who are already seen as important—by other canons. More simply, you are important if others who are already seen as important indicate that you are important. The problem with the *Backlink* and *PageRank* metrics is that they assume that backlinks are a reliable indication of importance or relevance. In those cases where authors of pages create links to other pages they see as valuable, this assumption may be true. There are, however, many organizations that actively cultivate backlinks by inducing Web-page creators to add a link to their page through incentives such as discounts on products, free software utilities, access to exclusive information, and so forth. Obviously, not all Web-page creators have equal access to the resources or the incentive to induce others to link to them.

The *Location Metric* uses location information from the URL to determine "next steps" in the crawl. "For example, URLs ending with '.com' may be deemed more useful than URLs with other endings, or URLs containing the string 'home' may be more of interest than other URLs." Even though the authors do not indicate what they see as more important, one can assume that these decisions are made when crawl heuristics are set for a particular spider. It may therefore be of great significance "where you are located" as to how important you are seen to be. With the URL as the basis of decision making, many things can aid you in catching the attention of the crawling spider, such as having the right domain name, being located in the root directory, and so forth. From this discussion on crawling metrics we can conclude that pages with many backlinks, especially backlinks from other pages with high backlink counts, which are at locations seen as useful or important to the crawling spider, will become targets for harvesting.

Another criterion that seems to guide spiders is breadth or depth of representation. If a spider's algorithm favors breadth (rather than depth), it would visit more sites (or hosts) but index them only partially. In the case of big sites such as America Online (AOL), Geocities, and so forth, spiders will index them at a rate of approximately 10–15%.[15] If your site is hosted on AOL or another big site, there is a good chance that it will not be included. Another reason that a site, and so all the pages on that server, may be excluded from search engine databases is that the owner/Webmaster of that server has excluded spiders through the robot exclusion standard by means of a "robots.txt" file.[16] This is often done because requests for pages from spiders may significantly increase the load on a server and reduce the level of service to all other users. CNN, for example, excludes all spiders from its site,[17] as do many sites that offer free Web-page space.[18] It is also important to note that the harvesting spiders of the search engines we looked at process only HTML files and in particular HTML tags. If important information on your Website is in other formats, such as Acrobat (pdf) files or represented by a graphic (gif) file, this information could be lost in the indexing process.[19]

Having said all of this, it ought to be acknowledged that most spider-based search engines do also allow autonomous submissions by Webmasters/designers. Software is available that automatically generates the required electronic formats and facilitates submission to a number of search engines simultaneously. Using this route has had very mixed results, according to the Webmasters we spoke to.

On Being Ranked

Indexing is but one hurdle to clear for the creators of Web pages who strive for recognition through search engines. Having been successful in the indexing game, their concern shifts to ranking. Many observe that to be noticed by a person doing a search, a Web page has to be ranked among the top 10 to 20 listed as hits. Because most search engines display the 10 most relevant hits on the first page of the search results, Web designers jealously covet those 10 or 20 top slots. The importance of ranking is regularly discussed by leading authors in the field of Web-site promotion:

> There is competition for those top ten seats. There is serious competition. People are trying to take away the top spots every day. They are always trying to fine-tune and tweak their HTML code and learn the next little trick. The best players even know dirty ways to "bump off" their competition while protecting their own sites (Anderson & Henderson, 1997).

Although we have not found large-scale empirical studies measuring the effects of ranking on the behavior of seekers, we observe anecdotally that seekers are likely to look down a list and then cease looking when they find a "hit." A study of travel agents using computerized airline reservations systems, which showed an overwhelming likelihood that they would select a flight from the first screenful of search results, is suggestive of what we might expect among Web users at large (Friedman & Nissenbaum, 1996). Indeed, if this were not the case it would be difficult to see why Webmasters are going to all the effort to get into the first screen—and there is significant evidence that they do, indeed, take it very seriously. Now it may be that it is not only the first screen but the second and third screen as well. Nevertheless, even though we cannot say without further research exactly where this line may be (and it may vary with topic, type of searcher, and so forth), we can propose that it does matter whether you are in the first few screens rather than much lower down in the order. One could also argue such a position from an information-overload point of view; we shall not pursue it here (Wurman, 1989).

Relevancy ranking is an enormously difficult task. Some researchers working on search technologies argue that relevancy ranking is currently the greater challenge facing search engines and that developments in technical know-how and sheer capacity to find and index sites has not nearly been matched by the technical capacity to resolve relevancy ranking. Besides the engineering challenges, experts must struggle with the challenge of approximating a complex human value (relevancy) with a computer algorithm. In other words, according to these experts, while we seem to be mastering the coverage issue, we continue to struggle with the issue of what precisely to extract from the enormous bulk of possibilities for a given search.[20]

Most ranking algorithms of search engines use both the position and the frequency of keywords as a basis for their ranking heuristics (Pringle et al., 1998). Accordingly, a document with a high frequency of keywords in the beginning of a document is seen as more relevant (relative to the keyword entered) than one with a low frequency lower down in the document. Other ranking schemes, like the heuristic used by Lycos, are based on so-called inlink popularity. The popularity score of a particular site is calculated based on the total number of other sites that contain links to that site (also refer to backlink value, discussed earlier). High link popularity leads to an improved ranking. As with the crawl metrics discussed earlier, one sees the standard or threshold of relevance being set by the big sites at the expense of equally relevant small sites.

The desire and battle for ranking have generated a field of knowledge called search engine design, which teaches how to design a Web page in order to optimize its ranking and combines these teachings with software to assess its ranking potential. On one end of the spectrum, practices that make reasonable use of prima facie reasonable heuristics help designers to optimize their Web pages' expected rankings when they are legitimately relevant to the person searching. On the other end of the spectrum, some schemes allow Web designers to manipulate, or trick, the heuristics—schemes such as relevancy (or keyword) spamming,[21] where Web-page designers "trick" the ranking algorithm into ranking their pages higher than they deserve to be ranked by means of keyword stuffing, invisible text, tiny text, and so forth. Such spamming activities doubly punish the innocent. If, for example, you design a Web page with a few graphic images at the beginning, followed somewhere toward the middle with text, you would be severely "punished" by the algorithm both because key terms are positioned relatively low down on the page and also because you would be competing for rank with those less, as it were, scrupulous in their designs.

Out of this strange ranking warfare has emerged an impossible situation: Search-engine operators are loath to give out details of their ranking algorithms for fear that spammers will use this knowledge to trick them.[22] Yet, ethical Web-page designers can legitimately defend a need to know how to design for, or indicate relevancy to, the ranking algorithm so that those who search find what is genuinely relevant to their searches.[23]

Beyond the challenge of second-guessing ranking algorithms, there may be yet another, more certain, method of getting results. Some producers of Web sites pursue other ways of elevating their ranking, ways that are outside

TABLE 1
Summary of criteria for indexing and ranking

Perspective	Reason for exclusion
Search engine: Indexing	
Directory-type search engines	(1) The human editor does not include your submission on the basis of criteria not generally known and apparently inconsistently applied.
Automatic-harvesting-type search engines	(1) Site not visited because of spider exclusion standard set by the Webmaster.
	(2) Site not in the crawl path of the spider (not sufficiently rich in backlinks).
	(3) Part of a large (often free) site that is only partially indexed.
	(4) Documents don't conform to HTML standard (pdf, gif, etc.).
Ranking (in top 10 when relevant)	(1) Did not buy the keyword or top spot.
	(2) Not high in inlink popularity (from and to site).
	(3) Relevant keywords not in meta tag or title.
	(4) Keyword spammers have pushed you down.
	(5) Important parts of your title are stop words.
	(6) Your pages have been altered (dumped off) through unethical practices by your competitors.
Seeker: Finding appropriate content	(1) Using only one search engine (sometimes a default that user is unaware of).
	(2) Inappropriate use of search criteria.

of the technical fray: They try to buy them. This subject is an especially sensitive one, and representatives of several major search engines indignantly deny that they sell search positions. Recently, however, in a much-publicized move, Alta Vista and Doublclick have invited advertisers to bid for positions in their top slots (Hansell, 1999). Yahoo! sells prominence indirectly by allowing Web owners to pay for express indexing. This allows them to move ahead in the 6-month queue. Another method for buying prominence—less controversial but not unproblematic—allows Web owners to buy keywords for purposes of banner ads. Amazon Books, for example, has a comprehensive arrangement with Yahoo!, and Barnes & Noble has one with Lycos. If a seeker submits a search to Yahoo! with the term "book" in it, or a term with a name that corresponds to an author's name or book title in the Amazon database, the seeker would get the Amazon banner (and URL) on his or her search result screen. This is also true for many other companies and products.

The battle for ranking is fought not only between search engines and Web masters/designers but also among organizations wishing for prominence. There is sufficient evidence to suggest that the fierce competition for both presence and prominence in a listing has led to practices such as one organization's retrieving a competitor's Web page, editing it so that it will not do well in the ranking, and resubmitting it as an updated submission, or one organization's buying a competitor's name as a keyword and then having the first organization's banner and URL displayed when a search is done on that keyword.[24]

In Table 1, we summarize the main points of our description, showing some of the ways search engine designers and operators commonly make choices about what to include in and exclude from their databases. These choices are embedded in human-interpreted decision criteria, in crawl heuristics, and in ranking algorithms.

Implications

We may wonder how all this affects the nature of Web users' experiences. Based on what we have learned so far about the way search engines work, we would predict that information seekers on the Web, whose experiences are mediated through search engines, are most likely to find popular, large sites whose designers have enough technical savvy to succeed in the ranking game, and especially those sites whose proprietors are able to pay for various means of improving their site's positioning. Seekers are less likely to find less popular, smaller sites, including those that are not supported by knowledgeable professionals.[25] When a search does yield these sites, they are likely to have lower prominence in rankings.

These predictions are, of course, highly general and will vary considerably according to the keywords or phrases with which a seeker initiates a search, and this, in turn, is likely to be affected by the seeker's competence with search engines. The nature of experiences of information seekers will also vary according to the search engines they choose. Some users may actively seek one search engine over others, but some will simply, and perhaps unknowingly, use a default engine provided by institutions or Internet service providers (ISPs).[26] We are unlikely to find much relief from these robust irregularities in meta search engines like Metacrawler, Ask Jeeves, and Debriefing because they base their results on existing search engines and normally accomplish their task by recognizing only higher-order search keys rather than first-order engines.[27] We note further that not only are most users unaware of these particular biases, they seem also to be unaware that they are unaware.

SHOULD WE LET THE MARKET DECIDE?

Readers may find little to trouble them in this description of search engine proclivities. What we have before us is an evolving marketplace in search engines: We ought to let producers of search engines do what they will and let users decide freely which they like best. Search engines whose offerings are skewed either because their selections are not comprehensive or because they prioritize listings according to highest bid will suffer in the marketplace. And even if they do not, the collective preferences of participants should not be second-guessed. As the representatives of Yahoo! we cited earlier have argued, users' reactions must remain the benchmark of quality: Dissatisfied seekers will defect from an inadequate search engine to another that does a better job of indexing and prioritizing. Thus will the best search engines flourish; the poor ones will fade away due to lack of use. McChesney (1997b, p.12) describes a comparable faith in the market mechanism as it applied to traditional broadcast media: "In the United States, the notion that commercial broadcasting is the superior system because it embodies market principles is closely attached to the notion that the market is the only 'democratic' regulatory mechanism, and that this democratic market is the essence of Americanism, patriotism, and all that is good and true in the world." Both McChesney (1999) and Schiller (1995), however, have criticized the idea that a media market best represents democratic ideals. In the case of search engines, we are, likewise, not optimistic about the promise of development that is shaped only by a marketplace.

As anyone who has used search engines knows, the dominant search engines do not charge seekers for the search service. Rather, the arrangement resembles that of commercial television where advertisers pay television stations for the promise of viewers. Similarly, search engines attract paid advertisements based on the promise of search usage. High usage, presumably, garners advertisers and high charges. To succeed, therefore, search engines must establish a reputation for satisfying seekers' desires and needs; this way they will attract seekers in the first place, and then will keep them coming back.[28] As a way of simplifying the discussion, however, we refer to the marketplace as a marketplace in search engines with seekers as the buyers. This strategy does not, as far as we have been able to tell, alter the substantive outcomes of the particular issues we have chosen to highlight.

We do not dispute the basic fact of the matter, namely that a marketplace for search engines (and seekers, if you will) is possible. It is also possible that such a market, reflecting discrepant degrees of satisfaction by seekers, will result in some search engines flourishing and others failing. Our dissatisfaction with this forecast is not that it cannot come true but what it would mean, from the perspective of social values and the social investment in the Internet, if it did. Why, the critic might ask, on what grounds, would we presume to override the wishes of users so as they are cleanly reflected in their market choices? Our reply to this challenge, which we try to keep as free from sentimental prejudices as possible, cites two main sources of concern. One is that the conditions needed for a marketplace to function in a democratic and efficient way are simply not met in the case of search engines. The other is our judgment that Web-search mechanisms are too important to be shaped by the marketplace alone. We discuss each in turn, the first one only briefly.

A virtue frequently claimed by defenders of the market mechanism is that participants are free to express their preferences through the choices they make among alternatives. Through their choices, incompetent inefficient suppliers are eliminated in favor of competent, efficient suppliers. As many critics have pointed out, however, this holds true only for markets in which those who supply goods or services have an equal opportunity to enter the market and communicate with potential customers, and in which those who demand goods and services are fully informed and act in a rational manner. Such an ideal market simply does not exist, and this is especially so in the case of search engines.

If we focus on the demand side first, we see that most users of the Web lack critical information about alternatives. Only a small fraction of users understand how search engines work and by what means they yield their results. It is misleading to suggest that these users are meaningfully expressing preferences or exercising free choice when they select from the alternatives. Though we lack systematic empirical evidence, the anecdotal results of asking people why they use or prefer one search engine to others is some version of "It finds what I'm looking for" and a shrug. Now, if one is searching for a specific product or service, it may be possible to know in advance how to determine that one has indeed found what one was looking for. When searching for information, however, it is difficult (if not impossible) to make such a conclusive assessment, since the locating of information also serves to inform one about that which one is looking for. This is an old information-retrieval problem—often expressed as "how do you know what you do not know until you know it"—with which information science scholars have been battling for many years. It seems unlikely that this would be different for search engines. In fact, the partiality of any search attempt (even if we assume a competent searcher) will magnify this problem in the context of search engines. Not only this, we would also claim that users tend to be ignorant about the inherent partiality present in any search engine search results (as explained earlier, in the technical overview). They tend to treat search-engine results the way they treat the results of library catalogue searches. Given the vastness of the Web, the close guarding of algorithms, and the abstruseness of the technology to most users, it should come as no surprise that seekers are unfamiliar, even unaware, of the systematic mechanisms that drive search engines. Such awareness, we believe, would make a difference. Although here, too, we came across no systematic empirical findings, we note that in spheres outside of the electronic media, people draw clear and definitive distinctions between information and recommendations coming from disinterested, as compared with interested, sources, between impartial advice as compared with advertisement.[29] And anecdotal experience bears this out, as when customers learned that Amazon Books, for example, had been representing as "friendly recommendations" what were in reality paid advertisements. Customers responded with great ire, and Amazon hastily retreated. The problem is equally complex on the supply side of the supposed market. We have already indicated the complex hurdles that need to be cleared to get listed and ranked appropriately. They all indicate that there simply is no level playing field by any stretch of the imagination. It seems clear that the "market will decide" view (problematic in most cases) is extremely problematic in this context. It is also doubtful that this can be resolved to the point where the market argument will become valid.

The question of whether a marketplace in search engines sufficiently approximates a competitive free market is, perhaps, subordinate to the question of whether we ought to leave the shaping of search mechanisms to the marketplace in the first place. We think this would be a bad idea.

Developments in Web searching are shaped by two distinct forces. One is the collective preferences of seekers. In the current, commercial model, search engines wishing to achieve greatest popularity would tend to cater to majority interests. While markets undoubtedly would force a degree of comprehensiveness and objectivity in listings, there is unlikely to be much market incentive to list sites of interest to small groups of individuals, such as individuals interested in rare animals or objects, individuals working in narrow and specialized fields or, for that matter, individuals of lesser economic power, and so forth. But popularity with seekers is not the only force at play. The other is the force exerted by entities wishing to be found.

Here, there is enormous inequality. Some enter the market already wielding vastly greater prowess and economic power than others. The rich and powerful clearly can influence the tendencies of search engines; their dollars can (and in a restricted way do already) play a decisive role in what gets found. For example, of the top 100 sites—based on traffic—just 6 are not .com commercial sites.[30] If we exclude universities, NASA, and the U.S. government, this number drops to two. One could reasonably argue that the United Nations site ought to generate at least enough traffic to be on the list if we consider that Amazon is in position 10 and *USA Today* in position 35. The cost to a search engine of losing a small number of searching customers may be outweighed by the benefits of pandering to "the masses" and to entities paying fees for the various forms of enhanced visibility. We can expect, therefore, that at least some drift will be caused by those wishing to be found, which, in turn, would further narrow the field of what is available to seekers of information, association, support, and services.[31]

It may be useful to think of the Web as a market of markets, instead of as just one market. When we seek, we are not interested in information in general; rather, we are interested in specific information related to our specific interests and needs. Seekers might be in the market for information about, for example, packaged tour holidays or computer hardware suppliers. For these markets, where we expect the demand for information to be great, we would expect the competition for recognition to be great as well. Companies would pay high prices for the keyword banners that will ensure them the top spot and a search will generate many hits for the seekers. In contrast, there are other, significantly smaller markets—for information about a rare medical condition or about the services of a local government authority or community.

In this market of markets, there is likely to be little incentive to ensure inclusion of these small markets and only a small cost (in loss of participation) for their exclusion. Although we do not have empirical evidence, we would expect the law of Pareto to apply (see Sen, 1985). We could imagine that a high percentage of search requests (say 80%, for argument's sake) are directed to a small percentage (say 20%) of the big markets, which would be abundantly represented in search results.[32] Only a small percentage of the search requests (say 20%) might be addressed to the large percentage (say 80%) of the smaller markets, which would be underrepresented. This scenario would explain the limited incentive for inclusion and relatively low cost of exclusion. We find this result problematic.

A market enthusiast does not find this result problematic. This is exactly what the market is supposed to do; the range and nature of choices are supposed to ebb and flow in response to the ebb and flow of the wants and needs of market participants—from varieties of salad dressings to makes of automobiles. Nevertheless, we resist this conclusion not because we are suspicious of markets in general—for cars and salad dressings, they are fine—but because maintaining the variety of options on the Web is of special importance. We resist the conclusion because we think that the value of comprehensive, thorough, and wide-ranging access to the Web lies within the category of goods that Elizabeth Anderson describes in her book *Values in Ethics and Economic* as goods that should not be left entirely (if at all) to the marketplace (Anderson, 1993).

Anderson constructs an elaborate argument defending the claim that there are ethical limitations on the scope of market norms for a range of goods (and services). Abstracting principles from cases that are likely to be noncontroversial in this regard—for example, friendship, persons, and political goods (like the vote)—she then argues that these principles apply to goods that are likely to be more controversial in this regard, such as public spaces, artistic endeavor, addictive drugs, and reproductive capacities. For some goods, such as cars, bottled salad dressings, and so on, "unexamined wants," expressed through the marketplace, are a perfectly acceptable basis for distribution. For others, including those that Anderson identifies, market norms do not properly express the valuations of a liberal democratic society like ours, which is committed to "freedom, autonomy and welfare" (Anderson, 1993, p. 141). Although it is not essential to our position that we uncritically accept the whole of Anderson's analysis, we accept at least this: that there are certain goods—ones that Anderson calls "political goods," including among them schools and public places—that must be distributed not in accordance with market norms but "in accordance with public principles" (Anderson, 1993, p. 159).

Sustaining the 80% of small markets that would be neglected by search engines shaped by market forces qualifies as a task worthy of public attention. Sustaining a full range of options here is not the same as sustaining a full range of options in bottled salad dressings or cars because the former enriches the democratic arena, may serve fundamental interests of many of the neediest members of our society, and more (on which we elaborate in the next section). We make political decisions to save certain goods that might fall by the wayside in a purely market-driven society. In this way, we recognize and save national treasures, historic homes, public parks, schools, and so forth. In this spirit, we commit to serving groups of people, like the disabled, even though (and because) we know that a market mechanism would not cater to their needs. (We make special accommodation for nonprofit efforts through tax exemption without consideration for popularity.) We see an equivalent need in the case of search engines.

In order to make the case convincing, however, we need to introduce into the picture a substantive claim, because our argument against leaving search engines fully to the mercy of the marketplace is not based on formal grounds—or at least, we do not see them. We base our case against leaving it to the market on the particular function that we see search engines serving and on the substantive vision of the Web that we think search engines (and search-and-retrieval mechanisms more generally) ought to sustain. We do not argue unconditionally that the trajectory of search engine development is wrong or politically dangerous in itself, but rather that it undermines a particular, normative vision of the Web in society. Those who do not share in this vision are unlikely to be convinced that search engines are different (in kind) from salad dressings and automobiles. The case that search engines are a special, political good presumes that the Web, too, is a special good.

THE FUTURE OF THE WEB AS A PUBLIC GOOD[33]

The thesis we here elaborate is that search engines, functioning in the manner outlined earlier, raise political concerns not simply because of the way they function, but also because the way they function seems to be at odds with the compelling ideology of the Web as a public good. This ideology portrays the fundamental nature and ethos of the Web as a public good of a particular kind, a rich array of commercial activity, political activity, artistic activity, associations of all kinds, communications of all kinds, and a virtually endless supply of information. In this regard the Web was, and is still seen by many as, a democratic medium that can circumvent the hegemony of the traditional media market, even of government control.

Over the course of a decade or so, computerized networks—the Internet and now the Web—have been envisioned as a great public good. Those who have held and promoted this vision over the course of, perhaps, a decade have based their claims on a combination of what we have already achieved and what the future promises. For example, with only a fraction of the population in the United States linked to the Internet, Al Gore (1995) promoted the vision of a Global Internet Infrastructure. This conception of the great public good—part reality, part wishful thinking—has gripped people from a variety of sectors, including scholars, engineers and scientists, entrepreneurs, and politicians. Each has highlighted a particular dimension of the Web's promise, some focusing on information, some on communication, some on commerce, and so on. Although we cannot enumerate here all possible public benefits, we highlight a few.

A theme that is woven throughout most versions of the promise is that the Web contributes to the public good by serving as a special kind of public space. The Web earns its characterization as public in many of the same ways as other spaces earn theirs, and it contributes to the public good for many of the same reasons. One feature that pushes something into the realm we call public is that it is not privately owned. The Web does seem to be public in this sense: Its hardware and software infrastructure is not wholly owned by any person or institution or, for that matter, by any single nation. Arguably, it does not even come under the territorial jurisdiction of any existing sovereign state.[34] There is no central or located clearinghouse that specifies or vets content or regulates overall who has the right of access. All those who accept the technical protocols, conform to technical standards (HTML, for example), and are able to connect to it may enter the Web. They may access others on the Web and, unless they take special precautions, they may be accessed. When I post my Web pages, I may make them available to any of the millions of potential browsers, even if, like a street vendor, I decide to charge a fee for entry to my page. The collaborative nature of much of the activity on the Web leads to a sense of the Web's being not simply unowned but collectively owned.

The Web fulfills some of the functions of other traditional public spaces—museums, parks, beaches, and schools. It serves as a medium for artistic expression, a space for recreation, and a place for storing and exhibiting items of historical and cultural importance, and it can educate. Beyond these functions, the one that has earned it greatest approbation both as a public space and a political good is its capacity as a medium for intensive communication among and between individuals and groups in just about all the permutations that one can imagine, namely, one-to-one, one-to-many, etc. It is the Hyde Park Corner of the electronic age, the public square where people may gather as a mass or associate in smaller groups. They may talk and listen, they may plan and organize. They air viewpoints and deliberate over matters of public importance. Such spaces, where content is regulated only by a few fundamental rules, embody the ideals of the liberal democratic society.

The idea of the Web as a public space and a forum for political deliberation has fueled discussions on teledemocracy for some time (Abramson et al., 1988; Arterton, 1987). The notion of the public sphere as a forum in which communicatively rational dialogue can take place unsullied by ideology has had one of its strongest proponents in Habermas (1989). Although there is no universal agreement among scholars on the extent of the effect the Web may have in the political sphere, several contributors to the debate have cited cases in which the Web appears to have had a decisive impact on the outcome. Douglas Kellner (1997) gives some examples: Zapatistas in their struggle against the Mexican government, the Tiananmen Square democracy movement, environmental activists who exposed McDonald's through the McLibel campaign, and the Clean Clothes Campaign supporting attempts of Filipino garment workers to expose exploitative working conditions.

We have not yet mentioned the perhaps dominant reason for conceiving of the Web as a public good, namely, its function as a conveyor of information. As a public

means of access to vast amounts of information, the Web promises widespread benefits. In this so-called information age, being among the information-rich is considered to be so important that some, like the philosopher Jeroen van den Hoven (1994, 1998), have argued that it makes sense to construe access to information as one of the Rawlsian "primary goods," compelling any just society to guarantee a basic, or reasonable, degree of it to all citizens. Growing use of the Web as a repository for all manner of information (e.g., government documents, consumer goods, scientific and artistic works, local public announcements, etc.) lends increasing weight to this prescription. The Web, according to the vision, is not intended as a vehicle for further expanding the gap between haves and have-nots, but for narrowing it (see, e.g., Civille, 1996; Hoffman & Novak, 1998).

The view of the Internet as a public good, as a globally inclusive, popular medium, fueled much of the initial social and economic investment in the medium and its supporting technology, convincing progressive politicians (or those who wish to appear progressive) to support it with investment and political backing.[35] The vision has also motivated idealistic computer scientists and engineers to volunteer energy and expertise toward developing and promulgating the hardware and software, from the likes of Jonathan Postel, one of the early builders of the Internet, who worked to keep its standards open and free,[36] to professionals and researchers volunteering in efforts to wire schools and help build infrastructure in poorer nations. These inclusive values were very much in the minds of creators of the Web like Tim Berners-Lee:

> The universality of the Web includes the fact that the information space can represent anything from one's personal private jottings to a polished global publication. We as people can, with or without the Web, interact on all scales. By being involved on every level, we ourselves form the ties which weave the levels together into a sort of consistency, balancing the homogeneity and the heterogeneity, the harmony and the diversity. We can be involved on a personal, family, town, corporate, state, national, union, and international levels. Culture exists at all levels, and we should give it a weighted balanced respect at each level.[37]

While the promise of the Web as a public space and a public good continues to galvanize general, political, and commercial support, many observers and scholars have cautioned that the goods are not guaranteed. The benefits of the vast electronic landscape, the billions of gigabytes of information, and the participation of millions of people around the world depend on a number of contingencies. Issuing one such caution, Lewis Branscomb (1996) calls for political effort to protect public interests against encroaching commercial interests. He worries about the enormous amount of money "invested in the new business combinations to exploit this consumer information market; the dollars completely swamp the modest investments being made in bringing public services to citizens and public institutions" (p. 27), urging federal, state, and local government to "develop and realize the many non-profit public service applications necessary for the realization of the 'promise of NII'" (p. 31).

Gary Chapman and Marc Rotenberg, writing in 1993 on behalf of the organization Computer Professionals for Social Responsibility, listed a number of problems that would need to be solved before the National Information Infrastructure would be capable of serving the public interest. Of particular relevance to us here is Chapman and Rotenberg's reference to Marvin Sirbu's (1992) call for "Development of standardized methods for information finding: White Pages directories, Yellow Pages, information indexes." Without an effective means of finding what you need, the benefits of an information and communication infrastructure like the Web are significantly diminished. We can conjure up analogies: a library containing all the printed books and papers in the world without covers and without a catalogue; a global telephone network without a directory; a magnificent encyclopedia, haphazardly organized and lacking a table of contents.

Search engines are not the only answer to this need, but they still are the most prominent, the one to which most users turn when they want to explore new territory on the Web. The power, therefore, that search engines wield in their capacity to highlight and emphasize certain Web sites, while making others, essentially, disappear, is considerable. If search engines systematically highlight Web sites with popular appeal and mainstream commercial purpose, as well as Web sites backed by entrenched economic powers, they amplify these presences on the Web at the expense of others. Many of the neglected venues and sources of information, suffering from lack of traffic, perhaps actually disappear, further narrowing the options to Web participants.

If trends in the design and function of search engines lead to a narrowing of options on the Web—an actual narrowing or a narrowing in what can be located—the Web as a public good of the particular kind that many envisioned is undermined. The ideal Web serves all people, not just some, not merely those in the mainstream. It is precisely the inclusivity and breadth that energized many to think that this technology would mean not just business as usual in the electronic realm, not merely a new tool for entrenched views and powers. The ideal Web would extend the possibilities for association, would facilitate access to obscure sources of information, would give voice to many of the typically unheard, and would preserve intensive and broadly inclusive interactivity.

In considering the effects of a biased indexing and retrieval system, our attention first was drawn to the seekers. It is from the perspective of seekers that we noted the systematic narrowing of Web offerings: There would be fewer opportunities to locate various types of information, individuals, and organizations, a narrowing of the full range of deliberative as well as recreational capabilities. If access to the Web is understood as access by seekers to all of these resources, then the outcome of biased search engines amounts to a shrinking of access to the Web. This perspective, however, does not represent all that is at stake. At stake is access to the Web in the shape of those, in addition, who would like to be found, to be seen and heard. Marc Raboy describes this dimensions of the new medium:

> The notion of "access" has traditionally meant different things in broadcasting and in telecommunications. In the broadcasting model, emphasis is placed on the active receiver, on free choice, and access refers to the entire range of products on offer. In the telecommunications model, emphasis is on the sender, on the capacity to get one's messages out, and access refers to the means of communication. In the new media environment, public policy will need to promote a new hybrid model of communication, which combines the social and cultural objectives of both broadcasting and telecommunications, and provides new mechanisms—drawn from both traditional models—aimed at maximizing equitable access to services and the means of communication for both senders and receivers (Raboy, 1998, p. 224).

The public good of the Web lies not merely in its functioning as a repository for seekers to find things, but as a forum for those with something (goods, services, viewpoints, political activism, etc.) to offer. The cost of a biased search-and-retrieval mechanism may even be greater for Web-site owners wishing to be found—the senders. Consider an example of just one type of case, someone seeking information about, say, vacation rentals in the Fiji Islands. Because one rental is all the person needs, he or she is likely to look down a list of options and stop looking when he or she finds it. There is no loss to the seeker even if it turns out that lower down on the list there are many other candidates meeting his or her criteria. The seeker has found what he or she needs. Those who are not found (because their lower ranking deprives them of attention or recognition) are offering, arguably, just as much value to the seeker. Our loss, in this case is twofold: One is that if continuing invisibility causes options to atrophy, the field of opportunity is thinned; the other is that many of those reaching out for attention or connection are not being served by the Web. If search mechanisms systematically narrow the scope of what seekers may find and what sites may be found, they will diminish the overall value of the Web as a public forum and as a broadly inclusive source of information.

Many have observed that to realize the vision of the Web as a democratizing technology or, more generally, as a public good, we must take the question of access seriously. We agree with this sentiment but wish to expand what the term covers. Access involves not merely a computer and a network hookup, as some have argued, nor, in addition, the skills and know-how that enable effective use. Access implies a comprehensive mechanism for finding and being found. It is in this context that we raise the issue of the politics of search engines—a politics that at present seems to push the Web into a drift that does not resonate with one of the historically driving ideologies.[38] We also believe we have shown why a rally to the market will not save the day, will not ensure our grand purpose. The question of how to achieve it is far harder.

SOME CONCLUSIONS AND IMPLICATIONS

We have claimed that search-engine design is not only a technical matter but also a political one. Search engines are important because they provide essential access to the Web both to those with something to say and offer and to those wishing to hear and find. Our concern is with the evident tendency of many of the leading search engines to give prominence to popular, wealthy, and powerful sites at the expense of others. This they do through the technical mechanisms of crawling, indexing, and ranking algorithms as well as through human-mediated trading of prominence for a fee. As long as this tendency continues, we expect these political effects will become more acute as the Web expands.

We regret this tendency not because it goes against our personal norms of fair play but because it undermines a substantive ideal—the substantive vision of the Web as an inclusive democratic space. This ideal Web is not merely a new communications infrastructure offering greater bandwidth, speed, massive connectivity, and more, but also a platform for social justice. It promises access to the kind of information that aids upward social mobility; it helps people make better decisions about politics, health, education, and more. The ideal Web also facilitates associations and communication that could empower and give voice to those who, traditionally, have been weaker and ignored. A drift toward popular, commercially successful institutions, through the partial view offered by search engines, seriously threatens these prospects. Scrutiny and discussion are important responses to these issues but policy and action are also needed—to fill that half-empty portion of the cup. We offer preliminary suggestions, calling for a combination of regulation through public policy as well as value-conscious design innovation.

The tenor of our suggestions is enhancement. We do not see that regulating and restricting development of commercial search engines is likely to produce ends that we would value—as it were, siphoning off from the half-full portion. This course of action is likely to be neither practically appealing nor wise, and might smack of cultural elitism or paternalism. Amartya Sen (1987, p. 9), commenting on existing schools of thought within the field of economics,

wrote: "It is not my purpose to write off what has been or is being achieved, but definitely to demand more." We take a similar stance in response to our study of Web search engines.

Policy

As a first step we would demand full and truthful disclosure of the underlying rules (or algorithms) governing indexing, searching, and prioritizing, stated in a way that is meaningful to the majority of Web users. Obviously, this might help spammers. However, we would argue that the impact of these unethical practices would be severely dampened if both seekers and those wishing to be found were aware of the particular biases inherent in any given search engine. We believe, on the whole, that informing users will be better than the status quo, in spite of the difficulties. Those who favor a market mechanism would perhaps be pleased to note that disclosure would move us closer to fulfilling the criteria of an ideal competitive market in search engines. Disclosure is a step in the right direction because it would lead to a clearer grasp of what is at stake in selecting among the various search engines, which in turn should help seekers to make informed decisions about which search engines to use and trust. But disclosure by itself may not sustain and enhance Web offerings in the way we would like it to—that is, by retaining transparency for those less popular sites to promote inclusiveness.

The marketplace alone, as we have argued, is not adequate. As a policy step, we might, for example, consider public support for developing more egalitarian and inclusive search mechanisms and for research into search and meta-search technologies that would increase transparency and access. Evidently, if we leave the task of charting the Web in the hands of commercial interests alone, we will merely mirror existing asymmetries of power in the very structure of the Web (McChesney, 1999). Although these and other policies could promise a fairer representation of Web offerings, a second key lies in the technology itself.

Values in Design

Philosophers of technology have recognized the intricate connection between technology and values—social, political, and moral values.[39] These ideas—that technological systems may embed or embody values—resonate in social and political commentary on information technology written by engineers as well as by philosophers and experts in cyberlaw (see, e.g., Friedman, 1997; Lessig, 1999; Nissenbaum, 1998). Translating these ideas into practice implies that we can build better systems—that is to say, systems that better reflect important social values—if we build them with an explicit commitment to values. With this article, the commitment we hope to inspire among the designers and builders of search engine technology is a commitment to the value of fairness as well as to the suite of values represented by the ideology of the Web as a public good.

Two technical approaches that appear to be attracting interest are not without drawbacks. One would increase segmentation and diversification. Search engines would become associated with particular segments of society—borders drawn perhaps according to traditional categories (sports, entertainment, art, and so forth). A problem with segmentation overall, however, is that it could fragment the very inclusiveness and universality of the Web that we value. The Web may eventually merely mirror the institutions of society with its baggage of asymmetrical power structures, privilege, and so forth.

The other approach is to develop individualized spiders that go out and search for pages based on individual criteria, building individualized databases according to individual needs.[40] There is, however, a significant "cost" in automatic harvesting via spiders that even the existing population of spiders imposes on system resources; this has already caused concern (see Kostner, 1995).

There is much interesting work under way concerning the technology of search engines that could, in principle, help: for example, improving the way individual pages indicate relevance (also referred to as metadata) (see Marchiori, 1998), refining overall search engine technology,[41] and improving Web resource presentation and visualization (see Hearst, 1997) and meta-search technology (see Lawrence & Giles, 1998). Although improvements like these might accidentally promote values, they hold greatest promise as remedies for the current politics of search engines if they are explicitly guided by values. We urge engineers and scientists who adhere to the ideology of the Web, to its values of inclusivity, fairness, and scope of representation, and so forth, to pursue improvements in indexing, searching, accessing, and ranking with these values firmly in their sights. It is good to keep in mind that the struggle to chart the Web and capture the attention of the information seekers is not merely a technical challenge, it is also political.

NOTES

1. In an online survey the NDP Group polled 22,000 seekers who accessed search engines to determine their satisfaction with the search engine. Ninety-six percent (96%) indicated that they were satisfied with the search results. This would seem to go against our argument. However, in another study done by researchers from British Telecom (BT), PC-literate but not regular users of the Internet found their search results disappointing and generally "not worth the effort" (Pollock & Hockley, 1997). This may indicate that a fairly high level of searching

skill is necessary to get what you want. We return to this issue when we discuss the market argument for the development of search engines.

2. Winner, L. 1980. Do artifacts have politics? *Daedalus* 109:121–136.

3. For those interested in more detail, the Web site http://www.searchenginewatch.com is a good place to start.

4. We are thinking here of the top 10 to 20 when it is a matter of actual relevancy. We later discuss the issue of spamming.

5. One could argue that it is also possible for a Web page to be found through portal sites, which are increasingly popular, though as a matter of fact, we think it would be highly unlikely that a link would be established through a portal site if it does not meet the indexing criteria for search engines.

6. We realize we have not listed all the means through which pages may be found. For example, one may access a page through an outlink from another page. The problem with such means is that they depend on somewhat unpredictable serendipity. One needs also to add that increasing numbers of alternatives are emerging as viable options, such as portal sites and keyword retrieval via Centraal's Real Name system (http://www.centraal.com). Nevertheless, the majority of those who access the Web continue to do it through search engines. There is no reason to believe that this would change in the foreseeable future.

7. We note, for readers who are aware of the debate currently raging over domain names, that an effective system of search and retrieval is a constructive response to the debate and would lessen the impact of whatever decisions are made. We argue that domain names are important in inverse proportion to the efficacy of available search mechanisms, for if individuals and institutions can easily be found on the basis of content and relevancy, there is less at stake in the precise formulation of their domain names. In other words, a highly effective indexing and retrieval mechanism can mitigate the effects of domain-name assignments.

8. A stop word is a frequently occurring word such as the, to, and we that is excluded because it occurs too often. Stop words are not indexed. This is not insignificant if one considers that the word "web" is a stop word in Alta Vista. So if you are a company doing Web design and have "Web design" in your title, you may not get indexed and will be ranked accordingly.

9. The <TITLE> tag is either created by the Web-page designer or deduced by a converter. For example, when you create an MSWord document and want to publish it on the Web, you can save it as HTML directly in the MSWord editor. In this case the MSWord editor assumes that the first sentence it can find in the document is the title and will place this in the <TITLE> tag in the HTML source code it generates.

10. Most of the directory-based search engines also use some form of automatic harvesting to augment their manually submitted database.

11. When parsing the page, the spider views the page in HTML format and treats it as one long string of words, as explained by Alta Vista: "Alta Vista treats every page on the Web and every article of Usenet news as a sequence of words. A word in this context means any string of letters and digits delimited either by punctuation and other non-alphabetic characters (for example, &, %, $, /, #, _, ~), or by white space (spaces, tabs, line ends, start of document, end of document). To be a word, a string of alphanumerics does not have to be spelled correctly or be found in any dictionary. All that is required is that someone type it as a single word in a Web page or Usenet news article. Thus, the following are words if they appear delimited in a document:

HAL5000, Gorbachevnik, 602e21, www, http, EasierSaidThanDone, etc. The following are all considered to be two words because the internal punctuation separates them: don't, digital.com, x–y, AT&T, 3.14159, U.S., All'sFairInLoveAndWar."

12. Page is one of the designers of Google, and the details presented here are the heuristics used by Google (at least the earlier version of these heuristics).

13. We are not claiming that this is a straightforward and uncontroversial metric. The decision about the "similarity" between the query term and the document is by no means trivial. Decisions on how to implement the determination of "similarity" can indeed be of significance to our discussion. However, we do not pursue this discussion here.

14. In the cases of Excite, Hotbot, and Lycos, there is evidence that this is a major consideration for determining indexing appeal—refer to http://www.searchenginwatch.com/webmasters/features.html. Exclusion, using this metric, is less likely for a search engine like Alta Vista, which goes for massive coverage, than for its smaller, more selective competitors.

15. For search-engine operators it is a matter of deciding between breadth and depth: Should many sites be partially indexed or few sites fully indexed, since they know a priori that they can not include everything? (Brake, 1997) Louis Monier, in a response to John Pike—Webmaster for the Federation of American Scientists site—indicated that Alta Vista indexed 51,570 of the estimated 300,000 pages of the Geocities site. This amounts to approximately 17% coverage. He thought this to be exceptionally good. Pike indicated that Alta Vista indexed 600 of their 6000 pages. (Refer to this discussion at http://www4.zdnet.com/anchordesk/talkback/talkback_11638.html and http://www4.zdnet.com/anchordesk/talkback/talkback_13066.html as well as to the *New Scientist* paper at http://www.newscientist.com/keysites/networld/lost.html.)

16. For a discussion of this standard, refer to http://info.webcrawler.com/mak/projects/robots/exclusion.html.

17. Another reason for excluding spiders from sites such as CNN is that their content is constantly in flux and one does not want search engines to index (and now cache) old content. Another issue worth noting here is that many search engines now have large caches to go along with their indexes.

18. Refer to the *New Scientist* paper at http://www.newscientist.com/keysites/networld/lost.html. The "cost" of a spider visit can be significant for a site. Responsible spider will request a page only every so many seconds. However, the pressure to index has induced what is termed "rapid fire." This means that the spider requests in rapid succession, which may make the server unavailable to any other user. Although there is a danger that this problem will worsen, there seems to be a generally optimistic view among experts that we will develop technical mechanisms to deal with it, for example, proposals to devise extensions to HTTP, or parallel spiders.

19. Although at present some spiders are unable to deal with features such as frames and are better with simple HTML files, there are spiders that have been developed that are now able to handle a variety of formats.

20. Lee Giles disputes this. He still considers indexing to be a huge problem.

21. Also referred to as spamdexing. Refer to http://www.jmls.edu/cyber/index/metatags.html for a reasonable discussion of this issue.

22. "To stay ahead of the game, the major search engines change their methods for determining relevancy rankings every few months. This is usually when they discover that a lot of people have learned the latest technique and are all sneaking into a side door. They also try to fool the tricksters . . . sometimes they put irrelevant pages at the top of the list just to cause confusion" (Patrick Anderson & Michael Henderson, editor & publisher, *Hits To Sales*, at http://www.hitstosales.com/2search.html).

23. At the WWW7 Conference, researchers in Australia devised an ingenious method for attempting to reverse-engineer the relevance-ranking algorithms of various commercial search engines, causing consternation and some outrage—see Pringle et al. (1998).

24. Lawsuits have been filed by Playboy Enterprises, Inc., and Estee Lauder Companies, Inc., challenging such arrangements between Excite, Inc., and other companies that have "bought" their respective names for purposes of banner ads. See Kaplan (1999).

25. "If you want the traffic and the exposure, *you are going to pay for the education or you are going to pay for the service.* There is no other way to do it. It is not easy. It is not magic. It takes time, effort, and knowledge. Then it takes continual monitoring to keep the position you worked so hard to get in the first place. Please do not misunderstand—the competition is fierce and severe for those top spots, which is why the search engines can charge so much money to sell keyword banners" (Anderson & Henderson, 1997, emphasis added).

26. Some large sites (universities, for example) allow users to submit keywords, which the site, in turn, submits to a particular default search engine (frequently Yahoo!). If users select "search" on the Netscape toolbar it takes them to the Netscape Web pages where they have a list of search engines. In this case Excite is the default search engine. There is clearly considerable advantage to being chosen as the default search engine on the Netscape or other equivalent Web page.

27. This is because, as Giles and Lawrence remarked in verbal consultation, there is a fair degree of convergence in the results yielded by various search engine algorithms and decision criteria.

28. One should also note that search engines also market themselves aggressively. They also establish agreements with other service providers to become defaults on their pages. Refer to footnote 26.

29. As noted by one of the reviewers, this is equally true outside the electronic media.

30. Refer to http://www.100hot.com for the latest list.

31. And engines that use link popularity for priority listing will be even more prone to reifying a mode of conservatism on the Web.

32. This guess is not far from reality, as searches for sex-related key terms are by far the most frequent—constituting perhaps as high a percentage as 80% of overall searches.

33. Our discussion of the Web would probably be more accurately addressed to the Internet as a whole. We think that the more inclusive discussion would only strengthen our conclusions but would probably introduce unnecessary complexity.

34. See Johnson and Post (1996). This article puts forward an extreme version of this view. We will not engage further in the debate.

35. Popular news media reflect the hold of this vision of the Web. In an article in *The New York Times* about the Gates Learning Foundation's recent donation for public-access computers to libraries, the gift is discussed in terms of bridging economic inequality and overcoming technical illiteracy. Librarians are quoted as enthusiastically reporting that the computers are used "to type (their) resumes, hunt for jobs, do schoolwork, research Beanie Babies, look up medical information, investigate their family roots, send E-mail and visit wrestling sites on the web" (Katie Hafner, *The New York Times*, 21 February 1999).

36. "A Net Builder Who Loved Invention, Not Profit," *The New York Times*, 22 October 1998.

37. Refer to http://www.w3.org/1998/02/Potential.html

38. Larry Lessig has argued that there has been an unacknowledged but significant shift in this ethos. See "The law of the horse: What cyberlaw might teach," *Harvard Law Review* 1999.

39. See, for example, L. Winner. "Do artifacts have politics?" *Daedelus* 109:121–136, 1980.

40. Individualized spiders such as *NetAttaché* are already available for as little as $50. Refer to http://www.tympani.com/store/NAProTools.html (Miller & Bharat, 1998).

41. Some cite Google as an example. This is a particularly interesting case, as Google started out as a search engine that was developed within an educational setting and moved into the for-profit sector. We think it would be very worthwhile to trace changes in the technology that might result from this move.

REFERENCES

Abramson, Jeffrey B., Arterton, F. C., and Orren, G. R. 1988. *The electronic commonwealth: The impact of new media technologies on democratic politics.* New York: Basic Books.

Anderson, Elizabeth. 1993. *Value in ethics and economics.* Cambridge, MA: Harvard University Press.

Anderson, Patrick, and Henderson, Michael. 1997. *Hits to Sales.* <http://www.hitstosales.com/2search.html>

Arterton, F. Christopher. 1987. *Teledemocracy: Can technology protect democracy.* Newbury Park, CA: Sage.

Brake, David. 1997. Lost in cyberspace. *New Scientist* 28 June. <http://www.newscientist.com/keysites/networld/lost.html>

Branscomb, Lewis. 1996. Balancing the commercial and public-interest visions. In *Public Access to the Internet*, eds. Brian Kahin and James Keller, 24–33. Cambridge, MA: MIT Press.

Chapman, Gary, and Rotenberg, Marc. 1993. The national information infrastructure: A public interest opportunity. *CPSR Newsletter* 11(2):1–23.

Cho, J., Garcia-Molina, H., and Page, L. 1998. Efficient crawling through URL ordering. *Seventh International World Wide Web Conference*, Brisbane, Australia, 14–18 April.

Civille, Richard. 1996. The Internet and the poor. In *Public access to the Internet*, eds. Brian Kahin and James Keller, 175–207. Cambridge, MA: MIT Press.

Friedman, B., ed. 1997. *Human values and the design of computer technology.* Chicago: University of Chicago Press.

Friedman, B., and Nissenbaum, H. 1996. Bias in computer systems. *ACM Transactions on Information Systems* 14(3):330–347.

Golding, Peter. 1994. The communications paradox: Inequality at the national and international levels. *Media Development* 4:7–9.

Gore, Al. 1995. Global information infrastructure. In *Computers, ethics and social values*, eds. D. Johnson and H. Nissenbaum, 620–628. Englewood Cliffs, NJ: Prentice Hall.

Habermas, Jurgen. 1989. *The structural transformation of the public sphere*, Trans. T. Burger and F. Lawrence. Cambridge, MA: Harvard University Press.

Hansell, S. 1999. AltaVista invites advertisers to pay for top ranking. *New York Times* 15 April.

Hearst, Marti. 1997. Interfaces for searching the Web. *Scientific American* March. <http://www.sciam.com/0397issue/039/hearst.html>

Hoffman, Donna L., and Novak, Thomas P. 1998. Bridging the racial divide on the Internet. *Science* 280:390–391.

Johnson, David R., and Post, David. 1996. Law and borders—The rise of law in cyberspace. *Stanford Law Review* 48(5):1367–1402.

Kaplan, C. 1999. Lawsuits challenge search engines' practice of "selling" trademarks. *New York Times* 12 February. <http://www.nytimes.com/library/tech/99/02/cyber/cyberlaw/12law.html>

Kellner, Douglas. 1997. Intellectuals, the new public spheres, and techno-politics. <http://www.gseis.ucla.edu/courses/ed253a/newDK/intell.htm>

Kostner, Martijn. 1995. Robots in the web: Threat or treat. <http://info.webcrawler.com>

Lawrence, S., and Giles, C. L. 1998. Inquirus, the NECI meta search engine. *Seventh International World Wide Web Conference*, Brisbane, Australia, 14–18 April. <http://www7.scu.edu.au/programme/fullpapers/1906/com1906.htm>

Lawrence, S., and Giles, C. L. 1999. Accessibility and distribution of information on the Web. *Nature* 400:107–109.

Lessig, Lawrence. 1999. *Code and other laws of cyberspace.* New York: Basic Books.

McChesney, Robert W. 1993. *Telecommunications, mass media and democracy.* Oxford, Oxford University Press.

McChesney, Robert W. 1997a. The mythology of commercial media and the contemporary crisis of public broadcasting. *Spry Memorial Lecture*, Montreal & Vancouver, 2 & 4 December.

McChesney, Robert W. 1999. Making media democratic. *Boston Review: New Democracy Forum.* <http://polisci.mit.edu/BostonReview/BR23.3/mcchesney.html>

McChesney, Robert W. 1997b. *Corporate media and the threat to democracy.* New York: Seven Stories Press.

McChesney, Robert W., and Herman, Edward S. 1997. *The global media: The new missionaries of corporate capitalism.* London: Cassell.

Marchiori, M. 1998. The limits of Web metadata, and beyond. *Seventh International World Wide Web Conference*, Brisbane, Australia, 14–18 April. <http://www7.scu.edu.au/programme/fullpapers/1896/com1896.htm>

Miller, R. C., and Bharat, K. 1998. SPHINX: A framework for creating personal, site-specific Web crawlers. *Seventh International World Wide Web Conference*, Brisbane, Australia, 14–18 April. <http://www7.scu.edu.au/programme/fullpapers/1875/com1875.htm>

Nissenbaum, H. 1998. Values in the design of computer systems. *Computers in Society* March: 38–39.

Office of the Vice President. 1995. Remarks as Delivered by Vice-President Gore to the Networked Economy Conference, 12 September.

Phua, V. 1998. *Towards a set of ethical rules for search engines.* MSc dissertation, London School of Economics.

Pollack, Andrew. 1995. A cyberspace front in a multicultural war. *New York Times* 7 August: C1, C6.

Pollack, Andrew, and Hockley, A. 1997. What's wrong with Internet searching. *D-Lib Magazine* March. <http://www.dlib.org/dlib/march97/bt/03pollack.htm>

Poster, Mark. 1995. CyberDemocracy: Internet and the public sphere. In *Internet Culture*, ed. David Porter, pp. 201–217. New York: Routledge. <http://www.hnet.uci.edu/mposter/writings/democ.html>

Pringle, G., Allison, L., and Dowe, D. L. 1998. What is a tall poppy among webpages. *Seventh International World Wide Web*

Conference, Brisbane, Australia, 14–18 April. <htpp://www7.scu.edu.au/programme/fullpapers/ 1872/com1872.htm>

Raboy, Marc. 1998. Global communication policy and human rights. In *A communications cornucopia: Markle Foundation essays on information policy* 218–242. Washington, DC: Brookings Institution Press.

Sen, Amartya. 1985. The moral standing of the market. *Social Philosophy & Policy* 2:2.

Sen, Amartya. 1987. *On ethics and economics*. Oxford: Blackwell.

Shapiro, Andrew. 1995. Street corners in cyberspace. *Nation* 3 July.

Schiller, Dan. 1995. Ambush on the I-way: Information commoditization on the electronic frontier. *BCLA Information Policy Conference*, Vancouver, 27–28 October.

Sirbu, Marvin. 1992. Telecommunications technology and infrastructure. Institute for Information Studies. In *A national information network: Changing our lives in the 21st century*, pp. 174–175. Nashville, TN, and Queenstown, MD: Institute for Information Studies.

Van den Hoven, Jeroen. 1994. Towards ethical principles for designing politico-administrative information systems. *Informatization in the Public Sector* 3:353–373.

Van den Hoven, Jeroen. 1998. Distributive justice and equal access: Simple vs. complex equality. *Computer Ethics: A Philosophical Inquiry*, London, December.

Wurman, R. S. 1989. *Information anxiety: What to do when information doesn't tell you what you want to know*. New York: Bantam Books.

Part III
Values and Technology

[18]

Do Artifacts Have Politics?

LANGDON WINNER

IN CONTROVERSIES ABOUT TECHNOLOGY AND SOCIETY, there is no idea more provocative than the notion that technical things have political qualities. At issue is
the claim that the machines, structures, and systems of modern material culture
can be accurately judged not only for their contributions of efficiency and productivity, not merely for their positive and negative environmental side effects,
but also for the ways in which they can embody specific forms of power and
authority. Since ideas of this kind have a persistent and troubling presence in
discussions about the meaning of technology, they deserve explicit attention.[1]

Writing in *Technology and Culture* almost two decades ago, Lewis Mumford
gave classic statement to one version of the theme, arguing that "from late neo-
lithic times in the Near East, right down to our own day, two technologies have
recurrently existed side by side: one authoritarian, the other democratic, the
first system-centered, immensely powerful, but inherently unstable, the other
man-centered, relatively weak, but resourceful and durable."[2] This thesis
stands at the heart of Mumford's studies of the city, architecture, and the history of technics, and mirrors concerns voiced earlier in the works of Peter
Kropotkin, William Morris, and other nineteenth century critics of industrial-
ism. More recently, antinuclear and prosolar energy movements in Europe and
America have adopted a similar notion as a centerpiece in their arguments.
Thus environmentalist Denis Hayes concludes, "The increased deployment of
nuclear power facilities must lead society toward authoritarianism. Indeed, safe
reliance upon nuclear power as the principal source of energy may be possible
only in a totalitarian state." Echoing the views of many proponents of appropriate technology and the soft energy path, Hayes contends that "dispersed solar
sources are more compatible than centralized technologies with social equity,
freedom and cultural pluralism."[3]

An eagerness to interpret technical artifacts in political language is by no
means the exclusive property of critics of large-scale high-technology systems.
A long lineage of boosters have insisted that the "biggest and best" that science
and industry made available were the best guarantees of democracy, freedom,
and social justice. The factory system, automobile, telephone, radio, television,
the space program, and of course nuclear power itself have all at one time or
another been described as democratizing, liberating forces. David Lilienthal, in
T.V.A.: Democracy on the March, for example, found this promise in the phos-

phate fertilizers and electricity that technical progress was bringing to rural Americans during the 1940s.[4] In a recent essay, *The Republic of Technology*, Daniel Boorstin extolled television for "its power to disband armies, to cashier presidents, to create a whole new democratic world—democratic in ways never before imagined, even in America."[5] Scarcely a new invention comes along that someone does not proclaim it the salvation of a free society.

It is no surprise to learn that technical systems of various kinds are deeply interwoven in the conditions of modern politics. The physical arrangements of industrial production, warfare, communications, and the like have fundamentally changed the exercise of power and the experience of citizenship. But to go beyond this obvious fact and to argue that certain technologies *in themselves* have political properties seems, at first glance, completely mistaken. We all know that people have politics, not things. To discover either virtues or evils in aggregates of steel, plastic, transistors, integrated circuits, and chemicals seems just plain wrong, a way of mystifying human artifice and of avoiding the true sources, the human sources of freedom and oppression, justice and injustice. Blaming the hardware appears even more foolish than blaming the victims when it comes to judging conditions of public life.

Hence, the stern advice commonly given those who flirt with the notion that technical artifacts have political qualities: What matters is not technology itself, but the social or economic system in which it is embedded. This maxim, which in a number of variations is the central premise of a theory that can be called the social determination of technology, has an obvious wisdom. It serves as a needed corrective to those who focus uncritically on such things as "the computer and its social impacts" but who fail to look behind technical things to notice the social circumstances of their development, deployment, and use. This view provides an antidote to naive technological determinism—the idea that technology develops as the sole result of an internal dynamic, and then, unmediated by any other influence, molds society to fit its patterns. Those who have not recognized the ways in which technologies are shaped by social and economic forces have not gotten very far.

But the corrective has its own shortcomings; taken literally, it suggests that technical *things* do not matter at all. Once one has done the detective work necessary to reveal the social origins—power holders behind a particular instance of technological change—one will have explained everything of importance. This conclusion offers comfort to social scientists: it validates what they had always suspected, namely, that there is nothing distinctive about the study of technology in the first place. Hence, they can return to their standard models of social power—those of interest group politics, bureaucratic politics, Marxist models of class struggle, and the like—and have everything they need. The social determination of technology is, in this view, essentially no different from the social determination of, say, welfare policy or taxation.

There are, however, good reasons technology has of late taken on a special fascination in its own right for historians, philosophers, and political scientists; good reasons the standard models of social science only go so far in accounting for what is most interesting and troublesome about the subject. In another place I have tried to show why so much of modern social and political thought contains recurring statements of what can be called a theory of technological politics, an odd mongrel of notions often crossbred with orthodox liberal, conservative, and socialist philosophies.[6] The theory of technological politics draws attention to the momentum of large-scale sociotechnical systems, to the response of modern societies to certain technological imperatives, and to the all too common signs of the adaptation of human ends to technical means. In so doing it offers a novel framework of interpretation and explanation for some of the more puzzling patterns that have taken shape in and around the growth of modern material culture. One strength of this point of view is that it takes technical artifacts seriously. Rather than insist that we immediately reduce everything to the interplay of social forces, it suggests that we pay attention to the characteristics of technical objects and the meaning of those characteristics. A necessary complement to, rather than a replacement for, theories of the social determination of technology, this perspective identifies certain technologies as political phenomena in their own right. It points us back, to borrow Edmund Husserl's philosophical injunction, *to the things themselves.*

In what follows I shall offer outlines and illustrations of two ways in which artifacts can contain political properties. First are instances in which the invention, design, or arrangement of a specific technical device or system becomes a way of settling an issue in a particular community. Seen in the proper light, examples of this kind are fairly straightforward and easily understood. Second are cases of what can be called inherently political technologies, man-made systems that appear to require, or to be strongly compatible with, particular kinds of political relationships. Arguments about cases of this kind are much more troublesome and closer to the heart of the matter. By "politics," I mean arrangements of power and authority in human associations as well as the activities that take place within those arrangements. For my purposes, "technology" here is understood to mean all of modern practical artifice,[7] but to avoid confusion I prefer to speak of technolog*ies,* smaller or larger pieces or systems of hardware of a specific kind. My intention is not to settle any of the issues here once and for all, but to indicate their general dimensions and significance.

Technical Arrangements as Forms of Order

Anyone who has traveled the highways of America and has become used to the normal height of overpasses may well find something a little odd about some of the bridges over the parkways on Long Island, New York. Many of the overpasses are extraordinarily low, having as little as nine feet of clearance at the curb. Even those who happened to notice this structural peculiarity would not be inclined to attach any special meaning to it. In our accustomed way of looking at things like roads and bridges we see the details of form as innocuous, and seldom give them a second thought.

It turns out, however, that the two hundred or so low-hanging overpasses on Long Island were deliberately designed to achieve a particular social effect. Robert Moses, the master builder of roads, parks, bridges, and other public works from the 1920s to the 1970s in New York, had these overpasses built to specifications that would discourage the presence of buses on his parkways. According to evidence provided by Robert A. Caro in his biography of Moses, the reasons reflect Moses's social-class bias and racial prejudice. Automobile-owning whites of "upper" and "comfortable middle" classes, as he called them, would be free to use the parkways for recreation and commuting. Poor people and blacks, who normally used public transit, were kept off the roads because the twelve-foot tall buses could not get through the overpasses. One consequence was to limit access of racial minorities and low-income groups to Jones Beach, Moses's widely acclaimed public park. Moses made doubly sure of this result by vetoing a proposed extension of the Long Island Railroad to Jones Beach.[8]

As a story in recent American political history, Robert Moses's life is fascinating. His dealings with mayors, governors, and presidents, and his careful manipulation of legislatures, banks, labor unions, the press, and public opinion are all matters that political scientists could study for years. But the most important and enduring results of his work are his technologies, the vast engineering projects that give New York much of its present form. For generations after Moses has gone and the alliances he forged have fallen apart, his public works, especially the highways and bridges he built to favor the use of the automobile over the development of mass transit, will continue to shape that city. Many of his monumental structures of concrete and steel embody a systematic social inequality, a way of engineering relationships among people that, after a time, becomes just another part of the landscape. As planner Lee Koppleman told Caro about the low bridges on Wantagh Parkway, "The old son-of-a-gun had made sure that buses would *never* be able to use his goddamned parkways."[9]

Histories of architecture, city planning, and public works contain many examples of physical arrangements that contain explicit or implicit political purposes. One can point to Baron Haussmann's broad Parisian thoroughfares, engineered at Louis Napoleon's direction to prevent any recurrence of street fighting of the kind that took place during the revolution of 1848. Or one can visit any number of grotesque concrete buildings and huge plazas constructed on American university campuses during the late 1960s and early 1970s to defuse student demonstrations. Studies of industrial machines and instruments also turn up interesting political stories, including some that violate our normal expectations about why technological innovations are made in the first place. If we suppose that new technologies are introduced to achieve increased efficiency, the history of technology shows that we will sometimes be disappointed. Technological change expresses a panoply of human motives, not the least of which is the desire of some to have dominion over others, even though it may require an occasional sacrifice of cost-cutting and some violence to the norm of getting more from less.

One poignant illustration can be found in the history of nineteenth century industrial mechanization. At Cyrus McCormick's reaper manufacturing plant in Chicago in the middle 1880s, pneumatic molding machines, a new and largely untested innovation, were added to the foundry at an estimated cost of $500,000. In the standard economic interpretation of such things, we would expect that this step was taken to modernize the plant and achieve the kind of efficiencies that mechanization brings. But historian Robert Ozanne has shown why the development must be seen in a broader context. At the time, Cyrus McCormick II was engaged in a battle with the National Union of Iron Molders. He saw the addition of the new machines as a way to "weed out the bad element among the men," namely, the skilled workers who had organized the union local in Chicago.[10] The new machines, manned by unskilled labor, actually produced inferior castings at a higher cost than the earlier process. After three years of use the machines were, in fact, abandoned, but by that time they had served their purpose—the destruction of the union. Thus, the story of these technical developments at the McCormick factory cannot be understood adequately outside the record of workers' attempts to organize, police repression of the labor movement in Chicago during that period, and the events surrounding the bombing at Haymarket Square. Technological history and American political history were at that moment deeply intertwined.

In cases like those of Moses's low bridges and McCormick's molding machines, one sees the importance of technical arrangements that precede the *use* of the things in question. It is obvious that technologies can be used in ways that enhance the power, authority, and privilege of some over others, for example, the use of television to sell a candidate. To our accustomed way of thinking, technologies are seen as neutral tools that can be used well or poorly, for good, evil, or something in between. But we usually do not stop to inquire whether a given device might have been designed and built in such a way that it produces a set of consequences logically and temporally *prior* to any of its professed uses. Robert Moses's bridges, after all, were used to carry automobiles from one point to another; McCormick's machines were used to make metal castings; both technologies, however, encompassed purposes far beyond their immediate use. If our moral and political language for evaluating technology includes only categories having to do with tools and uses, if it does not include attention to the meaning of the designs and arrangements of our artifacts, then we will be blinded to much that is intellectually and practically crucial.

Because the point is most easily understood in the light of particular intentions embodied in physical form, I have so far offered illustrations that seem almost conspiratorial. But to recognize the political dimensions in the shapes of technology does not require that we look for conscious conspiracies or malicious intentions. The organized movement of handicapped people in the United States during the 1970s pointed out the countless ways in which machines, instruments, and structures of common use—buses, buildings, sidewalks, plumbing fixtures, and so forth—made it impossible for many handicapped persons to move about freely, a condition that systematically excluded them from public life. It is safe to say that designs unsuited for the handicapped arose more from long-standing neglect than from anyone's active intention. But now that the issue has been raised for public attention, it is evident that justice requires a remedy. A whole range of artifacts are now being redesigned and rebuilt to accommodate this minority.

Indeed, many of the most important examples of technologies that have political consequences are those that transcend the simple categories of "intended" and "unintended" altogether. These are instances in which the very process of technical development is so thoroughly biased in a particular direction that it regularly produces results counted as wonderful breakthroughs by some social interests and crushing setbacks by others. In such cases it is neither correct nor insightful to say, "Someone intended to do somebody else harm." Rather, one must say that the technological deck has been stacked long in advance to favor certain social interests, and that some people were bound to receive a better hand than others.

The mechanical tomato harvester, a remarkable device perfected by researchers at the University of California from the late 1940s to the present, offers an illustrative tale. The machine is able to harvest tomatoes in a single pass through a row, cutting the plants from the ground, shaking the fruit loose, and in the newest models sorting the tomatoes electronically into large plastic gondolas that hold up to twenty-five tons of produce headed for canning. To accommodate the rough motion of these "factories in the field," agricultural researchers have bred new varieties of tomatoes that are hardier, sturdier, and less tasty. The harvesters replace the system of handpicking, in which crews of farmworkers would pass through the fields three or four times putting ripe tomatoes in lug boxes and saving immature fruit for later harvest.[11] Studies in California indicate that the machine reduces costs by approximately five to seven dollars per ton as compared to hand-harvesting.[12] But the benefits are by no means equally divided in the agricultural economy. In fact, the machine in the garden has in this instance been the occasion for a thorough reshaping of social relationships of tomato production in rural California.

By their very size and cost, more than $50,000 each to purchase, the machines are compatible only with a highly concentrated form of tomato growing. With the introduction of this new method of harvesting, the number of tomato growers declined from approximately four thousand in the early 1960s to about six hundred in 1973, yet with a substantial increase in tons of tomatoes produced. By the late 1970s an estimated thirty-two thousand jobs in the tomato industry had been eliminated as a direct consequence of mechanization.[13] Thus, a jump in productivity to the benefit of very large growers has occurred at a sacrifice to other rural agricultural communities.

The University of California's research and development on agricultural machines like the tomato harvester is at this time the subject of a law suit filed by attorneys for California Rural Legal Assistance, an organization representing a group of farmworkers and other interested parties. The suit charges that University officials are spending tax monies on projects that benefit a handful of private interests to the detriment of farmworkers, small farmers, consumers, and rural California generally, and asks for a court injunction to stop the practice. The University has denied these charges, arguing that to accept them "would require elimination of all research with any potential practical application."[14]

As far as I know, no one has argued that the development of the tomato harvester was the result of a plot. Two students of the controversy, William Friedland and Amy Barton, specifically exonerate both the original developers of the machine and the hard tomato from any desire to facilitate economic concentration in that industry.[15] What we see here instead is an ongoing social process in which scientific knowledge, technological invention, and corporate profit reinforce each other in deeply entrenched patterns that bear the unmistakable stamp of political and economic power. Over many decades agricultural research and development in American land-grant colleges and universities has tended to favor the interests of large agribusiness concerns.[16] It is in the face of such subtly ingrained patterns that opponents of innovations like the tomato harvester are made to seem "antitechnology" or "antiprogress." For the harvester is not merely the symbol of a social order that rewards some while punishing others; it is in a true sense an embodiment of that order.

Within a given category of technological change there are, roughly speaking, two kinds of choices that can affect the relative distribution of power, authority, and privilege in a community. Often the crucial decision is a simple "yes or no" choice—are we going to develop and adopt the thing or not? In recent years many local, national, and international disputes about technology have centered on "yes or no" judgments about such things as food additives, pesticides, the building of highways, nuclear reactors, and dam projects. The fundamental choice about an ABM or an SST is whether or not the thing is going to join society as a piece of its operating equipment. Reasons for and against are frequently as important as those concerning the adoption of an important new law.

A second range of choices, equally critical in many instances, has to do with specific features in the design or arrangement of a technical system after the decision to go ahead with it has already been made. Even after a utility company wins permission to build a large electric power line, important controversies can remain with respect to the placement of its route and the design of its towers; even after an organization has decided to institute a system of computers, controversies can still arise with regard to the kinds of components, programs, modes of access, and other specific features the system will include. Once the mechanical tomato harvester had been developed in its basic form, design alteration of critical social significance—the addition of electronic sorters, for example—changed the character of the machine's effects on the balance of wealth and power in California agriculture. Some of the most interesting research on technology and politics at present focuses on the attempt to demonstrate in a detailed, concrete fashion how seemingly innocuous design features in mass transit systems, water projects, industrial machinery, and other technologies actually mask social choices of profound significance. Historian David Noble is now studying two kinds of automated machine tool systems that have different implications for the relative power of management and labor in the industries that might employ them. He is able to show that, although the basic electronic and mechanical components of the record/playback and numerical control systems are similar, the choice of one design over another has crucial consequences for social struggles on the shop floor. To see the matter solely in terms of cost-cutting, efficiency, or the modernization of equipment is to miss a decisive element in the story.[17]

From such examples I would offer the following general conclusions. The things we call "technologies" are ways of building order in our world. Many technical devices and systems important in everyday life contain possibilities for many different ways of ordering human activity. Consciously or not, deliberately or inadvertently, societies choose structures for technologies that influence how people are going to work, communicate, travel, consume, and so forth over a very long time. In the processes by which structuring decisions are made, different people are differently situated and possess unequal degrees of power as well as unequal levels of awareness. By far the greatest latitude of choice exists the very first time a particular instrument, system, or technique is introduced. Because choices tend to become strongly fixed in material equipment, economic investment, and social habit, the original flexibility vanishes for all practical purposes once the initial commitments are made. In that sense technological innovations are similar to legislative acts or political foundings that establish a framework for public order that will endure over many generations. For that reason, the same careful attention one would give to the rules, roles, and relationships of politics must also be given to such things as the building of highways, the creation of television networks, and the tailoring of seemingly insignificant features on new machines. The issues that divide or unite people in society are settled not only in the institutions and practices of politics proper, but also, and less obviously, in tangible arrangements of steel and concrete, wires and transistors, nuts and bolts.

Inherently Political Technologies

None of the arguments and examples considered thus far address a stronger, more troubling claim often made in writings about technology and society—the belief that some technologies are by their very nature political in a specific way. According to this view, the adoption of a given technical system unavoidably brings with it conditions for human relationships that have a distinctive political cast—for example, centralized or decentralized, egalitarian or inegalitarian, repressive or liberating. This is ultimately what is at stake in assertions like those of Lewis Mumford that two traditions of technology, one authoritarian, the other democratic, exist side by side in Western history. In all the cases I cited above the technologies are relatively flexible in design and arrangement, and variable in their effects. Although one can recognize a particular result produced in a particular setting, one can also easily imagine how a roughly similar device or system might have been built or situated with very much different political consequences. The idea we must now examine and evaluate is that certain kinds of technology do not allow such flexibility, and that to choose them is to choose a particular form of political life.

A remarkably forceful statement of one version of this argument appears in Friedrich Engels's little essay "On Authority" written in 1872. Answering anarchists who believed that authority is an evil that ought to be abolished altogether, Engels launches into a panegyric for authoritarianism, maintaining, among other things, that strong authority is a necessary condition in modern industry. To advance his case in the strongest possible way, he asks his readers to imagine that the revolution has already occurred. "Supposing a social revolution dethroned the capitalists, who now exercise their authority over the production and circulation of wealth. Supposing, to adopt entirely the point of view of the anti-authoritarians, that the land and the instruments of labour had become the collective property of the workers who use them. Will authority have disappeared or will it have only changed its form?"[18]

His answer draws upon lessons from three sociotechnical systems of his day, cotton-spinning mills, railways, and ships at sea. He observes that, on its way to becoming finished thread, cotton moves through a number of different operations at different locations in the factory. The workers perform a wide variety of tasks, from running the steam engine to carrying the products from one room to another. Because these tasks must be coordinated, and because the timing of the work is "fixed by the authority of the steam," laborers must learn to accept a rigid discipline. They must, according to Engels, work at regular hours and agree to subordinate their individual wills to the persons in charge of factory operations. If they fail to do so, they risk the horrifying possibility that production will come to a grinding halt. Engels pulls no punches. "The automatic machinery of a big factory," he writes, "is much more despotic than the small capitalists who employ workers ever have been."[19]

Similar lessons are adduced in Engels's analysis of the necessary operating conditions for railways and ships at sea. Both require the subordination of workers to an "imperious authority" that sees to it that things run according to plan. Engels finds that, far from being an idiosyncracy of capitalist social organization, relationships of authority and subordination arise "independently of all social organization, [and] are imposed upon us together with the material conditions under which we produce and make products circulate." Again, he intends this to be stern advice to the anarchists who, according to Engels, thought it possible simply to eradicate subordination and superordination at a single stroke. All such schemes are nonsense. The roots of unavoidable authoritarianism are, he argues, deeply implanted in the human involvement with science and technology. "If man, by dint of his knowledge and inventive genius, has subdued the forces of nature, the latter avenge themselves upon him by subjecting him, insofar as he employs them, to a veritable despotism independent of all social organization."[20]

Attempts to justify strong authority on the basis of supposedly necessary conditions of technical practice have an ancient history. A pivotal theme in the *Republic* is Plato's quest to borrow the authority of *technē* and employ it by analogy to buttress his argument in favor of authority in the state. Among the illustrations he chooses, like Engels, is that of a ship on the high seas. Because large sailing vessels by their very nature need to be steered with a firm hand, sailors must yield to their captain's commands; no reasonable person believes that ships can be run democratically. Plato goes on to suggest that governing a state is rather like being captain of a ship or like practicing medicine as a physician. Much the same conditions that require central rule and decisive action in organized technical activity also create this need in government.

In Engels's argument, and arguments like it, the justification for authority is no longer made by Plato's classic analogy, but rather directly with reference to technology itself. If the basic case is as compelling as Engels believed it to be, one would expect that, as a society adopted increasingly complicated technical systems as its material basis, the prospects for authoritarian ways of life would be greatly enhanced. Central control by knowledgeable people acting at the top of a rigid social hierarchy would seem increasingly prudent. In this respect, his stand in "On Authority" appears to be at variance with Karl Marx's position in Volume One of *Capital*. Marx tries to show that increasing mechanization will render obsolete the hierarchical division of labor and the relationships of subordination that, in his view, were necessary during the early stages of modern manufacturing. The "Modern Industry," he writes, " . . . sweeps away by technical means the manufacturing division of labor, under which each man is bound hand and foot for life to a single detail operation. At the same time, the capitalistic form of that industry reproduces this same division of labour in a still more monstrous shape; in the factory proper, by converting the workman into a living appendage of the machine. . . ."[21] In Marx's view, the conditions

that will eventually dissolve the capitalist division of labor and facilitate prole-
tarian revolution are conditions latent in industrial technology itself. The differences between Marx's position in *Capital* and Engels's in his essay raise an
important question for socialism: What, after all, does modern technology make
possible or necessary in political life? The theoretical tension we see here mirrors many troubles in the practice of freedom and authority that have muddied
the tracks of socialist revolution.

Arguments to the effect that technologies are in some sense inherently political have been advanced in a wide variety of contexts, far too many to summarize
here. In my reading of such notions, however, there are two basic ways of
stating the case. One version claims that the adoption of a given technical system actually *requires* the creation and maintenance of a particular set of social
conditions as the operating environment of that system. Engels's position is of
this kind. A similar view is offered by a contemporary writer who holds that "if
you accept nuclear power plants, you also accept a techno-scientific-industrial-
military elite. Without these people in charge, you could not have nuclear
power."[29] In this conception, some kinds of technology require their social environments to be structured in a particular way in much the same sense that
an automobile requires wheels in order to run. The thing could not exist as an
effective operating entity unless certain social as well as material conditions
were met. The meaning of "required" here is that of practical (rather than logical) necessity. Thus, Plato thought it a practical necessity that a ship at sea have
one captain and an unquestioningly obedient crew.

A second, somewhat weaker, version of the argument holds that a given
kind of technology is strongly *compatible with*, but does not strictly require,
social and political relationships of a particular stripe. Many advocates of solar
energy now hold that technologies of that variety are more compatible with a
democratic, egalitarian society than energy systems based on coal, oil, and nuclear power; at the same time they do not maintain that anything about solar
energy requires democracy. Their case is, briefly, that solar energy is decentral-
izing in both a technical and political sense: technically speaking, it is vastly
more reasonable to build solar systems in a disaggregated, widely distributed
manner than in large-scale centralized plants; politically speaking, solar energy
accommodates the attempts of individuals and local communities to manage
their affairs effectively because they are dealing with systems that are more
accessible, comprehensible, and controllable than huge centralized sources. In
this view, solar energy is desirable not only for its economic and environmental
benefits, but also for the salutary institutions it is likely to permit in other areas
of public life.[23]

Within both versions of the argument there is a further distinction to be
made between conditions that are *internal* to the workings of a given technical
system and those that are *external* to it. Engels's thesis concerns internal social
relations said to be required within cotton factories and railways, for example;
what such relationships mean for the condition of society at large is for him a
separate question. In contrast, the solar advocate's belief that solar technologies
are compatible with democracy pertains to the way they complement aspects of
society removed from the organization of those technologies as such.

There are, then, several different directions that arguments of this kind can
follow. Are the social conditions predicated said to be required by, or strongly

compatible with, the workings of a given technical system? Are those conditions internal to that system or external to it (or both)? Although writings that address such questions are often unclear about what is being asserted, arguments in this general category do have an important presence in modern political discourse. They enter into many attempts to explain how changes in social life take place in the wake of technological innovation. More importantly, they are often used to buttress attempts to justify or criticize proposed courses of action involving new technology. By offering distinctly political reasons for or against the adoption of a particular technology, arguments of this kind stand apart from more commonly employed, more easily quantifiable claims about economic costs and benefits, environmental impacts, and possible risks to public health and safety that technical systems may involve. The issue here does not concern how many jobs will be created, how much income generated, how many pollutants added, or how many cancers produced. Rather, the issue has to do with ways in which choices about technology have important consequences for the form and quality of human associations.

If we examine social patterns that comprise the environments of technical systems, we find certain devices and systems almost invariably linked to specific ways of organizing power and authority. The important question is: Does this state of affairs derive from an unavoidable social response to intractable properties in the things themselves, or is it instead a pattern imposed independently by a governing body, ruling class, or some other social or cultural institution to further its own purposes?

Taking the most obvious example, the atom bomb is an inherently political artifact. As long as it exists at all, its lethal properties demand that it be controlled by a centralized, rigidly hierarchical chain of command closed to all influences that might make its workings unpredictable. The internal social system of the bomb must be authoritarian; there is no other way. The state of affairs stands as a practical necessity independent of any larger political system in which the bomb is embedded, independent of the kind of regime or character of its rulers. Indeed, democratic states must try to find ways to ensure that the social structures and mentality that characterize the management of nuclear weapons do not "spin off" or "spill over" into the polity as a whole.

The bomb is, of course, a special case. The reasons very rigid relationships of authority are necessary in its immediate presence should be clear to anyone. If, however, we look for other instances in which particular varieties of technology are *widely perceived* to need the maintenance of a special pattern of power and authority, modern technical history contains a wealth of examples.

Alfred D. Chandler in *The Visible Hand*, a monumental study of modern business enterprise, presents impressive documentation to defend the hypothesis that the construction and day-to-day operation of many systems of production, transportation, and communication in the nineteenth and twentieth centuries require the development of a particular social form—a large-scale centralized, hierarchical organization administered by highly skilled managers. Typical of Chandler's reasoning is his analysis of the growth of the railroads.

Technology made possible fast, all-weather transportation; but safe, regular, reliable movement of goods and passengers, as well as the continuing maintenance and repair of locomotives, rolling stock, and track, roadbed, stations, roundhouses, and other equipment, required the creation of a sizable administrative organization. It meant the employment of a set of managers to supervise these functional activities over an extensive geographical area; and the appointment of an administrative command of middle and top executives to monitor, evaluate, and coordinate the work of managers responsible for the day-to-day operations.

Throughout his book Chandler points to ways in which technologies used in the production and distribution of electricity, chemicals, and a wide range of industrial goods "demanded" or "required" this form of human association. "Hence, the operational requirements of railroads demanded the creation of the first administrative hierarchies in American business."[25]

Were there other conceivable ways of organizing these aggregates of people and apparatus? Chandler shows that a previously dominant social form, the small traditional family firm, simply could not handle the task in most cases. Although he does not speculate further, it is clear that he believes there is, to be realistic, very little latitude in the forms of power and authority appropriate within modern sociotechnical systems. The properties of many modern technologies—oil pipelines and refineries, for example—are such that over-whelmingly impressive economies of scale and speed are possible. If such systems are to work effectively, efficiently, quickly, and safely, certain requirements of internal social organization have to be fulfilled; the material possibilities that modern technologies make available could not be exploited otherwise. Chandler acknowledges that as one compares sociotechnical institutions of different nations, one sees "ways in which cultural attitudes, values, ideologies, political systems, and social structure affect these imperatives."[26] But the weight of argument and empirical evidence in *The Visible Hand* suggests that any significant departure from the basic pattern would be, at best, highly unlikely.

It may be that other conceivable arrangements of power and authority, for example, those of decentralized, democratic worker self-management, could prove capable of administering factories, refineries, communications systems, and railroads as well as or better than the organizations Chandler describes. Evidence from automobile assembly teams in Sweden and worker-managed plants in Yugoslavia and other countries is often presented to salvage these possibilities. I shall not be able to settle controversies over this matter here, but merely point to what I consider to be their bone of contention. The available evidence tends to show that many large, sophisticated technological systems are in fact highly compatible with centralized, hierarchical managerial control. The interesting question, however, has to do with whether or not this pattern is in any sense a requirement of such systems, a question that is not solely an empirical one. The matter ultimately rests on our judgments about what steps, if any, are practically necessary in the workings of particular kinds of technology and what, if anything, such measures require of the structure of human associations. Was Plato right in saying that a ship at sea needs steering by a decisive hand and that this could only be accomplished by a single captain and an obedient crew? Is Chandler correct in saying that the properties of large-scale systems require centralized, hierarchical managerial control?

To answer such questions, we would have to examine in some detail the moral claims of practical necessity (including those advocated in the doctrines of economics) and weigh them against moral claims of other sorts, for example, the notion that it is good for sailors to participate in the command of a ship or that workers have a right to be involved in making and administering decisions in a factory. It is characteristic of societies based on large, complex technological systems, however, that moral reasons other than those of practical necessity appear increasingly obsolete, "idealistic," and irrelevant. Whatever claims one may wish to make on behalf of liberty, justice, or equality can be immediately neutralized when confronted with arguments to the effect: "Fine, but that's no way to run a railroad" (or steel mill, or airline, or communications system, and so on). Here we encounter an important quality in modern political discourse and in the way people commonly think about what measures are justified in response to the possibilities technologies make available. In many instances, to say that some technologies are inherently political is to say that certain widely accepted reasons of practical necessity—especially the need to maintain crucial technological systems as smoothly working entities—have tended to eclipse other sorts of moral and political reasoning.

One attempt to salvage the autonomy of politics from the bind of practical necessity involves the notion that conditions of human association found in the internal workings of technological systems can easily be kept separate from the polity as a whole. Americans have long rested content in the belief that arrangements of power and authority inside industrial corporations, public utilities, and the like have little bearing on public institutions, practices, and ideas at large. That "democracy stops at the factory gates" was taken as a fact of life that had nothing to do with the practice of political freedom. But can the internal politics of technology and the politics of the whole community be so easily separated? A recent study of American business leaders, contemporary exemplars of Chandler's "visible hand of management," found them remarkably impatient with such democratic scruples as "one man, one vote." If democracy doesn't work for the firm, the most critical institution in all of society, American executives ask, how well can it be expected to work for the government of a nation—particularly when that government attempts to interfere with the achievements of the firm? The authors of the report observe that patterns of authority that work effectively in the corporation become for businessmen "the desirable model against which to compare political and economic relationships in the rest of society."[27] While such findings are far from conclusive, they do reflect a sentiment increasingly common in the land: what dilemmas like the energy crisis require is not a redistribution of wealth or broader public participation but, rather, stronger, centralized public management—President Carter's proposal for an Energy Mobilization Board and the like.

An especially vivid case in which the operational requirements of a technical system might influence the quality of public life is now at issue in debates about the risks of nuclear power. As the supply of uranium for nuclear reactors runs out, a proposed alternative fuel is the plutonium generated as a by-product in reactor cores. Well-known objections to plutonium recycling focus on its unacceptable economic costs, its risks of environmental contamination, and its dangers in regard to the international proliferation of nuclear weapons. Beyond these concerns, however, stands another less widely appreciated set of hazards—those that involve the sacrifice of civil liberties. The widespread use of plutonium as a fuel increases the chance that this toxic substance might be stolen by terrorists, organized crime, or other persons. This raises the prospect, and not a trivial one, that extraordinary measures would have to be taken to safeguard plutonium from theft and to recover it if ever the substance were stolen. Workers in the nuclear industry as well as ordinary citizens outside could well become subject to background security checks, covert surveillance, wiretapping, informers, and even emergency measures under martial law—all justified by the need to safeguard plutonium.

Russell W. Ayres's study of the legal ramifications of plutonium recycling concludes: "With the passage of time and the increase in the quantity of plutonium in existence will come pressure to eliminate the traditional checks the courts and legislatures place on the activities of the executive and to develop a powerful central authority better able to enforce strict safeguards." He avers that "once a quantity of plutonium had been stolen, the case for literally turning the country upside down to get it back would be overwhelming."[31] Ayres anticipates and worries about the kinds of thinking that, I have argued, characterize inherently political technologies. It is still true that, in a world in which human beings make and maintain artificial systems, nothing is "required" in an absolute sense. Nevertheless, once a course of action is underway, once artifacts like nuclear power plants have been built and put in operation, the kinds of reasoning that justify the adaptation of social life to technical requirements pop up as spontaneously as flowers in the spring. In Ayres's words, "Once recycling begins and the risks of plutonium theft become real rather than hypothetical, the case for governmental infringement of protected rights will seem compelling."[28] After a certain point, those who cannot accept the hard requirements and imperatives will be dismissed as dreamers and fools.

*   *   *

The two varieties of interpretation I have outlined indicate how artifacts can have political qualities. In the first instance we noticed ways in which specific features in the design or arrangement of a device or system could provide a convenient means of establishing patterns of power and authority in a given setting. Technologies of this kind have a range of flexibility in the dimensions of their material form. It is precisely because they are flexible that their consequences for society must be understood with reference to the social actors able to influence which designs and arrangements are chosen. In the second instance we examined ways in which the intractable properties of certain kinds of technology are strongly, perhaps unavoidably, linked to particular institutionalized patterns of power and authority. Here, the initial choice about whether or not to adopt something is decisive in regard to its consequences. There are no alternative physical designs or arrangements that would make a significant difference; there are, furthermore, no genuine possibilities for creative intervention by different social systems—capitalist or socialist—that could change the intractability of the entity or significantly alter the quality of its political effects.

To know which variety of interpretation is applicable in a given case is often what is at stake in disputes, some of them passionate ones, about the meaning of technology for how we live. I have argued a "both/and" position here, for it seems to me that both kinds of understanding are applicable in different circumstances. Indeed, it can happen that within a particular complex of technology—a system of communication or transportation, for example—some aspects may be flexible in their possibilities for society, while other aspects may be (for better or worse) completely intractable. The two varieties of interpretation I have examined here can overlap and intersect at many points.

These are, of course, issues on which people can disagree. Thus, some proponents of energy from renewable resources now believe they have at last discovered a set of intrinsically democratic, egalitarian, communitarian technologies. In my best estimation, however, the social consequences of building renewable energy systems will surely depend on the specific configurations of both hardware and the social institutions created to bring that energy to us. It may be that we will find ways to turn this silk purse into a sow's ear. By comparison, advocates of the further development of nuclear power seem to believe that they are working on a rather flexible technology whose adverse social effects can be fixed by changing the design parameters of reactors and nuclear waste disposal systems. For reasons indicated above, I believe them to be dead wrong in that faith. Yes, we may be able to manage some of the "risks" to public health and safety that nuclear power brings. But as society adapts to the more dangerous and apparently indelible features of nuclear power, what will be the long-range toll in human freedom?

My belief that we ought to attend more closely to technical objects themselves is not to say that we can ignore the contexts in which those objects are situated. A ship at sea may well require, as Plato and Engels insisted, a single captain and obedient crew. But a ship out of service, parked at the dock, needs only a caretaker. To understand which technologies and which contexts are important to us, and why, is an enterprise that must involve both the study of specific technical systems and their history as well as a thorough grasp of the concepts and controversies of political theory. In our times people are often willing to make drastic changes in the way they live to accord with technological innovation at the same time they would resist similar kinds of changes justified on political grounds. If for no other reason than that, it is important for us to achieve a clearer view of these matters than has been our habit so far.

REFERENCES
[1] I would like to thank Merritt Roe Smith, Leo Marx, James Miller, David Noble, Charles Weiner, Sherry Turkle, Loren Graham, Gail Stuart, Dick Sclove, and Stephen Graubard for their comments and criticisms on earlier drafts of this essay. My thanks also to Doris Morrison of the Agriculture Library of the University of California, Berkeley, for her bibliographical help.
[2] Lewis Mumford, "Authoritarian and Democratic Technics," *Technology and Culture*, 5 (1964): 1-8.
[3] Denis Hayes, *Rays of Hope: The Transition to a Post-Petroleum World* (New York: W. W. Norton, 1977), pp. 71, 159.
[4] David Lilienthal, *T.V.A.: Democracy on the March* (New York: Harper and Brothers, 1944), pp. 72-83.
[5] Daniel J. Boorstin, *The Republic of Technology* (New York: Harper & Row, 1978), p. 7.
[6] Langdon Winner, *Autonomous Technology: Technics-out-of-Control as a Theme in Political Thought* (Cambridge, Mass.: M.I.T. Press, 1977).
[7] The meaning of "technology" I employ in this essay does not encompass some of the broader definitions of that concept found in contemporary literature, for example, the notion of "technique"

in the writings of Jacques Ellul. My purposes here are more limited. For a discussion of the difficulties that arise in attempts to define "technology," see Ref. 6, pp. 8-12.

[8]Robert A. Caro, *The Power Broker: Robert Moses and the Fall of New York* (New York: Random House, 1974), pp. 318, 481, 514, 546, 951-958.

[9]*Ibid.*, p. 952.

[10]Robert Ozanne, *A Century of Labor-Management Relations at McCormick and International Harvester* (Madison, Wis.: University of Wisconsin Press, 1967), p. 20.

[11]The early history of the tomato harvester is told in Wayne D. Rasmussen, "Advances in American Agriculture: The Mechanical Tomato Harvester as a Case Study," *Technology and Culture*, 9 (1968): 531-543.

[12]Andrew Schmitz and David Seckler, "Mechanized Agriculture and Social Welfare: The Case of the Tomato Harvester," *American Journal of Agricultural Economics*, 52 (1970): 569-577.

[13]William H. Friedland and Amy Barton, "Tomato Technology," *Society*, 13:6 (September/October 1976). See also William H. Friedland, *Social Sleepwalkers: Scientific and Technological Research in California Agriculture*, University of California, Davis, Department of Applied Behavioral Sciences, Research Monograph No. 13, 1974.

[14]*University of California Clip Sheet*, 54:36, May 1, 1979.

[15]Friedland and Barton, "Tomato Technology."

[16]A history and critical analysis of agricultural research in the land-grant colleges is given in James Hightower, *Hard Tomatoes, Hard Times* (Cambridge, Mass.: Schenkman, 1978).

[17]David Noble, "Social Choice in Machine Design: The Case of Automatically Controlled Machine Tools," in *Case Studies in the Labor Process* (New York: Monthly Review Press, forthcoming).

[18]Friedrich Engels, "On Authority" in *The Marx-Engels Reader*, 2nd ed., Robert Tucker (ed.) (New York: W. W. Norton, 1978), p. 731.

[19]*Ibid.*

[20]*Ibid.*, pp. 732, 731.

[21]Karl Marx, *Capital*, vol. 1, 3rd ed., Samuel Moore and Edward Aveling (trans.) (New York: The Modern Library, 1906), p. 530.

[22]Jerry Mander, *Four Arguments for the Elimination of Television* (New York: William Morrow, 1978), p. 44.

[23]See, for example, Robert Argue, Barbara Emanuel, and Stephen Graham, *The Sun Builders: A People's Guide to Solar, Wind and Wood Energy in Canada* (Toronto: Renewable Energy in Canada, 1978). "We think decentralization is an implicit component of renewable energy; this implies the decentralization of energy systems, communities and of power. Renewable energy doesn't require mammoth generation sources of disruptive transmission corridors. Our cities and towns, which have been dependent on centralized energy supplies, may be able to achieve some degree of autonomy, thereby controlling and administering their own energy needs" (p. 16).

[24]Alfred D. Chandler, Jr., *The Visible Hand: The Managerial Revolution in American Business* (Cambridge, Mass.: Belknap, Harvard University Press, 1977), p. 244.

[25]*Ibid.*

[26]*Ibid.*, p. 500.

[27]Leonard Silk and David Vogel, *Ethics and Profits: The Crisis of Confidence in American Business* (New York: Simon and Schuster, 1976), p. 191.

[28]Russel W. Ayres, "Policing Plutonium: The Civil Liberties Fallout," *Harvard Civil Rights-Civil Liberties Law Review*, 10 (1975):443, 413-4, 374.

[19]

Towards ethical principles for designing politico-administrative information systems

M.J. van den Hoven

Department of Philosophy, Erasmus University Rotterdam, P.O. Box 1738, 3000 DR Rotterdam, The Netherlands. Phone: + 31 10 408 1157; fax +31 10 212 0448; email: hoven@filint.fwb.eur.nl

Abstract. Moral and political philosophers have thusfar shown remarkable little interest in the moral questions concerning socio-technological design, especially when compared to their efforts dedicated to socio-economic design. This general observation can be seen to apply to information technology (1) Langdon Winner has argued that we must repair this blind spot in contemporary normative theory and that we need to reflect upon ways of designing machines and systems which are responsive to our moral and political ideals, an activity referred to by him as 'political ergonomics'. Taking Winner's plea as a vantage point, I draw attention to some of the conceptual difficulties for a 'political ergonomics' of information systems in the public sector (2). One of the main difficulties is that information technology transforms our life-world and calls for the reconstruction of some of our central moral concepts, since the application of old concepts to new situations can be misleading and confusing (3). I suggest ways of reconceptualizing traditional conceptions of autonomy (4.1) and responsibility (4.2), privacy (4.3) and justice (4.4) in order to prevent them from misfiring in their application and to be able to specify mid-level principles for the design of public information infra-structures.

1. Introduction

Political and moral philosophers of the recent past have devoted much of their attention to the justification of ethical principles for the design of *socio-economic institutions*. A whole generation of political and moral philosophers indulged in thinking about a just and fair distribution of wealth and well-fare[1]. Health-care systems, educational programs, tax laws, population policies, development aid plans, social security benefits schemes have been extensively studied and new principles of fair distribution and just allocation of goods have been proposed and defended. However, normative theorists involved in this enterprise have focussed on the design of socio-economic institutions at the expense of giving attention to questions concerning design in *technology*. An overwhelming majority of them simply seem to have missed the point that by designing artifacts technology is an equally powerful force in shaping human possibilities or determining human destiny[2]. This seems

---

[1] John Rawls' epochal *A Theory of Justice* (1972) has contributed much to focus the attention of scholars in the field on this type of questions.

[2] See for strong arguments and illuminating examples to the effect that technical devices and

to have escaped their notice in the general form in which I have just stated it, but is has also escaped their attention that technology has become a paramount feature of the *objects* of their studies in healthcare, education, science, government, and politics and that in the case of information technology, the technology has even become part and parcel of the tools which society uses to regulate and steer itself and its component parts.

To make up for this peculiar blind spot in modern moral philosophy and political theory, Langdon Winner has recently called for the establishment of a new discipline, which he called "political ergonomics"[3]. The general aim of political ergonomics, as defined by Winner, is to develop ideas which facilitate the specification of 'a suitable fit between a good society and its instruments'[4]. Political ergonomists should help us 'to answer the question of how to design machines and systems which are responsive to our moral ideals'.

I think Winner is correct in calling attention to the moral and political issues of *socio-technological* design for two reasons. First, moral philosophy and political theory run the risk of becoming increasingly irrelevant by their aloofness, since technological change is a potent element in changing the conditions of social and political life. Secondly, if we would prove to be unable to specify which socio-technical arrangements are desirable or undesirable and why, we jeopardize our moral autonomy, and forego a precious opportunity to shape communal life.

2. Difficulties for a political ergonomics of information technology

The specification of 'a suitable fit between a good society and its instruments', and the articulation of 'principles for the design of systems which are responsive to our moral ideals' however, is not an easy task. Do we know what a good society is, and what our moral ideals amount to? And if we do, how can we squeeze practicable principles out of them? As Winner himself observed in a more recent article "As it ponders important social choices that involve the application of new technology, contemporary moral philosophy works within a vacuum"[5]. We do have some highly cherished words, some well-entrenched and catchy phrases like 'autonomy' and 'self-determination', 'liberty', 'justice as fairness', 'privacy' and 'the right to be let alone', 'responsibility'. But what do they mean to us now that the world has seen such great changes?

systems may impose important constraints on human activity, Langdon Winner's "Do Artifacts have Politics?", *The Whale and the Reactor. A Search for Limits in an Age of High Technology.* Chicago/London: University of Chicago Press, 1986. I agree with Winner that the idea of Technological Determinism is a much too strong claim. It tends to obscure the real and myriad decisons that are taken in the course of technical and social transformations. See for discussions about Technological Determinism *Does Technology Drive History? The Dilemma of Technological Determinism,* Merritt Roe Smith and Leo Marx (eds.). Cambridge, Mass.: The MIT Press, 1994.

[3]See L. Winner, "Political Ergonomics: Technological Design and the Quality of Public Life", Publication of the Wissenschaftszentrum Berlin für Sozialforschung, 1987, IIUG dp 87–87.

[4]*Op. cit.,* p. 20.

[5]See his "Citizen Virtues in a Technological Order", *Inquiry,* vol. 35, nos 3–4, 1992. Reprinted in E.R. Winkler and R.R. Coombs (eds.), *Applied Ethics.* Oxford: Basil Blackwell, 1993, 46–69.

The task sketched by Winner is no less difficult with respect to information technology than with respect to other technologies, perhaps more difficult[6]. The following conceptual problems must somehow be addressed. Like with other modern technologies thinking about information technology requires the twisting and overstretching of old concepts which usually results in moral perplexity and bewilderment. "Data-theft", "informational privacy", "virtual reality", "digital computer", "software engineering" are newcomers to the scene, and we have to find ways to accommodate them. We even may have to get to the level of ontological analysis, to figure out whether we are talking about things, facts, events, processes, or what other basic ontological categories you may wish to distinguish.

There is another peculiar feature of information technology which prompts conceptual disquiet[7]. Information technology is used to simulate, duplicate, and to take over many of the things that used to be done by human beings. In the introduction phase of the technology we often only wondered whether these cabinets with tubes and wires could really engage in reliable calculation, but now their functional equivalents are ubiquitous, cheap and the size of a cigar box, we realize that the digital computer is probably as close as we can get to a universal tool. And it is in this phase of the development, the permeation stage, that a different type of questions imposes itself upon us, questions about matters which are *central* to our existence. Now we have machines that calculate, we begin to wonder what the nature of calculation is. If *they* can do it, does that mean that *we* do it the same way they do it? Now we have machines that can draw conclusions from heaps of data, we begin to wonder what the nature of reasoning is, and ask ourselves whether we arrive at conclusions in the same way the computer does. Now we no longer need to interact face to face to communicate, we begin to wonder what the essence of communication is. Now the real thing is no longer required to give us the impression of it, because we are presented with its 'virtual counterpart', we may sometimes be at a loss about what is reality, what truth.

Another major obstacle to an easy resolution of our practical problems in the field of information technology is the fact that the knowledge that is involved is not only central to our existence, but is also *fundamental* (as it is in the case of biotechnology, nuclear technology), in a way the knowledge involved in steam technology and clockwork mechanics is not. Science at present has reached such a level of understanding of the universe that its application in the form of technology is bound to have upsetting consequences. We are enthusiastically tampering with the basic structures of life, and optimistically simulating consciousness and redesigning intelligence. Our technologies thus impinge on some of our most fundamental concepts[8].

Furthermore, we have to think about the impact of technology on ways of living,

---

[6]See for bibliographical references concerning ethics in the field of information technology: Terryl Ward Bynum, "A Computer Ethics Bibliography", *Metaphilosophy*, vol. 16, no. 4, 1985, 350–353; Joseph Behar, "Critique of Computer Ethics", *Journal of Information Ethics*, vol. 2, no. 2, 1993, 27–43. See also my "Computer Ethics: information technology, moral puzzlement and public policy". *Informatization and the Public Sector* vol. 2, no. 3, 1992, 259–265.

[7]See for this observation J. Moor, "What is Computer Ethics?", *Metaphilosophy*, Issue on Computers and Ethics vol. 16, no. 4 (1985), 266–275.

[8]For this reason High Technology can be said to exert a pressure to reflect. See R.C. Schank and

thinking and experiencing, whereas we can not be sure that the conditions under which we do so are not already tainted by the very developments the effects of which we want to reflect upon. We have to repair our vessel at sea.

Finally, we may even have to reconsider our major moral and political concepts and traditions[9]. It has been argued for example that technological and organizational complexity[10] require a new conception of responsibility, which may have repercussions for traditional legal doctrines of accountability and liability[11]. It has been argued that conceptions of democracy should be under constant review due to information technological innovations[12]. Individual autonomy seems to be the odd one out in a world of growing epistemic and economic interdependencies[13] and our views about privacy are at stake with the introduction of every new information technological gadget[14]. The idea of fair distribution of primary goods also comes up for reconstruction in an information society, as will be argued below[15].

3. Reconstruction

We may thus have to reconstruct our basic moral and political concepts to adapt them to the new technological practices. Conceptions of moral and political ideas are not unchanging verities but 'tools' for refining the material of experience and for solving problems. And like tools these conceptions can get worn out. Reconcep-

---

P. Childers, *The Cognitive Computer. On Language, Learning and Artificial Intelligence.* Wokingham, 1984, p. 216: "If, as Socrates maintained the unexamined life is not worth living, AI has made an important contribution to many people's lives. (...) They begin to analyze their thoughts and to examine their use of language in novel ways".

[9]See for a general discussion of this theme Q. Skinner's "Language and Political Change". In: Ball, Farr and Hanson (eds.), *Political Innovation and Conceptual Change*, Cambridge University Press, 1989. As a preface to Al Gore's "Infra-structure for the Global Village", a *Scientific American*'s editor puts it as follows: "The new technologies also redefine time and place in a manner that can confound the traditional legal concepts of property, ownership, originality, privacy and intellectual freedom. Government must address such issues, and it must also build a framework of policy that enables the economic and intellectual opportunities of the emerging technologies to be realized". *Scientific American* September 1991, p. 108.

[10]As Klaus Lenk has argued we have just begun to scratch the surface of this type of complexity. See "Conceptual Foundations of Information System Design in Public Administration". *Information Systems' Architecture and Technology*, ISAT 1992, M. Bazewicz (ed.). Wroclaw: Politechnika Wroclawska, 1992, 149–159.

[11]See John Ladd, 'Computers and Moral Responsibility: A Framework for an Ethical Analysis'. In: C. Gould, *The Information Web: Ethical and Social Implications of Computer Networking*. San Francisco: Westview Press, 1988.

[12]See for an overview of the literature Van de Donk and P.W. Tops, "Informatization and Democracy: Orwell or Athens?" In: *Informatization and the Public Sector* 2 (1992) 169–196.

[13]See John Hardwig, "Epistemic Dependence", *Journal of Philosophy* 82 (1985) p. 335–349.

[14]See C. Bennett, *Regulating Privacy*. Ithaca/London: Cornell University Press, 1992. Bennett observes that "This new technological context highlights the importance of continual updating, review, and amendment" (p. 246), and that it "continues to shape the agenda" concerning privacy issues, p. 247.

[15]See for a suggestion to this point, Danilo Zolo, *Democracy and Complexity*, Polity Press 1992.

tualizing them may be the only way to prevent them from misfiring in their application[16]. Conceptual change therefore is itself a species of political innovation[17]. The need for an ongoing process of conceptual adaptation and reconstruction was already articulated by the members of the Significs Movement and John Dewey[18]. Central to it is the idea that the world sometimes outpaces our conceptualisation of it, with potential for untoward outcomes and disastrous results.

A frivoulous example can make this clear. We know or we think we know that our classical red Bordeaux wines have to be served at 'room temperature'. We are wrong and right at the same time. The expression 'room temperature' stems from the time that apartments were not centrally heated and were on average colder than our modern houses. Applying the advice 'serve your Premier Cru Bordeaux wine at room temperature' to your beautiful Mouton-Rothschild 1976, will not optimalize your hedonistic calculus. If we want to get it right from an oenological point of view we should keep to the rule "serve your Classical Bordeaux wines at room temperature *anno 1890*; do not serve them at room temperature *anno 1990*". The concept of 'room temperature' in the context of wine tasting should be revised and adapted to a world that has seen technical progress. The same holds for our notions of autonomy (section 4.1), responsibility (section 4.2), privacy (section 4.3) and justice (section 4.4), as I will sketch out below.

4. Reconstruction of concepts and specification of principles

Taking Winner's manifesto for 'political ergonomics' as a new vantage point, I will suggest a) ways in which traditional conceptions have to be updated in order to be of service in solving some of the policy problems in the field of information technology, and b) mid-level moral principles that can provide guidance in the attempt to live up to our otherwise under-specified and non-descript moral ideals of autonomy, responsibility, privacy, and social justice in designing politico-administrative information systems. Furthermore I hope that the presented arguments illustrate the general claim that providing answers to questions concerning desirable socio-technological forms involves much more fundamental philosophical reflection on the core technology and its impacts on human lives than has been allowed for until now by the philosophical minimalism of political liberalism.

---

[16]The conceptual clarification should be especially sensitive, according to O. Höffe, to the fact that normative assessments rely on conceptualizations which predate the phenomena and experiences of a high tech society: "Während sich die Lebensverhältnisse grundlegend verändert haben, stammen die Begriffe und Prinzipien Ihrer sittlichen Beurteilung, stammen die Maßstäbe der Humanität und Gerechtigkeit immer noch aus der alteuropäische Gesellschaft". O. Hoffe, *Sittlich-politische Diskurse*, Frankfurt: Suhrkamp, 1981. See p. 14.

[17]Ball, Farr and Hanson (eds.), *Political Innovation and Conceptual Change*, Cambridge University Press, 1989, p. 2.

[18]See for Dewey, J. Campbell, "John Dewey's Method of Social Reconstruction". In: *The Community Reconstructs*. Urbana and Chicago: University of Illinois Press, 1992.

4.1. Autonomy[19]

The first major issue I would like to address concerns individual autonomy in an information society. Knowledge-based systems are replacing, supporting human activity in many areas. What are the moral repercussions for the less qualified and less knowledgeable people working with these systems? What is cognitive or epistemic autonomy in the light of a technology which makes disembodied expert knowledge widely available to people who are less experienced and less knowledgeable than the human experts that were consulted during the design and construction of the system? What does the Kantian injunction 'think for your self' mean in a world of endemic epistemic man-computer dependence? To what extent is it still admitted that our understanding should be our own, as John Stuart Mill put it[20]? Information technology seems to be the technology *par excellance* that invites us to what Kant has called 'selbstverschuldete Unmündigkeit', and forces conformity to a pre-ordained intelligence.

I will provide the outline of an analysis which strongly suggests that the user of information systems may not always be able to do what is required of him as a fully responsible human being by the traditional standards of cognitive autonomy. It seems that we must either arrange things in such a way as to prevent this type of situation from arising, or we must tune down our moral demands and grant that a changed world calls for different, and perhaps less stringent, norms of responsibility. The following analysis indicates that there may be a way of getting around this dilemma.

Two problems must be met in order to restore the user of information systems as a morally responsible and autonomous person who can be held fully accountable. The first problem is that he has only indirect control over the belief-acquisition process, i.e., he cannot freely decide to believe this rather than that. At stake here is the question whether *doxastic voluntarism* is false or true. I think there are good reasons to believe that it is false and that the will (*voluntas*) is ineffective with respect to the direct and voluntary acquisition of the contents of beliefs (*doxa*)[21]. In highly computerized work environments, to which I will refer as *artificial epistemic niches,* the system's output (in the form of a display reading of electronic instruments, a string of characters on the monitor, a red alert lamp) will give rise to associated beliefs. If one is presented with the fact that the display indicates 'pressure 500' one will come to believe *ceteris paribus* that the pressure is 500, and if the control system indicates a time lag for an incoming flight of 5 minutes and 32 seconds, the air traffic controler will come to believe *ceteris paribus* that the incoming flight is late by 5 minutes and 32 seconds. If the system indicates that the applicant has a criminal record, the street-level bureaucrat comes to believe that the applicant has a criminal past. If the system

---

[19]See also my "Moral Foundations of Systems Design". In: *Ethics and Systems Design. The Politics of Social Responsibility*. Preecedings of the International Federation of Information Processing (WG 9.1) Workshop, Cuba, Havanna 17–19 february 1994, Clement, Robinson, Suchman, Wagner (eds.). Vienna: Technical University Vienna, 1994. Pp. 57–63. And "Expert Systems and Epistemic Enslavement". In: *The Expert Sign: Semiotics of Culture and Organisation*. L.J. Slikkerveer et al. (eds.). Leiden: DSWO Press, 1993, 293–307.

[20]John Stuart Mill, *On Liberty*, Chapter III, par. 5.

[21]See my *Applied Ethics, Information Technology and Public Policy* (forthcoming).

indicates that the spotted car is registered as stolen, the police officer is bound to believe that the vehicle was stolen[22]. To the extent that we are unfree to choose or to decide to believe this rather than that, we cannot be blamed for believing this rather than that.

The second problem concerns the justification relation between user and system. Users may be epistemically dependent[23] upon the systems they are working with. A person is epistemically dependent on a system if his or her sufficient grounds for believing that the system has sufficient grounds to provide particular output as accurate and adequate, provides that person with sufficient grounds to believe that the outputted data are fully accurate and adequate.

> (ED) B is epistemically dependent on A with respect to p if and only if the following holds: If B has good reasons for believing A has good reasons for believing p, then B has good reasons for believing p.

Problems for intellectual and moral autonomy arise if epistemically dependent users and the system – "the tandem of system and user"[24] – are what I call, *narrowly embedded* in an organization, or in an institutional arrangement.

Military combat situations provide a paradigm case of narrowly embedded user-system tandems. The users of the computerized Aegis combat system of the USS *Vincennes*, which shot down an Iranian airliner, were narrowly embedded. The human operators mis-identified it as 'enemy aircraft', because of a design flaw in the human interface. They were unable to scrutinize the inside of the systems, they had to decide in split-seconds, on the basis of software that was so complex as to rule out mathematical proof of soundness, they could not question or quiz it, and they were unable to detect defeating information, except for the most obvious malfunctions, such as smoke coming out of the keybord. And even if they would have had the expertise and opportunity, it would have been useless, because investigations showed no software errors, or hardware malfunction in this case[25]. It was admitted after investigation that if the altitude of flying objects would have been represented in real time on the Aegis large screen display, the misidentification would probably not have occurred. The Chairman of the Joint Chiefs of Staff recommended "that some additional human engineering be done on the display screens" of the information system. We can say that

> (NE) A user is narrowly embedded in an artificial epistemic niche if and only if conditions of *invisibility, pressure, error, absence of discursive scrutiny* obtain.

Users who are both narrowly embedded and epistemically dependent upon a sys-

---

[22]See for the description of a tragic case, Forester and Morrison, *Computer Ethics. Cautionary Tales and Ethical Dilemmas in Computing.* Oxford: Basil Blackwell, 1990, p. 88.

[23]See for this notion, John Hardwig, *op. cit.*

[24]See Klaus Lenk, *op. cit.*

[25]Software errors were involved in the failing of the Partriot air defence system in the Gulfwar 1991, where an Iraqi Scud-missile killed 28 American soldiers at Dahran. See for an excellent empirical overview of fatal accidents Donald MacKenzie, "Computer related accidental death: an empirical exploration", *Science and Public Policy*, vol. 21, no. 4, 1994, pp. 233–248. Mackenzie's article provides many good examples of epistemically enslaved users.

tem are its epistemic slaves, they are *epistemically enslaved* vis-à-vis the system.

(EE) If a user B is epistemically dependent on system S, and B is narrowly embedded in an epistemic niche of which S is part, then B is epistemically enslaved vis-à-vis S.

Once the user has given in, there is no good reason for him to opt out. From the moral point of view he has painted himself into a corner. The moral consequences of this condition can thus be unpacked as follows:

(MR) If a user is epistemically enslaved vis-à-vis system S, then non-compliance with the system's output constitutes a form of moral risk taking the user cannot justify, at the moment of non-compliance.

Both problematic features of system use, the limited freedom in the belief *acquisition* process and the epistemic dependence or the limited freedom to *justify* one's beliefs once acquired, make clear that once a user enters an *artificial epistemic niche*, or establishes an epistemic relation with a system, his or her freedom to think for him or herself is severely limited.

The following cases may serve as further support for my claims and at same time show how these epistemic dependencies may manifest themselves in the field of public policy and public administration[26].

Case A. The computers on board NASA observation satellites during the 1970s and 1980s were programmed so as to reject ozone readings below a certain level. Policy makers and politicians and even global climate specialists were relying on the figures produced by the system. It was only when British scientists using ground-based equipment in the mid 1980s found a substantial decline in ozone levels that the world became aware of the imminent dangers to the environment. Had the NASA systems been able to provide us with the adequate data ten years earlier, the political approach to the problem could have been more adequate. The British scientists, in cooperation with computer specialists, were able to find defeating information to the received point of view. Policy makers would never have been able to do so by themselves, because they were epistemically dependent on the relevant information technology[27].

Case B. During the Vietnam War computers in the field were specifically programmed to tell Pentagon computers that raids over neutral Cambodia were actually raids over Vietnam. Policy makers in the White House therefore wrongly believed that they were getting the accurate picture of the combat situation. In retrospect Admiral Moorer, chairman of the Joint Chiefs, remarked: "It is unfortunate that we had to become slaves to those damned computers"[28].

---

[26]As MacKenzie observes (*Op. cit.*, p. 234) system failings or untoward outcomes of system use are more likely to be reported if a loss of lives is involved for the simple reason that deaths are more newsworthy than non-fatal injuries, or disregard for people's interests.

[27]Forrester and Morrison, *Computer Ethics. Cautionary Tales and Ethical Dilemmas in Computing.* Cambridge, Massachusetts: The MIT Press, 1990.

[28]Mosco, V., 1988, "Information in the Pay-per Society". In: *The Political Economy of Information*, (eds.) V. Mosco and Janet Wasko. Madison: The University of Wisconsin Press, 1988, p. 15.

4.2. Responsibility

These observations about epistemic dependence quite naturally give rise to the following reflections on responsibility and the design of information systems[29]. It would be strange to argue that we should stop using information systems we are epistemically dependent upon altogether, since in some cases it may be morally obligatory to use them without further questioning[30]. However, nothing "can remove from us the necessity of deciding whether someone (or something, MJVDH) is in a position to tell us the facts. It is our inalienable decision whom to believe on what and when. This being so, unquestioning deference to epistemic authority is a form of self-deception or bad faith"[31]. In order to curb the reduction of his cognitive autonomy, and his relativized responsibility, the user must be permitted to reflect *ex ante* upon the epistemic conditions, within the confines of which he or she will be working. Since the *locus* of responsibility can be seen to be primarily in the design of the environment where new beliefs are acquired, the major responsibility concerns the design of our 'artificial epistemic niches', and the drafting doxastic policies, which lead us out of epistemic enslavement. What Russell Hardin has observed with respect to institutional morality, seems therefore particularly appropriate for 'systems morality': "Institutional morality is a design issue: Morality must be built in"[32]. This does not mean that a *particular* morality must be built in, but rather that the system or epistemic artefact must be designed in such a way as to allow the user to work with it, while retaining his status as an autonomous person. The following deontic principle seems therefore an appropriate part of our doxastic policy:

> (SP) End-users ought to endorse the output of information systems they are epistemically dependent upon, and with which they know they will be operating under conditions of narrow embeddedness, only after a search for acceptability whose cost is proportional to the cost that could reasonably be expected if what is endorsed and acted upon should prove in any sense to be inadequate[33].

[29]I think that these suggestions are consonant with John Ladd's argument for the appropriateness of what he calls a 'comprehensive responsibility concept' (*Op. cit.*), which is non-exclusive, and forward looking and not blame oriented. Technical and organisational complexity have made traditional conceptions of responsibility obsolete. Responsibility, according to Ladd's proposal, is not apportioned by looking back and trying to establish which single individual was to blame, but by looking forward and seeing how those, whose actions can make a difference, can collectively prevent untoward outcomes and human suffering.

[30]See Daniel Dennett, "Information, Technology, and the Virtues of Ignorance", *Deadalus*, 115, 135–153.

[31]Michael Welbourne, *The Community of Knowledge*. New Jersey: Humanities Press, 1986, p. 70.

[32]Russel Hardin, "Institutional Morality", Paper for the meeting of the American Political Science Association, Washington, 4 September 1993.

[33]It has been pointed out to me by Ig Snellen that the proportionality clause implies that if the cost is too high, in case of applications that could bring about a substantial loss of human lives, the effort that should be put in to a search for reliability would be unrealistically demanding so as to effectively prevent implementation. I think this is a correct observation, but one that at the same time shows the adequacy of (SP), since it accounts for example for the hesitation or moratorium on the large-scale 'fly by wire' in civil aviation and similar cases. The stakes are too high, the risks of replacing good old servo-mechanics with digitalized control too high, given the reliability of the

A corrolary thesis for the responsibility of system designers can be formulated as follows:

> (SQ) System designers ought to allow users to work with systems in such a way as not to make it impossible for them to live up to their obligations as users, specified by (SP).

I take it that (SP) and (SQ) both support so-called 'participatory design approaches' to systems development, and the involvement of the 'potentially affected persons' in the design and maintenance-process of information systems[34].

4.3. Privacy

Another and equally troublesome concept which is frequently used in the context of debates about shaping information technological applications is that of privacy. The concept of privacy requires serious analysis, before we can try to spell out principles for the design of politico-administrative information systems. The concept of privacy is multifarious and hard to explicate[35]. After many years of debate there is still no clear picture of why privacy is important to us and how privacy claims are to be weighed against claims of state interest and average utility.

In reaction to the rise of computer technology and enhanced surveillance capabilities restraints on the processing of data about persons, in the name of privacy, is acknowledged in data-protection laws in many countries. Unfortunately our provisional understanding of the importance and nature of privacy as implied and codified in these regulations is constantly teased out by technical innovations and probed for consistency by attempts to come to international cooperation and harmonization in data protection. Lawyers, policy-makers and politicians are regularly at a loss about which claims to privacy make sense and which are exaggerated. The lack of a systematic and fundamental understanding of privacy has given rise to incrementalist public policy, incoherent law and regulations, and difficulties in adjudicating new technical developments.

If privacy is important at all, I think it is important to know why it is important. What is needed therefore is an answer to the question

> (Q1) Why is privacy at all important to persons in an information age?

To make (Q1) amenable to analysis we have to undo its glearing generality, and therefore I propose to rephrase it as follows:

> (Q2) What has personal information to do with the person it is about, so as to give her a claim against others with respect to the processing of it?

---

systems involved. Administrative decisions taken on the basis of information systems can have far-reaching consequences, but are most often reversible and can be compensated for, in case of errors. (SP) allows us to differentiate between the degree of involvement and participation of all affected persons in the development and maintenance process, depending on the stakes, in these cases.

[34] This outcome needs to be unpacked further. See for necessary conceptual distinctions for all affected persons and the structure of the design process, Klaus Lenk, *op. cit.*

[35] See my *Applied Ethics, Information Technology and Public Policy* (forthcoming) for a listing of privacy scholars confirming this observation.

Attempts at answering this question must be interpreted as attempts to reconstruct the self-understanding of individuals in a modern information society. It is an analytical attempt to look behind moral experiences of modern individuals, and to articulate the conditions that make them possible.

Sensible answers to (Q2), or reasoned accounts of why a person may have legitimate claims against others not to register and process representations of her and her properties, are hard to come by. Representations of persons may arise quite naturally in the course of interacting with other human beings, and indeed by interacting with epistemic artefacts, like computersystems. At first sight it seems that none of us has a right over any fact including facts about persons, to the effect that that fact shall not be known to others. As Stanley Benn has remarked, there seems to be "nothing intrinsically objectionable in observing the world, including its inhabitants, and in sharing one's discoveries with anyone who finds them interesting (...). The burden of justification lies with the advocate of restraint, not with the person restrained. It is not sufficient for someone simply to say that something pertains to him as a person and therefore shares his immunity; he needs a reason for saying so"[36].

Many answers to the question as to why privacy is important have been provided, but they all single out quite different reasons for thinking it is important. I will disregard the views which are austerely consequentialist, because I think they can be shown to be inadequate[37]. The set of possible answers is narrowed down further in present debates by two considerations. Firstly, there seems to be a fair amount of consensus about the formal properties of a right to privacy. The moral right to privacy is ususally construed as a *prima facie* negative claim right. Secondly, there is a fair amount of consensus about the fact that it has to do with constraints on the flow of information about persons. The latter feature is a clear result of the impact of information technology on society, because before the introduction of the computer the right to privacy was framed in spatio temporal terms as 'a right to be left alone'. It is now generally accepted that the notions of time and space are becoming less and less important in this context. These two constraints both point in the direction of the following circumscription of a moral right to privacy: A right to privacy on the part of a person with respect to particular type of information, implies an obligation on the part of others to refrain from processing that information if there is no prior consent by the data subject:

> (C5) If X has a moral right to privacy then others have a *prima facie* moral obligation to refrain from processing (acquiring and disseminating are here treated as limiting cases of processing) X's personal data D or information I without X's explicit consent.

Why it is important to have something like (C5) implemented is the question which should concern us here. If we want to make deliberations about the scope and application of the right to privacy transparant, we must be able to make this clear.

I can only present the gist of my argumentation here[38]. Information about a person

---

[36]See Stanley Benn, *A Theory of Freedom*. Cambridge: Cambridge University Press, 1988, pp. 271, 278.

[37]See my *Applied Ethics, Information Technology and Public Policy*, Erasmus University Rotterdam, 1995.

[38]*Ibidem*, for a detailed argument.

P, whether fully accurate or not, facilitates the formation of judgements about P[39]. The judgement of others about P, when it is brought to P's attention may bring about a change in his view of himself. This may happen basically in two distinct ways. First, when the judgment by others suggests that there exists a discrepancy between accepted identity norms and the way P looks upon himself, it tends to exert normative pressure in the direction of compliance with accepted identity norms. Secondly, and not unrelated to the foregoing, it can happen by making the subject look upon himself through the eyes of the beholder, thus establishing an element of determination from without[40].

To modern individuals living in a highly volatile socio-economic environment, and a great diversity of audiences and settings before which the individual makes its appearance, such *fixation* and rigging of identity is felt as a burden to moral experiment. The modern individual wants to be able to determine himself morally or to undo his previous determinations, on the basis of more profuse experiences in life, or additional factual information[41]. Informational privacy provides the leeway to do just that.

This conception of the person as being morally autonomous, as being the experimentator of his or her own moral career, provides us with a rationale for a moral right to informational privacy. It is compatible and as a matter of fact unifies all non-reductionist and non-consequentialist privacy conceptions[42]. We could therefore propose the following answer to (Q1) and (Q2):

> (IP) Privacy is important to a person P because it means exemption from other persons' systematically processing information about P in such a way as to give rise to judgements concerning P, the availability of which will interfere, or is likely to interfere, with P's experiments concerning his moral identity.

Data-protection laws thus provide forbearance against the fixation of one's moral identity by others than one's self and have the symbolic utility[43] of conveying to citizens that they are morally autonomous[44].

---

[39]See for a judgmental construal of the importance of privacy, J.L. Johnson, "Privacy, Liberty and Integrity", *Public Affairs Quarterly* 3, no. 3 (1989), pp. 15–34.

[40]As Isaiah Berlin has aptly put it: "I cannot ignore the attitude of others with Byronic disdain, fully conscious of my own intrinsic worth and vocation, or to escape into my inner life, for I am in my own eyes as others see me. I identify myself with the point of view of my milieu: I feel myself to be somebody or nobody in terms of my position and function in the social whole; this is the most 'heteronomous' condition imaginable". *Four Essays on Liberty*, Oxford: Oxford University Press, 1969, p. 156, n. 1. This theme is in different ways stressed by Rousseau, Schopenhauer, Simmel, G.H. Mead, and Erving Goffman.

[41]John Stuart Mill is deservedly famous for articulating this tenet of modern individualism in his plea for individuality as one of the most important elements of well-being. In: *On Liberty*: "If a person possesses any tolerable amount of common sense and experience, his own mode of laying out his existence is the best, not because it is the best in itself, but because it is his own mode". Harmondsworth: Penguin Books, 1977, 132–133.

[42]See my *Applied Ethics, Information Technology, and Public Policy* (forthcoming).

[43]See for the notion of 'symbolic utility', Robert Nozick, *The Nature of Rationality*, Princeton: Princeton University Press, 1993.

[44]It is important to note it is *moral* autonomy that is at stake here and not one's autonomy *simpliciter*. (IP) rules out tampering with one's biography to get a free-ride at the expense of the

One could object to this construal of privacy's importance that if the processed personal information would be fully accurate and relevant so as to give rise to judgements which do perfect justice to the moral identity of the data-subject, then there would be no reason to claim informational privacy. I think that the appropriateness of privacy claims could in this case still be upheld by arguing that it would be a matter of epistemic and moral luck that others get it right about the data-subject's moral identity, because at any given point in time it is virtually impossible to know who someone 'really' is. This answer may be subdivided in two lines of reasoning, a strong and and a weak one. The strong line of reasoning points to the interrelatedness of the privacy of the mental and informational privacy. Factual knowledge of another person or another person is always knowledge by description. The person P himself, however, does not only know the facts of his biography, but is the only person who is *acquainted* with the associated thoughts, desires and aspirations. However detailed and elaborate our files and profiles on P may be, we are never able to refer to the data-subject as he himself is able to do. Compare for example Bertrand Russell's remark:

> "(...) when we say anything about Bismarck, we should like, if we could, to make the judgement which Bismarck alone can make, namely the judgement of which he himself is a constituent. In this we are necessarily defeated since the actual Bismarck is unknown to us".[45]

The weaker line of reasoning would point out that, although it is not impossible to do justice to the person in principle, it is very difficult in practice, and requires a particular form of attention, which is ruled out by the current practices of computerized data-processing. Bernard Williams for example has pointed out that respecting a person involves 'identification' in a very special sense. Let us refer to it as 'moral identification':

> "(...) in professional relations and the world of work, a man operates, and his activities come up for criticism, under a variety of professional or technical titles, such as 'miner' or 'agricultural labourer' or 'junior executive'. The technical or professional attitude is that which regards the man solely under that title, the human approach that which regards him as a man who has that title (among others), willingly, unwillingly, through lack of alternatives, with pride, etc. (...) each man is owed an effort at identification: that he should not be regarded as the surface to which a certain label can be applied, but one should try to see the world (including the label) from his point of view"[46].

Moral identification thus presupposes knowledge of the point of view of the data-subject, which is concerned with what it is for a person to live that life. Persons have aspirations, higher-order evaluations and attitudes and they see the things they do in a certain light. Representation of this aspect of persons seems exactly what is missing when personal data are piled up in our databases and persons are represented in

---

public good, it excludes dishonesty which allows people to see to it that their autonomously formed preferences are satisfied, whatever they are.

[45]Bertrand Russell, *The Problems of Philosophy*. Oxford: Oxford University Press. Eighth impressions, 1978, p. 31. The context of Russell's remark is different from our present inquiry, but the distinction is relevant to my purposes.

[46]Bernard Williams, *Problems of the Self*. Cambridge: Cambridge University Press, 1973, p. 236.

administrative procedures[47]. The identifications made on the basis of our data fall short of respecting the individual person, because they will never match the identity as it is experienced by the data-subject. It fails because it does not conceive of the other on his own terms. Respect for privacy of persons can thus be seen to have an *epistemic* dimension. It is a way of acknowledging the 'impossibility' of really knowing other persons and of perceiving them on their own terms.

Even if we could get it right about moral persons at any given point in time, by exhibit of extraordinary emphathy and attention, then it is highly questionable whether the data-subject's experience of himself, as far as the *dynamics* of the moral person is concerned, can be captured. The person conceives of himself as trying to improve himself morally. The person can not be identified, not even in the weaker sense articulated by Williams, with something limited, definite and unchanging. This point was already eloquently made by the French Existentialist Gabriel Marcel:

> "(...) il faudra dire que la personne ne saurait être assimilée en aucune manière a un objet dont nous pouvons dire qu'il est là, c'est-à-dire qu'il est donné, présent devant nous, qu'il fait partie d'une collection par essence dénombrable, ou encore qu'il est un element statistique (...)"[48].

The person always sees itself as something that has to be overcome, not as a fixed reality but as something in the making, something that has to be improved upon:

> "Elle se saisit bien moins comme être que comme volonté de dépasser ce que tout ensemble elle est et elle n'est pas, un actualité dans laquelle elle se sent à vrai dire engagée ou impliqué, mais *qui ne la satisfait pas*: *qui n'est pas à la mesure de l'aspiration avec laquelle elle s'identifie*"[49].

As Marcel puts it, the individual's motto is not *sum* (I am) but *sursum* (higher). The human person has a tendency not to be satified, but always aspiring to improve himself. Always on his way, *Homo Viator*.

In conclusion we can say that privacy protection is a way of acknowledging our systematic inability to identify the datasubject as being the same as the moral self with which the datasubject identifies itself.

(PP) To the extent that a data-protection regulation is effective in realizing the rationale (IP) it can be said to support reasonable claims, to the extent it does not, claims to privacy ought to give way to claims of public interest and average utility.

(IP) has helped to focus on the informational character and epistemic rationale of privacy claims. It can be seen that privacy aims to protect specific vulnerabilities of persons as morally autonomous beings.

---

[47]See *Protection of personal data used for employment purposes*, Council of Europe, Recommendation No. R (89) 2, adopted by the Committee of Ministers on 18 January 1989, article 2: "(...) respect for human dignity relates to the need to avoid statistical dehumanisation by undermining the identity of employees through data-processing techniques which allow for profiling of employees or the taking of decisions based on automatic processing which concern them" (Explanatory Memorandum, para. 25). Quoted by B.W. Napier, "The Future of Information Technology Law", *Cambridge Law Journal*, 51, no. 1, 1992, p. 64.

[48]Gabriel Marcel, *Homo Viator*. Paris: Aubier, Editions Montaigne, 1944, p. 31. This neatly accomodates the fact that in French criminal law statistical evidence relating to persons is not allowed in court. I thank Daniele Bourcier for pointing this out to me.

[49]*Op. cit.*, p. 32.

4.4. Justice

The final question I will take up is the question of differential access and equal distribution of information. As I indicated in the opening section, normative theory has been dominated in the last two decades by the work of John Rawls. The aim of John Rawls in *A Theory of Justice* was to lay down the principles of justice to guide the design of the basic institutions of society. He arrived at the following principles:

1. Each person is to have an equal right to the most extensive total system of equal basic liberties compatible with a similar system of liberty for all.
2. Social and economic inequalities are to be arranged so that they are both (a) to the greatest benefit of the least advantaged, and (b) attached to offices and positions open to all under conditions of fair equality of opportunity.

The 'inequalities', and 'the least advantaged' mentioned in the second principle are to be individuated in terms of so-called 'primary goods'. The notion of a primary good however, is not unproblematic for several reasons. One of the reasons is discussed by Daniel Zolo. Zolo observes[50] that "The attention which Rawls, like all moralists, gives almost exclusively to the problem of distribution presupposes (...) that the essential goods – which he calls "social primary goods" – should be those which are "distributable". In complex societies, however, it seems on the contrary that those goods become primary which are the object of diffuse interests. Increasingly important are elements such as the environment, energy, demographic balance, information, scientific knowledge (...) all of them goods for which no system of apportionment or measurement can easily be envisaged"[51]. None of these objects of diffuse interests seems to play an important role in Rawls' Theory.

It is surprising to find that the issue of 'information' and 'information needs' is not explicitly addressed by Rawls, nor by the participants in the debates concerning his proposals[52]. If the notion of a primary good, is an adequate concept in framing our ideas about social justice and the design of the basic institutions of society, then information, or to be more precise 'access to the data relevant to an individual's legitimate purposes in life', should be considered as a serious candidate to be incorporated in the list of primary goods. If on the other hand the outcome of the debates about Rawls' proposal would suggest the inadequacy of the notion of a primary good, then I think we can safely say that there are at least variations among persons in their basic capabilities to use information to attain their aims. Variations in their natural or acquired information behaviour[53], variations also in the opportunities and circumstances to acquire relevant information, given the state of the technology[54]. The basic idea of equality is that society should to some extent indemnify people

[50]See for a suggestion to this point, Danilo Zolo, *Democracy and Complexity*, Polity Press 1992, p. 34.
[51]I thank Ignace Snellen for drawing my attention to Zolo's work.
[52]With the possible exception of Amartya Sen. His ideas about 'informational analysis' and 'moral principles' in the Dewey Lectures (1985) deserve further investigation in this context.
[53]Their capability to actively seek information, to make it available, to make sense of it, and draw relevant conclusions on the basis of it.
[54]Deborah Johnson discusses access to computing, computing expertise, and decision making

against poor outcomes that are the consequences of causes that are beyond their control. We may therefore conclude that the availability and distribution of both raw and intelligently organized data as a resource to individual citizens can no longer be ignored[55]. If they are ignored, this must be considered as a serious shortcoming of any substantive contribution to a theory of justice which is supposed to provide guidance in an information society.

I will argue that four considerations point to the primary goods status, in a Rawlsian sense, of information. Finally, I will formulate two principles of justice pertaining to the design of politico-administrative information systems.

The first argument for the primary good-status of information is a simple one. Citizens need it to function in societies in the post-industrial era. First of all, our economies are increasingly based on knowledge and information. This point is eloquently made by Peter Drucker: "The basic economic resource – 'the means of production' to use the economist's term – is no longer capital, nor natural resources (the economist's land), nor 'labour'. It is and will be knowledge"[56]. What holds for organisations and nation states equally applies to individuals: information is of crucial importance to attain either health or wealth and to critically evaluate the goals they have set themselves in life. Individual citizens need information: 1) to effectively seek their advantage in markets; 2) to participate in decisionmaking and democratic processes and to hold organisations and institutions accountable; 3) to fulfil their duties and responsibilities, exercise their rights and receive the services to which they are entitled; and 4) to attend to their own well-being and make sensible choices about their lives[57]. In short, an information infra-structure which provides citizens with the information they need[58] on an equal basis, is required if it is to be put into place at all.

The second (indirect) argument for the primary goods status of information draws upon Rawls' own listing of primary goods. What are examples of primary goods, according to Rawls? He mentions 'rights and liberties, powers and opportunities, income and wealth and finally self-respect, or the basis of self-respect[59]. Several objections may be raised against this list, but most important for my purpose here is that the list is not exhaustive. Rawls himself has indicated that there may be additional candidates to be included in the list, for example 'health', 'educated intelligence', and 'leisure'[60]. In short, it seems very well possible that Rawls or other

about computers. "Equal Access to Computing, Computing Expertise, and Decision Making About Computers". In: *Ethical Issues in Information Systems*, Dejoie, Fowler, Paradice (eds.). Boston: Boyd & Fraser Publishing Company, pp. 210–218. Access to these is in a way derivative. They are important because what is the topic of computing, processing, expertise, decision making is important. The issue of equality of access would never have come up if trivial games were the only things one could retrieve or down load.

[55]See Arthur L. Morin's well-documented argument for the public good's nature of Government Information, "Regulating the Flow of Data: OMB and the Control of Government Information", *Public Administration Review*, vol. 54, no. 5, 1994, 434–443.

[56]Peter Drucker, *Post-Capitalist Society*. Oxford: Butterworth-Heinemann Ltd, 1993, p. 7.

[57]See Jane Steele, "Information for Citizens", *Policy Studies* 1991 vol. 12, no 3, 47–55.

[58]See Al Gore's plea for information infrastructure, *op. cit.*

[59]*A Theory of Justice*, p. 313.

[60]See John Rawls, *Political Liberalism*. New York: Columbia University Press, 1993, p. 182, n. 9: "(...) if necessary the list of primary goods can in principle be expanded".

scholars of the theory of justice have overlooked candidates for primary goods. Why would information, now technology has contributed so much to its commodification, fail to qualify as a primary good?

A third argument is taken from Rawls' general characterization of a primary good. He provides us with the following characterizations of a primary good: 1) it is rational for a person K to want a primary good A, whatever K wants; 2) it is rational for K to prefer more rather than less of A; and 3) A has a use whatever K's rational plan of life: they have a 'use' in every rational plan of life in the sense of being normally necessary means to formulating, pursuing, and executing a rational plan incorporation any final ends whatsoever[61]. I think that these three criteria apply to large portions of the information available today from the storage capacity of government agencies; aggregated information on the environment, employment, healthcare risks, national safety, crime rates, political participation, education, economic prospects. Firstly, we all want information about these issues irrespective of what our goals in life may be. Secondly, it is more rational for a person to want more information than less, he always prefers to be better informed[62]. Thirdly, in order to think out, draw up, analyse and evaluate plans of life, careers, etc., information is the first thing needed. So it seems that relevant information is satifying all three general conditions of being a primary good.

Finally, another argument is provided by the overall characteristic of primary goods, namely the fact that they are required for rational persons of a Kantian variety to plan a rational life or to make rational choices. Information is the first thing you need if you want to make plans. Indeed the notions of rationality, planning, decision, choice and information are intimately related. Several functions of information in the lives of rational may be distinguished here. Information is valued for the fact that it is instrumental in adding alternatives to the choice set of the individual ($n + 100$ items in the tele-shop list instead of n on your local store's shelves), but its value also derives from its potential to help discriminate between alternatives and to reduce the number of unconnected preferences[63]. The classical example of unconnected preferences is Buridan's hungry ass. The animal died of starvation not because he was *merely indifferent* with respect to the two stacks of hay, but because his preference for eating over not-eating and his indifference between the two bundles were unconnected. Keith Dowding remarks:

---

[61]See for textual evidence of these characterizations, W.L. Sessions, "Rawls's concept and conception of primary good", *Social Theory and Practice*, vol. 7, 1981, p. 321, n.14, n.15, n.16.

[62]One could object that people, within the bounds of rationality, would prefer to remain ignorant about their genetic predispositions to serious illnesses, as for particular forms of Alzheimer's Disease. See, e.g., D.E. Ost, "The 'right' not to know", *The Journal of medicine and Philosophy*, 9, 1984; Mark Strasser, "Mill and the right to remain uninformed", *The Journal of Medicine and Philosophy*, 11, 1986. I think that choosing not to know the facts about one's physical condition is *pro tanto* irrational. However, it seems highly relevant whether knowing or not knowing can make a difference. Knowledge of a fully deterministic process seems less worth wanting if it causes anxiety and grief, especially when one's decisions are relatively robust, i.e., not likely to be revised in the light of new information.

[63]See for a discussion of the relation between choice and knowledge and information Keith Dowding, "Choice Its Increase and Its Value", *British Journal of Political Science* 22, 1992, 301–314.

M.J. van den Hoven / Ethical principles

In fact, the health market (...) offers good examples of unconnected preferences. Individuals do not generally have well-defined indifference curves over the primary characteristics of health care, for they are often ignorant of their own illnesses[64].

Individuals are not only often ignorant about their own illnesses, but also about their relevant physical properties, such as metabolism rates, ignorant about the circumstances and pertinent scientific knowledge (risk and ways to counter-act risk[65]). Increasing the amount of information available to individual citizens as rational persons may thus expand their choice set, thereby increasing the chance that they may be able to get what they want, and secondly, to help *connect* preferences defined in the choice set[66]. Furthermore information is valued for the fact that it helps people to coordinate actions. A mutually beneficial exchange opportunity may remain unexploited, because both parties are unaware of the opportunity. Discoordinated action in this case, is brought about by the discoordinated knowledge[67].

Summarizing my arguments for a primary good status of 'access to data relevant to one's legitimate purposes in life' we can say that there is the general and obvious, but nonetheless true observation, that the economies of the Western world are increasingly information-based. Secondly, the rationale behind the listing of primary goods provided by Rawls extends itself to information as a resource and perhaps even warrants the claim that access to information is a necessary condition to attain and enjoy the other primary goods explicitly mentioned by Rawls, such as health and freedom of speech. Thirdly, the criteria which Rawls provides for primary goods can be easily seen to apply to information as well. Fourthly, from the nature of information and its role in decision-making and choice it is evident that information is central to persons conceived of along Kantian lines as Rawls envisages them in his Theory of Justice. It therefore seems plausible to accept

(PG) Access to data relevant for citizens' legitimate purposes in life qualifies as a Rawlsian primary good.

It seems therefore reasonable to suppose that Rawls' principles of Justice apply to the design of the basic informational institutions such as the National Information Super-Highway and its international counterpart. Rawls principles have a clear bearing upon this issue. Slightly rephrased we can conclude:

(JI) Each person is to have an equal right to the most extensive total system of equal basic information liberties compatible with a similar system of liberty for all.

(JD) Informational inequalities are to be arranged so that they are both (a) to the great-

---

[64]Dowding, *op. cit.*, p. 310.

[65]Exposure to radioactivity, can be neutralized by increasing the intake of iodine, some effects of nicotine through smoking may be counter balanced by increasing intake of vitamine C. See for this discussion Norman Daniels, *Just Health Care*. Cambridge: Cambridge University Press, 1985. See especially pp. 159–162, the section on 'information and competency'. See also D.G. Mayo and R.D. Hollander (eds.), *Acceptable Evidence. Science and Values in Risk Management*. Oxford: Oxford University Press, 1991.

[66]Keith Dowding furthermore suggests an interesting relation between on the one hand citizen control over government provisions and unconnected preferences, *op. cit.* p. 313.

[67]E.F. Thomsen, *Prices and Knowledge: A Market-Process Perspective*. London: Routledge, 1992, p. 88 ff.

est benefit of those who are the least advantaged, and (b) attached to offices and positions open to all under conditions of fair equality of opportunity[68].

If it is plausible at all that the contracters in Rawls' Original Position would choose (1) and (2), then I think they will also choose (JI) and (JD). It has to be noted that it is possible to choose (JI) and (JD) without lifting the Veil of Ignorance, because choice of neither principle assumes that the contracters know any particular things about themselves, other than the things stipulated in the Original Position. Two further distinctions have to be made in order to qualify the object of allocation.

4.4.1. Information, data, access to data

If we subscribe to an egalitarian scheme, along Rawlsian lines, with respect to the distribution and dissemination of information, then the question remains 'How is this equality exactly to be framed?'. What do the information liberties do for us?

There is a useful distinction made in information sciences between data and information, that we have to take up at this point. Data are symbolic tokens which can be interpreted and appreciated by human beings. According to the ISO definition: they are "representations of facts, concepts and instructions in a formalized manner suitable for communication, interpretation or processing by human beings or by automatic means". Information is according to the ISO definition "the meaning that a human being assigns to data by means of the conventions applied to that data". If a string of characters is read, translated, in short, when human beings become aware of them as semantical entities, then the informational content is 'released' from the data. One can present people with data, without being able to make them soak up their intended meaning or informational content, let alone to increase their knowledge. One can bring a horse to a well without being able to make it drink. In this sense information as a primary good is comparable to that of self-respect as a primary good. Whereas one can provide its basis or the necessary conditions for self-respect, it seems impossible to see to it that people respect themselves[69]. So it seems as inappropriate to claim that government ought to see to it that people are informed, in the ISO sense, as it is to claim that government ought to see to it that people respect themselves.

One might argue, however, that there are some likelihoods and regularities that have to be taken into account if one wants to further a person's self-respect. Although providing someone with decent housing and employment is no guarantee that he will come to respect himself, it is *more probable* that he will come to think of himself as having the value that ought to be accorded to human beings, than when unemployed and badly housed. So, although there are certainly no hard and fast laws

---

[68]One might add that informational inequalities may also be allowed in cases of justified epistemic paternalism, i.e., cases where information is withheld from persons, because it is known that they jump to wrong conclusions on the basis of it. This may occur, as psychological research has shown, when people have to deal with probabilities. See A.I. Goldman, "Epistemic Paternalism". In: *Liaisons, Philosophy meets the Cognitive and Social Sciences*. Cambridge, Mass.: MIT Press, 1992.

[69]See, e.g., J. Elster, *Nuts and Bolts for the Social Sciences*. Cambridge: Cambridge University Press, 1989, p. 24: "Self-esteem is essentially a byproduct of actions undertaken for other ends- it cannot be the sole purpose of policy".

pertaining to the growth of selfrespect, there seem to be certain regularities which have to be taken into account. Now one could argue that the same holds for the transformation of data into meaningful information that will provide one with orientation in life. Information, knowledge, understanding may be what people ultimately want, the only things they can legitimately claim however are the things that increase the likelihood of their making sense of its raw material[70]: resources (data) and assistance (education and training) to learn to make sense of data (enhance cognitive capabilities).

4.4.2. Positionality of information, horizontal and vertical

There is a feature of the object of allocation which has to be taken into account if we are thinking about the role of government in designing public information systems. Information, however problematic its status as a good, seems to have many things in common with what is called a positional good. A positional good is one which a person values only on condition that not everyone has it[71]. Martin Hollis distinguishes between vertical and horizontal positional goods. Information and data may be either vertical or horizontal positional goods.

> (VP) Data D are vertically positional goods if and only if they derive their value to one particular person, or one particular group of users from the fact that there are no other persons or just a limited number of them that have access to D.
>
> (HP) Data D are horizontally positional if and only if they derive their value for a person (or group) x from the fact that 1) other data D' are either available to x or to some other person (or group) y, who interacts with x or 2) the same data D are available to some other person (or group) y, who interacts with x.

Government may decide to privatize the data flow in some sectors or fields, but it cannot defer the political ergonomics of information provision systems to the market, and waive its obligation to design a just framework for information services and provisions to citizens. Government is directly or indirectly responsible for the design of the public informational infrastructure on all levels.

The above made distinctions allow us to specify the following mid-level principles. We would like the politico-admininistrative information systems to be designed in such a way as to reduce the number of cases where data D, or information I, is only of value to P because no one else or only a small number of other people have it. This amounts to an 'obligation to effectively disseminate', and reduce unbalanced distribution of relevant data, and may be seen as a specification of (JI). On the other hand we would like to have our public information systems designed in such a way as to reduce the number of cases where a person or group of persons have some information, but lack some particular other pieces of information, that would give it its true value. It would be perverse to give someone a medical advice on a diskette in

---

[70]Taking into account for example the limited capabilities of human beings to process vast amounts of complex and badly structured information. See for a enlightening discussion on our cognitive limitations Christopher Cherniak, *Minimal Rationality*. Cambridge, Mass.: The MIT Press, 1986.

[71]See Martin Hollis, "Positional Goods". In: *Moral Philosophy and Contemporary Problems*, Philosophy, Supplement volume 22, 1987.

encoded form, without supplying the decode-program. Or to tell someone that he may come to collect his salary, without telling him when or where. Or to allow someone who is doing bibliographical research to use a libarary system that allows him only anonimized items. There is therefore a *prima facie* obligation to make interdepencies of this type in information repositories visible; the obligation of perspicuous representation. In the case of the above mentioned unconnected preferences, and discoordinated action, there is horizontal positional information involved. It is the information which respectively, when disseminated to the subject(s), would turn unconnected preferences into connected preferences, and discoordinated action into coordinated action. We end up therefore with the following two specified principles of justice for the design of databases and information infra-structures in general:

> (JV) Government has a *prima facie* obligation to reduce the amount of vertically positional data in public databases and information service provisions.
> (JH) Government has a *prima facie* obligation to see to it that databases and information service are designed and connected in such a way so as to perspicuously represent horizontal positionality and to articulate meta-knowledge concerning horizontally positional data.

5. Concluding remark

I have tried to show that the notions of autonomy, responsibility, privacy and distributive justice can be made to bear upon the design of politico-administrative information systems. More in particular I have tried, taking Langdon Winner's plea for 'political ergonomics' in systems design as a vantage point, to specify mid-level moral principles. These principles or principled statements, far from being absolute and ultimate results of reflection, should be used as fuel for collective moral debate and political deliberation, and should be made to cohere with our relevant moral intuitions and scientific views, if we have them[72].

---

[72]There is not much agreement in Ethics, but with respect to this way of proceeding in order to justify one's moral beliefs, there is considerable consensus. This procedure, sometimes referred to as 'the method of wide reflective equilibrium', brings together all relevant considerations, intuitions or well-considered judgments, highly corroborated scientific theories, juridical data, abstract moral principles or rules, into a discursive process of mutual adjustment, until a satifactory fit between them is established. See James Griffin "How we do Ethics Now". In: *Ethics*, A. Phillips Griffiths (ed.). Cambridge; Cambridge University Press, 1993, p. 165: "The best procedure for ethics (...) is the going back and forth between intuitions about fairly specific situations on the one side and the fairly general principles that we formulate to make sense of our moral practice on the other, adjusting either, until eventually we bring them all into coherence. This is, I think, the dominant view about method in ethics nowadays". See also Chapter 4 of my *Applied Ethics, Information Technology and Public Policy* (forthcoming).

[20]

Bias in Computer Systems

BATYA FRIEDMAN
Colby College and The Mina Institute
and
HELEN NISSENBAUM
Princeton University

From an analysis of actual cases, three categories of bias in computer systems have been developed: preexisting, technical, and emergent. Preexisting bias has its roots in social institutions, practices, and attitudes. Technical bias arises from technical constraints or considerations. Emergent bias arises in a context of use. Although others have pointed to bias in particular computer systems and have noted the general problem, we know of no comparable work that examines this phenomenon comprehensively and which offers a framework for understanding and remedying it. We conclude by suggesting that freedom from bias should be counted among the select set of criteria—including reliability, accuracy, and efficiency—according to which the quality of systems in use in society should be judged.

Categories and Subject Descriptors: D.2.0 [**Software**]: Software Engineering; H.1.2 [**Information Systems**]: User/Machine Systems; K.4.0 [**Computers and Society**]: General

General Terms: Design, Human Factors

Additional Key Words and Phrases: Bias, computer ethics, computers and society, design methods, ethics, human values, standards, social computing, social impact, system design, universal design, values

INTRODUCTION

To introduce what bias in computer systems might look like, consider the case of computerized airline reservation systems, which are used widely by travel agents to identify and reserve airline flights for their customers. These reservation systems seem straightforward. When a travel agent types in a customer's travel requirements, the reservation system searches

This research was funded in part by the Clare Boothe Luce Foundation.

Earlier aspects of this work were presented at the 4S/EASST Conference, Goteborg, Sweden, August 1992, and at InterCHI '93, Amsterdam, April 1993. An earlier version of this article appeared as Tech. Rep. CSLI-94-188, CSLI, Stanford University.

Authors' addresses: B. Friedman, Department of Mathematics and Computer Science, Colby College, Waterville, ME 04901; email: b_friedm@colby.edu; H. Nissenbaum, University Center for Human Values, Marx Hall, Princeton University, Princeton, NJ 08544; email: helen@phoenix.princeton.edu.
Permission to make digital/hard copy of part or all of this work for personal or classroom use is granted without fee provided that the copies are not made or distributed for profit or commercial advantage, the copyright notice, the title of the publication, and its date appear, and notice is given that copying is by permission of the ACM, Inc. To copy otherwise, to republish, to post on servers, or to redistribute to lists, requires prior specific permission and/or a fee.

a database of flights and retrieves all reasonable flight options that meet or come close to the customer's requirements. These options then are ranked according to various criteria, giving priority to nonstop flights, more direct routes, and minimal total travel time. The ranked flight options are displayed for the travel agent. In the 1980s, however, most of the airlines brought before the Antitrust Division of the United States Justice Department allegations of anticompetitive practices by American and United Airlines whose reservation systems—Sabre and Apollo, respectively—dominated the field. It was claimed, among other things, that the two reservations systems are biased [Schrifin 1985].

One source of this alleged bias lies in Sabre's and Apollo's algorithms for controlling search and display functions. In the algorithms, preference is given to "on-line" flights, that is, flights with all segments on a single carrier. Imagine, then, a traveler who originates in Phoenix and flies the first segment of a round-trip overseas journey to London on American Airlines, changing planes in New York. All other things being equal, the British Airlines' flight from New York to London would be ranked lower than the American Airlines' flight from New York to London even though in both cases a traveler is similarly inconvenienced by changing planes and checking through customs. Thus, the computer systems systematically downgrade and, hence, are biased against international carriers who fly few, if any, internal U.S. flights, and against internal carriers who do not fly international flights [Fotos 1988; Ott 1988].

Critics also have been concerned with two other problems. One is that the interface design compounds the bias in the reservation systems. Lists of ranked flight options are displayed screen by screen. Each screen displays only two to five options. The advantage to a carrier of having its flights shown on the first screen is enormous since 90% of the tickets booked by travel agents are booked by the first screen display [Taib 1990]. Even if the biased algorithm and interface give only a small percent advantage overall to one airline, it can make the difference to its competitors between survival and bankruptcy. A second problem arises from the travelers' perspective. When travelers contract with an independent third party—a travel agent—to determine travel plans, travelers have good reason to assume they are being informed accurately of their travel options; in many situations, that does not happen.

As Sabre and Apollo illustrate, biases in computer systems can be difficult to identify let alone remedy because of the way the technology engages and extenuates them. Computer systems, for instance, are comparatively inexpensive to disseminate, and thus, once developed, a biased system has the potential for widespread impact. If the system becomes a standard in the field, the bias becomes pervasive. If the system is complex, and most are, biases can remain hidden in the code, difficult to pinpoint or explicate, and not necessarily disclosed to users or their clients. Furthermore, unlike in our dealings with biased individuals with whom a potential victim can negotiate, biased systems offer no equivalent means for appeal.

Although others have pointed to bias in particular computer systems and have noted the general problem [Johnson and Mulvey 1993; Moor 1985], we know of no comparable work that focuses exclusively on this phenomenon and examines it comprehensively.

In this article, we provide a framework for understanding bias in computer systems. From an analysis of actual computer systems, we have developed three categories: preexisting bias, technical bias, and emergent bias. Preexisting bias has its roots in social institutions, practices, and attitudes. Technical bias arises from technical constraints or considerations. Emergent bias arises in a context of use. We begin by defining bias and explicating each category and then move to case studies. We conclude with remarks about how bias in computer systems can be remedied.

1. WHAT IS A BIASED COMPUTER SYSTEM?

In its most general sense, the term bias means simply "slant." Given this undifferentiated usage, at times the term is applied with relatively neutral content. A grocery shopper, for example, can be "biased" by not buying damaged fruit. At other times, the term bias is applied with significant moral meaning. An employer, for example, can be "biased" by refusing to hire minorities. In this article we focus on instances of the latter, for if one wants to develop criteria for judging the quality of systems in use—which we do—then criteria must be delineated in ways that speak robustly yet precisely to relevant social matters. Focusing on bias of moral import does just that.

Accordingly, we use the term bias to refer to computer systems that *systematically* and *unfairly discriminate* against certain individuals or groups of individuals in favor of others. A system discriminates unfairly if it denies an opportunity or a good or if it assigns an undesirable outcome to an individual or group of individuals on grounds that are unreasonable or inappropriate. Consider, for example, an automated credit advisor that assists in the decision of whether or not to extend credit to a particular applicant. If the advisor denies credit to individuals with consistently poor payment records we do not judge the system to be biased because it is reasonable and appropriate for a credit company to want to avoid extending credit privileges to people who consistently do not pay their bills. In contrast, a credit advisor that systematically assigns poor credit ratings to individuals with ethnic surnames discriminates on grounds that are not relevant to credit assessments and, hence, discriminates unfairly.

Two points follow. First, unfair discrimination alone does not give rise to bias unless it occurs systematically. Consider again the automated credit advisor. Imagine a random glitch in the system which changes in an isolated case information in a copy of the credit record for an applicant who happens to have an ethnic surname. The change in information causes a downgrading of this applicant's rating. While this applicant experiences unfair discrimination resulting from this random glitch, the applicant could have been anybody. In a repeat incident, the same applicant or others with similar ethnicity would not be in a special position to be singled out. Thus, while the system is prone to random error, it is not biased.

Second, systematic discrimination does not establish bias unless it is joined with an unfair outcome. A case in point is the Persian Gulf War, where United States Patriot missiles were used to detect and intercept Iraqi Scud missiles. At least one software error identified during the war contributed to systematically poor performance by the Patriots [Gao 1992]. Calculations used to predict the location of a Scud depended in complex ways on the Patriots' internal clock. The longer the Patriot's continuous running time, the greater the imprecision in the calculation. The deaths of at least 28 Americans in Dhahran can be traced to this software error, which systematically degraded the accuracy of Patriot missiles. While we are not minimizing the serious consequence of this systematic computer error, it falls outside of our analysis because it does not involve unfairness.

2. FRAMEWORK FOR ANALYZING BIAS IN COMPUTER SYSTEMS

We derived our framework by examining actual computer systems for bias. Instances of bias were identified and characterized according to their source, and then the characterizations were generalized to more abstract categories. These categories were further refined by their application to other instances of bias in the same or additional computer systems. In most cases, our knowledge of particular systems came from the published literature. In total, we examined 17 computer systems from diverse fields including banking, commerce, computer science, education, medicine, and law.

The framework that emerged from this methodology is comprised of three overarching categories—preexisting bias, technical bias, and emergent bias. Table I contains a detailed description of each category. In more general terms, they can be described as follows.

2.1 Preexisting Bias

Preexisting bias has its roots in social institutions, practices, and attitudes. When computer systems embody biases that exist independently, and usually prior to the creation of the system, then we say that the system embodies preexisting bias. Preexisting biases may originate in society at large, in subcultures, and in formal or informal, private or public organizations and institutions. They can also reflect the personal biases of individuals who have significant input into the design of the system, such as the client or system designer. This type of bias can enter a system either through the explicit and conscious efforts of individuals or institutions, or implicitly and unconsciously, even in spite of the best of intentions. For example, imagine an expert system that advises on loan applications. In determining an applicant's credit risk, the automated loan advisor negatively weights applicants who live in "undesirable" locations, such as low-income or high-crime neighborhoods, as indicated by their home addresses (a practice referred to as "red-lining"). To the extent the program

ACM Transactions on Information Systems, Vol. 14, No. 3, July 1996.

334   •   Batya Friedman and Helen Nissenbaum

Table I.   Categories of Bias in Computer System Design

These categories describe ways in which bias can arise in the design of computer systems. The illustrative examples portray plausible cases of bias.

1. Preexisting Bias
Preexisting bias has its roots in social institutions, practices, and attitudes.
When computer systems embody biases that exist independently, and usually prior to the creation of the system, then the system exemplifies preexisting bias. Preexisting bias can enter a system either through the explicit and conscious efforts of individuals or institutions, or implicitly and unconsciously, even in spite of the best of intentions.

1.1. Individual
Bias that originates from individuals who have significant input into the design of the system, such as the client commissioning the design or the system designer (e.g., a client embeds personal racial biases into the specifications for loan approval software).

1.2 Societal
Bias that originates from society at large, such as from organizations (e.g., industry), institutions (e.g., legal systems), or culture at large (e.g., gender biases present in the larger society that lead to the development of educational software that overall appeals more to boys than girls).

2. Technical Bias
Technical bias arises from technical constraints or technical considerations.

2.1 Computer Tools
Bias that originates from a limitation of the computer technology including hardware, software, and peripherals (e.g., in a database for matching organ donors with potential transplant recipients certain individuals retrieved and displayed on initial screens are favored systematically for a match over individuals displayed on later screens).

2.2 Decontextualized Algorithms
Bias that originates from the use of an algorithm that fails to treat all groups fairly under all significant conditions (e.g., a scheduling algorithm that schedules airplanes for take-off relies on the alphabetic listing of the airlines to rank order flights ready within a given period of time).

2.3 Random Number Generation
Bias that originates from imperfections in pseudorandom number generation or in the misuse of pseudorandom numbers (e.g., an imperfection in a random-number generator used to select recipients for a scarce drug leads systematically to favoring individuals toward the end of the database).

2.4 Formalization of Human Constructs
Bias that originates from attempts to make human constructs such as discourse, judgments, or intuitions amenable to computers: when we quantify the qualitative, discretize the continuous, or formalize the nonformal (e.g., a legal expert system advises defendants on whether or not to plea bargain by assuming that law can be spelled out in an unambiguous manner that is not subject to human and humane interpretations in context).

Table I. *Continued*

These categories describe ways in which bias can arise in the design of computer systems. The illustrative examples portray plausible cases of bias.

3. Emergent Bias

Emergent bias arises in a context of use with real users. This bias typically emerges some time after a design is completed, as a result of changing societal knowledge, population, or cultural values. User interfaces are likely to be particularly prone to emergent bias because interfaces by design seek to reflect the capacities, character, and habits of prospective users. Thus, a shift in context of use may well create difficulties for a new set of users.

3.1 New Societal Knowledge

Bias that originates from the emergence of new knowledge in society that cannot be or is not incorporated into the system design (e.g., a medical expert system for AIDS patients has no mechanism for incorporating cutting-edge medical discoveries that affect how individuals with certain symptoms should be treated).

3.2 Mismatch between Users and System Design

Bias that originates when the population using the system differs on some significant dimension from the population assumed as users in the design.

3.2.1 Different Expertise

Bias that originates when the system is used by a population with a different knowledge base from that assumed in the design (e.g., an ATM with an interface that makes extensive use of written instructions—"place the card, magnetic tape side down, in the slot to your left"—is installed in a neighborhood with primarily a nonliterate population).

3.2.2 Different Values

Bias that originates when the system is used by a population with different values than those assumed in the design (e.g., educational software to teach mathematics concepts is embedded in a game situation that rewards individualistic and competitive strategies, but is used by students with a cultural background that largely eschews competition and instead promotes cooperative endeavors).

embeds the biases of clients or designers who seek to avoid certain applicants on the basis of group stereotypes, the automated loan advisor's bias is preexisting.

2.2 Technical Bias

In contrast to preexisting bias, technical bias arises from the resolution of issues in the technical design. Sources of technical bias can be found in several aspects of the design process, including limitations of computer tools such as hardware, software, and peripherals; the process of ascribing social meaning to algorithms developed out of context; imperfections in pseudorandom number generation; and the attempt to make human constructs amenable to computers, when we quantify the qualitative, discretize the continuous, or formalize the nonformal. As an illustration, consider again the case of Sabre and Apollo described above. A technical constraint imposed by the size of the monitor screen forces a piecemeal presentation of flight options and, thus, makes the algorithm chosen to rank flight options critically important. Whatever ranking algorithm is used, if it systematically places certain airlines' flights on initial screens and other airlines' flights on later screens, the system will exhibit technical bias.

2.3 Emergent Bias

While it is almost always possible to identify preexisting bias and technical bias in a system design at the time of creation or implementation, emergent bias arises only in a context of use. This bias typically emerges some time after a design is completed, as a result of changing societal knowledge, population, or cultural values. Using the example of an automated airline reservation system, envision a hypothetical system designed for a group of airlines all of whom serve national routes. Consider what might occur if that system was extended to include international airlines. A flight-ranking algorithm that favors on-line flights when applied in the original context with national airlines leads to no systematic unfairness. However, in the new context with international airlines, the automated system would place these airlines at a disadvantage and, thus, comprise a case of emergent bias. User interfaces are likely to be particularly prone to emergent bias because interfaces by design seek to reflect the capacities, character, and habits of prospective users. Thus, a shift in context of use may well create difficulties for a new set of users.

3. APPLICATIONS OF THE FRAMEWORK

We now analyze actual computer systems in terms of the framework introduced above. It should be understood that the systems we analyze are by and large good ones, and our intention is not to undermine their integrity. Rather, our intention is to develop the framework, show how it can identify and clarify our understanding of bias in computer systems, and establish its robustness through real-world cases.

3.1 The National Resident Match Program (NRMP)

The NRMP implements a centralized method for assigning medical school graduates their first employment following graduation. The centralized method of assigning medical students to hospital programs arose in the 1950s in response to the chaotic job placement process and on-going failure of hospitals and students to arrive at optimal placements. During this early period the matching was carried out by a mechanical card-sorting process, but in 1974 electronic data processing was introduced to handle the entire matching process. (For a history of the NRMP, see Graettinger and Peranson [1981a].) After reviewing applications and interviewing students, hospital programs submit to the centralized program their ranked list of students. Students do the same for hospital programs. Hospitals and students are not permitted to make other arrangements with one another or to attempt to directly influence each others' rankings prior to the match.

ACM Transactions on Information Systems, Vol. 14, No. 3, July 1996.

Table II.   The Simplest Case of Rank-Order Lists in which the Desires of Students and
Programs are in Conflict (Reprinted from Williams et al. [1991], by permission of the *New
England Journal of Medicine*)

Rank Order	Student I	Student II	Program A	Program B
1	Program A	Program B	Student II	Student I
2	Program B	Program A	Student I	Student II

Note: Each program in this example has a quota of one position.

With the inputs from hospitals and students, the NRMP applies its
"Admissions Algorithm" to produce a match.

Over the years, the NRMP has been the subject of various criticisms. One
charges that the Admissions Algorithm systematically favors hospital
programs over medical students in cases of conflict [Graettinger and
Peranson 1981b; Roth 1984; Sudarshan and Zisook 1981; Williams et al.
1981]. Consider the example developed by Williams et al., which we
reproduce:

> To generate a match from Table II, the NRMP algorithm first attempts
> a so-called 1:1 run, in which concordances between the first choice of
> students and programs are matched (this table was constructed so that
> there would be none). The algorithm then moves to a 2:1 run, in which
> the students' second choices are tentatively run against the programs'
> first choices. Both students are matched with their second-choice pro-
> grams. This tentative run becomes final, since no students or program
> is left unmatched. Matching is completed; both programs receive their
> first choices, and both students their second choices.
>
> The result of switching the positions of the students and programs in
> the algorithm should be obvious. After the 1:1 run fails, the 2:1 run
> under a switch would tentatively run the programs' second choices
> against the students' first choices, thus matching both programs with
> their second-choice students. Matching is again completed, but on this
> run, both students receive their first choices, and the programs . . .
> receive their second choices [Williams et al. 1981, p. 1165].

Does such preference for hospital programs reflect bias? We are inclined
to answer yes because in cases of conflict there does not appear to be a good
rationale for favoring hospital programs at the expense of students. Moreover, Graettinger and Peranson provide grounds for assessing the type of
bias. They write, "The constraint inherent in the NRMP algorithm, in
which preference is given to hospital choices when conflicts in rankings
occur, duplicates what happens in an actual admissions process without a
computerized matching program" [Graettinger and Peranson 1981b, p.
526]. Elsewhere, they write:

> Changing the [Admissions] algorithm would imply changing the
> NRMP's role from one of passive facilitator to one in which the NRMP
> would be intervening in the admissions process by imposing a different

result than would be obtained without the matching program. This is not the role for which the NRMP was intended [p. 526].

Thus, if the algorithm systematically and unfairly favors hospital over student preferences, it does so because of design specifications and organizational practices that predate the computer implementation. As such, the NRMP embodies a preexisting bias.

Earlier versions of the NRMP have also been charged with bias against married couples in cases where both the husband and wife were medical students. When the NRMP was originally designed, few such couples participated in the medical match process. Beginning, however, in the late 1970s and early 1980s more women entered medical schools, and not surprisingly, more married couples sought medical appointments through the NRMP. At this point, it was discovered that the original Admissions Algorithm placed married couples at a disadvantage in achieving an optimal placement as compared with their single peers [Roth 1984; 1990]. Roth describes the problem as follows:

> Prior to the mid-1980s, couples participating in the match were required to specify one of their members as the "leading member," and to submit a rank ordering of positions for each member of the couple; that is, a couple submitted two preference lists. The leading member was matched to a position in the usual way, the preference list of the other member of the couple was edited to remove distant positions, and the second member was then matched if possible to a position in the same vicinity as the leading member. It is easy to see how instabilities [nonoptimum matches] would often result. Consider a couple whose first choice is to have two particular jobs in Boston, and whose second choice is to have two particular jobs in New York. Under the couples algorithm, the leading member might be matched to his or her first choice job in Boston, whereas the other member might be matched to some undesirable job in Boston. If their preferred New York jobs ranked this couple higher than students matched to those jobs, an instability would now exist [Roth 1990, p. 1528].

In this example, once the leading member of the couple is assigned a match in Boston no other geographic locations for the couple are considered. Thus, a better overall match with a hospital in New York is missed. The point here is that the bias—in this case emergent bias—against couples primarily emerged when a shift occurred in the social conditions, namely, when husband and wife medical students increasingly participated in the match process.

Compare the above two charges of bias with a third one, which accuses the NRMP of bias against hospitals in rural areas because of a consistent placement pattern over the years in which urban hospitals are far more successful in filling their positions than rural ones [Roth 1984; Sudarshan and Zisook 1981]. The Admissions Algorithm does not take into account geographic distribution when determining a match, considering only the ranked preferences of hospitals and students. Because the best teaching hospitals tend to be in urban areas, the urban areas tend to fill their positions far more effectively, and with better students, than rural hospitals. Observing this uneven distribution some have concluded that the NRMP is biased against rural hospitals in favor of urban ones. Is this so?

While we are committed to a stance against injustice, we do not think the distinction between a rationally based discrimination and bias is always easy to draw. In some cases, reasonable people might differ in their judgments. In this case, we ourselves would shy away from viewing this as a bias in the system because we think this discrimination can be defended as having a reasonable basis. Namely, the discrimination reflects the preferences of match participants, and it is reasonable in our view for employment decisions to be determined largely by the choices of employers and employees.

Bias in the NRMP is particularly troubling because of the system's centralized status. Most major hospitals agree to fill their positions with the NRMP assignments. Thus, for an individual or couple to elect not to participate in the NRMP is tantamount to forgoing the possibility of placement in most hospital programs. In this manner, centralized computing systems with widespread use can hold users hostage to whatever biases are embedded within the system.

3.2 A Multilevel Scheduling Algorithm (MLSA)

In timeshare computer systems many individuals make use of a single computer. These systems face a common problem of how to schedule the processing demands of the many individuals who make use of the processor at the same time. When posed with how to share equitably a limited resource, accepted social practice often points toward a first-come, first-serve basis. But the practical shortcomings of this approach are readily apparent. Imagine a person who uses the computer for interactive editing. Such work entails many small jobs that take very little time to process. Should another user with a large job requiring several minutes or hours of computation come along, the first user would experience a noticeable delay between execution of editing commands. Likely enough, frustrations would run high, and users would be dissatisfied. Thus, a balance must be struck between providing a reasonable response time and relatively efficient computation speed of large and long-running programs.

Proposed by F. J. Corbato in the 1960's, the MLSA represents one algorithm to address this balance [Corbato et al. 1962]. This algorithm was implemented in the CTSS timesharing system and in Multics. In brief, the MLSA works as follows. When a new command is received, it is executed for up to a quantum of time. If the process is not completed in that quantum of time, then the process is placed in a queue for "longer-running processes." Other new commands, if present, then are processed. Only when there are no new commands does the processor return to the process left in the queue for longer-running processes. Execution of this process is continued for a larger quantum of time. If the process is not completed in this larger quantum of time, then it is placed in yet another queue of "even longer running processes." And again, the processor returns to execute any new commands and, after that, any processes in the queue for longer-running processes. Only when there are no new commands and the queue for longer-running processes is empty will the processor look to the queue of even longer running processes for unfinished processes. In this manner the MLSA gives processing attention to all processes as quickly as possible that are beginning a new command. Thus, assuming the system is not saturated with too many users, short-running processes are speedily processed to completion. At the same time, however, in principle a long-running process could wait all day to finish.

Does the balance between response time and computation speed of long-running programs achieved by the MLSA systematically disadvantage some users? To help answer this question, consider a situation in which many people use a timeshare system at the same time on a regular basis. Of these individuals, most use relatively small programs on relatively short tasks, such as the interactive editing mentioned above. However, one or two individuals consistently use the system to execute long-running programs. According to the MLSA, the long-running programs of these individuals will necessarily end up with a lower priority than the short-running tasks of the other users. Thus, in terms of overall service from the processor, these individuals with long-running programs are systematically disadvantaged. According to Corbato (electronic communication, December 17, 1993), in response to this situation, some users with long-running programs uncovered the MLSA's strategy and developed a counterstrategy: by using a manual button to stop execution of a long-running process and a moment later restarting the process from where it left off, users effectively ran their long-running tasks in small chunks. Each small chunk, of course, was placed by MLSA into the top priority queue and executed speedily.

Having established systematic discrimination in the MLSA, we next ask whether this systematic discrimination is unfair. Consider that in other sorts of mundane queuing situations, such as movies or banks, we generally perceive that the "first-come first-served" strategy is fairest. It is also true that we can appreciate alternative strategies if they can complement and replace the strategy. In supermarkets, for example, we can appreciate express checkouts. But we likely would perceive as unfair a checkout system in which customers with fewer than, say, 10 items in their baskets could push ahead of anyone else in the line with more than ten items. Similarly, it seems to us that by systematically favoring short jobs, the MSLA violates the fairness preserved in the "first-come first-served" strategy.

While a human context gave rise to the need for the scheduling algorithm, it is important to understand that there was no prior bias against individuals with longer-running jobs. That is, the algorithm's bias did not arise from social factors, say, to dissuade users from large computational projects or to encourage interactive editing and debugging. Had this been the case, the bias would be preexisting. Rather the bias is technical, for the algorithm arose in the attempt to satisfy a difficult technical requirement to allocate a scare resource. It does so by giving processing attention to all processes as quickly as possible.

Another algorithm might have eluded the MLSA's form of technical bias by balancing response time and long-running computations in a manner that did not lead to systematic disadvantage for individuals with long-running programs. However, we also recognize that in the attempt to strike a balance between two apparently conflicting claims on a processor, it may not be possible to achieve a solution that is completely fair to all of those using the system. In cases like the MLSA, an awareness may be needed that one group is disadvantaged by the system, and an attempt made to minimize that disadvantage from within the system or to address it by some other means.

3.3 The British Nationality Act Program (BNAP)

Before discussing bias in the BNAP, a bit of history. In 1981 the Thatcher government passed the British Nationality Act as a means to redefine British citizenship. The act defined three new categories: British citizenship, citizenship of the British Dependent Territories, and British overseas citizenship. Only full British citizens in the first category would have the right to live in Britain. While the Thatcher government and some British citizens defended the act, others raised objections. For example, within Britain, according to *The London Times*, "The Labour Shadow Cabinet . . . decided to oppose the Bill on the grounds that it contains elements of racial and sexual discrimination" [Berlins and Hodges 1981, p. 1]. Similarly, in India, the *Hindustan Times* reported (quoted by Fishlock [1981]):

> Racial discrimination, by whatever name or device, is still discrimination of the most reprehensible kind. The Bill formalizes and legitimates racism toward people of a different hue which reflects the xenophobic paranoia that afflicts a section of British society today. The proposed three tiers of citizenship are a fine sieve which will allow into Britain only those of the desired racial stock.

Beginning in 1983, M. J. Sergot and his colleagues at the Imperial College, University of London, undertook to translate the British Nationality Act into a computer program so that "consequences of the act can be determined mechanistically" [Sergot et al. 1986, p. 370].[1] Critics have charged BNAP of gender bias. Consider the following. One of the most compelling grounds for establishing British citizenship is to have at least one parent who is a British citizen. As specified in Section 50-(9) of the British Nationality Act itself and imple-

---

[1] Although the program authors [Sergot et al. 1986] state "It was never our intention to develop the implementation of the act into a fully functional program" (p. 371), it is difficult to take their disclaimer entirely seriously. For in the same text the authors also state (as noted above) that their goal is to translate the British Nationality Act so that "the consequences of the act can be determined mechanistically" (p. 370), and they place their work in the context of other legal expert systems designed for use with real users.

mented in BNAP, "a man is the 'father' of only his legitimate children, whereas a woman is the 'mother' of all her children, legitimate or not" [Sergot et al. 1986, p. 375]. Consider then the instance of an unmarried man and woman who live together with the children they have jointly conceived. If the mother is a British citizen, and the father is not, then the children have one parent who is considered a British citizen. But if the situation is reversed (that is, if the father is a British citizen, and the mother is not), then the children have no parents who are considered British citizens. Thus the British Nationality Act is biased against the illegitimate descendants of British men. Accordingly, to the extent the BNAP accurately represents the British Nationality Act, the program embodies preexisting bias.

Two further concerns with the BNAP can be understood in terms of emergent bias. First, the system was designed in a research environment, among people with sophisticated knowledge of immigration law. Its users, however, are likely to be at best paralegal or immigration counselors in Britain, if not lay persons in foreign countries with only limited access to British legal expertise. A problem thus arises for nonexpert users. Some of the program's queries, for example, require expert knowledge to answer. More generally, nonexperts advising British citizen hopefuls are not alerted to alternative legal frameworks that complement the British Nationality Act. Thus nonexperts—particularly in developing countries— would be inclined to accept decisively the BNAP's response to their client's situation. In such ways, the BNAP comes to act as an instrument of bias against the nonexperts and their clients. Because this bias arises from a shift in the population using the system from the one apparently held in mind by the system's creators (from expert to nonexpert users) we identify this bias as emergent.

Another source for emergent bias can arise in the following way. At the time of the BNAP's initial implementation (1983) no mechanism was built into the program to incorporate relevant case law as it came into being [Sergot et al. 1986]. Should the accumulation of case law lead to changes in the way the Act is interpreted—say, by granting new subgroups British citizenship—BNAP would systematically misinform members of this subgroup regarding their status as British citizens [Leith 1986]. Again, we identify this bias as emergent because it depends on a shift in the social context, in this instance one concerning knowledge within the legal community. Emergent bias poses a potential problem for any legal expert system, especially in a society where legal systems depend on evolving case law. Indeed, to varying degrees, any expert system (independent of content area) that does not possess a reasonable mechanism for integrating new knowledge may be vulnerable to a similar form of emergent bias.

4. CONSIDERATIONS FOR MINIMIZING BIAS IN COMPUTER SYSTEM DESIGN

As our framework helps delineate the problems of bias in computer systems, so does it offer ways to remedy them. But, before saying more along these lines, it is important to address two potential concerns that the reader may have about the framework itself.

First, as we have noted earlier, computer systems sometimes help implement social policies on which reasonable people can disagree regarding whether the policies are fair or unfair. Does the NRMP, for example, embody a bias against rural hospitals? Other examples might include affirmative-action hiring programs, tax laws, and some federal funding programs. According to our framework, would computer systems that help implement such discriminative policies embody bias? The answer follows the initial (controversial) question—namely, "Is the policy under consideration fair or unfair?" Does affirmative action, for example, help redress past unfairness or not? The answer to most of these questions is beyond the scope of this article. But we do say that if unfairness can be established in the system's systematic discrimination, then the charge of bias follows.

Second, although we have talked about bias in computer systems, the presence of bias is not so much a feature inherent in the system independent of the context of use, but an aspect of a system in use. This distinction can be seen clearly in an example of emergent bias. Consider the case of an intelligent tutoring system on AIDS whose intended users are to be college students. Here, a high degree of literacy can be assumed without incurring bias. In contrast, the same level of literacy cannot be assumed without introducing bias in designing a system to provide AIDS education in a public space such as a shopping mall or metro station. For in such public spaces less educated people would be at an unfair disadvantage in using the system. Or consider again the case of technical bias with the MLSA (which favors users with short jobs over long jobs). While technical bias is embedded in the program, the bias is a phenomenon of the system in use, in a context wherein users with short and long jobs outpace the system's capacity.

Remedying bias from a practical perspective involves at least two types of activities. One, we need to be able to identify or "diagnose" bias in any given system. Second, we need to develop methods of avoiding bias in systems and correcting it when it is identified. We offer below some initial directions this work could take.

Toward minimizing preexisting bias, designers must not only scrutinize the design specifications, but must couple this scrutiny with a good understanding of relevant biases out in the world. The time to begin thinking about bias is in the earliest stages of the design process, when negotiating the system's specifications with the client. Common biases might occur to populations based on cultural identity, class, gender, literacy (literate/less literate), handedness (right-handed/left-handed), and physical disabilities (e.g., being blind, color-blind, or deaf). As the computing community develops an understanding of these biases, we can correspondingly develop techniques to avoid or minimize them. Some current computer systems, for instance, address the problem of handedness by allowing the user to toggle between a right- or left-handed configuration for user input and screen display. Similarly, systems could minimize bias due to color blindness by encoding information not only in hue, but in its intensity, or in some other way by encoding the same information in a format unrelated to color. In addition, it can prove useful to identify potential user populations which might otherwise be overlooked and include representative individuals in the field test groups. Rapid prototyping, formative evaluation, and field testing with such well-conceived populations of users can be an effective means to detect unintentional biases throughout the design process.

Technical bias also places the demand on a designer to look beyond the features internal to a system and envision it in a context of use. Toward preventing technical bias, a designer must envision the design, the algorithms, and the interfaces in use so that technical decisions do not run at odds with moral values. Consider even the largely straightforward problem of whether to display a list with random entries or sorted alphabetically. In determining a solution, a designer might need to weigh considerations of ease of access enhanced by a sorted list against equity of access supported by a random list.

Minimizing emergent bias asks designers to envision not only a system's intended situations of use, but to account for increasingly diverse social contexts of use. From a practical standpoint, however, such a proposal cannot be pursued in an unbounded manner. Thus, how much diversity in social context is enough, and what sort of diversity? While the question merits a lengthy discussion, we offer here but three suggestions. First, designers should reasonably anticipate probable contexts of use and design for these. Second, where it is not possible to design for extended contexts of use, designers should attempt to articulate constraints on the appropriate contexts of a system's use. As with other media, we may need to develop conventions for communicating the perspectives and audience assumed in the design. Thus, if a particular expert system because of its content matter, goals, and design requires expert users to be used effectively, this constraint should be stated clearly in a salient place and manner, say, on one of the initial screens. Third, system designers and administrators can take responsible action if bias emerges with changes in context. The NRMP offers a good example. Although the original design of the Admissions Algorithm did not deal well with the changing social conditions (when significant numbers of dual-career couples participated in the match), those responsible for maintaining the system responded conscientiously to this societal change and modified the system's algorithm to place couples more fairly [Roth 1990].

That said, even if a designer successfully detects bias in a proposed design, and has ideas on how to eradicate or minimize it, a client may be reluctant to remedy the bias for a variety of reasons. For example, airlines executives whose companies serve national and international routes may knowingly support the bias in an automated reservation system that favors on-line flights. Situations such as these put designers in a difficult spot. What ought they to do if a client actually wants a bias to be present? Is it the designer's responsibility to speak out against a client, or is it simply to tow the line and produce a system, bias and all?

Readers who have followed discussions of professional ethics will be familiar with similar dilemmas. A quick answer is not possible, but one thing is clear. In order for designers to take an effective stand against a client regarding biased systems, it will be important for designers to find support for such action from their professional community. The criteria of reliability and safety offer a perspective on this point. Through extensive discussion and solid technical work, the computing community over the recent years has recognized that good systems must be judged on criteria that include reliability and safety. Such consensus provides individual system designers with substantial backing if and when they are required to make their cases to skeptical clients or employers. Something similar is needed for bias. The more the computing community explicitly recognizes bias as a feature of computer systems that is worth addressing and minimizing, the more individual designers will have clout in shaping the practice of computing in the work place and elsewhere.

While we advocate serious attention to bias in system design, we also recognize there are limits to what system designers can accomplish. Some biases extend beyond computing to larger societal problems. An empirical result from work by Huff and Cooper [1987] on gender-bias in the design of educational software provides a helpful illustration. In their study, subjects were asked to propose designs for software to teach seventh graders the correct use of commas. One group of subjects was asked to design the software for seventh-grade boys, the second group to design for seventh-grade girls, and the third group to design for seventh-graders, gender unspecified. Huff and Cooper report that along a number of dimensions the designs proposed by subjects in the gender-unspecified group closely resembled the designs proposed by subjects who designed for boys and were significantly different from the designs proposed by subjects who designed for girls. This study illustrates how preexisting biases, in the form of expectations about what software will appeal to each gender, coupled with the implicit assumption that the generic "user" of software is likely to be male, can influence design and give rise to bias in software. Huff and Cooper report, furthermore, that many of their subjects were aware of and had expressed open concern about how computers were frequently perceived to be in the male domain. We thus infer that in this case the biased designs were unintended and, instead, reflected gender-biases deeply rooted in the culture at large. While creating nongender-biased educational software contributes to addressing the larger social problems tied to gender bias and computing, resolving problems like gender bias go beyond system design. More broadly, where biases in the larger society flourish, bias-free system design forms but one part of a movement to a more equitable society.

5. CONCLUSION

Because biased computer systems are instruments of injustice—though admittedly, their degree of seriousness can vary considerably—we believe that freedom from bias should be counted among the select set of criteria according to which the quality of systems in use in society should be judged. The methods delineated here can be used to assess and minimize bias in the design of systems. Concern with bias in system design and experience with these methods can be integrated with other software engineering methods as part of the standard for a computer science curriculum.

As with other criteria for good computer systems, such as reliability, accuracy, and efficiency, freedom from bias should be held out as an ideal. As with these other criteria, this ideal might be difficult if not impossible to achieve. Nonetheless, in practice we must approach actively the task of minimizing bias in our designs. Furthermore, as a community we must hold our designs accountable to a reasonable degree of freedom from bias against which negligence can be judged.

ACKNOWLEDGMENTS

We thank our research assistant Mark Muir for help with aspects of this analysis. We thank F. J. Corbató, John Ellis, Deborah Johnson, James Moor, John Mulvey, Peter Neumann, and Alvin Roth for discussions concerning bias; and we thank Rob Kling and anonymous reviewers for their comments on this article. We extend our appreciation to CSLI, Stanford University, for use of their facilities during December, 1993.

REFERENCES

BERLINS, M. AND HODGES, L. 1981. Nationality Bill sets out three new citizenship categories. *The London Times* (Jan. 15), 1, 15.

CORBATÓ, F. J., MERWIN-DAGGETT, M., AND DALEY, R. C. 1962. An experimental time-sharing system. In *Proceedings of the Spring Joint Computer Conference*. Spartan Books, 335–344.

FISHLOCK, T. 1981. Delhi press detect racism in Nationality Bill. *The London Times* (Jan. 20).

FOTOS, C. P. 1988. British Airways assails U.S. decision to void CRS agreement with American. *Aviat. Week Space Tech.* (Oct. 24), 78.

GAO. 1992. Patriot Missile defense: Software problem led to system failure at Dhahran, Saudi Arabia. GAO/IMTEC-92-26, U.S. General Accounting Office, Washington, D.C.

GRAETTINGER, J. S. AND PERANSON, E. 1981a. The matching program. *New Engl. J. Med. 304*, 1163–1165.

GRAETTINGER, J. S. AND PERANSON, E. 1981b. National resident matching program. *New Engl. J. Med. 305*, 526.

HUFF, C. AND COOPER, J. 1987. Sex bias in educational software: The effect of designers' stereotypes on the software they design. *J. Appl. Soc. Psychol. 17*, 519–532.

JOHNSON, D. G. AND MULVEY, J. M. 1993. Computer decisions: Ethical issues of responsibility and bias. Statistics and Operations Res. Series SOR-93-11, Dept. of Civil Engineering and Operations Research, Princeton Univ., Princeton, N.J.

LEITH, P. 1986. Fundamental errors in legal logic programming. *Comput. J. 29*, 225–232.

MOOR, J. 1985. What is computer ethics? *Metaphilosophy 16*, 266–275.

OTT, J. 1988. American Airlines settles CRS dispute with British Airways. *Aviat. Week Space Tech.* (July 18).

ROTH, A. E. 1984. The evolution of the labor market for medical interns and residents: A case study in game theory. *J. Pol. Econ. 92*, 6, 991–1016.

ROTH, A. E. 1990. New physicians: A natural experiment in market organization. *Science 250*, (Dec. 14), 1524–1528.

SERGOT, M. J., SADRI, F., KOWALSKI, R. A., KRIWACZEK, F., HAMMOND, P., AND CORY, H. T. 1986. The British Nationality Act as a logic program. *Commun. ACM 29,* 370–386.

SHIFRIN, C. A. 1985. Justice will weigh suit challenging airlines' computer reservations. *Aviat. Week Space Tech.* (Mar. 25), 105–111.

SUDARSHAN, A. AND ZISOOK, S. 1981. National resident matching program. *New Engl. J. Med. 305,* 525–526.

TAIB, I. M. 1990. Loophole allows bias in displays on computer reservations systems. *Aviat. Week Space Tech.* (Feb.), 137.

WILLIAMS, K. J., WERTH, V. P., AND WOLFF, J. A. 1981. An analysis of the resident match. *New Engl. J. Med. 304,* 19, 1165–1166.

Received May 1994; revised February 1995; accepted August 1995

[21]

Method in computer ethics: Towards a multi-level interdisciplinary approach

Philip Brey
University of Twente, The Netherlands

Abstract. This essay considers methodological aspects of computer ethics and argues for a multi-level interdisciplinary approach with a central role for what is called disclosive computer ethics. Disclosive computer ethics is concerned with the moral deciphering of embedded values and norms in computer systems, applications and practices. In the methodology for computer ethics research proposed in the essay, research takes place at three levels: the disclosure level, in which ideally philosophers, computer scientists and social scientists collaborate to disclose embedded normativity in computer systems and practices, the theoretical level, in which philosophers develop and modify moral theory, and the application level, that draws from research performed at the other two levels, and at which normative evaluations of computer systems and practices takes place.

1. Computer ethics: Aim, scope and method

This essay considers the role of method in computer ethics and proposes that a particular methodology for doing computer ethics that is multi-level and interdisciplinary and assigns a special role to the moral deciphering of embedded normativity or values in computer systems, application and practices. In this section, the methodological issues for computer ethics are introduced by relating them to the aim and scope of computer ethics. In section 2, a particular approach within computer ethics is discussed, which is called disclosive computer ethics. It is an approach that centers on the deciphering of embedded normativity in computer systems, application and practices. In section 3, the multi-level interdisciplinary methodology for doing computer ethics that is the topic of this paper is outlined, building on the discussions in the previous sections. The paper ends with a brief concluding section.

In his by now classical essay "What is computer ethics?" Jim Moor proposed that the central aim of computer ethics is to formulate policies to guide individual and collective action in the use of computer technology (Moor 1985). I agree with this proposal, with the addition that not just the use of computer technology, but also other practices that involve computing technology, such as its development or management, require the formulation of policy guidelines. When we conceive of computer ethics in this way, it is clear that it is a branch of *applied ethics*. Whereas its counterpart, theoretical ethics, is concerned with general aspects of morality, applied ethics is concerned with the study of morality in particular domains of human practice. Moreover, the aim of applied ethics is

not merely to arrive at well-supported moral analysis, but also to use such analyses to affect the discourse, policies and practices that are prevalent in its domain of study.

The *scope* of computer ethics includes individual and collective practices that somehow essentially involve computers. This includes practices like the use, development, regulation, management, advocacy and advertisement of computer technology. Also included should be the products of such actions, e.g., computer systems and software, manuals, advertisements, and laws and policies regulating the use of computers. These products deserve special mention because their moral properties may be analyzed independently from a consideration of the actions that have lead to them. For example, a law regulating the copying of software may be analyzed for its moral content independently of an analysis of any actions that led to the adoption of the law.

Having defined what I see as the aim and scope of computer ethics, I will now proceed to discuss various *methods* used within it, with the aim of identifying different research activities involved in contemporary computer ethics research. To begin with, computer ethics, like other branches of applied ethics, often involves the application of existing moral theory to practices that are under study (Van Den Hoven 1997). So *the application of moral theory* is certainly one of the central activities in computer ethics. For example, the question of what amount of protection should be granted to software developers against the copying of their programs may be answered by applying consequentialist or natural law theories of property, and the question of what actions governments should take in helping citizens have access to computers may be answered by applying Rawls's principles of justice.

Applying moral theory is only part of what computer ethicists do, however. As Jim Moor (1985) has pointed out, the changing settings and practices that emerge with new computer technology may yield new values, as well al require the reconsideration of old values. There may also be new moral dilemma's because of conflicting values that suddenly clash when brought together in new settings and practices. It may then be found that existing moral theory has not adequately theorized these values and value conflicts. Privacy, for example, is now recognized by many computer ethicists as requiring more attention than it has previously received in moral theory. In part this is due to reconceptualizations of the private and public sphere brought about by the use of computer technology, which has resulted in inadequacies in existing moral theory about privacy. It is therefore fitting for computer ethicists to contribute to the development of moral theory about privacy. In general, it is part of the task of computer ethics to *further develop and modify existing moral theory* when existing theory is insufficient or inadequate in light of new demands generated by new practices involving computer technology.

Part of the work done in computer ethics is the development of ethical theory and its application to practices involving computer technology. Both these activities are *normative*, in that they are concerned with proposing, defending, analyzing or applying normative concepts and principles. I want to claim, however, that a large part of the research in computer ethics is not normative in this sense, but is instead *descriptive*: it is concerned with describing aspects of reality and with proposing, defending, analyzing or applying descriptive concepts and principles.

The importance of descriptive research has been noted to some extent by Jim Moor (1985), who has claimed that "much of the important work in computer ethics is devoted to proposing conceptual frameworks for understanding ethical problems involving computer technology" (p. 266). Moor clearly holds that a large part of the conceptual work needed for doing computer ethics is found in the analysis of descriptive concepts. For example, Moor holds that to arrive at a policy for protecting computer programs, descriptive conceptual questions must first be answered such as "What is a computer program?" and "Can programs really be owned?". So a third important research activity for computer ethics is *conceptual analysis of descriptive concepts and adequate description of relevant empirical facts.*

2. Hidden morality and disclosive computer ethics

I want to argue that there is still a fourth important research activity in computer ethics, one that has not been recognized sufficiently by Moor. Moor seems to presume that computer ethics is in large part about solving preexisting moral problems. He claims: "A typical problem in computer ethics arises because there is a policy vacuum about how computer technology should be used." In such a case, the work that is to be done is the conceptual clarification and description of the practice that generates the moral problem. However, I want to claim that a large part of work in computer ethics is not about the clarification of practices that have already generated moral controversy, but rather about *revealing the moral import of practices that appear to be morally neutral.* Many designs and uses of computer systems, I want to claim, have important moral properties, that remain hidden because the technology and its relation to the context of use are too complex or are insufficiently well-known. It is part of the job of computer ethics to make computer technology and its uses transparent, in a way that reveals its morally relevant features.

The notion that computer technology can have moral properties is an extension of the notion that it can have political properties (Winner 1980; Sclove 1995; Pfaffenberger 1992; Akrich 1992). As Winner (1980) has argued, technological artifacts and systems function much like laws, by constraining behavior and serving as frameworks for public order. Richard Sclove has made the same point by identifying technical artifacts as elements of social structure. Sclove defines the social structure of a society as its 'background features that help define or regulate patterns of human interaction. Familiar examples include laws, dominant political and economic institutions, and systems of cultural belief' (1995, p. 11). He argues that technologies should also be included in this list, because they have the same kinds of structural effects as these other elements of social structure. Technologies are, for example, capable of coercing individuals to behave in certain ways, may provide opportunities and constraints, may affect cultural belief systems, and may require certain background conditions for them to function properly. Many such structural effects of technology may be analyzed from a moral point of view.

Much recent work in computer ethics is centrally concerned with the moral deciphering of computer technology. Friedman and Nissenbaum (1997), for example, is a study of bias in computer systems (see also Brey 1998). Biases in computer systems are usually not recognized, but Friedman and Nissenbaum try to reveal the existence of bias by describing computer systems with bias and by bringing into view the possible unjust consequences of such systems. Similarly, Brey (1999, 1998) is concerned with the consequences of the design of computer systems for the autonomy of users. A large part of the research in these papers is concerned with revealing the potential impacts of computer designs on the autonomy of users, and much less attention is devoted to theorizing and applying moral principles of autonomy. Other examples are Nissenbaum (1997), revealing the moral importance of practices of registering public information, Blanchette (1998), revealing the importance of trust relations in cryptographic protocols and payment mechanisms, Introna and Nissenbaum (2000), who decipher the hidden politics of search engines, Agre and Mailloux (1997), who reveal the implications for privacy of Intelligent Vehicle-Highway Systems, and Tavani (1999), who analyzes the implications of data mining for privacy. The major contribution of all this research is not so much found in the development or application of ethical theory, but rather in the description of computer technology and related practices in a way that reveals their moral importance.

The importance of this mode of analysis in computer ethics justifies the introduction of a label by which it may be named. I propose to call this approach *disclosive computer ethics*. Disclosive studies in computer ethics are hence studies concerned with disclosing and evaluating embedded normativity in computer systems, applications and practices.

Admittedly, the description of technologies and practices so as to reveal their moral importance presupposes that one can already discern what is and what is not morally important, and hence that relevant moral values have already been formulated before analysis comes off the ground. However, this does not mean that one must already be equipped with moral theories before disclosive analysis can take place. The (potential) moral importance of designs or practices is already sufficiently established if it is shown that these designs or practices yield, for example, an unequal distribution of power or of goods, that they diminish privacy or freedom (according to common-sense notions of these terms), that they affect social relations or statuses, or that they touch on other important moral values that are widely shared in society. Therefore, a more precise moral evaluation can wait until after disclosive analysis.

Thus, a disclosive study in computer ethics may take the form of a two-stage process. In the first stage of analysis, some technology (*X*) is analyzed from the point of view of a relevant moral value (*Y*) (where *Y* is, e.g., privacy, justice, freedom, etc.), which is only given a loose, common-sense definition. This analysis may yield a tentative conclusion that certain features of *X* tend to undermine (or perhaps sustain) *Y* in particular ways. For example, it may be found that search engines in use on the Internet tend to undermine informational privacy, where informational privacy is defined loosely as the control that individuals have over the disclosure of information about their person. This analysis may prompt a second stage in which theories of informational privacy are applied and perhaps further developed so as to arrive at a more specific normative evaluation of the privacy-aspects of search engines, that can also be used to arrive at policy guidelines regarding their design, use and regulation.

Of course, it is also possible to do disclosive analysis in a more theory-driven way. In the above example, one would then start with a moral theory of informational privacy that would contain specific moral principles, and then analyze the manner in which search engines uphold or fail to uphold these principles. Optionally, this analysis could again result in a set of policy recommendations regarding the privacy-aspects of search engines.

These two approaches are both acceptable varieties of disclosive computer ethics. There are, however, at least two reasons why a theory-driven variety may ultimately be less preferable. First, a theory-driven approach tends to makes the acceptance of a disclosive analysis dependent on the acceptance of a particular moral theory. For example, a study that shows that existing search engines violate a particular conception of informational privacy found in theory *T* may not convince someone that search engines raise issues for informational privacy if that person rejects *T*. That person might have been convinced by an analysis that had started with a loose definition of informational privacy, and proceeded to show that search engines pose a problem for informational privacy according to this loose definition.

Second, a theory-driven approach will already contain preconceptions about the technology or practice that is under scrutiny, because it already employs a highly theoretical vocabulary in the analysis of observable phenomena, that may include empirical presuppositions. It may therefore come to observations that are as based in part on preconceptions in the theory that is applied, at points where more neutral descriptions may be preferable. In conclusion, there are good reasons not to choose a theory-driven approach in disclosive computer ethics if given the choice.

Finally, the question should be raised *what* moral values and norms are to be studied in disclosive analyses. I propose they should preferably be moral values and norms that are broadly supported throughout society, because computer systems or applications that violate them are clearly morally unacceptable. Some values that fit this criterion that have successfully been investigated in past studies in disclosive computer ethics are justice (or fairness), autonomy (or freedom), democracy, and privacy. So for example, a disclosive study of fairness in the design of an electronic credit rating system would start with a broad, common-sense definition of fairness and then proceed to investigate if there are groups that are treated unfairly by the system according to the definition of fairness used.

3. The need for multi-level interdisciplinary research

Disclosive computer ethics requires an approach that is multi-level and interdisciplinary. It is multi-level in that research is to take place at various stages or levels. Three such levels can be discerned. First, there is the *disclosure level*, which is the initial level at which disclosive computer ethics research takes place. At this level, some type of computer system or software is analyzed from the point of view of a relevant moral value like privacy or justice. Second, there is the *theoretical level*, which is the level at which moral theory is developed and refined. This was identified in section 1 as one of the core tasks of computer ethics. This rather fundamental research, on issues like informational privacy or the relation between distributive justice and information, may be motivated by new practices involving computer technology, and may use concrete examples to support its claims, but aims to come to generalizations that abstract from specific technologies or practices. Third, there is the *application level*, in which, in varying degrees of specificity and concreteness, moral theory is applied to analyses that are the outcome of research at the disclosure level.

Whereas computer ethics research at the theoretical level only requires philosophical expertise and may be carried out by philosophers, this is not so for research at the disclosure and application levels. Research at the disclosure level often requires considerable technical expertise, and often also require expertise in social science for the analysis of the way in which the functioning of systems is dependent on human actions, rules and institutions. So ideally, research at the disclosure level is a cooperative venture between computer scientists, social scientists and philosophers. Or else, it should be carried out by researchers with an adequate interdisciplinary background.

Research at the application level may be argued to be a philosopher's job again, as applying moral theory (e.g., weighing moral principles against considered moral judgments) seems to make an appeal to mostly philosophical skills (Van Den Hoven 1997). However,

even if bringing moral theory in agreement with moral judgments, empirical facts, scientific claims and other relevant sources of information is a activity that mostly appeals to philosophical skills, the information that must be processed in this task largely of a nonphilosophical kind. Philosophers engaged in this activity must therefore have a solid grasp of the social, legal and technical aspects of the technology or practice on which they are to pass moral judgments, or should opt to work with experts in these areas.

The above three-layer model applies to disclosive approaches in computer ethics. Nondisclosive computer ethics normally follows a two-stage model that only includes the theoretical and application levels. Nondisclosive approaches are typically concerned with issues where it is already clear that the technologies or practices involved raise moral questions, and the aim is to try to answer these questions. In such studies, the technologies and practices are usually fairly transparent, but resolving the moral issues they raise turns out to be a challenge. For example, in studies on the ethics of anonymous speech on-line, it will usually be clear in advance what practices are at issue and what role technology plays in making them possible, so there is not much work to be done at the disclosure level. Instead, most work will typically be done at the application level, in weighing and combining existing moral theory (e.g., on the ethics of anonymity) with the specifics of the case at hand.

4. Conclusion

Disclosive computer ethics constitutes a much needed approach in computer ethics that deviates from traditional approaches in applied ethics that usually neglect embedded normativity in technological systems and practices, and still often concentrate on formulating and applying moral theory. As has been argued, disclosive computer ethics should preferably not be theory-driven and should focus on four key values: justice, autonomy, democracy, and privacy. The proposed disclosive method may well be generalized to other areas of applied ethics in which technology plays an important role.

The methodology required for disclosive computer ethics is a multi-level interdisciplinary one, in which research takes place at three levels: the disclosure level, in which philosophers, computer scientists and social scientists collaborate to disclose embedded normativity in computer systems and practices, the theoretical level, in which philosophers develop and modify moral theory, and the application level, at which individuals with good philosophical skills and a broad relevant background knowledge work on normative evaluations of computer systems and practices, drawing from research performed at the other two levels. Nondisclosive computer ethics research does not involve a disclosure level, but is a two-level process, involving an application level and a theoretical level. It is not involved with revealing moral issues, but has its focus on an attempt to (further) clarify and resolve them.

References

P. Agre and C. Mailloux. Social Choice about Privacy: Intelligent Vehicle-Highway Systems in the United States. In B. Friedman, editor, *Human Values and the Design of Computer Technology*, Cambridge University Press, 1997.

M. Akrich. The Description of Technical Objects. In W. Bijker and J. Law, editors, *Shaping Technology/Building Society: Studies in Sociotechnical Change*. MIT Press, 1992.

J. Blanchette. *On the Social Discourse of Cryptology*, Paper presented at CEPE'98, London School of Economics and Political Science, 14–15 December, 1998.

P. Brey. New Media and the Quality of Life. *Techné: Journal of the Society for Philosophy and Technology*, 3: 1–23, 1997.

P. Brey. The Politics of Computer Systems and the Ethics of Design. In J. van den Hoven, editor, *Computer Ethics: Philosophical Enquiry*. Rotterdam University Press, 1998.

P. Brey. Worker Autonomy and the Drama of Digital Networks in Organizations. *Journal of Business Ethics*, 22: 15–25, 1999.

G. Dworkin. *The Theory and Practice of Autonomy*. Cambridge University Press, Cambridge, 1988.

B. Friedman and H. Nissenbaum. Bias in Computer Systems. In B. Friedman, editor, *Human Values and the Design of Computer Technology*. Cambridge University Press, 1997.

T. Hill. *Autonomy and Self-Respect*. Cambridge University Press, 1991.

J. van den Hoven. Computer Ethics and Moral Methodology. *Metaphilosophy*, 28: 234–248, 1997.

L. Introna and H. Nissenbaum. The Public Good Vision of the Internet and the Politics of Search Engines. In R. Rogers, editor, *Preferred Placement. Knowledge Politics on the Web*. Jan van Eyck Akademie Editions, Maastricht, 2000.

J. Moor. What is Computer Ethics? *Metaphilosophy*, 16: 266–275, 1985.

H. Nissenbaum. Can We Protect Privacy in Public? In J. van den Hoven, editor, *Computer Ethics: Philosophical Enquiry*. Rotterdam University Press, 1998.

B. Pfaffenberger Technological Dramas. *Science, Technology, and Human Values*, 17: 282–312, 1992.

J. Rawls. *A Theory of Justice*. Harvard University Press, 1971.

R. Sclove. *Democracy and Technology*. Guilford Press, New York, 1995.

H. Tavani. Informational Privacy, Data Mining, and the Internet. *Ethics and Information Technology*, 1: 137–145, 1999.

L. Winner. Do Artifacts have Politics? *Daedalus*, 109: 121–136, 1980.

Part IV
Responsibility and Professionalism

[22]

Human Agency and Responsible Computing: Implications for Computer System Design

Batya Friedman
Mills College, Oakland, California

Peter H. Kahn, Jr.
University of Houston, Houston, Texas

To understand and promote responsible computing, this paper highlights the importance of analyses based on human agency. We first examine whether computers can be moral agents. Then we draw on research in human factors, cognitive science, and instructional technology to examine how three types of computing practices can be problematic from the perspective of human agency. The first involves anthropomorphizing a computational system, the second, delegating decision making to a computational system, and the third, delegating instruction to a computational system. Throughout this discussion, we provide alternative design goals and methods by which responsible computing can be enhanced as a shared vision and practice within the computing community.

Societal interest in responsible computing perhaps most often arises in response to harmful consequences that can result from computing. For instance, consider the frustration and economic loss incurred by individuals and businesses whose computer systems have been infected by the Internet worm or other computer viruses. Or consider the physical suffering and death of the cancer patients who were overradiated by Therac-25, or of civilians accidentally bombed in the Persian Gulf war by "smart" missiles gone astray. Largely in reaction to events like these, we have in recent years seen a surge of interest in preventing or at least minimizing such harmful consequences. But if responsible computing is to be understood as something more than a form of damage control, how are we to understand the term? Moreover, how can responsible computing be promoted within the computing community?

In this article, we address these questions by highlighting the importance of analyses based not only on consequences of acts, but agency—on what and why some things can be held morally responsible for action. We shall first examine whether computers can be such things. While our discussion here will be largely philosophical (and somewhat condensed as each piece may well be familiar to the reader), a compelling position on whether computers can be moral agents provides an important starting point for our central task. We seek to understand how, from the moral perspective, we should conceive of the human relationship to computational systems, and to provide sketches of how to build on that conception to promote responsible computing through system design. To this end, we will examine how three types of computing practices can be problematic from the perspective of human agency. The first involves anthropomorphizing a computational system, the second, delegating decision making to a computational system, and the third, delegating instruction to a computational system.

CAN COMPUTERS BE MORAL AGENTS?

To understand the place and urgency of the question of whether computers can be moral agents, consider the issues raised by computer-based closed-loop drug administration systems. In critical care medicine, these automated systems are designed to monitor and, when necessary, adjust the administration of a variety of drugs for patients in an intensive care unit. Such

Address correspondence to Batya Friedman, Clare Boothe Luce Asst. Professor of Computer Science, Dept. of Mathematics and Computer Science, Colby College, Waterville, ME 04901.

8   J. SYSTEMS SOFTWARE   Batya Friedman and Peter H. Kahn, Jr.
         1992; 17:7–14

computer-based systems are touted for their increased effectiveness over human-administered drug therapy, for their safety, and for their usefulness in reducing nursing demands [1, 2]. However, these systems, although currently recommended for use, pose ethical problems. For instance, Snapper [3] suggests that such a computer-based system "may not be able to check as many variables as could a doctor at the bedside and so may administer the wrong drug when a doctor would administer the correct drug" (p. 289). Or such a computer-based system may not be programmed to account for a particular atypical case, and so may administer the wrong drug when an experienced doctor would administer the correct drug. In such situations, can the computer-based closed-loop drug administration system itself be held, even in part, morally responsible for the decision to administer a wrong drug? Stated more generally, can a computational system be a moral agent and thus be held morally responsible for a decision?

Toward addressing this question, consider two cases. While hiking in the mountains, Y is crushed by a falling boulder and killed. In case one, the boulder was dislodged by a slight shifting and settling of the land on which it balanced. In case two, the same boulder was dislodged by a push from X, who desired to kill Y, believed the push would cause the boulder to fall on Y, understood that a boulder of such weight would kill Y, and freely chose to perform the act. The cases are the same in that some "thing" caused a boulder to fall, killing Y. But the cases are fundamentally different in that only in the second case was the act of dislodging the boulder the result of an intentional act. This distinction between the cases highlights a philosophical position that for a thing to be held morally responsible it must be capable of intentionality, which, at a minimum, refers to the capability of having or experiencing beliefs, desires, understandings, intentions, and volition [4, 5]. Given, then, that people but not land are usually considered psychologically capable of intentional states, only X (but not the land) could be held morally responsible for the death of Y. Moving now to the question at hand: If we accept that intentional states are a prerequisite for a thing to be held morally responsible, then a subset of the above question—can a computational system be a moral agent and thus be held morally responsible for a decision?—can be framed as follows: Can a computational system be considered to have intentional states?

Much of the literature in artificial intelligence would have us think it so, or at least have us think it possible. One classic framing of this position can be traced to McCarthy [6], who proposed some decades ago that machine intentionality is equivalent to human intentionality. For example, in one of his well-known analogies, McCarthy claimed that a thermostat has beliefs (of whether a room is too hot or cold) that lead to intended action (turning the heater off or on). Such intentional states, according to McCarthy, are equivalent to that of a human who can have beliefs (of whether a room is too hot or cold) that lead to intended action (taking a sweater off or putting one on).

There are two ways to understand such a position that equate machine intentionality with human intentionality. Both will frame our analyses of computer system design. In the first, whatever we may call intentionality and think we may experience in terms of feelings, beliefs, understandings, free will, or an underlying sense of self or personhood are epiphenomenal, meaning such experiences play no authentic causal role in our actions. In the second, it is claimed that machines have (or with increased technological advancements will have) psychological states similar or identical to those which comprise human intentionality (in a nonepiphenomenal sense). In other words, the first reduces humans to the status of computers, while the second raises computers to the status of humans.

Both ways of understanding are problematic. Granted, it may be that humans ultimately will never be able to prove conclusively that what we take to be intentionality is not epiphenomenal, for the position draws on a radical skepticism that calls into question every means we might have to undermine it. The argument is similar to one that charges that you, the reader, are nothing but a brain in a vat [7], prodded at this very moment with electrical stimulation to induce you to think that you are reading this essay, and that you have the thoughts, feelings, and experiences that you do. Anything you might try to say to counter this position (e.g., "I think therefore I am," or less formally, "But I know deep down inside myself that that is not true") can be counterargued with the claim that your knowledge has simply been induced by electrical stimulation.

It is a far cry, however, from not being able to prove this position conclusively false to believing, with good reason, that it is true. Phenomenologically, humans experience intentional states and believe they have beliefs, understandings, and free will. If such intentionality is epiphenomenal, it is difficult to understand biologically and psychologically why or how it ever originated within our species. Moreover, it would be virtually impossible to live in this world without taking our intentional states seriously. We would, for instance, have to abandon such beliefs that a difference exists between accidental and intended harm (since the belief in intended action is epiphenomenal), that persons can lose weight, climb hills, or read books if they so choose (since the belief in free choice is epiphenomenal), and so on for the countless intentional states that pervade our lives. Indeed, even the desire to understand how intentionality is epiphenomenal presupposes a validity to intentionality, to such psychological constructs as desire and understanding that lead to the intended action to provide an alternative explanation. The point here is that without positive evidence to the contrary, which this first position based on a radical skepticism does not provide, humans have good reason to believe that human intentionality plays an authentic causal role in our actions.

The second way of understanding the proposition that equates human intentionality with machine intentionality, that machines have states similar or identical to those which comprise human intentionality, has been substantively critiqued by Searle [8]. His Chinese room argument is well known:

> Consider a language you don't understand. In my case, I do not understand Chinese. To me Chinese writing looks like so many meaningless squiggles. Now suppose I am placed in a room containing baskets full of Chinese symbols. Suppose also that I am given a rule book in English for matching Chinese symbols with other Chinese symbols. The rules identify the symbols entirely by their shapes and do not require that I understand any of them. Imagine that people outside the room who understand Chinese hand in small bunches of symbols and that in response I manipulate the symbols according to the rule book and hand back more small bunches of symbols. Now, the rule book is the "computer program." The people who wrote it are "programmers," and I am the "computer." The baskets full of symbols are the "data base".... Now suppose that the rule book is written in such a way that my "answers" to the "questions" are indistinguishable from those of a native Chinese speaker.... All the same, I am totally ignorant of Chinese. And there is no way I could come to understand Chinese in the system as described, since there is no way that I can learn the meanings of any of the symbols. Like a computer, I manipulate symbols, but I attach no meaning to the symbols. (p. 26)

In other words, because computational systems are purely formal (syntax), and because purely formal systems have no means to generate intentionality (semantics), computational systems do not have intentionality.

Searle's position has generated a great deal of debate, including 26 commentaries, since it appeared in 1980 [9], and continued more recently by Churchland and Churchland [10]. While this is not the place to review the many arguments and counterarguments in the debate, in our view and the view of others, Searle has defended his position well against his critics. This is not to say that minds and their intentional states might not someday be realized in materials or structures other than biological brains. But it is to say that computers as we can conceive of them today are not such materials or structures.

Thus we have argued, however briefly, for three propositions: 1) intentionality is a necessary condition of moral agency; 2) we can, with confidence, believe that human intentionality plays an authentic causal role in our actions; and 3) a computer system as we can conceive of it today in material and structure cannot have intentionality. From these three propositions, it follows that humans, but not computational systems, are capable of being moral agents, and that humans, but not computational systems, are capable of being morally responsible for computer-mediated actions and consequences.

DESIGN TO SUPPORT HUMAN AGENCY AND RESPONSIBLE COMPUTING

Based on this line of reasoning, we propose that responsible computing often depends on humans' clear understanding that humans are capable of being moral agents and that computational systems are not. However, as anticipated by the above discussion, this understanding can be distorted in one of two ways. In the first type of distortion, the computational system diminishes or undermines the human user's sense of his or her own moral agency. In such systems, human users are placed into largely mechanical roles, either mentally or physically, and frequently have little understanding of the larger purpose or meaning of their individual actions. To the extent that humans experience a diminished sense of agency, human dignity is eroded and individuals may consider themselves to be largely unaccountable for the consequences of their computer use. Conversely, in the second type of distortion the computational system masquerades as an agent by projecting intentions, desires, and volition. To the extent that humans inappropriately attribute agency to such systems, humans may well consider the computational systems, at least in part, to be morally responsible for the effects of computer-mediated or computer-controlled actions.

Accordingly, to support humans' responsible use of computational systems, system design should strive to minimize both types of distortion. That is, system design should seek to protect the moral agency of humans and to discourage in humans a perception of moral agency in the computational system. How might design practices achieve these goals? Given that little research exists that addresses this question directly, we seek to provide some initial sketches by examining three types of computer practices.

Anthropomorphizing the Computational System

Anthropomorphic metaphors can be found in some of the definitions and goals for interface design. For

10 J. SYSTEMS SOFTWARE
1992; 17:7-14

Batya Friedman and Peter H. Kahn, Jr.

example, some interfaces are designed to "use the process of human–human communication as a model for human–computer interaction" ([11], p. 86), to "interact with the user similar to the way one human would interact with another" ([11], p. 87), or to be "intelligent" where intelligence is based on a model of human intelligence. When such anthropomorphic metaphors become embedded in the design of a system, the system can fall prey to the second type of distortion by projecting human agency onto the computational system.

Moreover, even in unsophisticated designs of this type, there is some evidence that people do attribute agency to the computational system. For example, Weizenbaum [12] reported that some adults interacted with his computer program DOCTOR with great emotional depth and intimacy, "conversing with the computer as if it were a person" (p. 7). In a similar vein, some of the children Turkle [13] interviewed about their experiences with an interactive computer game called Merlin that played Tic-Tac-Toe attributed psychological (mental) characteristics to Merlin. For example, children sometimes accused Merlin of cheating, an accusation that includes a belief that the computer has both the intention and desire to deceive. In another example, Rumelhart and Norman [14] attempted to teach novices to use an editing program by telling the novices that the system was like a secretary. The novices drew on this human analogy to attribute aspects of a secretary's intelligence to the editing system and assumed (incorrectly) that the system would be able to understand whether they intended a particular string of characters to count as text or as commands.

While these examples of human attribution of agency to computational systems have largely benign consequences, this may not always be the case. Consider Jenkins' [15] human factors experiment that simulated a nuclear power plant failure. In the experiment, nuclear power plant operators had access to an expert system to aid them in responding to the plant failure. Although previously instructed on the expert system's limitations, the "operators expected that the expert system implemented in the computer 'knew' about the failures of the cooling system without being told. The system [however] was neither designed nor functioned as an automatic fault recognition system" (p. 258). Jenkins attributed this overestimation of the system's capabilities to the power plant operators' expectations for the expert system to know certain information, presumably the type of information that any responsible human expert would know or attempt to find out in that situation.

Because nonanthropomorphic design does not encourage people to attribute agency to the computational system, such designs can better support responsible computing. To clarify what such design looks like in practice, consider the possibilities for interface design. Without ever impersonating human agency, interface design can appropriately pursue such goals as learnability, ease and pleasure of use, clarity, and quick recovery from errors. In addition, nonanthropomorphic interface design can employ such techniques as novel pointing devices, nonanthropomorphic analogies, speech input and output, and menu selection. Or consider the characteristics of another plausible technique: direct manipulation. According to Jacob [16], direct manipulation refers to a user interface in which the user "seems to operate directly *on* the objects in the computer rather than carrying on a dialogue *about* them" (p. 166). For example, the Xerox Star desktop manager adapted for systems such as the Apple Macintosh uses images of standard office objects (e.g., files, folders, and trash cans) and tasks to represent corresponding objects and functions in the editing system [17]. In this environment, disposing of a computer file is achieved by moving the image of the file onto the image of the trash can, akin to disposing of a paper file by physically placing the file in a trash can. There is no ambiguity in this direct manipulation interface as to who is doing the acting (the human user) and what the user is acting upon (objects in the computational system). The defining characteristics of direct manipulation suggest that this technique would not lead to projecting human agency onto the system. This is because direct manipulation involves physical action on an object as opposed to social interaction with an other as an underlying metaphor. Additionally, direct manipulation seeks to have the human user directly manipulate computational objects, thereby virtually eliminating the possibility for the human user to perceive the computer interface as an intermediary agent.

Nonanthropomorphic design considerations fit within a larger vision for interface design that is already part of the field. For example, Shneiderman [18] draws on Weizenbaum [12] to advocate design that "sharpen[s] the boundaries between people and computers . . . [for] human–human communication is a poor model for human–computer interaction" (p. 434). More recently, Shneiderman [19] writes that "when an interactive system is well designed, it almost disappears, enabling the users to concentrate on their work or pleasure" (p. 169). Winograd and Flores [20] similarly advocate the design of nonanthropomorphic computer tools that provide a transparent interaction between the user and the resulting action. "The transparency of interaction is of utmost importance in the design of tools, including computer systems, but it is not best achieved by attempting to mimic human faculties" (p. 194). When a transparent interaction is achieved, the user is freed from the details of using the tool to focus on the task at

J. SYSTEMS SOFTWARE 11
1992; 17:7-14

hand. The shared vision here is for the interface to "disappear," not to intercede in the guise of another "agent" between human users and the computational system.

Delegating Decision Making to Computational Systems

When delegating decision making to computational systems, both types of distortions can occur. The discussion that follows examines these distortions in the context of the APACHE system [21, 22]. More generally, however, similar analyses could be applied to other computer-based models and knowledge-based systems such as MYCIN [23] or the Authorizer's Assistant used by the American Express Corporation [24].

APACHE is a computer-based model implemented but not yet used clinically that determines when to withdraw life support systems from patients in intensive care units. Consider the nature of the human computer relationship if APACHE, used as a closed-loop system, determines that life support systems should be withdrawn from a patient, and then turns off the life support systems. In ending the patient's life the APACHE system projects a view of itself to the medical personnel and the patient's family as a purposeful decision maker (the second type of distortion). Simultaneously, the system allows the attending physician and critical care staff to distance or numb themselves from the decision making process about when to end another human's life (the first type of distortion).

Now, in actuality, at least some of the researchers developing APACHE do not recommend its use as a closed-loop system, but as a consultation system, one that recommends a course of action to a human user who may or may not choose to follow the recommendation [21]. These researchers write: "Computer predictions should never dictate clinical decisions, as very often there are many factors other than physiologic data to be considered when a decision to withdraw therapy is made" (p. 1096). Thus, used as a consultation system, APACHE functions as a tool to aid the critical care staff with making difficult decisions about the withdrawal of therapy. Framed in this manner, the consultation system approach seems to avoid the distortions of human agency described above: the consultation system does not mimic purposeful action or inappropriately distance the medical staff from making decisions about human life and death.

In practice, however, the situation can be more complicated. Most human activity, including the decision by medical personnel to withdraw life support systems, occurs in a web of human relationships. In some circumstances, because a computational system is embedded in a complex social structure human users

may experience a diminished sense of moral agency. Let us imagine, for instance, that APACHE is used as a consultation system. With increasing use and continued good performance by APACHE, it is likely that the medical personnel using APACHE will develop increased trust in APACHE's recommendations. Over time, these recommendations will carry increasingly greater authority within the medical community. Within this social context, it may become the practice for critical care staff to act on APACHE's recommendations somewhat automatically, and increasingly difficult for even an experienced physician to challenge the "authority" of APACHE's recommendation, since to challenge APACHE would be to challenge the medical community. But at this point the open-loop consultation system through the social context has become, in effect, a closed-loop system wherein computer prediction dictates clinical decisions.

Such potential effects point to the need to design computational systems with an eye toward the larger social context, including long-term effects that may not become apparent until the technology is well situated in the social environment. Participatory design methods offer one such means [25, 26]. Future users, who are experienced in their respective fields, are substantively involved in the design process. As noted at a recent conference [27], Thoresen worked with hospital nurses to design a computer-based record-keeping system. In the design process, nurses helped to define on a macro level what institutional problems the technology would seek to solve, and on a micro level how such technological solutions would be implemented. From the perspective of human agency, such participatory design lays the groundwork for users to see themselves as responsible for shaping the system's design and use.

Delegating Instruction to Computational Systems

Instructional technology programs that deliver systematically designed computer-based courseware to students can suffer from the first type of distortion—computer use that erodes the human user's sense of his or her own agency. Often absent from this type of instructional technology is a meaningful notion of the student's responsibility for learning. Johnsen and Taylor [28] have discussed this problem in a paper aptly titled "At cross-purpose: instructional technology and the erosion of personal responsibility." According to Johnsen and Taylor, instructional technology "define[s] responsibility operationally in the context of means/ends rationality. The singular responsibility for a student's education becomes identified with the success of the program" (p. 9). They further point to the logical conclusion of this educational view for students, parents, teachers, and government: failure to educate comes to mean that

12   J. SYSTEMS SOFTWARE
        1992; 17:7-14

Batya Friedman and Peter H. Kahn, Jr.

the instructional technology failed to teach, not that students failed to learn.

As an example of this type of instructional technology, consider how the GREATERP intelligent tutoring system (described in [29]) for novice programmers in LISP handles students' errors. When GREATERP determines the student has entered "incorrect" information, the tutor interrupts the student's progress toward the student's proposed solution (viable or not) and forces the student to backtrack to the intelligent tutor's "correct" solution. Thus GREATERP assumes responsibility not only for student learning but also for preventing student errors along the way and for the process of achieving a solution. In so doing, this intelligent tutoring system—and other comparable instructional technology programs—can undermine the student's sense of his or her own agency and responsibility for the educational endeavor.

In contrast, other educational uses of computing promote students' sense of agency and active decision making. For example, just as consultation systems can to some degree place responsibility for decision making on the human user, so educational uses of computer applications software (e.g., word processors, spreadsheets, data bases, microcomputer-based labs) can place responsibility for learning on the student. With computer applications students determine when the applications would be useful and for what purposes, and evaluate the results of their use. Moreover, the social organization of school computer use can contribute to students' understanding of responsible computing. As with participatory design, consider the value of student participation in creating the policies that govern their own school computer use. For example, as discussed in a recent article by Friedman [30], students can determine the privacy policy for their own electronic mail at school. To establish such a privacy policy, "students must draw on their fundamental understandings of privacy rights to develop specific policies for this new situation. In turn, circumstances like these provide opportunities for students not only to develop morally but to make decisions about a socially and computationally powerful technology, and thus to mitigate a belief held by many people that one is controlled by rather than in control of technology." Through such experiences, students can learn that humans determine how computer technology is used and that humans bear responsibility for the results of that use.

CONCLUSION

We argued initially that humans, but not computers (as they can be conceived today in material and structure),

are or could be moral agents. Based on this view, we identified two broad approaches by which computer system design can promote responsible computer use. Each approach seeks to minimize a potential distortion between human agency and computer activity. First, computational systems should be designed in ways that do not denigrate the human user to machine-like status. Second, computational systems should be designed in ways that do not impersonate human agency by attempting to mimic intentional states. Both approaches seek to promote the human user's autonomous decision making in ways that are responsive to and informed by community and culture.

What we have provided, of course, are only broad approaches and design sketches. But if we are correct that human agency is central to most endeavors that seek to understand and promote responsible computing, then increased attention should be given to how the human user perceives specific types of human–computer interactions, and how human agency is constrained, promoted, or otherwise affected by the larger social environment. In such investigations, it is likely that research methods can draw substantively on existing methods employed in the social-cognitive and moral-developmental psychological fields. Methods might include 1) semistructured hypothetical interviews with participants about centrally relevant problems [31-35]; 2) naturalistic and structured observations [36-38]; and 3) semistructured interviews based on observations of the participant's practice [39-41]. Of note, some anthropologists [42] and psychologists [43] working in the area of human factors have with some success incorporated aspects of these methods into their design practices.

A final word needs to be said about the role of moral psychology in the field of computer system design. As increasingly sophisticated computational systems have become embedded in social lives and societal practices, increasing pressure has been placed on the computing field to go beyond purely technical considerations and to promote responsible computing. In response, there has been, understandably, a desire to know the "right" answer to ethical problems that arise, where "right" is understood to mean something like "philosophically justified or grounded." We agree that there is an important place for philosophical analyses in the field. But philosophy seldom tells us how or why problems relevant to a philosophical position involving computing occur in practice, let alone what can most effectively resolve them. Such issues require empirical data that deal substantively with the psychological reality of humans. Thus, by linking our technical pursuits with both philosophical inquiry and moral-psychological research, responsible computing can be enhanced as a shared vision and practice within the computing community.

REFERENCES

1. P. Bednarski, F. Siclari, A. Voigt, S. Demertzis, and G. Lau, Use of a computerized closed-loop sodium nitroprusside titration system for antihypertensive treatment after open heart surgery, *Crit. Care Med.* 18, 1061–1065 1990).

2. S. McKinley, J. F. Cade, R. Siganporia, O. M. Evans, D. G. Mason, and J. S. Packer, Clinical evaluation of closed-loop control of blood pressure in seriously ill patients, *Crit. Care Med.* 19, 166–170 (1991).

3. J. W. Snapper, Responsibility for computer-based errors, *Metaphilosophy* 16, 289–295 (1985).

4. G. E. Scott, *Moral Personhood: An Essay in the Philosophy of Moral Psychology*, State University of New York Press, Albany, New York, 1990.

5. J. R. Searle, *Intentionality*, Cambridge University Press, Cambridge, England, 1983.

6. J. McCarthy, Ascribing mental qualities to machines, in *Philosophical Perspectives on Artificial Intelligence* (M. Ringle, ed.), Humanities Press, Needham Heights, MA, 1979.

7. A. Zuboff, The story of a brain, in *The Mind's I* (D. R. Hofstadter and D. C. Dennett, eds.), Basic Books, Inc., New York, 1981.

8. J. R. Searle, Is the brain's mind a computer program? *Sci. Am.* 262, 26–31 (1990).

9. J. R. Searle, Minds, brains and programs, *Behav. Brain Sci.* 3, 417–458 (1980).

10. P. M. Churchland and P. S. Churchland, Could a machine think? *Sci. Am.* 262, 32–37 (1990).

11. R. E. Eberts and C. G. Eberts, Four approaches to human computer interaction, in *Intelligent Interfaces: Theory, Research and Design* (P. A. Hancock and M. H. Chignell, eds.), Elsevier Science Publishers, New York, 1989.

12. J. Weizenbaum, *Computer Power and Human Reason*, W. H. Freeman & Company, New York, 1976.

13. S. Turkle, *The Second Self: Computers and the Human Spirit*, Simon & Schuster, New York, 1984.

14. D. E. Rumelhart and D. A. Norman, Analogical processes in learning, in *Cognitive Skills and Their Acquisition* (J. R. Anderson, ed.), Lawrence Erlbaum Associates, Hillsdale, NJ, 1981.

15. J. P. Jenkins, An application of an expert system to problem solving in process control displays, in *Human-Computer Interaction* (G. Salvendy, ed.), Elsevier Science Publishers, New York, 1984.

16. R. J. K. Jacob, Direct manipulation in the intelligent interface, in *Intelligent Interfaces: Theory, Research and Design* (P. A. Hancock and M. H. Chignell, eds.), Elsevier Science Publishers, New York, 1989.

17. D. C. Smith, C. Irby, R. Kimball, W. Verplank, and E. Marslem, Designing the user interface, *Byte* 7, 242–282 (1982).

18. B. Shneiderman, *Designing the User Interface: Strategies for Effective Human-Computer Interaction*, Addison-Wesley Publishing Company, Reading, Massachusetts, 1987.

19. B. Shneiderman, Designing the user interface, in *Computers in the Human Context: Information Technology, Productivity, and People* (T. Forester, ed.), The MIT Press, Cambridge, Massachusetts, 1989.

20. T. Winograd and F. Flores, *Understanding Computers and Cognition: A New Foundation for Design*, Addison-Wesley Publishing Company, Reading, Massachusetts, 1986.

21. R. W. S. Chang, B. Lee, S. Jacobs, and B. Lee, Accuracy of decisions to withdraw therapy in critically ill patients: clinical judgment versus a computer model, *Crit. Care Med.* 17, 1091–1097 (1989).

22. J. E. Zimmerman, ed., APACHE III study design: analytic plan for evaluation of severity and outcome, *Crit. Care Med.* 17 (Part 2 Suppl), S169–S221 (1989).

23. E. H. Shortliffe, Medical consultation systems: designing for doctors, in *Designing for Human-Computer Communication* (M. E. Sime and M. J. Coombs, eds.), Academic Press, New York, 1983.

24. C. L. Harris *et al.*, Office automation: making it pay off, in *Computers in the Human Context: Information Technology, Productivity, and People* (T. Forester, ed.), The MIT Press, Cambridge, Massachusetts, 1989.

25. P. Ehn, *Work-oriented Design of Computer Artifacts*, Lawrence Erlbaum Associates, Hillsdale, New Jersey, 1989.

26. J. Greenbaum and M. Kyng, eds., *Design at Work: Cooperative Design of Computer Systems*, Lawrence Erlbaum Associates, Hillsdale, New Jersey, 1990.

27. A. Namioka and D. Schuler, eds., *Proceedings from the Conference on Participatory Design 1990*, Computer Professionals for Social Responsibility, Palo Alto, California, 1990.

28. J. B. Johnsen and W. D. Taylor, At cross-purpose: instructional technology and the erosion of personal responsibility, paper presented at the annual meeting of the American Educational Research Association, New Orleans, April 1988.

29. R. Kass, Student modeling in intelligent tutoring systems —implications for user modeling, in *User Models in Dialog Systems* (A. Kobsa and W. Wahlster, eds.), Springer-Verlag, New York, 1989.

30. B. Friedman, Social and moral development through computer use: a constructivist approach, *J. Res. Comput. Educ.* 23: 560–567 (1991).

31. W. Damon, *The Social World of the Child*, Jossey-Bass, San Francisco, 1977.

32. L. Kohlberg, Stage and sequence: the cognitive-developmental approach to socialization, in *Handbook of Socialization Theory and Research* (D. A. Goslin, ed.), Rand-McNally, Chicago, 1969.

33. J. Piaget, *The Child's Conception of the World*, Routledge & Kegan Paul, London, 1929.

34. J. Piaget, *The Moral Judgment of the Child*, Routledge & Kegan Paul, London, 1932.

14   J. SYSTEMS SOFTWARE
            1992; 17:7–14

Batya Friedman and Peter H. Kahn, Jr.

35. E. Turiel, *The Development of Social Knowledge: Morality and Convention*, Cambridge University Press, Cambridge, England, 1983.

36. R. DeVries and A. Goncu, Interpersonal relations in four-year dyads from constructivist and Montesorri programs, *J. Appl. Dev. Psychol.* 8, 481–501 (1987).

37. B. Friedman, Societal issues and school practices: An ethnographic investigation of the social context of school computer use, paper presented at the annual meeting of the American Educational Research Association, Boston, April 1990 (ERIC Document Reproduction Service No. ED 321 740).

38. L. P. Nucci and M. Nucci, Children's responses to moral and social conventional transgressions in free-play settings, *Child Dev.* 53, 1337–1342 (1982).

39. R. DeVries, Children's conceptions of shadow phenom-

ena, *Gen. Soc. Gen. Psychol. Monographs* 112, 479–530 (1986).

40. L. P. Nucci and E. Turiel, Social interactions and the development of social concepts in preschool children, *Child Dev.* 49, 400–407 (1978).

41. G. B. Saxe, *Culture and Cognitive Development: Studies in Mathematical Understanding*, Lawrence Erlbaum Press, Hillsdale, New Jersey, 1990.

42. L. A. Suchman, *Plans and Situated Actions: The Problem of Human–Machine Communication*, Cambridge University Press, Cambridge, England, 1987.

43. C. Allen and R. Pea, Reciprocal evolution of research, work practices and technology, in *Proceedings from the Conference on Participatory Design 1990* (A. Namioka and D. Schuler, eds.), Computer Professionals for Social Responsibility, Palo Alto, 1990.

[23]

Informatics and Professional Responsibility*

Donald Gotterbarn, *East Tennessee State University, USA*

Keywords: computer ethics, informatics, professional responsibility

ABSTRACT: *Many problems in software development can be traced to a narrow understanding of professional responsibility. The author examines ways in which software developers have tried to avoid accepting responsibility for their work. After cataloguing various types of responsibility avoidance, the author introduces an expanded concept of positive responsibility. It is argued that the adoption of this sense of positive responsibility will reduce many problems in software development.*

INTRODUCTION

In the summer of 1991 a major telephone outage occurred in the United States because an error was introduced when three lines of code were changed in a multi-million-line signaling program. Because the three-line change was viewed as insignificant, it was not tested. This type of interruption to software systems is too common. Not only are systems interrupted but sometimes lives are lost because of software problems. A New Jersey inmate under computer-monitored house arrest removed his electronic anklet. "A computer detected the tampering. However, when it called a second computer to report the incident, the first computer received a busy signal and never called back."[1] While free, the escapee committed murder. In another case innocent victims were shot to death by the French police acting on an erroneous computer report.[2] In 1986 two cancer patients were killed because of a software error in a computer controlled X-ray machine. Given the plethora of these kinds of stories, it is not surprising that informatics and computing have not enjoyed a positive image.

---

* An earlier version of this paper was written for inclusion in S. Rogerson and T. W. Bynum, eds., *Computer Ethics and Professional Responsibility*, Blackwell, (in press). Prepublished here with permission from the author and the editors.

Address for correspondence: Donald Gotterbarn, Professor, Computer and Information Sciences, East Tennessee State University, Box 70711, Johnson City, TN 37614, USA; gotterba@access.etsu.edu (email).

Published by Opragen Publications, POB 54, Guildford GU1 2YF, UK. http://www.opragen.co.uk

D. Gotterbarn

How can such problems result from the actions of moral software developers? The existence of such cases is a problem, but that is not my major concern in this paper; rather my concern is the narrow concept of responsibility which contributes to these disasters. I argue that, although informatics has been undergoing a rapid development, there has been only minimal corresponding development in the concept of responsibility as it applies to computing practitioners (CPs). Computing is an emerging profession that will not succeed until it has expanded its sense of responsibility. I describe a broader concept of responsibility that is consistent with professionalism in computing.

The focus of cases like the ones cited above is computer failures. In the early days of computing, CPs sought immunity from blame for their failure to develop reliable systems. CPs developed their own special language. Flaws in computer programs were not errors introduced by the programmer but were "bugs" found in the program. Notice how the emphasis is on finding the "bug" and not on determining how it got into the program or taking preventative action so that similar "bugs" will not get into future programs. Another favorite exculpatory euphemism used by CPs is "computer error". "I am not to blame. It was a computer error." The developer sometimes attempts to avoid responsibility for undesirable events by assigning the responsibility to the client who failed to adequately specify what was "really" needed. If the specifications are precise and the client cannot be used to exempt the developer from responsibility, the fact that "no program can be proven to be error free" is used to excuse critical system failures. And as a last resort, one can simply appeal to the complexity of the system. Complex systems are expected to fail. This is like the engineering concept of an "inevitable or normal accident". This concept holds that as the complexity of a system increases so does the likelihood of an accident. The accident should not be attributed to anyone's errors or failures to act. The implication of all of these excuses is that the responsibility for these events is borne by the computer or the complexity of the system rather than being borne by the developer of the computer system. This side-stepping of responsibility by software developers is based on inaccurate computer science. The problem here is more than bad science, these excuses are used to justify the development of systems that are detrimental to society and these excuses inhibit the development of computing as a profession.

The news media like to emphasize catastrophic cases of software development. This emphasis sometimes misleads us into ignoring questions of responsibility in more common cases of software development. Let us look at a common example in computing which can be used to illustrate a fuller, more positive concept of responsibility.

AN INADEQUATE INTERFACE

Fred Consultant, a computer consultant, developed several quality computer systems for the national government of NewLand. He attributed the quality of some of his systems to the good working relationship he had established with potential system users. The government of NewLand has an unnecessarily complex accounting system.

The system has so much overhead that administering it wastes significant amounts of taxpayer's money. Jim Midlevel, a local manager of this accounting system, understood where the waste was in the system. Even though he did not understand the day-to-day procedures of the system, he was able to design modifications to the systems which would significantly reduce the overhead costs of running it. Jim convinced his upper level management to implement his modifications to the system. Because of Fred's previous accomplishments his company was given the contract to write the first stage of the more efficient accounting system that will be used by the government and will save taxpayers a considerable amount of money. Fred met with Jim to discuss the system and carefully studied the required inputs and outputs of the revised system. Fred asked one of his best software engineers, Joanne Buildscreen to design the user interface for the system. Joanne studied the required inputs to the system and built an interface for the revised system. The system was developed and shown to Jim Midlevel. Jim was satisfied that the accounting system and the interface contained all of the functionality described in the requirements. The system passed its acceptance test which proved that all stated requirements had been met. The system was installed, but the user interface was so hard to use that the complaints of Jim's staff were heard by his upper level management. Because of these complaints, upper level management decided that it would not invest any more money in the development of the revised accounting system. To reduce staff complaints they would go back to the original more expensive accounting system.

What is the net result of the development effort described in this case? There is now a general ill will toward Fred's company and NewLand's officials do not give his company many contracts. The original, expensive, accounting program is back in place. The continued utilization of this program is a significant burden on the taxpayers. The situation is worse than it had been before this project was undertaken, because now there is little chance of ever modifying the system into a less expensive system.

SIDE-STEPS: AVOIDING OR DODGING RESPONSIBILITY

One of the first questions to be asked about this undesirable situation is "Who is responsible?" Generally this question is associated with seeking someone to blame for the problem. One of the reasons why the "blame-game" is so popular is that once it has been decided who is to blame, no one else needs to feel accountable for the problem. Finding a scapegoat to bear the blame for all others who may be involved is just as popular a model in computing as it is in literature.

I believe that there are two primary reasons why CPs side-step the assignment of responsibility, especially after a system failure or a computer disaster. Both of these reasons are errors grounded in misinterpretations of responsibility. These erroneous reasons are the belief that software development is an ethically neutral activity and belief in a malpractice model of responsibility.

D. Gotterbarn

Ethical Neutrality

The first error is that responsibility is not related to a CP because computing is understood by many CPs as an ethically neutral practice. There are a number of factors which contribute to this mistake. One factor contributing to why CPs find it reasonable to look elsewhere for someone to blame is the way we train them in the university. We train CPs to solve problems; and the examples we use, such as finding the least common multiple (LCM) for a set of numbers, portrays computing as merely a problem-solving exercise. The primary goal of the exercise is to solve the problem exactly as it is presented to the CP. All energy (and responsibility) is focused on finding a solution in an almost myopic fashion. This is analogous to the way people approach crossword puzzles. Solving the puzzle is an interesting exercise, but it generally lacks any significant consequences. There is no responsibility beyond solving the puzzle, other than properly disposing of the paper on which it is written. The same assumptions are made about solving computing problems.

The crossword-puzzle approach to computing problems leads to a failure to realize that computing is a service to the user of the computing artifact. This failure makes it easy to assign blame elsewhere. If there is no responsibility, there is no blame or accountability. The failure to see one's responsibility has other significant consequences. One result of the crossword-puzzle view is seen when we consider the real case of a programmer who was asked to write a program that would raise and lower a large X-ray device above the X-ray table, moving the machine to various fixed positions on a vertical support pole. The programmer wrote and tested his solution to this puzzle. It successfully and accurately moved the device to each of the positions from the top of the support pole to the top of the table. The difficulty with this narrow problem-solving approach was shown when, after installation, a X-ray technician told a patient to get off the table after a X-ray was taken and then the technician set the height of the device to "table-top-height". The patient had not heard the technician and was later found crushed to death between the machine and the table top. The programmer solved a puzzle but didn't consider any consequences of his solution to the user. If the programmer had considered the broader context, rather than limiting his attention to moving the X-ray machine on the pole, then he might have required an additional confirmation when moving the machine to the table top.

This first misunderstanding of responsibility is dangerous in that it is used to justify a lack of attention to anything beyond the job specification. The absurd degree to which this side-step can be taken is illustrated in the following real case. A defense contractor was asked to develop a portable shoulder-held anti-aircraft system. The specifications required that the shoulder-held system be capable of destroying a particular type of attack helicopter at 1000 yards with 97% efficiency. The system the contractor developed did effectively destroy incoming helicopters. Its kill rate was better than a 97%. It also had another feature. Because of a software error, the shoulder held missile launcher occasionally overheated to the extent that it burned off vital portions of the anatomy of the person holding the launcher. The extent of the burns killed the person who launched the missile. The government was, of course, dissatisfied with the product and declined to make the final payment to the contractor. The company took the government to court over the final payment. The company owners declared that they should be paid and that they are not responsible for the deaths because the system they developed "is in full compliance with the specifications given to them by the user". The contractors viewed this problem like a crossword puzzle. They solved a crossword puzzle exactly as it was presented to them, and they denied any further responsibility.

Diffuse Responsibility

The second side-step error is based on the belief that responsibility is best understood using a malpractice model which relates responsibility to legal blame and liability. It is important to find the correct parties to blame in order to bring legal action against them. Generally the concept of blame is tied to a direct action which brought about the undesirable event. A typical approach to determining blame is to isolate the event which immediately preceded and was causally related to the undesirable event, and then blaming the party who brought about the preceding event. In the case of NewLand's inadequate interface, Joanne's design of the interface screens was the direct cause of the user's dissatisfaction with the system. Joanne's screens were the immediate cause of the dissatisfaction so the tendency is to blame her. If the blame is both severe and public, then others will feel excused from responsibility for the unhappy event.

Joanne will not want to bear the blame and will point to other people's failures as contributing to the problem. This leads to the belief that one can avoid responsibility if the blame can be diffused by being widely distributed. This second side-step is based on the claim that individual software developers are too far from the event which causes the problem. It also distributes the blame so widely that it becomes negligible or cannot be clearly attributed.

This side-step is a paradoxical denial of responsibility since it starts by identifying multiple locations of failure of responsibility, namely the particular irresponsible acts of each member of the development team. This diffusion technique might be used in the Inadequate Interface case. Fred did not behave responsibly because he did not adequately understand the nature of the task.. Jim, because of his lack of specific system details, should have coordinated the development activities with the system users. Joanne should have shown preliminary screen designs to the system users. Everyone failed to meet his or her responsibilities. This distribution of failure is then used to deny legal fault or blame. The absurdity is that this identification of multiple individuals failing to meet their system development obligations is also used to deny each individual's responsibility. Like the first side-step, this diffusion of responsibility is a very dangerous practice. It follows from the diffusion side-step that whenever there are many people contributing to a project, no individual will be held accountable for their contributions to the project. If I am not responsible, then I have no prior commitment to do a competent job or worry about the overall quality of a product.

D. Gotterbarn

The diffusion of responsibility has a corollary which Ladd[3] has called "task responsibility", which ties responsibility to one narrowly defined task. An example of task responsibility can be generated by giving more details from the "Inadequate Interface" case. What was the problem that made the interface unusable? The multiple input screens used in the new accounting system did contain fields for all the required data, but the input sequence on the screens was not consistent with the structure of the input forms used by the clerks. To enter the data from a single input form, the clerks had to go back and forth between several screens. Using task responsibility, Joanne would maintain that it is "not her job" to get copies of the input forms. If "they" wanted the sequence of the data on the screens to match the input forms, then "someone" should have provided her with sample input forms. It is not her job to get the forms.

The association of responsibility with blame leads to a variety of excuses for not being accountable. These excuses include:

a. Absence of a direct and immediate causal link to the unacceptable event,[4]
b. Denial of responsibility since a responsible act conflicts with one's own self-interest,[5]
c. Responsibility requires the ability to do otherwise but CPs do most of their work in teams and for large organizations,[6]
d. Lack of strength-of-will to do what one thinks is right,[5]
e. Blaming the computer,[4]
f. Assuming that science is ethically neutral,
g. Microscopic vision.[7]

Both the neutrality and the diffusion side-stepping approaches to responsibility are inconsistent with efforts to professionalize computer science and engineering. Any profession should be strongly motivated to pursue the good of society. It should understand its primary function as a service to society. To professionalize computing, therefore, we need to revisit the concept of responsibility, separating it from the legal concept of blame, and separating it from direct and immediate causes of undesirable events. What sense of responsibility would meet these objections and mitigate the urge for side-stepping?

POSITIVE AND NEGATIVE RESPONSIBILITY

The philosophical concept of "responsibility" is very rich and is frequently tied to philosophical conundrums like "free will". Philosophers have long been concerned about the relationship between individual responsibility and free will. This concern derives in part from the implicit connection of the concept of blame with the concept of responsibility. If people have no free will then it is difficult to blame them for their actions. In opposition to this dependency of "responsibility" on the concept of blame and liability, Ladd distinguished the traditional sense of responsibility – which he calls "negative responsibility" from "positive responsibility". Negative responsibility deals with or looks for that which exempts one from blame and liability. An exemption from blame is an exemption from moral responsibility and an exemption from liability is an exemption from legal responsibility. Negative responsibility is distinguished from positive responsibility.

The concept of positive responsibility is consistent with many philosophies. One can extend Ladd's concept of positive responsibility to be justifiable under most philosophical theories. Positive responsibility can be grounded in any of the classical and contemporary theories. Such theories can be organized into a matrix created by the intersection of two of the following dimensions: rules/consequences and collective/individual.[8]

	RULES	CONSEQUENCES
COLLECTIVE	Collective rule-based	Collective consequentialist
INDIVIDUAL	Individual rule-based	Individual consequentialist

The emphasis in positive responsibility is on the virtue of having or being obliged to have regard for the consequences of his or her actions on others. We can place this sense of positive responsibility in each quadrant of the matrix. This sense of responsibility can be founded in: collective rule-based ethics based on the logic of the situation; individual rule-based ethics based on universal duties applicable to all;[9] collective consequentialists like Mill providing the greatest good for the greatest number; or individual consequentialists like Adam Smith who maintain that the social welfare is advanced by individuals doing good acts which have good consequences for society. No matter which ethical theory is used to justify positive responsibility, the focus of positive responsibility is on what ought to be done rather than on blaming or punishing others for irresponsible behavior.

Positive responsibility is not exclusive. It does not seek a single focus of blame. Negative responsibility, on the other hand, seeks a single focus of blame who, once found, exonerates all others from blame. With positive responsibility, saying that Joanne is responsible and should be held accountable for her failings does not exclude Fred. A virtue of positive responsibility is that several people can be responsible to varying degrees. Not only can we attribute responsibility to Fred, but we can say that he bears more of the responsibility in this case because he knew that Jim was only working with limited knowledge of the system.

This point illustrates a second and more significant virtue of positive responsibility, namely that it does not require either a proximate or direct cause. This extension of causal influence beyond the immediate and proximate cause is more consistent with assigning responsibility in the disasters that affect computing. Nancy Leveson,[10] in her article about the technical difficulties of the Therac-25 X-ray machine which led to multiple deaths, concludes that because of the involvement of many hands, responsibility for the Therac-25 incidents cannot be assigned. Leveson uses a limited-negative concept of responsibility and after identifying failures of multiple software

D. Gotterbarn

engineering practices refers to the deaths that resulted as "accidents". Nissenbaum[11] correctly criticized such an approach to responsibility when she said, "If we respond to complex cases by not pursuing blame and responsibility, we are effectively accepting agentless mishaps and a general erosion of accountability." The positive sense of responsibility allows the distribution of responsibility to software development teams, designers, etc. and can apply the concept of responsibility even to large development teams. In the Therac-25 case there may not be a single locus of blame, but under positive responsibility the developers are still responsible.

Any preliminary definition of responsibility starts from the presumption that others are affected by the outcomes of CPs' particular actions or failures to act. This presumption is embodied in many codes of ethics of computing associations. Such codes tend to organize responsibilities by the roles of the people involved. Most codes talk about the CPs' responsibilities to other professionals, to the client or employer, and to society in general. Only a few codes include the obligations of CPs to students. Although such codes try to recognize most of these relationships, most of them make the mistake of not distinguishing employers, clients, and users. In Joanne's case, her employer was Fred, the client was Jim, and the users were the accounting clerks. Because she stood in different relations to each of these parties, she owed them different and perhaps conflicting obligations. Some recent codes, such as the Software Engineering Code of Ethics and Professional Practice (SE)[12] provide the CP with techniques for adjudicating between conflicting obligations.

There are two types of responsibilities owed in all of these potential relations. One type of positive responsibility is technically based and the other positive responsibility is based on values. These two types of positive responsibility are both necessary for a concept of professional responsibility.

Positive responsibility points both forward and backward. It points backward when it identifies unmet obligations and what people ought to have done. Fred had an obligation to meet with the clerks to understand the structure of the interface they would need. This sense of responsibility goes beyond the malpractice model. Responsibility is more than just blame, there should also be some lessons learned from failures of responsibility. Thus there should be some lessons learned from the Inadequate Interface case. As a result of this event, Fred is responsible for preventing similar system's development failures in the future. Knowledge of this kind of failure and its consequences also places responsibility on other computer practitioners and places responsibilities on the profession of computing as a whole. For example, the activity of establishing computing standards of practice is justified by the forward looking sense of positive responsibility of the CP and the responsibility of the profession.

A RESPONSE TO AVOIDANCE

The concept of positive responsibility can be used to address several of the responsibility-avoidance techniques referred to earlier. This broader concept of responsibility meets the diffusion side-step and the positive aspect of this concept of responsibility meets the malpractice side-step.

Positive Responsibility and the Profession of Computing

Computing is an emerging profession. Computing already bears several of the marks of a profession. In order for computing to be a profession there must be some agreement among its members of goals and objectives or ideology. This agreement is of two kinds. One is technological and the other kind is moral. These match technical positive responsibility and moral positive responsibility. In accordance with the malpractice model, a CP has a responsibility to conform to good standards and operating procedures of the profession. These are generally minimal standards embodied in software development models and model software engineering curricula. This kind of technical knowledge and skill does not distinguish a technician from a professional. To make this distinction one must go beyond mere technical positive·responsibility.

A Broader Sense of Responsibility

In a profession, the members pledge to use their skills for the good of society and not to merely act as agents for the client doing whatever a client asks. This commitment is generally embodied in a professional organization's code of ethics. To be a professional, one assumes another layer of responsibility beyond what has been described in positive responsibility. The professional commits to a "higher degree of care" for those affected by the computing product. Most occupations have a principle of "due care" as a standard. For example, a plumber is responsible that the results of his work will not injure his customers or users of the plumbing system. But the plumber does not bear the responsibility to advise the customer of potential negative impacts a new system may have on the customer's business, customer's quality of life, or the environment. The concern to maximize the positive effects for those affected by computing artifacts goes beyond mere "due care", mere avoidance of direct harm. The addition of this layer of responsibility to positive responsibility is what is necessary to change a computing practitioner into a computing professional. The inadequate interface met the contract specifications, but it did not meet the user's needs. Although the system technically was capable of doing all the required functions and met Jim Midlevel's requests, the computing professional had the responsibility to be sure that the system met the user's needs. The forward looking sense of positive responsibility also means that the computer professional has the obligation to meet with upper-level management in order to convince them to re-instate the new accounting system. The computing professional has an obligation to the client, the users and the taxpayers.

This broader sense of responsibility goes beyond the malpractice model. It incorporates moral responsibility and the ethically commendable. This concept of professional responsibility can be used to address the above-mentioned ways used to deny accountability. This sense of responsibility provides a way to address distributed responsibility as well as diffusion of collective responsibility. The ability to deal with

D. Gotterbarn

collective responsibility is important because it enables meaningful discussion of the "professional responsibility" of organizations which produce software and organizations which represent computing professionals. It is clear that the computing disasters mentioned at the beginning of this paper would not have occurred if computing practitioners understood and adopted the positive sense of professional responsibility. The recent development by software engineers of a code of ethics and professional practice[12] is an attempt to define for them this sense of professional responsibility.

REFERENCES

1   Joch, A. (1995) How Software Doesn't Work. *Byte*, December: 48-60
2   Vallee, J. (1982) *The Network Revolution*, And/Or Press, Berkeley, CA, USA.
3   Ladd, J. (1988) Computers and Moral Responsibility: A Framework for an Ethical Analysis, in: Gould, Carol (ed.) *The Information Web: Ethical and Social Implications of Computer Networking*, Westview Press.
4   Dunlop, C., et. al. (1991) Ethical Perspectives and Professional Responsibility, in: King, R. (ed.) *Computerization and Controversy: Value Conflicts and Social Choices*, Academic Press, California, USA.
5   Harris, C.E., et. al., eds. (1995) *Engineering Ethics: Concepts and Cases*, Wadsworth, USA.
6   Johnson, D. (1994) *Computer Ethics*, Prentice Hall., USA.
7   Davis, M. (1989) Explaining Wrongdoing, *Journal of Social Philosophy*, Spring/Fall: 74-90.
8   Laudon, K. (1995) Ethical Concepts and Information Technology, *Communications of the ACM* **38** (12): 33-40.
9   Ross, W.D. (1969) *Moral Duties*, Macmillan, USA.
10 Leveson, N., et. al. (1993) An Investigation of the Therac-25 Accidents, *IEEE Computer Magazine* **26**: 18-41.
11 Nissenbaum, H. (1994) Computing and Accountability, *Communications of the ACM* **37**: 73-80.
12 SE "Software Engineering Code of Ethics and Professional Practice", adopted by the IEEE-CS and the ACM. (1998) http://computer.org/computer/code-of-ethics.pdf. Also republished in *Science and Engineering Ethics* 7(2): 231-238.

[24]

Do Engineers have Social Responsibilities?

DEBORAH G. JOHNSON

ABSTRACT *Most American engineers believe that they have a responsibility for the safety and well-being of society, but whence does this responsibility arise? What does it entail? After describing engineering practice in America as compared with the practice of other professions, this paper examines two standard types of accounts of the social responsibilities of professionals. While neither provides a satisfactory account of the social responsibilities of American engineers, several lessons are learned by uncovering their weaknesses. Identifying the framework in which professional rights and responsibilities are justified, I argue that an end or primary good is the starting place for conceptualising a profession, and justifying its existence and shape. Too little attention has been paid to the end(s) of engineering. The social responsibilities of American engineers as defined in the present system of engineering are ambiguous and weak. I indicate how the case for assigning American engineers stronger social responsibilities must be made by starting with the end(s) of engineering. I argue that, at present, American engineers do not have social responsibilities as engineers, though they do have social responsibilities as persons.*

Introduction

Few American engineers would deny that they have a responsibility for human welfare and safety. Indeed, the codes of most American engineering associations proclaim this, and many put forward this responsibility as paramount [1]. The hard part comes in specifying whence this responsibility arises and what exactly it calls for in the way of behaviour.

'Responsibility' is not a very precise notion and what we mean when we speak of 'social responsibilities' is even less clear. The literature on engineering ethics consistently suggests that American engineers see themselves as having four basic types of duties: (1) duties to society; (2) duties to employers; (3) duties to clients; and (4) duties to co-professionals or professional organisations. I will use 'the social responsibilities' of engineers to refer to their duties to protect the safety and welfare of society. While I do not want to 'jump the gun' on an answer to the question of this paper, the kind of behaviour we seem to have in mind when we use this phrase includes such actions as: refusing to work for a particular company or on a particular project; blowing the whistle on wrong-doing or illegality; speaking out publicly against a proposed project; and contributing one's services to worthy, non-profit groups.

In using 'social responsibilities' in this way, I believe I will be staying close to H. L. A. Hart's notion of 'role-responsibility'. Hart wrote that

> ... whenever a person occupies a distinctive place or office in a social organization, to which specific duties are attached ... he is properly said to be responsible for the performance of these duties, or for doing what is necessary to fulfil them. Such duties are a person's responsibilities. [2]

22   *D. G. Johnson*

He also explained:

> what distinguishes those duties of a role which are singled out as responsibilities is that they are duties of a relatively complex or extensive kind, defining a 'sphere of responsibility' requiring care and attention over a protracted period of time . . . [3]

Of course, when it comes to the social responsibilities of American engineers, what is at issue is not so much the duties attached to an engineer's job for a particular employer, but rather the duties attached to the role of engineer. What responsibilities come with being an engineer in America? What actions or kinds of actions may be said to be necessary to fulfil these responsibilities?

A careful reading of the literature on engineering ethics suggests that philosophers and others are generally after two things in their accounts of the social responsibilities of engineers. First, they want to explain why engineers have social responsibilities at all. This question is interesting in its own right, but more often than not, it is pursued with the presumption that clarity on this matter will yield clarity on what it is that engineers ought to do in particular situations. This is the second thing that seems to be sought by engineering ethicists, an account specifying what is called for by an engineer's social responsibility. This specification would give meaning to what are otherwise just platitudes about protecting society—good public relations statements for the profession.

To be sure, the recent work on engineering ethics has provided useful insight and the dialogue has become increasingly more sophisticated. However, the accounts provided have not been wholly successful in achieving what is aimed for.

I begin here by identifying some special features of engineering practice in America as compared with that of other professions. I critically examine two types of accounts that are often given of the social responsibilities of professionals. After finding fault with these as they apply to engineering, I try to use the lessons learned from these failures to outline the framework in which social-professional responsibilities are justified. My analysis suggests that an end or primary good at which a profession aims is the starting place for conceptualising a profession and justifying its rules of practice. Using this insight, I argue that American engineers do not have social responsibilities *as engineers*. Rather, they have social responsibilities as persons—persons with special expertise and positions in organisations through which they often contribute to projects with the potential to cause harm. I also argue that the case can probably be made for assigning special social responsibilities to American engineers *qua engineers*, but that this will necessitate changes in the way engineering is structured in America.

Engineering Practice

The literature on engineering ethics is filled with comparisons between American engineers and the 'classic' professionals, doctors and lawyers. The most striking difference that comes to light is that engineers generally work as employees (of very large corporations or government agencies) and, as such, have little autonomy individually. As well, they have no single unifying professional organisation and, consequently, have little power as a group. Historically, their alliance with and dependence on the business world has always interfered with engineers' being able to establish a unified professional organisation [4].

Another characteristic of the work of American engineers as opposed to that of doctors and lawyers is its relatively fragmented nature [5]. Engineers most often work on small parts of much larger, highly complex projects. Their authority is limited to the small segment, with someone else (often not an engineer) having the designated responsibility for the whole project. Doctors and lawyers, on the other hand, typically (though not always) treat whole patients or clients, and follow a case from start to finish.

Moreover, it is said that engineers are more distant from the ultimate effects of their activities. They may labour on a project at certain stages of its development and then never see the product until it appears in the market place, having no involvement in how it is used, distributed or advertised. Doctors, on the other hand, see in their patients the direct result of their decisions, and lawyers know whether they have won or lost cases, furthered or impeded the interests of their clients. It has even been argued that the engineer's distance from the effects of her work tends to diffuse her sense of responsibility [6].

It is worth noting that all three of these differences between doctors and lawyers, on the one hand, and engineers, on the other, are less sharp today in America than ever before, not because engineering is changing, but because medicine and law are. Many American lawyers now work in large corporate law firms or for big companies, and many American doctors now work for hospitals or health maintenance organisations. In both cases they may be expected to protect the interest of their employer, to take orders, follow company policies. They have much less autonomy than professionals in private practice. Indeed, it may be that, in the future, American doctors and lawyers will look to engineers to learn how to manage their social responsibilities in the corporate and bureaucratic context.

If one is suspicious of using doctors and lawyers as the norm for professionals, engineering can be compared to other professions. University professors, journalists and clergy, for example, seem closer to engineers in that they generally work as employees within organisations which have hierarchical structures and complex divisions of labour. Even so, there is a marked difference in the degree of the autonomy that these professionals have as compared with American engineers. For all three of these types of professionals—journalists, professors and clergy—there has been some social recognition of the need for autonomy and a granting of special privilege to accommodate this need. American clergy have the privilege of confidentiality with those who come to them for help; professors have academic freedom. American journalists do not exactly have the legal 'right' to protect their sources, but there is significant social acceptance when they refuse to reveal a source. These legal or quasi-legal protections recognise that members of these professions have an allegiance to something beyond their employers—to truth, knowledge, God. They recognise the value of allowing members of these professions to maintain that allegiance.

Engineers have nothing comparable. They have no special legal or quasi-legal protection to do or refrain from doing anything *because they are engineers*. Of course, they have protections which all employees have, e.g. they cannot be ordered to do what is illegal, but they have nothing more.

This lack of special privilege or protection has meant that at the very heart of the professional life of American engineers (more so than any of the other professions just mentioned) is a tension between the engineer's need for autonomy and the demands for organisational loyalty made by employers. The tension can be characterised, as well, as that between having the status of an employee versus the status of a professional [7]. Engineers need autonomy because they have special knowledge. If they are to use that knowledge in a responsible manner and for the good of society,

24   *D. G. Johnson*

they must have the power to do so. However, as they work for corporations with complex organisational structures and decision-making procedures, and as these large organisations need co-ordination of their various parts, it would seem that engineers must often simply do what they are told.

It is no surprise, then, that the one topic which has received the most attention in the engineering ethics literature has been whistle-blowing [8]. Acts of whistle-blowing are acts in which individuals opt against loyalty to their employer, in favour of protecting society.

A number of recommendations for changes in engineering have emerged from discussions of whistle-blowing. Most of these aim at empowering engineers to speak out more freely when they are concerned about the safety or legality of a project. There is recognition that the scales are now weighted against protecting society in that engineers who opt against loyalty to their employer do so at personal peril. They are harassed, lose their jobs and cannot get new ones because they have been labelled 'trouble-makers', or are accused of being crazy. Some of the proposed changes aim at making it possible for engineers to speak out with less risk, for example, through corporate ombudsmen, anonymous hotlines or with legal protection against being fired [9]; others aim at providing support for those who take the risk and speak out, by strengthening professional organisations so that they might intervene and investigate, or by providing legal services or ethics awards to engineers in trouble for speaking out [10]. Yet other recommendations aim at changing the profession more fundamentally by changing the education of engineers, increasing the role of licensing or creating a system like tenure for engineers [11].

What is clear in all of this is that, while American engineers see themselves as having social responsibility, they practise in a system in which their autonomy is constrained and they are expected to act for the interests of their employers. Hence, even though they may see themselves as having social responsibility, it is especially difficult for them to act accordingly.

Deducing the Social Responsibilities of Engineers

When one has conflicting duties, it seems reasonable to expect that a better under-standing of the roots of those duties might yield some insight into how they should be balanced. An understanding of the roots of an engineer's duty to protect society ought to give us some clues as to what this duty entails, when it overrides, when it can be overridden and so on. Much of the philosophical literature on the social responsibilities of engineers is aimed at providing such an account by showing how the social responsibilities of engineers are deduced from or implied in a general moral principle or a broad moral theory.

The list of accounts of the social responsibilities of engineers (including those hinted at as well as those explicitly argued for) is probably as long as the list of kinds of moral theories. I will focus here on two types of accounts: those that employ social contract theory and those that appeal to a principle of ordinary morality. While both types of accounts seem to capture an intuition that one might have about the origins of social responsibilities, neither provides a satisfactory account of the social responsibilities of engineers. Each account is, nevertheless, revealing in its misfit with engineering.

Many sociological analyses of professions allude to a hypothetical social contract between society and each profession, and a number of philosophers have explicitly argued for such an account of professional ethics [12]. On these accounts, we are to think of the rights and responsibilities of professionals as arising from social arrangements; social arrangements hypothetically agreed to because they are in the rational self-interest of both parties. Society grants special privileges to the professional (and, thereby, to members of the profession) in exchange for the promise by the profession that it will maintain certain standards of behaviour, and that its members will practise in ways that benefit society.

This account of the relationship between society and a profession does not quite work for American engineering, but in order to see why, it is helpful to try to make the case. We can hypothesise a contract between American engineers and American society in which engineers are granted the right to practise engineering, in exchange for the promise that they will practise in ways that are good for society or, at least, not in ways that are harmful. In support of this account, one might point out how engineers cannot do what they do without the benefit of a good deal of social apparatus, e.g. the laws of the state, the economic system, educational institutions. Of course, society benefits by receiving the new technologies engineers create, for they presumably make life better, easier or more efficient. So both parties give something and receive something. For our purposes the important part is that engineers agree to take on the burden of responsibility for the safety and well-being of society (as it is affected by their work) in exchange for the benefits provided by the state and for the right to practise engineering.

So the argument goes. However, when we press key points in this analysis, the account falters. The first problem arises from the fact that the right referred to in the hypothetical contract is not granted just to engineers. It is not engineers *per se* who are allowed to build bridges, airplanes, skyscrapers, etc. In principle, anyone who adheres to the regulations (and, of course, has the necessary resources) can do these things. In fact, in America, it is primarily corporations (employing engineers) that undertake such projects, financing them under contract with other corporations or governments.

The distinction between licensed and non-licensed engineers in America is important here, for many American regulations require that a licensed engineer sign the plans for a building, airplane, etc. before it can be built. In signing, the licensed engineer attests to the fact that the plans meet regulatory requirements and ordinary standards of safety. Thus, licensed engineers do have a right (or power) which ordinary persons do not. However, licensed engineers make up a small segment of the American engineering profession [13]. An account that only explained why licensed engineers have social responsibilities would be a rather weak account.

A second problem arises with the social contract account because on such an account engineers would be promising to do something which they do not have the capacity to do. To be sure, engineers have the most appropriate expertise to estimate the risks of the technologies they design, build and monitor, and they are often in positions from which they can see that a technology is unsafe or counter to the welfare of society. Still, as explained earlier, American engineers typically have little or very circumscribed power. They do not have the final say about what is built, put on the market, taken off the market and so on. Hence, they cannot promise to protect the safety and well-being of society.

It might be argued that my analysis has so far been aimed at individual engineers as the bearers of responsibility and, instead, we should think of the social contract being made between society and the profession as a whole. Thus, we would say that the profession of engineering acquires the social contract rights and responsibilities as a collective, and these rights and responsibilities could be managed in some way other than by distributing them to individual engineers. This is a theoretical possibility. The profession might create a set of mechanisms for self-regulation, ensuring that it lives up to its part of the bargain. In fact, however, American engineering is not structured this way. There are mechanisms by which engineers can influence the regulatory process affecting engineering activities, but few of these are controlled by engineering professional associations, and there is no single unified organisation of American engineers. In other words, engineering in America is not structured as if the profession collectively bore responsibility.

These problems aside, social contract theories are better understood as theories of justice than as theories which establish responsibilities. Social contract theories help us to understand what just social arrangements look like and, as such, provide the basis for a critique of extant arrangements. For example, American engineers might argue that the extant system is unfair because American engineers must now take enormous personal and professional risks to avoid contributing to harm; that is, to act morally or responsibly. As mentioned earlier, incidents of whistle-blowing show that engineers who refuse to work on projects or report wrongdoing lose their jobs, are accused of being crazy, and find it difficult to get new jobs because their reputations have been damaged. Their point, put in social contract terms, would be either that the terms of the extant contract (prevailing arrangements) are not fair, or that society is not living up to its part of what would otherwise be a fair contract. There ought to be more support, they would argue, for engineers who put their social responsibilities first; indeed, there ought to be a system of employment in which engineers have more power and can speak out without risk.

Social contract theory allows us to see the role of engineer (and other professional roles) as socially designated clusters of rights and responsibilities, and it allows us to ask whether the rights and responsibilities assigned to a profession or professional role are fair. It is important to note here that justice does not require that the role of engineer be constituted in a particular way. It does not even require, for example, that engineers have more autonomy. Justice requires only that *if* we assign engineers broad responsibilities for safety, we also give them commensurate power, and *if* we expect engineers to take greater risks than the ordinary person for the welfare of society, then we let them know about this before they enter the profession. We could just as well redefine the role of engineer to that of mere employee. I do not advocate this; my point is only that justice imposes certain constraints on how we constitute the role. It does not necessitate a particular assignment of rights and responsibilities.

So, while social contract theory is useful in understanding engineering, it does not tell us what are the social responsibilities of American engineers.

A second type of account deduces the social responsibilities of engineers from a general principle of ordinary morality. Alpern takes this tack in "Moral Responsibility of Engineers" [14]. He begins by asserting what he takes to be a principle of ordinary morality which would not be questioned, namely that "other things being equal, it is morally wrong to harm others". Alpern then restates the principle with some qualifications as follows: "Other things being equal, one should exercise due care to avoid contributing to significantly harming others". Though he does not spell out the reasons for these qualifications, they are not difficult to infer. Typically, engineers do not engage in activities which directly cause harm to others. Even when they work on weapon systems, they do not aim at or intend to harm people. At most, we can say that engineers perform actions which contribute (in complex causal sequences) to the occurrence of events which harm people. They may do this by either their action or inaction.

Moreover, it is impossible for individuals to altogether avoid contributing to events which result in harm to others. We cannot always foresee how our actions will interact with other events and actions, and what the ultimate results will be. Even when we can, sometimes we must do things which we know will result in harm to others, because the benefits of doing so outweigh the harm done or because another duty takes priority, and so on. Nevertheless, Alpern insists, while we cannot altogether avoid making causal contributions to events which cause harm to others, we should exercise due care, especially when the harm will be significant.

He goes on to try to specify more what he means by due care and to do this he proposes a corollary to the first principle, the 'corollary of proportionate care'. According to this corollary, "when one is in a position to contribute to greater harm or when one is in a position to play a more critical part in producing harm than is another person, one must exercise greater care to avoid so doing" [15].

It is this corollary that gets Alpern to the obligations of engineers. Since engineers are in a position to contribute to greater harm than others, they must exercise "greater care". Since the projects on which engineers work have a greater potential to significantly harm people, "practising engineers can be held to a higher standard of care; that is, it can be demanded that they be willing to make greater sacrifices than others for the sake of the public welfare" [16].

Just what Alpern means by "exercising care" is not clear as he slips into the language of "making greater sacrifices" and being held to a "higher standard of care". No doubt, he has in mind whistle-blowing and other acts of dissent with one's employer, but it is unfortunate that the account is vague on the very question which it aims to answer—what exactly do engineers have a responsibility to do?

The appeal of this account is two-fold. It places the social responsibilities of engineers on the firm foundation of a fundamental principle of ordinary morality, and it suggests a resolution of the separatist controversy [17]. The separatist controversy surrounds the question whether the rules by which one operates in a professional role are consistent with or exceptions to the rules of ordinary morality. On Alpern's account we are able to explain how the standards of professionals are both different from and the same as standards of conduct for all persons. The general principle is not unique; it applies to all. On the other hand, that general principle implies special things for people in special situations. Engineers are in a special position because their work and knowledge allow them to contribute to (potential) harm in a way that ordinary persons do not. This potentially greater contribution means greater responsibility.

Nevertheless, while Alpern's account has this appeal, it does not quite accomplish what it intends. The major problem is that it does not show why engineers *qua engineers* have a special responsibility. It is an account of the responsibility of all those who are in positions in which they make contributions to significant harm. Anyone, according to the principle, who is in a position to contribute to significant harm, has an obligation to take greater care.

Indeed, the principle can be used to move responsibility away from engineers, to managers and corporate executives. As pointed out earlier, engineers typically are not nearly as powerful as managers or company executives. The latter have most of the decision-making authority. Thus, while engineers are in positions to contribute to significant harm, their superiors make greater, more powerful contributions. By

Alpern's corollary, managers and corporate executives must exercise due care or be held to a higher standard of care.

The emphasis on contributing to harm also skews our attention away from the important issue in engineering. The calculations which must be made in engineering have more to do with 'risk' of harm than with actual harm. Engineers thinking about the potential effects of their work must ask themselves about the risks and trade-offs in the projects to which they contribute. The issue is not "will I be contributing to significant harm?", but rather "how much risk will there be?", "is the risk worth the benefit to be gained?" and "what is an acceptable degree of risk?"

De George recognises this point in his piece on the Pinto case and argues that, while engineers have expertise in identifying and calculating risks, they certainly do not have expertise in deciding what is an acceptable or unacceptable risk [18]. These are decisions which, De George argues, should be made directly or indirectly by society, presumably by government and the marketplace. Others have argued that these are decisions which should be made by those who will be put at risk. Executives in Ford made them in the Pinto case by estimating what they thought the public was willing to accept. Thus, De George argues that the engineers involved in the Pinto case did what they should have done. They reported to management their concerns about the placement of the petrol tank, and recommended a part which would make the car safer. It was then up to management to decide if the part should be installed. Management, judging the market, decided against installation of the part.

Similarly, Roger Boisjoly as an employee of Morton Thiokol reported his concerns about the seal on the rocket boosters months, weeks and moments before the shuttle disaster. He then backed off as management made the final decision [19].

De George's point does not, by any means, undermine Alpern's proportionality thesis. If anything, De George seems to be presupposing some sort of connection between one's power to affect a situation and one's responsibility to take care, but he sees this connection as putting a heavy responsibility on managers and corporate executives, rather than engineers. Of course, this need not be an either/or matter. Both engineers, and managers and corporate executives, may be responsible. The point is simply that persons other than engineers also make contributions to engineering achievements and to technologies which may cause significant harm.

Alpern's account is not and cannot be an account of the social responsibilities of engineers for he has not identified anything distinctive about engineering which gives rise to special responsibilities. Without this we are left with the idea that engineers may have responsibilities with regard to their work, but these responsibilities are human and non-professional. They apply to all persons who contribute to significant harm. This is not the unique domain of engineers.

The attempt to deduce the social responsibilities of engineers from a fundamental principle of ordinary morality such as the edict "do no harm" seems to capture something in our intuitions about social responsibility, in particular that our responsibilities should parallel our proportionate causal contribution. Nevertheless, Alpern's account does not establish the claim that engineers have social responsibilities because they are engineers.

Both types of accounts examined above fail, then, to provide a satisfactory account of the social responsibilities of American engineers. It is important to note, at this point, that even if American engineers have no 'special' social responsibilities as engineers, they will have social responsibilities as persons—persons with varying degrees of power, making varying contributions to potentially dangerous events.

Before we conclude that this is all they have, however, a change of tactics is in order. Let us examine a normative framework often used in applied professional ethics.

Getting the Framework Right, not Missing the Middle

Gewirth argues that there are two levels of justification in professional ethics [20]. We justify individual actions in roles, by showing that they are in accordance with the rules of an institution. However, we must also show that the institution—its rules and practices—is morally justified. A profession is such an institution. It is a set of rules and practices which give shape to rights and responsibilities. If we fail to bring engineering into our analysis of engineers' social responsibilities, we fail to come to grips with the institutional level of justification and we fail to understand what it means to act in a professional role.

Gewirth proposes specific criteria that a morally justified institution must fulfil, but whether we accept his criteria or not, it seems clear that we will have to appeal to something beyond a profession—fundamental principles or primary goods to justify the professon's very existence, as well as its character. The end or good at which the profession aims plays an important role here as the conceptual starting place for understanding a profession and justifying its practices. Consider, for example, justification in medical-professional ethics. We may justify a doctor's actions by appealing to the rights and duties of doctors; for example, a doctor's refusal to assist a patient in committing euthanasia is justified on grounds that the doctor has a duty never to intentionally bring about the death of a patient. This duty, in turn, must be justified. It must be justified as part of a system of medical practices; and that system—the system of practices which constitute the profession of medicine—is justified ultimately by its serving human health.

There are, then, three levels of analysis: the level of analysis in which we consider what a particular individual acting in a professional role ought to do; the level of analysis in which we consider what the rules or practices of a profession ought to be; and the level of analysis dealing with our highest goods or principles. We justify conclusions drawn at each of the first two levels, at least in part, by appealing to an analysis at the next level. We justify individual actions in a role by appealing to the rights and responsibilities attached to the role, and we justify the system of rights and responsibilities—professional practices—by appealing to a primary good or fundamental principle.

Once we recognise distinct levels of analysis in professional ethics, it becomes clear that the middle level, which is the level of 'professional' or institutional arrangements, is often missed, in particular when an appeal is made directly to a fundamental principle or primary good. Alpern's account is a good example of this. He misses the middle level because he tries to deduce the duties of individual engineers directly from a principle of ordinary morality, a principle which functions at the highest level in the sense that it is understood to transcend all other considerations. Alpern fails to recognise that there might be a system of rules in between the highest principle and an individual's responsibilities. In effect, he fails to recognise a place for professions, and professional rights and responsibilities. This is precisely why his account fails as an account of the social responsibilities *of engineers*.

Applied philosophers working on professional ethics often seem captivated with the idea that there must be a deductive relationship between the levels of analysis [21]. Even those who acknowledge the middle level seem taken with the idea that from a primary good or fundamental principle of morality, we can 'deduce' the middle level; that is, we can deduce what the rules or practices of a profession *must* be (and from these, in turn, we can deduce what an individual ought to do in a given situation).

While I will not give an account of the precise nature of the relationship between the levels, it seems misleading to think of it as 'deduction'. Among other things, deduction implies that one and only one conclusion can be drawn. However, when we move from one level to another in professional ethics, the connection is not so tight. The good which a profession serves does not necessitate that the profession be structured in one and only one way. For example, in the case of law, the good that justifies the existence of the profession is justice, but in America we have adopted a system based on advocacy and, consequently, have given lawyers appropriate rights and responsibilities, essential to an advocacy system. However, other systems that serve justice are possible—systems in which lawyers have quite different rights and responsibilities. Thus, while one cannot understand the rights and responsibilities of lawyers in America without understanding how they serve justice, we cannot deduce the American system merely from 'justice'. The rules defining the rights and responsibilities of American lawyers can only be understood as part of a system with a particular approach to justice [22].

When this point is missed and the presumption is made that the practices of a profession are deducible from a fundamental principle or primary good, the importance of the middle level is missed again. The significance of cultural and historical factors shaping professions, shaping the systems of rules which define the rights and responsibilities of professionals, is missed. It is presumed, instead, that professions must (morally) be the way they are.

Once we let go of the idea of deduction in the relationship between levels of analysis, we can admit that alternative systems of practices (institutional arrangements) may be consistent with a primary good or fundamental principle [23]. This means, among other things, that when it comes to justifying the rights and responsibilities of a profession, we may show that one set of practices is a sensible, even coherent and consistent system for achieving a certain end; we may even be able to show that some systems of professional rights and responsibilities are better than others, but we will not be able to 'deduce' these rights and responsibilities in the sense of showing that they must be this or that way and only this or that way.

At the same time, while a fundamental principle or primary good does not necessitate a particular system of professional rights and responsibilities, it may significantly constrain the possibilities. That is, the good which directs the very being of the profession may rule out certain arrangements. For example, in medicine it would be antithetical to the very idea of human health if doctors were allowed to take organs from healthy patients or remove limbs upon request (without at least some special conditions being met).

In seeking an account of the social responsibilities of a profession or its members, we must work at the middle level. We must seek an understanding of a profession as a set of social arrangements which must be justified by something higher, but not completely determined by the higher good or principle. We must also understand that such a system might require members to do things not expected or required of non-members.

Do Engineers have Special Social Responsibilities?

Now let us return to the question of this paper which should now read; Do American engineers have special social responsibilities because they are engineers? To answer this question, we must look to the middle level engineering. There are two different questions we might be asking: Does the system of engineering in America assign special social responsibilities to engineers?, or; Should we assign stronger, special social responsibilities to American engineers?

If we ask the first question, the answer seems to be that the system of practices in America today is, at best, ambiguous. For the most part, it does not recognise or assign special social responsibilities to engineers because they are engineers. The descriptive analysis of engineering practice in America provided earlier indicates that the extant system gives mixed signals. The codes of the American engineering professional associations indicate that engineers have a duty to protect the public and this duty is paramount, but the institutions in which engineers work give quite a different message, as does the law. The institutions in which American engineers typically work put great emphasis on loyalty to the company or agency, rather than on commitment to the good of society. If there is reference to social responsibilities in these contexts, the rhetoric suggests that social responsibilities are fulfilled by organisational accomplishments, e.g. the corporation producing something that society needs, or the government agency protecting the public rather than professional commitment. In American law, engineers are rarely held liable, except for gross cases of malpractice, and even in these cases, it is most often a company, not an individual engineer that is liable.

Even if we look to popular attitudes about the social responsibilities of American engineers, we do not find a very clear picture. In some cases of whistle-blowing, for example, public response has been quite mixed on whether the whistle-blower did the right thing or was disloyal to his/her employer. Even the attitudes of engineers and engineering professional organisations towards whistle-blowers have been mixed.

The substance of an answer to the second question—Should stronger, special social responsibilities be assigned to American engineers?—has not yet been provided, though the framework in which the case must be made has been sketched. We would have to begin with the good or goods at which engineering aims, and show how assigning stronger social responsibilities to engineers would further this good (or goods).

Unfortunately, American engineers have not, at least in recent years, focused much on the end of engineering. Several historical accounts of engineering suggest that in the early days of engineering (during the late nineteenth and early twentieth centuries), engineers saw themselves as "the saviors of society" [24]. They believed that they were engaged in an enterprise which would solve many of humanity's social problems, and would make life easier and better. No doubt some engineers still believe this, but it is not an idea that has had prominence in the professional discussions or activities of engineers, nor in public debate about engineering.

The most likely candidates for the ends of engineering are human well-being and safety. While these are broad and general concepts, the same could be said of health and justice as the ends of medicine and law, respectively. They cannot be expected fully to determine the shape of the profession, but they can and should focus the organisation and culture of the profession. While recognition of human welfare and safety as the ends of engineering may not decide debates on complex issues such as whether engineers should work on weapons systems, it would shape such debates by defining the terms in which they take place. Indeed, keeping in mind that human well-being and safety are the ends of engineering makes clear that such questions are appropriate for discussion within the profession. Such questions become matters of professional importance and not just matters of personal conscience.

32   *D. G. Johnson*

Moreover, recognition of human well-being and safety as the ends of engineering would provide grounds for rejecting a view of engineers as 'guns for hire'. When engineers are understood to be the tools or means for ends which are to be chosen by others (whether the others be clients or government or the market), then engineers are essentially 'guns for hire' [25]. All responsibility for engineering projects lies, in effect, with those who hire engineers and with the government in so far as it regulates engineering endeavours. On such a view, engineers are expected to cease to be moral when they act as engineers [26].

I do not claim to have shown that the 'guns for hire' view of engineering is wrong; nor do I claim to have shown that engineers should have stronger social responsibilities. I argue only that arguments for either view should be framed in a context in which the end (or ends) of engineering are the starting place.

The Social Responsibilities of Engineers

Answering the initial questions of this paper—do American engineers have social responsibilities? whence do they arise? what do they entail?—has turned out to be a much more complicated matter than it first appeared. The answer that emerges from the preceding analysis is that American engineers today do not have special social responsibilities as engineers. This does not, however, mean that they have no social responsibilities whatsoever. Engineers are persons, persons with special knowledge, acting in employee roles. Their knowledge and their positions allow them to contribute to complex technological endeavours that have consequences. As persons they bear responsibility for their contributions to these endeavours.

So, Alpern was sort of right. He was right about engineers as persons, but not as professionals. We cannot derive special social responsibilities for engineers from engineering because it is not a strongly role-differentiated profession, to use Goldman's term [27]. Engineering is not structured so as to require of non-licensed engineers that they do or refrain from doing anything more or less than others (who are not engineers).

It may be helpful, then, to draw a sharp distinction between professional and social responsibilities. In both cases a person bears responsibility for the consequences of her behaviour. When the source of the responsibility comes directly from the rules of the profession (and only indirectly from being a person), it is professional responsibility, and when the source of the responsibility comes directly from being a person, it is social responsibility.

Alpern does not quite see this and, therefore, puts the emphasis in the wrong place. That is, he emphasises the degree of harm that can be done by engineering endeavours and the degree of contribution that engineers make to these endeavours. Both of these are important, but they are not unique or even intrinsic to engineering. We cannot say that all engineers contribute to harm or that engineering, by its very nature, involves significant harm. We can only say that when people are in situations in which they might contribute to significant harm, as engineers often are, they should take care. In other words, the edict, do no harm or take care when you are doing something with potential harm, has implications for many engineers [28].

Deborah G. Johnson, Department of Science and Technology Studies, Rensselaer Polytechnic Institute, Troy, New York 12180, USA.

NOTES

[1] See for example: *Code of Ethics* of the National Society of Professional Engineers (as revised, 1979); *Code of Ethics of Engineers* of the Accreditation Board of Engineering and Technology (approved, 1977); and *Fundamental Canons* of the American Society of Civil Engineers (adopted 1976).

[2] H. L. A. HART (1968) *Punishment and Responsibility: Essays in the Philosophy of Law* (New York, Oxford University Press), p. 212.

[3] Ibid., p. 213.

[4] EDWIN LAYTON (1971, 1986) *The Revolt of the Engineers: Social Responsibility and the American Engineering Profession* (Baltimore, John Hopkins University Press), Chapter 1.

[5] MICHAEL W. MARTIN & ROLAND SCHINZINGER (1989) *Ethics in Engineering*, 2nd edn (New York, McGraw Hill Book Company), p. 77; ANTHONY D. ROBBI (1973) Social Ethics and the Modern Engineer, *Annals of the New York Academy of Science*, 196(10), pp. 461–464; A. MICHAEL BAKER (1985) Ethical and Legal Disputes Involving Corporate Engineers, *IEEE Technology and Society Magazine*, pp. 10–20; JOHN LADD (1982) Collective and Individual Moral Responsibility in Engineering: Some Questions, *IEEE Technology and Society Magazine*, pp. 3–10.

[6] BAKER, op. cit., p. 10.

[7] LAYTON, op. cit.

[8] See for example: ROBERT M. ANDERSON et al. (1980) *Divided Loyalties: Whistle-Blowing at BART* (West Lafayette, Indiana, Purdue University); FREDERICK ELLISTON et al. (1985) *Whistleblowing: Managing Dissent in the Workplace* (New York: Praeger Publishers); ALAN WESTIN (1980) *Whistleblowing* (New York, McGraw Hill); FREDERICK ELLISTON (1982) Anonymous Whistleblowing, *Business & Professional Ethics Journal*, 12, pp. 39–58; GENE G. JAMES (1983) In Defense of Whistleblowing, in: MICHAEL HOFFMAN & JENNIFER MOORE MILLS (Eds) *Business Ethics: Readings and Cases in Corporate Morality* (New York, McGraw Hill), pp. 249–260; JAMES C. PETERSEN & DAN FARRELL (1986) *Whistleblowing: Ethical and Legal Issues in Expressing Dissent* (Dubuque, Iowa: Kendall/Hunt).

[9] See: NORMAND M. LAURENDEAU (1982) Engineering Professionalism: The Case for Corporate Ombudsmen, *Business & Professional Ethics Journal*, 21, pp. 35–45; and ALFRED G. FELIU (1985) The Role of the Law in Protecting Scientific and Technical Dissent, *IEEE Technology and Social Magazine*, pp. 3–10.

[10] STEPHEN H. UNGER (1987) Would Helping Ethical Professionals get Professional Societies in Trouble? *IEEE Technology and Society Magazine*, pp. 17–20.

[11] See: DONALD E. WILSON (1982) Social Mechanisms for Controlling Engineer's Performance, in: ALBERT FLORES (ed.) *Designing for Safety: Engineering Ethics in Organizational Contexts* (Troy, NY, Rensselaer Polytechnic Institute); CAROLINE WHITBECK (1987) The Engineer's Responsibility for Safety: Integrating Ethics Teaching into Courses in Engineering Design, presented at the ASME Winter Annual Meeting, Boston, MA, December 13–18; STEPHEN H. UNGER (1982) *Controlling Technology: Ethics and the Responsible Engineer* (New York, Holt, Rinehart and Winston).

[12] See: LISA NEWTON (1982) The Origin of Professionalism: Sociological Conclusions and Ethical Implications, *Business & Professional Ethics Journal*, 14, pp. 33–43; and ROBERT F. LADENSON (1980) The Social Responsibilities of Engineers and Scientists: A Philosophical Approach, in DANIEL L. BABCOCK & CAROL ANN SMITH (Eds) *Proceedings: Values and the Publics Works Professional* (Chicago: American Public Works Association).

[13] According to DONALD E. WILSON, using 1980 data, 300,000 engineers were licensed in the United States out of 1.5 million or more (see [11]).

[14] KENNETH D. ALPERN (1983) Moral Responsibility of Engineers in Large Organizations, *Business & Professional Ethics Journal*, 22, pp. 39–48.

[15] Ibid., p. 41.

[16] Ibid., p. 41.

[17] BENJAMIN FREEDMAN (1978) A Meta-ethics for Professional Morality, *Ethics*, 89, pp. 1–19; (1981) What Really Makes Professional Morality Different: Response to Martin, *Ethics*, 91, pp. 626–630; MIKE W. MARTIN (1981) Rights and the Meta-Ethics of Ordinary Morality, *Ethics*, 91, pp. 619–625; Professional and Ordinary Morality: A Reply to Freedman, *Ethics*, 91, pp. 631–633.

[18] RICHARD T. DE GEORGE (1983) Ethical Responsibilities of Engineers in Large Organizations, *Business & Professional Ethics Journal*, 11, pp. 1–14.

[19] ROGER BOISJOLY (1987) The Challenger Disaster: Moral Responsibility and the Working Engineer, *Books and Religion*, March/April.

[20] ALAN GEWIRTH (1986) Professional Ethics: The Separatist Thesis, *Ethics*, 96(2), pp. 282–300.

34   *D. G. Johnson*

[21] For a discussion of the problems with this deductive model, see: ARTHUR L. CAPLAN (1983) Can Applied Ethics Be Effective in Health Care and Should It Strive to Be? *Ethics*, 93 (2), pp. 311–319.

[22] ALAN GOLDMAN (1980) *The Moral Foundations of Professional Ethics* (Totowa, NJ, Rowman and Littlefield).

[23] REX MARTIN (1985) makes a similar point when he argues that Rawlsian principles of justice do not dictate any particular political system (*Rawls and Rights* [Lawrence, Kansas, University of Kansas Press]). They constrain the possibilities, but the principles may be instantiated in a variety of forms of constitutional governments.

[24] SAMUEL FLORMAN (1976) *The Existential Pleasures of Engineering* (New York, St Martin's Press).

[25] SAMUEL FLORMAN (1978) comes very close to taking this position in: Moral blueprints: On regulating the ethics of engineers, *Harper's*, October, pp. 30–33. He does not think that engineers should impose their moral views on the world and is, therefore, reluctant to let them decide which projects they will work on.

[26] DEBORAH JOHNSON (1990) The Social and Professional Responsibility of Engineers, *Annals of the New York Academy of Sciences*, 577, pp. 106–114.

[27] GOLDMAN, op. cit.

[28] A very early draft of this paper was written as part of a Hastings Center Project entitled 'Moral Responsibilities and Moral Decisions in Science and Engineering' funded by the Ethics and Values in Science and Technology Program of the National Science Foundation in 1983. Later versions were significantly improved by comments from Ed Hackett, Rex Martin, Michael Davis and Jim Nickel, and by discussion generated when a draft of the paper was presented as part of the Philosophy Department Speaker Series at Dartmouth College in May 1989.

[25]

COMPUTING AND ACCOUNTABILITY

Helen Nissenbaum

teacher stands before her sixth-grade class demanding to know who shot the spitball in her ear. She threatens punishment for the whole class if someone does not step forward. Eyes are cast downward and nervous giggles are suppressed as a boy in the back row slowly raises his hand.

The boy in the back row has answered for his actions. We do not know whether he shot at the teacher intentionally or merely missed his true target, whether he acted alone or under goading from classmates, or even whether the spitball was in protest for an unreasonable action taken by the teacher. While all of these factors are relevant to determining a just response to the boy's action, the boy, in accepting responsibility for his action, has fulfilled the valuable social obligation of accountability.

In an increasingly computerized society, where computing, and its broad application, brings dramatic changes to our way of life, and exposes us to harms and risks, accountability is very important. A community (a society or professional community) that insists on accountability, in which agents are expected to answer for their work, signals esteem for high-quality work, and encourages diligent, responsible practices. Furthermore, where lines of accountability are maintained, they provide the foundations for just punishment as well as compensation for victims. By contrast, the absence of accountability means that no one answers for harms and risks. Insofar as they are regretted, they are seen as unfortunate accidents—consequences of a brave new technology. As with accidents due to natural disasters such as hurricanes and earthquakes, we sympathize with the victims' losses, but do not demand accountability.

This article maintains that accountability is systematically undermined in our computerized society—which, given the value of accountability to society, is a disturbing loss. While this systematic erosion of accountability is not an inevitable consequence of computerization, it is the inevitable consequence of several factors working in unison—an overly narrow conceptual understanding of accountability, a set of assumptions about the capabilities and shortcomings of computer systems, and a willingness to accept that the producers of computer systems are not, in general, fully answerable for the impacts of their products. If not addressed, this erosion of accountability will mean that computers are "out of control" in an important and disturbing way. This article attempts to explain why there is a tendency toward diminished accountability for the impacts, harms, and risks of computing, and it offers recommendations for reversing it.

My concern over accountability has grown alongside the active discussion within and about the computer profession regarding the harms and risks to society posed by computers and computerized systems. These discussions appeal to computer professionals,[1] to the corporate producers of computer systems, and to government regulators, to pay more heed to system safety and reliability in order to reduce harms and risks [1, 12-14, 16, 18, 22, 28]. Lives and well-being are increasingly dependent on computerized systems. Greater numbers of life-critical systems such as aircarft, spacecraft, other transportation vehicles, medical treatment machines, military equipment, and communications systems are controlled by computers. Increasing numbers of "quality-of-life-critical" systems, from the vast information systems (IS) supporting infrastructures of governments, corporations, and high finance, to community networks [21] and workplace systems [2], down to personal conveniences such as telephones, microwaves and toys, are controlled by computers. Consequently, lives, wellbeing, and quality-of-life, are vulnerable to poor system design and failure.

While this vulnerability gives compelling grounds for directing greater attention to system safety, reliability, and sound design, and for the technical strategies for overcoming shortcomings, it also indicates the need for greater accountability for failures, safety, risk, and harm. Why? Because those who are answerable for harms or risks are the most driven to prevent them. In this way, accountability serves as a powerful tool for bringing about better practices, and consequently more reliable and trustworthy systems. Accountability means there will be someone, or several people, to answer not only for the malfunctions in life-critical systems that cause or risk grave injuries and cause infrastructure and large monetary losses, but even for the malfunctions that cause individual losses of time, convenience, and contentment. Yet because of barriers generated by the contexts in which computer systems are produced, and assumptions about computing and its limitations, accountability for the harms and risks mediated by computing is becoming elusive. How does this occur? To understand how the barriers to accountability arise, some clarification of key concepts is needed.

Accountability, Blame, and Responsibility

For centuries, philosophers and legal scholars have sought to understand accountability and the related concepts of responsibility, blame, and liability, through definitions, prototypical cases, and sets of conditions that would capture their meanings and provide clear grounds for legal principles.[2] Take the concept of responsibility: A common denominator

in most analyses of responsibility are two conditions that determine whether someone is responsible for a harm: (1) a causal condition, and (2) a mental condition (that lawyers refer to as *mens rea*). According to the causal condition a person's actions (or omissions) must have *caused* the harm; according to the mental condition, the person must have *intended* (decided), or *willed* the harm.[3] For example, a person who intentionally installs the Explode virus on her employer's computer is responsible for extensive damage to files because her *intentional* actions were *causally* responsible for the damage.

The concepts of accountability, liability, and blame, extend somewhat farther than the scope suggested by the two preceding conditions. Take for example, the mental condition. Blame for harm is not limited to cases in which an individual willed, or intended it. Recall the case of Robert Morris's Internet Worm. Although the widespread harm it caused was a result of an unintended bug in Morris's code, few were willing to exonerate Robert Morris on the grounds that he had not directly intended the harm he, in fact, wrought. This case illustrates how the mental condition can be weakened to include even unintended harm, if the harm is brought about through negligence, carelessness, or recklessness. In general, if a person fails to take precautions of which he is capable, and that any reasonable person with normal capacities would have taken in those circumstances, then he is not excused from blame merely because he did not intend the outcome. We refer to this generalized version of the mental condition, which includes intent to harm, as well as negligence and recklessness, as "the fault condition" [5].

The causal condition, too, can be weakened to cover cases in which an

agent's actions were not *the* cause, but merely one significant causal factor among a number of others. For example, we may blame a person whose actions, in conjunction with those of another, causes harm. We may even blame a person who causes injury while acting under someone else's orders. These variations on the two conditions, though truer to realistic notions of blame and responsibility, make drawing lines difficult. In an actual case, a judgment over whether an individual is blameworthy can depend on numerous factors particular to that case.

Responsibility and blameworthiness are only a part of what is covered when we apply the robust and intuitive notion of accountability—the notion exemplified by the boy in the back row "stepping forward." When we say someone is accountable for a harm, we may also mean that he or she is liable to punishment (e.g., must pay a fine, be censured by a professional organization, go to jail), or is liable to compensate a victim (usually by paying damages). In most actual cases these different strands of responsibility, censure, and compensation converge because those who are to blame for harms are usually those who must "pay" in some way or other for them. There are some important exceptions, including for example, the case of parents who must answer for injuries caused by their children's reckless behavior, or insurance companies who must cover damages caused by their clients. Strict liability is another. In its bearing on the goal of maintaining accountability in a computerized society, strict liability is of great importance.

To be strictly liable for a harm is to be liable to compensate for it even though one did not bring it about through faulty action. (In other words, one "pays for" the harm even though the fault condition is not satisfied.) This form of liability, which is found in the legal codes of most countries, typically applies to the producers of mass-produced consumer goods, to the producers of potentially harmful goods, and to owners of "ultrahazardous" property. For example, even if they have taken a normal degree of care, milk

---

[1]Here and elsewhere, I use the term "computer profession" very broadly to refer to the loose community of people who dedicate a significant proportion of their time and energy to building computer and computerized systems, and to those engaged in the science, engineering, design, and documentation of computing.

[2]For excellent, and more thorough, contemporary discussions, see for example [5, 7, 8].

[3]A precondition for blameworthiness, especially relevant to the legal domain, is that a person be in possession of certain mental capacities, including the capacities to distinguish right from wrong, and to control his or her actions. Since the issue of mental capacity has no bearing on computing and accountability, I will take it no further.

producers are strictly liable for illness caused by spoiled milk; owners of dangerous animals (for example, tigers in a circus) are strictly liable for injuries caused by escaped animals even if they have taken precautions to restrain them. Although critics of strict liability argue that it is unjust—because people are made to pay for harms that were not their fault—supporters respond that strict liability is nevertheless justified because it contributes significantly to the good of society. It serves a paramount public interest in protecting society from potentially harmful or hazardous goods and property, and provides incentive to sellers of consumer products and owners of potentially hazardous property to take *extraordinary* care. It assures compensation for victims by placing the risk on those best able to pay, and those best able to guard against the harm. And it reduces the cost of litigation by eliminating the onerous task of proving fault.

Four Barriers to Accountability

Accountability is obscured when we apply these conceptual understandings to the types of contexts in which computer systems are produced, combined with commonly held views about the nature of computing—both its capabilities and limitations. The barriers I will discuss are: 1) The problem of "many hands"—because computer systems are created predominantly in organizational settings, 2) Bugs—because bugs not only cause problems but commonly are conceived of as a fact of programming life, 3) The computer as scapegoat—because it can be convenient to blame a computer for harms or injuries, and 4) Ownership without liability—because in the clamor to assert rights of ownership over software, the responsibilities of ownership are neglected. These barriers to accountability can lead to harms and risks for which no one is answerable and about which nothing is done.

1. The problem of many hands. Most computer systems in use today are the products not of single programmers working in isolation, but of groups, collectives, or corporations. They are produced by teams of diverse individuals, that might include designers, engineers, programmers, writers, psychologists, graphic artists, managers, and salespeople. Consequently, when a system gives rise to harm, the task of assigning responsibility, the problem of identifying who is accountable, is exacerbated and obscured because responsibility, characteristically understood in terms of a single individual, does not easily generalize to collective action. In other words, while our conceptual understanding of accountability directs us in search of "the one" who must step forward (for example, the boy in the back row answering for the spitball), collective action presents a challenge.

Where a mishap is the work of "many hands," it can be difficult to identify who is accountable because the locus of decision making (the "mental condition") is frequently different from the mishap's most direct causal antecedent; that is, cause and intent do not converge. Take for example, a bad course of action taken by a political leader, which was based on the word of a trusted adviser. Although the action is taken by the leader, the adviser's word has been a decisive factor. How do we figure the adviser's role into the question of accountability? Further, with the collective actions characteristic of corporate and government hierarchies, decisions and causes themselves are fractured. Boards of directors, task forces, or committees, make decisions jointly, sometimes according to a majority vote. It is the collective efforts of a team that give rise to a product. When high-level decisions work their way down from boards of directors to managers, from managers to employees, ultimately translating into actions and consequences, it is difficult to trace precisely the source of a given problem. As a result, the connection between outcome and the one who is accountable is difficult to make. The problem of many hands, also known as the problem of collective responsibility, is not unique to computing but plagues other technologies, big business, government, and the military [4, 5, 11, 25, 27].

Computing is vulnerable to the obstacles of many hands because, first, as noted earlier, most software systems in use are produced in institutional settings, whether in small and middle-sized software development companies, or large corporations, government agencies and contractors, or educational institutions. (Some cynics argue that institutional structures are designed precisely to avoid accountability.) Second, computer systems themselves—usually not monolithic—are constructed out of segments, or modules. Some systems include code from earlier versions, while others borrow code from different systems entirely. When systems grow in this way, sometimes reaching huge and complex proportions, there may be no single individual who grasps the whole system, or keeps track of all the individuals who have contributed to its various components (See [10, 28].) Third, performance in a wide array of mundane and specialized computer-controlled machines—from rocket ships to refrigerators—depends on the symbiotic relationship of machine with computer system. When things go wrong, it can be difficult to discern whether the call goes to the manufacturers of the machine or to the producers of the computer software.

To see the problem of many hands in action, recall the case of the Therac-25, a striking example of the way many hands can obscure accountability, and at the same time a stark reminder of the practical importance of accountability. In a series of mishaps, now quite familiar to the computer community, the Therac-25, a computer-controlled radiation treatment machine, massively overdosed patients in six known incidents. (The primary sources for my discussion are Leveson and Turner's excellent and detailed account [13] and an earlier paper by Jacky [9].) These overdoses, which occurred over a two-year period from 1985 to 1987, caused severe radiation burns which in turn caused death in three cases, and irreversible injuries (one minor, two very serious) in the other three. Built by Atomic Energy of Canada Limited (AECL), the Therac-25 was the further development in a line of medical linear accelerators which destroy cancerous tumors by irradiating them with accelerated electrons and X-ray photons. Computer controls were far more prominent in the Therac-25, both because the machine had been designed from the ground up with computer controls in mind, and because the safety of the machine was largely left to software. Whereas earlier models had included hardware safety mechanisms and interlocks, designers of the Therac-25 did not duplicate software safety mechanisms with hardware equivalents.

The origin of the malfunction was traced not to a single source, but to numerous faults, including (among others) at least two significant software coding errors ("bugs"), and a faulty microswitch. The impact of these faults was exacerbated by the absence of hardware interlocks, obscure error messages, inadequate testing and quality assurance, exaggerated claims about the reliability of the system in AECL's safety analysis, and, in at least two cases, negligence on the parts of the hospitals where treatment was administered. In one instance monitors enabling technicians to observe patients receiving treatment were not operating at the time of malfunction; in another, the clinic kept poor treatment records. Aside from the important lessons in safety engineering that the case of Therac-25 provides, it offers a lesson in accountability—or rather the breakdown of accountability due to "many hands."

If we apply standard conceptions of accountability to identify who should step forward and answer for the injuries, we see an intricate web of causes and decisions. Since we can safely rule out intentional wrongdoing, we must try to identify causal agents who were also negligent or reckless. If none can be identified, we conclude that the mishaps were truly accidental, that no one is responsible, no one is to blame. First, consider the causal antecedents: AECL designers, safety engineers, programmers, machinists, corporate executives, hospital administrators, physicians, physicists, and technicians. Since each group bore a significant causal relationship to the existence and character of the machine, it is reasonable to examine their rela-

tionship to the malfunction, the massive overdoses, deaths and injuries. The machine technicians, who entered the doses and push buttons, are the most direct causal antecedents. The others are more distant. In one of the most chilling anecdotes, a machine technician is supposed to have responded to the agonized cries from a patient by flatly denying that it was possible he had been burned.

Although the machine technicians are most closely causally linked to the outcomes, they are not necessarily accountable. The second condition on responsibility directs the search to faulty action (the fault condition). According to Leveson and Turner's account, which spotlights the work of software engineers and quality assurance personnel, there is evidence of inadequate software engineering and testing practices, as well as a failure in the extent of corporate response to signs of a problem. The safety analysis was faulty in that it systematically overestimated the system's reliability, and evidently did not consider the role software failure could play in derailing the system as a whole. Computer code from earlier Therac models was used on the Therac-25 system and assumed unproblematic because no similar injuries had resulted. Further investigation showed that although the problems had always been present, because earlier models had included mechanical interlocks, they simply had not surfaced.

The practical implications of diminished accountability are tragically clear in the deaths and injuries at six different locations where Therac-25 accelerators were used. Until the physicist Fritz Hager, at Tyler Hospital, Tyler, East Texas took it upon himself to trace the source of the problem, and many months later, the FDA stepped in, insisting on a regimen of upgrades and improvements, early responses to reports of problems were lackluster. AECL was slow to react to requests to check the machine, understand the problem, or to remediate (for example by installing an independent hardware safety system). Even after a patient filed a lawsuit in 1985 citing hospital, manufacturer, and service organization as responsible for her injuries, AECL's

follow up was negligible. For example, no special effort was made to inform other clinics operating Therac-25 machines about the mishaps. (Because the lawsuit was settled out of court, we do not learn how the law would have attributed liability.)

In sum, the Therac-25, a complex computer-controlled system, whose malfunction caused severe injury, provides an example of the way many hands can lead to an obscuring of accountability. Because no individual was both an obvious causal antecedent and decision maker, it was difficult, at least on the face of it, to identify who should have stepped forward and assumed responsibility. Collective action of this type provides excuses at all levels, from those low down in the hierarchy who are "only following orders," to top-ranking decision makers who are only distantly linked to the outcomes.

We should not, however, confuse the *obscuring* of accountability due to collective action, with the *absence* of blameworthiness. Even Leveson and Turner, whose detailed analysis of the Therac-25 mishaps sheds light on both the technical aspects as well as the procedural elements of the case, appear unwilling to probe the question of accountability. They refer to the malfunctions and injuries as "accidents" and say they do not wish "to criticize the manufacturer of the equipment or anyone else." [13] Contrary to Leveson and Turner's own assessment of what they were doing, in identifying inadequate software engineering practices and corporate response, I think their analysis produces at the very least an excellent starting place for attributing accountability. If we consistently respond to complex cases by not pursuing blame and responsibility, we are effectively accepting agentless mishaps and a general erosion of accountability.

2. Bugs. To say that bugs in software make software unreliable and can cause systems to fail and be unsafe is to state the obvious. However, it is not quite as obvious how the way we think about bugs affects considerations of accountability. (I use the term "bug" to cover a variety of types of software errors including modeling, design, and coding errors.) The

Even when we factor out sheer incompetence, **bugs in significant number are endemic to programming.** *They are the natural hazards of any substantial system.*

inevitability of bugs escapes very few computer users and programmers and their pervasiveness is stressed by most software, and especially safety, engineers. The dictum, "There is always another software bug," [13] especially in the long and complex systems controlling life-critical and quality-of-life-critical technologies, captures this fact of programming life. Errors in complex functional computer systems are an inevitable presence in ambitious systems [3]. Many agree with the claim that "errors are more common, more pervasive, and more troublesome, in software than in other technologies," and that even skilled program reviewers are apt to miss flaws in programs [18]. Even when we factor out sheer incompetence, bugs in significant number are endemic to programming. They are the natural hazards of any substantial system.

While this way of thinking about bugs exposes the vulnerability of complex systems, it also creates a problematic mind-set for accountability. On the one hand the standard conception of responsibility directs us to the person who either intentionally or by not taking reasonable care causes harm. On the other, the view of bugs as inevitable hazards of programming implies that while harms and inconveniences caused by bugs are regrettable, they cannot—except in cases of obvious sloppiness—be helped. In turn, this implies that it is unreasonable to hold programmers, systems engineers and designers, accountable for imperfections in their systems.

An illustrative parallel can be drawn from the annals of bridge building and the collapse of the Tacoma Narrows bridge. Analysts tend to agree that although the bridge collapsed because of its defective design, no one should be blamed for it,

because it was built according to the best specifications of the day and did not fall short of the state of knowledge in civil engineering. By contrast, in the case of the Challenger, another oft-cited case, critics blame NASA for their recklessness in going ahead with the launch in spite of known limitations of the O-Rings. Insofar as we accept bugs as an inevitable byproduct of programming, we will tend to draw parallels between bug-related failures and the collapse of the Tacoma Narrows Bridge: no one need "step forward" and be accountable. The problem with this as a blanket approach is that we are likely to miss the cases that more closely parallel the Challenger, in which it is important that someone "step forward" and be accountable. A more discerning approach to bugs in a system would better enable us to discriminate the "natural hazards," from those that with reasonable effort and good practices, could have been avoided. I would go further and say that even for the bugs that persist, despite reasonable efforts and good practices, there should be accountability, for reasons to be revealed in the section on recommendations.

3."It's the computer's fault": The computer as scapegoat. It is likely that most of us have experienced the bank clerk explaining an error, the ticket agent excusing lost bookings, the students justifying a late paper, by blaming the computer. But while the practice of blaming a computer, on the face of it, appears reasonable and even felicitous, it is a barrier to accountability because, having found one explanation for an error or injury, the further role and responsibility of human agents may be underestimated.

Let us try to understand why, in the first place, blaming a computer

appears plausible by applying the conceptual analysis of blame discussed earlier : cause and fault. Consider first the causal condition: Computer systems frequently function as mediators of interactions between machines and humans, and between one human and another. This means, first, that human actions are distanced from their causal impacts, including harms and injuries, and second, the computer's action is the more direct causal antecedent. Thus the first condition on blameworthiness is satisfied by the computer. But causal proximity is not sufficient. We do not, for example, excuse a murderer on grounds that it was the bullet entering the victim's head and not he who was directly responsible for the victim's death.

The mental condition must be satisfied too. Here, computers present a curious challenge and temptation. As distinct from many other inanimate objects, computers perform tasks previously performed by humans in positions of responsibility. They calculate, decide, control, and remember. For this reason, and perhaps even more deeply rooted psychological reasons [26], people attribute to computers and not to other inanimate objects (like bullets) the array of mental properties, such as intentions, desires, thought, preferences, that make humans responsible for their actions. Where a loan adviser approves a loan to an applicant who subsequently defaults on the loan, or a doctor prescribes the wrong antibiotic and a patient dies, or an intensive care attendant incorrectly assesses the prognosis for an accident victim and denies the patient a respirator, we hold accountable the loan adviser, the doctors, and the attendant. Now replace these human agents with the computerized loan adviser, the expert systems (ES)

Accountability, and *the responsible practice of* **computing, are social values worth sustaining** *and, when necessary, rehabilitating.*

MYCIN, and APACHE (a computer system that predicts a patient's chance of survival [6]). While on the face of it, it may seem reasonable to associate the blame with the *functions* even though they are now performed by computer systems and not humans, the result of not working out alternative lines of accountability means ultimately a loss of accountability for that function. (For other discussions and proposed solutions see [11, 15, 23].)

We can fairly easily explain some of the cases in which people blame computers. In the first place there are cases in which an agent, by blaming a computer, is obviously shirking responsibility. In the second place, there are cases in which an agent cites a computer because he is genuinely perplexed about who is responsible. For example, when an airline reservation system apparently malfunctions, it may be that accountability is already so obscured that the computer is indeed the most salient agent. In these cases, the computer serves as a stopgap for something elusive, the one who is, or should be, accountable. In the remaining cases, in which computers perform functions previously performed by humans who were held accountable for their actions, we need to rescue accountability. It is important that the ethical issue of who is accountable not hang in the balance on an answer to the metaphysical question of whether computers really decide, calculate, intend, and think. We need to adjust the lines of accountability to identify other humans who will be accountable to the impacts of these systems.

4. Ownership without liability. The issue of property rights over computer software has sparked active and vociferous public debate. Should program code, algorithms, user interface ("look-and-feel"), or any other aspects of software be privately

ownable? If yes, what is the appropriate form and degree of ownership—trade secrets, patents, copyright, or a new (*sui generis*) form of ownership devised specifically for software? Should software be held in private ownership at all? Some have clamored for software patents, arguing that protecting a strong right of ownership in software, permitting owners and authors to "reap rewards," is the most just course. Others urge social policies that would place software in the public domain, while still others have sought explicitly to balance owners' rights with broader and longer-term social interests and the advancement of computer science [17, 19, 24]. Significantly absent in these debates is any reference to owners' responsibilities.[4]

While ownership implies a bundle of rights, it also implies responsibilities. Along with the privileges of ownership comes responsibility. If a tree branch on private property falls and injures a person under it, if a pet Doberman escapes and bites a passerby, its owners are accountable. Holding owners responsible makes sense from a perspective of social welfare because owners are typically in the best position to directly control their property. In the case of software, its owners (usually the producers) are in the best position to directly affect the quality of the software they release to the public. Yet the trend in the software industry is to demand maximal property protection while denying, to the extent possible, accountability.

This is expressed in, for example, the license agreements that accompany almost all mass-produced consumer software which usually includes a section detailing the

producers' rights, and another negating accountability. Accordingly, the consumer merely licenses a copy of the software application and is subject to various limitation on use and access to it. The disclaimers of liability are equally explicit: "In no event will Danz Development Corporation, or its officers, employees, or affiliates be liable to you for any consequential, incidental, or indirect damages . . . "; "Apple makes no warranty or representation, either expressed or implied, with respect to software, its quality, performance, merchantability, or fitness for a particular purpose. As a result, this software is sold 'as is,' and you, the purchaser are assuming the entire risk as to its quality and performance." The Apple disclaimer goes on to say, "In no event will Apple be liable for direct, indirect, special, incidental, or consequential damages resulting from any defect in the software or its documentation, even if advised of the possibility of such damages."

Maintaining Accountability in a Computerized Society— Recommendations

An underlying premise of this article—and one I hope is shared with readers—is that accountability, and the responsible practice of computing, are social values worth sustaining and when necessary, rehabilitating. We have seen how features of the organizational contexts in which computer systems and computerized systems are created, and broadly held views about the power and limitations of computing can erode accountability for risks and injuries; namely, many hands, bugs, computers-as-scapegoat, and ownership without liability. Rehabilitating accountability in a computerized society does not, however, imply an obsession with pinning the blame on someone, or an insistence that someone be punished no matter what.

---

[4]For an exception see Samuelson's recent discussion of liability for defective information [20].

Rather, it recommends an approach to harms, injuries, and risks, that is cognizant of the contexts and assumptions that are apt to obscure accountability. We should hold on to the assumption that someone is accountable, unless after careful investigation, we conclude that the malfunction in question is, indeed, no one's fault.

Beyond this general approach to rehabilitating accountability, I propose three specific lines of approach to promote accountability—one conceptual, the other two practical. The recommendations are addressed to the professional community—those actively engaged in the computing profession, their professional organizations, and the institutions that educate them. They are addressed also to policy makers, and to all of us living in this increasingly computerized society. With lines of accountability recovered, responsibility for the impacts of computing will, we hope, become as clear to the computing profession and the rest of society, as to the boy in the back row taking the first step forward toward accountability.

1. Keep accountability distinct from liability to compensate. The problem of many hands is profound and unlikely to yield easily to any general, or slick, solution. Greater success, at least for the present, is likely to come from careful case-by-case analysis, in which accountability is determined according to the details of a specific situation. A good system of liability offers a *partial* solution because, while we wrestle with the conceptual puzzles of blame and accountability, at least the needs of victims are being addressed.

Liability, however, is not the same as accountability. It ought not be accepted as a substitute for it because this would further obscure accountability. Liability is grounded in the plight of a victim. Its extent, usually calculated in terms of a sum of money, is determined by the degree of injury and damage suffered by the victim. For example, when harm is the result of collective action, because the weight of compensation can be shared, its burden on each agent is considerably eased. Furthermore, since compensation is victim-

centered, identifying one satisfactory source of compensation lets others "off the hook." By contrast, accountability is grounded in the nature of the action, and the relationship of the agent to an outcome. (Recall the causal and fault conditions.) If several individuals are collectively responsible, we hold each fully accountable because many hands ought not make the burden of accountability light. Further, holding one individual accountable does not let others off the hook because several individuals may all be fully accountable for a harm.[5] From the general annals of engineering ethics, the fatal calculation of Ford executives in which they offset the value of life and injury against the cost of improving the Pinto's design, we see an example in which considerations of liability were primary. Had they been thinking about accountability to society and not merely liability, they would surely have reached a different conclusion.

2. Clarify and vigorously promote a substantive standard-of-care. A growing literature, including several of the articles cited earlier (for example, [13, 18]) discusses guidelines for producing safer and more reliable computer systems. Among these guidelines is a call for simpler design, a modular approach to system building, formal analysis of modules as well as the whole, meaningful quality assurance, independent auditing, built-in redundancy, and excellent documentation. If such guidelines were to evolve into a standard of care, taken seriously by the computing profession, promulgated through educational institutions, urged by professional organizations, and even enforced through licensing or accreditation (a controversial issue), better and safer systems would be the direct result. Another result of a standard of care would be a nonarbitrary means of determining accountability. The standard of care provides a tool to distinguish between malfunctions (bugs) due to

[5]Compare this to the judge's finding in the "Red Hook Murder." Even though it was almost certainly known which one of the three accused pulled the trigger, the court viewed all three as equal and "deadly conspirators" in the death of Patrick Daley.

inadequate practices and those that occur in spite of a programmer or designer's best efforts. A standard of care provides a tool for distinguishing the analogs of the Tacoma Narrows Bridge, from those of the Challenger space shuttle. For example, had the guidelines discussed by Leveson and Turner been known at the time the Therac-25 was created, we would have been able to conclude that the developers of the system were accountable for the injuries. In not meeting these standards they were negligent.

A standard of care could also be of benefit to systems engineers working within large organizations. It would provide an explicit measure of excellence that functions independently of pressures imposed by the organizational hierarchy.

3. Impose strict liability for defective consumer-oriented software, as well as for software whose impact on society and individuals is great. Strict liability would shift the burden-of-accountability to the producers of defective software and thereby would address an anomaly (perhaps even a paradox) in our current system of liability. We have seen, on the one hand, that strict liability is a way of assuring that the public is protected against the potential harms of risky artifacts and property. On the other hand, while the prevailing lore portrays computer systems as prone to error in a degree surpassing most other technologies, most producers of software explicitly deny accountability for harmful impacts of their products, even when they malfunction. Software seems, therefore, to be *precisely* the type of artifact for which strict liability is necessary—assuring compensation for victims, and sending an emphatic message to producers of software to take *extra*ordinary care to produce safe and reliable systems.

Conclusion

In the twentieth century B.C. the Code of Hammurabi declared that if a house collapsed and killed its owner, the builder of the house was to be put to death. In the twentieth century A.D. many builders of computer software would deny responsibility and pass the "entire risk" to the user. While the centuries have placed a distance between the harsh punishments meted out by Hammurabi's Code and contemporary legal codes, the call for accountability remains a standard worth restoring, and one whose achievement would be a source of professional pride. ◪

References

1. Borning, A. Computer system reliability and nuclear war. *Commun. ACM 30,* 2 (1987), 112–131.
2. Clement, A. Computing at work: Empowering action by 'low-level users.' *Commun. ACM 37,* 1 (Jan. 1994) (this issue).
3. Corbato, F.J. On building systems that will fail. *Commun. ACM 34,* 9 (1991), 73–81.
4. De George, R. Ethical responsibilities of engineers in large organizations: The Pinto case. In *Collective Responsibility,* L. May and S. Hoffman, Eds., 1991, Rowman and Littlefield, pp. 151–166.
5. Feinberg, J. Collective responsibility. In *Doing and Deserving,* J. Feinberg, Ed., 1970, Princeton University Press, Princeton, N.J.
6. Fitzgerald, S. *Hospital Computer Predicts Patients' Chances of Survival.* The *Miami Herald,* 1992, Miami, p. 6J.
7. Hart, H.L.A. *Punishment and Responsibility.* Clarendon Press, Oxford, 1968.
8. Hart, H.L.A. and Honore, T. *Causation and the Law.* Second ed., Clarendon Press, Oxford, 1985.
9. Jacky, J. Safety-critical computing: Hazards, practices, standards and regulations. Unpublished manuscript. University of Washington, 1989.
10. Johnson, D.G. and Mulvey, J.M. *Computer Decisions: Ethical Issues of Responsibility and Bias.* Statistics and Operations Research Series, Princeton University, 1993.
11. Ladd, J. Computers and moral responsibility: A framework for an ethical analysis. In *The Information Web: Ethical and Social Implications of Computer Networking,* C.C. Gould, Ed. Westview Press, Boulder, Colo. 1989.
12. Leveson, N. Software safety: Why, what, and how. *Comput. Surv. 18,* 2 (1986), 125–163.
13. Leveson, N. and Turner, C. An investigation of the Therac-25 accidents. *Computer 26,* 7 (1993), 18–41.
14. Littlewood, B. and Strigini, L. The risks of software. *Sci Am.* (1992), 62–75.
15. Moor, J. What is computer ethics? *Metaphilosophy 16,* 4 (1985), 266–275.
16. Neuman, P.G. Inside RISKS. *Commun. ACM.*
17. Nissenbaum, H. Should I copy my neighbor's software? *Comput. Philos.* To be published.
18. Parnas, D., Schouwen, J. and Kwan, S.P. Evaluation of safety-critical software. *Commun. ACM 33,* 6, (1990), 636–648.
19. Samuelson, P. *Adapting Intellectual Property Law to New Technologies: A Case Study on Computer Programs.* National Research Council, 1992.
20. Samuelson, P. Liability for defective information. *Commun. ACM 36,* 1 (1993), 21–26.
21. Schuler, D. Community networks: Building a new partipatory medium. *Commun. ACM 37,* 1 (Jan. 1994) (this issue).
22. Smith, B. The limits of correctness. Center for the study of language and information, Rep. CSLI-85-35, Stanford, 1985.
23. Snapper, J.W. Responsibility for computer-based errors. *Metaphilosophy 16* (1985), 289–295.
24. Stallman, R.M. The GNU manifesto. *GNU Emacs Manual,* 1987, 175–84.
25. Thompson, D. The moral responsibility of many hands. In *Political Ethics and Public Office.* Harvard University Press, Cambridge, Mass. 1987, pp. 40–65.
26. Turkle, S. *The Second Self.* Simon & Schuster, Inc., New York, 1984.
27. Velasquez, M. Why corporations are not morally responsible for anything they do. In *Collective Responsibility,* L. May and S. Hoffman, Eds. Rowman and Littlefield, 1991, pp. 111–131.
28. Weizenbaum, J. On the impact of the computer on society. *Science 176,* 12 (1972), 609–614.

CR Categories and Subject Descriptors: D.2.5 [**Software Engineering**]: Testing and Debugging; D.4.5 [**Operating Systems**]: Reliability; K.1 [**Computing Mileux**]: The Computer Industry—*standards;* K.4.1 [**Computers and Society**]: Public Policy Issues—*human safety, regulation;* K.5.0 [**Legal Aspects of Computing**]: General; K.7.m [**The Computing Profession**]: Miscellaneous—*codes of good practice;* ethics; K.7.3 [**The Computing Profession**]—*testing, certification, and licensing*

General Terms: Human Factors, Legal Aspects

Additional Key Words and Phrases: Liability, responsibility

About the Author:
HELEN NISSENBAUM is associate director of the Center for Human Values. Her research interests in computer ethics include property rights over software, the value dimensions of computing, accountability, and privacy. **Author's Present Address:** University Center for Human Values, Marx Hall, Princeton University, Princeton, NJ 08540. Email: helen@phoenix.princeton.edu

Permission to copy without fee all or part of this material is granted provided that the copies are not made or distributed for direct commercial advantage, the ACM copyright notice and the title of the publication and its date appear, and notice is give that copying is by permission of the Association for Computing Machinery. To copy otherwise, or to republish, requires a fee and/or specific permission.

© ACM 0002-0782/94/100 $3.50

Using the New ACM CODE OF ETHICS IN Decision Making

Ronald E. Anderson
Deborah G. Johnson
Donald Gotterbarn
Judith Perrolle

Historically, professional associations have viewed codes of ethics as mechanisms to establish their status as a profession or as a means to regulate their membership and thereby convince the public that they deserve to be self-regulating. Self-regulation depends on ways to deter unethical behavior of the members, and a code, combined with an ethics review board, was seen as the solution. Codes of ethics have tended to list possible violations and threaten sanctions for such violations. ACM's first code, the Code of Professional Conduct, was adopted in 1972 and followed this model. The latest ACM code, the Code of Ethics and Professional Conduct, was adopted in 1992 and takes a new direction.

ACM and many other societies have had difficulties implementing an ethics review system and came to realize that self-regulation depends mostly on the consensus and commitment of its members to ethical behavior. Now the most important rationale for a code of ethics is an embodiment of a set of commitments of that association's members. Sometimes these commitments are expressed as rules and sometimes as ideals, but the essential social function is to clarify and formally state those ethical requirements that are important to the group as a professional association. The new ACM Code of Ethics and Professional Conduct follows this philosophy.

Recent codes of ethics emphasize socialization or education rather than enforced compliance. A code can work toward the collective good even though it may be a mere distillation of collective experience and reflection. A major benefit of an educationally oriented code is its contribution to the group by clarifying the professionals' responsibility to society.

A code of ethics holds the profession accountable to the public. This tends to yield a major payoff in terms of public trust. In Frankel's words, "To the extent that a code confers benefits on clients, it will help persuade the public that professionals are deserving of its confidence and respect, and of increased social and economic rewards" [8].

The final and most important function of a code of ethics is its role as an aid to individual decision making. In the interest of facilitating better ethical decision making, we have developed a set of nine classes that describe situations calling for ethical decision making. These cases address in turn the topics of intellectual property, privacy, confidentiality, professional quality, fairness or discrimination, liability, software risks, conflicts of interest, and unauthorized access to computer systems.

Within each case we begin with a scenario to illustrate a typical ethical decision point and then lay out the different imperatives (principles) of the new Code of Ethics that pertain to that decision. There are 24 principles in the Code and each case analysis calls on at least two or three different principles to evaluate the relevant ethical concerns. Each of the principles is relevant to at least one scenario, and some principles apply to several situations. The purpose of these case analyses is to provide examples of practical applications of the new ACM Code of Ethics.

Case 1: Intellectual Property

Jean, a statistical database programmer, is trying to write a large statistical program needed by her company. Programmers in this company are encouraged to write about their work and to publish their algorithms in professional journals. After months of tedious programming, Jean has found herself stuck on several parts of the program. Her manager, not recognizing the complexity of the problem, wants the job completed within the next few days. Not knowing how to solve the problems, Jean remembers that a coworker had given her source listings from his current work and from an early version of a commercial software package developed at another company. On studying these programs, she sees two areas of code which could be directly incorporated into her own program. She uses segments of code from both her coworker and the commercial software, but does not tell anyone or mention it in the documentation. She completes the project and turns it in a day ahead of time. (Adapted from a scenario by Dave Colantonio and Deborah Johnson.)

The Code addresses questions of intellectual property most explicitly in imperative 1.6: "Give proper credit for intellectual property . . . Specifically, one must not take credit for other's ideas or work . . ." This ethical requirement extends the property rights principle (1.5) that explicitly mentions copyrights, patents, trade secrets and license agreements. These restrictions are grounded in integrity (1.3) and in the need to comply with existing laws (2.3).

Jean violated professional ethics in two areas: failure to give credit for another's work and using code from a commercial package that presumably was copyrighted or in another

ACM CODE OF ETHICS AND PROFESSIONAL CONDUCT

On October 16, 1992, ACM's Executive Council

voted to adopt a revised Code of Ethics.

The following imperatives and explanatory guidelines

were proposed to supplement the Code as contained

in the new ACM Bylaw 17.

Commitment to ethical professional conduct is expected of every voting, associate, and student member of ACM. This Code, consisting of 24 imperatives formulated as statements of personal responsibility, identifies the elements of such a commitment.

It contains many, but not all, issues professionals are likely to face. Section 1 outlines fundamental ethical considerations, while Section 2 addresses additional, more specific considerations of professional conduct. Statements in Section 3 pertain more specifically to individuals who have a leadership role, whether in the workplace or in a volunteer capacity, for example with organizations such as ACM. Principles involving compliance with this Code are given in Section 4.

The Code is supplemented by a set of Guidelines, which provide explanation to assist members in dealing with the various issues contained in the Code. It is expected that the Guidelines will be changed more frequently than the Code.

The Code and its supplemented Guidelines are intended to serve as a basis for ethical decision making in the conduct of professional work. Secondarily, they may serve as a basis for judging the merit of a formal complaint pertaining to violation of professional ethical standards.

It should be noted that although computing is not mentioned in the moral imperatives section, the Code is concerned with how these fundamental imperatives apply to one's conduct as a computing professional. These imperatives are expressed in a general form to emphasize that ethical principles which apply to computer ethics are derived from more general ethical principles.

It is understood that some words and phrases in a code of ethics are subject to varying interpretations, and that any ethical principle may conflict with other ethical principles in specific situations. Questions related to ethical conflicts can best be answered by thoughtful consideration of fundamental principles, rather than reliance on detailed regulations.   ▶

way protected by law. Suppose that Jean only looked at her coworker's source code for ideas and then completely wrote her own program; would she still have an obligation to give credit? Our answer is yes, she should have acknowledged credit to her coworker in the documentation. There is a matter of professional discretion here, because if the use of another's intellectual material is truly trivial, then there probably is no need to give formal credit.

Jean's use of commercial software code was not appropriate because she should have checked to determine whether or not her company was authorized to use the source code before using it. Even though it is generally desirable to share and exchange intellectual materials, using bootlegged software is definitely a violation of the Code.

Those interested in additional discussions on this subject should refer to the numerous articles by Pamela Samuelson on intellectual property in *Communications*. Also recommended are [2, 7, 17].

Case 2: Privacy

Three years ago Diane started her own consulting business. She has been so successful that she now has several people working for her and many clients. Their consulting work included advising on how to network microcomputers, designing database management systems, and advising about security.

Presently she is designing a database management system for the personnel office of a medium-sized company. Diane has involved the client in the design process, informing the CEO, the director of computing, and the director of personnel about the progress of the system. It is now time to make decisions about the kind and degree of security to build into the system. Diane has described several options to the client. Because the system is going to cost more than they planned, the client has decided to opt for a less secure system. She believes the information they will be storing is extremely sensitive. It will include performance evaluations, medical records for filing insurance claims, salaries, and so forth.

With weak security, employees

working on microcomputers may be able to figure out ways to get access to this data, not to mention the possibilities for on-line access from hackers. Diane feels strongly that the system should be much more secure. She has tried to explain the risks, but the CEO, director of computing and director of personnel all agree that less security will do. What should she do? Should she refuse to build the system as they request? (Adapted from [14]).

In the Code of Ethics, principle number 1.7 deals with privacy and 1.8 with confidentiality. They are integrally related but the privacy principle here is the most explicit. The Guidelines of the Code say that computer professionals are obligated to preserve the integrity of data about individuals "from unauthorized access or accidental disclosure to inappropriate individuals." The Code also specifies that organizational leaders have obligations to "verify that systems are designed and implemented to protect personal privacy and enhance personal dignity" (3.5), and to assess the needs of all those affected by a system (3.4).

The company officials have an obligation to protect the privacy of their employees, and therefore should not accept inadequate security. Diane's first obligation is to attempt to educate the company officials, which is implied by imperative 2.7 to promote "public understanding of computing and its consequences." If that fails, then Diane needs to consider her contractual obligations as noted under imperative 2.6 on honoring assigned responsibilities. We do not know the details of Diane's contract, but she may have to choose between her contract and her obligation to honor privacy and confidentiality.

Additional perspectives and discussion on the privacy obligations of computer professionals can be found in [5, 6, 14, 23]. We also recommend proceedings of the latest conference on Computers, Freedom and Privacy [13].

Case 3: Confidentiality

Max works in a large state department of alcoholism and drug abuse. The agency administers programs

for individuals with alcohol and drug problems, and maintains a huge database of information on the clients who use their services. Some of the data files contain the names and current addresses of clients.

Max has been asked to take a look at the track records of the treatment programs. He is to put together a report that contains the number of clients seen in each program each month for the past five years, length of each client's treatment, number of clients who return after completion of a program, criminal histories of clients, and so on. In order to put together this report, Max has been given access to all files in the agency's mainframe computer. After assembling the data into a new file that includes the client names, he downloads it to the computer in his office.

Under pressure to get the report finished by the deadline, Max decides he will have to work at home over the weekend in order to finish on time. He copies the information onto several disks and takes them home. After finishing the report he leaves the disks at home and forgets about them (adapted from [14]).

This scenario resembles the previous one that dealt with privacy considerations. However, it raises several additional issues. From the Code of Ethics, principles 1.7 on privacy and 1.8 on confidentiality apply. Imperative 2.8 on constraining access to authorized situations is also central to a computer user's decisions in this type of situation. Additionally, the Code specifies that organizational leaders have obligations to "verify that systems are designed and implemented to protect personal privacy and enhance personal dignity," (3.5) and it also states that they should specify appropriate and authorized uses of an organization's resources (3.3).

The government agency should have had policies and procedures that protected the identity of its clients. Max's relatives and friends might accidentally discover the files and inappropriately use the information to harm the reputation of the clients. The files that Max worked with for his report did not need to have any names or other information in the records that made it possible to easily identify individuals. The

1. General Moral Imperatives.
As an ACM member I will . . .

1.1 Contribute to society and human well-being
This principle concerning the quality of life of all people affirms an obligation to protect fundamental human rights and to respect the diversity of all cultures. An essential aim of computing professionals is to minimize negative consequences of computing systems, including threats to health and safety. When designing or implementing systems, computing professionals must attempt to ensure that the products of their efforts will be used in socially responsible ways, will meet social needs, and will avoid harmful effects to health and welfare.

In addition to a safe social environment, human well-being includes a safe natural environment. Therefore, computing professionals who design and develop systems must be alert to, and make others aware of, any potential damage to the local or global environment.

1.2 Avoid harm to others
"Harm" means injury or negative consequences, such as undesirable loss of information, loss of property, property damage, or unwanted environmental impacts. This principle prohibits use of computing technology in ways that result in harm to any of the following: users, the general public, employees, employers. Harmful actions include intentional destruction or modification of files and programs leading to serious loss of resources or unnecessary expenditure of human resources such as the time and effort required to purge systems of computer viruses.

Well-intended actions, including those that accomplish assigned duties, may lead to harm unexpectedly. In such an event the responsible person or persons are obligated to undo or mitigate the negative consequences as much as possible. One way to avoid unintentional harm is to carefully consider potential impacts on all those affected by decisions made during design and implementation.

To minimize the possibility of indirectly harming others, computing professionals must minimize malfunctions by following generally accepted standards for system design and testing. Furthermore, it is often necessary to assess the social consequences of systems to project the likelihood of any serious harm to others. If system features are misrepresented to users, coworkers, or supervisors, the individual computing professional is responsible for any resulting injury.

In the work environment the computing professional has the additional obligation to report any signs of system dangers that might result in serious personal or social damage. If one's superiors do not act to curtail or mitigate such dangers, it may be necessary to "blow the whistle" to help correct the problem or reduce the risk. However, capricious or misguided reporting of violations can, itself, be harmful. Before reporting violations, all relevant aspects of the incident must be thoroughly assessed. In particular, the assessment of risk and responsibility must be credible. It is suggested that advice be sought from other computing professionals. (See principle 2.5 regarding thorough evaluations.)

1.3 Be honest and trustworthy
Honesty is an essential component of trust. Without trust an organization cannot function effectively. The honest computing professional will not make deliberately false or deceptive claims about a system or system design, but will instead provide full disclosure of all pertinent system limitations and problems.

A computer professional has a duty to be honest about his or her own qualifications, and about any circumstances that might lead to conflicts of interest.

Membership in volunteer organizations such as ACM may at times place individuals in situations where their statements or actions could be interpreted as carrying the "weight" of a larger group of professionals. An ACM member will exercise care to not misrepresent ACM or positions and policies of ACM or any ACM units.

1.4 Be fair and take action not to discriminate
The values of equality, tolerance, respect for others, and the principles of equal justice govern this imperative. Discrimination on the basis of race, sex, religion, age, disability, national origin, or other such factors is an explicit violation of ACM policy and will not be tolerated.

Inequities between different groups of people may result from the use or misuse of information and technology. In a fair society, all individuals would have equal opportunity to participate in, or benefit from, the use of computer resources regardless of race, sex, religion, age, disability, national origin or other such similar factors. However, these ideals do not justify unauthorized use of computer resources nor do they provide an adequate basis for violation of any other ethical imperatives of this code.

1.5 Honor property rights including copyrights and patents
Violation of copyrights, patents, trade secrets and the terms of license agreements is prohibited by law in most circumstances. Even when software is not so protected, such violations are contrary to professional behavior. Copies of software should be made only with proper authorization. Unauthorized duplication of materials must not be condoned.

1.6 Give proper credit for intellectual property
Computing professionals are obligated to protect the integrity of intellectual property. Specifically, one must not take credit for other's ideas or work, even in cases where the work has not been explicitly protected, for example by copyright or patent.

1.7 Respect the privacy of others
Computing and communication technology enables the collection and exchange of personal information on a scale unprecedented in the history of civilization. Thus there is increased potential for violating the privacy of individuals and groups. It is the responsibility of professionals to maintain the privacy and integrity of data describing individuals. This includes taking precautions to ensure the accuracy of data, as well as protecting it from unauthorized access or accidental disclosure to inappropriate individuals. Furthermore, procedures must be established to allow individuals to review their records and correct inaccuracies.

This imperative implies that only the necessary ▶

agency should have removed the identifying information from the files it allowed Max to use. If that procedure had been followed, it would not have mattered that Max copied the file to his computer. Thus the organizational context created many ethical issues for Max, but unfortunately he was not attentive to these ethical issues ahead of time.

Further reading on this subject can be found in [12, 15, 20]. Discussions of computer-related procedures to maintain the confidentiality of data from specific sources also are available from other professional associations such as the American Medical Association and the American Statistical Association.

Case 4: Quality in Professional Work

A computer company is writing the first stage of a more efficient accounting system that will be used by the government. This system will save taxpayers a considerable amount of money every year. A computer professional, who is asked to design the accounting system, assigns different parts of the system to her staff. One person is responsible for developing the reports; another is responsible for the internal processing; and a third for the user interface. The manager is shown the system and agrees that it can do everything in the requirements. The system is installed, but the staff finds the interface so difficult to use that their complaints are heard by upper-level management. Because of these complaints, upper-level management will not invest any more money in the development of the new accounting system and they go back to their original, more expensive system (adapted from [10]).

The Code of Ethics advocates that computer professionals "strive to achieve the highest quality in both process and products" (2.1). Imperative 3.4 elaborates that users and those affected by a system have their needs clearly articulated.

We presume that in this case the failure to deliver a quality product is directly attributable to a failure to follow a quality process. It is likely that most of the problems with this interface would have been discov-

ered in a review process, either with peers or with users, which is promoted by imperative 2.4. When harm results, in this case to taxpayers, the failure to implement a quality process becomes a clear violation of ethical behavior.

For recent discussions of ethics cases that deal with software quality, see [11].

Case 5: Fairness and Discrimination

In determining requirements for an information system to be used in an employment agency, the client explains that, when displaying applicants whose qualifications appear to match those required for a particular job, the names of white applicants are to be displayed ahead of those of nonwhite applicants, and names of male applicants are to be displayed ahead of those of female applicants (adapted from Donald Gotterbarn and Lionel Diemel).

According to the general moral imperative on fairness, an ACM member will be "fair and take action not to discriminate." In this case the system designer is being asked to build a system that, it appears, will be used to favor white males and discriminate against nonwhites and females. It would seem that the system designer should not simply do what he or she is told but should point out the problematic nature of what is being requested and ask the client why this is being done. Making this inquiry is consistent with 2.3 (to respect existing laws) and 2.5 (to give thorough evaluations) and 4.1 (to uphold and promote the Code of Ethics).

If the client concludes that he or she plans to use the information to favor white males, then the computer professional should refuse to build the system as proposed. To go ahead and build the system would be a violation not only of 1.4 (fairness), but of 2.3 (respecting existing laws) and would be inconsistent with 1.1 (human well-being) and 1.2 (avoiding harm).

For further discussion of the topic of bias see [9, 16, 21].

Case 6: Liability for Unreliability

A software development company

has just produced a new software package that incorporates the new tax laws and figures taxes for both individuals and small businesses. The president of the company knows that the program has a number of bugs. He also believes the first firm to put this kind of software on the market is likely to capture the largest market share. The company widely advertises the program. When the company actually ships a disk, it includes a disclaimer of responsibility for errors resulting from the use of the program. The company expects it will receive a number of complaints, queries, and suggestions for modification.

The company plans to use these to make changes and eventually issue updated, improved, and debugged versions. The president argues that this is general industry policy and that anyone who buys version 1.0 of a program knows this and will take proper precautions. Because of bugs, a number of users filed incorrect tax returns and were penalized by the IRS (adapted from scenario V.7 in [18]).

The software company, the president in particular, violated several tenets of the ACM code of ethics. Since he was aware of bugs in the product, he did not strive to achieve the highest quality as called for by 2.1. In failing to inform consumers about bugs in the system, principle 2.5 was also violated.

In this instance the risks to users are great in that they have to pay penalties for mistakes in their income tax which are the result of the program. Companies by law can make disclaimers only when they are "in good conscience." The disclaimer here might not meet this legal test, in which case imperative 2.3 would be violated. As a leader in his organization the president is also violating 3.1, for he is not encouraging his staff to accept their social responsibilities.

Issues of software liability have been discussed by [19, 22].

Case 7: Software Risks

A small software company is working on an integrated inventory control system for a very large national shoe manufacturer. The system will

amount of personal information be collected in a system, that retention and disposal periods for that information be clearly defined and enforced, and that personal information gathered for a specific purpose not be used for other purposes without consent of the individual(s). These principles apply to electronic communications, including electronic mail, and prohibit procedures that capture or monitor electronic user data, including messages, without the permission of users or *bona fide* authorization related to system operation and maintenance. User data observed during the normal duties of system operation and maintenance must be treated with strictest confidentiality, except in cases where it is evidence for the violation of law, organizational regulations, or this Code. In these cases, the nature or contents of that information must be disclosed only to proper authorities (See 1.9)

1.8 Honor confidentiality

The principle of honesty extends to issues of confidentiality of information whenever one has made an explicit promise to honor confidentiality or, implicitly, when private information not directly related to the performance of one's duties becomes available. The ethical concern is to respect all obligations of confidentiality to employers, clients, and users unless discharged from such obligations by requirements of the law or other principles of this Code.

2. More Specific Professional Responsibilities.

As an ACM computing professional I will . . .

2.1 Strive to achieve the highest quality, effectiveness and dignity in both the process and products of professional work

Excellence is perhaps the most important obligation of a professional. The computing professional must strive to achieve quality and to be cognizant of the serious negative consequences that may result from poor quality in a system.

2.2 Acquire and maintain professional competence

Excellence depends on individuals who take responsibility for acquiring and maintaining professional competence. A professional must participate in setting standards for appropriate levels of competence, and strive to achieve those standards. Upgrading technical knowledge and competence can be achieved in several ways: doing independent study; attending seminars, conferences, or courses; and being involved in professional organizations.

2.3 Know and respect existing laws pertaining to professional work

ACM members must obey existing local, state, province, national, and international laws unless there is a compelling ethical basis not to do so. Policies and procedures of the organizations in which one participates must also be obeyed. But compliance must be balanced with the recognition that sometimes existing laws and rules may be immoral or inappropriate and, therefore, must be challenged.

Violation of a law or regulation may be ethical when that law or rule has inadequate moral basis or when it conflicts with another law judged to be more important. If one decides to violate a law or rule because it is viewed as unethical, or for any other reason, one must fully accept responsibility for one's actions and for the consequences.

2.4 Accept and provide appropriate professional review

Quality professional work, especially in the computing profession, depends on professional reviewing and critiquing. Whenever appropriate, individual members should seek and utilize peer review as well as provide critical review of the work of others.

2.5 Give comprehensive and thorough evaluations of computer systems and their impacts, including analysis of possible risks

Computer professionals must strive to be perceptive, thorough, and objective when evaluating, recommending, and presenting system descriptions and alternatives. Computer professionals are in a position of special trust, and therefore have a special responsibility to provide objective, credible evaluations to employers, clients, users, and the public. When providing evaluations the professional must also identify any relevant conflicts of interest, as stated in imperative 1.3.

As noted in the discussion of principle 1.2 on avoiding harm, any signs of danger from systems must be reported to those who have opportunity and/or responsibility to resolve them. See the guidelines for imperative 1.2 for more details concerning harm, including the reporting of professional violations.

2.6 Honor contracts, agreements, and assigned responsibilities

Honoring one's commitments is a matter of integrity and honesty. For the computer professional this includes ensuring that system elements perform as intended. Also, when one contracts for work with another party, one has an obligation to keep that party properly informed about progress toward completing that work.

A computing professional has a responsibility to request a change in any assignment that he or she feels cannot be completed as defined. Only after serious consideration and with full disclosure of risks and concerns to the employer or client, should one accept the assignment. The major underlying principle here is the obligation to accept personal accountability for professional work. On some occasions other ethical principles may take greater priority.

A judgment that a specific assignment should not be performed may not be accepted. Having clearly identified one's concerns and reasons for that judgment, but failing to procure a change in that assignment, one may yet be obligated, by contract or by law, to proceed as directed. The computing professional's ethical judgment should be the final guide in deciding whether or not to proceed. Regardless of the decision, one must accept the responsibility for the consequences. However, performing assignments "against one's own judgment" does not relieve the professional of responsibility for any negative consequences. ▶

gather sales information daily from shoe stores nationwide. This information will be used by the accounting, shipping, and ordering departments to control all of the functions of this large corporation. The inventory functions are critical to the smooth operation of this system.

Jane, a quality assurance engineer with the software company, suspects that the inventory functions of the system are not sufficiently tested, although they have passed all their contracted tests. She is being pressured by her employers to sign off on the software. Legally she is only required to perform those tests which had been agreed to in the original contract. However, her considerable experience in software testing has led her to be concerned over risks of the system. Her employers say they will go out of business if they do not deliver the software on time. Jane contends if the inventory subsystem fails, it will significantly harm their client and its employees. If the potential failure were to threaten lives, it would be clear to Jane that she should refuse to sign off. But since the degree of threatened harm is less, Jane is faced by a difficult moral decision (adapted from [10]).

In the Code of Ethics, imperative 1.2 stresses the responsibility of the computing professional to avoid harm to others. In addition, principle 1.1 requires concern for human well-being; 1.3 mandates professional integrity, and 2.1 defines quality as an ethical responsibility. These principles may conflict with the agreements and commitments of an employee to the employer and client.

The ethical imperatives of the Code imply that Jane should not deliver a system she believes to be inferior, nor should she mislead the client about the quality of the product (1.3). She should continue to test, but she has been told that her company will go out of business if she does not sign off on the system now. At the very least the client should be informed about her reservations.

For additional discussion of software risks, [3, 22] are suggested.

Case 8: Conflicts of Interest

A software consultant is negotiating a contract with a local community to design their traffic control system. He recommends they select the TCS system out of several available systems on the market. The consultant fails to mention that he is a major stockholder of the company producing TCS software.

According to the Guidelines, imperative 2.5 means that computer professionals must "strive to be perceptive, thorough and objective when evaluating, recommending, and presenting system descriptions and alternatives." It also says that imperative 1.3 implies a computer professional must be honest about "any circumstances that might lead to conflicts of interest." Because of the special skills held by computing professionals it is their responsibility to ensure that their clients are fully aware of their options and that professional recommendations are not modified for personal gain.

Additional discussion on conflict of interest appears in [1, 25].

Case 9: Unauthorized Access

Joe is working on a project for his computer science course. The instructor has allotted a fixed amount of computer time for this project. Joe has run out of time, but he has not yet finished the project. The instructor cannot be reached. Last year Joe worked as a student programmer for the campus computer center and is quite familiar with procedures to increase time allocations to accounts. Using what he learned last year, he is able to access the master account. Then he gives himself additional time and finishes his project.

The imperative to honor property rights (1.5) has been violated. This general, moral imperative leads to imperative 2.8, which specifies that ACM members should "access communication resources only when authorized to do so." In violating 2.8 Joe also is violating the imperative to "know and respect existing laws" (2.3). As a student member of the ACM he must follow the Code of Ethics even though he may not consider himself a computing professional.

For additional reading see [4, 24,]. The most current material on this subject is likely to be found in [13].

Conclusion

These nine cases illustrate the broad range of issues a computer scientist may encounter in professional practice. While the ACM Code does not precisely prescribe what an individual must do in the situations described, it does identify some decisions as unacceptable. Often in ethical decision making many factors have to be balanced. In such situations computer professionals have to choose among conflicting principles adhering to the *spirit* of the Code as much as to the *letter*.

The ACM Code organizes ethical principles into the four categories: general moral imperatives; more specific professional responsibilities, organizational leadership imperatives, and compliance. Some may find it helpful to sort out the ethical issues involved in other ways. For example, the context of practice is relevant. Those in industry may encounter different issues from those in government or education. Those who are employed in large corporations may experience different tensions than those who work in small firms or who are self-employed. But whether working in private practice or in large organizations, computer professionals must balance responsibilities to employers, to clients, to other professionals, and to society, and these responsibilities can come into conflict. Our range of cases illustrates how one can use the general principles of the Code to deal with these diverse types of situations.

The reader may wonder why we did not have a whistle-blowing case. In a prototypical scenario, a professional has to take action which threatens the employer after concluding that the safety or well-being of some other group must take priority. Three of our cases—5, 6, 7—dealt with whistle-blowing indirectly. In all three cases, the computing professional served an outside client rather than an employer. This adds other dimensions to whistle-blowing. In Case 5, suppose the system designer learns that his client plans to use the database to discriminate and he refuses to design the system. Later he finds that a friend of his designed the system as the client wanted. He would then have to decide whether

2.7 **Improve public understanding of computing and its consequences**

Computing professionals have a responsibility to share technical knowledge with the public by encouraging understanding of computing, including the impacts of computer systems and their limitations. This imperative implies an obligation to counter any false views related to computing.

2.8 **Access computing and communication resources only when authorized to do so**

Theft or destruction of tangible and electronic property is prohibited by imperative 1.2—"Avoid harm to others." Trespassing and unauthorized use of a computer or communication system is addressed by this imperative. Trespassing includes accessing communication networks and computer systems, or accounts and/or files associated with those systems, without explicit authorization to do so. Individuals and organizations have the right to restrict access to their systems so long as they do not violate the discrimination principle (see 1.4).

No one should enter or use another's computing system, software, or data files without permission. One must always have appropriate approval before using system resources, including .rm57 communication ports, file space, other system peripherals, and computer time.

3. Organizational Leadership Imperatives.

As an ACM member and an organizational leader, I will . . .

3.1 **Articulate social responsibilities of members of an organizational unit and encourage full acceptance of those responsibilities**

Because organizations of all kinds have impacts on the public, they must accept responsibilities to society. Organizational procedures and attitudes oriented toward quality and the welfare of society will reduce harm to members of the public, thereby serving public interest and fulfilling social responsibility. Therefore, organizational leaders must encourage full participation in meeting social responsibilities as well as quality performance.

3.2 **Manage personnel and resources to design and build information systems that enhance the quality of working life**

Organizational leaders are responsible for ensuring that computer systems enhance, not degrade, the quality of working life. When implementing a computer system, organizations must consider the personal and professional development, physical safety, and human dignity of all workers. Appropriate human-computer ergonomic standards should be considered in system design and in the workplace.

3.3 **Acknowledge and support proper and authorized uses of an organization's computing and communications resources**

Because computer systems can become tools to harm as well as to benefit an organization, the leadership has the responsibility to clearly define appropriate and inappropriate uses of organizational computing resources. While the number and scope of such rules should be minimal, they should be fully enforced when established.

3.4 **Ensure that users and those who will be affected by a system have their needs clearly articulated during the assessment and design of requirements. Later the system must be validated to meet requirements.**

Current system users, potential users and other persons whose lives may be affected by a system must have their needs assessed and incorporated in the statement of requirements. System validation should ensure compliance with those requirements.

3.5 **Articulate and support policies that protect the dignity of users and others affected by a computing system**

Designing or implementing systems that deliberately or inadvertently demean individuals or groups is ethically unacceptable. Computer professionals who are in decision-making positions should verify that systems are designed and implemented to protect personal privacy and enhance personal dignity.

3.6 **Create opportunities for members of the organization to learn the principles and limitations of computer systems**

This complements the imperative on public understanding (2.7). Educational opportunities are essential to facilitate optimal participation of all organizational members. Opportunities must be available to all members to help them improve their knowledge and skills in computing, including courses that familiarize them with the consequences and limitations of particular types of systems. In particular, professionals must be made aware of the dangers of building systems around oversimplified models, the improbability of anticipating and designing for every possible operating condition, and other issues related to the complexity of this profession.

4. Compliance with the Code.

As an ACM member I will . . .

4.1 **Uphold and promote the principles of this Code**

The future of the computing profession depends on both technical and ethical excellence. Not only is it important for ACM computing professionals to adhere to the principles expressed in this Code, each member should encourage and support adherence by other members.

4.2 **Treat violations of this code as inconsistent with membership in the ACM**

Adherence of professionals to a code of ethics is largely a voluntary matter. However, if a member does not follow this code by engaging in gross misconduct, membership in ACM may be terminated. ◘

This Code and the supplemental Guidelines were developed by the Task Force for the Revision of the ACM Code of Ethics and Professional Conduct: Ronald E. Anderson, chair, Gerald Engel, Donald Gotterbarn, Grace C. Hertlein, Alex Hoffman, Bruce Jawer, Deborah G. Johnson, Doris K. Lidtke, Joyce Currie Little, Dianne Martin, Donn B. Parker, Judith A. Perrolle, and Richard S. Rosenberg. The Task Force was organized by ACM/SIGCAS and funding was provided by the ACM SIG Discretionary Fund.

to "blow the whistle" on his ex-client. These and similar types of situations are indeed important, if not common, for computer professionals. (For more prototypical situations see discussion of the Bart case and [19] on SDI.)

In all of the cases presented, we portrayed individuals acting in constrained situations. Ethical decisions depend on one's institutional context. These environments can facilitate or constrain ethical behavior. Leadership roles can set the tone and create work environments in which computer professionals can express their ethical concerns. It is significant that leadership responsibilities were demonstrated in nearly all of our nine cases. In some instances, the problem could be resolved by following the imperatives in the Code that apply to leaders. In other cases, the problem was created by a lack of ethical leadership, and the individual professional had to make a personal decision on how to proceed.

Several ethical topics were not specifically interpreted in either the Guidelines or in our cases. For instance, specific requirements of integrity for research in computing and computer science were not detailed. Nor were specific suggestions offered for maintaining professional development. These should be among the tasks of the ACM leadership to address with future additions to the Guidelines.

Other ethical issues, such as software copyright violation, were addressed but not with sufficient detail relative to their salience to the field of computing. These issues, as well as new issues not yet imagined, will confront the field of computing in the future. Not only will the Guidelines need to be updated, but there will be a need for writing and interpreting more cases typical of the ethical decisions of computing professionals. Those with special ethical computing situations are encouraged to share them with us and with others in order to foster more discussion and attention to exemplary ethical decision-making. **◰**

References
1. Bayles, M.D. *Professional Ethics.* Wadsworth, Belmont, Calif., 1981.
2. Bynum, T.W., Maner, W. and Fodor, J., Eds. *Software Ownership and Intellectual Property Rights.* Research Center on Computing and Society, Southern Connecticut State University, New Haven, Conn. 06515, 1992.
3. Clark, D. *Computers at Risk: Safe Computing in the Information Age.* National Research Council, National Academy Press, Washington, D.C., 1990
4. Denning, P.J., Ed. *Computers under Attack: Intruders, Worms and Viruses.* Addison-Wesley, Inc., Reading, Mass., 1990.
5. Dunlop, C. and Kling, R., Eds. *Computerization and Controversy: Value Conflicts and Social Choices.* Academic Press, New York, N.Y., 1991.
6. Flaherty, D. *Protecting Privacy in Surveillance Societies.* University of North Carolina Press, Chapel Hill, N.C., 1989.
7. Forester, T. Software theft and the problem of intellectual property rights. *Comput. Soc. 20,* 1 (Mar. 1990), 2–11.
8. Frankel, M.S. Professional Codes: Why, How, and with What Impact? *J. Bus. Ethics 8* (2 and 3) (1989), 109–116.
9. Frenkel, K.A. Women and computing. *Commun. ACM 33,* 11 (Nov. 1990), 34–46.
10. Gotterbarn, D. Computer ethics: Responsibility regained. *National Forum* (Summer 1991).
11. Gotterbarn, D. Editor's corner. *J. Syst. Soft. 17* (Jan. 1992), 5–6.
12. Guynes, C.S. Protecting statistical databases: A matter of privacy. *Comput. Soc. 19,* 1 (Mar. 1989), 15–23.
13. IEEE Computer Society Press. *Proceedings of the Second Conference on Computers, Freedom and Privacy.* (Los Alamitos, Calif.), IEEE Computer Society Pres, 1992.
14. Johnson, D.G. *Computer Ethics,* Second Ed. Prentice Hall, Englewood Cliffs, N.J., 1993.
15. Laudon, K.C. *Dossier Society: Value Choices in the Design of National Information Systems.* Columbia University Press, New York, N.Y., 1986.

16. Martin, C.D. and Murche-Beyma, E., Eds. In *Search of Gender Free Paradigms for Computer Science Education*. International Society for Technology in Education, Eugene, Ore., 1992.

17. National Research Council. *Intellectual Property Issues in Software*. National Academy of Sciences, Washington, D.C., 1991.

18. Parker, D., Swope, S. and Baker, B. Ethical conflicts in information and computer science. Techology and Business. Wellesley, Mass. QED Information Sciences, 1990.

19. Parnas, D.L. SDI: A violation of professional responsibility. *Abacus 4*, 2 (Winter 1987), 46–52.

20. Perrolle, J.A. *Computers and Social Change: Information. Property, and Power*. Wadsworth, Belmont, Calif., 1987.

21. Perrolle, J. Conversations and trust in computer interfaces. In *Computers and Controversy*. Dunlop and Kling, Eds., 1991.

22. Pressman, R.S. and Herron, R. *Software Shock: The Danger and the Opportunity*. Dorsett House, 1991.

23. Salpeter, J. Are you obeying copyright law? *Technol. Learning 12*, 8 (1992), 12–23.

24. Spafford, G. Are computer hacker break-ins ethical? *J. Syst. Softw. 17* (Jan. 1992).

25. Stevenson, J.T. *Engineering Ethics: Practices and Principles*. Canadian Scholars Press, Toronto, 1987.

Note: A more extensive list of references for each of the nine specific cases, as well as general discussions of professional ethics, can be obtained by writing Ronald E. Anderson, 909 Social Sciences Bldg., University of Minnesota, Minneapolis, MN 55455. Both the ACM Code of Ethics and the bibliography are available on the Internet from acm.org using anonymous ftp or mailserve. The files are under the SIGCAS Forum and called code_of_ethics.txt and ethics_biblio.txt.

Permission to copy without fee all or part of this material is granted provided that the copies are not made or distributed for direct commercial advantage, the ACM copyright notice and the title of the publication and its date appear, and notice is give that copying is by permission of the Association for Computing Machinery. To copy otherwise, or to republish, requires a fee and/or specific permission.

Part V
Privacy and Surveillance

[27]

Are Computer Hacker Break-ins Ethical?*

Eugene H. Spafford

Department of Computer Sciences, Purdue University, West Lafayette, Indiana

Recent incidents of unauthorized computer intrusion have brought about discussion of the ethics of breaking into computers. Some individuals have argued that as long as no significant damage results, break-ins may serve a useful purpose. Others counter that the break-ins are almost always harmful and wrong. This article lists and refutes many of the reasons given to justify computer intrusions. It is the author's contention that break-ins are ethical only in extreme situations, such as a life-critical emergency. The article also discusses why no break-in is "harmless."

INTRODUCTION

On November 2, 1988, a program was run on the Internet that replicated itself on thousands of machines, often loading them to the point where they were unable to process normal requests [2–4]. This INTERNET WORM program was stopped in a matter of hours, but the controversy engendered by its release has raged ever since. Other incidents, such as the "wily hackers"[1] tracked by Cliff Stoll [5], the "Legion of Doom" members who are alleged to have stolen telephone company 911 software [6], and the growth of the computer virus problem [7–10] have added to the discussion. What constitutes improper access to computers? Are some break-ins ethical? Is there such a thing as a "moral hacker" [11]?

It is important that we discuss these issues. The continuing evolution of our technological base and our increasing reliance on computers for critical tasks suggest that future incidents may well have more serious consequences than those we have seen to date. With human nature as varied and extreme as it is, and with the technology as available as it is, we must expect to experience more of these incidents.

In this article, I will introduce a few of the major issues that these incidents have raised, and present some arguments related to them. For clarification, I have separated several issues that often have been combined when debated; it is possible that most people agree on some of these points once they are viewed as individual issues.

WHAT IS ETHICAL?

Webster's Collegiate Dictionary defines ethics as "the discipline dealing with what is good and bad and with moral duty and obligation." More simply, it is the study of what is right to do in a given situation—what we ought to do. Alternatively, it is sometimes described as the study of what is good and how to achieve that good. To suggest whether an act is right or wrong we need to agree on an ethical system that is easy to understand and apply as we consider the ethics of computer break-ins.

Philosophers have been trying for thousands of years to define right and wrong, and I will not make yet another attempt at such a definition. Instead, I will suggest that we make the simplifying assumption that we can judge the ethical nature of an act by applying a deontological assessment: regardless of the effect, is the act itself ethical? Would we view that act as sensible and proper if everyone were to engage in it? Although this may be too simplistic a model (and it can certainly be argued that other ethical philosophies may also be applied), it is a good first approximation for purposes of discussion. If you are unfamiliar with any other formal ethical evaluation method, try applying this assessment to the points I raise later in this article. If the results are obviously unpleasant or dangerous in the large, then they should be considered unethical as individual acts.

Address correspondence to Eugene H. Spafford, Dept. of Computer Sciences, Purdue University, West Lafayette, IN 47907-1398.

* An earlier version of this paper appeared as [1].

[1] Many law-abiding individuals consider themselves *hackers*—a term formerly used as a compliment. The press and general public have co-opted the term, however, and it is now commonly viewed as pejorative. Here, I will use the word as the general public now uses it.

42   J. SYSTEMS SOFTWARE   Eugene Spafford
         1992; 17:41–47

Note that this philosophy assumes that right is determined by actions, not results. Some ethical philosophies assume that the ends justify the means; our society does not operate by such a philosophy, although many individuals do. As a society, we profess to believe that "it isn't whether you win or lose, it's how you play the game." This is why we are concerned with issues of due process and civil rights, even for those espousing repugnant views and committing heinous acts. The process is important no matter the outcome, although the outcome may help to resolve a choice between two almost equal courses of action.

Philosophies that consider the results of an act as the ultimate measure of good are often impossible to apply because of the difficulty in understanding exactly what results from any arbitrary activity. Consider an extreme example: the government orders 100 cigarette smokers, chosen at random, to be beheaded on live nationwide television. The result might well be that many hundreds of thousands of other smokers would quit cold turkey, thus prolonging their lives. It might also prevent hundreds of thousands of people from ever starting to smoke, thus improving the health and longevity of the general populace. The health of millions of other people would improve because they would no longer be subjected to secondary smoke, and the overall impact on the environment would be favorable as tons of air and ground pollutants would no longer be released by smokers or tobacco companies.

Yet, despite the great good this might hold for society, everyone, except for a few extremists, would condemn such an act as immoral. We would likely object even if only one person were executed. It would not matter what the law might be on such an issue; we would not feel that the act was morally correct, nor would we view the ends as justifying the means.

Note that we would be unable to judge the morality of such an action by evaluating the results, because we would not know the full scope of those results. Such an act might have effects, favorable or otherwise, on issues of law, public health, tobacco use, and daytime TV shows for decades or centuries to follow. A system of ethics that considered primarily only the results of our actions would not allow us to evaluate our current activities at the time when we would need such guidance; if we are unable to discern the appropriate course of action prior to its commission, then our system of ethics is of little or no value to us. To obtain ethical guidance, we must base our actions primarily on evaluations of the actions and not on the possible results.

More to the point here, if we attempt to judge the morality of a computer break-in based on the sum total of all future effect, we would be unable to make such a judgement, either for a specific incident or for the general class of acts. In part, this is because it is so difficult to determine the long-term effects of various actions and to discern their causes. We cannot know, for instance, if increased security awareness and restrictions are better for society in the long term, or whether these additional restrictions will result in greater costs and annoyance when using computer systems. We also do not know how many of these changes are directly traceable to incidents of computer break-ins.

One other point should be made here: it is undoubtedly possible to imagine scenarios where a computer break-in would be considered to be the preferable course of action. For instance, if vital medical data were on a computer and necessary to save someone's life in an emergency, but the authorized users of the system could not be located, breaking into the system might well be considered the right thing to do. However, that action does not make the break-in ethical. Rather, such situations occur when a greater wrong would undoubtedly occur if the unethical act were not committed. Similar reasoning applies to situations such as killing in self defense. In the following discussion, I will assume that such conflicts are not the root cause of the break-ins; such situations should very rarely present themselves.

MOTIVATIONS

Individuals who break into computer systems or who write vandalware usually use one of several rationalizations for their actions. (See, for example, [12] and the discussion in [13].) Most of these individuals would never think to walk down a street, trying every door to find one unlocked, then search through the drawers of the furniture inside. Yet these same people seem to give no second thought to making repeated attempts at guessing passwords to accounts they do not own, and once into a system, browsing through the files on disk.

These computer burglars often give the same reasons for their actions in an attempt to rationalize their activities as morally justified. I present and refute some of the most commonly used ones; motives involving theft and revenge are not uncommon, and their moral nature is simple to discern, so I shall not include them here.

The Hacker Ethic

Many hackers argue that they follow an ethic that both guides their behavior and justifies their break-ins. This hacker ethic states, in part, that all information should be free [11]. This view holds that information belongs to everyone and there should be no boundaries or restraints to prevent anyone from examining information. Richard Stallman states much the same thing in

Are Break-ins Ethical?   J. SYSTEMS SOFTWARE   **43**
                                                                          1992; 17:41–47

his GNU Manifesto [14]. He and others have stated in
various forums that if information is free, it logically
follows that there should be no such thing as intellectual property, and no need for security.

What are the implications and consequences of such
a philosophy? First and foremost, it raises some disturbing questions of privacy. If all information is (or
should be) free, then privacy is no longer a possibility.
For information to be free to everyone and for individuals to no longer be able to claim it as property means
that anyone may access the information if they please.
Furthermore, as it is no longer property of any individual, anyone can alter the information. Items such as
bank balances, medical records, credit histories, employment records, and defense information all cease to
be controlled. If someone controls information and
controls who may access it, the information is obviously not free. But without that control, we would no
longer be able to trust the accuracy of the information.

In a perfect world, this lack of privacy and control
might not be cause for concern. However, if all information were to be freely available and modifiable,
imagine how much damage and chaos would be caused
in our real world! Our whole society is based on
information whose accuracy must be assured. This
includes information held by banks and other financial
institutions, credit bureaus, medical agencies and professionals, government agencies such as the IRS, law
enforcement agencies, and educational institutions.
Clearly, treating all their information as "free" would
be unethical in any world where there might be careless
and unethical individuals.

Economic arguments can be made against this philosophy, too, in addition to the overwhelming need for
privacy and control of information accuracy. Information is not universally free. It is held as property
because of privacy concerns, and because it is often
collected and developed at great expense. Development
of a new algorithm or program or collection of a
specialized data base may involve the expenditure of
vast sums of time and effort. To claim that it is free or
should be free is to express a naive and unrealistic view
of the world. To use this to justify computer break-ins
is clearly unethical. Although not all information currently treated as private or controlled as proprietary
needs such protection, that does not justify unauthorized access to it or to any other data.

The Security Arguments

These arguments are the most common ones offered
within the computer community. One argument is the
same as that used most often to defend the author of the
INTERNET WORM program in 1988: break-ins illus-

trate security problems to a community that will otherwise not note the problems.

In the WORM case, one of the first issues to be
discussed widely in Internet mailing lists dealt with the
intent of the perpetrator—exactly why the worm program had been written and released. Explanations put
forth by members of the community ranged from simple accident to the actions of a sociopath. Many said
that the WORM was designed to reveal security defects
to a community that would not otherwise pay attention.
This was not supported by the testimony of the author
during his trial, nor is it supported by past experience
of system administrators.

The WORM author, Robert T. Morris, appears to
have been well known at some universities and major
companies, and his talents were generally respected.
Had he merely explained the problems or offered a
demonstration to these people, he would have been
listened to with considerable attention. The month before he released the WORM program on the Internet,
he discovered and disclosed a bug in the file transfer
program *ftp*; news of the flaw spread rapidly, and an
official fix was announced and available within a matter
of weeks. The argument that no one would listen to his
report of security weaknesses is clearly fallacious.

In the more general case, this security argument is
also without merit. Although some system administrators might have been complacent about the security of
their systems before the WORM incident, most computer vendors, managers of government computer in-
stallations, and system administrators at major colleges
and universities have been attentive to reports of security problems. People wishing to report a problem with
the security of a system need not exploit it to report it.
By way of analogy, one does not set fire to the neighborhood shopping center to bring attention to a fire
hazard in one of the stores, and then try to justify the
act by claiming that fireman would otherwise never
listen to reports of hazards.

The most general argument that some people make is
that the individuals who break into systems are performing a service by exposing security flaws, and thus
should be encouraged or even rewarded. This argument
is severely flawed in several ways. First, it assumes
that there is some compelling need to force users to
install security fixes on their systems, and thus computer burglars are justified in "breaking and entering"
activities. Taken to extremes, it suggests that it would
be perfectly acceptable to engage in such activities on a
continuing basis, so long as they might expose security
flaws. This completely loses sight of the purpose of the
computers in the first place—to serve as tools and
resources, not as exercises in security. The same reasoning would imply that vigilantes have the right to

44   J. SYSTEMS SOFTWARE
          1992; 17:41–47

Eugene Spafford

attempt to break into the homes in my neighborhood on a continuing basis to demonstrate that they are susceptible to burglars.

Another flaw with this argument is that it completely ignores the technical and economic factors that prevent many sites from upgrading or correcting their software. Not every site has the resources to install new system software or to correct existing software. At many sites, the systems are run as turnkey systems—employed as tools and maintained by the vendor. The owners and users of these machines simply do not have the ability to correct or maintain their systems independently, and they are unable to afford custom software support from their vendors. To break into such systems, with or without damage, is effectively to trespass into places of business; to do so in a vigilante effort to force the owners to upgrade their security structure is presumptuous and reprehensible. A burglary is not justified, morally or legally, by an argument that the victim has poor locks and was therefore "asking for it."

A related argument has been made that vendors are responsible for the maintenance of their software, and that such security breaches should immediately require vendors to issue corrections to their customers, past and present. The claim is made that without highly-visible break-ins, vendors will not produce or distribute necessary fixes to software. This attitude is naive, and is neither economically feasible nor technically workable. Certainly, vendors should bear some responsibility for the adequacy of their software [15], but they should not be responsible for fixing every possible flaw in every possible configuration.

Many sites customize their software or otherwise run systems incompatible with the latest vendor releases. For a vendor to be able to provide quick response to security problems, it would be necessary for each customer to run completely standardized software and hardware mixes to ensure the correctness of vendor-supplied updates. Not only would this be considerably less attractive for many customers and contrary to their usual practice, but the increased cost of such "instant" fix distribution would add to the price of such a system and greatly increase the cost borne by the customer. It is unreasonable to expect the user community to sacrifice flexibility and pay a much higher cost per unit simply for faster corrections to the occasional security breach, assuming it is possible for the manufacturer to find those customers and supply them with fixes in a timely manner—something unlikely in a market where machines and software are often repackaged, traded, and resold.

The case of the INTERNET WORM is a good example of the security argument and its flaws. It further stands as a good example of the conflict between ends and means valuation of ethics. Various people have argued that the WORM's author did us a favor by exposing security flaws. At Mr. Morris's trial on Federal charges stemming from the incident, the defense attorneys also argued that their client should not be punished because of the good the WORM did in exposing those flaws. Others, including the prosecuting attorneys, argued that the act itself was wrong no matter what the outcome. Their contention has been that the result does not justify the act itself, nor does the defense's argument encompass all the consequences of the incident.

This is certainly true; the complete results of the incident are still not known. There have been many other break-ins and network worms since November 1988, perhaps inspired by the media coverage of that incident. More attempts will possibly be made, in part inspired by Mr. Morris's act. Some sites on the Internet have restricted access to their machines, and others were removed from the network; other sites have decided not to pursue a connection, even though it will hinder research and operations. Combined with the many decades of person-hours devoted to cleaning up after the worm, this seems a high price to pay for a claimed "favor."

The legal consequences of this act are also not yet known. For instance, many bills have been introduced into Congress and state legislatures over the last three years in part because of these incidents. One piece of legislation introduced into the House of Representatives, HR-5061, entitled "The Computer Virus Eradication Act of 1988," was the first in a series of legislative actions that have the potential to affect significantly the computer profession. In particular, HR-5061 was notable because its wording would prevent it from being applied to true computer viruses.[2] The passage of similar well-intentioned but poorly-defined legislation could have a major negative effect on the computing profession as a whole.

The Idle System Argument

Another argument put forth by system hackers is that they are simply making use of idle machines. They argue that because some systems are not used at a level near their capacity, the hacker is somehow entitled to use them.

This argument is also flawed. First of all, these systems are usually not in service to provide a general-

---

[2] It provided penalties only in cases where programs were introduced into computer systems; a computer virus is a segment of code attached to an existing program that modifies other programs to include a copy of itself [7].

Are Break-ins Ethical?   J. SYSTEMS SOFTWARE   45
                                                          1992; 17:41-47

purpose user environment. Instead, they are in use in commerce, medicine, public safety, research, and government functions. Unused capacity is present for future needs and sudden surges of activity, not for the support of outside individuals. Imagine if large numbers of people without a computer were to take advantage of a system with idle processor capacity: the system would quickly be overloaded and severely degraded or unavailable for the rightful owners. Once on the system, it would be difficult (or impossible) to oust these individuals if sudden extra capacity were needed by the rightful owners. Even the largest machines available today would not provide sufficient capacity to accommodate such activity on any large scale.

I am unable to think of any other item that someone may buy and maintain, only to have others claim a right to use it when it is idle. For instance, the thought of someone walking up to my expensive car and driving off in it simply because it is not currently being used is ludicrous. Likewise, because I am away at work, it is not proper to hold a party at my house because it is otherwise not being used. The related positions that unused computing capacity is a shared resource, and that my privately-developed software belongs to everyone, are equally silly (and unethical) positions.

The Student Hacker Argument

Some trespassers claim that they are doing no harm and changing nothing—they are simply learning about how computer systems operate. They argue that computers are expensive, and that they are merely furthering their education in a cost-effective manner. Some authors of computer viruses claim that their creations are intended to be harmless, and that they are simply learning how to write complex programs.

There are many problems with these arguments. First, as an educator, I claim that writing vandalware or breaking into a computer and looking at the files has almost nothing to do with computer education. Proper education in computer science and engineering involves intensive exposure to fundamental aspects of theory, abstraction, and design techniques. Browsing through a system does not expose someone to the broad scope of theory and practice in computing, nor does it provide the critical feedback so important to a good education [16, 17]; neither does writing a virus or worm program and releasing it into an unsupervised environment provide any proper educational experience. By analogy, stealing cars and joyriding does not provide one with an education in mechanical engineering, nor does pouring sugar in the gas tank.

Furthermore, individuals "learning" about a system cannot know how everything operates and what results

from their activities. Many systems have been damaged accidently by ignorant (or careless) intruders; most of the damage from computer viruses (and the INTERNET WORM) appear to be caused by unexpected interactions and program faults. Damage to medical systems, factory control, financial information, and other computer systems could have drastic and far-ranging effects that have nothing to do with education, and could certainly not be considered harmless.

A related refutation of the claim has to do with knowledge of the extent of the intrusion. If I am the person responsible for the security of a critical computer system, I cannot assume that *any* intrusion is motivated solely by curiosity and that nothing has been harmed. If I know that the system has been compromised, I must fear the worst and perform a complete system check for damages and changes. I cannot take the word of the intruder, for any intruder who actually caused damage would seek to hide it by claiming that he or she was "just looking." To regain confidence in the correct behavior of my system, I must expend considerable energy to examine and verify every aspect of it.

Apply our universal approach to this situation and imagine if this "educational" behavior was widespread and commonplace. The result would be that we would spend all our time verifying our systems and never be able to trust the results fully. Clearly, this is not good, and thus we must conclude that these "educational" motivations are also unethical.

The Social Protector Argument

One last argument, more often heard in Europe than the United States, is that hackers break into systems to watch for instances of data abuse and to help keep "Big Brother" at bay. In this sense, the hackers are protectors rather than criminals. Again, this assumes that the ends justify the means. It also assumes that the hackers are actually able to achieve some good end.

Undeniably, there is some misuse of personal data by corporations and by the government. The increasing use of computer-based record systems and networks may lead to further abuses. However, it is not clear that breaking into these systems will aid in righting the wrongs. If anything, it may cause those agencies to become even more secretive and use the break-ins as an excuse for more restricted access. Break-ins and vandalism have not resulted in new open-records laws, but they have resulted in the introduction and passage of new criminal statutes. Not only has such activity failed to deter "Big Brother," but it has also resulted in significant segments of the public urging more laws and

46 J. SYSTEMS SOFTWARE
1992; 17:41-47

more aggressive law enforcement—the direct opposite of the supposed goal.

It is also not clear that these hackers are the individuals we want "protecting" us. We need to have the designers and users of the systems—trained computer professionals—concerned about our rights and aware of the dangers involved with the inappropriate use of computer monitoring and record keeping. The threat is a relatively new one, as computers and networks have become widely used only in the last few decades. It will take some time for awareness of the dangers to spread throughout the profession. Clandestine efforts to breach the security of computer systems do nothing to raise the consciousness of the appropriate individuals. Worse, they associate that commendable goal (heightened concern) with criminal activity (computer break-ins), thus discouraging proactive behavior by the individuals in the best positions to act in our favor. Perhaps it is in this sense that computer break-ins and vandalism are most unethical and damaging.

CONCLUSION

I have argued here that computer break-ins, even when no obvious damage results, are unethical. This must be the considered conclusion even if the result is an improvement in security, because the activity itself is disruptive and immoral. The results of the act should be considered separately from the act itself, especially when we consider how difficult it is to understand all the effects resulting from such an act.

Of course, I have not discussed every possible reason for a break-in. There might well be an instance where a break-in might be necessary to save a life or to preserve national security. In such cases, to perform one wrong act to prevent a greater wrong may be the right thing to do. It is beyond the scope or intent of this paper to discuss such cases, especially as no known hacker break-ins have been motivated by such instances.

Historically, computer professionals as a group have not been overly concerned with questions of ethics and propriety as they relate to computers. Individuals and some organizations have tried to address these issues, but the whole computing community needs to be involved to address the problems in any comprehensive manner. Too often, we view computers simply as machines and algorithms, and we do not perceive the serious ethical questions inherent in their use.

However, when we consider that these machines influence the quality of life of millions of individuals, both directly and indirectly, we understand that there are broader issues. Computers are used to design, analyze, support, and control applications that protect and guide the lives and finances of people. Our use

(and misuse) of computing systems may have effects beyond our wildest imagining. Thus, we must reconsider our attitudes about acts demonstrating a lack of respect for the rights and privacy of other people's computers and data.

We must also consider what our attitudes will be towards future security problems. In particular, we should consider the effect of widely publishing the source code for worms, viruses, and other threats to security. Although we need a process for rapidly disseminating corrections and security information as they become known, we should realize that widespread publication of details will imperil sites where users are unwilling or unable to install updates and fixes.[3] Publication should serve a useful purpose; endangering the security of other people's machines or attempting to force them into making changes they are unable to make or afford is not ethical.

Finally, we must decide these issues of ethics as a community of professionals and then present them to society as a whole. No matter what laws are passed, and no matter how good security measures might become, they will not be enough for us to have completely secure systems. We also need to develop and act according to some shared ethical values. The members of society need to be educated so that they understand the importance of respecting the privacy and ownership of data. If locks and laws were all that kept people from robbing houses, there would be many more burglars than there are now; the shared mores about the sanctity of personal property are an important influence in the prevention of burglary. It is our duty as informed professionals to help extend those mores into the realm of computers.

REFERENCES

1. E. H. Spafford, Is a computer break-in ever ethical? *Info. Tech. Quart.* IX, 9-14 (1990).
2. D. Seeley, A tour of the worm, In *Proceedings of the Winter 1989 Usenix Conference*, The Usenix Association, Berkeley, CA, 1989.
3. E. H. Spafford, The internet worm: crisis and aftermath. *Commun. ACM* 32, 678-698 (1989).
4. E. H. Spafford, An analysis of the internet work. In *Proceedings of the 2nd European Software Engineering Conference* (C. Ghezzi and J. A. McDermid, eds.), Springer-Verlag, Berlin, Germany, 1989, pp. 446-468.
5. C. Stoll, *Cuckoo's Egg*, Doubleday, New York, 1989.

---

[3]To anticipate the oft-used comment that the "bad guys" already have such information: not every computer burglar knows or will know *every* system weakness—unless we provide them with detailed analyses.

Are Break-ins Ethical?

J. SYSTEMS SOFTWARE   **47**
1992; 17:41-47

6. John Schwartz, The hacker dragnet, *Newsweek* 65, (April, 1990).

7. E. H. Spafford, K. A. Heaphy, and D. J. Ferbrache, *Computer Viruses: Dealing with Electronic Vandalism and Programmed Threats*, ADAPSO, Arlington, Virginia, 1989.

8. L. Hoffman, ed., *Rogue Programs: Viruses, Worms, and Trojan Horses*, Van Nostrand Reinhold, City, 1990.

9. D. J. Stang, *Computer Viruses*, 2nd ed., National Computer Security Association, Washington, DC, 1990.

10. P. J. Denning, ed., *Computers Under Attack: Intruders, Worms, and Viruses*. ACM Books/Addison-Wesley, Reading, Massachusetts, 1991.

11. B. J. Baird, L. L. Baird, Jr., and R. P. Ranauro, The moral cracker? *Comp. Sec.* 6, 471-478 (1987).

12. W. Landreth, *Out of the Inner Circle: a Hacker's Guide to Computer Security*, Microsoft Press, New York, 1984.

13. Adelaide, J. P. Barlow, R. J. Bluefire, R. Brand, C. Stoll, D. Hughes, F. Drake, E. J. Homeboy, E. Gold-

stein, H. Roberts, J. Gasperini (JIMG), J. Carroll (JRC), L. Felsenstein, T. Mandel, R. Horvitz (RH), R. Stallman (RMS), G. Tenney, Acid Phreak, and Phiber Optik, Is computer hacking a crime? *Harper's Magazine* 280, 45-57 (March 1990).

14. R. Stallman, The GNU Manifesto, in *GNU EMacs Manual*, Free Software Foundation, Cambridge, MA, 1986, pp. 239-248.

15. M. D. McIlroy, Unsafe at any price, *Info. Techn. Quart.* IX, 21-23 (1990).

16. P. J. Denning, D. E. Comer, D. Gries, M. C. Mulder, A. Tucker, A. J. Turner, and P. R. Young, Computing as a discipline, *Commun. ACM* 32, 9-23 (1989).

17. A. B. Tucker, B. H. Barnes, R. M. Aiken, K. Barker, K. B. Bruce, J. T. Cain, S. E. Conry, G. L. Engel, R. G. Epstein, D. K. Lidtke, M. C. Mulder, J. B. Rogers, E. H. Spafford, and A. J. Turner, *Computing Curricula 1991*, IEEE Society Press, Piscataway, NJ, 1991

[28]

A moral approach to electronic patient records

N. B. FAIRWEATHER and S. ROGERSON

Centre for Computing and Social Responsibility, Faculty of Computing Sciences and Engineering, De Montfort University, The Gateway, Leicester, LE1 9BH, UK; e-mail: ccsr@dmu.ac.uk

Abstract. This paper seeks to establish a morally appropriate balance between the various moral standards that are in tension in the field of Electronic Patient Records (EPRs). EPRs can facilitate doctorpatient relationships, however at the same time they can undermine trust and so harm the doctorpatient relationship. Patients are becoming increasingly reluctant to tell their own doctor everything that is relevant. A number of moral principles and the question of consent to release of records are considered here. There is also explicit mention of the principles for the treatment of the EPRs of the dead. A number of tensions between principles are explored, including that between privacy and promotion of welfare, both in an emergency and in more routine situations. The discussion also includes the tension between access and the right to not know about a condition that may undermine, for example, self-esteem; and the tensions between principles that arise when epidemiology, public health surveillance and healthcare evaluation are conducted. Suggestions are made about an appropriate balance between the principles. It is suggested that the patient's right to informed consent should be dominant.

Keywords: Electronic patient records; Health informatics; Medical ethics; Privacy; Medical data access

1. Context

Healthcare computing (also called medical informatics) is one of the fastest growing areas of information and communication technology (ICT) application. ICTs have been applied in healthcare to performance indicators, financial (including insurance) systems, paramedical support, emergency services, electronic patient records, computer aided diagnosis, clinical governance, remote surgery, research support and hospital management. The implementation of information systems in healthcare is inevitably ethically charged and moving at a faster pace than ethical consideration of those developments. Developments in the exchange of electronic patient records are a particularly strong theme in the implementation of information systems in healthcare. Thus, in the United Kingdom, NHSnet, a national health information network has been established for some years (p. 307) [1], yet adequate security infrastructures for it are *still* some way off [2; see also (pp. 6–9) 3].

All uses of ICT in healthcare should ideally promote, and must certainly not conflict with, the fundamental principles of medical ethics. There is a widespread consensus around the principles of beneficence, nonmaleficence, and respect for patient autonomy within medical ethics, and substantial acceptance of the principle of distributive justice (p. 38) [4]. Beneficence can be taken as meaning a duty to promote good and to act in the best interest of the patient and the health of society.[†] Nonmaleficence indicates a duty to do no harm to patients. Respect for patient autonomy can be interpreted as a duty to protect and foster a patient's free, uncoerced choices. Finally, distributive justice implies ensuring that the costs and benefits of healthcare are fairly distributed, and according to some theories ensuring that the relationship between the distribution of costs and benefits is fair.

At a philosophical level, certain of the principles are more closely associated with particular positions in general ethics: thus autonomy might be associated with deontologism and beneficence with consequentialism. Such an association is, however, simplistic. As Beauchamp and Childress (p. 110) [4] say, 'Many different theories lead to similar action-guides and ... It is possible from several of these standpoints to defend roughly the same principles, obligations, rights, responsibilities, and virtues'. Many plausible consequentialist theories, for example, would give rise to a deep concern for autonomy.

Whatever the level of agreement about these principles of medical ethics, there may at times be a tension between the duties implied by these various principles; and between them and other principles, either derived from them, or with other strong moral support. It may appear inadequate to start from a basis of principles that at times are in tension, but since no claim to have identified the perfect moral theory has even come close to having been proven, there is, in our opinion, no better starting point available, and the questions at hand are too urgent to wait for a convincing proof of the perfect ethical theory to be discovered.

While this paper is interested in principles, it is not attempting to develop the perfect principles no matter how impractical; our position, rather, is that practicality is one factor that needs to be considered, along with principles, perhaps through 'The method of wide reflective equilibrium' (p. 449) [5], after Rawls and Griffin).

This paper considers one aspect of healthcare computing, electronic patient records (EPRs). It identifies a viable moral approach to EPRs taking into account the ethical principals discussed. EPRs enable some or all of the medical history of patients to be computerized. They offer new methods of storing, duplicating, manipulating and communicating medical and non-medical information of all kinds, including text, images, and recordings of sound, video and tactile senses (p. 4) [6], (p. 2) [7]. Thus they can be more powerful and flexible than paper-based systems. They allow providers, payers and patients to interact more efficiently, and in ways that improve health and can be life enhancing. Perhaps for these reasons, governments appear to favour national healthcare infrastructures with 'longitudinal' patient records, which cover a patient's complete medical history [8] from the womb (or perhaps even before conception) to the grave.

2. Inappropriate balances

The centrality of trust to the doctorpatient relationship can to some extent be gauged by the fact that ensuring patients will find medical professionals trustworthy provides a substantial part of the reasoning for regulation of medical

---

[†]It should be recognized that 'promoting good', 'acting in the best interest of the patient' and 'acting in the best interest of the health of society' give beneficence different senses in different contexts.

professions (p. 7) [4]. EPRs can facilitate doctor–patient relationships through the use of computerized notes, which the doctor and the patient can share and contribute to. However, at the same time EPRs can harm the doctor–patient relationship and undermine trust. For example, in the US, medical data clearinghouses sell patient data to a range of organizations including insurance companies, police departments, employers and drug companies (p. 91) [9]. In doing so they have the potential to reduce the cost of healthcare, and thus support the beneficent aim of medicine.† However, the knowledge that data may be widely distributed and sold means that patients are becoming increasingly reluctant to tell their own doctors everything about their symptoms and the possible causes of them (p. 89) [9, 10], (p. 6) [7].

The potential for severe damage to the relationship between doctors and patients if privacy is not adequately protected has been well known for some time (see, for example, (p. 177) [11], (p. 78) [12]). The relationship depends heavily on confidentiality, and patients withholding information about their symptoms and possible causes of them can damage the quality, and hence (paradoxically) the efficiency of care.

There has not been enough work on defining ethically appropriate procedures and criteria for disclosures to the vast array of potential secondary users of health data such as managed care evaluators, insurance companies, and drug companies. The locations of the boundaries of morally legitimate trade in medical information have not been sufficiently explored. More work is also needed on ensuring that data is completely anonymized when traded, even where patients have rare medical conditions and other unusual attributes (perhaps unusually high levels of educational qualification) that make them easy to identify when these facts are combined (see (pp. 2, 7) [13]). The aim of this paper is to stimulate further debate about EPRs and to encourage others to participate in this essential work.

3. Other research into the problem

The single most important answer to the problem that has been produced hitherto by other researchers is the Opinion of the European Group on Ethics *Ethical Issues of Healthcare in the Information Society* [6], which like this paper, 'confines itself to the ethical [considerations] of the use of person identifiable personal health data' (p. 3) [6], (emphasis removed). The 'Opinion' identified a number of relevant 'value conflicts in the provision of healthcare' including 'effectiveness versus confidentiality', 'privacy versus the collective good' and 'efficiency versus beneficence' (p. 9) [6].

Since that 'Opinion', further (less comprehensive) research has been published [7], [14, 15, 16], providing further insights that have been taken into account in this paper. Alpert [9] has made another substantial contribution on these issues. However, Alpert concentrates on the tension between privacy and needs to 'maximize appropriate access to personal information' (p. 75), and in doing so reaches solutions that do not give enough weight to the influence of other moral principles.

The contribution of this paper differs from previous work by taking an interdisciplinary approach with insights from information systems and from

---

†Potentially in either the individual or social senses of the principle of beneficence, depending how health care is paid for.

moral philosophy, and by taking on board a wider range of sources, including material that has become available since previous work in this fast-moving field. It identifies and considers a larger number of relevant tensions between moral standards than previous work, but unlike Wagner *et al.* (p. 10) [6] is not committed to the view that 'Trust is a fundamental ethical value in itself', rather seeing strong grounding for trust in other, more fundamental, values. We further believe calls for closed networks that restrict access whilst operating globally (p. 11) [6] to be unsustainable. The failure of the 'Opinion' of Wagner *et al.* to explicitly recognize the problems that can be caused by doctor–patient records being inappropriately widely available is an especially serious shortcoming that this paper seeks to rectify.

4. Principles

As already stated, three of the most widely accepted principles of medical ethics are beneficence, nonmaleficence, and respect for patient autonomy. Thus there is a fiduciary responsibility on doctors towards patients 'of acting only in the patient's best interests' (p. 79) [12] which implies a duty normally to keep medical records private, as would be required by the Hippocratic oath, where it is still taken.

Others have argued that 'Electronically based patient records . . ., are . . . patient analogues' (p. 105) [17], and because of this the promotion of autonomy requires allowing control for the patient over their analogue. We are not entirely convinced by this argument. Patients certainly have an interest[†] in what happens to their records after they are dead; yet their autonomy cannot be promoted once they are dead, even if their 'analogue' persists as if they were alive. Concern for privacy derived from the promotion of autonomy as applied to a patient analogue appears to be too limited in scope.

Breaches of the duty of confidentiality can leave doctors subject to being disciplined by their professional body, and prosecution in many legal systems (p. 7) [16]. The fiduciary relationship extends to health information professionals (p. 105) [17] and thus, 'The health care informatician should respect the privacy of individuals, groups or organizations and should know that any breach of their privacy through the utilization of their data without their authorization or consent constitutes a considerable threat to their person' (p. 384) [18]. The principle that consent must be properly informed is well established in medical ethics (pp. 142–157) [4]. However, this is not enough, because it must be remembered that there are times when individuals are required to give 'consent' on pain of being excluded from significant benefits. It may even be that continued employment may on occasion be effectively dependent on giving such 'consent' [19], although it is more common for such benefits as gaining employment or securing life insurance to be conditional on releasing medical data in some jurisdictions. A requirement that access to private information be with 'consent' would not be enough on its own to ensure that such access is morally correct.

Further, there are times when it is morally appropriate for access to be given without consent having been obtained from the data subject. These

---

[†]At minimum an anticipatory interest while they are still alive: we will not explore here the question of whether the dead still have interests.

circumstances may arise when the patient is unconscious and cannot give permission, or when there is an overriding public interest (such as to prevent the spread of a communicable disease by tracing carriers; see also (p. 8) [16]). When consent cannot be obtained from the data subject, access should only be with the consent 'of a duly empowered legal authority acting with due process of the law' (p. 336) [20]. This requirement for legal sanction is, like 'consent', not enough on its own. In a regime that is corrupt, arbitrary, liable to prejudiced discrimination, totalitarian or otherwise acting beyond its moral authority; legal sanction may be given in circumstances where it should not, or denied when it should be given.

Privacy is not an all-or-nothing concept. A person never has either complete privacy (even the sole inhabitant of an abundantly fertile island will feel the impact of global climate change, which has been caused by other people), nor utter lack of privacy (even in the most humiliating imprisonment, some of the prisoner's thoughts remain private). Privacy can, as with those two extremes, relate either to the ability of others to make an impact on your life ('associative privacy': [21]), or to knowledge about you ('informational privacy': (p. 340) [22]). Very often, but not always, both types of privacy are closely intertwined in practice (knowledge about my life would enable you to have impacts on it, while many of the impacts that you can make on my life leave you with the knowledge that my life has been affected in that way). This paper is more centrally concerned with privacy regarding knowledge about the subject.

The degree of privacy could, in principle, be different for each piece of knowledge about a person (insofar as it makes sense to talk in terms of discrete pieces of knowledge). For each piece of knowledge about an individual, x, the degree of privacy would be determined by how many, and which, other individuals and organizations had access to the knowledge at what effective cost ('cost' here should not be thought of solely in financial terms, but also in terms of time and effort, the risk of effective sanctions, whether from the law or others, etc.). Thus for each piece of knowledge, greatest privacy is achieved when nobody but you knows it, and no amount of resources (not even use of extensive torture facilities) could cause it to be revealed. Similarly, for each piece of knowledge, zero privacy would be when everybody who will ever live knows that about you: thus zero privacy is not achievable in respect to any single item of knowledge, although near-zero privacy in respect of some items of knowledge is possible for such world famous people as the late Diana, Princess of Wales.

According to Nevado LLandres (p. 76) [12], it is 'quite clear to everyone that under no circumstances should the use of databases diminish the right of the patient to the privacy and confidentiality of his data'. However, the use of databases is diminishing the practical extent of privacy and confidentiality. It may be that the *right* has not been diminished, but evidence suggests that the extent of *respect* of the right is declining. Violations of medical privacy may be easier than ever before because of the very efficiency of computerized systems, so that we are now in an age when 'Neither physicians nor patients can assume that rules regulating the use of patient information will effectively stop potential breaches of confidentiality' [19]. The extent and severity of damage to the privacy and broader well-being of a patient [23] whose confidentiality is violated may be proportionately greater because of the amount of data held within an

EPR and the ease with which it can be replicated, distributed and data-matched.

Consideration of the principle of beneficence suggests that the best interests of patients are served (1) by improvements in care at reasonable and affordable cost; (2) by reductions in cost resulting in more care being provided for the same expenditure; and (3) by reductions in cost enabling the same care to be provided for less cost, freeing up resources to promote patient welfare in other fields.

Gritzalis *et al.* argue (p. 385) [18] that 'The user of a medical computer system will not design systems that can come to originate considerable harm to the health of the patient or the reputation of the health care professional'. However, the *potential* for considerable harm is virtually inevitable with medical computer systems, because even the best-designed system meeting all appropriate standards for safety-critical systems is liable to have the potential for being a contributory factor in considerable harm when in the hands of someone evil and technically proficient.

Distributive justice also plays an important role in medical ethics, and requires that the various outputs of healthcare (including medical well being), and the costs to achieve them, be fairly distributed.

4.1. *The fair information principles*

According to Kluge (p. 336) [20], there has been 'a remarkable convergence' in regulation of medical informatics 'towards a uniform position centred in the so-called "fair information principles"'. These principles are, in brief: openness, limitation of collection, limitation of disclosure, limitation of use, security and access (see also (p. 90) [24] where these principles are re-worked into a more coherent, but less widely accepted, list of seven principles). Each of these is considered in turn.

- **Openness** is strongly associated with respect for patient autonomy, as without knowledge of 'the existence of an electronic data-bank' or 'the kind of information it contains' (p. 336) [20] it is simply impossible for the patient to make autonomous decisions on relevant questions (which may include whether to seek medical attention for an injury sustained in a particularly embarrassing way, for example). Respect for patient autonomy requires that patients be educated about the nature of EPRs and their rights (p. 13) [6], and be able to effectively articulate their views.
- The principle of '**limitation of collection**' is an aspect of the more general requirement to respect privacy, requiring that data only be collected and held if they are 'necessary to achieve the legitimate aims' of the information system, and have been collected using 'ethically defensible' procedures (p. 336) [20].
- '**Limitation of disclosure**' is essentially another way of expressing the privacy questions relating to consent for disclosure of data as discussed previously.
- '**Limitation of use**' relates to considerations both of privacy and autonomy, this time requiring that the uses to which data are put are limited to those which are 'duly empowered legitimate purposes' of the information system (p. 336) [20]. Clearly, any restriction on the extent of distribution and use of information about individuals promotes privacy. Autonomy is promoted by limitations of use, because they enable the data subject (the patient, for medical data) to give (or decline to give) consent to the purposes to which the data actually will be put.

- **Security** is essential to privacy in practice. In a world in which a significant proportion of people seek information to which they are not entitled,[†] the only way to make sure that an item of knowledge is available to a limited number of people and organizations is to employ data security systems. These systems must be capable of withstanding sophisticated (and simple) attacks by those seeking to breach the security, since there have been successful attempts to breach security of EPR systems in the past (p. 11) [16].

- **'Access'**, as a 'fair information principle' is concerned with the right of the *data subject* to gain access to the data about them, and to correct it if it is inaccurate, incomplete, or contains irrelevant material (p. 336) [20]. The Shipman murder case in the UK, however, suggests that correction of records should not be technically possible without the agreement of two doctors. Access to data about himself or herself would enable an individual to ensure that beneficence were maintained, at least in their respect as an individual (see also below on how 'access' may at times be in tension with beneficence).

Kluge argues (pp. 338–339) [20] that EPRs are an analogue of the patient in a kind of nominal decision-space and as such should be treated according to ethical standards that mirror the standards that apply to treatment of the physical patient. In this light Kluge argues (p. 340) [20] that the 'fair information principles' are 'Not the ultimate justification of an ethical course of action, but a heuristic move that is adopted for the sake of inferential brevity', when the right course of action is more correctly inferred from more basic moral principles. It is also clear, as Kluge points out (p. 340) [20] that, for all their usefulness, there are circumstances in which the right course of action may run counter to the 'fair information principles'.

4.2. The dead

There has been remarkably little consideration of moral obligations with respect to the dead [26], but the issue is in practice inescapable when considering electronic patient records: a high proportion of the entries on an EPR are likely to relate to the period immediately before death.

In the only legal system with which we are sufficiently familiar (the English), the dead have no right to have their good name protected from defamation. It may be said that the dead no longer have rights, because they can no longer make claims, when 'the content of a system of rights is historically conditioned by the making of claims' (p. 64) [27]. However, we are interested in morality, not the law, when not all morality is rights-based; not all rights are claim-rights [28]; and 'there is a distinction to be made between *having* claims and *making* claims. The mere fact that someone claims something is not sufficient to establish it as his right' while 'someone may have a claim relative to me whether or not he makes the claim or is even able to make a claim'. (p. 64) [27].[†]

It may be argued that the dead 'are no longer morally significant persons', and thus the only basis for respect towards the dead is the 'psychological harm to the living relatives' [29]. While we are not convinced that this is the only basis, this basis alone could give rise to substantial obligations with respect to the

[†]In a recent survey, over 30% of the respondents agreed, or strongly agreed that "It is acceptable for me to use other employees' access codes with their permission to access data normally hidden from me" (pp. 28–29) [25].

treatment of the dead. People do like to think well of the dead, and could be anxious, for example, that some aspects of a patient record remained confidential, rather than be allowed to tarnish a reputation.

Most of us do care about what happens to our body and our reputation after our death. This suggests that how we treat the dead may be morally important independent of the effect on relatives, at the very least because those who are alive are anxious not to be treated the same way. It is also worth remembering that the relationship of medicine to the dead is decidedly ambiguous: much medical knowledge (especially anatomy) has been derived from treatment of corpses which in other contexts would be clearly unacceptable, while at times medicine appears to be working flat-out to prevent death at all costs.

Furthermore, the EPRs of the dead, like EPRs of the living, can have direct relevance to knowledge about the medical status of other family members. This gives rise to particular problems, however, with the dead, which are considered below.

5. Tensions between and within principles

In practice there can be a need to provide timely access to as much relevant data as possible to allow the correct treatment of a patient, and especially in an emergency. 'An accurate medical record helps the health care team avoid unintended complications by alerting them to a patient's condition and current treatment ... [therapeutic] drugs ... carry the risk of significant side effects and may interact negatively with other medications.' [19] Electronic patient records can facilitate such timely access as is needed, but in an emergency access to the EPR may be needed (p. 7) [16], possibly even by a paramedic who does not have 'full' medical training, or by a doctor acting outside their field of medicine. Even more difficult cases arise when the only timely treatment available would be given by somebody who is not employed in any of the medical or related professions, and not subject to the associated enforcement of professional standards, but rather has received brief training in emergency life support. This need for access could apply when the patient has never met the person accessing his/her EPR, when the patient is unconscious and next of kin cannot be contacted sufficiently quickly. How can sufficient access to data be provided to such people without access to the EPR being open to all?

Although there is a need to provide timely access to as much relevant data as possible, patients should have the ability to allow selective access to their records. For example a woman who has had an abortion may visit a doctor for treatment of an ailment that cannot possibly be related: she should have the right to withhold from the doctor such especially sensitive information that is not relevant to the matter at hand [30]; contra (p. 10) [6]. There are, of course, practical difficulties attached to patients making judgements about whether aspects of their history are relevant. However, EPRs can provide a greater potential for patient control in these matters, because a computer program can assess the likely relevance given other inputs (for example of current symptoms) before it even suggests to the patient that revealing a particular item of data may be beneficial.

The 'fair information principle' of 'access', while often being a useful way of maintaining beneficence (see above), can at times be in tension with other aspects of beneficence. Patients should also have the right to *not* be informed of some medical facts where, for example the fact may undermine self-esteem and the way in which they live their lives (such as genetic data or information about terminal illness).[†] Where genetic data or data about infectious diseases is present that may be undermining in this way, family members also have the right to *not* be informed in the same way. While normally this would not be a problem (as EPRs are personally confidential among adults), there is particular cause for concern with the EPRs of minor children. Another possible cause for concern would be if relatives were to be allowed control of the EPRs of the deceased. It is appropriate for somebody to be appointed to uphold the interests of the deceased with respect to their EPRs. This cannot, however, normally be a relative of the deceased, because if it were, an exception would have to be made whenever the record contained data that could also be undermining to the family member. If such a procedure were followed, the making of such an exception would be tantamount to acknowledging the existence of the very data from which it was intended to protect the family member. A different procedure, outlined below, is needed.

There are further difficulties with genetic data and data about infectious diseases that are likely to be passed between family members. There is a mismatch between *individual* control over the collection and storage of EPRs and *individual* access to EPRs (on the one hand), and information that applies to a group of family members (on the other) (p. 1) [14]. One often cannot prevent such information about oneself being gathered, stored, or accessed as part of a family member's EPR. Worse, 'in some cases', such as where a genetic condition only affects one gender, 'the information has greater significance for others than it has for the one from whom it was gathered' (p. 2) [14].

Electronic access to patient data can also be beneficial in a variety of settings where inaccurate interpretation of hand-written messages can have harmful effects. For example, electronic transmission of prescriptions with digital signatures can prevent some cases of potentially dangerous incorrect dispensing.

It is not in any way a matter of controversy that 'notations of a psychiatric illness carry the risk of potential discrimination that could destroy the patient's current and future employment if the information is insufficiently protected' [19]. It would not, equally, be a matter of dispute that medical notes relating to a number of other types of symptoms or hinting at a number of other types of illness or medical procedures could cause similar harm if revealed to current or prospective employers. While this problem has not been entirely created by digitization of patient records, the increases in ease of duplication, manipulation and communication of records that digitization has enabled; make disclosure of more information and to more people than ever before very real prospects. The prospect of unauthorized access to records has also been increased by digitization.

Epidemiology, public health surveillance, and healthcare evaluation, each seek to promote the health of society. In the era of ICTs each encourages the collation

---

[†]This right may appear paradoxical, in that if rights were only exercised at the request of the right-holder, this right could never be successfully exercised. However, as stated above, having such a claim does not require an individual to be in a position to actually make such a claim: a right can exist even if no individual is ever in a position to decide whether to exercise it. It is worth noting that beyond having a right to not be informed, *R v Mid Glamorgan Family Health Services Authority and another, ex parte Martin* [31] holds that a patient does not have the right to access to medical records under such circumstances.

and comparison of many disparate facts about as large a proportion of the relevant population as practical (while the limits of the relevant population may not always be easy to discern, encouraging a wide interpretation). The databases so generated can be used, for example, 'to trace long-term effects of certain drugs, trajectories of particular diseases, [and] outcomes of particular medical interventions' (p. 5) [6]. They could also detect unusually high death rates, detecting some multiple murders (as in the Shipman murders), and flawed practice (as with the Bristol babies case in the UK). The large databases so used can give rise to a tension between the privacy of some individuals and the health of another group which may, or may not, overlap the group whose privacy is at stake. Clearly, principles relating to distributive justice are at stake here. There is also the possibility that data collected for epidemiological or scientific research might provide information relevant to the potential treatment of an individual, giving rise to a tension between the health of an individual and their own privacy (p. 231) [32].

Due to considerations such as the principle of beneficence,[†] in healthcare there is a need to cut costs that are not inevitable costs of treatment where this can be done without harming treatment. Electronic transfer of patient records offers the potential to save money when compared to traditional methods (p. 308) [1], freeing resources for 'front-line' patient care. As all security and privacy technologies come with associated costs, there is a direct tension here between privacy and financial goals.

The categorization and profiling of patients by managed care evaluators, insurance companies and the like also has the potential to enable cost savings, but may enable discriminatory or exclusionary effects that can run counter to the principle of nonmaleficence for some, even while promoting beneficence for others.[‡] Thus principles of distributive justice could be violated at the same time as the principle of nonmaleficence.

It should be apparent that 'the user of medical software assumes the social responsibility of utilizing it to promote the quality of the health care provided to the patient and the moral obligation to question whether or not its use is beneficial to the patient' (p. 384) [18]. However, such concerns of immediate benefit to particular patients might be in tension with the potential benefits to other patients of more comprehensive testing, etc. The issues here are exactly the same as more typical medical trials.

6. Striking a balance

It is clear that a balance must be struck so that EPRs might realize their potential beneficial status, whilst ensuring the risk of harm is minimized. The main elements of this balance are discussed in this section. Further research may in due course disturb the current reflective equilibrium between the various principles which are in tension and between the principles and questions of practicality.

A patient's right to informed consent should be dominant, and in order to enable this, education about these issues should be available to patients (cf (pp. 10, 13) [6]). All patients should, following the 'fair information principle' of

---

[†]In the social sense, and in the individual sense if there is individual payment for treatment.
[‡]In the individual sense of the principle of beneficence, and in the social sense if the categorization is widespread.

openness (p. 336) [20], have practical access to information about the existence of all databases with medically relevant information about themselves. There are rare exceptions. The first exception is where the knowledge about the very presence of a record in a particular database itself (regardless of content) may undermine self-esteem and the way in which the patient lives their life.[†] The second exception is when knowledge about the existence of a record in a database may seriously jeopardize the health of others, seriously jeopardize an investigation into a serious crime, or have a similar impact.

A patient should have effective control over his/her data and the ability to prevent any casual distribution that might be harmful to himself or herself, ensuring EPRs maintain nonmaleficence.[‡] There may need to be exceptions again, for example to combat contagion, but where the patient has at least an ordinary degree of rationality, strenuous efforts should be made at persuasion before release of the information is taken out of the individual's control.[§] Where a patient does not have the degree of rationality routinely present among adults, his/her representative (parent or guardian in the case of a young child) should have the control that the patient would normally have. We agree with Barroso (p. 4) [16], and certain jurisdictions, that 'If a child is regarded as mature enough to make conscious decisions in relation to the confidentiality of personal information, the law should ... recognize this and the child should have the right to make the decision'.

Upon death, the executors of the estate should be able to exert control over the dead person's EPR [33], except when the executors are family members, in which case a special 'patient record executor' should be appointed in all cases: it should thus be standard practice for wills to appoint a 'patient record executor' at the same time as the will is written if the executors are family members. The patient record executor (whether the same person as the general executor or not) should have most of the rights over the records that the deceased would have had (without any restrictions that may have been in place over records knowledge of which might have harmed the, now deceased, patient). Given that most patients never express any opinion about their records, and that when opinions are expressed, they are usually concern for privacy or about 'consent' to release records, it is not anticipated that the patient record executor would be called upon in any but the most exceptional cases. Further consideration is needed on whether they should have the right to correct records. On the one hand an incorrect record can no longer harm the patient's health, and the possibility of introducing inaccuracies is much greater than when the patient can be consulted.[¶] On the other hand, inaccurate data concerning the dead might harm living family members. Individualization of data (see below) may ease this tension somewhat.

[†]It is recognized that this exception could allow authorities with ill will to ignore the principle: there needs to be protection to ensure that this exception genuinely only applies when stated. Further, it may be worthwhile for there to be a procedure for routinely asking *all* citizens what their attitude would be to knowledge of such sorts, and for recording such attitudes in advance of them becoming relevant.
[‡]In the case where a patient does not know of the existence of data, due to the considerations in the preceding paragraph, the restrictions on the distribution of such data should be at least as strong as those on data that the patient does know about.
[§]We will leave to one side the operational details of what would constitute sufficiently strenuous efforts, since this paper is not about operational details.
[¶]Further information might possibly be added as a result of a post-mortem, or as further knowledge is gained through other sources.

Given the existence in EPRs of genetic data and data about infectious diseases that also apply to other family members, we suggest that information gathered should be 'as individualized as possible (e.g. not recording [the identity of] siblings, parents, offspring)' (p. 4) [14]. This will, however, reduce the amount of benefit that can be gained from some instances of genetic testing (thus inhibiting beneficence[†] to some extent). We have not, as yet, resolved all of the questions of how to reconcile this with the need to prevent the spread of infectious disease.

Where epidemiological data is required (including kinds that cannot be individualized while still maintaining their epidemiological relevance), anonymized data collection should be employed, employing suitable encryption and an anonymizing gatekeeper [15].

There needs to be safeguards to ensure that declining to give consent to access records (in employment and insurance contexts for instance) does not harm the patient unduly. This will have serious implications for employers who have been accustomed to health screening that enables them to decline to employ the disabled; and for insurers who have hitherto given cheaper or more comprehensive cover to those with a 'clean bill of health'.

Patients should have the ability to allow selective access to their records, being assisted to make informed choices about when it may be appropriate to reveal information they would normally prefer to remain confidential.

The appropriate scope for EPRs, and patients' rights with respect to their own medical information should be clearly defined. Prohibitions on certain sorts of uses of data and what principles should govern legitimate access to and use of personal health and medical data and information also need to be clearly enunciated in a way that ensures they are respected. In societies such as those that presently exist in the industrialized world, legislation is likely to be the most appropriate mechanism for such definition and enunciation. In societies where property is a dominant concern for the law, clarification of the ownership of patient data is vital. Mechanisms for the enforcement of applicable laws and oversight of use and access must be in place, adequately resourced and effective.

Harm to the doctor/patient relationship should not be taken lightly. While doctors have on occasion exaggerated the intimacy of the doctor/patient relationship; it is normally advantageous for such intimacy to be promoted,[‡] if patients are to be appropriately treated. Healthcare providers and funders and other potential recipients of medical data should understand the impact of receipt of data on the doctorpatient relationship (cf (p. 13) [6]), and be aware that the knowledge that data is being collected may bias the data in ways that dramatically reduce its value.[§] Against this background, recipients of data should ensure (1) that whenever possible data is only collected in ways that are not individually identifiable (including by combining with other data sets); (2) that the data collected is the absolute minimum required for the purposes at hand, which are themselves morally scrupulous; and (3) that the advantages of use and

---

[†]In the social sense, and in the individual sense for as yet unidentified individuals.
[‡]Although not by a reduction in the inhibitions and knowledge of the patient.
[§]Both by inhibiting patients from revealing symptoms and other medically relevant information, and by inducing doctors to avoid recording, or disguise the recording, of especially sensitive information. Such biases would render any subsequent statistical analysis of the data unreliable in unpredictable ways.

further distribution of data are weighed against the potential for harm to individuals and to the data stream of such use.

7. Implementation

While this paper does not focus on implementation, it must be explicitly recognized that there are serious issues in the implementation of Electronic Patient Records. These are briefly discussed in this section.

The movement of EPRs over the Internet, intranets and extranets raises particular concerns. The further (in terms of logical steps rather than physical distance) data is from its original source, the greater the risks of duplication, falsification, inaccuracy, manipulation and unauthorized distribution. There has been little effective control over data use over computer networks, with high levels of security for dial-in and Internet links. While encryption of data in transmission, and in storage, can ease these problems [34] (cf (p. 11) [6]) it is logically impossible for it to solve them: to be interpreted, data must be decrypted, yet 'passwords are considered by many to be awkward and unnecessary' and 'Re-establishing network connections can take so long that busy clinical staff avoid logging off between transactions' (p. 6) [3]. Another problem is that inappropriate 'insider access to medical records' has led to violations of privacy for some years [19]. While it may be possible to foster a good security culture, the first step is to recognize that purely technical 'solutions' are insufficient.

There should be clearly defined limits of access for each type of authorized person. When implemented, systems should provide security alarms linked to all functions that involve an element of browsing, copying or reporting [34], and record who has accessed sensitive information [19; (p. 3) 35].

While other issues are mentioned below, it is important to remember that manipulation, use or abuse of healthcare information is not needed to cause harm. The mere suspicion that information might be, or might have been, leaked can cause harm [19] (cf [8]) whether by inhibiting the doctor/patient relationship or by meaning that records are incomplete.

Another issue is accuracy of the original data. Health care workers 'may be highly capable and competent, but if they lack the training necessary to use the program correctly, they may cause irreparable harm; [thus] the ideal we seek is that the user introduce clinically accurate data into the computer' (pp. 76) [12]. However, that ideal may well not be achieved, with the potential for serious detriment to the health and wider well being of the patient.

7.1. *Inaccurate data*

According to Nevado LLandres (pp. 77) [12] 'if ... erroneous or inadequate symptoms were introduced [ie input], then the responsible party is the physician'. However, this leaves substantial problems. A requirement to guarantee adequate input of symptoms could lead to doctors conducting unnecessary duplicate tests with direct adverse consequences to patient welfare, and consequences through unnecessary expenditure. Further, it is quite possible for electronic patient records to be altered by someone (for example a technician) who is not medically qualified: responsibility thus cannot fall entirely on medical professionals. Worse, it is possible for an inaccurate record to persist long after the person who was morally responsible for the introduction of the inaccuracy has ceased to practice: indeed, such inaccuracies could remain relevant to the (mis-)treatment of a patient long after the culpable person has died. While this was possible with paper records, the greater willingness to trust information that arrives in electronic form, the greater durability, the ease of reproduction, the ease of searching, and the greater distribution offered by electronic records all exacerbate the problem.

Another particular problem arises when there are suspicions about the privacy of the patient record. 'Failure to record significant diagnoses and therapies ... puts patients at risk.' [19], yet because of the fear that patients may be harmed if records do not remain private, 'the practice of keeping 'double' records for patients [with psychiatric diagnoses] ... has become widespread. Alternatively some clinicians ... have created 'code language' to obscure the true content of clinical interactions' from those who were not present in the consulting room [19]. While there may be legal protection of the privacy of the patient record in many jurisdictions, such protections are not sufficient if there are still suspicions on the part of either the patient or their doctor that records will not remain sufficiently private for a long time. In both the USA and the UK, such suspicions would currently be well founded.

8. Conclusions

This paper has focused on the ethical issues surrounding the growing existence and use of electronic patient records. The tensions between conflicting needs have been discussed. A morally defensible approach to EPRs has been suggested which can be summarized as follows:

- A patient's right to informed consent should be dominant: thus education about these issues should be available to patients, along with information about the existence of all databases with medically relevant information about the patient (with some minor exceptions).
- A patient should normally have effective control over his/her data and the ability to prevent any casual distribution that might be harmful, ensuring EPRs maintain nonmaleficence. There need to be safeguards to ensure that declining to give consent to access records does not harm the patient unduly.
- Patients should have the ability to allow selective access to their records.
- The EPRs of the dead should be treated with the same consideration as those of the living.
- In contemporary industrialized societies, legislation should clearly define the appropriate scope for EPRs, and ownership of patient data. It should clarify what principles should govern legitimate access to and use of personal health and medical data and information, and patients' rights with respect to their own medical information. There should be prohibitions on certain sorts of uses of data. Mechanisms for the adequate enforcement of applicable laws and oversight of use and access must be in place.
- Healthcare providers and funders and other potential recipients of medical data should understand the range of impacts of all sorts of medical data sharing, including on the requirement for openness in the doctor-patient relationship (both if patients are to be appropriately treated and if accurate data is to be collected) (cf (p. 13) [6]).

EPRs are indicative of a society that is increasingly dependent upon ICTs. The impact of this morally sensitive application of ICTs cannot and should not be ignored. We urge those involved in the creation, use and promotion of EPRs to consider our suggestions.

References
1. POULOUDI, A. and WHITLEY, E. A., 1996, Privacy of Electronic Medical Records: understanding conflicting concerns in an interorganizational system. In *ETHICOMP96: III International Conference Values and Social Responsibilities of the Computer Science: Proceedings*, Volume 1, edited by P. Barroso Asenjo, T. W. Bynum, S. Rogerson, and L. Joyanes, (Madrid, Spain: Pontificial University of Salamanca in Madrid), 307–327.
2. SCHNEIDER, P., 1998 Europeans ready for privacy law. In *Healthcare Informatics* June 1998, 137–138. Online at http://www.healthcare-informatics.com/issues/1998/06_98/interntl.htm, accessed 09 March 1999.
3. GAUNT, P. N., 2000, Practical approaches to creating a security culture. Paper at *The 8th Working Conference of the IMIA WG4: Security of the Distributed Electronic Patient Record (EPR)*, Victoria, BC, Canada, 21–24 June 2000.
4. BEAUCHAMP, T. and CHILDRESS, J., 1994, *Principles of biomedical ethics*, fourth edition, (New York, USA: Oxford University Press).
5. HOVEN, VAN DEN, J., 1996, Computer Ethics and Moral Methodology. In *ETHICOMP96: III International Conference Values and Social Responsibilities of the Computer Science: Proceedings*, Volume 1, edited by P. Barroso Asenjo, T. W. Bynum, S. Rogerson, and L. Joyanes, (Madrid, Spain: Pontificial University of Salamanca in Madrid), 444–453.
6. WAGNER, I. LENOIR, N., QUINTANA TRIAS, O., MARTINHO DA SILVA, P., MCLAREN, A., SORDA, M., HERMERÉN, G., HOTTOIS, G., MIETH, D., RODOTA, S., SCHROTEN, E. and WHITTAKER, P., 1999, *Ethical Issues of Healthcare in the Information Society*. Opinion of the European Group on Ethics in Science and New Technologies to the European Commission. Opinion 13, 30 July 1999. Online at http://europa.eu.int/comm/sg/sgc/ethics/en/opinion13.pdf, accessed 30 November 1999.
7. MAURO, V., 1999, Patient Privacy and Economic Interests: raising issues in health telematics. *ETHICOMP99 Look to the Future of the Information Society: Proceedings of the 4th ETHICOMP International Conference on the Social and Ethical Impacts of Information and Communications Technologies*, edited by A. D'Atri, A. Marturano, S. Rogerson and T. W. Bynum (Rome, Italy: Libera Università Internazionale degli Studi Sociali Guido Carli).
8. SCHNEIDER, P., 1997 InSecurity: how safe are your data? In *Healthcare Informatics*, April 1997. Online at http://www.healthcare-informatics.com/issues/1997/04_97/safe.htm, accessed 09 March 1999.
9. ALPERT, S. A., 1998, Health care information: access, confidentiality, and good practice. In *Ethics Computing and Medicine*, edited by K. W. Goodman (Cambridge, UK: Cambridge University Press), 75–101.
10. UTILITY CONSUMER'S ACTION NETWORK, 1999, Fact Sheet # 8: How Private Is My Medical Information? Online at http://www.privacyrights.org/FS/fs8-med.htm, accessed 18 January 2000.
11. ANNAS, G. J., 1989, *The Rights of Patients: the basic ACLU guide to patient rights*, second edition. (Carbondale, IL, USA: Southern Illinois University Press).
12. NEVADO LLANDRES, M. A., 1998, Ethical problems caused by the use of informatics in medicine. In *Ethics and Information Technology*, edited by G. Collste, (Delhi, India: New Academic Publishers).
13. BARBER, B. and ROGERS, R., 2000, Response to comments on first working document on 'Guidance for handling personal Health data in International applications in the context of the EU Data Protection Directive'. Online at http://forum.afnor.fr/afnor/WORK/AFNOR/GPN2/S95I/PRIVATE/DOC/00033ann.pdf, accessed 14 June 2001.
14. CAVANAUGH, T. A., 1999, Genetics and the fair use of electronic information. In *ETHICOMP99 Look to the Future of the Information Society: Proceedings of the 4th ETHICOMP International Conference on the Social and Ethical Impacts of Information and Communications Technologies*, edited by A. D'Atri, A. Marturano, S. Rogerson and T. W. Bynum (Rome, Italy: Libera Università Internazionale degli Studi Sociali Guido Carli).
15. VLUG, A., 1999 Double encryption of anonymized electronic data interchange. In *ETHICOMP99 Look to the Future of the Information Society: Proceedings of the 4th ETHICOMP International Conference on the Social and Ethical Impacts of Information and Communications Technologies*, edited by A. D'Atri, A. Marturano, S. Rogerson and T. W. Bynum (Rome, Italy: Libera Università Internazionale degli Studi Sociali Guido Carli).

16. BARROSO ASENJO, P., 1999, Ethical problems generated by the use of informatics in medicine. In *ETHICOMP99 Look to the Future of the Information Society: Proceedings of the 4th ETHICOMP International Conference on the Social and Ethical Impacts of Information and Communications Technologies*, edited by A. D'Atri, A. Marturano, S. Rogerson and T. W. Bynum (Rome, Italy: Libera Università Internazionale degli Studi Sociali Guido Carli)

17. KLUGE, E.-H. W., 1998, Fostering a security culture: a model code of ethics for health information professionals. *International Journal of Medical Informatics*, **49,** 105–110.

18. GRITZALIS, D., TOMARAS, A., KATSIKAS, S. and KEKILOGLOU, J., 1990, Medical Data Protection: a proposal for a deontology code (HIDEC, Health Informaticians' Deontology Code). *Journal of Medical Systems*, **14,** 375–386.

19. CLAGETT, C., POVAR, G. and MORIN, K., 1996, Documenting sensitive information poses dilemma for physicians. In *ACP Observer* (December). Also at http://www.acponline.org/journals/news/dec96/sensinfo.htm, accessed 15 December 1999.

20. KLUGE E.-H. W., 1994, Health Information, the Fair Information Principles and Ethics. *Methods of Information in Medicine* **33,** 336–345.

21. DeCEW, J. W., 1997,. *In Pursuit of Privacy: Law, Ethics and the Rise of Tecnology* (Cornell University Press), as quoted p341 in Spinello and Tavani, 2001 [22].

22. SPINELLO, R. A. and TAVANI, H. T., 2001, Introduction to Chapter Four: privacy in cyberspace. In *Readings in CyberEthics*, edited by Spinello and Tavani (Sudbury, MA, USA: Jones and Bartlett), 339–348.

23. ORAM, A., 1999, A wronged individual. Message sent to email list med-privacy@essential.org. Online at http://lists.essential.org/1999/med-privacy/msg00010.html, accessed 09 March1999.

24. KLUGE, E.-H. W., 2000, Professional codes for electronic HC record protection: ethical, legal, economic and structural issues. *International Journal of Medical Informatics*, **60,** 85–96.

25. PRIOR, M., ROGERSON, S., FAIRWEATHER, N. B, BUTLER, L. and DIXON, S., 1999, *Is IT Ethical? 1998 ETHICOMP Survey of Professional Practice* (Sidcup: Institute for the Management of Information Systems).

26. FLORIDI, L., 1998, Information Ethics: on the philosophical foundation of computer ethics. Paper at *ETHICOMP98, but not present in Proceedings of ETHICOMP98: The Fourth International Conference on Ethical Issues of Information Technology*, edited by J. van den Hoven, S. Rogerson, T. W. Bynum, and D. Gotterbarn (Rotterdam, Netherlands: Erasmus University Rotterdam). Online at http://www.wolfson.ox.ac.uk/~floridi/ie.htm, accessed 20 January 2000.

27. GOLDING, M. P., 1981, Obligations to future generations. In *Responsibilities to Future Generations: Environmental Ethics*, edited by E. Partridge, (Buffalo, NY, USA: Prometheus Books), reprinted from *The Monist* **56** (Jan 1972).

28. HOFELD, W. N., 1920, *Fundamental Legal Conceptions as Applied in Judicial Reasoning, and Other Legal Essays*, edited by W. W. Cook, (New Haven, USA: Yale University Press).

29. FIESER, J. and DOWDEN, B., (eds), 1998, Moral Personhood. In *The Internet Encyclopedia of Philosophy*. Online at http://www.utm.edu/research/iep/p/personho.htm, accessed 20 January 1999.

30. PAUL, L., 1999 Europe: managed care principles gaining ground. In *Healthcare Informatics*, March 1999. Online at http://www.healthcare-informatics.com/issues/1999/03_99/international.htm, accessed 09 March 1999.

31. *R v Mid Glamorgan Family Health Services Authority and another, ex p Martin* [1995] 1 All ER, 357.

32. GERARDI, L., 1998, Data Medical Privacy Act: an Italian lacking. Some remarks. In *Proceedings of ETHICOMP98: The Fourth International Conference on Ethical Issues of Information Technology*, edited by J. van den Hoven, S. Rogerson, T. W. Bynum, and D. Gotterbarn (Rotterdam, Netherlands: Erasmus University Rotterdam), 231–234.

33. KARANJA, S. K., 1995, *The Role of Legal Regulation in the Social Shaping of New Information Technologies: the computerised health data card (CHDC) as a case study*. Online at http://www.uio.no/~stephenk/thesis.htm, accessed 24 January 2000.

34. HAYS, M., 1997, A model for security. Sidebar in Schneider, 1997 [8].

35. SAFRAN, C. and GOLDBERG, H., 2000, Electronic Patient Records and the Impact of the Internet. Paper at *The 8th Working Conference of the IMIA WG4: Security of the Distributed Electronic Patient Record (EPR)*, Victoria, BC, Canada, 21–24 June 2000.

[29]

Privacy and the Varieties of Informational Wrongdoing

Jeroen van den Hoven
Erasmus University

Introduction

The privacy issue lies at the heart of an ongoing debate in nearly all Western democracies between liberalists and communitarians over the question how to balance individual rights and collective goods. The privacy issue is concerned more specifically with the question how to balance the claims of those who want to limit the availability of personal information in order to protect individuals and the claims of those who want to make information about individuals available in order to benefit the community. This essential tension emerges in many privacy discussions, e.g. undercover actions by the police on the Internet, use of closed circuit television in public places, making medical files available for health insurance purposes or epidemiological research, linking and matching of databases to detect fraud in social security, soliciting information about on-line behaviour of Internet users from access providers in criminal justice cases.

Communitarians typically argue that the community benefits significantly from having knowledge about its members available. According to communitarians, modern Western democracies are in a deplorable condition, and our unquenchable thirst for privacy serves as its epitome. Who could object to having his or her data accessed if honourable community causes are served? Communitarians also point out that modern societies exhibit high degrees of mobility, complexity and anonymity. As they are quick to point out, crime, free riding and the erosion of trust are rampant under these conditions. Political philosopher Michael Walzer observes that, 'Liberalism is plagued by free-rider problems, by people who continue to enjoy the benefits of membership and identity while no longer participating in the activities that produce these benefits. Communitarianism, by contrast, is the dream of a perfect free-riderlessness' (Walzer, 1995, p.63).

The modern nation states with their complex public administrations need a steady input of personal information to function well or to function at all. In postindustrial societies 'participation in producing the benefits' often takes the form of making information about oneself available. Those who are responsible for managing the public goods therefore insist on removing constraints on access to personal information and tend to relativise the importance of privacy of the individual.

Jeroen van den Hoven

Panoptic Technologies and the Public Good

Information technology's applications - panoptic technologies, as Oscar Gandy and Jeffrey Reiman call them (Gandy & Reiman, 1993) - ranging from active badges, intelligent vehicle highway systems (IVHS), closed circuit television (CCTV) to database mining techniques, encourage government agencies, public administrators and business firms to pursue the communitarian dream of perfect free-riderlessness. It is the logic of the public goods problem that contributes to the initial plausibility of their aspirations.

Many public administration problems can be characterised as free-rider problems: law enforcement, tax collection, implementation of environmental policy. The general description of a free-rider problem is that it is a situation where a number of persons contribute to the production and maintenance of a public good, where each person individually has an incentive to profit from the public good without making the necessary contribution to its production or maintenance. When too many persons ride free, i.e. benefit without contributing, the means fall below the minimum required and the public good can no longer be produced or sustained, so it disappears altogether. For example, all citizens in a country have to contribute to the budget for the protection of the environment in order to sustain particular environmental programs, but if too many persons profit from a healthier environment without paying their eco-tax, the basis for a sustained environmental policy will eventually crumble.

The free-rider problem manifests itself in many areas and has the structure of the prisoner's dilemma. The prisoner's dilemma is a strategic choice situation, where the optimal result is individually inaccessible, and the only equilibrium is suboptimal. In the free-rider problem, as in the prisoner's dilemma, we need some way of constraining the egoistic motives, which are individually rational but do not lead to Pareto optimal results. One way for optimal results to ensue is to see to it that cooperation is in itself so highly valued by the parties involved so as to affect the pay-off matrix in the right direction. This is sometimes referred to as the 'internal solution' to the dilemma. Philosophers and game theorists have proposed ways to avoid the worst outcome by following strategies of constrained maximisation (Gauthier, 1986). Public administration, however, has to deal with free-riders without assuming unrealistic levels of self-constraint in the population. Therefore, government agencies try to discourage free-riders by excluding non-contributors or by tracking them down and punishing them, that is by affecting the pay-off matrix by external solutions. But as, De Jasay observes:

> (...) it is not non-exclusion that makes retaliation impossible (for there may be other ways of punishing the free-rider than by excluding him), but anonymity of the free-rider. Clearly in a small group it is easier to spot the free rider and sanction him in one of many possible ways once

31

he is identified than in a large group, where he can hide in the crowd'.
(1989, p.149)

Free-rider problems can only take on socially unacceptable forms if the provider of the public good does not know who rides free and cannot determine who the free-riders are. An increase in relevant identifying information increases chances of retaliation, by alleviating the problem of anonymity. Information technology (IT) is ideally suited to uncover identities of free-riders. Mobile computing, ID-chip cards and palmtop computers allow street-level bureaucrats to verify information on site so as to increase the effectiveness of public administration and law enforcement procedures. Often millions of dollars of community money can be saved by simple and cheap database applications. IT provides the cost efficient means to affect the pay-off matrix of free-riders and thereby establish results that are superior in terms of social utility.

In the market sector the logic of the situation is the same in principle. In a society of strangers trust and the means to establish normative status and moral reputation are of paramount importance. By means of 'credentials' (on-line searchable databases, front-end verification) and 'ordeals' (polygraphs, log-in procedures, biometrical identification) we try to compensate for our ignorance about those with whom we have encounters and dealings.[1] Information technology is expected to give us techniques of perfect information, by reducing transactions and information cost dramatically and by reducing the risks of commerce among strangers, so as to approximate levels of trust associated with smaller, traditional and less volatile communities.

Both in the private as well as in the public sector IT is seen as the ultimate technology to resolve the problem of anonymity. Information and communication technology therefore presents itself as the technology of the logistics of exclusion and access-management to public goods and goods involved in private contracts. Whether IT really delivers the goods is not important for understanding the dynamics of the use of personal data. The fact that it is widely believed to be effective in this respect is, I think, sufficient to explain its widespread use for these purposes. The game-theoretical structure and the calculability of community gains make the arguments in favour of overriding privacy seem clear, straightforward and convincing.

But the communitarian interpretation of our modern moral predicament goes deeper than just pointing to crime, fraud and free-riding in a liberal individualistic society. It questions the very viability of the liberal conception of the self on behalf of which privacy is claimed and which is central to much of modern ethical theory and political philosophy. The liberal self is - as Michael Sandel calls it - an 'unencumbered self': a self that makes its choices, including choices about its own goals and identity, in isolation and far removed from a community. But individuation does not precede association. The liberal conception of the self does not account for the constitutive attachments that precede the formation of identities. The liberal conception of the self is unrealistically voluntaristic, disengaged and radically unsituated, as Charles Taylor and Seyla Benhabib have argued. The liberal self is an autonomous bricoleur of identities and symbolic personal information, which claims for itself the elbow room to shape itself in splendid isolation from a pre-existing community of speech and action, while reducing the risk of being unmasked, exposed and caught in inconsistencies by others.

From a communitarian point of view the idea of a moral right to privacy therefore seems doubly wrong. First of all, the autonomous subject of the moral right is a figment of enlightenment philosophy and it does not exist strictly speaking. Secondly, the protection it offers is not worth wanting.

In the final section I will provide a characterisation of some of the main features of the liberal self on which defences of a moral right to privacy can to be based. In the first part of the paper (sections 2–6) I shall argue that we can and should deconstruct the privacy notion, and that we must distinguish at least three types of moral wrongdoing on the basis of personal information that have nothing to do with privacy,[2] but nevertheless justify data protection. I thus suggest a broad and revisionary conception according to which claims to data protection or to constraints on access to personal information can be identified on the basis of the types of moral reasons for such claims.

I think the following types of moral reason for data protection can be distinguished: 1) information-based harm; 2) informational inequality; 3) informational injustice; and 4) encroachment on moral autonomy. In many cases where we want epistemic or cognitive access to ourselves and our data restricted, we do not want to be 'left alone' or to be 'private', but we want to prevent others from wronging us by making use of knowledge about us. We want fair treatment, equality of opportunity and do not want to be harmed or discriminated against.

Only the fourth type of moral reason can be identified exclusively with privacy in a strict sense. It is important to note that not all cases where data protection is justified are privacy cases, although in all cases where privacy (in a narrow sense) is at stake, data protection is justified. On this broader conception of informational wrongdoing and data protection, privacy interests are identified with interests in moral autonomy, i.e. the capacity to shape our own moral biographies, to reflect on our moral careers, to evaluate and identify with our own moral choices, without the critical gaze and interference of others. Where moral reasons of this type can be used appropriately, we can say that privacy is at issue. I will deal with this type of moral reason in the final section.

Data protection regimes (like that of the European Community) and their application to specific types of situations and sectors can thus be justified on the basis of the values of preventing harm, achieving equality of opportunity, realising justice and safeguarding moral autonomy. In practice we may find that some of them apply to the same cases and that data protection in these cases is morally overdetermined. I think it is still important to be able to distinguish analytically between these different types of moral reasons for the protection of personal information, and to have a fine-grained account of moral reasons for data protection, because it enables us to weigh competing claims more carefully.

Both liberals and communitarians can acknowledge the validity of the moral reasons to justify data protection concerned with harm, equality and justice, although they would disagree about the validity of justifications for restricting access to personal data which are premised on appeals to moral autonomy and the disputed liberal conception of the self associated with it. In practice we will find both liberals and communitarians agreeing on data protection laws and their applications, since - as this account from informational wrongdoing shows - the essentially contested concept of the self need not always be involved.

Information-Based Harm

The first type of moral reason for data protection is concerned with the prevention of harm, more specifically harm which is done to persons by making use of personal information about them. The fact that personal information is used to inflict harm or cause serious disadvantages to individuals does not necessarily make such uses violations of a moral right to privacy. Cyber criminals and malevolent hackers are known to have used computerised databases and the Internet to get information on their victims in order to prepare and stage their crimes. The most important moral problem with 'identity theft', for example, is the risk of financial and physical damages. One's bank account may be plundered and one's credit reports may be irreversibly tainted so as to exclude one from future financial benefits and services. Stalkers and rapists have used the Net and on-line databases to track down their victims, and they could not have done what they did without tapping into these resources. In an information society there is a new vulnerability to information-based harm. The prevention of information-based harm provides government with the strongest possible justification for limiting the freedom of individual citizens. Policies that encourage rigorous security measures must be put in place to protect citizens against information-based harm. This seems to be a matter of security and not of privacy. No other moral principle than John Stuart Mill's harm principle is needed to justify limitations of the freedom of persons who cause threaten to cause, or are likely to cause, information-based harm to people. Protecting personal information, instead of leaving it in the open, diminishes the likelihood that people will come to harm, analogous to the way in which restricting the access to fire arms diminishes the likelihood that people will be shot in the street. We know that if we do not establish a legal regime that constrains citizens' access to weapons, the likelihood that innocent people will be shot increases. In information societies information is comparable to guns and ammunition.

Informational Inequality

The second type of moral reason to justify data protection is concerned with equality and fairness. Several authors have pointed out that privacy may be disappearing as a foundational moral value in the West. According to Calvin Gottlieb, the laws safeguarding privacy don't work because 'people don't want them to work in far too many situations' (1996, p.156). One reason for this development is that people welcome the benefits (convenience, discounts, knowledge) that information technology can give them in exchange for the use of their personal data. More and more people are keenly aware of the benefits a market for personal data can provide. If a consumer buys coffee at the shopping mall, information about that transaction can be generated and stored. Many consumers realise that every time they come to the counter to buy something they can also sell something, namely, information about their purchase or transaction, the so-called transactional data. Likewise, sharing information about ourselves on the Net with websites, browsers, autonomous agents may pay off in terms of more and more adequate information (or discounts and convenience) later. Many privacy concerns have been and will be resolved in quid pro quo practices and private contracts about the use and secondary use of personal data. But although a market mechanism for trading personal data seems to be kicking in on a global scale, not all individual consumers are aware of this economic opportunity, and if they are, they are not always trading their data in a transparent and fair market environment. Moreover, they do not always know what the implications are of what they are consenting to when they sign a contract. We simply cannot assume that the conditions of the developing market for personal data guarantee fair transactions by independent standards. Data protection laws should be put in place in order to guarantee equality and a fair market for personal data. Data protection laws in these types of cases typically protect individual citizens by requiring openness, transparency, participation and notification on the part of business firms and direct marketeers to secure fair contracts.

Informational Injustice

A third and important moral reason to justify the protection of personal data is concerned with justice in a sense which is associated with the work of the political philosopher Michael Walzer.

Michael Walzer has objected to the simplicity of Rawls' conception of primary goods and universal rules of distributive justice by pointing out that

35

'there is no set of basic goods across all moral and material worlds, or they would have to be so abstract that they would be of little use in thinking about particular distributions' (1983, p.8). Goods have no natural meaning, their meaning is the result of socio-cultural construction and interpretation. In order to determine what is a just distribution of the good, we have to determine what it means to those for whom it is a good. In the medical, the political, the commercial spheres there are different goods (medical treatment, political office, money) which are allocated by means of different allocative or distributive practices: medical treatment on the basis of need; political office on the basis of desert; and money on the basis of free exchange. What ought to be prevented, and often is prevented as a matter of fact, is dominance of particular goods. Walzer calls a good dominant if the individuals that have it, because they have it, can command a wide range of other goods. A monopoly is a way of controlling certain social goods in order to exploit their dominance. In that case advantages in one sphere can be converted as a matter of course to advantages in other spheres. This happens when money (commercial sphere) could buy you a vote (political sphere) and would give you preferential treatment in health care (medical), would get you a university degree (educational), etc. We resist the dominance of money – and other social goods for that matter (land, physical strength) – and think that political arrangements allowing for it are unjust. No social good X should be distributed to men and women who possess some other good Y merely because they possess Y and without regard to the meaning of X.

What is especially offensive to our sense of justice, Walzer argues, is the allocation of goods internal to sphere A on the basis of the distributive logic or the allocation scheme associated with sphere B; secondly, the transfer of goods across the boundaries of separate spheres; and, thirdly, the dominance and tyranny of some goods over others. In order to prevent this, the 'art of separation' of spheres has to be practised, and 'blocked exchanges' between them have to be put in place. If the art of separation is effectively practised and the autonomy of the spheres of justice is guaranteed, then 'complex equality' is established. One's status in terms of the holdings and properties in one sphere are irrelevant – ceteris paribus – to the distribution of the goods internal to another sphere.

Walzer's analysis also applies to information, I claim. The meaning and value of information are local, and allocative schemes and local practices that distribute access to information should accommodate local meanings and should therefore be associated with specific spheres. Many people do not object to the use of their personal medical data for medical purposes, whether these are directly related to their own personal health affairs, to those of their family, perhaps even to their community or the world population at large, as long as they can be absolutely certain that the only use that is made of the data is to cure people from diseases. They do object, however, to their medical data

Jeroen van den Hoven

being used to disadvantage them socio-economically, to discriminate against them in the workplace, refuse them commercial services, deny them social benefits, or turn them down for mortgages or political office on the basis of their medical records. They do not mind if their library search data are used to provide them with better library services, but they do mind if these data are used to criticise their tastes and character. They would also object to informational cross-contaminations when they would benefit from them, as when the librarian might advise them of a book on low-fat meals on the basis of knowledge of their medical record and cholesterol values, or a doctor might pose questions on the basis of the information that one has borrowed a book from the public library about AIDS.

We may thus distinguish another form of informational wrongdoing: 'informational injustice', that is, disrespect for the boundaries of what we may refer to, following Michael Walzer, as 'spheres of justice' or 'spheres of access'. I think that what is often seen as a violation of privacy is often more adequately construed as the morally inappropriate transfer of data across the boundaries of what we intuitively think of as separate 'spheres of justice' or 'spheres of access.'

Spheres of Access

This construal of constraints on access to personal information in terms of social spheres[3] captures an important aspect of what people find threatening and problematic about information technology: the fact that it facilitates the violation, blurring or annihilation of boundaries between separate social realms or provinces of meaning. Several moral philosophers and sociologists have written about social differentiation using the intuitively plausible but somewhat nondescript notion of social 'spheres', 'domains' or 'fields'. The massive literature on social differentiation may provide us with useful insights into how social reality is carved up and how information management is practised in order to maintain the integrity and functional unity of what Walzer refers to as spheres of justice. Although there are differences in vocabularies, sociologists and philosophers including Erving Goffman, Bourdieu and Luhman and Walzer have made very much the same point about the separateness, segregation, autonomy and integrity of audiences, fields and systems, domains and spheres.

According to Pierre Bourdieu, in highly differentiated societies the social cosmos is made up of a number of such relatively 'autonomous social microcosms' or 'fields', such as the artistic field, the religious field, the economic field, which all follow specific logics and are irreducible to each other. A field is a network of objective relations between agents or institutions (positions), which are defined by their present/potential situation (situs) in the structure of distribution of species of power (or capital). One's place in this relational space determines one's access to the specific profits that are at stake in the field. The question of the delineation of the boundaries of the field is a very difficult one, if only because it is always at stake in the field itself. Boundaries can only be determined by an empirical investigation. It is only by studying them that you can assess how concretely they are constituted, where they stop, who gets in and who does not, and whether at all they form a field.

Michael Philips, following Walzer, proposes a moral theory on the basis of the distinction between different social domains and the articulation of domain-specific standards: 'Domain-specific standards regulate activities and relationships in specific domains of social life. Individuating by roles, examples of domains include the family, the educational system, the scientific community, the criminal justice system, the medical system, the economic system, the political system, and so forth' (Philips, 1994, pp. 95 ff).

There are also core standards, which regulate a single category of action across all domains. Philips takes the prohibition against lying as an example. The single category of action involved here is 'information exchange'. But there is no general standard 'do not lie'. Information exchange is regulated differently in different domains; there is a cluster of regulations governing information exchanges in various domains.

Seyla Benhabib has made a distinction between two types of communitarian thinking, integrationist and participatory (1992, pp. 77 ff). According to the former, only the recovery of a coherent value scheme can solve the problems of individualism, anomie, egotism and alienation in modern societies. Participationists see the problems of modernity not in fragmentation or a loss of belonging and solidarity but in a loss of political agency and efficacy. This loss may be a consequence, she surmises, of certain contradictions between the various spheres, which diminishes one's possibilities for agency in one sphere on the basis of one's position in another sphere (as, for example, when the right to vote is made dependent upon income). Social differentiation is not the problem that participationist communitarianism attempts to overcome; it is the reduction of contradictions and tensions between spheres and the articulation of non-exclusive principles of membership among the spheres (Benahabib, 1992, pp. 77-78).

Data protection, as a set of normative constraints on information exchange, is an instrument of the art of separation and the design of blocked exchanges, and an important rationale is that it can establish an interesting level of social justice, political agency and efficacy by diminishing the tensions among spheres and further complex equality.

Encroachment on Moral Autonomy

Information-based harm, informational inequality and informational injustice are the three types of moral reasons to protect personal data for both liberalists and communitarians. They are framed in moral terms which should be

Jeroen van den Hoven

acceptable to both liberalists and communitarians. One other reason for protecting personal data is what I think is the privacy concern in a strict sense.

I think that philosophical theories of privacy which account for its importance in terms of the moral autonomy,[4] i.e. the capacity to shape our own moral biographies, to reflect on our moral careers, to evaluate and identify with our own moral choices, without the critical gaze and interference of others and a pressure to conform to the 'normal' or socially desired identities, provides us with a bridging concept between the privacy notion and a liberalist conception of the self. Such a construal of privacy's importance, or core value, will limit the range of application of the privacy concept, but may invigorate its value, if the underlying conception of the self is vindicated. Privacy, conceived along these lines, would only provide protection to the individual in his quality of a moral person engaged in self-definition and self-improvement against the normative pressures which public opinions and moral judgments exert on the person to conform to a socially desired identity. Conformism is a real threat. Information about Bill, whether fully accurate or not, facilitates the formation of judgments about Bill. Judgments about Bill, when he learns about them, suspects that they are made, fears that they are made, may bring about a change in his view of himself, may induce him to behave differently than he would have done without. There are several mechanisms of what Von Wright referred to as 'normative pressure' operative here.[5]

To modern contingent individuals, who have cast aside the ideas of historical and religious necessity, living in a highly volatile socio-economic environment and a great diversity of audiences and settings before which they make their appearance, the fixation of one's moral identity by means of the judgments of others is felt as an obstacle to 'experiments in living', as Mill called them. The modern liberal individual wants to be able to determine himself morally or to undo his previous determinations, on the basis of more profuse experiences in life, or additional factual information.[6] Data protection laws can provide the leeway to do just that. Data protection laws thus provide protection against the fixation of one's moral identity by others than oneself and have the symbolic utility of conveying to citizens that they are morally autonomous.[7]

A further explanation for the importance of respect for moral autonomy may be provided along the following lines. Factual knowledge of another person is always knowledge by description. The person himself, however, does not only know the facts of his biography, but is the only person who is acquainted with the associated thoughts, desires and aspirations. However detailed and elaborate our files and profiles on Bill may be, we are never able to refer to the data-subject as he himself is able to do. We may only approximate his knowledge and self-understanding. Bernard Williams has pointed out that respecting a person involves 'identification' in a very special sense, which I refer to as 'moral identification', which has a static and a dynamic dimension:

> ...in professional relations and the world of work, a man operates,
> and his activities come up for criticism, under a variety of professional or
> technical titles, such as 'miner or 'agricultural labourer' or 'junior
> executive'. The technical or professional attitude is that which regards the
> man solely under that title, the human approach that which regards him
> as a man who has that title (among others), willingly, unwillingly,
> through lack of alternatives, with pride, etc. ...each man is owed an
> effort at identification: that he should not be regarded as the surface to
> which a certain label can be applied, but one should try to see the world
> including the label) from his point of view. (1973, p. 236)

Moral identification thus presupposes knowledge of the point of view of
the data-subject and a concern with what it is for a person to live that life.
Persons have aspirations, higher order evaluations and attitudes, and they see
the things they do in a certain light. Representation of this aspect of persons
seems exactly what is missing when personal data are piled up in our databases
and persons are represented in administrative procedures.[8] The identifications
made on the basis of our data fall short of respecting the individual person,
because they will never match the identity as it is experienced by the data-
subject. It fails because it does not conceive of the other on his own terms.
Respect for privacy of persons can thus be seen to have a distinctly epistemic
dimension. It represents an acknowledgment that it is impossible really to
know other persons as they know and experience themselves. Even if we could
get it right about moral persons at any given point in time, by exhibit of
extraordinary empathy and attention, then it is highly questionable whether
the data-subject's experience of himself, as far as the dynamics of the moral
person are concerned, can be captured and adequately represented. The person
conceives of himself as trying to improve himself morally. The person cannot
be identified, not even in the sense articulated by Bernard Williams, with
something limited, definite and unchanging. This point was made by the
French existentialist Gabriel Marcel: '...il faudra dire que la personne ne saurait
etre assimilee en aucune maniere a un objet dont nous pouvons dire qu'il est
la, c'est-a-dire qu'il est donne, present devant nous, qu'il fait partie d'une
collection par essence denombrable, ou encore qu'il est un element
statistique...' (1944, p. 31).[9]

The person always sees itself as becoming, as something that has to be
overcome, not as a fixed reality, but as something in the making, something that
has to be improved upon: 'Elle se saisit bien moins comme etre que comme
volonte de depasser ce que tout ensemble elle est et elle n'est pas, une actualite
dans laquelle elle se sent a vrai dire engagee ou implique, mais qui ne la satisfait
pas: qui n'est pas a la mesure de l'aspiration avec laquelle elle s'identifie' (Marcel,
p. 32). As Marcel puts it, the individual's motto is not *sum* (I am) but *sursum*
(higher). The human person has a tendency not to be satisfied, but he or she is

Jeroen van den Hoven

always aspiring to improve him or herself, always on his or her way, homo viator.[10]

It is clear that this construal of privacy implies a disengaged, unsituated and 'punctual' self. At the end of his very perceptive paper on privacy and intelligent vehicle highway systems (Reiman, 1997, pp. 182–183) Jeffrey Reiman observes that there is a profound link between liberalism, privacy and conceptions of the self: 'The liberal vision is guided by the ideal of the autonomous individual, the one who acts on principles that she has accepted after critical review, rather than simply absorbing them unquestioned from outside. Moreover, the liberal stresses the importance of people making sense of their own lives... and has an implicit trust in the transformational and ameliorative possibilities of private inner life.'

Communitarians have always felt themselves comfortably supported by Aristotle in their critique of this liberalist conception of the individual and its relation to the community. Aristotle has traditionally been interpreted as exalting the community and public realm over the private and the individual. Judith Swanson persuasively argues, however, that privacy plays an important role in Aristotle's political philosophy. In her attempted historical reconstruction she articulates an interesting position on privacy and the self that could satisfy both communitarians and liberalists. The rationale of privacy for Aristotle is to enable one to turn away in order to achieve moral excellence. Insofar as private activity requires pulling away from the drag of common opinion, the public should foster privacy, that is, not sites but activities that cultivate virtue without accommodating or conforming to common opinion.[11]

I have tried to give a broad and revisionary account of moral reasons for data protection. Protecting privacy here is proposed as a way of acknowledging our systematic inability to identify the data-subject as being the same as the moral self with which the data-subject identifies himself in his sincere attempts to reflect upon what is good and right. Justifying data protection on grounds of privacy is to ask for a 'moral time out', that is, not a time out from morality, but a time out from the prevailing social morality. It can be granted only if and insofar as it is used for moral reflection and self-improvement. Communitarians and guardians of the public good should now decide what the best way is to pursue the dream of perfect free-riderlessness, sticks or carrots.

Notes

1. For the distinction between 'credentials' and 'ordeals', see Steven L. Nock (1993), *The Costs of Privacy, Surveillance and Reputation in America.* Aldine de Gruyter, New York.

2. I first proposed this in a seminar at the University of Virginia in the summer of 1996. I thank Judi Decew, Jim Childress, Joe Kupfer for their comments.

3. Ferdinand Schoeman (1992) (*Privacy and Social Freedom*, Cambridge) introduced the notion of 'spheres of access' or 'spheres of life' in the privacy literature. He contends that different domains of life deserve protection from various kinds of intrusion (p. 157): 'We can begin to think about a sphere of life by identifying a sphere as defined by an associational tie. One important function of privacy is to help maintain both the integrity of intimate spheres as against more public spheres and the integrity of various public spheres in relation to one another'. Geoffrey Brown (1989) (*The Information Game: Ethics in a Microchip World*, New York) has proposed along these lines that access to particular information about person P should be systematically related in the appropriate way to the network of social relationships in which P stands to others, by virtue of their place in the role structure. An invasion of privacy can be said to have occurred wherever the flow of information becomes divorced from the social role structure, what Brown labels a 'Short Circuit Effect'. According to Brown, privacy is important because it allows one to manage one's role identity. If someone accepts a particular social role (P acts as a doctor; P gives a lecture; P borrows a book in the public library), this person thereby assents to the appropriateness of an associated pattern of information exchange.

4. Joe Kupfer (1987) has made a similar proposal in his 'Privacy, Autonomy and Self-concept', *American Philosophical Quarterly*, Vol. 24, No. 1 pp. 81–89. Privacy, according to Kupfer, enables '...self-knowledge, self-criticism, and self-evaluation. This sort of control over self-concept and self is a second-order autonomy.'

5. Judith DeCew (1997) has also identified the prevention of 'pressure to conform' as one of the important rationales of privacy protection: *In Pursuit of Privacy*, Cornell University Press, Ithaca, NY.

6. Kierkegaard (1986) identified 'irony' as the originating concept of the modern individual; it is the 'liberty of the subject to refuse any determination proposed to him or projected onto him. It is absolute freedom: the capacity to say No without limit and without qualification'. See L. Mackey, *Points of View: Readings of Kierkegaard*, University Presses of Florida, Tallahassee, p. 133.

7. For the notion of 'symbolic utility', see Robert Nozick (1993), *The Nature of Rationality*, Princeton University Press, Princeton, NJ.

8. See Protection of Personal Data Used for Employment Purposes, Council of Europe, Recommendation No. R (89) 2, adopted by the Committee of Ministers on 18 January 1989, article 2: '...respect for human dignity relates to the need to avoid statistical dehumanisation by undermining the identity of employees through data-processing techniques which allow for profiling of employees or the taking of decisions based on automatic processing which concern them' (Explanatory Memorandum, para. 25). Quoted by B.W. Napier (1992), "The Future of Information Technology Law", *Cambridge Law Journal*, Vol. 51, No. 1, p. 64.

9. Gabriel Marcel (1944), *Homo Viator*, Paris: Aubier, Editions Montaigne, p. 31. This neatly accommodates the fact that in French criminal law statistical evidence relating to persons is not allowed in court. I thank Daniele Bourcier for pointing this out to me.

10. This is only part of Marcel's diagnosis of the modern subject. His work is in part a way of remedying its deficiencies.

11. Swanson notes: '...in Aristotle's view, every human being has a right to privacy insofar as everyone from children to the slavish to the philosophical should be granted ...opportunities to cultivate the most virtue of which they are capable. But this right may sometimes require denying some persons (for example, children, law breakers) freedom to make choices, or it may circumscribe their choices; and it does not grant the eligible merely the freedom to choose, but also the resources and thus the encouragement or direction to choose virtuously'. (1992, p. 7, n. 17).

References

Benahabib, S. (1992). *Situating the Self.* Routledge, New York.

De Jasay, A. (1989). *Social Contract, Free Ride: A Study of the Public Goods.* Clarendon Press, Oxford.

Gandy, O.H. (1993). *The Panoptic Sort: A Political Economy of Personal Information.* Westview Press, Boulder, CO; Rowman and Littlefield, London.

Gauthier, D. (1986). *Morals by Agreement.* Oxford University Press, Oxford.

Gottlieb, C., (1996) 'Privacy: A Concept Whose Time Has Come and Gone' in Lyon and Zureik (eds), *Computer, Surveillance and Privacy.* University of Minnesota Press, Minneapolis, MN.

Philips, M. (1994). *Between Universalism and Skepticism: Ethics as Social Artifact.* Oxford University Press, Oxford.

Reiman, J. (1997) in 'Driving to the Panopticon: A Philosophical Exploration of the Risks to Privacy Posed by the Information Technology of the Future', *Critical Moral Liberalism.* Rowman and Littlefield, Lanham, MD, pp. 169–188.

Swanson, J.A. (1992). *The Public and the Private in Aristotle's Political Philosophy.* Cornell University Press, Ithaca, NY.

Walzer, M., (1983) *Spheres of Justice.* Basil Blackwell, Oxford.

Walzer, M. (1995). ' The Communitarian Critique of Liberalism' in A. Etzioni (ed.), *New Communitarian Thinking.* University of Virginia Press, Charlottesville, VA.

Williams, B. (1973). *Problems of the Self.* Cambridge University Press, Cambridge.

[30]

PROTECTING PRIVACY IN AN INFORMATION AGE: THE PROBLEM OF PRIVACY IN PUBLIC

HELEN NISSENBAUM

INTRODUCTION

There is growing awareness as well as resentment of the routine practice of recording, analyzing, and communicating information about individuals as they act and transact in the normal course of their commercial and public lives. The information in question is taken into the possession of and used by whomever collects it and from there may be transmitted – usually electronically, usually for fee or favor – to others – second parties, third parties, fourth parties, and so on. While philosophical theories have long acknowledged the relationship between privacy and information about persons, and have argued for limits on allowable practices of information gathering, analyzing, and sharing as a means of protecting privacy, their efforts have primarily applied to intimate and sensitive information.

While not denying the importance of protecting intimate and sensitive information, this paper insists that theories of privacy should also recognize the systematic relationship between privacy and information that is neither intimate nor sensitive and is drawn from public spheres. The significance of this information for privacy has emerged in recent decades as a result of contemporary surveillance practices enabled by advances in information technology, creating what I here call the problem of privacy in public.[2] As

---

[1] I am grateful to many colleagues who generously contributed to this paper with excellent comments and suggestions: Phil Agre, Judith Wagner DeCew, Jodi Halpern, David Heyd, Jerry Kang, John Kleinig, Gary Marx, David Orentlicher, Kristen Shrader-Frechette, Jeroen van den Hoven, and Tom Vogt. I am also indebted to anonymous reviewers for *Law and Philosophy* for careful reading and several wise suggestions.

[2] Anita Allen recently drew my attention to a discussion in Allen, A., *Uneasy Access* (Totowa, New Jersey: Rowman & Littlefield, 1988), Chapter 5, in which

observed in 1985 by Larry Hunter, a computer scientist, "Our revolution will not be in gathering data – don't look for TV cameras in your bedroom – but in analyzing the information that is already willingly shared."[3]

In the course of this paper I will argue that privacy in public, which in the past has been explicitly excluded or merely neglected by many of the most highly-regarded and often-cited philosophical and legal works on privacy, is a genuine privacy interest that is worthy of study as well as protection.

The discussion proceeds as follows. After surveying circumstances and activities that give rise to the problem of privacy in public, I offer an explanation for why predominant and influential theoretical accounts of privacy have failed to deal explicitly with it. Following this, in what may be seen as the core of the paper, I identify the features of contemporary surveillance practices that are central to viewing these practices as genuine concerns for any normative theory of privacy. In the concluding sections of the paper, I consider how we may absorb privacy in public into comprehensive theories of privacy. Although I do not provide such a theory myself, I suggest that resources are already present in some existing theories – for example, in work by Ferdinand Schoeman and, more recently, by Judith DeCew.[4] I also clear the way for such a theory by showing how certain barriers that, in the past, have seemed insurmountable may be overcome.

---

she discusses whether, and when, it is reasonable to expect that privacy will be respected in public spaces. She argues that even in public places like hiking trails, subway cars, or bars, people ought to be free of invasive surveillance. She also considers sexual harassment in public spaces and the public display of pornography to be activities that violate privacy in public. Also, see Helen Nissenbaum, "Toward an approach to privacy in public: the challenges of information technology," *Ethics and Behavior* 7 (3) (1997), pp. 207–219, where I introduce the concept of privacy in public.

[3] Larry Hunter, "Public Image," *Whole Earth Review* (January, 1985). Reprinted in Deborah Johnson and Helen Nissenbaum, *Computers, Ethics, and Social Values* (Englewood Cliffs: Prentice Hall, 1995), p. 294.

[4] In their various writings but see, especially, Judith Wagner DeCew, *In Pursuit of Privacy: Law, Ethics, and the Rise of Technology* (Ithaca: Cornell University Press, 1997) and Ferdinand Schoeman, *Privacy and Social Freedom* (Cambridge: Cambridge University Press, 1992).

I. THE PROBLEM OF PRIVACY IN PUBLIC

My interest in the problem of protecting privacy in public is motivated by circumstances in the real world that are obviously problematic for most people, and have frequently been reported in public and popular mass media.[5] These circumstances are that even, and especially, in the public arena, people have become targets of surveillance at just about every turn of their lives. In transactions with retailers, mail order companies, medical care givers, daycare providers, and even beauty parlors, information about them is collected, stored, analyzed and sometimes shared. Their presence on the planet, their notable features and all their momentous milestones are dutifully recorded by agencies of federal, state and local government including birth, marriage, divorce, property ownership, driver's licenses, vehicle registration, moving violations, parenthood, and, finally, their demise. Into the great store of information, people are identified through name, address, phone number, credit card numbers, social security number, passport number, and more; they are described by age, hair color, eye color, height, quality of vision, mail orders and on site purchases, credit card activity, travel, employment history, rental history, real estate transactions, change of address,[6] ages and numbers of children, and magazine subscriptions.[7] The dimensions are endless.

In several ways, information technology is essentially implicated in this relentless gathering of information. In the first place, computerized databases have provided for it the right kind of home. Information that is drawn from the physical world is harbored

---

[5] For example, see "Goals Clash in Shielding Privacy," *The New York Times*, October 28, 1997, "In Prison, Free to Get Information," *The New York Times*, October 20, 1997, "On Line, High-Tech Sleuths Find Private Facts," *The New York Times*, September 15, 1997, *No More Privacy: All About You*, Films for the Humanities and Sciences, Inc., Princeton: 1993. "The Death of Privacy," *Time*, August 25, 1997, Col. 150 No. 8.

[6] H. Jeff Smith, in *Managing Privacy: Information Technology and Corporate America* (Chapel Hill: The University of North Carolina Press, 1994), reports that post offices release lists to owners of target marketing consisting of the names and addresses of individuals who complete National Change of Address cards.

[7] Molecular biologists predict that one day, in the not too distant future, a computer chip will be capable or recording each individual's complete DNA sequence in something analogous to a bar-code.

562   HELEN NISSENBAUM

in electronic databases, which give these records the permanence, malleability and transportability that has become the trademark of information technology. Without information technology, the gatherers and users of information would be able neither to conduct surveillance (that is, gather the data), nor create databases of great magnitude and power, nor extract the information that motivates these activities. Roughly forty years ago, this application of information technology to the creation of computerized databases mainly by government and other large organizations, was the first to attract concern among policy analysts, journalists and fiction writers.

In the unfolding of recent developments in information technology, and especially comprehensive digital electronic networks, there is another means by which information may be harvested. In contemporary, technologically advanced societies, it is commonplace for large sectors of populations to participate, in varying degrees, in electronically networked interactions. Governments, as well as individual and institutional agents of the private sector, encourage such participation by their explicit expressions of approval, by progressively increasing the ease of access, as well as speed and declining prices (for example, through the World Wide Web), and at the same time creating the possibility for more and more to be done by electronic means. Once in the electronic sphere, the tracks of people's activities may be recorded directly into electronic databases. Electronic transactions, even carefree meanderings (popularly referred to as "browsing" and "surfing") may be captured and recorded.[8] Information like email addresses, system characteristics, and a trail of network-based activities are not only effortlessly recorded, but easily combined with information from the physical world. In this activity information technology is doubly implicated

---

[8] One of the devices for doing so, affectionately called "cookies", is coming under fire from perspectives both of security and privacy. Cookies are small programs that are transmitted from one site to another (usually from a web page to a web browser) for the purpose of conveying information about a user's system configuration, usage information, as well as other information that a user voluntarily provides to the cookie.

as it acts as the medium for transactions as well as repository for the information.[9]

In addition to these two means by which information technology facilitates surveillance, there is yet another layer of surveillance that builds upon them. Where most of the activities earlier described involved the collecting of information by an agency, organization, or individual with whom a person interacts directly, this new layer involves secondary users and suppliers who acquire information from other sources, either the primary sources or other secondary sources. These secondary, or second-order purveyors of information include credit bureaus – and the so-called "super-bureaus" – medical insurance bureaus, and list brokers.[10] Although some of the information supplied to agents of secondary collection is drawn from the private sector, including banks, credit card companies, and retailers, much is drawn from government records. No longer is it necessary to send a person to a court house to copy these records, painstakingly, into databases.

The electronic format offers great convenience and flexibility; databases may be searched for individual records or entire databases may be transferred via digital electronic networks. Some government agencies are fast understanding that their computerized records may be a source of significant revenue.[11] But even when they have balked at the idea of releasing information electronically, courts have forced them to do so.[12] Secondary harvesting of information is held deeply under suspicion not only because it is seen as the significant driver of the unquenchable thirst for information about persons as well as its seemingly endless supply, but also because people perceive it to be illegitimate. This uncontrolled harvesting of public information has not escaped the notice of scholars and advocates of policy, who consider it a serious problem for

---

[9] Partly because of this, the battle over encryption is so hard fought, with privacy advocates arguing that access to the full capabilities of encryption should be available to individuals.

[10] For example, TRW Credit Data, Equifax and Trans Union, the three major (super) credit bureaus.

[11] See Iver Peterson, "Public Information, Business Rates: State Agencies Turn Data Base Record Into Cash Cows," *The New York Times*, July 14, 1997.

[12] Higg-A-Rella, Inc. v. County of Essex; 141 N.J. 35 (1985).

privacy that public as well as corporate policy has not adequately addressed.

Although the privacy concerns of data subjects have not been completely ignored in the policy arena, they are more often noticed as a result of a highly publicized media event than as a result of thoughtful public deliberation over the need for privacy. A case in point is the Video Privacy Protection Act (known commonly as the "Bork Bill"). When a national newspaper published the video rental records of Robert Bork during Senate Hearings for his nomination as Associate Justice for the Supreme Court, congress hastily responded with the Video Privacy Act.[13] The result is a body of policy that is piecemeal and inconsistent.[14]

As disturbing as the practices of public surveillance are, they seem to fall outside the scope of predominant theoretical approaches to privacy, which have concerned themselves primarily with two aspects of privacy – namely, maintaining privacy against intrusion into the intimate, private realms, and protecting the privacy of individuals against intrusion by agents of government. Philosophical and legal theories of privacy offer little by way of an explicit justificatory framework for dealing with the problem of privacy in public. Indeed, with only a few exceptions, work within these traditions appears to suffer a theoretical blind spot when it comes to privacy in public, for while it has successfully advanced our understanding of the moral basis for privacy from some of the traditionally conceived threats, such as violation of the personal sphere, abuse of intimate information, protection of the private individual against government intrusion, and protection of, say doctor-patient, lawyer-

---

[13] In *Managing Privacy*, H. Jeff Smith describes a parallel situation in the business world where corporate policy on privacy is fragmented and not always internally consistent. One company's privacy policies, usually devised in isolation from those of other companies, may differ enormously in what they allow and disallow with the information they gather. They frequently do not admit to being driven by any underlying "right to privacy," but prefer to portray their policies as being driven by prudence and public perception. Corporations continue to resist public policy that would impose governmental regulation on their use of information about persons.

[14] See Smith, *Managing Privacy*, and Priscilla M. Regan, *Legislating Privacy: Technology, Social Values and Public Policy* (Chapel Hill: The University of North Carolina Press, 1995).

client and similar special relationships, it has not kept abreast of the privacy issues that have developed in the wake of advanced uses of information technology.

Although Hunter, in the passage quoted earlier, may have understated the extent to which the sheer growth in data gathering affects privacy and the extent to which technological means allows intrusion into and surveillance of even private, enclosed spaces,[15] he accurately predicted not only that *analysis* of information will be a major source of privacy invasion, but that because the information analyzed is willingly shared, people are, in some sense, complicit in the violation of their own privacy. Accordingly, although the traditional topics covered by philosophical discussions remain important both for their historical significance and their present urgency and seriousness, they no longer cover the full extent of a need for privacy protection in our information age where the practice of public surveillance, record keeping, and information analysis seems to be growing not only without apparent limit but so completely out of the control of those who are its subjects.

This paper's emphasis on theoretical and conceptual foundations of privacy – not public or business policy – does not preclude consideration of important practical implications. In particular, I would suggest that the absence of a clearly articulated philosophical base is not of theoretical interest only, but is at least partially responsible for the inconsistencies, discontinuities and fragmentation, and incompleteness in the framework of legal protections and in public and corporate policy. It may be useful to consider the practical import of an inadequately developed conceptual scheme in terms of an actual case – the case of Lotus Marketplace.

In April 1990, Lotus Development Corporation, a developer and marketer of popular software, and Equifax Inc., one of the "big three" companies that collect and sell information about consumer financial transactions,[16] announced their intention to produce a database called "Lotus Marketplace: Households" which would contain actual and inferred information about approximately 120 million individuals in the United States. It would include name, address, type of dwelling, marital status, gender, age, household income,

---

[15] In legal terms, what may be referred to as a person's "curtilage".

[16] The other two are TRW and Trans Union Credit Information.

566 HELEN NISSENBAUM

lifestyle, and purchasing propensity. The two companies expected the database, which was to have been recorded and sold in the format of a CD-ROM, to be widely adopted by marketers and mailing companies.[17] Grassroots opposition, including an estimated 30,000 letters of protest, led company executives to announce, in January 1991, that they were canceling the project. Even as privacy advocates and individual participants trumpeted victory for privacy, executives insisted that their actions were prompted only by negative publicity and public misunderstanding and not by a conviction of wrongdoing. They insisted that their product would not have violated privacy.

Though hailed as a victory for privacy, the legacy of Lotus Marketplace Households for the course of data gathering has been negligible; current practices far surpass it in scope and magnitude. This result suggests that in the absence of well understood and clearly articulated normative principles, the decision to withdraw Lotus Marketplace Households, by itself, provides a scant basis for dealing with subsequent challenges.[18] There was no common agreement that here was an effort that violated privacy, or an understanding of the reasons why it violated privacy. The same may be said for the other individual victories that the dogged efforts of policy advocates have yielded. With no underlying thread to tie one effort to another, each must be fought on its own terms; the fate of privacy in public remains in the hands of those with the most energy and with the strongest lobbies; it does not reflect underlying values at all.

II. WHY PRIVACY IN PUBLIC IS DISMISSED

Before responding directly to the challenge of producing principles by which Lotus Marketplace Households and similar efforts may be judged violations of privacy, I consider the reasons why many influential philosophical theories of privacy may not have addressed

---

[17] Other industry analysts were also very encouraging. An interesting example is Esther Dyson, now head of the Electronic Frontier Foundation, in "Data is Dandy," *Forbes* (April, 1990), p. 180.

[18] Helen Nissenbaum, "Toward an Approach to Privacy in Public: Challenges of Information Technology".

directly the cluster of issues raised by widespread public surveillance. If privacy in public *does* constitute a genuine privacy interest, then not only is it important to construct the much needed justificatory framework, but also to ask why philosophical and normative theories of privacy have either explicitly dismissed the idea of any genuine privacy interest in public, or merely have overlooked it.[19]

A variety of factors have shaped normative theories of privacy, making them more responsive to some types of problems and constraints and less responsive to others. Examining these theories with a view to understanding why specifically they either neglect or dismiss the normative force of privacy in public, three factors (there may be others) emerge, which I have labeled, respectively, conceptual, normative, and empirical.

Conceptual

To many, the idea that privacy may be violated in public has an oddly paradoxical ring. One likely source of this response is the way the terms "public" and "private" have been used in political and legal theory. Although their respective meanings may vary from one context to another (and I take it this assertion is relatively uncontroversial among scholars in these areas), the terms are almost always used as a way to demarcate a strict dichotomy of realms.[20] In some contexts, for example, the term "private" indicates the realm of familial and other personal or intimate relations, while the term "public" indicates the civic realm or realm of community outside

---

[19] I should qualify. First, there are elements in existing theories, even those that do not directly address the problem of privacy in public, that I will show are relevant to it. Second, several writers have written about privacy in ways that overlap with my concern with "privacy in public." As mentioned earlier, these include Ferdinand Schoeman and Judith DeCew. Specific references to their works are given in subsequent footnotes.

[20] I do not mean to suggest that there is universal agreement among scholars either about the strictness of the dichotomy or the meaning of the respective concepts. Stanley J. Benn and Gerald F. Gauss (eds.), *Public and Private in Social Life* (London and Canberra: St. Martin's Press, 1983), suggest that although the concepts of private and public serve to organize norms of access, agency and interest, the dichotomy is not as clear and consistent as some would have us believe. For example, a context can be conceived as both public and private: for example, a living room in a house is considered private in relation to the outside, but public in relation to bedrooms in the house.

of this personal one. In some contexts, "public" indicates the realm of governmental institutions in contrast with the realm of "private" citizens or "private" institutions (such as corporations). In relation to law, the term "private" generally marks a distinctive area dedicated to settling scores between people in their capacities as private citizens, in contrast with "public" law, which generally covers disputes in which officials or agencies of government are involved. In a similar vein Judith W. DeCew observes,

> The public/private distinction has sometimes been taken to reflect differences between the appropriate scope of government, as opposed to self-regulation by individuals. It has also been interpreted to differentiate political and domestic spheres of life. These diverse linguistic descriptions capture overlapping yet nonequivalent concepts. Nevertheless they share the assumption that there is a boundary marking off that which is private from that which is public.[21]

For the majority of theorists, it follows seamlessly that the concept and value of privacy corresponds with, or applies to, the sphere of the private alone. In the past few decades, therefore, the issues most vigorously pursued in philosophical and legal work on privacy, the defenses of privacy most thoroughly articulated, are remarkably consonant with these dichotomies – as I briefly illustrate below.

Following the lines of the private/public dichotomy as it identifies distinctive realms of individual citizens and private sector institutions versus governmental agents and institutions, there is a substantial body of work by philosophers, as well as legal and political theorists, scholars and advocates of policy, and novelists, who have viewed privacy as an effective way to keep government out of the lives of private individuals and institutions. Historically, this impulse has made perfect sense in light of government's enthusiasm for using computerized databases as a means of storing records of information about people. Certainly government had the resources and manpower as well as the need to apply the power of computing to the substantial corpus of personal information that it routinely collects.[22] In 1965, when, in the name of efficiency and efficacy, the

---

[21] Judith DeCew, *In Pursuit of Privacy: Law, Ethics, and the Rise of Technology*, p. 10.

[22] David Heyd pointed out to me, the word "statistics" is derived from the word "state". Government involvement in the practice of collecting information about populations, such as in census-taking, goes back many centuries, and is

Social Science Research Council, proposed a Federal Data Center to coordinate government statistical information, critics were immediately alert to the political and personal threat implicit in this proposal.[23]

A great deal of the research and scholarship on privacy that immediately followed this period focused on privacy as a means of maintaining the traditionally valued balance of power between government and private individuals. This work connects the concept and value of privacy with the considerable body of theoretical work on the relationship of individuals in political society to government. It has been able to promote the value of privacy by showing that privacy is an important means by which individuals may sustain power, liberty, and autonomy against potentially overwhelming forces of government. Being able to draw on traditional thinking about the balance of power, has helped advocates and scholars gain support for public policy to constrain and control government record-keeping practices. Powerful fictional images such as Big Brother, developed in George Orwell's novel *1984*, together with observed experiences of life under totalitarian regimes, have lent credence to the practical efforts of privacy advocates.

In parallel with the private/public dichotomy that marks distinct realms of the intimate or sensitive, on the one hand, and the non-intimate, on the other, there is a considerable body of work by philosophers and others argues for protection of intimate and sensitive realms against intrusion by government or any other individual or collective agent. This work assumes the existence of distinctive realms of the personal, familial, and intimate, on the one hand, contrasted with the public, on the other. Scholars interested in this form of privacy protection emphasize the importance of a realm to which people may go, from which others are excluded. They

---

even discussed in the Bible. Alan Westin, *Privacy and Freedom* (New York: Atheneum, 1965), Priscilla Regan, *Legislating Privacy*, and Kenneth Laudon, *Dossier Society: Value Choices in the Design of National Information Systems* (New York: Columbia University Press: 1986) all discuss aspects of privacy protection against government intrusion.

[23] See Priscilla Regan, *Legislating Privacy: Technology, Social Values, and Public Policy*, for an excellent discussion of privacy policy. Regan pinpoints the SSRC's 1965 proposal as a key point in the history of privacy policy with respect to records of information about people.

conceive of this realm in terms of a secure physical space, in terms of a private psychological space, or even in terms of a class of information that is sensitive or intimate over which one would have supreme control.

Those who emphasize the importance of an intimate zone or sphere would say that defending the integrity of this private realm is a means of enhancing other goods, such as autonomy, liberty, personal relationships, and trust. Defenders suggest these goods may be either necessarily or empirically dependent on an individual's having sovereignty over an intimate realm.[24] Thus, theorists invest privacy with value by showing that privacy preserves these universally recognized values.

In this section, I have tried to show that the dichotomy between private and public naturally leads to certain lines of inquiry into privacy. While the dichotomy between public and private has yielded some important insights into the role and value of privacy, it has diverted attention from others. It does so by establishing conceptual categories that are not only hard to bridge but carry with them the implication that privacy is an interest we need protect in the private realm alone and, by implication, that privacy in public makes little sense at all. To the extent that a public-private dichotomy drives the direction of theory and policy, it naturally leads to a concentration on the private sphere alone and – mistakenly, I think – has made the idea of privacy in public seem paradoxical.

Normative

If conceptions of the public-private dichotomy have implicitly or explicitly affected the agenda for privacy theory by placing some issues in the limelight and others backstage, modes of normative argumentation have lent plausibility to certain dimensions of the privacy interest while seeming to expose others as indefensible. Claims for the protection of privacy in public have fallen into the second category as they have appeared fatally vulnerable to a

---

[24] Julie Innes in her book, *Privacy, Intimacy and Isolation* (New York and Oxford: Oxford University Press, 1992) articulates one such view of privacy in which intimacy is a defining charactersitic. Also, see Nissenbaum, "An Approach to Privacy In Public," for a fuller discussion of approaches to privacy that have focused on privacy as a protection for the intimate realm.

persistent and apparently "knock-down" objection which refers to overriding competing interests. How so?

It is common for theorists and advocates of privacy to agree that while privacy is an important interest it must be balanced against other, competing interests. (This strategy is, of course, not unique to privacy.) While theorists, in their distinctive ways, have argued that privacy ought to be protected, they have understood that protecting privacy for one person inevitably leads to restraints on the freedom of another or others, or may even result in harms to them. Even those generally sympathetic to the idea of a moral right to privacy have been ready to moderate the exercise of this right in light of some of these competing claims. Privacy in public is frequently a victim of such balancing as it regularly succumbs to the apparently overwhelming weight of competing interests.

A crisp version of this objection may be found in Jeffrey Reiman's paper, "Privacy, Intimacy and Personhood."[25] Reiman, who characterizes privacy as a social practice involving "a complex of behaviors that stretches from refraining from asking questions about what is none of one's business to refraining from looking into open windows one passes on the street"[26] and who argues that privacy is essential for the formation of a conception of the self, nevertheless concedes that the social practice of privacy "does not assert the right never to be seen even on a crowded street."[27] This concession, in one form or another, is at bottom of the persistent normative objection that has so effectively blocked attempts to protect privacy in public.

The power of this widely used rejoinder rests in a foundation of considerations that have been intuitively compelling to many. One is that claims in favor of privacy in public affect information that is ostensibly innocuous, namely, information we would not normally judge to be sensitive or intimate. This being so, it does not take much for a person's claim to privacy with respect to this information to be outweighed by countervailing claims, even ones that themselves are not terribly weighty. Another consideration is that if people make

---

[25] Jeffrey Reiman, "Privacy, Intimacy and Personhood," *Philosophy & Public Affairs* 6 (1) (1976), pp. 26–44

[26] Reiman, "Privacy, Intimacy and Personhood," pp. 43–44.

[27] Reiman, "Privacy, Intimacy and Personhood," p. 44.

572   HELEN NISSENBAUM

no effort to cover, hide, or remove themselves, or information about themselves, from public view, if they willingly yield information into the public domain, then they have "let the cat out of the bag." It is unreasonable of them to think that, having let the information out, they can subsequently shift course and "get it" back, suppress it.[28] If, for example, you stroll downtown wearing a red sweater, then you have freely exposed the information that you were wearing a red sweater at a certain time and date. It is unreasonable to expect that this information may later be suppressed.

Not only is this unreasonable, but it is wrong because it imposes an unacceptable restraint on the freedom of others. If you have chosen to expose yourself and information about yourself in public view with the result that others have access to you, or to information about you without intruding upon your private realm, then any restrictions on what they may observe, record and do with this information cannot be justified. In the case of your red sweater, you could not, for example, expect others to avert their gaze so as not to see what you were wearing. You could not stop them remembering what you were wearing, nor prevent them from telling others about it. Such requirements would amount to an excessive restraint on the freedoms of others to observe, speak (about your red sweater), and possibly even profit from so doing. Applying the relevant phrase in legal discourse, a critic might say that because in a public area we have no "reasonable expectation of privacy," we have no right to limit access of others to the information we there expose.

These considerations have held enormous power in theoretical discussions of privacy and, to my knowledge, have rarely been directly challenged.[29] In Charles Fried's influential paper on privacy, for example, although he defends a robust moral and legal right to privacy, he is equally explicit about its limits. On the one hand he argues that a right to privacy, a right to control information about oneself, ought to be secured through law because: "By using the public, impersonal and ultimate institution of law

---

[28] The idea behind trade secrets is similar. A secret earns legal protection only if owners take adequate measures to keep it out of the public eye.

[29] Again, Schoeman, discussed later, is a notable exception. Also see Jeffrey Reiman, "Driving to the Panopticon: A Philosophical Exploration of the Risks to Privacy Posed by the Highway Technology of the Future," *Santa Clara Computer and High Technology Law Journal* (Volume 11, Number 1, March 1995).

to grant persons this control, we at once put the right to control as far beyond question as we can and at the same time show how seriously we take that right."[30] On the other hand, although a right to privacy would be recognized by law, it would extend only over a limited, conventionally designated, area of information, "symbolic of the whole institution of privacy".[31] According to Fried, this designated area, whose content may differ considerably from society to society, would include intimate or sensitive information, and exclude the so-called "public" sphere from its scope of protection. Fried's rationale for the "inevitable fact that privacy is gravely compromised in any concrete social system" is because of "the inevitably and utterly just exercise of rights by others ... ".[32]

For similar reasons, Larry Hunter grants that "although we consider it a violation of privacy to look in somebody's window and notice what they are doing, we have no problem with the reverse: someone sitting in his living room looking *out* his window."[33] Consequently, placing any restraint on such activity would constitute an unacceptable restraint on liberty – again a manifestation of the "knock down" normative argument.

In the practical arena, as well as in the theoretical realm, public surveillance is indignantly defended on grounds that it is unreasonable to prevent others from perceiving, noticing, and talking about the goings-on in public realms. This form of argument is favored for protecting the commercial interest in data collection. In the case of Lotus Marketplace Households, executives defending the proposed product, cited considerations like these. Denying legal or moral wrongdoing they argued that only information from the public domain would be used, no private realms would be breached, and no information deemed sensitive or intimate would be included.

Versions of the knock-down argument frequently appear in case law. In *California v. Greenwood*,[34] for example, which has been cited as a precedent in many subsequent cases involving (of all things) people's right to privacy in their garbage, the Supreme Court

---

[30] Charles Fried "Privacy," *The Yale Law Journal* (Volume 77), p. 493.

[31] Fried, "Privacy," pp. 488–489.

[32] Fried, "Privacy," p. 487.

[33] Larry Hunter, "Public Image," p. 295.

[34] 486 U.S. 35, 108 S.Ct. 1625, 100 L. Ed. 2d 30 (1988).

ruled that police had not violated the Fourth Amendment when they arranged for Greenwood's trash collector to segregate his trash and turn it over to them for inspection. The court majority offered the following consideration,

Accordingly, having deposited their garbage "in an area particularly suited for public inspection and, in a manner of speaking, public consumption, for the express purpose of having strangers take it," respondents could have no reasonable expectation of privacy in the inculpatory items that they discarded.[35]

In another case, *United States v. Scott*,[36] the court defended the actions of IRS agents, who had reassembled documents which the defendant had shredded into 5/32-inch strips before disposing of them in the garbage, arguing,

In our view, shredding garbage and placing it in the public domain subjects it to the same risks regarding privacy, as engaging in a private conversation in public where it is subject to the possibility that it may be overheard by other persons. Both are failed attempts at maintaining privacy whose failure can only be attributed to the conscious acceptance by the actor of obvious risk factors. In the case of the conversation, the risk is that conversation in a public area may be overheard by a third person. In the disposal of trash, the risk is that it may be rummaged through and deciphered once it leaves the control of the trasher. In both situations the expectation of privacy has been practically eliminated by the citizen's own action. Law enforcement officials are entitled to apply human ingenuity and scientific advances to collect freely available evidence from the public domain.[37]

In *Florida v. Riley*,[38] this time not involving garbage, the Supreme Court decided that police had not conducted an illegal search when an officer observed from a helicopter, at a height of 400 feet, what he thought were marijuana plants. In a separate but concurring opinion, Justice O'Connor wrote, "I agree that police observation of the greenhouse in Riley's curtilage from a helicopter passing at an altitude of 400 feet did not violate an expectation of

---

[35] This case and a series of related cases are discussed in LaFave, W.R. *Search and Seizure: A Treatise on the Fourth Amendment*, Third Edition, Volume 1 (St. Paul, Minn.: West Publishing Co., 1996).

[36] 975 F.2d 927 (1st Circ. 1992).

[37] Quoted from LaFave, *Search and Seizure*, p. 603.

[38] 488 U.S. 445; 109 S. Ct. 693; 1989 U.S. LEXIS 580; 102 L. Ed. 2d 835; 57 U.S.L.W. 4126.

privacy" that society is prepared to recognize as 'reasonable.'[39,][40] She argued that in the same way it is unreasonable to expect police to shield their eyes so as to avoid seeing into private property from public thoroughfares, so is it unreasonable for citizens to expect to be free of aerial observation at altitudes where the "public travel with sufficient regularity."[41]

In sum, I have tried to show that attempts to define and defend privacy in public, both in theory and in practice, have been undermined by versions of an argument from competing interests that I call the normative knock-down argument. It is so named because it has had a compelling hold over philosophers, policy-makers, and judges, as well as the commercial interests that benefit from its use.

Empirical

In this section, I outline a third explanation why theorists have seemed to overlook the problem of privacy in public. I suggest that the divergence of philosophical theory from popular resentment of surveillance practices is due, in significant measure, to critical changes which philosophical theory has not yet absorbed because, quite simply, prior to key developments in information technology, the problem did not exist in a compelling form. People could count on virtual anonymity even as they traversed the public arena. We see this assumption at work as the fictional detective, Alexander Gold, interrogates a murder suspect,

"You certainly sounded as though you hated him enough to kill him."
"Not hated, Mr. Gold, despised. If I had killed him, would I have told you how I felt?"
"Maybe. You could be trying reverse psychology."
"Yes, but Professor Moriarty, you know that I know that you really know that I really know . . ." Kirsch let his voice fade away.
Alexander had to smile. "All right. Let's talk about something else. Where were you when Talbott was killed."
"Jogging. In Central Park."
"Witnesses?"

---

[39] *Katz v. United States*, 389 U.S. 347, 361 (1967).

[40] *Florida v. Reilly* (O'Connor, J. concurring).

[41] One of the anonymous reviewers for *Law and Philosophy* points out that newly developed method of government surveillance, for example, through walls, makes this issue even more pressing and problematic.

"Hundreds." ...
"So you have an alibi."
"Not exactly...."[42]

Seen by hundreds, noticed by none. Most people reasonably make this assumption: either that they are not noticed, or that any single observer can observe and harbor only discrete bits of information.[43] As such, not only would the information be sparse and disjointed but it would be limited by what any single human brain could reasonably and efficiently hold. An individual going about his daily activities does not worry about undue surveillance even if he is observed by one person, on April 4 1997, to be wearing chinos, a blue polo shirt and loafers and to be tall and blond. By another, he is observed purchasing three cases of wine from the local liquor store. By a third he is overheard discussing his son's progress with his school teacher. Later that day, by a fourth, is observed participating in a march for gay and lesbian rights. All these activities occur in the public eye; all may be observed, even noted. No single one of these instances of being observed is necessarily threatening or intrusive.

What has changed? Key advances in computer technology have clearly affected our facility with information. These advances include an exponential decline in the cost of computer storage and processing coupled with vast increments in power, the capacity to create large and complex but decentralized databases on networks of minicomputers and PCs, the use of expert systems for processing data, and the cooperative handling of data both within and among institutions.[44] These developments in information technology and practices have meant that: a) there is virtually no limit to the amount of information that can be recorded, b) there is virtually no limit to the scope of analysis that can be done – bounded only by human ingenuity, and c) the information may be stored virtually forever. These capabilities combined with alert and intelligent observation

---

[42] Herbert Resnicow, *The Gold Solution* (New York: St. Martin's Press, 1983), pp. 116–117.

[43] I exclude here special cases such as when suspects are surveilled by law enforcement officers, with a special purpose, such as, hoping to catch them in the act of purchasing a shipment of heroin.

[44] I draw on H.M. Deitels' characterization of the period of 1970s to the present, which he describes as the "Fourth Generation of information technology." This is discussed in Smith, *Managing Privacy*, pp. 180–181.

have contributed to the practices and modes of surveillance familiar to us.[45]

The effects of these advances are felt along various dimensions. In the public arena, not only may the amount of information increase enormously, but information that was once scattered and transient may now be ordered, systematized, and made permanent. We can do things with the information, such as merge and compare real-time observations with past records, compare those with the records of others, and communicate any of this, at lightening speed, across networks. Mr. Kirsch would have his alibi, and we would have a fuller and more systematic picture of the conservatively dressed father protagonist going about his business on April 4. I discuss the implications of these practices in more detail later in the paper.

An arena in which these changes have been acutely felt is that of public records. According to the Freedom of Information Act,[46] all governmental records, except those covered by a specified set of exceptions, including The Privacy Act of 1974, are freely available for public access. Even though some records of information about people are covered by The Privacy Act, there are many classes of records with information about persons, such as birth, death and marriage records, drivers records, real estate ownership records, court records, and more, that are public. Prior to computerization and advanced networking capabilities, access to these public records was costly in time and effort. Anyone seeking information from these records would be required to travel to wherever the records were housed, such as Courts and Departments of Motor Vehicles, and painstakingly search for and copy the information they needed. Such effort created de facto protection, serving to limit access and, therefore, exposure.

The computerization of public records has made them available with far less effort, either directly from respective government agencies responsible for collecting them, or from intermediaries who have gathered and organized them. As a consequence, these records

---

[45] James Rule also credits changes in social organization, now driven by large anonymous institutions, along with people's desire to be treated as individuals. See James Rule, et al., "Preserving Individual Autonomy in an Information-Oriented Society," in Lance Hoffman (ed.), *Computer Privacy in the Next Decade* (New York: Atheneum: 1980), pp. 65–87.

[46] F.O.I.A. 5 U.S. Code, sec 552, 1966, strengthened in 1974 and 1976.

578   HELEN NISSENBAUM

are public in a far more thoroughgoing sense than ever before. In two
cases that have come before the New Jersey Supreme Court, court
opinions have acknowledged that the mode by which information is
made public (as in computerized versus paper records) may affect
the actual degree of publicity of these so-called "public" records.[47]
In a similar vein, those who have advocated for limiting access
to Drivers' Records have argued that when the decision to allow
public access to these records was made, the implications of such
records being public was quite different from what they presently
are. In public deliberations, privacy advocates have suggested that
we ought to re-evaluate the meaning of a public record, including
such key issues as the criteria of access to records and the grounds
for classifying a given database as public. Representatives of other
sectors including marketers, information brokers, and media organizations sharply disagree with such suggestions.[48] This important
debate is beyond the scope of this paper.

In review: As a third explanation for neglect of the problem of
privacy in public, I have suggested that until powerful information
technologies were applied to the collection and analysis of information about people, there was no general and systematic threat to
privacy in public. Privacy, as such, was well-enough protected by
a combination of conscious and intentional efforts (including the
promulgation of law and moral norms) abetted by inefficiency. It is
not surprising, therefore, that theories were not shaped in response
to the issue of privacy in public; the issue did not yet exist.

III. SHOULD WE PROTECT PRIVACY IN PUBLIC?

To this point, my purpose has been to explain why conceptions
of privacy developed by predominant philosophical and normative
theories have not accounted for encroachments on privacy occurring
in so-called "public" realms. For reasons that are conceptual, norma-

---

[47] See Higg-A-Rella, Inc. v. County of Essex. 141 N.J. 35 (1985) and Doe V.
Poritz, 142 N.J. 1 (1995), discussed in greater detail in Nissenbaum, "Toward an
Approach to Privacy in Public: Challenges of Information Technology," op. cit.

[48] For example, as debated at the Public Hearings of the Information Task Force
Information Policy Committee Working Group on Privacy, held on January 26–
27, 1994, Washington DC.

tive and empirical in origin, these theories lack mechanisms to deal with conflicts involving privacy in public and have generally not taken up hard questions about surveillance in non-intimate realms to determine when such surveillance is morally acceptable and when not. Implicit in my discussion so far has been an assumption that now bears direct examination, that normative theories of privacy *ought* to be concerned with privacy in public, that contemporary experience with information technology offers compelling reasons to *expect* from theory that it provide a means of understanding the problem of privacy in public as well as a means for adjudicating it.

A *prima facie* case for caring about public surveillance is that it stirs popular indignation, worry and resentment. The 30,000 letters of protest against Lotus Marketplace Households expressed these reactions as do poll results, such as a 1990 poll showing 90% of respondents agreeing that consumers are being asked to provide excessively personal information. (57% found it a major problem, 33% a minor problem.)[49] Individual concerns are registered in various ways as shown in the segment below quoted from the RISKS Forum Digest:

Recently ... several firms have started abusing the power of the Internet to publish large databases of personal information without permission. This is impolite, and in many cases it can even be dangerous.

True story: recently, I followed a lead from MacUser magazine to a web page for dealing with spam e-mailers. That page suggested that one of the first steps to take was to contact services that track people's e-mail addresses. With growing horror, I connected to page after page on the list and located myself in their databases. Some services listed far more than just name and e-mail address. My home address and phone number were accessible from the same record. Two services even had a facility to show a map of my neighborhood and the location of my house in it.

The widespread dispersal of information of this sort, without prior consent, is a serious invasion of privacy."[50]

While invectives like this may signal a morally relevant need, they may also be read as expressions of mere preference, or desire,

---

[49] Smith, *Managing Privacy*, p. 125.

[50] Jon Handler, submitted to RISKS Forum Digest, DEC 23, 1996. RISKS is a moderated bulletin board whose purpose is to publicize and resolve computer-related risks. It is held in high regard within the community of security experts and software engineers.

580   HELEN NISSENBAUM

or even worse, as muddle-headedness. Two noted contributors to
the literature on privacy, William Parent and Tom Gerety, would
explain it as the latter. Both Parent and Gerety assume the burden
of sharpening and clarifying the concept of privacy. Gerety worries
that the problem for the concept of privacy;

comes not from the concept's meagerness but from its amplitude, for it has a
protean capacity to be all things to all lawyers. . . . A legal concept will do us little
good if it expands like a gas to fill up the available space.[51]

While he characterizes privacy as an "island of personal
autonomy,"[52] he limits the scope of this autonomy to the "intimacies
of personal identity."[53] Parent defines a right to privacy that covers
only information that is both personal in nature and not anywhere
documented in a public place, for example, reported in a newspaper.
About all other information, he concludes that it "cannot without
glaring paradox be called private."[54] Thus, for Parent and Gerety,
popular judgment aside, public surveillance would not to be a matter
that is covered by a right to privacy.

I suggest, contrary to approaches like Gerety's and Parent's, that
although an important purpose of philosophical theory is to introduce greater conceptual rigor, a normative theory that strays too
far from ordinary usage and popular sentiment is thereby rendered
unhelpful, or worse, irrelevant. Yet there is still work to be done,
for even if we reject the narrow definitional accounts of theorists
like Parent and Gerety, we are not thereby committed to embracing
widespread indignation as, in itself, sufficient reason for admitting
that moral violation has occurred in the activities of public surveillance and data harvesting. We may regard public expression as a
sign, as strongly suggestive, of something more than preference and
mere opinion – more so if it is consistent and fairly widespread –
and we must seek a greater understanding of its source. Only then

---

[51] Tom Gerety, "Redefining Privacy," Harvard Civil Rights-Civil Liberties Law
Review, 12 (2) (1977), p. 234.

[52] Gerety, "Redefining Privacy," p. 271.

[53] Gerety, "Redefining Privacy," p. 281.

[54] William Parent, "Privacy, Morality, and the Law," *Philosophy & Public
Affairs* 12 (5) (1983), p. 271. See also DeCew, *In Pursuit of Privacy: Law, Ethics,
and the Rise of Technology*, especially Chapter 2, for a careful critique of Parent's
position.

will we be adequately guided toward a conclusion about whether privacy in public is a legitimate part of the moral right to privacy, and if so, under what conditions. To suggest a moral basis for expressions of popular indignation we must show that popular reaction plumbs human needs that are deeper and more universal than "mere" preferences and desires.

It is with this purpose that I explore two key aspects of public data harvesting. One is the practice of shifting information from one context to another – usually from the context in which it was collected, to another context.[55] A second is the set of practices involving collection, collation, and combination of information drawn from diverse sources in activities, known variously as "data mining", "profiling", "matching", and the like. Although the problematic nature of the second set of practices overlaps with first – because it involves the shifting of information from one context to another – it involves an additional concern, which I later elaborate. I will argue that these two aspects of public surveillance make privacy in public an issue which adequate theories of privacy must cover, alongside the issues that have traditionally been acknowledged as part of their territory.

IV. PRIVACY AND CONTEXTUAL INTEGRITY

Most people have a robust sense of the information about them that is relevant, appropriate, or proper to particular circumstances, situations, or relationships. When information is judged appropriate for a particular situation it usually is readily shared; when appropriate information is recorded and applied appropriately to a particular circumstance it draws no objection. People do not object to providing to doctors, for example, the details of their physical condition, discussing their children's problems with their children's teachers, divulging financial information to loan officers at banks, sharing with close friends the details of their romantic relationships. For the myriad transactions, situations and relationships in which people engage, there are norms – explicit and implicit – governing how much information and what type of information is fitting for

---

[55] A term that has entered the vocabulary of on-line discussions, for this, is "data creeping."

them. Where these norms are respected I will say that contextual integrity[56] is maintained; where violated, I will say that contextual integrity has been violated.

Norms governing the appropriateness of information to a context may mark some information as appropriate for it and some information as inappropriate. It may be appropriate to expect an employee, for example, to yield a great deal of information to an employer concerning past employment and education, but inappropriate to have to provide information about, say, marital status or sexual orientation. Citizens routinely provide a great deal of information to government agencies and consider it appropriate to do so, but they are careful about what information they are willing to provide to which agencies. And there is some information, such as religious affiliation, which they are likely to resist giving to any government agency at all. Family members know us well, but prying relatives may rankle us by asking the details of our romantic entanglements. These twinges of indignation are not necessarily reserved for demands for personal, sensitive, or intimate information. They occur even when a store clerk requires one's name and address for a cash transaction, as was standard practice at branches of Radio Shack, or when on-line services ask for information about one's off-line life, as a subscription to the electronic version of *The New York Times* requires of potential subscribers by insisting they complete a questionnaire asking not only for their names and electronic identification, but also for mailing address, gender, age, and household income.

About the norms governing specific relationships and situations, and who determines these norms – whether by mutual agreement, by authority of one of the participants, through the shaping influence of culture and society – a great deal could and should be said. Although I do not here have a ready theory about contexts and the particular norms associated with them, it is critical to the position on privacy in public that I articulate in this paper, that such a theory be considered plausible. Furthermore, at least some of the norms of contextual integrity must be shown to originate from sources other than mere

---

[56] A similar idea has been proposed by the philosopher Jeroen van den Hoven. He uses the term, "spheres of access," to cover essentially the same idea as "contextual integrity."

convention, must be seen as protecting something of independent value to individuals, or to society, or to both. For if the norms of contextual integrity express only the conventions of the day, then critics may argue that it is simply a matter of time before people will become accustomed to the new order brought about by information technology and readily accept the new privacy conventions of public surveillance. Just as, according to Justice O'Connor, airplanes have changed the norms of privacy vis-a-vis surveillance from the air, so new norms will emerge regarding the collection and use of information about persons. Objections to all the various forms of public surveillance described in the first section of this paper will cease.[57]

Existing philosophical work on privacy, though it does not address the issue exactly as defined in the previous paragraph, lends credibility to the idea of independent value protected by norms of contextual integrity. James Rachels, for example, argues that a right to privacy ought to include the right not only to control whether information is shared, but when and with whom it is shared. In having the power to share information discriminately, people are able to define the nature and degree of intimacy of various relationships:

The same general point can be made about other sorts of human relationships: businessman to employee, minister to congregant, doctor to patient, husband to wife, parent to child, and so on. In each case, the sort of relationship that people have to one another involves a conception of how it is appropriate for them to behave with each other, and what is more, a conception of the kind and degree of knowledge concerning one another which it is appropriate for them to have.[58]

The capacity to define the nature and degree of closeness of relationships is an important aspect of personal autonomy, Rachels argues, and ought to be protected. Having to enter relationships or settings with little or no control over what is known about one, may lead to a

---

[57] I am grateful to Philip Agre for prodding me into seeing that simply asserting the presence of norms is not grounds enough for rejecting a new practice that violates the norms. We need further to show that the norms are more than "mere" convention and that they protect something of genuine value to individuals or society or both. Ferdinand Schoeman, in *Privacy and Social Freedom* (Cambridge: Cambridge University Press, 1992), Chapter 10, introduces a similar concept in his discussion and literary exploration of "spheres of life."

[58] James Rachels, "Why Privacy is Important," *Philosophy & Public Affairs* 4 (4) (1975), p. 328.

584   HELEN NISSENBAUM

sense of having been demeaned, embarrassment, disempowerment, or even fear.

Schoeman sees similar value in respecting norms of contextual integrity. He writes,

People have, and it is important that they maintain, different relationships with different people. Information appropriate in the context of one relationship may not be appropriate in another.[59]

And elsewhere he illustrates this point,

A person can be active in the gay pride movement in San Francisco, but be private about her sexual preference vis-a-vis her family and coworkers in Sacramento. A professor may be highly visible to other gays at the gay bar but discreet about sexual orientation at the university. Surely the streets and newspapers of San Francisco are public places as are the gay bars in the quiet university town. Does appearing in some public settings as a gay activist mean that the person concerned has waived her rights to civil inattention, to feeling violated if confronted in another setting?[60]

People's judgments that privacy has been violated concur more systematically with breaches of contextual integrity than with breaches of only intimate or sensitive realms. Although they may ascribe special status to the latter, they do not thereby accept that outside of this special realm no norms of privacy apply; they do not accept that outside this special realm information is detachable from its context and is – we might say – "up for grabs." This attitude is reflected in the indignation that may follow as simple a gesture as a stranger asking a person his or her name in a public square. By contrast, even if information is quite personal or intimate, people generally do not sense their privacy has been violated when the information requested is judged relevant to, or appropriate for, a particular setting or relationship. And this is why traditional theories of privacy, which take as their guideposts the dichotomy of private versus public, asserting that privacy is morally violated only when private information or the private sphere is inappropriately revealed,

[59] Ferdinand Schoeman, "Privacy and Intimate Information," in F. Schoeman (ed.), *Philosophical Dimensions of Privacy: An Anthology* (Cambridge: Cambridge University Press, 1984), p. 408.

[60] F. Schoeman, "Gossip and Privacy" in R.F. Goodman and A.B. Ze'ev (eds.), *Good Gossip* (University Press of Kansas, 1994), p. 73.

diverge from popular judgment which takes contextual integrity as its benchmark. Whereas the former considers privacy norms as relevant only to private or intimate information, the latter considers privacy norms as potentially relevant to any information.

In the public surveillance currently practiced, information is routinely shifted from one sphere to another, as when, for example, information about your supermarket purchases is sold to a list service for magazine subscriptions. At times, the shift may cross not only contextual lines but temporal lines as information collected in the past – sometimes a very long time past – is injected into a current setting. (Unlike human memory, which fades, computer memory lasts indefinitely.)

When the actress Rebecca Shaefer was murdered and police discovered that her murderer had traced her whereabouts through drivers' records, people were not only outraged by the murder but indignant over the means by which her attacker had traced her. As a result, State Departments of Motor, which have become a fertile source of information routinely collected from licensed drivers and owners of registered vehicles, have become an irritant to privacy advocates as well as individuals who are aware of widespread trade in their computerized records. Public indignation stirred by Shaefer's murder, and similar perceived breaches, led to passage of the Drivers' Privacy Protection Act of 1993[61] which places some restrictions on the sale of these records. Critics still argue that these restrictions do not go far enough.[62]

It is commonplace for information deemed not to be "sensitive" to be freely shifted about, transmitted, exchanged, transferred, and sold. Those who engage in these practices seem to assume that the information in question has been dislodged from its contextual attachments and therefore "up for grabs". Discomfort with

---

[61] 103rd Congress, H.R. 3365.

[62] In another driver-related case, privacy advocates worry about E-ZPass, the electronic toll system operating on toll roads and bridges in the East Coast of the United States, operated by the Triborough Bridge and Tunnel Authority. Electronic devices installed in a motor vehicle transmit information about identity for billing purposes. Critics worry that information about drivers' whereabouts may be used in unrelated contexts. Apparently, the New York Police Department successfully fought against a requirement that records be closed to access except via subpoenas.

586 HELEN NISSENBAUM

the practices involving the shifting around of information reflects a far different perspective: it suggests that people judge norms of contextual integrity, and consequently privacy, to have been violated even when the information in question is not sensitive or intimate. People resent the rampant and unauthorized distribution of information about themselves not only when they violate the integrity of an intimate and personal realm, but when they violate contextual integrity. In violating contextual integrity they strike at an important aspect of why people care about privacy.

V. AGGREGATION

At the heart of contemporary data harvesting is the activity known variously as "profiling", "matching" "data aggregation" and "data mining" in which disparate records, diverse sources of information about people, are aggregated to produce databases with complex patterns of information. Smith describes a number of cases. For example, A.T.&T. creating specialty directories for customers[63] based on the aggregated record of their 800 calls; Citicorp's analyzing the credit card purchases of customers in order to sell profiles to others;[64] banks that Smith studied creating an expert system to categorize individuals into profile groups by pooling information about them that the banks held; super-bureaus collecting "information available in many places – from regular credit bureaus (both major and independent), drivers' license and motor vehicle records, voter registration lists, Social Security number lists, birth records, court records, etc.,"[65] in order to devise comprehensive profiles about individuals that would indicate such things as: purchasing power (credit card activity index, estimated income, fixed payments, etc.), purchasing activity (active accounts, bank debits, etc.), shopping data, and demographic data (job, marriage status, dwelling type, gender, market segment, etc.).[66]

Data aggregation is by no means limited to the private sector. Used for some time by law enforcement and the Drug Enforce-

---

[63] Smith, *Managing Privacy*, p. 185.

[64] Smith, *Managing Privacy*, p. 186.

[65] Smith, *Managing Privacy*, p. 124.

[66] Smith, *Managing Privacy*, pp. 114–115.

ment Agency, the enterprising San Diego County government has engaged in the practice for commercial purposes. It created and sold a CD-ROM disk containing the records – including name, address, telephone number, occupation, birthplace, birthdate, and political affiliation – of 1.25 million of its voters.[67]

Data subjects and the harvesters of information alike are keenly aware of the qualitative shift that can occur when individual bits of data are compiled into profiles. From the perspective of the data gatherers, this capability is one of the most exciting advances that information technology enables. Institutions in both the public and private sectors, including law enforcement, financial, and marketing, either take advantage of compiled data directly, or buy these products from others – like credit bureaus and list brokers – who specialize in gathering data from primary sources and organizing it into useful and potentially profitable forms. Information belies the adage about sewing silk purses out of sows ears, for out of worthless bits information we may sew assemblages that are rich in value. Assemblages are valuable for the very reasons that their subjects resent them.

When challenged, supporters and beneficiaries of profiling frequently resort to what I earlier called the normative "knock down" argument. They argue that there are no good reasons to prohibit these activities when the information in question is "out there" and people have made no effort to hide it from view. To prohibit the collection and aggregation of this information would violate the freedom of those who would observe, record, and aggregate it. Because the "cat is out of the bag" already, there is no good reason to stifle the ingenuity of entrepreneurs who would sell and thereby profit from this information. If these entrepreneurs choose to share what they have learned with others, it would violate their freedom of expression to stop them.[68] Accordingly, any sentiment expressed against profiling should be treated as such, namely as a sentiment, not as an overriding moral consideration.

If defenders of aggregation are correct that no private zones are violated, that the information they use has been provided freely and not under duress, that it is neither stolen nor leaked, then what

---

[67] Smith, *Managing Privacy*, p. 190.

[68] This sort of rhetoric was present during the Lotus Marketplace incident.

588   HELEN NISSENBAUM

could be the privacy interest that is thwarted by the practice of aggregation?

Even if we grant these defenders of data aggregation their premises, their conceptions of aggregation – whether sincere or disingenuous – seem to miss something important about it. It misses whatever element distinguishes the activity of a person casually looking out his or her window observing the passing scene and the activities described below in a continuation of the paragraph quoted earlier from Hunter's paper:

> Consider what happens if I write down everything I see out my window, and all my neighbors do, too. Suppose we shared notes and compiled the data we got just by looking out our own windows. When we sorted it all out, we would have detailed personal profiles of everyone we saw. If every move anyone made in public were recorded, correlated, and analyzed, the veil of anonymity protecting us from constant scrutiny would be torn away. Even if that record were never used, its very existence would certainly change the way we act in public.[69]

The difference between casually observing the passing scene out of one's window, which seems perfectly harmless, and the surveillance Hunter has imagined, which seems definitely sinister, is not merely one of degree. In the passage below, James Boyle in his book, *Shamans, Software, and Spleens*, draws attention to a similar concern,

> Why do supermarkets offer their preferred customers discounts just for running an electronic card through a scanner on their way past the checkout? Because technology now permits the store to keep a precise record of those customers' purchases and to correlate it with demographic information about them. Advertisers will soon know everything from our individual brand-name preferences for toilet paper to the odds that a middle-class family on a particular street will buy Fig Newtons on a Wednesday. If you are what you eat, then manufacturers will soon have the information technology to know exactly what you are. This commercially driven intrusion has not reached Orwellian proportions – at least, not yet. Nevertheless, information technology has the capacity, if not to *end* privacy, then to redefine what we mean by the term.[70]

While the magnitude, detail, thoroughness and scope are important characteristics of the surveillance described in the two passages,

---

[69] Hunter, L. "Public Image," p. 295.

[70] James Boyle, *Shamans, Software, and Spleens* (Cambridge: Harvard University Press, 1996), pp. 3–4.

they alone do not account for a sense that a moral line has been crossed. There are two further considerations that bear mentioning. First, that the process of compiling and aggregating information almost always involves shifting information taken from an appropriate context and inserting it into one perceived not to be so. That is, the violation of contextual integrity is part of the reason critics find data aggregation to be morally offensive. A second consideration, striking closer to the core of the practice of profiling, is that while isolated bits of information (as generated, for example, by merely walking around in public spaces and not taking active steps to avoid notice) are not especially revealing, assemblages are capable of exposing people quite profoundly.

The value of aggregates is that they are multidimensional and as such provide more information than pictures that are less filled out. Beyond this, however, an aggregate can incorporate a richer portrait of the individual than even the bits taken together (i.e. the whole being more than the sum of parts) as it may include not only information explicitly given but information inferred from that which has been given. As Jeffrey Reiman observes,

... by accumulating a lot of disparate pieces of public information, you can construct a fairly detailed picture of a person's private life. You can find out who her friends are, what she does for fun or profit, and from such facts others can be inferred, whether she is punctual, whether she is faithful, and so on.[71]

If we know, for example, that someone has purchased a home pregnancy test, we can infer with some degree of certainty the nature of activities in which she has recently engaged; if a person has registered as a Republican we can infer with some degree of certainty how he or she would react to a range of social and political issues; if someone owns a house in affluent Palo Alto, we can infer his or her minimum financial holdings. In other words, portraits may provide descriptive access to an individual, multiple forms of identification, and a sense of what they care about.

The picture of a person that a profile provides can, for the reasons given, be broad, deep and traverse time. These pictures may be rich enough to reveal aspects of an individual's character,

---

[71] Jeffrey H. Reiman, "Driving to the Panopticon: A Philosophical Exploration of the Risks to Privacy Posed by the Highway Technology of the Future," *Santa Clara Computer and High Technology Law Journal* 11 (1) (1995).

590   HELEN NISSENBAUM

to ground predictions about their propensities, and even suggest
ways of manipulating them. One provider of such a service boasts
as follows:

> With a 98% compliance rate, our registered users provide us with specific infor-
> mation about themselves, such as their age, income, gender and zip code. And
> because each and every one of our users have verifiable e-mail addresses, we
> know their data is accurate – far more accurate than any cookie-based counting.
>
> Plus, all of our user information is warehoused in a sophisticated database, so
> the information is stable, accessible and flexible.
>
> Depending on your needs, we can customize user groups and adjust messages
> to specific segments, using third-party data or additional user-supplied informa-
> tion. So you can expand your targeting possibilities.
>
> What's more, because they're New York Times on the Web subscribers, our
> users are affluent, influential and highly engaged in our site.[72]

Demographic profiles, financial profiles, and consumer profiles
identify people as suitable targets for proposed "treatments." Used
in this way, a profile may be seen as a device that offers a way of
targeting people as the likely means to fulfilling someone else's end.

In sum, the two preceding sections argue that the negative reactions to public surveillance are due at least in part to characteristics
of public surveillance that are genuinely morally objectionable.
One is that public surveillance practices regularly violate norms
of contextual integrity when information readily revealed in one
context, and public with respect to it, is transmitted to, and revealed
in, another. The importance of integrity of contexts, which has been
recognized in relation to intimate and sensitive realms, has not been
sufficiently acknowledged in other realms. Also morally objectionable are the activities integral to public surveillance practices known
as profiling, data aggregation, and data mining, which provide the
means to reach, target, and possibly manipulate their subjects.

VI. PRIVACY IN PUBLIC: A GENUINE PRIVACY INTEREST

I began this paper by suggesting that philosophical theories of
privacy, in responding primarily to the threat of governmental
intrusion into privacy and to the threat of any intrusions into the

---

[72] Advertisement, *The New York Times*, Monday July 14, 1997.

personal, intimate realms, fail to respond to an important and growing challenge to privacy. My purpose has been to argue that public surveillance, which many theorists have denied a central place, ought often to be construed as a violation of genuine privacy interests. Although I have criticized predominant theories of privacy for neglecting this important privacy interest, I rely on the considerable insights developed in these theories to show why even in the public sphere individuals have legitimate privacy interests. It also remains for the courts as well as further theoretical work to develop criteria for distinguishing between those acts of public surveillance that seem not to violate privacy and those that do.

Among the essential contributions that these theories make is drawing the connection between privacy and other values. For many, privacy is valuable, is worth protecting as either a moral or legal right, or both, because it functions to protect and promote other important ends.[73] Alan Westin, for example, in his influential book *Privacy and Freedom*, asserts that privacy promotes important human ends in a democratic, free society: it enhances personal autonomy (which he understands as "the desire to avoid being manipulated or dominated wholly by others"[74]), it creates a protected realm for emotional release, provides a context in which an individual can "exert his individuality on events",[75] and the creates the possibility of limited and protected communication. Ruth Gavison offers another persuasive account of the essential role privacy plays in safeguarding or promoting other deeply held values including liberty of action, "mental health, autonomy, growth, creativity, and the capacity to form and create meaningful human relations".[76] Several other exemplary works on privacy offer analogous insights, demonstrating the value of privacy both for individuals and society. Although I articulate my analysis in terminology drawn primarily from Westin and Gavison, it is not necessarily tied to the details of their theories.

---

[73] This claim is not incompatible with the stronger claims that some make about privacy, that it is valuable not only because it is instrumental in achieving other ends but as an end in itself.

[74] Alan F. Westin, *Privacy and Freedom* (New York: Atheneum, 1967), p. 33.

[75] Ibid., p. 36.

[76] Ruth Gavison, "Privacy and the Limits of the Law," p. 442.

592   HELEN NISSENBAUM

These approaches have in common a version of the idea that
privacy protects a "safe haven", or sanctuary, where people may
be free from the scrutiny and possibly the disapprobation of others.
Within these private spheres people are able to control the terms
under which they live their lives.[77] By exercising control over
intimate and sensitive information about themselves, people may
exercise control over the way they portray themselves to others,
especially those others with whom they engage in lasting relationships. These two forms of privacy, namely, control over information
and control over access, are among the conditions for a free society
and, among other things, enhance people's capacity to function as
autonomous, creative, free agents.

In the world before powerful computers, virtually limitless
storage capacity, software for information management, and network capabilities, privacy was well enough protected by safeguarding sensitive information and intimate spheres against unwanted
intrusion. Through a relatively narrow range of prohibitions, privacy
was afforded a decent level of protection because, as discussed in
the section on empirical reasons for the neglect of privacy in public,
the prohibitions themselves were abetted by conditions such as the
limits of human memory, polite indifference, and inconvenience.

But these conditions no longer hold. In their place we have
powerful information technology coupled with an insatiable desire
to know – whatever now may be useful to someone, somewhere, or
what may become so in the future. Information is fluid and comprehensive; cleverly devised profiles constitute a powerful tool for
understanding people, influencing their behavior, and even manipulating them. Those who are not fully aware what or how much
others know about them are more easily targeted or manipulated.
Those with greater awareness and understanding may be able to
protect their privacy more effectively, but at the expense of developing a wariness, self-consciousness, suspicion, and even tentativeness
in their relations with others. DeCew describes this as "a chilling

---

[77] John Kleinig reminds me that even these freedoms are limited. One cannot,
for example, claim protection for spousal abuse on grounds that it occurs in
private.

effect" on behavior.[78] The values that were once relatively well shielded through the fortification of the intimate realm are now vulnerable via other, supposedly public, approaches. Because there is more at stake in an individual's controlling even non-intimate information, it is no longer self-evident that the balance must favor the freedom of those who seek to observe and record when weighed against the privacy interests of those who are observed.

These considerations support the view that popular reaction to public surveillance is not merely a reflection of popular – possibly irrational – sentiment but a recognition that prominent elements of public surveillance constitute a genuine moral violation of privacy. Reasons for protecting privacy in public are quite similar to reasons for protecting privacy of the more traditional kind because values placed in jeopardy from invasions of the intimate realm are also jeopardized by various forms of public surveillance practiced today. As noted earlier, these values are wide-ranging, including individual values such as autonomy, liberty, individuality, capacity to form and maintain intimate relations, mental health, creativity, personal growth; as well as social values such as a free and democratic society. Those who engage in contemporary practices of public surveillance have discovered a novel way to eavesdrop, to spy on, to learn more about people than they have a legitimate right to know. And preventing this constellation of intrusions is one of the fundamental protections that privacy offers.

VII. IMPLICATIONS FOR POLICY

The purpose of this paper has been to present a case for extending or revising existing philosophical theory, or developing new theories, that would accommodate privacy in public. I hope to have succeeded in this. Although the purpose has not been to recommend or craft specific privacy policies, I would like, in these concluding paragraphs, to consider whether a recognized interest in privacy in public could have any power to shift the course of privacy policy in the United States, which at present, gives no systematic consideration to it.

---

[78] Judith Wagner DeCew, *In Pursuit of Privacy: Law, Ethics, and the Rise of Technology* (Ithaca: Cornell University Press, 1997) p. 64.

594   HELEN NISSENBAUM

I see two means. One would be to emphasize the principle of contextual integrity in order to weaken the influence of the private-public dichotomy in setting the agenda for privacy, policy as well as theory. The idea of contextual integrity and the norms emerging from it ought not be utterly foreign. There is, after all, ample precedent in relationships that explicitly call for confidentiality such as physician to patient, clergyman to congregant, and so on. We can view these relationships and contexts that call for confidentiality as instances of a more general requirement of contextual integrity. We may likewise view the Video Privacy Protection Act as giving legal protection to the video rental context, also an extension of the familiar professional settings. Building upon such cases, we might extend application of a principle of contextual integrity further to cover various settings such as medical insurance bureaus, charitable organizations to which one has donated, some as mundane as supermarkets, and more.[79]

Some privacy advocates object to the approach just described – a "sectoral" approach – favoring a second, "omnibus" approach. This second approach accords a strong, comprehensive right to privacy which grants control to individuals over all information about themselves irrespective of context. The European Union's privacy initiative, scheduled to take effect in 1998, is considered an example of this approach.[80] Recognizing a fundamental right to privacy shifts the burden away from individuals having to demonstrate the importance of maintaining control over various especially sensitive categories of information onto potential gatherers and users of information, who would need to demonstrate a critical need for the information. Although it is important to show that there are feasible policy mechanisms for protecting privacy in public, I will not pursue the details of these options here.

Before concluding, I will consider a possible objection to the protection of privacy in public, namely the objection I earlier called, the normative "knock-down" argument. Are we in a position to

---

[79] This takes us into the territory of hard-fought battles over whether integrity would be more aptly protected through opt-in versus opt-out. Opt-in, in my view, is far truer to privacy requirements but I will not take up the matter here.

[80] This is the approach that is incorporated in the European Union Privacy Directive which is scheduled to take effect in 1998.

better understand this argument, and more important, will we be able to defend privacy in public against it?

As we have seen, those who invoke a normative knock-down argument against protecting privacy in public usually point out that the information in question is neither intimate nor sensitive. They also say that because the information in question has been freely exposed in public by its subjects, it is unreasonable and wrong for their subjects to claim a right to prevent access to it or use of it.

In responding to such an argument I would suggest, first, that some of its power is based on an equivocation on the "it" to which subjects have supposedly given implicit consent. While shoppers in a supermarket have implicitly consented to fellow shoppers seeing the contents of their shopping carts – they do not expect fellow shoppers *not* to look – they have neither implicitly nor explicitly agreed to others collecting the information and selling it to third, fourth, etc. parties so that the data may be warehoused, mined, and assembled, so that their behavior may be modeled and manipulated. Just as someone buying a pregnancy test in a drugstore may have no choice but to expose this bit of information to fellow shoppers, they have not thereby acceded to unrelenting publication of their sexual behavior.

A detractor may still balk. To incorporate protection for privacy in public into law and public policy is, nevertheless both unrealistic and unreasonable. Even if the moral authority of the normative "knock-down" argument has been undermined, its practical force remains evident in Reiman's warning. The challenge remains that if one is willing to be open, and behave openly, it would be an oppressive society that enforced norms of privacy that entailed a right never to be seen on a crowded street. The burden placed on others cannot interfere with the normal activities of their daily lives, we cannot expect in general, as Justice O'Connor wrote about police officers in particular, that people "shield their eyes when passing by."[81]

Although it seems both impossible and wrong to impose so great a burden on people in order to protect privacy in public, it is not impossible to articulate other measures of protection that are not overly burdensome and at the same time do not unduly compromise

---

[81] 488 U.S. 445; 109 S. Ct. 693; 1989 U.S. LEXIS 580; 102 L. Ed. 2d 835; 57 U.S.L.W. 4126 (O'Connor, J., concurring).

what is valuable in privacy in public. This would involve recognizing the distinction between exposing something for observation, on the one hand, and yielding control over it, on the other. Although at first this may seem practically difficult or even impossible, a model for policy based in recognizing such a distinction may be found in another area of discourse – intellectual property. Two central mechanisms for protecting intellectual property, patent and copyright, are devised expressly for the purpose of allowing something to be exposed (in this case, the works of intellectual labor) without yielding control over it. While I do not support the position, sometimes put forward, of privacy as a form of self-ownership[82] (a debate for another occasion), I suggest that for purposes of crafting reasonable policy, the practical mechanisms developed in the service of intellectual ownership, which are socially entrenched and for the most part successful, may serve well for the purpose of protecting privacy.

This paper has argued for a right to privacy that would encompass privacy in public. Although it does not articulate a theory from which this extended right can be derived, it has advanced principles to guide the development of such a theory, principles according to which activities that, in the past, have fallen outside the scope of many influential legal and philosophical theories, may be judged relevant to a moral right to privacy. I have in mind here, the principle of contextual integrity and the principle that no information is genuinely "up for grabs", available for purposes such as aggregation, profiling, and data mining. These principles offer criteria for discriminating from among the various forms of public surveillance and record-keeping those that constitute moral violations of privacy and those that do not.

5 Ivy Lane
University Center for Human Values
Princeton University
Princeton, NJ 08544
U.S.A.

---

[82] See for example Laudon, K. "Markets and Privacy," *Communications of the ACM* 39 (9) (1996).

[31]

Privacy, the Workplace and the Internet

Seumas Miller
John Weckert

ABSTRACT. This paper examines workplace surveillance and monitoring. It is argued that privacy is a moral right, and while such surveillance and monitoring can be justified in some circumstances, there is a presumption against the infringement of privacy. An account of privacy precedes consideration of various arguments frequently given for the surveillance and monitoring of employees, arguments which look at the benefits, or supposed benefits, to employees as well as to employers. The paper examines the general monitoring of work, and the monitoring of email, listservers and the World Wide Web. It is argued that many of the common justifications given for this surveillance and monitoring do not stand up to close scrutiny.

KEY WORDS: email, internet, monitoring, privacy, surveillance, workplace, World Wide Web

The coming into being of new communication and computer technologies has generated a host of ethical problems, and some of the more pressing concern the moral notion of privacy. Some of these problems arise from new possibilities of data collections, and software for computer monitoring. For example, computers can now combine and integrate data bases provided by polling and other means to enable highly personalised and detailed voter profiles. Another cluster of problems revolves around the threat to privacy posed by the new possibilities of monitoring and surveillance. For example, telephone tapping, interception of electronic mail messages, minute cameras and virtually undetectable listening and recording devices give unprecedented access to private conversations and other private communications and interactions. Possibly the greatest threat to privacy is posed by the possibility of combining these new technologies and specifically combining the use of monitoring and surveillance devices with certain computer software and computer networks, including the Internet.

Concerns about the use of computer technology to monitor the performance and activity of employees in the workplace are not new (see Garson, 1988; and Zuboff, 1988), and are widely discussed from a variety of perspectives, frequently in computer ethics texts. Johnson (1995), and Forester and Morrison (1991) raise questions regarding the monitoring of work, while Langford (1995) and Severson (1997) both discuss the monitoring of employees email. The works just cited mention arguments both from the point of view of employers and employees. Parker et al. take a different approach (1990). Their discussion is based on a survey taken of attitudes towards monitoring both employees email and computer usage. Similar surveys have also been reported recently by Loch et al. (1998) and Hawk (1994). There are also a number of sociological examinations, including those by Perrolle (1996) and Rule (1996). An argument from the employees' point of view, highlighting employees' problems and concerns is given by Nussbaum (1989). A number of other important discussions are considered later in this paper.

These discussions are useful, but their purposes are different from the current one in this paper. Applied ethics is interdisciplinary by nature, so questions must be examined from a variety of perspectives. Some of the works just cited highlight the problems or perceived problems, some report on what people actually believe, and some give a sociological analysis. The concern in this paper is to examine the question of employee monitoring from a philosophical point of view. Hence the emphasis is on analysis and argument, not on original empirical research.

Provision of an adequate philosophical account of the notion of privacy is a necessary precursor to setting the proper limits of intrusion by the various new technologies. Such an account of privacy would assist in defining the limits to be placed on unacceptably intrusive applications of new technologies. Moreover it would do so in such a way as to be sensitive to the forms of public space created by these technologies and not unreasonably impede those new possibilities of communication and information acquisition which are in fact desirable. As always it is important to balance the rights of individuals against the needs of the community. On the one hand there is a fundamental moral obligation to respect the individual's right to privacy, on the other hand there are the legitimate requirements of, for example, employers to monitor the performances of their employees, and law enforcement agencies to monitor the communications and financial transactions of organised crime. Moreover the working out of these ethical problems is relativised to a particular institutional and technological context. The question as to whether email, for example, ought to be assimilated to ordinary mail depends in part on the nature of the technology in question and the institutional framework in which it is deployed. Perhaps email messages sent on a company owned computer network ought to be regarded as public communications within the organisation however personal their content. These email messages, unlike ordinary mail, are always stored somewhere in the backup system owned by the company and are therefore accessible to the dedicated company cybersleuth (Magney, 1996). In this paper the discussion will be restricted to the notion of privacy with reference to computer monitoring in the workplace. First, an outline of the general notion of privacy.

The notion of privacy has proven to be a difficult one to adequately explicate. One account which has been influential is that by Parent:

> Privacy is the condition of not having undocumented personal knowledge about one possessed by others. . . . [P]ersonal knowledge . . . consists of facts about a person which most individuals in a given society at a given time do not want widely known about themselves (Parent, 1992, p. 92).

A problem with this definition is that personal knowledge and, therefore, privacy, is completely relativised to what people in a particular society, at a particular time, are prepared to disclose about themselves. Accordingly, if in some society everyone is prepared to disclose everything about themselves to everyone else, then they are still, on this account, in a condition of privacy. But they are surely not in a condition of privacy. Rather, they have chosen to abandon such a condition.

Presenting an alternative account is not easy, however, there are a number of general points that can be made (Miller, 1997; Benn, 1988; Warren and Brandeis, 1890). First, the notion of privacy has both a descriptive and a normative dimension. On the one hand privacy consists of not being interfered with, or having some power to exclude, and on the other privacy is held to be a moral right, or at least an important good. Most accounts of privacy acknowledge this much. For example, Warren and Brandeis gave an early and famous definition in terms of the right to be let alone. Naturally the normative and the descriptive dimensions interconnect. What ought to be must be something that realistically could be. The normative dimension of privacy is not a fanciful thing. The proposition must be rejected that the extent and nature of the enjoyment of rights to individual privacy is something to be determined by the most powerful forces of the day, be they market or bureaucratic forces. But it is equally important to avoid utopian sentimentality; it is mere self-indulgence to pine after what cannot possibly be.

Second, privacy is a desirable condition, power or moral right that a person has in relation to other persons and with respect to the possession of information by other persons about him/herself or the observation/perceiving of him/herself by other persons. The kind of "interference" in question is cognitive or perceptual (including perhaps tactile) interference.

Third, the range of matters regarded as private embraces much of what could be referred to as a person's inner self. A demand – as opposed to a request – by one person to know all about another person's thoughts, beliefs, emotions, and bodily sensations and states would be regarded as unacceptable. Naturally there are conditions under which knowledge concerning another person's inner self are appropriate. A doctor, counsellor, psychoanalyst or psychiatrist may need to know about a patient's bodily sensations and states, in so far as this was necessary for successful treatment and in so far as the patient had consented to be treated. Nevertheless such information while no longer unavailable to the doctor or other care worker, would still be unavailable to others, and for the care worker to disclose this information would constitute a breach of confidentiality, except perhaps to another who may be required to assist in the treatment.

Fourth, a person's intimate personal relations with other people are regarded as private. So while a lover might be entitled to know his/her lover's feelings toward him/her, others would not be so entitled. Indeed there would typically be an expectation that such information would not be disclosed by a lover to all and sundry.

Fifth, certain facts pertaining to objects I own, or monies I earn, are held to be private, at least in most Western societies, simply in virtue of my ownership of them. Ownership appears to confer the right not to disclose information concerning the thing owned. Or at least there is a presumption in favour of non-disclosure; a presumption that can be overridden by, for example, the public interest in tax gathering.

Sixth, certain facts pertaining to a person's various public roles and practices, including one's voting decisions are regarded as private. These kinds of facts are apparently regarded as private in part by virtue of the potential, should they be disclosed, of undermining the capacity of the person to function in these public roles or to compete fairly in these practices. If others know how I vote, my right to freely support a particular candidate might be undermined. If business competitors have access to my business plans they will gain an unfair advantage over me. If a would-be employer knows my sexual preferences he or she may unfairly discriminate against me.

Seventh, and more generally, a measure of privacy is necessary simply in order for a person to pursue his or her projects, whatever those projects might be. For one thing reflection is necessary for planning, and reflection requires privacy. For another, knowledge of someone else's plans can enable those plans to be thwarted. Autonomy requires a measure of privacy.

Equipped with this working account of privacy, including a basic taxonomy of the kinds of information regarded as private, let us now consider a number of ethical issues posed by computer monitoring and surveillance in the workplace.

Employers clearly have some rights in seeing that their employees are working satisfactorily. It is not only in the employer's interests that the required tasks are performed efficiently and well. It is also in the interests of other employees and in the interests of the general public. Employees do not want to have to work harder to support lazy or incompetent colleagues. Consumers do not want to buy sub-standard or overpriced products. But it does not follow from this that employees have no right to privacy when at work. Unfortunately, although some may say fortunately, the widespread use of computers has made workplace surveillance very easy.

Does this monitoring and surveillance matter? It is often defended by employers, who argue that it is in the interests of all. Employees who are not performing well are weeded out. Those doing their job well can be rewarded on objective criteria. In addition, and probably most importantly, it leads to more efficient and profitable businesses. But there are other important things in life besides efficiency and profitability. In particular, there is the right to privacy. As was indicated above, privacy considerations take a number of forms. All of these are conceivably relevant to employees in their place of work.

The existence of the right to privacy, and related rights such as confidentiality and autonomy, is sufficient to undermine extreme views such as the view that employees ought to be under surveillance every minute of the working day, or that should they be in a situation where every minute of the working day they suspect that they might be under surveillance, or that there should there be surveillance of a nature or extent in respect of which the employees are ignorant. These extreme situations involve unjustified invasions of privacy. Employers have certain rights in respect of their employees, but there is no general and absolute right to monitor and control employees. This is obvious from the fact that employers are restricted in a whole range of ways by the rights of employees. Employers cannot imprison or rob their employees, and flogging, in order to improve productivity, is not generally condoned. The reason, obviously, why employers cannot imprison or rob (or flog), is that these activities are violations of a human's rights, and the fact that someone is your employee does not confer the right to violate those rights. Even in cases where explicit contracts have been agreed to, there are limits to which either party can go in order to ensure that the other party adheres to that contract.

So much is obvious. What is less obvious is the extent to which an employer can justifiably infringe an employee's right to privacy. It has already been argued that there is a right to privacy, and, other things being equal, employees have this right. The violation of the employee's right to privacy of concern in this paper, is that posed by the electronic surveillance and monitoring of an employee's activities made easy by current computer technology, particularly networking. Keystrokes can be monitored for speed and accuracy, and the work on your screen may be brought up on the screen of another without your knowledge. Common software for accessing the Internet logs all activity, so that a record is kept of all visits to all sites, and email, listservers and so on can monitored. A supervisor can fairly easily find who did what on the Internet. Notwithstanding these technical possibilities of infringing privacy, protection of privacy is high on the list of principles supported by many professional computing association codes of ethics (Barroso, 1997). A good example is found in the Association for Computing Machinery (ACM) code:

Computing and communication technology enables the collection and exchange of personal information on a scale unprecedented in the history of civilization. Thus there is increased potential for violating the privacy of individuals and groups. It is the responsibility of professionals to maintain the privacy and integrity of data describing individuals . . .

This imperative implies that only the *necessary amount of personal information* [emphasis added] be collected in a system, that retention and disposal periods for that information be clearly defined and enforced, and that personal information gathered for a specific purpose not be used for other purposes without consent of the individual(s). These principles apply to electronic communications, including electronic mail, and prohibit procedures that capture or monitor electronic user data, including messages, without the permission of users or bona fide authorization related to system operation and maintenance (1992).

(This code, it should be noted, is the code of a professional computing body, and hence is aimed at computer professionals who often have access to private information stored electronically, in their daily work of creating, managing and maintaining computer systems and networks. There is no implication that *only* computer professionals have responsibilities with respect to individual privacy.)

The quotation above makes it appear that employee monitoring by computer technology is frowned upon by the ACM, and that computer professionals should have no part of it, either in developing necessary software or involvement in the monitoring itself. It could be argued, however, that this surveillance of employees falls within the class of a "necessary amount of personal information"; necessary to the well-functioning of a business. In order to assess the justifiability of computer monitoring, first some arguments for it will be considered, followed by a consideration of a number of criticisms.

Employees, as well as having at least a prima facie right to privacy, are also accountable to their employers because their employers have a right to a reasonable extent and quality of work output for the wages and salaries that they pay, and it is in the employees' interests (as well as the interests of employers) that their employers make a profit. Given potential conflict between these rights, perhaps an employees' right to privacy, *qua* employee, can, in a range of circumstances, be overridden. Three related types of justification are given, in terms of employers, customers, and employees. The most obvious is that with better monitored employees, profitability is greater, although this is sometimes couched in terms of better quality customer service. For example, "quality of service telemarketing monitoring" is the way that the Telemarketing Association portrays employee monitoring (*Direct Marketing*, 1993). The Computer Business and Equipment Manufacturers' Association puts it like this:

> the measurement of work by computer is a legitimate management tool that should be used wisely. Used appropriately, monitoring and related techniques, such as incentive pay or promotion based on productivity, can increase both an organizations effectiveness and the employee's ability to advance (Lund, 1992, p. 54).

Here the emphasis is not just on the employer, it is particularly on the benefit to the employee.

An interesting approach to computer monitoring is presented by DeTienne. She argues that this monitoring can be, not only quite benign, but useful to employees:

> Not only will these computers keep closer tabs on employees, but based on this added information, the computer will be able to help employees do their jobs more effectively. . . .
> Information gathered via computer monitoring will increasingly be used to coach employees. Currently, many organisations use the information gathered as a basis for criticism. Companies will begin to realize that it is more motivating for employees to be coached rather than reproached (1993).

So the claim is that computer monitoring of employees has multiple benefits, at least potentially. It improves the quality of goods and services, and so is good for customers; it makes businesses more efficient, so profits rise, which benefits employers; and it helps employees get higher pay and promotion, and assists them in doing their jobs better. Given all these benefits,

why is it questioned? There are two types of reasons, one type based on the unacceptable consequences to the organisation of monitoring and surveillance. Such consequences include ill health, stress and lowering of morale. The other type of reason concerns the harm to employees, including as a harm, infringement of employees' rights to privacy. Other harms relate to employees' well-being. There is evidence that computer monitored employees suffer health, stress and morale problems to a higher degree than other employees (Bewayo, 1996; Aiello and Kolb, 1996). If it does indeed generate these sorts of problems, then these problems must be weighed against the benefits. It might be countered that if the problems are too great, then monitoring will not make organisations more efficient, and so the practice will stop. Alternatively, the organisations who practice it will not be able to attract good employees, and so will be forced to discontinue it. One weakness of this counter is that workers are not always free to pick and choose their employers, particularly in times and places of high unemployment. Many will almost certainly prefer to work under conditions which they do not like, than to not work at all. Another flaw in the argument is that it is not necessarily true that practices which are detrimental to health and morale will lead to less efficiency, at least not in the short term. For example, forcing workers to work for long hours without rest over extended periods could increase productivity in the short term, but lead to longer term health problems. Raising the levels of stress through continual monitoring could have the same effect. If the work requires a relatively low level of skill, and if there is unemployment, workers are easily replaceable. Treating workers in this fashion may not be good for a businesses' long term viability or profitability, but many businesses are not around for long. If the motive is short term profitability, long term effects are irrelevant. More importantly, treating workers in this fashion may be good for the profitability, long and short term, of that particular business. The problem may be the long term ill effects on the business sector in general, or on the specific industry sector in question.

The moral objection to computer monitoring

is based on the principle that a right cannot be infringed without very good reason. It would be rare that greater efficiency or profitability would constitute such a good reason. There clearly are times when a person's privacy rights can be overridden. An unconscious and unconsenting hospital patient, for example, may need constant monitoring, but that is for the patient's own good. A prison inmate might also need constant monitoring, but that might be for the protection of the community. Monitoring of employees however, does not, in most circumstances, secure these fundamental rights to life and protection.

A defender of computer monitoring might argue that the moral problem only arises if employees have no input into the establishing of the monitoring system, or if they are not fully aware of its scope and implications. If these conditions are satisfied, there is no moral problem, because the employee has, in effect, consented to the system's use, by accepting employment under those conditions.

While this has some initial attraction, on closer examination it is not so plausible. One reason is the same as that discussed in connection with health and morale. When unemployment is high, or if the person badly needs a job, there is not much force in consent. It is rather a case of economic coercion. A second problem is that even if people do consent to some sort of treatment, it does not follow that it is moral to treat them in that manner. Slavery cannot be justified on the grounds that some slaves may not have minded their condition too much if they knew nothing better, and if they had always been taught that slavery was the natural order of things. Likewise, violation of privacy cannot be condoned simply because some employees are willing to accept it.

What can be made of the argument that employee monitoring can be to the benefit of the employees themselves. Their privacy is violated, but it is in a good cause. Three benefits to the employee have been suggested. One is that it can, if used properly, help them to improve their work practices. This might be true, but it would at best only justify short term monitoring, and only with the employee's consent. Perhaps the techniques and satisfaction of clumsy lovers could be

improved by information gained from spying on their activities, but that hardly seems to justify spying. A second benefit is said to be that employees can be assessed on purely objective criteria, say number and accuracy of keystrokes. While objectivity is good, assessment of an employee's worth will usually have a substantial subjective element as well. A highly responsible or experienced person who types slowly may well improve the productivity of others. So at best this is a weak justification for infringement of privacy. Finally, it is argued that this monitoring will help get rid of "dead wood", workers who are not doing their fair share of the work. This will not only be good for the employer, but also for the other employees. However, while none of us want to support lazy and incompetent colleagues, it is not clear that this will not have countervailing effects, namely, on the hardworking and competent workers also thus monitored. There could, of course, be limited and targeted monitoring where there was good reason to believe that particular employees were not meeting reasonable standards. This would seem to be a far more reasonable policy. However this is clearly not *general* monitoring and surveillance of the kind being discussed here. Supporting such colleagues is not good, but violation of privacy would, to many, seem even worse. (For discussion of these three points see De Tienne, 1993; Lund, 1992; and Fenner and Lerch, 1993.)

A stronger argument for employing surveillance is the control of crime in the workplace, especially theft and financial fraud. Law enforcement agencies can have rights which override those of individuals in certain circumstances when it is in the public interest. Theft and fraud in the workplace are still theft and fraud, so some surveillance can be justified in order to apprehend culprits.

Another form of monitoring, perhaps less worrying, but often discussed, is that of monitoring employees' email. While this might be thought to be akin to opening private mail or listening in to private conversations, the argument is that because the system on which the email operates is owned by the employers, they have a right to read any messages (see Loch et al. 1992 for a discussion of a survey on this issue). But do they? The fact that two people are conversing in my house does not give me an automatic right to listen to what they are saying. But what if the two people are my employees? Does this make a difference? One argument that it does not, might go as follows: All I am paying for is my employees' labour. What they say to customers might be my business, but what they say to each other is not if it does not obviously and directly harm the business. Perhaps the cases are not analogous, because in the email case they are using my equipment, while in the other they are not. But what they say is still none of my business even if the consequences of what they say might be. The fact that they are continually having conversations might be overloading the equipment or hindering the work of others or themselves. Accordingly, banning or limiting private conversations might be justified. But this would not justify *monitoring* conversations. Perhaps this still misses the point. How will I know if the email is being used for private discussions unless I monitor it? I will not know unless I am told. But if no problems are being caused by overuse and so on, then there is no need to worry. If no harm is being caused by personal email, either to the computing equipment or to productivity, then monitoring what is said can have no purpose, except perhaps to satisfy curiosity. This is hardly a justification for violating a right. If there are problems such as the overloading of the system or inadequate work levels, then some steps may need to be taken, but even here actually reading messages would rarely be necessary. There could be a limit put on the length or number of messages, or the productivity of employees in question could be investigated. Employing people does not confer the right to monitor their private conversations, whether those conversations be in person or via email.

It might still be argued that what one employee says to a second employee might be my business as employer, if their conversation is work related. But even this cannot in general be correct. Consider the following three situations. First, if the two employees are, say, doctors in a private hospital, then their work related conver-

sation might need to be protected by confidentiality. Second, what an employee is saying to a 'customer' might be protected by confidentiality, for example in the case of a lawyer working for a large corporation. In these circumstance a professional employee, that is, one who is a member of what is commonly thought of as a profession, for example, a medical doctor, lawyer or accountant, will need to be treated differently from a non-professional. Third, even non-professional employees need a measure of autonomy – conferred by privacy in the sense of non-interference and non-intrusion – in respect of one another and the public, if they are to take responsibility for their jobs and their performance in those jobs. Taking responsibility in this sense involves "being left alone" to do, or fail to do, the tasks at hand. Far from having the effect of ensuring that people do not make mistakes, intrusive and ongoing monitoring and surveillance might have the effect of causing employees to underperform because they are never allowed to take responsibility for outcomes, and therefore become lazy or engage in corrupt practices. Consider in this connection a salesman trying to convince a customer to buy a house, or a mechanic trying to figure out what is wrong with a car, or a supervisor trying to instruct a new clerk. The conception of employees that those who favour monitoring or surveillance tend to have in mind seem to be those doing menial, repetitive jobs that do not require any autonomy or individual initiative or judgment in order to be performed.

The discussion so far in relation to the Internet, has concerned only email, but of course Internet access involves much more than just email. Some employees have, on their employer's computing equipment, almost unlimited access to material, particularly through the World Wide Web (WWW). Is it an unjustified invasion of privacy for employers to monitor their employees activity on the WWW, to check on the sites visited? Given costs, particularly in processing time, associated with activity on the WWW, some restrictions seem quite justifiable. It would be difficult to condemn an employer who prohibited access except for work-related tasks. Given general knowledge of this prohibition, the periodic checks of the sites accessed by employees is not unreasonable. More interesting problems arise in situations where employees require very free access in order to do their jobs properly, for example, many people involved in education. Universities, typically, allow their staff completely unfettered Internet access. Does the university then have a right to know how its employees are using this access? In general it would seem not. From a privacy perspective, there is no problem with restricting access to certain sites by the use of software. Monitoring sites visited, however, is not such an acceptable way of restricting access. Monitoring someone's use of the Internet in this way is a bit like monitoring library use, and it is instructive to look at how the library profession views the privacy issue.

Librarians have long been concerned about maintaining the privacy of library users' reading habits. The American Library Association puts its concern this way:

> The ethical responsibilities of librarians . . . protect the privacy of library users. Confidentiality extends to "information sought or received, and materials consulted, borrowed, acquired," and includes database search records, reference interviews, circulation records, interlibrary loan records, and other personally identifiable uses of library materials, facilities, or services (*ALA Policy Manual*, 1996).

Why have librarians traditionally been so concerned about privacy? The reading habits of library users are the business of nobody except the user, but that in itself is not too important. My preference for unsugared, black tea rather than the sweet, white variety is also the business of nobody but me and the person making it for me, but worrying about the privacy of this information seems a bit extravagant. While much information about users which is stored in library databases might not be much more important than my preference in tea, in general, reading habits do reveal a little more about a person. It can been argued that what someone reads is very close to what he or she thinks, and therefore the ability to discover what is read is, in effect, the ability to find out what is thought.

It is not difficult to imagine situations where governments, advertising agencies or other groups could make use of this information for purposes which were not beneficial to the individual. For example, according to Million and Fisher, in the United States the Moral Majority attempted to obtain the names of school districts and individuals who had borrowed a film on sexual maturity from the Washington State Library (1986). Sometimes of course it might be beneficial to the community, for example when law enforcement agencies need information for criminal investigations. Borrowers, however, can be harmed if their records are not kept private. The burden of proof should be on those who want records made public, or at least available. The privacy of the individual can be overridden, but only to protect more important individual rights, or for the sake of very significant public goods (for further discussion see Weckert and Adeney, 1997).

Given that university librarians are part of the library profession, according to their own code of ethics, they are bound to keep library records private, including the borrowing records of university staff. From a professional librarian's point of view then, it would be an invasion of privacy for the university to check on an employee's borrowing record, even though the library is university owned and operated. It is difficult to see where the relevant difference lies is between the library and the Internet in this instance. Both are sources of information.

One complicating factor which rears its head in the context of email and Internet monitoring is vicarious libality, that is, the liability an employer might have for the actions of his or her employees. *Black's Law Dictionary* defines it thus:

> The imposition of liability on one person for the actionable conduct of another, based solely on a relationship between the two persons. Indirect or imputed legal responsibility for acts of another; for example, the liability of an employer for the acts of an employee . . . (1990).

Given this, it seems irresponsible of an employer not to monitor the email of employees or their use of the Internet in general. If this does not happen, the employer could be liable for breaches of the law with respect to, for example, defamation, copyright infringement and obscene material (Cutler, 1998). It does not follow from this however, that an employer has the right to monitor employee activity on the Internet which the employee could reasonably expect to be private. It does though, strengthen an employer's right to insist that his or her computing equipment is not to be used for anything apart from legitimate work related purposes. This policy must, of course, be made clear. It also might call into question the appropriateness of maintaining vicarious liability in some of these contexts. At any rate, the general point to be made here is that where an employer allows private email and other Internet activity, his vicarious liability does not necessarily legitimise monitoring of that activity.

Finally, should employers be able to monitor listservers which are on their computer systems? For employers in general, this will probably be a rare situation, but not for universities. Suppose that a university runs courses by distance education, something which is becoming increasingly common. The lecturer and students decide to establish a listserver to facilitate discussion, and to help overcome the isolation often felt by distance education students. Does the university have a right to monitor activity on that listserver without notifying the participants? It might be argued that they do, because the listserver is public in the same sense that a university lecture theatre is, and so any authorised university person has access. The analogy however, is not good. If someone enters a lecture theatre, he or she is there for all to see. There is no question of secrecy. Suppose now that the university monitors lectures, not by having staff attend, but rather by secretly installing cameras and microphones. The analogy here is closer, but the monitoring does not seem so benign. It might be objected that in the listserver case there is nothing secret. The university monitor enrols, so it is not too difficult to discover the monitoring. Just look to see who is enrolled. But that is not the point. If there is to be monitoring, the onus for making it public should not be on those monitored, but on those monitoring.

Drawing an analogy between listservers and lecture theatres is misleading in any case. While it is true that authorised university staff can attend lectures in university owned buildings without violating anyone's right to privacy, nothing follows from this about secret listserver monitoring. Normally university lectures are not private. Anyone can come and listen. The situation changes a little with tutorials, where there is more interaction, and at private discussion between a lecturer and a student. It is not so clear that the university would be justified in authorising someone to monitor tutorials, without the tutors and students knowledge, or to monitor private student-lecturer discussions. The claim that this is justified simply because these activities are taking place on university property is dubious at best. Listservers seem more like tutorials than lectures. There is some privacy. One cannot just look and see what is happening, as is possible with a newsgroup. One must enrol. Secret monitoring of class listservers then, can be seen as a violation of privacy rights, just as secret monitoring of tutorials would be.

Workplace monitoring is a practice which requires much more examination. Employers need an efficient and competent workforce in order to survive in a competitive environment, and customers demand and deserve high quality goods and services. The employees who produce these goods and services have a responsibility to work to the best of their ability for the financial reward that they receive, but they do not forfeit their rights to privacy by virtue of being employees. Although workplace monitoring can be justified in some circumstances, privacy is a moral right, and as such there is a presumption against its infringement. This paper has argued that some of the common justifications given for this monitoring do not withstand close scrutiny.

A number of questions remain to be researched, both empirical and analytical. One of these questions is the relationship between monitoring and trust in the workplace. It would appear that monitoring is a sign or distrust, and perhaps employees who know that they are being monitored, and hence not trusted, will become less trustworthy, in which case they will require more monitoring. Superficially at least, it appears that monitoring could precipitate a breakdown in trust, which in the longer term would probably lead to a less efficient workforce. But this requires investigation. Another issue is the role of vicarious liability in the violation of individual employee privacy. It seems that the current law (in countries which have it), or its interpretation, encourages, or even necessitates employee monitoring which is morally questionable. Perhaps the law requires modification in the light of contemporary computer technology. Privacy is perhaps the topic most discussed by those concerned about the social and ethical implications of computer technology. It deserves to be.

References

ACM Code of Ethics and Professional Conduct: 1992, Section 1.7. http://www.acm.org/constitution/code.html (Read 25 July, 1998).

Aiello, John R. and Kathryn, J. Kolb: 1996, 'Electronic Performance Monitoring: A Risk Factor for Workplace Monitoring', in S. L. Sauter and L. R. Murphy, (eds.), *Organisational Risk Factors for Job Stress* (American Psychological Association), pp. 163–179.

ALA Policy Manual: 1996, Section Two (Position and Public Policy Statements), 52.4 Confidentiality of Library Records, gopher://ala1.ala.org:70/00/alagophviii/policy.hb (Read 25 July 1998).

Barroso Asenjo, P.: 1997, 'Key Ethical Concepts for the Internet and for Ethical Codes of Computer Professionals', *Australian Computer Journal* 29, 2–5.

Benn, S. A.: 1988, *Theory of Freedom* (Cambridge University Press, Cambridge).

Bewayo, E.: 1996 , 'Electronic Management: Its Downside Especially in Small Business', in J. Kizza (ed.), *Social and Ethical Effects of the Computer Revolution* (McFarland and Co., Jefferson, NC), pp. 186–199.

Black, Henry Campbell: 1990, *Black's Law Dictionary*, 6th edition (West Publishing Co., St. Paul, MN), p. 1566.

Cutler, P. G.: 1998, 'E-mail: Employees and Liability', *Chemistry in Australia* (March, 1), 30–31.

DeTienne, K. B.: 1993, 'Big Brother or Friendly Coach', *Futurist* 27, 33–37.

Direct Marketing: 1993, 'Telephone Monitoring Heads to Congress', (August 6), 6. Quoted in M. Levy,

'Electronic Monitoring in the Workplace: Power Through the Panopticon', http://bliss.berkeley.edu/impact/students/mike/mike_   paper.html (Read 25 July 1998).

Fenner, Deborah B. and F. Javier Lerch: 1993, 'The Impact of Computerized Performance Monitoring and Prior Performance Knowledge on Performance Evaluation', *Journal of Applied Social Psychology* 23, 573–601.

Forester, Tom and Perry Morrison: 1991, *Computer Ethics: Cautionary Tales and Ethical Dilemmas in Computing* (MIT Press, Cambridge, MA).

Garson, Barbara: 1988, *The Electronic Sweatshop* (Simon and Schuster, New York).

Hawk, Stephen, R.: 1994, *Journal of Business Ethics* 13, 949–957.

Johnson, Deborah G.: 1994, *Computer Ethics*, Second edition (Prentice Hall, Upper Saddle River, NJ).

Langford, Duncan: 1995, *Practical Computer Ethics* (McGraw-Hill, Maidenhead, Berkshire).

Loch, Karen D., Sue Conger and Effy Oz: 1998, 'Ownership, Privacy and Monitoring in the Workplace: A Debate on Technology and Ethics', *Journal of Business Ethics* 17, 653–663.

Lund, J.: 1992, 'Electronic Performance Monitoring: A Review of the Research Issues', *Applied Ergonomics* 23, 54–58.

Magney, J.: 1996, 'Computing and Ethics: Control and Surveillance Versus Cooperation and Empowerment', in J. Kizza (ed.), *Social and Ethical Effects of the Computer Revolution* (McFarland and Co., Jefferson, NC), pp. 200–209.

Miller, S.: 1997 'Privacy and the Internet', *Australian Computer Journal* 29, 12–15, for a similar discussion of the notion of privacy.

Million, A. C. and K. N. Fisher: 1986, 'Library Records: A Review of Confidentiality Laws and Policies', *Journal of Academic Librarianship* 11, 346–349.

Nussbaum, Karen: 1991, 'Computer Monitoring a Threat to the Right to Privacy?', reprinted in Roy Dejoie, George Fowler and David Paradice, *Ethical Issues in Information Systems* (Boyd and Fraser Publishing Company, Boston).

Parent, P. "Privacy": 1992, in E. E. Cohen (ed.), *Philosophical Issues in Journalism* (Oxford University Press, New York), pp. 90–99.

Parker, Donn B., Susan Swope and Bruce N. Baker: 1990, *Ethical Conflicts In Information and Computer Science, Technology, and Business* (QED Information Sciences, Inc., Wellesley, MA).

Perrolle, Judith A.: 1996, 'Privacy and Surveillance in Computer-Supported Cooperative Work', in

David Lyon and Elia Zureik (eds.), *Computers, Surveillance, and Privacy* (University of Minnesota Press, Minneapolis), 47–65.

Rule, James, B.: 1996, 'High-Tech Workplace Surveillance: What's Really New?', in David Lyon and Elia Zureik (eds.), *Computers, Surveillance, and Privacy* (University of Minnesota Press, Minneapolis), pp. 66–76.

Severson, Richard J.: 1997, *The Principles of Information Ethics* (M.E. Sharp, Armonk, NY).

Warren, S. and L. Brandeis: 1890, 'The Right to Privacy', *Harvard Law Review* **4**, 193–220.

Weckert, J. and D. Adeney: 1997, *Computer and Information Ethics* (Greenwood Publishing Group, Westport, Conn.).

Zuboff, Shoshana: 1988, *In the Age of the Smart Machine: The Future of Work and Power* (Basic Books, New York).

ARC Special Research Centre for
Applied Philosophy and Public Ethics,
Wagga Wagga,
Australia.

[32]

Surveillance in Employment: The Case of Teleworking

N. Ben Fairweather

ABSTRACT. This paper looks at various ways teleworking can be linked to surveillance in employment, making recommendations about how telework can be made more acceptable. Technological methods can allow managers to monitor the actions of teleworkers as closely as they could monitor "on site" workers, and in more detail than the same managers could traditionally. Such technological methods of surveillance or monitoring have been associated with low employee morale. For an employer to ensure health and safety may require inspections of the teleworkplace. When the teleworkplace is in the home, there may be an invasion of privacy associated with such inspections, that could be perceived and resented as surveillance. A problem of telework is that teleworkers may feel isolated. Methods to counter this could be associated with further forms of surveillance, and fear of such surveillance may inhibit them from reaching their potential as methods to counter isolation. The idea that teleworking may also allow communications to be intercepted by third parties is also looked at. Some, but not all, of the issues considered are applicable, to some extent, in non-teleworked employment situations. The overall conclusion of the paper is that the potential exists for surveillance to be associated with telework. Fears of such surveillance may turn actors against telework. However, much can be done to reduce such fears.

KEY WORDS: Computer Based Performance Monitoring, Electronic Performance Monitoring, employment, health and safety, home workers, interception of communications, monitoring, surveillance, telecommuting, telework

N. Ben Fairweather is Research Fellow in the Centre for Computing and Social Responsibility at De Montfort University, Leicester. He has published articles in Business Ethics: European Review and Communications of the ACM, and numerous conference proceedings.

ABBREVIATIONS: ASCII – American Standard Code for Information Interchange; CBPM – Computer Based Performance Monitoring; ICTs – Information and Communications Technologies

1. Introduction

This paper takes as a starting point the idea that "outside of special contexts, revelation of self is not . . . desirable" (Schoeman, 1984, p. 404). While there is no doubt that employers have a legitimate interest in a certain amount of monitoring of their employees, to ascertain that they are not paying an employee to do nothing, there is also no doubt that the employee is not a slave – the employee should not be required to reveal their whole self to the employer: in other words there is scope for some privacy. The special contexts where revelations of intimate information are desirable quite clearly do not include normal employer-employee situations. They are: intimate relationships, crises, and freely chosen revelation of personal information (such as publication of diaries or consultation with professionals) where it is clear there is no expectation of an intimate relationship (Schoeman, 1984, p. 405). To allow intimate information to remain private, workers and teleworkers should not normally have personal communications under surveillance by their employer, and the employer should not routinely monitor the nature or content of a worker's home life or the length of time employees spend on visits to the toilet.

1.1. *Telework*

Some types of telework can also be called telecommuting, and while I would contend that not all telework is telecommuting, the central concerns of this paper are ones that apply in the types of telework that could be called telecommuting. Telecommuting can be defined as using information and communications technologies (ICTs) to bring work to the worker, rather than require them to go to the work.

Telework can give substantial benefits both to employers and to many employees. "By shifting the workplace from a traditional office to the home, employers can potentially make considerable savings in the costs of office space . . . including office rental" (Odgers, 1994), which could amount to more than UK£21,000 per year for a single employee in some circumstances (Parkinson, 1995, p. 3). Telework offers opportunities for productivity improvements (Stanworth and Stanworth, 1991, pp. 21–24) as workers no longer suffer from the tiredness associated with physical commuting and are removed from many of the distractions of a traditional office (but a total absence of such "distractions" may cause problems of isolation – see below).

The time saved that previously would have been used commuting could either be used entirely by the teleworkers for the non-work parts of their life, giving them a substantial benefit, or could be (partly) used to give longer working hours, of benefit to the employer, while the cost of commuting often can also be saved, and there are a number of other potential advantages (European Telework Online, 1996?).

However, "Home based telework is inappropriate for some people – for example those who have poor personal motivation and are not 'self starters'", and telework from home requires sufficient space and freedom from disturbance to be available in the home, and not all tasks are appropriate for telework (European Telework Online, 1996?).

2. **Traditional management**

There has, in many situations, been a marked reluctance by managers to allow the introduction of telework. One of the most important factors behind this has been a fear that traditional ways of controlling workers are not suitable in teleworking situations. It has thus been suggested that management by objectives is introduced, "allowing employees autonomy to organise their own work". However this "can lead to managers fearing a loss of control over subordinates, especially those who adopt a traditional managerial style" (both quotes Symes, 1995, p. 5). A survey of U.K. managers' opinions has shown that many feel that home based workers would be inclined to under-perform (European Telework Online, 1996?). This should hardly be surprising, given that when.

> the social turmoil of the 1960's and 1970's erupted across the business landscape, and as women joined the ranks of management in unprecedented numbers, the power relationship of organization to worker, and the demand for conformity and compliance remained as strong as ever. (Brown, 1996, p. 1238)

Traditionally, it has been possible for many managers to monitor time of arrival and departure by simple observation, without any thought or effort. It has been such a "natural" way of monitoring staff that even in situations where management by results has, formally, been adopted; it is difficult for managers to resist expressing disapproval at workers arriving in the office "late" in the morning. Equally, managers have traditionally been able to monitor what particular employees are doing at any given time by visiting them at their desks and looking over their shoulder. When managers are resistant to change, they are likely to be especially resistant to changes that as a side effect require a change in management methods.

2.1. *Surveillance*

The controls exercised by typical enterprises in the post industrial revolution capitalist economy have been called "surveillance" (Lyon, 1994, p. 34; Dandeker, 1990, p. 157; see also Foucault, 1977, p. 207, p. 221), because the need to maintain control of such aspects as promotion practices, wage scales and job categorisations has required the collection of "objective" data on employees, rather than relying on personal relationships. There is some merit in this description, because the workplace in a capitalist economy through most of the twentieth century has been a place where the activities of the individual have been subject to a high degree of control and monitoring by supervisors and managers. It has not been acceptable for the worker to do what they think right, or what would benefit the enterprise most, or even to fulfil their task in the best way they can: supervisors and managers have required workers to work in particular uniform ways, even when those methods do not match the talents of the individual workers. Equally times of arrival and departure have been recorded automatically, to provide "objective" data.

However, these methods differ from what we characteristically call surveillance of individuals, in that normally there is interest in only part of the worker's life, albeit a large part: the time they are at work, further, there is nothing surreptitious about them.

3. Close technological monitoring

In the last years of the twentieth century, computer software packages for the first time enable Computer Based Performance Monitoring (CBPM) (also known as Electronic Performance Monitoring, Electronic Work Monitoring and Electronic Monitoring Systems (Aiello and Shao, 1993, p. 1011)). This significantly expands the scope of management to collect and process data on their workers. The technologies for CBPM have had quite wide application even without being associated with telework, with tens of millions of workers evaluated by measures derived from such systems (Aiello and Kolb, 1995, p. 163).

Such technological methods allow a manager to maintain as close an awareness of the actions of teleworkers as they ever could if the workers had been at the same location as the manager without the use of CBPM (Brown, 1996, p. 1239). Indeed it is possible for managers to

monitor teleworking employees in more detail than the same managers could traditionally. "The availability of technology based access may even lead decision makers to seek out information they would not have asked for in person." (Lally, 1996, pp. 1222–1223) While traditionally, managers usually could only spend a small proportion of their time on the monitoring part of their responsibilities, and could not pay attention to all of the workers they were managing at any given time, CBPM allows constant monitoring of all the employees it is applied to without taking much time or effort for the manager (Aiello and Shao, 1993, p. 1011).

Methods include monitoring the number of key-strokes a data-entry clerk makes in an hour, the length of telephone calls (Utility Consumers' Action Network, 1997), "the time between phone calls, and the time an individual spends away from his or her desk" (Spinello, 1995, p. 10).

3.1. Trades unions

Trades unions have a number of key concerns about telework. One of these is that collective bargaining may become impossible with dispersed and isolated workers, especially with workers that have never worked at a large company office (Odgers, 1994). They are also worried that out-of-hours work and requirements to be available on-call may be introduced without payments at levels that are currently normal for such contracts (Odgers, 1994).

Trades unions have strong opposition to electronic monitoring, in part because of its use in data entry workplaces, where workers have complained of tenosynovitis because of the relentless pace of work expected (Bibby, 1996). However, they have resisted technological monitoring in other circumstances, including monitoring of telephone calls (Browne, 1995).

3.2. Monitoring of communications

The practice of monitoring workers' communication "has been long-standing practice in many industries" (Brown, 1996, p. 1240). It is wide-spread, and is carried out in an "anthoritative" and in some cases covert fashion by "A growing number of firms such as Pillsbury, UPS, and Intel Corporation" (Spinello, 1997). For example, "Kmart Corporation . . . has adopted a policy that allows the company to review all E-mail messages, and every employee is informed of this policy at orientation meetings" (Samuels, 1996). It is not restricted to the United States, either: "One of the biggest problems faced by all staff in BT [British Telecommunications PLC] is the growth in the use of remote monitoring. . . . This is carried out in the workplace, either by remotely monitoring telephone calls or . . . the voicebox etc." (Browne, 1995)

Among the key reasons for a business to claim the right to intercept or inspect employees communications, one – ownership of the system – is dealt with later, while the other two principal reasons claimed are the prevention of misuse and quality control, which are dealt with now.

Misuse. "Companies that . . . inspect their employees' e-mail messages . . . maintain [that it] can help prevent blatant misuse of the corporation's E-mail system" (Spinello, 1997).

Such monitoring, is not limited to email, however. Monitoring of telephone conversations is also routine in many work situations, and can equally be applied to telework.

There are two broad types of "misuse" that monitoring is designed to counter, personal use, and directly harmful use. I will deal first with personal use.

Fear that communication is being monitored may make employees less likely to "waste company time by conversing with friends and relatives" (Spinello, 1997). However, in a society where employees live alone, or with others who are in paid employment, each working eight hour days, these employees "often have no choice but to conduct some personal business from their offices" (and, by extension, in the case of tele-workers, their teleworkplace) (Spinello, 1997). In such cases, there should be a reasonable *prima facie* expectation of privacy in such dealings. The need to conduct personal business during work hours is especially strong for those working conven-

tional hours, which are the only opening hours of many of the offices that they need to deal with in their private lives.

Many teleworkers will be working less conventional hours, and so will not feel the pressure to conduct personal business in working hours so severely. However, for those working full-time, the sheer length of the working week may make conducting personal business outside working hours difficult. Moreover, in conducting personal business, there is a regular requirement to be available to take telephone calls throughout normal working hours: many of the offices that a person deals with in their private life cannot cope with a requirement to only call at certain hours of the day.

In such circumstances, it is unreasonable for an employer to expect that no use at all is made of company time and resources for private business that remains private. However, when use for private business is significantly detrimental to the performance of the job that the employer has paid for, or uses a valuable quantity of resources, it is reasonable for an employer to take action, which might include monitoring.

The enunciation of the restricted circumstances in which monitoring might be appropriate because of excessive private use, does not however, tell us anything about monitoring to counter use which directly harms.

There can be little doubt that "if employees know that E-mail is monitored they are less likely to divulge valuable trade secrets through this medium, . . . or even use E-mail for illegal or fraudulent purposes." (Spinello, 1997) This may cause employers to claim the right to monitor communications. This is not, however, the end of the story. Most of us would not consider it acceptable if all of our post were read, which is why there are laws against such interception of post. Rogerson (1998, p. 23) suggests that "Organisations must consider the principle of proportionality where a balance has to be struck between the legitimate needs of an organisation . . . and the fundamental right of an individual to privacy". Spinello provides a clear and appropriate indication of how that balance should be struck:

The civil liberties of innocent people should not be suppressed because a few rogue employees might abuse those liberties. If a corporation has legitimate suspicions that someone is using its E-mail systems for illegal, untoward or frivolous reasons, it should investigate and take any necessary action (Spinello, 1997).

When there are no such suspicions, the possibility of such abuse of the systems should not outweigh the reasonable expectation of employees to be trusted by their employer.

Quality control. Companies that inspect their employees' e-mail messages "also claim that E-mail monitoring is an important means of quality control in some businesses where its workers are engaged in frequent E-mail contact with customers or suppliers." (Spinello, 1997) Similarly, "The pretext given by BT" for monitoring of staff telephone calls "is that it is to improve the quality of service to the customer by identifying areas of further staff development and training requirements" (Browne, 1995). Once again, a comparison with conventional mail is instructive: only trainees would expect all of their outgoing letters from their workplace to be monitored. This must give rise to the suspicion that close technological monitoring takes place more because it is technologically easy then because there is any great need for it. "It is seen by the members as very sinister and an obvious invasion of their privacy – especially when managers have the ability to listen in on private conversations. The moves have been resisted by the CWU [Union]" (Browne, 1995). It is also important to note that on 25th June 1997, the European Court of Human Rights ruled that workers have a "reasonable expectation" of privacy in making and receiving telephone calls at work (Bunyan, 1997), and it is reasonable to expect that this applies equally to emails and other communications at work (Campbell, 1997).

3.3. Consequences of monitoring

One worry with all types of surveillance and monitoring is that they give power over those

monitored to those who carry out the monitoring, which may be greater than the power it is appropriate for them to have, especially when they come to know intimate information about the monitored (Fried, 1968, p. 216).

A particular issue is where an employee works with a number of managers, or where an employee's communications are monitored by someone other than their line-manager. In such circumstances, there is a distinct possibility that information will fall into inappropriate hands within the organisation (Spinello, 1997). This can cause a variety of problems, including breaches of internal security and giving knowledge that amounts to organisational power to those who do not deserve it.

More typical, however, is concern that "It is . . . a method of total control which makes the individual totally 'visible' for the entire workday" (Brown, 1996, p. 1242) and as such it is seen as "a serious threat to employees privacy" (Browne, 1995).

Studies have linked "psychological illnesses such as anxiety, depression and nervous breakdown to the stress induced by continuous computer monitoring of workplace performance" (Brown, 1996, p. 1242).

Monitoring is particularly likely with email, one of the technologies most closely associated with telework, because "unlike . . . other forms of communication E-mail technology [almost automatically] provides an easy means of saving and inspecting messages for many years." (Spinello, 1997). With other forms of communication, the setting up of recording and monitoring may be relatively complex and time consuming. With email messages already in ASCII code, using a computer to search large numbers of emails for mentions of particular words is as easy as searching in a document being word-processed.

The fear that intimate or organisational information may fall into the wrong hands may lead those who are subject to surveillance or monitoring "to be constantly apprehensive and inhibited" in actions and communication that may be monitored. "There is always an unseen audience, which is the more threatening because of the possibility that one may forget about it and let down his guard, as one would not with a visible audience." (Fried, 1968, p. 216)

Even apart from circumstances where the worker has a fear about what damage can be done to them, or what unjustified power might be acquired by those monitoring communications, there are reasons to be worried about surveillance being an invasion of privacy. As Fried points out (1968, p. 216):

> where any intimate revelation may be heard by monitoring officials, it loses the quality of a gesture of love or friendship. Thus monitoring, in depriving one of privacy, destroys the possibility of bestowing the gift of intimacy, and makes impossible the essential dimension of love and friendship.

While Manning (1997, p. 821) argues "the sharing of information is merely a consequence of trust and caring which is part of intimate relationships", that does not make monitoring less serious for her, because "such surveillance is . . . a violation of my self qua worker. If, as a worker in company *X*, I am not considered trustworthy or competent enough to do my job without surveillance, my sense of myself is diminished."

Given the links with psychological illness, it is not surprising that where technological methods have been introduced for such detailed monitoring or surveillance, they have in some cases been associated with very low employee morale, where in the worst cases workers claim their plight is equivalent to "'working as a slave and being whipped, not in our bodies but in our minds'" (Bibby, 1996; see also Odgers, 1994). Even in the best cases "The monitored . . . is denied the sense of self-respect inherent in being trusted" (Fried, 1968, p. 216; Manning, 1997, p. 818).

The possibility of low morale among teleworking employees could dissuade an employer from implementing telework when they might otherwise be in favour. While it is possible to avoid the low morale associated with close monitoring by implementing telework without technological monitoring, not all employers are aware of the practicality of so doing.

4. Working conditions: health and safety

In the United Kingdom, as in many other wealthy societies, there are considerable legal obligations on the employer to ensure that workplaces are safe. In societies where there is little practical choice available about whether to work for an employer or not this provides a vital manifestation of a clear moral right to a means to obtain an income that does not endanger health. It is also clear that the teleworkplace counts as a workplace for such maters, both as a matter of morality, and as a matter of law (e.g. Odgers, 1994).

4.1. *Unions*

Trades unions have worries about the effect of telework on union surveillance of working conditions. Thus Unions are worried that telework combined with looking after children could reduce legitimate pressure for workplace nurseries, despite many parents being unable to combine telework and parenting without a nursery place (Odgers, 1994) (this is because some work will combine with childcare more easily, and different children need different amounts of attention).

Teleworking also makes it more difficult for the union to monitor health and safety in the workplace, because "Access to union occupational health and safety delegates . . . is likely to be difficult", and it is more difficult for isolated workers to refuse to work in ways that are unsafe (Odgers, 1994), because of a lack of colleagues close at hand to offer support.

Additionally, some will argue that if the equipment used by a teleworker has not been physically provided by the employer, responsibility for the safe functioning of that equipment does not fall on the employer, but on the supplier of the equipment and/or the user (Odgers, 1994). If responsibility were to fall initially on the supplier, it would also be possible for a supplier to claim that misuse was not their responsibility in a way that it is impossible for an employer that also has responsibility for training to claim. If responsibility were to fall on the individual, trades unions are likely to be worried that this "privatisation of responsibility" (Odgers, 1994) would spread to traditional workplaces.

4.2. Employers

For an employer to meet their legal requirement to ensure health and safety may well require inspections of the teleworkplace (Odgers, 1994; Union of Communication Workers, 1992?, p. 7).

When the teleworkplace is in the home, there may be an invasion of privacy associated with such inspections. Where a teleworker also has links with a trades union, it then becomes possible for visitors to spot trade union literature that could be sent to the home rather than a central office of an employer hostile to unions. Any type of materials present in the home, including religious symbols or dress could be seen in this way. Similarly, when, as in the United Kingdom, discrimination on grounds of sexuality is legally permitted, the presence of other adult household members of the same gender as the employee, or evidence of their existence, could cause problems. Even when the employee is careful to avoid such occurrences, other household members may accidentally leave things in plain sight, or they could be observed by the visitor making reasonable use of the toilet (or seeking to use that as an excuse for further invasion of privacy). Thus concerns about surveillance by employers may be placed on the whole household, in a way that could constitute an invasion of privacy for the whole household.

When so much information may be gleaned from home visits, their frequent or unannounced occurrence may cause substantial fears. Unlike with traditional management techniques, there is the potential for the whole of the employee's life to come under scrutiny. If they are used at all systematically, such visits (when unannounced or frequent) can be seen to amount to surveillance, even if their primary purpose is to monitor health and safety.

Occasional pre-announced visits should accomplish as much as frequent or unannounced ones in maintaining health and safety standards. There is one slight exception to this, when employees wilfully disguise risks they are running to hide them in announced visits. Such hiding of risks itself would, *ceteris paribus*, be evidence that the employee knows they are breaking procedures, in a way which morally can be seen as constituting taking responsibility for the risks they are running. The principal exception, where hiding of risks would not constitute the individual worker taking responsibility for risks, is when there is implicit or explicit pressure to break procedures or connivance in such breaches from the employer. For this reason, it is perfectly reasonable for employees to see frequent or unannounced visits as surveillance even when not used systematically, and it is also reasonable for frequent or unannounced visits to be resented by employees.

An additional issue of concern for employers of teleworkers may be that physical isolation means employees no longer have the opportunity to informally learn good working practices from each other (Odgers, 1994).

5. Supply of equipment

There are two basic types of situation that need to be considered when looking at the financing of equipment and teleworkplace costs in teleworking. The first situation is where telework generates substantial benefits for an employer (whether through a need for less office accommodation, or some other route), or is for some other reason at the instigation of the employer. Under these circumstances, a strong moral obligation falls upon the employer to ensure that the teleworker is not worse off by working under arrangements that give unusual benefits to the employer (Odgers, 1994), and the employer should pay for the full costs, including for office space in the home, even when providing the space has not caused the employee out-of-pocket expenditure.

The second situation is where teleworking is permitted by an employer largely as a concession to particular individuals who wish to telework, at the individuals' instigation. In such a situation, the employer may question "whether they can shift the burden of workstations onto users in exchange for the privileges and benefits for working from home." (Girard, 1998) Where this results in substantial savings for the employer, it is appropriate that those savings are spent to offset some or all of the out of pocket expenses of teleworking employees. A crucial consideration here, however, must be that teleworkers are able to return to the central work-place. This would require that equipment and space at the central workplace are available for possible returning former teleworkers to use. Such space and equipment will also involve costs, and thus savings to the employer may be reduced (however, it would be reasonable for such space to be less than the amount of office space that the total number of teleworkers would be allocated if they were not teleworking, and thus some savings could still be made).

To start to meet this obligation to meet the costs[1] of the teleworking employee, some employers may provide equipment. Further, there are indications (Girard, 1998) that it is cheaper for the employer to provide a computer and associated equipment than to support employee-owned computers. However, employers providing computers with software pre-loaded opens up the possibility that meeting such an obligation simultaneously enables employers to include software that enables reports to automatically be sent to the employer by CBPM systems, as well as data that could indicate what non-work activities computers are used for. A particular concern is that such surveillance by employer-supplied equipment could be conducted without the employee knowing that the equipment is capable of being used as such a tool of surveillance. This suggests that perhaps a better solution is for the worker to order equipment to be delivered direct from suppliers, but at the employers expense.

This is a particular instance of a broader problem: "some organizations contend that because they own the computer resources, the hardware, software, and networks on which E-mail messages are transmitted, they should have an unconditional right to control and monitor the contents of those messages." but "By this logic the corporation would have the right to inspect everything written with a company pen!"

(Spinello, 1997). Further, the European Court of Human Rights was quite clear that ownership does not permit surveillance, in rejecting the U.K. Government's case that taps of telephones were not in breach of human rights where telephones were government property (Bunyan, 1997).

6. Isolation

One of the recognised problems associated with telework is that teleworkers may feel isolated. Thus the "Australian Public Service Home Based Work Interim Award" (1994), an agreement negotiated by trades unions, established the presumption that the teleworker would spend "at least two-fifths of his/her usual weekly hours of duty at the office based site" (Odgers, 1994).

6.1. *Video*

Methods to counter isolation may include the provision of video-conferencing facilities (Union of Communication Workers, 1992?, p. 1; Cook, 1995). A side effect of video-conferencing is that whatever is in the background may be seen. As with home visits for health and safety purposes, anything or anyone present in the home could come to the notice of managers, if they appear in the view of an working video camera. Again, even when the employee is careful, other household members may accidentally leave things within the view of the camera, or move through vision showing something that the employee wishes to keep private from the employer. Again, fear of surveillance by the employer may affect the whole household, with the possibility of that being an invasion of privacy for the whole household.

Ways of avoiding surveillance as a side effect of video conferencing include allowing the teleworker complete control about when the camera is one, but this could still give rise to problems if the camera were left accidentally on. A more reliable method is for the teleworkplace to be in a room that is only used as the teleworkplace.

Telework may make use of technologies other than video conferencing to reduce isolation:

With regard to the effects of isolation, in the Inverness Experiment, as well as the video link already described, an electronic mail system was also provided. This enabled the teleworkers to receive general updates on events within the Unit and also Union information (Cook, 1995).

These other forms of communication are particularly important in more typical cases of telework, where the telecommunications costs of video links are a more significant factor that they are for a telecommunications business.

6.2. *Peer-to-peer communication*

Another method to counter feelings of isolation among teleworkers is to facilitate peer-to-peer communication, "many interactions in the workplace intersperse business and personal information; this often happens inadvertently as workers discuss what's new in their personal lives as they conduct business." (Spinello, 1997) Such interactions have the potential to make even the most boring jobs bearable. Furthermore, such informal communication can provide the breeding ground for ideas about how work processes could be improved, and waste reduced: or in more initiative – based employment, the opportunity for creative ideas to be worked out.

If such peer-to-peer communication is facilitated through video-conferencing, e-mail or telephone calls at the employer's expense, there again may be a strong potential for surveillance of such peer-to-peer communication. Managers may have a fear of such communication, as it enables workers to share stories detrimental to the image of the manager, or co-ordinate complaints. Equally, such time spent not at the primary work task could be seen by managers as wasted time. These worries in turn may lead managers to pay particular attention to peer-to-peer communications.

If employees are aware (or even suspect) that peer-to-peer communication is being monitored by managers, they may be less willing to use it, even if they do not intend to use it in ways that would worry management. This is because it is quite easy for the subject of conversations (or

exchanges of emails) to drift, or the other party to the conversation to raise issues that you would rather not discuss, when even saying that you are unwilling to discuss them could be revealing. Thus it should be clear that "an individual has a prima facie right to the confidentiality of his or her E-mail communications." (Spinello, 1997) If teleworkers are at all reluctant to use, or inhibited in their use of, the means supplied for peer-to-peer communication it will not work effectively as a way to counter isolation and generate creativity.

7. Interception by Third Parties

By definition, teleworking requires the use of information and communications technologies. Where this is associated with employment, most of these communications will be between the employee and the employer. The most natural ways for such communications to be made are as ordinary telephone conversations, emails and documents attached to emails. This, however, leaves open the possibility that such communications may be intercepted by third parties (Girard, 1998). Competitors may seek to intercept such communications for competitive advantage (Odgers, 1994). Obviously the relevance of this will vary according to the type of work that the teleworker is carrying out, but even when the teleworker's own work is not so sensitive, there is always the possibility that other employees and business associates may send them sensitive information unaware that the teleworker is off-site, and using non-secure telecommunications networks. Similarly, security agencies, such as the United States operation at Menwith Hill in England may seek to intercept communications in the name of public welfare (including for purely commercial reasons) (Davies, 1998): even if the communications are between members of a different public from the one whose welfare is the claimed justification of the interception.

Technologically, strong "public key" encryption should render useless such interception. However, governments and security agencies are still seeking to keep such high-grade encryption out of commercial and public hands, unless there are key recovery methods that could be used by security agencies to gain easy access to the content of messages (Department of Trade and Industry, 1998, especially paragraph 14). One fear associated with encryption with the possibility of key recovery is that the keys may be obtained by precisely those (including competitors) against whose interceptions the communication was encrypted. So long as secure public key encryption without centralised key recovery is not available; businesses are right to be wary of communicating sensitive information to and from teleworkers. Even when secure encryption is available, it is possible that it will not be used sufficiently consistently, especially if operation requires even a slight amount of extra work on the part of employees.

8. Conclusion

Whether or not the technologies associated with telework are actually used to conduct surveillance, the potential for them to be so used exists. Fears of such use, in turn, may set potential teleworkers, employers of teleworkers, and trades unions against this mode of employment, regardless of whether such fears are justified. However, much can be done by employers to reduce such fears.

Note

[1] Whether full or partial payment of out of pocket, or total costs, as applicable.

References

Aiello, J. R. and Y. Shao: 1993, 'Electronic Performance Monitoring and Stress: The Role of Feedback and Goal Setting', in M. J. Smith and G. Salvendy (eds.), *Human-Computer Interaction: Applications and Case Studies* (Elsevier Science Publishers, Amsterdam), pp. 1011–1016.

Aiello, J. R. and K. J. Kolb: 1995, 'Electronic Performance Monitoring: A Risk Factor for Workplace Stress', in S. L. Sauter and L. R.

Murphy (eds.), *Organizational Risk Factors for Job Stress* (American Psychological Association, Washington, DC), pp. 163–179.

Bibby, A.: 1996, *Trade Unions and Telework*: Report produced for the International Trade Secretariat FIET, Autumn 1996 at http://www.eclipse.co.uk/pens/bibby/fietrpt.html accessed 04.03.1998.

Brown, W. S.: 1996, 'Technology, Workplace Privacy and Personhood', *Journal of Business Ethics* **15**, 1237–1248.

Browne, N.: 1995 (Delegate and Branch Chair, Union of Communications Workers), 'Conclusions', in N. Browne, *Teleworking Conference Report: "WORKING ON THE INFOBAHN" Teleworking & The Labour Movement*. Conference held at Manchester, England, 13.01.1995. At http://www.humanities.mcmaster.ca/~misc2/telwkcon.htm, accessed 21.10.1997, also as "Teleworking Conference Report by Nic Browne (Part 2)" http://opus.freenet.vancouver.bc.ca/labour/women/women_an.txt accessed 21.10.1997.

Bunyan, N.: 1997, 'Ex-police chief wins phone tapping case', *Daily Telegraph*, 26.06.1997, U.K. News.

Campbell, D.: 1997, 'Europe spikes spooks' e-mail eavesdrop bid', *The Guardian*, 15.10.1997, Online.

Cook, E.: 1995 (National Officer, Union of Communications Workers), 'The Teleworking Directory Enquiry Experiment at Inverness', in N. Browne, *Teleworking Conference Report: "WORKING ON THE INFOBAHN" Teleworking & The Labour Movement*. Conference held at Manchester, England, 13.01.1995. At http://www.humanities.mcmaster.ca/~misc2/telwkdir.htm, accessed 21.10.1997, also at "Teleworking Conference Report by Nic Browne (Part 2)" http://opus.freenet.vancouver.bc.ca/labour/women/women_an.txt accessed 21.10.1997.

Dandeker, C.: 1990, *Surveillance, Power and Modernity: Bureaucracy and Discipline from 1700 to the Present Day* (Polity, Cambridge).

Davies, S.: 1998, 'EU Simmers Over Menwith Listening Post', *Daily Telegraph*, 16.07.1998, *Connected* p. 6.

Department of Trade and Industry: 1998, *Secure Electronic Commerce Statement* 27.04.1998 (Department of Trade and Industry, London) at http://www.dti.gov.uk/CII/ana27p.html accessed 30.07.1998.

European Telework Online: 1996?, 'Teleworking – Telework (Telecommuting): the Benefits', at http://www.eto.org.uk/faq/faq03.htm accessed 04.03.1998.

Foucault, M.: 1979, *Discipline and Punish: the Birth of the Prison*, A. Sheridan (tr.) (Penguin, Harmondsworth).

Fried, C.: 1968, 'Privacy', *Yale Law Journal* 77, 475–493. As reprinted under the title 'Privacy [A moral analysis]' in F. D. Schoeman (ed.): 1984, *Philosophical Dimensions of Privacy: An Anthology* (Cambridge University Press, Cambridge).

Girard, J.: 1998 'Should Home Computers be Used for Telecommuting?', *North America Network Service Providers, Remote Access, Mobile Business Strategies, Network Business Management*, and *Telecommuting and Remote Access*, each 02.02.1998, Document number KA-030-5078 (Gartner Group, Stamford, CT) at http://advisor.gartner.com/inbox/articles/iheadline5.html accessed 23.03.1998, but not accessible online 30.07.1998.

Lally, L.: 1996, 'Privacy versus Accessibility: The Impact of Situationally Conditioned Belief', *Journal of Business Ethics* 15, 1221–1226.

Lyon, D.: 1994, *The Electronic Eye: The Rise of Surveillance Society* (Polity, Cambridge).

Manning, R. C.: 1997, 'Liberal and Communitarian Defenses of Workplace Privacy', *Journal of Business Ethics* 16, 817–823.

Odgers, G.: 1994, 'Occupational Health and Safety and Industrial Relations' (Union Research Centre on Organisation and Technology, Melbourne) at http://teloz.latrobe.edu.au/testra/pgandpip/isochs2.html accessed 03.03.1998.

Parkinson, A.: 1995, 'Teleworking in Britain', in G. Hollinshead (ed.), *Work and Employment*, Issue 4, *Teleworking* (Bristol Business School, University of the West of England, Bristol), pp. 2–3.

Rogerson, S.: 1998, *Ethical Aspects of Information Technology: Issues for Senior Executives* (Institute of Business Ethics, London).

Samuels, P.: 1996, 'Who's Reading Your E-Mail? Maybe the Boss', *The New York Times*, 12.05.1996, p. F11 as reported in Spinello, 1997.

Schoeman, F. D.: 1984, 'Privacy and Intimate Information', in F. D. Schoeman (ed.), 1984, *Philosophical Dimensions of Privacy: An Anthology* (Cambridge University Press, Cambridge).

Spinello, R. A.: 1995, *Ethical Aspects of Information Technology* (Prentice-Hall, Englewood Cliffs, NJ).

Spinello, R. A.: 1997, 'The Case for E-Mail Privacy', paper presented at The Second Annual Ethics and Technology Conference, Chicago, 06–07.06.1997. At http://www.cmsu.edu/englphil/spinello.htm, accessed 21.10.1997.

Stanworth, J. and Stanworth, C.: 1991, *Telework: The Human Resource Implications* (Institute of Personnel Management, London).

Symes, C.: 1995, 'Teleworking – A Critical Perspective', in G. Hollinshead (ed.), *Work and Employment*, Issue 4, *Teleworking* (Bristol Business School, University of the West of England, Bristol), pp. 4–5.

Union of Communication Workers: 1992?, Pamphlet: *The Teleworking Directory Enquiry Experiment at Inverness* (Union of Communication Workers, London).

Utility Consumers' Action Network: 1997, 'Fact Sheet # 7: Employee Monitoring: Is There Privacy in the Workplace?', at http://www.privacyrights.org/fs/fs7-work.html, accessed 05.03.1998.

Centre for Computing and Social Responsibility,
Faculty of Computing Sciences and Engineering,
De Montfort University,
The Gateway,
Leicester, LE1 9BH,
U.K.

Part VI
What Computers Should Not Do

[33]

Are There Decisions Computers Should Never Make?

James H. Moor

The possibility may seem exhilirating or it may seem repugnant, but the possibility should be carefully considered. The possibility is that computers may someday (and perhaps to a limited extent already do) serve not merely as tools for calculation or consultation but as full-fledged decision makers on important matters involving human welfare. In examining this possibility I hope to avoid computerphilia and computerphobia and argue for an empirical approach as a significant component in our assessment of computer activity and its effects. I wish to focus on the issue of decision making because it is in this area that computers have the greatest potential for influencing and controlling our lives. In determining what limits, if any, we should place on the use of computers, we must consider whether there are decisions computers should never make.

Do Computers Make Decisions?

It can be objected that asking whether there are decisions computers should never make begs an important question, i.e., whether computers are the sort of thing which can make decisions at all. Before considering this objection, it is useful to distinguish between two senses of making a decision. In the *narrow* sense 'making a decision' refers to the arrival at a decision, i.e., to the selection of a course of action. Processes leading up to the decision are ignored. For example, if one is asked to pick any card during a card trick, then simply selecting a card constitutes making a decision. In the *broad* sense 'making a decision' refers not only to the decision but to processes leading up to the decision as well. Thus, in the broad sense making a decision may involve investigating possible courses of action, evaluating alternative strategies and selecting a course of action based on this investigation and evaluation. For example, in playing checkers one makes a decision by considering various possible moves, weighing the advantages and disadvantages of each and finally selecting a move based on this analysis.

Now, the objection above can be put more precisely. Computers might make decisions (or at least be used to make decisions) in the narrow sense of the term, but computers are not the sort of thing which can make decisions in the broad sense. In other words, computers might make decisions in the sense that one can flip a coin to make decisions, but computers are not the sort of thing which can investigate and evaluate alternative strategies in order to select a course of action.

I believe this objection is mistaken. Perhaps its initial plausibility stems from understanding a computer simply as a calculator of arithmetic operations. However, computer activity can be understood in many other ways.[1] One of the most common ways of understanding computer activity is in terms of the execution of an ordinary computer program. In describing this activity, programmers often use decision making language. For instance, a programmer might say that at a certain point in the execution of a program the computer decides whether an inputed string of characters matches another string of characters. Of course, such uses of 'decides' and its cognates might be discounted as nothing more than technical jargon. But there are other situations in which computer activity can be understood as a complex analysis of information resulting in the selection of a course of action. In such cases, decision making language often has a very natural application.

As an example, consider A. L. Samuel's now classic program for playing checkers.[2] The computer using Samuel's program not only plays checkers, but improves its game with experience. The computer understood as a checker player is naturally described as a decision maker. When its turn comes, the computer must decide what move to make. Moreover, if the computer is to play checkers well, it must base its decisions upon sophisticated decision making processes. As Samuel points out, "There exists no known algorithm which will guarantee a win or a draw in checkers, and the complete explorations of every possible path through a checker game would involve perhaps 10^{40} choices of moves which, at 3 choices per millimicrosecond, would still take 10^{21} centuries to consider."[3] The computer, using Samuel's program, makes its decision not unlike human players in that it looks ahead a few moves and evaluates the possible resulting board positions, but it differs from the human decision maker in the manner in which it evaluates board positions. The computer evaluates a board position in terms of a polynomial each term of which represents a parameter of the game, i.e., some configuration of pieces and squares. By playing lots of games, sometimes with itself as an opponent, the computer learns which parameters are important. By altering the weights of the parameters and trying different parameters from a stockpile of them, the computer's evaluation mechanism becomes better and better. Although the computer played poor checkers initially, through competition the computer's abilities improved to the point that it beat a human checker playing champion.[4]

The fact that the computer uses a polynomial to determine its selection of moves does not show that the computer is not a decision maker, for a human player could make his decisions in the same manner though certainly not as quickly. Indeed, a computer playing checkers is a very clear illustration of a computer making a decision in the broad sense. The computer must analyze the situation, discover what courses of action are available, evaluate the options, and select a course of action based on its information. This is a paradigm of decision making.

One might attempt to buttress the original objection that computers cannot make decisions by assuming that decision making must be done consciously. Certainly we are conscious of much of our decision making, but it is important to realize that we are not conscious of much of it as well. For example, each of us often decides what food to eat or which clothes to wear without being even slightly aware of why a particular decision is made. Much money is invested in marketing research to discover those factors, those "hidden persuaders" as Vance Packard once called them, which can affect our decision making without our being aware of them. Sometimes we can make decisions without even being aware that decisions are being made. For instance, unless we happen to reflect on the situation later, we can make many complex driving decisions in heavy traffic, perhaps while thinking about something else, without being conscious of our own decision making (in the narrow or the broad sense). Since our consciousness of our own decision making can vary from being much aware to completely unaware, consciousness of decision making should not be regarded as an essential feature of decision making.

Finally, it might be argued that it is not computes which make decisions but rather humans who *use* computers to make decisions. But, this point confuses the *power* to make decisions with the *ability* to make decisions. The power to make decisions involves being in the appropriate situation and having the authority to make decisions. For instance, at any time, only one person has the power to make United States presidential decisions although many people may have the ability to make such decisions. The source of this power comes from an election by the people under the Constitution. The fact that we use the president to make decisions is compatible with the president being a decision maker. Similarly, we can delegate decision making power to computers, and the fact that we use computers in this way is compatible with computers being decision makers.

I believe it is important to understand computer activity in some contexts as decision making not only because it is so, but because to see it otherwise tends to minimize our appreciation for the potential impact of computers on our society. To delegate decision making power is to delegate control. Ultimately, the issue is what aspects of our lives, if any, computers should control.

220   NATURE AND SYSTEM

HOW COMPETENT CAN COMPUTER DECISION MAKING BE?

If one grants that at least in principle computers are able to make decisions, it remains a question what kinds of decisions computers can make competently. Since computers are not limited to making random, fixed, or arbitrary decisions, as the checker playing computer illustrates, it may seem that there are no limits to computer decision making. But, the results of logic clearly indicate some limitations. If one accepts Church's thesis that algorithmic computability of a function is equivalent to Turing machine computability of it, then limits of Turing machines are limits of computers. Specifically, the results of the halting problem show that there are decisions even universal Turing machines cannot make effectively, viz., there is no universal Turing machine which can decide for every Turing machine whether or not it will halt. The trouble with this type of limitation is that it seems to apply to humans as well as to computers. Moreover, if one were to seriously set out to decide whether or not sufficiently complex Turing machines would halt, computers, though not infallible, would likely be better at the job than humans.

Therefore, the issue is not whether there are some limitations to computer decision making but how well computer decision making compares with human decision making. In order to make the matter most interesting, I will limit the class of computers to those sorts of electronic and mechanical devices which are ordinarily considered to be computers, i.e., for the purposes of this paper, I wish to specifically rule out considering human beings as computers and considering computers as persons.[5] Are there, then, decisions which (nonperson) computers could never make as well as humans?

I believe the simple, honest answer is that nobody really knows whether computers can possibly match or exceed human ability at decision making. I wish to advocate an empiricist's position on the question of computer decision making and on the question of computer intellectual abilities in general. My claim is:

(1) It is essentially an empirical matter what a computer's level of ability is for a given intellectual activity.

(2) It is possible to gather evidence to determine a computer's level of ability for a given intellectual activity.

(3) For most kinds of intellectual activities it is still unknown whether or not computers will one day match or exceed human levels of ability.

As a corollary of my general empiricist's position, I want to maintain that for most kinds of decision making, it is still a very open empirical question whether computers will ever have levels of ability which match or exceed human levels. I regard my view as nothing more than common sense; but common sense seems to be somewhat uncommon on this matter. For instance, some would challenge my view on the grounds that it is not an empirical matter at all. With regard to decision making, I have already responded to this kind of objection. Others who grant that there is an empirical component involved often suggest that the matter is already settled. For instance, in 1958 Herbert Simon and Allen Newell, prominent artificial intelligence researchers, asserted that "there are now in the world machines that think, that learn and that create. Moreover, their ability to do things is going to increase rapidly until—in the visible future—the range of problems they can handle will be coextensive with the range to which the human mind has been applied."[6] Artificial intelligence workers have clearly demonstrated that computers can possess certain kinds of intellectual abilities. To an amazing extent, today's computers can solve problems, recognize patterns, play games, prove theorems, and use natural language.[7] Nevertheless, it is just a brute fact that computers do not now possess anywhere near the general intelligence of an average human being, and there is no strong evidence that in the visible future the range of problems they will be able to handle will be coextensive with the range to which the human mind has been applied. The enthusiasm of artificial intelligence researchers for their work is commendable, but at this time the results of their labors do not establish that computers will one day match or exceed human levels of ability for most kinds of intellectual activities.

Some of the critics of artificial intelligence research would also disagree with my view. Hubert Dreyfus concludes his analysis of such research by stating: "Thus, insofar as the question whether artificial intelligence is possible is an empirical question, the answer seems to be that further significant progress in Cognitive Simulation or in Artificial Intelligence is extremely unlikely."[8] Dreyfus appeals both to the fact that work in these areas sometimes fails and to a phenomenological analysis which he takes to show that there are nonprogrammable human capacities involved in all forms of intelligent behavior.[9] The argument about failures in early endeavors is not very persuasive since it can be launched against any science in its early stages. The more interesting argument is his phenomenological appraisal which emphasizes, I think correctly, that when we engage in perceptual and intellectual activities, we usually have a global recognition of the situation and can pull out the essential features even in ambiguous contexts. For instance, if I utter the sentence 'Christopher Columbus had global recognition which no computer has ever had' we can all immediately grasp several meanings of the sentence and know which are related to this discussion and which are puns; and yet, we are not aware of any extensive analysis leading up to this understanding. Computers clearly lack such facility with language. Although today's computers can handle some perceptual and linguistic ambiguities, on the whole computers are very much inferior to people on such matters. Computers are not good punsters. Nevertheless, these phenomonelogical and factual points are not adequate to establish Dreyfus' conclusion that there are nonprogrammable capacities involved in all forms of intelligent behavior. What appears unlawlike, even capricious, at one level may be perfectly lawlike at another. It remains a possibility that activities of which we are not aware, but which underlie intelligent behavior, can be expressed in terms of computable functions. If this is the case, then computers might one day carry them out.

A task which may seem unprogrammable is the selection of appropriate hypotheses in science. But for certain families of molecules a computer using the program DENDRAL is an expert in identifying the molecular structure which best explains data produced by mass spectrometers. The computer is an expert in doing this even when compared with the best human performance.[10] On the other hand, for most of chemistry the computer's performance in selecting appropriate hypotheses is at the novice level or worse. The point is that there is enough evidence from artificial intelligence research to be suspicious of dogmatic claims that computers will never be able to accomplish certain feats of intelligence; yet, today there is not nearly enough evidence to support the conclusion that computers will someday match or exceed human intellectual ability in general or human decison making ability in particular.

How Can Computer Decision Making Competence Be Judged?

Empirical investigation will allow us to refine our judgments about the nature of computer abilities, but what sort of evidence counts? Since competence is the ability to perform at a given level of accomplishment, obviously the computer's performance will be one important source of evidence in evaluating competence. With regard to decision making, two features of the performance are relevant: (i) the decision making record and (ii) the justifications offered for the decisions. These two types of evidence will carry various weights depending upon the kind of decision making and the circumstances in which it is made.

Specifically, I wish to distinguish two extremes of decision making: decision making under clear standards and decison making under fuzzy standards. Many cases of decision making lie between these two extremes. In making decisions under clear standards every decision (or series of decisions) can be clearly classified as either correct or incorrect. For example, deciding which horse to bet on to win a race is a decision made under clear standards. The horse will either win or not win. After a number of such decisions, preferably made in a variety of situations, the decision maker will have established a clear record of correct decisions vs. incorrect decisions. In the case of decision making under clear standards the justifications offered for decisions are usually not very important in evaluating competence. If the bettor routinely picks winning horses, it hardly matters if he is unable to produce justifications for his decisions. If he cannot pick winning horses, justifications for decisions are small consolation. However, if the decision making record is not available or for some reason is not trusted, then certainly the justifications given for the decisions can be important in evaluating decision making under clear standards.

In decision making under fuzzy standards at least some of the possible decisions (or series of decisions) will be difficult to classify as correct or incorrect. For many people deciding which career to pursue is an example of decision making under fuzzy standards. The fuzzier the standards are the more difficult it is to establish a clear record of correct decisions vs. incorrect decisions, and the more important it is to provide some justifications for the decisions. For instance, it may be impossible to determine how many 'correct' and 'incorrect' grades a professor gives, but one can evaluate his decision making by checking his justifications for assigning individual grades.

The checker playing computer is making decisions under clear standards in that a series of decisions about moves either leads to a win or it does not. It is impressive that the computer has beaten a checker playing champion; but in order to really establish its competence, the computer would have to establish a substantial record of play against a variety of opponents.

Some computers can make decisions under fuzzy standards and can offer justifications for their decisions. For instance, consider MYCIN, an interactive program that "uses the clinical decision criteria of experts to advise physicians who request advice regarding the selection of appropriate antimicrobial therapy for hospital patients with bacterial infection.'[11] Advice of this kind has practical importance because often drug therapy has to be recommended before a positive identification of the bacteria can be made and because not every physician is a specialist in the subject. The computer asks the physician for information about the situation including the results of laboratory tests. The computer will give its conclusions about the identities of the organisms; and upon asking a few more questions about the patient's allergies, renal and hepatic status, the site(s) of the infection, etc., the computer will formulate and recommend therapy. MYCIN contains a set of over 200 production rules each of which state a set of preconditions and a conclusion or action to be taken if the preconditions occur. The production rules not only give the computer a basis for decisions, but allows it to offer justifications for its decisions. The computer can explain either why certain information is important in terms of its goals or how it arrives at its conclusions. Thus, a physician has a check on the computer's competence without knowing the computer's overall decision making record. The decision making record cannot be completely clear since even experts disagree about what is a 'correct' or on 'incorrect' decision in some cases, e.g., in recommending certain therapies. Nevertheless, in a preliminary evaluation, MYCIN's therapy recommedations were acceptable to the experts in 75% of the cases.[12] The workers on the MYCIN project hope to increase the computer's competence in this type of decision making and to extend the production rule methodology to other areas.[13] But whatever abilities computers may eventually acquire using the production rule approach, the MYCIN program illustrates that a computer's performance can be such that one can evaluate the computer's competence even in decision making under fuzzy standards.

Another kind of evidence about a computer's competence in decision making results from an analysis of the internal operation of the computer, perhaps in terms of a computer program. This kind of evidence is not essential, at least not in principle; for if the performance is good enough, it will provide a sufficient basis for a justified inductive inference about the computer's competence.[14] We often infer that other humans are competent decision makers without having any information about their internal operation except indirectly through performance. Nevertheless, as a practical matter it certainly can be very useful to have such information, e.g., in those situations in which a justification for a decision is an important piece of evidence but which the computer can not provide as part of its performance. Obviously, in the development stage one must pay close attention to the program for even the most novice programmer knows that a well-thought-out program may not result in the performance expected and a performance which is good in general may be the result of a program with hidden "bugs."

Usually it is not very helpful in assessing a computer's competence at decision making to simply ask whether the computer makes its decisions on the same basis (in the sense of internal operation) that humans do. The answer can almost always be "yes" or "no" depending upon how the activity is described. Yes, the computer checker player is like a human checker player in that it looks ahead a few moves. Or no, the computer checker player is not like a human checker player in that it uses a polynomial to evaluate board positions.[15] What is crucial is that the basis be capable of reliably generating a reasonable level of performance (including producing justifications when relevant). Indeed, if a computer does exceed human competence in decision making, it is very likely the basis for its decisions will be different from the human basis.

ARE THERE DECISIONS COMPUTERS SHOULD NEVER MAKE?

The empirical position I am advocating undercuts a lot of argumentation about which decisions computers should and should not make. Joseph Weizenbaum states:

> What could be more obvious than the fact that, whatever intelligence a computer can muster, however it may be acquired, it must always and necessarily be absolutely alien to any and all authentic human concerns. The very asking of the question, "What does a judge (or a psychiatrist) know that we cannot tell a computer?" is a monstrous obscenity. That it has to be put into print at all, even for the purpose of exposing its morbidity, is a sign of the madness of our times.

Computers can make judicial decisions, computers can make psychiatric judgments. They can flip coins in much more sophisticated ways than can the most patient human being. The point is that they ought not be given such tasks. They may even be able to arrive at "correct" decisions in some cases—but always and necessarily on bases no human being should be willing to accept.[16]

Weizenbaum claims that computers are outsiders to human affairs just as humans are sometimes outsiders to other human cultures. Outsiders will have bases for decisions which "must be inappropriate to the context in which the decision is to be made."[17] But this argument confuses lack of information with lack of competence. There may be good reasons not to grant outsiders the power to make some decisions, but there is no reason in principle why an *informed* outsider cannot be a competent decision maker. A physician who is an outsider may be more competent to make medical decisions than anybody in a primitive tribe. A computer which never has a bacterial infection may be very competent in making decisions about them.

Weizenbaum does not make it clear whether by "bases" he means the internal operation of the computer or the sorts of justfications it could give for making its decisions. But for neither case has he demonstrated that they must always and necessarily be such that human beings should not accept them. Weizenbaum's examples—judicial decisions and psychiatric judgments—are cases of decision making under fuzzy standards. It is possible to evaluate a computer's competence in these areas by paying close attention to the sorts of justifications the computer gives for its decisions. It is at least conceivable that the computer might give outstanding justifications for its decisions ranging from detailed legal precedents to a superb philosophical theory of justice or from instructive clinical observations to an improved theory of mental illness so that the competence of the computer in such decision making was considered to be as good or better than the competence of human experts. Empirically this may never happen but it is not a necessary truth that it will not.

Perhaps more importantly, an empirical attitude challenges an uncritical acceptance of computer competence. It is far too easy to try to justify a decision by simply saying "the computer says so." Such a reply should carry no weight unless the computer's competence has been rigorously tested. It is always relevant to raise two competency questions when computer decision making occurs—"What is the nature of the computer's (alledged) competence?" and "How has the competence been demonstrated?" A company spokesman might announce that a computer has decided there should be a 20% layoff when in fact the computer has done nothing more than determine which 20% of the firm's employees has least seniority. The problem is not just that one group might deceive another about the computer's competency but that even immediate users of the computer may take the computer's word too uncritically. In a nuclear age in which some of the decision making about whether to launch missles is in part made by computers, the possibility of deception about computer competency is a matter of great importance.

Thus, the first step in determining what kinds of decisions computers should and should not make at particular times is to determine what kinds of decisions computers can and cannot make competently at those times. But, there remains a question of values. Even if someday computers are competent to make a wide range of important decisions, should certain kinds of decision making be forbidden to computers? I believe that the proper answer suggests itself when considering why the following three maxims, though initially plausible, are really unsatisfactory.

DUBIOUS MAXIM #1 _Computers should never make any decisions which humans want to make._ This is a somewhat plausible maxim since we obviously enjoy the pleasure and freedom involved in making many of the decisions which affect our lives. A computer could competently decide which shoe a person should put on first in the morning, but clearly such a meaningless intrusion into a person's affairs would greatly reduce the quality of his life. However, this maxim is unsatisfactory in general because there can be other factors which outweigh the benefits of the freedom and pleasure humans derive from doing the decision making. For example, even if humans would like to make certain medical decisions, it might be the case that a computer existed which could make them far better. If the computer's diagnosis and suggestions for treatment would result in a significant savings of lives and reduction of suffering compared with human decision making on the subject, then there is a powerful moral argument for letting computers decide.

DUBIOUS MAXIM #2 _Computers should never make any decisions which humans can make more competently._ This also seems like a very reasonable maxim. We do not want the computer to make life-or-death medical decisons if the computer is less competent than human decision makers. But again the maxim is too limited because it neglects other considerations. Some activities, e.g., certain kinds of factory work or prolonged space travel, may be so boring, time-consuming, or dangerous that it would be morally better to use computers, even if this involved sacrificing some competency in decision making, in order to spare humans from enduring such experiences.

DUBIOUS MAXIM #3 _Computers should never make any decisions which humans cannot override._ This maxim seems most reasonable of all especially if it is set against a background of numerous science fiction tales in which computers take control and humans become their slaves. But there could be situations in which it would be morally better to make it impossible, at least practically speaking, for humans to override computer decisions. Suppose that when people drive cars, tens of thousands of people are killed in automobile accidents, hundreds of thousands are injured, and millions of dollars are lost in property damage. But when computers drive cars, not only are human transportation needs carried out more efficiently but there is a substantial reduction in deaths, injuries, and property damage. Further suppose in those cases in which humans override computer driving decisions, the accident rate soars. Under such circumstances there is a persuasive moral and prudential argument to have computers do the decison making and not to allow humans to override their decisions.

What I am advocating is that we regard computer decision making instrumentally. For particular situations we must determine whether using computer decision makers will better promote our values and accomplish our goals. The maxims above suggest important considerations but are inadequate as general rules because situations may arise in which the consequences are far better if the maxims are violated. This approach is a natural extension of the empiricist's position described earlier. Within the context of our basic goals and values (and the priorities among them) we must empirically determine not only the competence of the computer decision maker but the consequences of computer decision making as well.

This instrumental view of the value of computer decision making leads to the answer to the question what decisions computers should never make. Computers should never decide what our basic goals and values (and priorities among them) should be. These basic goals and values, such as the promotion of human life and happiness, decrease in suffering, search for truth and understanding, etc., provide us with the ultimate norms for directing and judging actions and decision making. By definition there are not further goals and values by which to evaluate these. Since we want computers to work for our ends, we obviously want to prohibit computers from deciding to change these ultimate norms, e.g., promoting computer welfare at the expense of human welfare or taking inconsistency to be the mark of good reasoning.

To prohibit computers from making decisons about basic goals and values (and the priorities among them) is, of course, not to limit computer decision making very much. Our basic goals and values remain fairly constant and humans rarely decide to change them. Thus, there is a wide range of possible decision making which computers one day might justifiably perform. Nevertheless, I believe there is a very legitimate concern that increased computerization of our society will lead to dehumanization of our lives. The proper root of this concern is not that computers are necessarily incompetent or inherently evil. It may be the case that one day computers will make the major decisions about the operations of our society better than humans with the result that the quality of human life is substantially improved. The root of concern about increased computerization should be focused on the issue of responsibility. By assumption, the kind of computers under discussion are not persons; and although they are causally responsible for their decisions, they are not legally or morally responsible for their decisions. One cannot sue a computer. Therefore, humans have not only an initial responsibility, but a continuing responsibility to raise the competency and value questions whenever computer decision making is at issue. First, what is the nature of the computer's competency and how has it been demonstrated? Secondly, given our basic goals and values why is it better to use a computer decision maker in a particular situation than a human decision maker? The danger is that our responsibility can be easily undermined by strong pressures, e.g., economic incentives, not to investigate and answer these questions. The dehumanization which results can either be in the form of computers making decisions which humans should make or vice versa. Of course, if the delegation of decision making power is carried out responsibly, we may be creating a much more humane society. Some of the most humanistic decisions may well come from decision makers which are not human.

Dartmouth College

NOTES

1. On one level a computer is nothing more than a physical system and can be explained as such. For the computer to perform even simple arithmetic calculations, we must interpret its actvities symbolically. Obviously, there is a wide range of possible interpretations. See James H. Moor, "Explaining Computer Behavior," *Philosophical Studies,* 34 (1978): 325-27.

2. A. L. Samuel, "Some Studies In Machine Learning Using the Game of Checkers," *Computers and Thought,* ed. Edward A. Feigenbaum and Julian Feldman (New York: McGraw-Hill, 1963), pp. 71-105.

3. Samuel, p. 72.

4. Samuel, pp. 103-105.

5. I want to separate the question of computers being persons from the main issue because I believe interesting results follow about computer decision making without raising matters of civil rights. The set of computers I am considering will have members which may be very good at particular kinds of decision making but no one member of the set will have sufficient variety of decision making abilities (among other things) to be considered a person.

6. H. A. Simon and A. Newell, "Heuristic Problem Solving: The Next Advance in Operations Research," *Operations Research* 6 (1958): 8.

7. For a nice summary of artificial intelligence work see Patrick Henry Winston, *Artificial Intelligence* (Reading, Mass.: Addison-Wesley, 1977).

8. Hubert Dreyfus, *What Computers Can't Do* (New York: Harper and Row, 1972), p. 197.

9. Dreyfus also has an argument based on the digital/analogue distinction. See James H. Moor, "Three Myths of Computer Science," *The British Journal of Philosophy of Science,* 29 (1978): 213-22.

10. E. A. Feigenbaum, B. G. Buchanan and J. Lederberg, "On Generality and Problem Solving: A Case Study Using the DENDRAL Program," *Machine Intelligence,* 6, ed. B. Meltzer (Edinburgh: Edinburgh University Press, 1971), p. 165.

11. Edward H. Shortliffe, Randall Davis, Stanton G. Axline, Bruce G. Buchanan, C. Cordell Green, and Stanley N. Cohen, "Computer-Based Consultations in Clinical Therapeutics: Explanation and Rule Acquisition Capabilities of the MYCIN System," *Computers and Biomedical Research* 8 (1975): 303.

12. *Ibid.*, p. 318.

13. Randall Davis, Bruce Buchanan, and Edward Shortliffe, "Production Rules as a Representation for a Knowledge-Based Consultation Program," *Artificial Intelligence* 8 (1977): 15-45.

14. James H. Moor, "An Analysis of the Turing Test," *Philosophical Studies* 30 (1976): 249-57.

15. The difference between doing artificial intelligence and cognitive simulation is not a sharp distinction. It is a matter of emphasis and level of description of the computer activity.

16. Joseph Weizenbaum, *Computer Power and Human Reason* (San Francisco: W. H. Freeman, 1976), pp. 226-27.

17. Weizenbaum, p. 226.

[34]

Computers in control: Rational transfer of authority or irresponsible abdication of autonomy?

Arthur Kuflik

Department of Philosophy, University of Vermont, 70 South Williams St, Burlington, VT 05401, USA

Abstract. To what extent should humans transfer, or abdicate, "responsibility" to computers? In this paper, I distinguish six different senses of 'responsible' and then consider in which of these senses computers can, and in which they cannot, be said to be "responsible" for "deciding" various outcomes. I sort out and explore two different kinds of complaint against putting computers in greater "control" of our lives: (i) as finite and fallible human beings, there is a limit to how far we can acheive increased reliability through complex devices of our own design; (ii) even when computers are more reliable than humans, certain tasks (e.g., selecting an appropriate gift for a friend, solving the daily crossword puzzle) are inappropriately performed by anyone (or anything) other than oneself. In critically evaluating these claims, I arrive at three main conclusions: (1) While we ought to correct for many of our shortcomings by availing ourselves of the computer's larger memory, faster processing speed and greater stamina, we are limited by our own finiteness and fallibility (rather than by whatever limitations may be inherent in silicon and metal) in the ability to transcend our own unreliability. Moreover, if we rely on programmed computers to such an extent that we lose touch with the human experience and insight that formed the basis for their programming design, our fallibility is magnified rather than mitigated. (2) Autonomous moral agents can reasonably defer to greater expertise, whether human or cybernetic. But they cannot reasonably relinquish "background-oversight" responsibility. They must be prepared, at least periodically, to review whether the "expertise" to which they defer is indeed functioning as he/she/it was authorized to do, and to take steps to revoke that authority, if necessary. (3) Though outcomes matter, it can also matter how they are brought about, and by whom. Thus, reflecting on how much of our lives should be directed and implemented by computer may be another way of testing any thoroughly end-state or consequentialist conception of the good and decent life. To live with meaning and purpose, we need to actively engage our own faculties and empathetically connect up with, and resonate to, others. Thus there is some limit to how much of life can be appropriately lived by anyone (or anything) other than ourselves.

Introduction

Technology is typically conceived as the instrument, not the master, of human will.[1] Now for the first time, however, technological devices are being called upon to "make decisions", not merely to implement them. This development conjures up the vision of a whole new age in which (a significant proportion of) decision-making responsibility in such areas as transportation, communication, health care, and military defense is transferred from human minds to "machine minds". Can it be *morally right* to put computers "in control"? Indeed, insofar as automated decision-making systems might be able to achieve demonstrably greater reliability than even the best human decision-makers, how could it be right *not* to do so?

There are, I believe, two broad spheres of potentially growing computer-dominion: (i) computers programmed to govern the operations of other technolo-gical devices such as factories, trains, planes, weapons; (ii) computers programmed to make decisions that bear *directly* on the conduct of human affairs – e.g., in such areas as management of the economy, medical diagnosis and prescription, prospecting for mineral resources, criminal investigation.[2]

Machines that regulate the behavior of other machines are, so to speak, "meta-machines". Machines programmed to address typically human decision-making predicaments – so-called "expert systems" – could of course, be reserved for a purely advisory, rather than an official, policy-determining role. But as the putative expertise of these so-called "expert systems" grows, people may come to rely on them in much the same way as they rely on fellow humans who, by virtue of their expertise – e.g. in medicine or economics – are elevated to authoritative decision-making roles (e.g. Director of the Food and Drug Administration, Chair of the Federal Reserve). In addition, whenever alternative sources of expert advice are absent, computer-generated decisions may come to enjoy de facto authority by default.

Should we be morally concerned about a growing reliance on computerized "decision-making"? Of course, *humanly* made decisions have not always been well-advised. But, wise or unwise, they were decisions for which humans – whether they fully realized it or not – bore the ultimate moral responsibility. And given our own finiteness and fallibility, how well can we manage to transcend ourselves through complex devices of our own construction? If we are now at the dawn of an age in which machines are to play an increasingly significant decision-making role – and with greater reliability than humans ever did or could achieve – must we rethink and revise our notions of human autonomy and accountability?

Clarifications: "Decision-making"; "Responsibility"

Perhaps the first thing to note is that the description – "making decisions, not merely implementing them" is a bit misleading. In making their decisions, today's computers *are* (at the same time) implementing humanly made decisions – decisions about *how* to make various kinds of decisions – about which factors to take into account and according to which problem-solving strategies. We might express this point by characterizing computer-made decisions as *secondary* or subordinate, in contrast with the more *fundamental* decisions made by their human designers and programmers.

The morally important point is that it is *the humans* who make these more fundamental decisions – the humans who design the computers and the humans who write the programs that embody the proposed problem-solving strategies[3] – not the machines which run those programs– who must bear the ultimate moral responsibility for what subsequently takes place. The decisions that computers make, if they are making decisions at all, are implementational not fundamental.[4]

Thus, as with all previous technologies – programmed computers are really just instruments (albeit vastly more complex) of human will. Why then does it seem so natural to say that new technologies are "making computers responsible for more and more decisions"? I suggest that the term 'responsible' is multiply ambiguous.

Six senses of 'Responsible'

Sometimes, to say that a computer *is responsible* for a certain decision is to say no more than that it (1)

is the proximate cause of the decision's being made (cf. "the hurricane-force winds are responsible for the felling of the old oak tree") or that it (2) plays a certain role in a functional system (cf. "decomposing bacteria are responsible for the recycling of nitrogen in a forest ecosystem", "the heart is responsible for pumping blood through the circulatory system of a human being").

These morally "thin" notions of "responsibility" – which might be dubbed (1) **"causal-responsibility"** and (2) **"functional-role responsibility"** – contrast with a number of "thicker" senses which are often used in connection with moral agents:

The individuals we consider to be morally responsible agents are appropriately subject to a very complex interaction: when their conduct impacts upon others in certain ways, not only is it appropriate for them to be asked to give an explanatory account of themselves (computers might be asked to do this as well) but – in what may well be a long and open-ended discussion – to provide *good* reason for their comportment, to assess the force of reasons they had not previously considered, to be willing in some cases to acknowledge the insufficiency of their own reasons and the greater force of reasons not previously considered, to explain mitigating factors and ask for forgiveness, and – failing a show either of good reason or good excuse – to apologize and look for ways of making amends. We might call this (3) **"moral accountability responsibility"**.

Pondering this sense of 'responsibility' might prompt us to wonder just how much more complex our technological creations would have to become in order to be "morally accountable persons" in their own right. As we shall soon see, this is a question which for present purposes can be bracketed. But it would seem to be a mistake – something akin to racism – to judge *a priori* that *only* flesh and blood, carbon-based, organic entities could ever be respected as morally accountable agents. The point here is that it is not appearance or the composition of one's "body" but how one actually functions that should be the basis both for moral respect and moral-responsibility ascription.

In yet a fourth sense of 'responsible', we might say that a person who is appropriately subject to the kind of interaction just indicated (a person capable of being held responsible) and who takes care to consider the impact of his or her behavior on others, in light of good and relevant moral reasons, is a "responsible" person, (or at least, someone who, in the case at hand, has behaved in a "responsible" way). In this (4) **honorific** sense of 'responsible', the clear contrast is with 'irresponsible'. In the previous sense of 'responsible', however, the contrasting case would be someone (or something) *not* to be regarded as either responsible (in the current honorific sense) *or* irresponsible. Even to be irresponsible, one must be capable of being held responsible (in sense (3)) in the first place.

Another familiar sense of 'responsible' has to do with the fact that we are not self-sufficient beings, islands unto ourselves. There is a morally justifiable division of humanly important roles and tasks. A person who justifiably plays a particular role or has been justifiably assigned a particular task is said to be "responsible" for performing in that role or completing that task. We might call this **(5) "role-responsibility"**: – it appears to be an amalgam of senses (2) and (3).

There is, I think, at least one more way of using the term 'responsible' for which our present context of discussion provides a particularly germane illustration: suppose we designed a computer-controlled technological process with no option of human intervention in the event of malfunction. Clearly, we *are* both causally (sense (1)) and morally (sense (3)) responsible for that arrangement. If it is demonstrably more reliable than a comparable system that includes the option of human override, then we will merit commendation and admiration as responsible agents (in the honorific sense (4)); if it is demonstrably less reliable, we may be subject to appropriate criticism. But suppose instead that we had built a system in which we retained oversight and the option of either backing up the system, or shutting it down, in the event of failure. (Compare: when power steering in one's car fails, the wheel can still be turned, albeit with greater difficulty, manually.) As in the first case, we would certainly be both causally and morally "responsible" for the performance of that system. But it would also be fair to say that in contrast with the first system, this was a system in which humans had retained for themselves a more "responsible" role. This sixth kind of responsibility might be called **(6) "oversight responsibility"**. It is a special form of "role-responsibility" – where the role is to review the performance of someone (*or* something) else and either to back up, override, or suspend the other party's performance of his/her/its role. This leads us to formulate the –

Key Issue: How much responsibility (in either sense (2) or sense (5)), could responsible (in sense (3)) human beings responsibly (sense (4)) allocate to a computer, *without* at the same time *reserving* to themselves oversight-responsibility (sense (6))?

I believe that responsible moral agents (in senses (3) and (4)) can never fully relinquish this oversight responsibility (sense (6)). In the final two sections of this paper, I defend this point and apply it to various cases: computers in control of jet planes, of doomsday machines, of the general governance of human society.

Questions: Central and incidental

To what extent can computerized systems controlling complex functional technologies be made reliable? How competently can various "expert systems" eventually perform? These are questions for computer science, rather than moral philosophy, but they do seem to bear centrally on the moral question of how far responsible human beings can responsibly go in transferring decision-making functionality to computers. At the same time, it is tempting to ask other questions, less central to the present concern. For example – Do computers really have thoughts, make decisions, etc.? Are they capable of genuine "consciousness"? Is it possible to perform certain kinds of mental functions without actually being "conscious" or "self-conscious"? These are fascinating questions in the philosophy of mind. It would be impossible to do them justice within the scope of the present discussion. Our main focus here is the moral-philosophical question of how much we should rely on computers to control events. To a significant extent, I think we can explore the question of what a reasonable and responsible policy might look like quite *apart from* how the question of computer-consciousness is settled.[5] So, leaving aside the question of computer consciousness and granting, for the sake of argument, that computers can be made highly reliable, at least two moral questions loom into view –

A. What are the *morally relevant considerations* we must take into account in deciding whether to assign computers a decision-making role (– knowing full well that we, *not* the computers, are ultimately accountable for the good or bad results of such an arrangement)?
B. If we do decide to give computers a measure of "control", *on what terms* should we do so? As reasonable and responsible human agents, to what extent must we maintain a kind of higher-order control over these control mechanisms? to what extent may we altogether usher ourselves from the scene and make computer-control *immune* to human *review* and *revocation*?

Factors to consider: (i) Competence and reliability

It is generally acknowledged that computers have certain advantages – greater processing speed, larger data storage, superior stamina (as John Ladd puts it, "They do not have to sleep or take coffee breaks"[6]). On the other hand, there seems to be a striking consensus in support of the idea that reliance on complex functional software in safety-critical contexts raises significant concerns:

Large software programs are difficult to test and correct under the best of conditions. Correcting one error can introduce new errors. A programmer cannot try out all possible combinations of unexpected input events.[7]

Testing only exercises a small proportion of the possible situations that the program may have to handle ... For even small amounts of software the number of possible paths far exceeds the number which could realistically be tested. For example, a recent module comprising 100 lines of assembly code was analyzed and found to contain 38 million possible paths, of which 500,000 could be followed with valid input data.[8]

"We believe that there are severe restrictions on the levels of confidence that one can justifiably place in the reliability of software ... The most obvious is testing: running the program, directly observing its behavior and removing bugs whenever they show up ... Unfortunately, this approach works only when the reliability requirements are fairly modest (say, in the range of one failure every few years) when compared with the requirements often set for critical applications ... In the time spans for which it is feasible to test, assurance of the safety would fall many orders of magnitude short of what is needed.[9]

Basically, the large number of states of most realistic software makes exhaustive testing impossible; only a relatively small part of the state space can be covered. Although research has resulted in improved testing techniques, no great breakthroughs are on the horizon, and mathematical arguments have been advanced for their impossibility.[10]

Moreover, even if software could be estimated to perform correctly in a huge percentage of cases, that would not translate into reasonable confidence about its safety:

There are very serious risks in reliance on software in safety-critical applications. A seemingly innocuous addition to the software could have disastrous effects not discovered in testing. Never trust anyone who says such failures can never happen.[11]

In reality, an attempt to fix a bug sometimes fails. It may even introduce an entirely novel fault. Because nothing would be known about the new bug, its effect on the reliability of the system would be unbounded ... the system might not even be as reliable as it was before the bug was found.[12]

We don't have the technology yet to tell if the programs have been adequately tested. We don't know what 'adequately tested' means. We can't predict what errors are left after testing, what their frequency is, or what their impact will be. If, after testing over a long period, the program has not crashed, then it is assumed to be okay. That presupposes that they will have generated all of the sort of data that will come at it in real life – and it is not clear that that will be true.[13]

"Many physical systems are fundamentally continuous in that they are described by 'well-behaved' functions – that is, very small changes in stimuli produce very small differences in responses. In contrast the smallest possible perturbation to the state of a digital computer (changing a bit from 0 to 1, for instance) may produce a radical response. A single incorrect character in the specification of control program for an Atlas rocket, carrying the first U.S. interplanetary spacecraft, *Mariner I*, ultimately caused the vehicle to veer off course. Both rocket and spacecraft had to be destroyed shortly after launch.[14]

Another notable property of software is its sensitivity to small errors. In conventional engineering, every design and manufacturing dimension can be characterized by a tolerance. One is not required to get things exactly right ... The use of a tolerance is justified by the assumption that small errors have small consequences. It is well-known that in software, trivial clerical errors can have major consequences. No useful interpretation of tolerance is known for software. A single punctuation error can be disastrous, even though fundamental oversights sometimes have negligible effects.[15]

Physical continuity in analog systems also makes them easier to test than software ... A small change in circumstances results in a small change in behavior: a few tests can be performed at discrete points in the data space, and continuity can be used to fill in the gaps. This approach does not work for software, which can fail in bizarre ways anywhere in the state space of inputs; the failure behavior need not be related in any way to normal behavior.[16]

In light of these difficulties, efforts have been made to employ a method already used in connection with hardware – increasing the reliability of the overall system by building a certain redundancy into the constituent elements. In respect to software, however, the usefulness of this approach is more problematic:

Another method now widely used (in avionic and railroad control applications, for instance) to achieve high reliability is fault tolerance, or protective redundancy. A typical way of applying redundancy is to have different design teams develop several versions of the program. The hope is that if teams make mistakes, the errors will be different. Each version of the program provides its "opinion" of the correct output. The outputs pass to an adjudicative phase, which produces a single output that would be correct if the majority of versions gave the correct result ... To measure the reliability of fault-tolerant software, it is necessary to gauge the statistical correlation between failures of the different versions. Unfortunately, the task turns out to be as hard as trying to measure the reliability by treating the whole system as a single entity – and we have seen the difficulty of doing that.[17]

Experiments with general software fault-tolerance techniques based on redundancy have shown that programmers often make the same mistakes and that independently coded software does not necessarily fail independently. In addition mathematical analysis and models have demonstrated limitations in the actual amount of reliability improvement possible using this approach.[18]

... every experiment with this approach that has checked for dependencies between software failures has found that independently written software routines do not fail in a statistically independent way ... In fact, the added complexity of providing fault tolerance in this fashion may itself cause runtime failures, just as it can in hardware redundancy.[19]

The launch of the first space shuttle was delayed at the last minute by a software problem. For reliability, the shuttle used four redundant primary avionics computers, each running the same software, along with a fifth backup computer running a different system ... despite great attention to reliability, there was still a software failure ... this particular problem arose from the additional complexity introduced by the redundant systems designed to achieve reliability ... and the bug was introduced during maintenance to fix a previous problem.[20]

No doubt, methods for ascertaining and improving the "reliability" of complex functional software, in safety-critical contexts, will continue to be refined.[21] It is tempting to suppose that new technology can be responsibly introduced just in case it reflects "state of the art reliability", the "best that can be achieved". But statements such as those cited above, raise the question of when it is appropriate to conclude that the best that can be done is *not* good enough. Where life and limb are potentially at stake, how can we know that complex software is "fit for human consumption"?

Two responses seem appropriate: First, we must, for the time being, concentrate computer control technology in predominantly *non*-safety-critical applications (e.g., running a fully robotic manufacturing process). Second, in safety-critical applications, where direct, continuous human control would be still less reliable, we may yet have to allow for human override

and/or back-up responses. (For further discussion of this issue, see *Computers in Control*, p. 178.)

A powerful illustration of this point is provided by the well-known case of a 66-year old Texas patient to whom a fatally excessive dose of radiation-therapy was computer-administered. The overdose was caused by a "software glitch" in the Canadian made Therac 25 linear accelerator. "In a circumstance unanticipated by the program code, when an operator tried to correct an erroneous command and re-entered the information in "edit" mode, the machine dispensed a much higher radiation level than intended."[22] Tragically, a machine technician evidently responded to "the agonized cries" by "flatly denying that it was possible he had been burned"![23] A morally more responsible use of this tragically flawed technology would have featured highly alert, feedback-responsive nurses, doctors and radiation technicians. By no means, should anyone involved have left the computer to its own, unchallengeable operation. The point here is *not* that the radiation therapy should have been administered manually but rather that – in response to patient feedback – humans should have been ready, able and willing to shut the machine down.[24]

Turning now to the use of computers in the operation of "expert systems" – such as programs for diagnosing disease – a typical assessment is that such programs "are blind to larger contexts, and they have difficulty deciding where the boundary of the domain lies and when something outside it might be significant."[25] Nevertheless, operating within "narrow technical domains", and taken as purely advisory rather than as authoritative, such systems may be worthwhile. (Durbase, for example – a prescription monitoring system – is one reasonably successful, advisory program that alerts doctors to the fact that patients have been issued prescriptions in medically problematic combinations.)

Even when complex programs are utilized as "aids", serious safety problems may ensue. As Henry Petroski explains in relation to "Computer Aided Design (CAD)", when stress analysis had to be done manually, the process would be "limited by the sheer time it would consume and structures would be generally overdesigned from the start and built that way". But now,

The computer can be used to analyze these structures through special software packages and ... to calculate the sizes of various components of the structure so that it has minimum weight since the maximum stresses are acting in every part of it. That is called optimization. But should there be an oversimplification or an outright error in translating the designer's structural concept to the numerical model that will be analyzed through the automatic and unthinking calculations of the computer, then the results of the computer analysis might have very little relation to reality. And since the engineer himself presumably has no feel for the structure he is designing, he is not likely to notice anything suspicious about any numbers the computer produces ... thus far the computer has been as much an agent of unsafe design as it has been a super brain ... the illusion of its power over complexity has led to more and more of a dependence on the computer to solve problems eschewed by engineers with a more realistic sense of their own limitations than the computer can have of its own.[26]

To sum up: We *can* correct for some of our own shortcomings by availing ourselves of the computer's peculiar assets (e.g., larger memory, faster processing speed, greater stamina). At the same time, however, there may be limits to our ability to transcend ourselves through complex devices of our own construction: limits that have at least as much to do with *our own finiteness and fallibility* as with whatever limitations may be inherent in silicon and metal. Moreover, if we rely on programmed computers to such an extent that we lose touch with the human experience and insight that formed the basis for their programming design, our fallibility is likely to be magnified rather than mitigated.

Factors to consider: (ii) Beyond competence and reliability

Competence and reliability are by no means the only factors that are worth taking into consideration. Thus a computer-controlled system may even be *less* reliable than a humanly controlled arrangement and still be *more* justifiable on balance. If mistakes would not seriously affect life and health, if the work in question would be tedious and unrewarding (mental labor, no less than physical, can be monotonous and deadening to human sensibility) then computer-controlled automation of the process may well be the most humane policy.

But even when a computer-governed procedure is *more* competent and reliable than the unaided human activity, the reasonable course may be to *eschew* computerization. Clearly, there are other kinds of considerations at work here. Imagine the following fully automated system: stored with information about the persons you know and love, it works out a highly reliable answer to the question, "what is it that person P does not yet have – and that would make P

happy on her/his next birthday?"; it then electronically mail-orders the gift in question and transfers funds from your bank account to the relevant vendor – thus obviating the need for you to spend more than a few seconds typing in (or voicing in) the relevant request (e.g., "birthday gift for Mom"). It is plausible to suppose that such a system (call it "Gift-Perfect") would miss much of the point of gift-giving. For while it is a good thing when someone one cares about receives something pleasing, useful, worthwhile, etc., it is also important that the gift reflect a measure of self-investment and involvement. Otherwise it could not symbolically express the right kind of connection and caring.

This is not to suggest that *all* that matters is how much one knocks oneself out. We can imagine someone who has gone to great lengths to get a gift that might well please himself but which bears no connection to the other person's good. Although he has put a great deal of himself into the giving of the gift, he has put little or no effort into thinking about the other person. So in gift-giving, self-involvement and effort do matter, but only to the extent that they reflect a sincere desire to relate to the other person's situation and state of mind.[27]

On the seemingly more trivial side, suppose a computer could be programmed to successfully work through a crossword puzzle more quickly, accurately and completely than one could do so oneself. This would hardly warrant one's abdication in favor of the computer. The whole point of such puzzles is to do them. One can hardly get the fun and challenge of trying to figure them out oneself, by giving them to a computer to do instead.

To sum up: Underlying these two examples is a serious philosphical point: our lives cannot be meaningfully lived *by others* (whether human or machine); to live with meaning and purpose, we need, at least to some extent, to actively engage ourselves, our *faculties* and abilities (as even the trivial example of the crossword puzzle suggests), and we need to *empathetically* connect up with, and resonate to, others (as the less trivial meditation on the art of gift-giving suggests).

Thus, reflecting on how much of our lives should be computer-directed and computer-implemented is one way of exploring deeper value questions. Here we might draw a parallel with a well-known philosophical thought-experiment: imagine a life filled entirely by satisfying but non-veridical experiences, put in our heads by a so-called "experience machine". To the extent that we are disturbed by the prospect of living this kind of life, we discover how deeply we value the possibility of deriving our satisfactions from veridical experiences and authentic activities. In a similar vein, this exploration of which activities might be transferred to computers is a *philosophical thought-experiment* that not only tests some of our ideas about responsibility but helps reveal to us how deeply we care about engaging ourselves and connecting to one another.

Computers in control: On what terms?

If and when it *is* wise to rely on computer generated decisions or to put computers in control of certain events, it is *we* humans who must decide as much. And it is we humans who must bear the ultimate responsibility for that decision. The question remains – whether in yet another sense of the term – we must remain "responsible" – i.e. alert and responsive to developments that defeat the purpose of relying on the computer in the first place. Or, could it be reasonable and responsible, even in morally significant, safety-critical contexts, to transfer a kind of unconditional (i.e., non-reviewable, non-revocable) "authority" to a computerized decision-system?

I believe that morally responsible human beings *ought to maintain a kind of "higher-order control" over the moral quality of their lives and their environs.*[28] I call this "autonomous moral functioning". In clarification of what this amounts to, there are two points worth emphasizing. (1) The morally autonomous life is not one of ceaseless reflection, deliberation, etc. For often it is unreasonable to deliberate at length or even at all. If a person discerns good reason for not securing further information or entertaining further argument, then he or she *is* acting in a rationally self-monitoring way. (2) Moral autonomy is not to be equated with self-sufficiency. Indeed, in a complex world, it is difficult to believe that anyone is always the best judge of every possible morally relevant matter. Thus, the ideal of moral autonomy is perfectly compatible with a "division of moral labor". A morally autonomous person is prepared to acknowledge that in certain cases someone else may be in a better position to gather morally relevant information or even to give that information a suitably empathetic and disinterested attention.

The crucial point is that whatever the autonomous person does or refrains from doing – whether she deliberates at length or not at all, whether she decides entirely on her own or relies on the knowledge or judgment of another – she is prepared to justify, on morally reasonable grounds, the course which she has taken.

Still there may be some question about how it is possible to maintain this higher-order control over one's own conduct without becoming hopelessly lost in thought and deliberation. I suggest that the autonomous moral agent will preserve autonomy in two ways: (a) by a more or less continuous, but essentially passive, receptivity to particularly significant developments that might warrant a change in his moral course; (b) by periodic full-scale reviews of his life and the principles on which it is based. On the one hand, the autonomous person is almost always "alive to" prominent signs or indicators that his life-course is not what it should be; and on the other hand, he is prepared to step back, though only from time to time, to engage in a more deliberate and thorough assessment.

Thus the autonomous person is able to monitor the moral quality of his or her life without having to defer life itself in favor of all-consuming deliberation and reflection. Let me now attempt to apply this bit of moral theory to the computer-decision-making context.

It might be objected that if, and/or when, decision by computer is statistically more reliable than human decision-making (e.g., in the guiding of a passenger jet) then responsibility really ought to be transferred from humans to computers, and *without* the option of human intervention or override. And if that is so, then the proper description of the matter really is "humans abdicate moral responsibility in favor of computers."

I would argue that this fails to put the matter in proper perspective. To be sure, we have granted for the sake of argument, that the computers we humans have designed and programmed, can be – perhaps even now are – statistically more reliable than humans in the same role. But even such "meta-machines" are fallible; they are not incapable of deviating from optimal performance. And if that is so, then the proper description of the matter really is "humans abdicate moral responsibility in favor of computers." (Indeed, it is hard to see how we fallible humans could ever have sufficient reason for believing that we had identified, let alone created, an infallible mechanism for making and implementing morally fundamental decisions).

And there are two kinds of deviations from optimal performance: subtle and gross. It might be unreasonable for a pilot to override what to all appearances was a normal flight pattern (on the ground, say, that he was a bit bored or thought he saw some way to improve fuel efficiency by 5%).[29] But when a computer malfunctions, however rare such occasions might be, the deviation from acceptable performance may be painfully obvious – the plane takes a sudden nosedive away into a densely populated area; or, in approaching Los Angeles, it maintains an altitude insufficient to clear the San Gabriel Mountains, and is presently heading directly into the side of (12,000 foot) Mount Baldy.[30]

While it might well be wrong of a human agent to override the computer in the normal course of the computer's operations (e.g., in an attempt to achieve somewhat greater fuel efficiency), a grossly deviant performance (e.g., heading into the side of a mountain) would be quite another matter. To stand idly by while a machine is on the verge of destroying innocent life *would* be wrong. (It would be foolish to sit idly by and say, "The computer has decided that the optimal path is to crash into the side of this mountain. Since the computer is more reliable than we are, we must adhere to its edicts!") From the claim that the computer can be designed to operate with greater reliability on the whole, it simply *does not follow that it is more reliable in every kind of reliably identifiable safety-critical situation.*[31]

Here we should distinguish between having an (i)(a) unlimited prerogative to override on the one hand and having a (i)(b) well-defined "special-contingency" override option on the other. That the computer is more reliable "overall" but less reliable in certain clearly identifiable situations, strongly suggests that appropriately skilled, responsible humans should retain a well-defined, special-contingency override option. We can also distinguish (ii)(a) "situational override" (whether "broadly discretionary" or "special contingency") from what I have been calling (ii)(b) "background oversight responsibility." Even if, in rare cases, it were advisable to give up the option of situational override, it is quite another matter to abdicate autonomy altogether by relinquishing the option of making even a periodic review and when appropriate, "revoking" the computer's role-responsibility. Humans who are qualified to assess a computer system's reliability and who are entitled to delegate to it a significant safety-critical role, must also be – barring a subsequent diminution in their own faculties that would render them non-responsible – both qualified to review the subsequent performance of the system, and responsible for terminating the arrangement if and when human safety considerations so warrant.[32]

So there are two points to make here: first, even when computers are overall more reliable than humans, special contingency override may (at least in some cases) still be appropriate.[33] Secondly, and more importantly, even when it is not reasonable to retain the option of "special contingency" override, humans who are responsible moral agents cannot reasonably abdicate their background oversight responsibility: i.e., their option of periodically reviewing and, when appropriate, either revising or even "revoking" the computer's decision-making role.

I suggest that situations of this sort are by no means new to us. What we have here is the familiar problem of how to conduct ourselves in relation to "experts" who are nevertheless fallible.

Here is a parallel example from another area of our lives: doctor-patient relations. When we take ourselves to a highly accomplished, well-recommended physician we do place a certain amount of confidence in his or her diagnostic and prescriptive abilities. But do we, or more crucially, *should* we, literally abdicate our own decision-making responsibility? If the physician is intoxicated, rambles incoherently about long-ago experiences, prescribes bizarre treatments (sexual intimacy with the physician, for example!), then we will surely conclude that this particular human "expert system" is malfunctioning in a grossly deviant way, not fulfilling the purpose for which one had delegated a kind of conditional decision-making authority in the first place.

Thus responsible, morally autonomous human agents will defer to greater expertise – when a reasonably informed and considered judgment establishes that they are in the presence of such expertise – but they will *maintain a certain level of background oversight* – of being "on the uptake" for relatively obvious signals that the "expert" is not functioning as the expert he/she/it can be. So the habit of deferring to expertise is not equivalent either to an abdication of moral responsibility or to the alienation of autonomous moral judgment.

One of the oldest mistakes in philosophy – going back at least as far as *The Republic* of Plato – is to suppose that once we have identified the greatest available expertise, unconditional obedience is warranted. One of the earliest lessons of moral and political wisdom was that absolute authority is dangerous and that even "experts" ought to be placed within an appropriate system of "checks and balances".[34]

An apparent counter-point

In "Are There Decisions Computers Should Never Make?"[35] James Moor characterizes the claim that "computers should never make decisions which humans cannot override" as a "dubious maxim."[36] Moor suggests that we look at the matter "instrumentally" – if computer decision-makers operate more competently than human decision-makers, then we should rely on them. Thus, Moor's discussion would *appear* to pose a challenge to the view defended here. But Moor goes on to make two additional points which, as I shall argue, raise a reasonable doubt as to whether there really is any disagreement between Moor and myself:

1. Moor warns that widespread decision-making by computers might "dehumanize" our lives (p. 129). Though the term is not explicated, Moor seems to have in mind something like the point I tried to make in connection with gift-giving: to have a

machine pick out the gift for one's spouse or parent could easily rob the gift-giving of its deeper human significance. In other words, even when computers are "instrumentally" superior, there may be intrinsic value in humans, rather than computers, engaging in certain activities (including decision-making activities) (see *Beyond Competence and Reliability*, p. 178).

2. Moor insists that humans, not computers, must decide on the values which computers, however competently, will be programmed to promote. Thus he writes, "Computers should never decide what our basic goals and values (and priorities among them) should be" (p. 129). And he goes on to conclude that "...humans have not only an initial responsibility, but a *continuing responsibility* (emphasis added here) to raise the competency and value questions whenever computer decision making is at issue." (loc.cit.) This is, I believe, tantamount to the view defended here,[37] namely, that the people who design and/or rely upon computers, must not abdicate their fundamental "oversight responsibility." The difference (if there is any) is that I have argued this point on general grounds, having to do with the nature of rational and responsible autonomous moral agency (see *Computers in Control*, p. 178), rather than on the specific ground that "increased computerization" could lead to "dehumanization."

To sum up

Whether or not a decision-making computer system is on the whole more reliable than humanly directed operation, it can still make good sense to design the system in a way that preserves the option of human override for special situations in which safety-endangering computer error is likely to be grossly obvious, and suitably trained and knowledgeable personnel can trigger the override mechanism after corroborating one another's perception. Where human safety is concerned, the speed, stamina, etc. of computers must be combined with the human virtues of moral judgment, pattern recognition, flexibility and resourcefulness in unexpected and ambiguous situations, etc. But even when such "special contingency" override is *not* appropriate, the people who delegate decision-making responsibility to computers cannot reasonably relinquish "background oversight responsibility." If humans are sufficiently equipped with reason to have responsibly delegated such role-responsibility to a computer (or a doctor, etc.) in the first place, then humans must be equipped, and prepared, to review and revoke that delegation of

responsibility should things not work out as envisioned. To fail to retain such oversight responsibility, would be tantamount to an indefensible abdication of their responsibility as autonomous moral agents.[38]

Epilogue: A futuristic vision – computers in ultimate control

Science fiction writers often dream of a distant future in which the creations "outperform" their creators. Outperform in which domains? Which activities? Such creatures might be no more than

(i) ultra-sophisticated robots, more accurate and reliable in every technically demanding task – motor coordination, perception, information storage, recall, computation. etc.

But what if they were

(ii) beings who not only think, but hope, fear, love and care – *and* who unfalteringly do what is just and kind – our *moral*, not merely technical, superiors?

In the first scenario, we might, I suppose, regard such creations as super-tools. yet there are many activities we would still reserve to ourselves. For what, after all, is the point of living our lives? Not merely to be instruments for the production of certain kinds of results, but to (i) engage our faculties, and (ii) resonate to one another – i.e., to lead a life and to live with one another.

In the second scenario, we might be hard-pressed to know what to do: would we usher ourselves from the scene, altogether abdicating in favor of them? or would we – inverting the relationship between creator and creation – faithfully strive to serve *them* (as many now think of themselves in relation to what they take to be an all-wise and loving deity?)[39]

I wonder if either of these responses is sufficiently resonant to what morality is about. It is just possible that our role, as morally decent people, is not to strive for the production of morally perfect beings performing morally perfect deeds (leaving us with the choice, in scenario (ii), of either becoming completely obedient servants or else checking out altogether). I wonder if a morally decent person's role might not be simpler – to do the best one can do to lead one's own life honestly and justly and kindly, and at the same time, to encourage the capacity for conscientious living in anyone else so capable.

Reflecting on our cybernetic futures may be another way of coming to appreciate the implausibility of a thoroughly end-state or consequentialist conception of morality.

Notes

1. Frederick Ferré, for example, defines technology as "the practical implementation of intelligence", *Philosophy of Technology* (Englewood Cliffs: Prentice-Hall, 1988). Of course, the advent of a new technology also has a way of influencing, and to some extent reshaping, what people want.
2. For an optimistic survey of what has been, and might yet be, accomplished in this area, see Raymond Kurzweil, *The Age of Intelligent Machines* (Boston: MIT Press, 1990). For skepticism, see Hubert Dreyfus and Stuart Dreyfus, *Mind over Machine: The Power of Human Intuition and Expertise in the Era of the Computer* (New York: Free Press, 1989).
3. That many different humans are typically involved can make it more difficult for each to recognize his/her share of the responsibility. For a fuller account of the difficulties in getting people to acknowledge responsibility when an operational computer is the product of many different hands, see Helen Nissenbaum, "Computing and Accountability", *Proceedings of the ACM*, January 1994.
4. James Moor has pointed out to me that programmed computers can evolve beyond their original programs and so whatever decision-making was originally made by humans may not be very germane. It seems to me, however, that if it is humans who programmed the self-reprogramming computer to be capable of this "evolution" (or programmed the computer that programmed the computer . . .), then in some sense those humans must still bear the ultimate responsibility for what ensues.
5. See Roger Penrose, *The Emperor's New Mind* (Oxford: Oxford University Press, 1989) for a case against the possibility of machine consciousness. See the works of Daniel C. Dennett for the opposite case. For a still more recent defense of eventual computer consciousness see Ray Kurzweil, *The Age of Spiritual Machines, When Computers Exceed Human Intelligence* (New York: Viking, 1999), chapter eleven. Kurzweil conjectures that by the year 2029, computers will be so evolved as to "claim to be conscious" and their claims will be "largely accepted."
6. "Computers and Moral Responsibility" in *The Information Web: Ethical and Social Implications of Computer Networking*, edited by Carol Gould (Boulder: Westview Press, 1989).
7. Ian Barbour, *Ethics in an Age of Technology*, (San Francisco: Harper Collins, 1993) p. 164.
8. Martyn Thomas, chair of Praxis Systems, which produces special high reliability software for Britain's Air Force, quoted in "Is America Ready to 'Fly by Wire'?", *The Washington Post*, April 2, 1989, p. C3.
9. Bev Littlewood and Lorenzo Strigini, "The Risks of Software" in *Scientific American*, November 1992, reprinted in *Computers, Ethics and Social Values* (Englewood Cliffs: Prentice Hall, 1995), edited by Deborah Johnson and Helen Nissenbaum, p. 434.
10. Nancy G. Leveson, *Safeware: System Safety and Computers* (Reading, Mass.: Addison-Wesley, 1995), p. 29.
11. Peter Neumann, S.R.I. International, a specialist in software engineering who "has documented hundreds of software failure cases in the aerospace and other industries", *The Washington Post*, loc. cit.
12. Littlewood and Strigini, op. cit., loc. cit., p. 435.
13. Mike Hennell, Department of Statistics and Computational Mathematics at Liverpool University, "an authority on software reliability", as quoted in *The Washington Post*, April 2, 1989, loc. cit.
14. Littlewood and Strigini, op. cit., loc. cit, p. 433.
15. David L. Parnas, A. John van Schouwen, and Shu Po Kwan, "Evaluation of Safety-Critical Software" in Johnson and Nissenbaum, op. cit., p. 441.
16. Leveson, op. cit., p. 33.
17. Littlewood and Strigini, op. cit., loc. cit., pp. 435–436.
18. Leveson, op. cit., p. 158.
19. Leveson, op. cit., pp. 434, 436.
20. Alan Borning, "Computer System Reliability and Nuclear War", originally in *Communications of the ACM* 30, 2, reprinted in Johnson and Nissenbaum, op. cit., p. 410.
21. A terminological caveat – Nancy Leveson has urged that "reliability" not be equated with "safety." For "software reliability is defined as compliance with the requirements specification, while most safety critical software errors can be traced to errors in the requirements – that is, to misunderstandings about what the software should do." (op. cit., p. 29). Indeed, while "Reliability engineers often assume that reliability and safety are synonymous . . . this assumption is true only in special cases . . . many accidents occur without any component failure – the individual components were operating exactly as specified or intended, that is, without failure. The opposite is also true – components may fail without a resulting accident." (op. cit., p. 164) These points are well-taken. For purposes of the present discussion, however, the expression "software reliability" is used in a less technical and more colloquial way: thus when we ask about the extent to which we can reasonably *rely* on software *in* safety-critical contexts, we are not merely concerned with the extent to which the program can be expected to operate as specified; we are also concerned with the extent to which we can determine whether a program has been (and/or can be) specified in a way that is sufficiently responsive to the circumstances that could endanger human life and limb. On this point, Alan Borning has noted that "There are many examples of errors arising from incorrect or incomplete specification. One such example is a false alert in the early days of the nuclear age . . . when on October 5, 1960, the warning system at NORAD indicated that the United States was under massive attack by Soviet missiles with a certainty of 99.9 percent. It turned out that the Ballistic Missile Early Warning System (BMEWS) radar in Thule, Greenland, had spotted the *rising moon*. Nobody had thought about the moon when specifying how the system should act." (op. cit., loc. cit., p. 410).
22. "Software and Safety" in *The Washington Post*, April 2, 1989, p. C3.
23. Here I quote from Helen Nissenbaum's "Computing and Accountability", *Communications of the ACM*, January 1994; Nissenbaum draws on the definitive account of Leveson and Turner, "An Investigation of the Therac-25 Accidents", *Computer*, 1993. 26(7), pp. 18–41. Leveson also analyzes this incident at length in Appendix A ("Med-

ical Devices: The Therac-25 Story") of her book, *Safeware: System Safety and Computers*, cited previously.

24. Here it might be suggested that we resort to physical "barriers" or limitations: e.g., that we only deploy machines whose hardware design is such that very large doses of radiation will not be administered, no matter how "unreliable" the *software* putatively "governing" the machine. This wouldn't stop patients from receiving more moderate overdoses accumulating to their detriment over longer periods of time, but it could avert a single catastrophe. The extent to which such strategies can be helpful will depend on the specifics of the physical system at issue. In the case of a jet plane on automatic pilot, for example, there seems to be no comparable "barrier" solution to insure, for example, that the plane not crash into mountainsides or tall buildings.

25. Ian Barbour, op. cit., p. 170; see also Dreyfus and Dreyfus, op. cit.

26. *To Engineer is Human* (New York: Random House, 1992), pp. 194–195.

27. In the well-known O'Henry story, "The Gift of the Magi", two people exchange gifts at great cost to themselves; unfortunately, the cost each has incurred renders the gift received from the other no longer of any material use. If end-results didn't matter at all, the story would lose most of its poignance and pathos; it would just be another laughable version of the "Alphonse and Gaston" routine: two silly men ushering one another through the door with pompous ceremoniousness are nevertheless unable to go anywhere because neither will go until the other goes first.

28. Here I follow my essay, "The Inalienability of Autonomy", *Philosophy & Public Affairs* 13(4): 271–298, Fall 1984.

29. The problem of boredom is not to be overlooked, however; while problems arising from fully automated systems can be mitigated if humans also have a role to play, the "human-machine interface" must be carefully designed. If human operators have nothing to do but intervene in rare, catastrophic emergency situations, they may become too inactive and inattentive to be able to respond quickly and skillfully if and when the time arrives. This suggests that while not constantly intervening and overriding, the humans who oversee a computer's safety-critical operation must nevertheless have meaningfully active roles (e.g., putting questions to the computer, collecting data on the state of the machine) to keep them adequately informed and sufficiently alert. See, for example, Nancy Leveson, op. cit., Chapter 5, section 2 ("The Need for Humans in Automated Systems") and Chapter 6 ("The Role of Humans in Automated Systems").

30. It has been suggested to me that, given the reliability of the computer, we should suppose not that the plane is heading into the side of the mountain, but that the pilot is hallucinating. No doubt there are cases in which this might be so. And in any event it might be sensible to design the system so that the override option could only be activated with the concurrence of two or more authorized crew members (who would first have to input their respective personal code numbers). But in the presently imagined case, we have only to note several other factors that would make the hypothesis non-credible. Suppose the pilot who takes

himself to be seeing the plane heading toward the side of the mountain seeks corroboration – not only from the co-pilot, but from flight attendants, passengers who have flown planes, et al – and they all report that they see the plane heading toward the side of the mountain. Of course, the only way for the plane to clear the mountains is for it to be presently cruising *above* 12,000 feet! Absent information about a special drug administered to everyone aboard that could have this kind of hallucinogenic effect, and *given* the aforementioned facts about the essential non-debuggability of complex functional programs, it is far more reasonable to suppose that the program is malfunctioning than that all these people are hallucinating. Someone might suggest that the pilot is hallucinating about the existence and reliability of these other witnesses. But so long as we are allowed to indulge in skeptical doubt so radical, the "extreme reliability" of the flight-control software itself should not be spared from the category of the potentially delusional.

31. "Human operators are included in complex systems because, unlike computers, they are adaptable and flexible ... Humans are able to look at tasks as a whole and to adapt both the goals and the methods to achieve them. Thus, humans evolve and develop skills and performance patterns that fit the peculiarities of a system very effectively, and they are able to use problem solving and creativity to cope with unusual and unforeseen situations. For example, the pilot of a Boeing 767 made use of his experience as an amateur glider pilot to land his aircraft safely after a series of equipment failures and maintenance errors caused the plane to run out of fuel while in flight over Canada. Humans can exercise judgment and are unsurpassed in recognizing patterns, making associative leaps, and operating in ill-structured, ambiguous situations." Leveson, op. cit, pp. 100–101, citing the work of W.B. Rouse and N.M. Morris, "Conceptual design of a human error tolerant interface for complex engineering systems" in G. Mancini, G. Johannsen and L. Martensson, eds. *Analysis, Design, and Evaluation of Man-Machine Systems*, pp. 281–286 (Pergamon Press, New York, 1986).

32. Here I follow the line of argument presented in my article, "The Inalienability of Autonomy", loc. cit, where it was directed against abdication in favor of fellow-humans, to make the case against abdication in favor of sophisticated programmed computers as well.

33. Leveson has suggested a number of possible guidelines for safer design of the "HMI" – i.e., the "human-machine interface." Among these are – "Design the HMI to augment human abilities, not replace them." "Involve operators in design decisions and safety analysis throughout development." "Design for error tolerance: (a) make errors reversible ... (b) provide time to reverse them, and (c) provide compensating (reversing) actions." "Provide adequate feedback to keep operator in the loop." "Allow the operator to maintain manual involvement and to update mental models, maintain skills, and preserve self-confidence." "Do not permit overrides of potentially safety-critical failures ... until all data has been displayed and perhaps not until the operator has acknowledged seeing it." "Train operators to understand how the system functions and to think flex-

ibly when solving problems." "Train for general strategies (rather than specific responses) to develop skills for dealing with unanticipated events." "Provide practice in problem solving." op. cit., pp. 485–488.

34. For a recent application of this same idea we have only to turn to an Op.-Ed. page essay *NY Times*, February 1, 1994, p. A 17) by Valery Yarynich, "a retired colonel in the Russian Strategic Rocket Forces, who spent his career working on command and control systems." Yarynich was commenting on a previous piece that alleged the existence of a secret computerized launching system that "in theory would enable Russia to fire its nuclear arsenal even if its top commanders had been killed." He was at pains to deny that any such "doomsday machine" had been set up. Instead, Yarynich insisted that the capacity to strike back even after top leaders had been incapacitated did obtain but in the form of a special crew of *human beings*, situated deep underground and subject to a three-point system of checks and balances. I believe that Yarynich was rightly uncomfortable with the idea of a computerized weapons system beyond all human reconsideration.

35. Nature and System I (1979), 217–229, reprinted in *Ethical Issues in the Use of Computers*, edited by Deborah Johnson and John W. Snapper.

36. p. 121 in Johnson and Snapper. Subsequent citations are to this edition.

37. See *Clarifications*: "*Decision-making*"; "*Responsibility*", p. 173 and *Computers in Control*, p. 178.

38. It might be objected that the conclusions of this paper fail to take seriously the paper's own admonition against the prejudice that "only flesh and blood, carbon-based, organic entities" could be responsible moral agents. See *Clarification*: "*Decision-making*"; "*Responsibility*", p. 173. I believe that nothing in the foregoing discussion tells against the possibility that computers could evolve to the point of being plausibly regarded as moral agents in their own right, though it must also be acknowledged that they are not there yet. The thrust of the argument against vesting irrevocable authority in computers is based, as I suggest above, on the same reflections that tell against vesting such authority in a fellow human.

39. Here it might be suggested that humans would not be serving the superior machines but merely just trusting them. Perhaps so. But the scenario envisioned has those "superior" machines so much wiser and more reliable that they would be revered by humans as the ultimate authority on everything that mattered. Humans would be not merely taking advice but in a sense obeying the "superior" beings. As noted above, this would be much like the relationship some people have to a deity: service, not in the sense of slavery, but in the sense of reverent obedience.

[35]

On Becoming Redundant or What Computers Shouldn't Do

JAMES LENMAN

ABSTRACT   *I argue here that the development of machines that provide for us what we could previously provide for ourselves may sometimes be a dubious blessing. For the value of many goods is not independent of the way in which they are produced and in particular of the human contribution to their production. With a large range of goods it may matter to us both that people rather than machines contribute to their production and that we ourselves make some such contribution. We have a need to be constructively engaged in the service of our own and one another's ends. We also have an interest both in the extent to which the society in which we live includes all its members in such engagement and the extent to which the goods we enjoy are the fruits of such inclusive human endeavour. A significant and shared human contribution to the meeting of our needs is itself one of our deepest needs. These thoughts are developed primarily with reference to the values found in art, conversation and work.*

I

1. How There Stopped Being Composers

Can a computer compose and perform great music? This question defined one of the major research projects of twenty-first century work on Artificial Intelligence. While it was underway, needless to say, plenty of philosophers and such went on at great length how it couldn't be done. Only then of course it *was* done, quite quickly, in the closing two decades of the century. In the year 2000 there was perhaps a small amount of music of the highest order of beauty and power — the finest works of Bach and the handful of others who had composed anything comparable. A few days might have sufficed to listen to the lot. Not so by 2100 — by then the creative musical efforts of human beings had been swamped: the compositional system BRANDENBURG VII was found to have stored in its memory a body of its own music, all of extraordinary power and beauty, that would require some 24,000,000 hours of listening time. And BRANDENBURG VII was only an early model. By 2150 the human professions of composer and musician were little more than a memory.

2. How There Stopped Being Scientists

This was trickier. At the end of the twentieth century there were already machines to do many of the labours that had previously exercised scientists. Calculation was so delegated and the generation of predictions from complex theories largely a matter of computer modelling. But the creative generation of hypotheses and the direction of the whole enterprise could surely, it was thought, never be done by any but human minds.

2   *J. Lenman*

But, as progress was made in AI, it turned out in practice there was less and less in the way of "creative" bits for the human scientist to do. By 2200 there was *nothing* for her to do. Huge mechanised laboratories in Southern Asia and Africa functioned more or less autonomously, constantly enlarging human knowledge, though increasingly it was true that no human actually knew the "knowledge" they were busily stockpiling.

3. How There Stopped Being Conversations

In 1950 Alan Turing had argued that a machine was intelligent if you couldn't tell it was a machine [1]. If conversing with the machine was just like conversing with a human person, that was enough. By 2100 the problem of constructing computers that easily passed this test was more or less solved. Talking to a computer could be just like talking to a human being — at least as far as what was *said* went; but this only began to have major practical implications in the twenty-third century. By this time technological advance had removed the need for such natural *fora* for social life as the school, the market and the workplace. Few people now had to leave their homes to work, to shop or to learn. More and more, the only reason one had to go out was that one was lonely. More and more however, people asked themselves — why bother, simply for someone to talk to? If it was *conversation* you wanted, after all, there was plenty of software to meet your needs without the risk and inconvenience of human interaction. The art of conversation did not quite die but it became something you could do on your own.

4. How There Stopped Being Sex

Our sexual needs, of course, gave us a reason to go out and encounter other people that no computer, however conversationally gifted, could meet. Or so it seemed. Virtual reality machinery had been a favourite of science fiction since the late twentieth century. But the pace of actual development was slower than many had hoped. It was only in the twenty-fourth century that certain especially intractable technical obstacles were finally solved — and all, of course, by mechanised engineers. In that century it at last became possible to offer people the experience of erotic engagement with the partner of their dreams without having to go through the fraught rituals of introduction and courtship.

5. How There Stopped Being People

Virtual sex, it goes without saying, doesn't make you pregnant. But that was hardly a difficulty. By this time reproductive technology had taken all the mess and pain out of having children. You had simply to supply an egg or some sperm to the Population Institute and they would do the rest. Sanitised parenthood was only a phonecall away. Only, for some reason, in the course of the twenty-fifth century fewer and fewer people, as they sat alone in automated homes they had now no reason to leave, could any longer be bothered . . . By the year 2600 most of these homes were empty.

Finally in the year 3000, a dream of science fiction finally came true: intelligent extraterrestrials arrived on Earth. To their surprise they found a highly technologically advanced civilisation but nobody at home. A vast array of self-sustaining automatic machinery was churning away, composing symphonies, proving mathematical theorems and so on to no apparent purpose. Filed away on the memories of these machines the aliens discovered the whole strange history of that extinct and eccentric species, *Homo Sapiens* [2].

II

We are all familiar enough with the sort of AI-buffery which enthuses effusively about how we may expect, as time passes, more and more of what we now have to do ourselves to be open to delegation to machines. Such speculation is apt to meet with a some scepticism. This scepticism may be well-motivated but perhaps there is always a certain idleness in *a priori* reflections over where the future development of science will or will not take us. For the sake of argument the foregoing story assumes that many of the wildest dreams of technological utopianism are satisfied [3], not with a view to begging those questions but simply in order to raise others.

While this gloomy little tale is not a very likely story, I hope that some of the thoughts it may suggest are not entirely idle. The question I am, in particular, concerned to dramatise is this: take certain central human goods and imagine those goods to survive but with the human contribution to them dispensed with. How much do we lose by this? The plausible answer in the cases I have considered is that we lose a great deal. The object of the exercise is to advance our understanding of why and how we value the things we do, and that concern is far from idle.

Thus suppose the supply of music became swamped with artificial music in the way the story imagines. Would we have good reason to be alarmed by such a prospect? After all, this music is just like "real" music. Wouldn't this all be rather splendid: bottomless supplies of Bach — or something just as good — endlessly on tap?

That's quite a tricky question to think clearly about and things may be easier if we focus first on the *third* episode of the story — the end of *conversation*. This case is easier because it seems quite clear that anyone who thinks a computer can be a satisfactory conversational partner must surely just misunderstand *what a conversation is*. Of course there is no *one* thing a conversation is but many of the things we do in conversations get their point from the fact that we have them with *another human being*.

Thus we chat, you and I: you got your pay rise? — splendid, I am delighted for you; you have been ill? — I commiserate; we compare some philosophical thoughts and argue a bit; we reminisce a little and you tell some stories about your youthful misadventures before we met; we notice the weather and gripe about it; we compare notes on who we do or do not fancy rotten in the latest soap; we plan a fishing trip at the weekend — should we invite so-and-so along? — he's nice enough but a bit boring; I love your hair that way — and say so; have you seen *Gladiator*? — yes? — you thought it was junk? — certainly, but, as junk goes, it was great fun; here is a joke I heard . . .

Of course if a computer can pass a Türing Test, you can have such a conversation with it just as you can with me. The computer can fool you into thinking it is human. But then you are being fooled. Machines do not have youthful misadventures — perhaps they can recount them but not truthfully; they aren't amused by jokes and don't fancy anyone; they don't care about your pay rise, your illness or the weather; nobody bores them and they don't go fishing; all movies leave them cold and they

4   *J. Lenman*

don't have any hair. So while you can imagine yourself in my story chatting happily away with the box in the corner, you are not doing at all what you are doing when you have a real conversation. You can *talk* to a machine but you cannot, for example, *cheer it up* or *wind it up* or *chat it up*. The machine is not your friend; it neither likes nor dislikes you; cannot be interested or bored, amused or unamused, impressed or unimpressed, attracted or repelled. It hasn't got a life and it isn't interested in yours.

We can of course imagine people *settling for* artificial conversation if it were readily available just as we sometimes settle for masturbation in place of lovemaking. But the difference is plausibly of the same order in both cases. It's the difference between fantasy and real human engagement — and this is not a difference that the mere verisimilitude of the fantasy can be expected to dissolve. The *fourth* episode is after all the easiest to think about of all — is lovemaking better than masturbation? (The unavoidable positive answer need not, in either case, be conditional on our ability readily to tell the two apart.)

So we can fairly easily understand why virtual conversations are not the same or as good as real ones. Turning to the parallel question about music, can we now see how best to answer it? Nearly, but I think another intermediate step may help. Let us focus initially on the rather easier case of *literature*. Imagine our first episode so reworked that it is *writers* being put out of a job. Here we may be helped on our way by what we've already noticed. For while literary enterprise is not the *same* as conversation, it is by no means *discontinuous* with it [4]:

> When evening comes I return home and go into my study, and at the door I take off my daytime dress covered in mud and dirt, and put on royal and curial robes; and then decently attired I enter the courts of the ancients, where affectionately greeted by them, I partake of that food which is mine alone and for which I was born; where I am not ashamed to talk with them and inquire the reasons of their actions; and they out of human kindness answer me, and for hours at a stretch I feel no worry of any kind; I forget all my troubles, I am not afraid of poverty or of death. I give myself up entirely to them. And because Dante says that understanding does not constitute knowledge unless it is retained in the memory, I have written down what I have learned from their conversation and composed a short work . . . [5]

If Machiavelli's picture of reading as a form of conversation is to some degree a literary conceit it is only because *continuity* is exaggerated into *identity*. The writing and reading of literature is after all the same phenomenon of human verbal communication at a greater distance and on a larger scale.

Once again it needs to be stressed that of course there is no *one* thing we are doing when we write something — the person who produces a literary text is seeking to put her thoughts in order on a subject that she cares something about. She is perhaps aiming to understand her thoughts and feelings, certainly to communicate them, perhaps to exorcize them. She expects, and hopes, that others too will care; that they will read and respond to what she writes: be provoked or inspired or amused; that perhaps some of them will give a little back and take the conversation further. She is moved by a wish to participate in a conversation that is larger than a table in a bar, a conversation with a history and a direction, that comes from, and is heading, somewhere; and where what she writes may influence that direction. It matters to her that we read her words and what we think of them.

Think now of any great works of art — Shakespeare's plays will do. Imagine learning that you have been tricked: *Shakespeare* is the name of a fancy computer and the *Complete Works* on your bookshelf is an improbably successful experiment in computer-generated literature. Or, since we need to generalise to the case of music, imagine the same shocking discovery made about the *St Matthew Passion* (it takes a bit of imagining but, for the sake of argument, indulge me). How would you feel about these works now? Will you take the book — or CD — down from the shelf and discard it in disgust or will you go on valuing it just as you previously have?

This is a difficult question. I think it might help to think first of a less bizarre case. Consider the changing attitude to the Bible of someone, raised as a Christian, who loses his faith. For such a person the Bible may remain a very rich book. But it is *no longer the book he thought it was*. What he had thought the Word of God is now taken to be merely the words of men and deeply misleading words at that. But perhaps the book still has a certain value. Firstly because, *qua* the words of men, there may be much in it that he still thinks beautiful and wise, albeit nothing he now thinks divine. It is also, secondly, a text that cannot but continue to resonate given the deep ways in which it is woven into history, both his own personal history and that of the culture he was born into. The value and importance of the book is utterly transformed and massively diminished but some value — perhaps in this case rather a lot — remains.

Now give him a second shock. He learns that the Bible is not even the words of men but a computer-generated text, smuggled into the ancient Near East by Martians with a quirky sense of humour. The work's historical significance nonetheless persists. St Paul, it turns out, was only a virtual author but not so Augustine or Dante or Bunyan — this is still going to be a fairly special book. And this sort of consideration will apply to some degree when we play this game with any of the greatest works in our history: that's a major factor that complicates things when we think about the Bach and Shakespeare cases.

Having identified this consideration let's take it out of the picture. Forget the Bible, Shakespeare, Bach and think of a piece of poetry or music that is five minutes old. It is, we will suppose, quite astonishing, as astonishing as Shakespeare or Bach. But it is also artificial, produced by a machine that can come up with a thousand more such pieces just as astonishing in a few minutes. How much would it interest you?

This need not be the same as the question how much would it *move* you? It might move you quite a lot and that not really be the point. A bird might, after all, be moved (insofar as birds are properly spoken of as moved) by synthesized sounds that mimic perfectly the mating call of its kind — but these are not the sounds it needs to hear. Human artistic performance is of course a far more complex matter than the songs and courtship displays of other species (though there may well be complexities in these that would surprise us). But it is implausible to suppose the two are altogether discontinuous — think of music and dance not in the somewhat rarefied context of ballets and string quartets but in that of a dancehall. The interests these forms may serve and emotions they may nourish are far more diverse than merely those bound up simply in courtship but they are unmistakably human interests and human emotions and that is plausibly why they matter to us as they do. What seem to be human words move us because they *seem* to be human words and interest us because we take it that is what

6   *J. Lenman*

they *are*. If the appearance is only a trick then they should not and very plausibly *would* not interest us in the same ways [6]. They are as different from the real thing — and in the same way — as virtual sex is from real lovemaking. It's not that virtual sex cannot be great fun, merely that it's ultimately somewhat second-rate.

What of my story's second episode? I suspect the things we need to say here will not be discontinuous with what has been said already, but I will not here attempt to formulate them. Let this be an exercise for the reader.

III

In domains such as conversation, sex and art, it matters to us not only that the inputs we receive have a human source but that we ourselves affirm our own humanity through contributions of our own. It matters too that these contributions be needed and valued by others in ways the products of machinery are not.

It may prove illuminating to turn here to the *zero*-th part of the story, the part that *isn't* science fiction and that I didn't need to tell. The replacement of human beings by machinery that does the same thing better, faster, cheaper is something that is *already* happening on a large scale. Of course much of what machinery already does for us is undoubtedly grim and unrewarding work that it would be silly to romanticise. And of course the whole process may leave us economically better off in aggregate though that is small comfort to those such processes leave too impoverished, typically, for their leisure to have much positive value. That is an important worry about distributive justice — what we might call a *product-distributive* concern — but there is another source of worry — a *process-distributive* worry, we might say — that is more continuous with the rest of this essay. This is concerned, not with the question of who is to be included, and to what degree, in the sharing out of the *end product* of economic activity but rather with who is included, and to what degree, in sharing the *activity itself*.

The worry is that, while technology can to some extent liberate us from our needs, this is something at which it can be *too* successful. The project of living is the endlessly multiple project of meeting human needs, the need for love, for friendship, for beauty and creative activity and exploratory engagement with the world, the need to be of use to others and to oneself. The meaning of our lives emerges from the way we go about meeting these needs and the patterns of significance we construct around the shape they give to these same lives. We differ, of course, in the relative evaluative salience we bestow on such needs. Perhaps, if there is enough else in our lives we, or some of us, can get along without working. Undoubtedly there are wealthy playboys who are happy enough. But the life of a wealthy playboy has ultimately only limited appeal. "But what use am I to anyone?" must, for many, become a question it is hard to ignore.

Unlike the wealthy playboy we engage in labours that make us necessary to others and to ourselves. People, as Kant insisted are not *merely* means [7] but means is nonetheless one of the most important things we are. *Whose* ends, after all are we? We are not simply ends but *our own* ends, the ends that we ourselves live largely in the service of. When we are not ourselves the means to our own — and one another's — ends, our capacity to value ourselves and what we do is diminished and undermined. To see people *merely as ends* is too dehumanize them no less surely, if perhaps less obviously, than to see them merely as means [8].

At this point an imaginary reader has an objection.

> You have told us a story about why we would not be happy about the music
> we listen to, the books we read, the conversational and erotic input we receive
> being artificial, the work of machinery. You then, in the last section, bring
> these reflections home to what you call the zero-th episode — the business of
> growing automation displacing human workers, where these are not poets or
> composers but, for example, assembly line workers. But here your argument
> becomes strained. I'm happy to grant that I don't want to spend my time
> listening to computer-generated symphonies and reading computer-generated
> novels. But why should it matter to me if, for example, much of the labour
> that goes into making the car I drive is automated? It may be essential to the
> sort of good a piece of music or a conversation is that it involves engagement
> with other human beings but a car is just a car. I care how fuel-efficient or fast
> or safe or stylish it is. But why should I care about the humanity of the agency
> that makes it?

Qua consumer, this objector suggests, there is no reason why I should prefer a
machine-built car to one built by people. This may seem right. But notice that it also
plausibly right that, if I think of myself merely as a *consumer* of books, music, scientific
knowledge, I'll not be too worried about the origins of *these* goods either and I'll not be
very impressed by the foregoing argument that these things matter [9]. Only we *don't*
think of ourselves merely as consumers of these latter things any more than, unless
there is something very badly amiss, we think of ourselves merely as consumers of the
words of our friends and the bodies of our lovers. We readily divide the world into
groups called "producers" and "consumers" and it is easy to forget that these are not
distinct groups of people. But of course a conversation is not a game where some of
us — the "producers" — say things to which others — the "consumers" — passively
listen. Neither indeed is that large conversation, the cultural life of our species. And
neither, it might be maintained, is our *economic* life.

We do however far more readily think of ourselves merely as consumers of motor
cars, refrigerators or communications infrastructure. We are also, we readily acknowledge, others things: we are moral agents and citizens, members of communities variously conceived. But we too easily conceive of the economic domain as amoral and
apolitical and hence of our economic agency as simply separate from these other and
larger dimensions. The question of course, and it is a very old one now, is how far we
should accept this separation. That is the question which my imagined objector has
begged.

Consider a very simple society. This society consists of a single family — say a moderately sizeable extended family. At first, everybody has to work flat out to keep the
community fed. But, after a bit, human inventiveness renders this project less and less
demanding. Of course, there are many reasons why this might be welcomed. Leisure as
such need be no problem: there's always after all music, poetry, philosophy, science,
sport, and the simple satisfactions of keeping one another company. Economic needs
are not our *only* needs. It is no part of my aim to dispute this.

Let us suppose, however, that there is still work for these people to do, albeit
significantly less than previously. There are now two broad options for this society:

8   *J. Lenman*

1. ELF: An *exclusive labour force*: here the workload for those who work remains considerable but fewer people now work. Because my immediate concern with the *process-distributive* issues we'll simply assume, for simplicity, that under the ELF option the end product of this labour is more or less equally shared. Everybody eats but not everybody works.
2. ILF: An *inclusive labour force*: here everybody continues to work but the workload per person is much reduced; here the saving gets made in number of hours worked rather then number of people working.

The ILF option clearly seems fairer than ELF, particularly, it might seem, for those who, on the latter arrangement do all the work [10]. But, I think we can also plausibly maintain, ILF may be better *for everybody*.

We will suppose this simple economy produces only a single kind of product — *the meal*. (They live in a cave in a perfect climate needing neither clothes nor fuel; they have no enemies and their way of life is simple enough to obviate the need for most domestic chores.) It now seems worth discriminating between two different kinds of meal:

M1. a meal one had oneself some share in the making of;
M2. a meal in which one had no such share.

M1 and M2 are not intrinsically different sorts of goods but the extrinsic difference between them is salient and important. In the light of the what has been said already, we may readily suppose there to be a clear difference in the significance of these two goods *vis à vis* the consumer's self-respect, his sense of one's own worth as a participant in the overall economic enterprise of his society. For some of the ways in which we respect ourselves and one another seem intimately bound up with the value we place on participation, cooperation and the sharing of contribution in the context of economic and social endeavour [11]. So, while it may make good sense for those who do all the work in ELF to prefer something more like ILF, it makes good sense not *only* to *them* but to *everybody*.

This oversimplifies of course. There is certainly nothing particularly demeaning to me — on the contrary — if you invite me to your home and cook my dinner. But this supposes that the exchange is not one sided. In showing hospitality to friends we operate within a relationship governed by norms of reciprocity and rough equality of contribution. So it is natural that I will bring wine, aim to return your invitation and so forth. It is when I am unable to, or am prevented from, making a contribution of my own that my self-respect suffers. A clearer analogy to what I have in mind in speaking of an ELF would be a dinner party where everyone brings something along that they have prepared themselves — everyone, that is, *except you*. Except in special circumstances, that may make the meal an uncomfortable occasion for you.

And plausibly not only for you. So, staying with our simple society, we might want to fine-tune this discrimination further. Rather than just classifying meals into types M1 and M2 we want to make a *three way* distinction between:

M1a. a meal which, along with everyone in else in one's community, one had a share in the making of;
M1b. a meal one had a share in the making of but that one shares with others who had none;
M2. a meal one had oneself no share in the making of.

Not only is it plausible to think that M1 is a different sort of commodity from M2 and a preferable one; we may also plausibly suppose that M1a is different from and preferable to M1b. We can clearly distinguish them and, *qua* moral agents and citizens, we have every reason for so ranking them. For *qua* moral agents and citizens it plausibly matters, or should matter, to us whether the economic life we share with others is exclusive or inclusive in character. When it is too exclusive its flavour may be soured — like that of a conversation in which someone is being ignored.

Now consider a more complex, real society. Consider the *whole* range of economic goods produced, exchanged and consumed in the United Kingdom (or wherever you may live) [12]. Call a bundle of such goods consumed by an individual over a period of time (a lifetime say) a *supermeal*. So defined, supermeals are, quite trivially, the *only* such goods we consume. But of course there are *three kinds of supermeals*:

S1a. a supermeal which, along with everyone [13] else in one's community, one had a share in the making of;

S1b. a supermeal one had a share in the making of but that one shares with others who had none;

S2. a supermeal one had oneself no share in the making of.

The points made about meals now translate directly to the case of supermeals. Supermeals of type S1 are preferable to those of type S2; and supermeals of type S1a to those of type S1b. In an exclusionary economy the package of consumer goods I consume is not the same sort of good — it represents the common endeavour of a *part* of the economic community. Or rather simply of the economy, for such an economy is not happily described as an economic *community*. Its wealth is not something we can celebrate as a society but a more private blessing.

S1b will perhaps worry some. Do we properly think of ourselves as *sharing* our supermeals? The answer, I think, is in important ways, *Yes*. I do not, even when I eat in company, literally share the food on my plate but its consumption is not then a private affair but part of an activity shared with others, an activity whose value is plausibly not unaffected by its exclusive or inclusive character in terms of the S1a/S1b distinction. Insofar as we have an atomistic understanding of the agent *qua* consumer, a more general affirmative answer may seem doubtful. If, on the other hand, we are disposed to follow Humboldt and Rawls in affirming the idea of a:

> social union founded upon the needs and potentialities of its members [through which] each person can participate in the total sum of the realized natural assets of the others. [14]

it is far less doubtful.

What of cars? Well your car is, trivially, part of a supermeal. And there are three kinds of car:

C1a. a car which is part of supermeal of type S1a;

C1b. a car which is part of a supermeal of type S1b;

C2. a car which is part of a supermeal of type S2.

If it is plausible that supermeals of type S1a are preferable to those of type S1b, then we may plausibly conclude that cars of type C1a are preferable to those of type C1b.

Notice that in fact it may make of itself no difference here who has or has not taken a share in the labour of making *the car*. Rather our conclusion is that it makes a difference to the value of the car who has or has not taken a share in the manufacture of the *whole range of goods* produced in a given community. When we think, in isolation, of the value of a car, this difference may still seem, intuitively, very small. But when we think of the differences in the value of cars and all the other goods we consume summed into the difference in the value of a supermeal, it may plausibly be thought far less so. We might express this by saying that it is not merely *qua* consumers that we value our cars or we might prefer to say that there is rather *more to* being a consumer even of cars than we might have supposed. I don't much care — either way the objection of my imaginary reader is met.

IV

Human lives, I have suggested, are structured around the project of meeting human needs and our sense of the value in our lives is informed by the quality of our participation in this project. When we find ourselves disengaged from this project our sense of this value is accordingly undermined. Though our needs may still, after a fashion, be met, we no longer participate adequately in the enterprise of meeting them. Moreover the shared human contribution to the meeting of our needs is itself something we value. Indeed it is itself one of our needs. The project of *meeting human needs* is not the same as and cannot without loss be replaced by the project of simply *having our needs met*.

These points were seen to have obvious application to speculative science fiction cases where the human contribution to the meeting of our more manifestly social and cultural needs is displaced by machinery. But they may also, I have argued, be very relevant to considering how we should view less fanciful cases where the human contribution to what may seem more mundane economic activity is so displaced. In both cases, the lives of many of us may be improved in the currency of convenience but only at a certain cost in the currency of significance [15].

James Lenman, Department of Philosophy, University of Glasgow, Glasgow G12 8QQ, UK.

NOTES

[1] A. M. TURING (1950) Computing machinery and intelligence, *Mind* 59.

[2] I won't attempt to list the half-remembered science fiction stories this fantasy echoes.

[3] Things are complicated if we start to suppose the machines in my story are in fact people in their own right and themselves become members of our moral community. For the sake of my argument, assume that this does not arise — it helps to suppose that the machines concerned with music, science, conversation, sex, etc. are discrete, specialised systems. Again I mean to beg no questions, merely to simplify an argument concerned with different questions.

[4] On this point see further NOËL CARROLL (1992) Art, intention and conversation in Gary Iseminger (ed.): *Intention and Interpretation* (Philadelphia, Temple University Press).

[5] NICCOLÒ MACHIAVELLI in a letter to Francesco Vettori, quoted in ROBERTO RIDOLFI (1963) *The Life of Niccolò Machiavelli* (translated by Cecil Grayson) (London, Routledge and Kegan Paul).

[6] Cf. ANTHONY O'HEAR (1995) Art and technology: an old tension in Roger Fellows (ed.): *Philosophy and Technology* (Cambridge, Cambridge University Press).

[7] See pp. 63–67 of the *Groundwork* (Second Edition pagination).

[8] On these thoughts, cf. BERNARD SUITS (1978) *The Grasshopper: games, life and utopia* (Edinburgh, Scottish Academic Press), chapter 15 and David Gauthier's discussion of Suits in his (1986) *Morals by Agreement* (Oxford, Clarendon Press), pp. 330 ff.

[9] This point comes out clearly in CARROLL, op. cit.

[10] This may be an oversimplification resulting from my putting aside of the product-distributive issue. The bleak reality may be that we are all too sensitive to the advantage of excluding people from their share in *process* insofar as it *legitimizes* their exclusion from their share in the *product*.

[11] Cf. GAUTHIER, op. cit., pp. 335–336.

[12] There are problems with taking the nation-state as the "unit" here that I disregard in the interests of simplicity.

[13] I ignore complications about the status of the old and the young.

[14] JOHN RAWLS (1972) *A Theory of Justice* (New York, Oxford University Press), p. 523. (For Humbolt see Rawls' own footnote.) Cf. also p. 529.

> The division of labour is overcome not by each becoming complete in himself but by willing and meaningful work within a just social union of social unions in which all can freely participate as they incline.

[15] I wish to thank the University of Glasgow and the United Kingdom's Arts and Humanities Research Board for funding a year's study leave during which this paper was completed. Thanks too to Emily Brady, Michael Hammond, Matthew Kieran, John O'Neill, Vernon Pratt and Elizabeth Telfer for valuable feedback.

Part VII
Morality and Machines

[36]

MEN, MACHINES, MATERIALISM, AND MORALITY

Peter T. Manicas

Recent philosophical literature has exhibited considerable interest in the ancient doctrine of materialism. In this paper I shall raise some of the questions connected with this doctrine, but I shall discuss them primarily in a moral context. Except for a few notable exceptions, for example, the brief final chapter of J. J. C. Smart's recent and excellent new book, *Philosophy and Scientific Realism* (The Humanities Press, New York, 1963), there has been surprisingly little discussion in recent years of the possible moral aspects of the materialist thesis.

In particular, the questions to which I shall address myself are these: (1) Should materialism be rejected on moral grounds? (2) Assuming that science were one day to construct a reproduction of a man (an artifact) sufficiently exact to be "conscious," what might or should be the metaphysical and moral consequences? To answer the first question, it will only be necessary to show that morality is possible assuming materialism to be correct, though, of course, a dualistic or spiritualistic basis of morality must be abandoned. In answering this first question, I shall also try to clear away some common confusions. The second question raises a plethora of difficult problems, regarding both my assumption and its consequent. But I believe that the thesis of materialism comes down to the question: Would we or rather should we admit a "sufficiently" complex "robot" to the moral community? [1]

I

Following Smart, by materialism I mean the view which maintains that there are no irreducible psychical entities over and above those entities called for in physics, present or future. Smart, as well as Herbert Feigl and others, have argued that this thesis is a metaphysical one and cannot

---

[1] Cf. Hilary Putnam's conclusion: "... the question: Are robots conscious? calls for a decision, on our part, to treat robots as fellow members of our linguistic community, or not to so treat them" (in "Robots: Machines or Artificially Created Life?" *Journal or Philosophy*, November 12, 1964, p. 690). The arguments of Putnam's valuable paper, which came to my attention after my essay was completed, seem to support my thesis even though Putnam claims that materialism is trivially false.

be settled exclusively by empirical or linguistic considerations.[2] It is further held by these writers that the principles of parsimony and determinism weigh heavily in favor of materialistic monism.[3]

If this issue is "metaphysical" and could be settled — if such disputes are "settled" — by appealing to principles, then a case against materialism can be made by arguing that certain moral principles preclude its acceptance. Thus while for "science," parsimony and determinism are important — or even essential — principles (or presuppositions), morality, too, depends upon certain principles which, it might be argued, count against materialism. Moreover, if indeterminism, dualism, and spiritualism are compatible with the body of scientific knowledge — and they are — perhaps the principles necessary for morality ought to be given greater weight. Such moral principles or moral postulates might include, for example: the Kantian postulates of God, freedom, and the immortal soul; the Christian and Roycean principles of Love, Atonement, and the "Community of Spirits"; the much less theological but widely held presupposition that man, as a person and not a thing, is an end in himself with intrinsic value; or finally, the simple notion that man has a certain dignity or sanctity, which uniquely characterizes him.

If we accept materialism, these moral postulates must be abandoned, once and for all; but without some such principles, morality is impossible. Indeed, "you make science's principles absolute and you make of man a machine; you seek explanation and simultaneously rob him of dignity and moral worth." [4]

This claim, it might be noticed, conjoins two distinguishable aspects of morality. First, there is the charge that materialism *because* it is mechanistic and therefore deterministic, robs man of moral autonomy. Machines are not responsible agents. Secondly, it charges that the unique value which, for morality must be attributed to humans as persons, ends-

---

[2] Few philosophers argue that the issue is empirical; even Feigl's (imaginary) autocerebroscope leaves room for parallelism. See his "The 'Mental' and the 'Physical'," *Minnesota Studies in the Philosophy of Science*, Volume II, Minneapolis, 1958, p. 456 and p. 461. A great many philosophers, however, do insist that linguistic considerations may be decisive. In this paper, I assume, without argument, that though linguistic considerations are relevant, they are not conclusive for either position.

[3] Parsimony eliminates parallelism since the mental realm becomes superfluous. It also eliminates objective idealism since we need not assume God or the Absolute. Determinism rules out most (if not all) varieties of interactionism. On this latter point see Feigl, "The 'Mental' and the 'Physical'," esp. pp. 376-379.

[4] This sort of claim, we shall assume, rejects materialism because it makes morality impossible, not because it denies the existence of God, or the immortal soul. In other words, the complaint is directed not at the "irreligion" of materialism but at its immoral implications.

in-themselves, or as intrinsically valuable beings is made impossible by denying that men have an irreducible "inner being," "self," or mental and spiritual existence. Again, though machines have value, it is instrumental at best.

Let us consider the first charge. Mechanism and determinism, which in the first place need to be distinguished, are frequently and perhaps rightly associated with materialism. But materialism does not *have* to be either mechanistic or deterministic. In other words, while many materialisms, those of Democritus, Hobbes, La Mettrie, and Elliot, for example, were both deterministic and mechanistic, materialism does not *entail* mechanism nor determinism.[5] Moreover, both mechanism and determinism are compatible with nonmaterialisms of various types, monistic and dualistic. Thus, the moral side to questions of determinism ought to be viewed independently of materialism-monism-dualism. If determinism, in some sense, is to be accepted, then, if it causes moral problems,[6] it causes them for dualists as well as materialists. If determinism is to be rejected, then, while it might count against many presently formulated variations of materialism, it would not in itself be decisive against all types of materialism.

I take it that the second claim — that materialism robs human beings of their intrinsic moral worth — bears far more weight for the moral rejection of materialism. Though this point of attack has traditionally been associated with religiously oriented philosophies, it is by no means confined to such views. It is, most likely, the raison d'être of the distinction between "persons" and "things."

A general observation might first be made. While it is all too often overlooked, the philosophical theory called materialism in no way changes men. Indeed, how can any theory, philosophical or otherwise, change the facts as they are? Men protest when they feel pain, they choose when they can. No philosophical or scientific theory by itself will or could alter this. It is of course true that a theory may alter the ways in which we explain and understand those facts and it is also true that this understanding might provide a basis for new policies and decisions. But the world is what it is and not another thing. If materialism is a scientifically plausible or perhaps *true* description of the way the world is, then that is the way it is and nothing about it has changed by knowing this.

---

[5] See, e.g., Smart, "Materialism," *Journal of Philosophy*, October, 1963. I add that it would also be possible to formulate materialism so that some special variety of brain transformation is uncaused. (This does not, of course, seem likely).

[6] While the present writer is in agreement with those who have argued that determinism causes no moral problems, I do not defend this thesis in this paper. I do not mainly because a moral rejection of materialism is irrelevant of this question.

More specifically, the point is that individual persons — James, Jack, and Penelope — carry on various activities, seek certain ends, respond in many ways, have thoughts, feelings, troubles, and joys, whether or not we philosophers accept or deny materialism. But if this is the case, how is man robbed of his dignity, moral worth (or freedom) by materialism? If man has dignity, it must be because we *find* value in the fact that he *is* a feeling, thinking, creative being, not because his feeling, thinking, and creativity is an irreducible something, a transcendently bestowed and ghostly power.

This argument should not be taken to mean that accepting or denying materialism makes no difference. In the second part of the paper I give my reasons for believing it makes a great deal of difference. The argument does mean that we must begin with the world as a brute fact, then attempt to account for it, and then finally, given this knowledge, to try to remake it in accordance with our aims.

It may now be insisted, however, that while men are what they are, if we accept materialism as correct, then we must see them as machine-like creatures. Admittedly, they are then creatures which are most complex, but nonetheless, they become, in principle at least, entirely explainable in terms of physics. Thus while men may, in degree of complexity, differ from lower animals and from "things," there is no longer any good reason to consider them as particularly unique, sacred, or intrinsically valuable existents. Why, then, treat men morally at all? Use them and discard them without compunction. Morality must be nonsense after all.

This sort of argument has, I think, two major flaws. First, it fails to acknowledge the proper locus of human morality, and second, it collapses the distinction between the maxims, precepts, or rules which govern human behavior and the justification or rationale for these maxims.

Though I cannot prove this, there is good reason to believe that human values are *created* by human beings. Then morality, as we humans understand it, depends only upon our *willingness* as valuing creatures to seek a harmony of values which includes the values of other valuing beings. Materialism does not make morality nonsense. Morality becomes nonsense when man fails to find value in the values of others.

Secondly, as Smart points out (in *op. cit.*, p. 3), "principles of conduct are by no means unambiguously determined by our general philosophy." That is, our metaphysic does not *entail* specific maxims, even though it does limit the ways in which we can justify those maxims. This means that conflicting precepts could be justified by the same metaphysic and that identical precepts could be supported by incompatible metaphysics. To use obvious examples, two defenders of a teleological universe might promote conflicting rules of conduct for the same reasons. One could insist that conduct X — treat men as equals — manifested the *Logos,* the other maintaining that conduct not-X was its proper manifestation. On the other hand, and here the examples are legion, a mechanistic materialist like Democritus could and did promote many precepts which were identical to his idealistic and dualistic contemporary, Plato. Thus if a materialist decides to adopt the precepts of Christianity, e.g., Love thy brother as thyself, he may. To be sure, the brotherhood of man could not be rooted in God, but it could be grounded in matter, as Plato's famous allegory of the metals suggests. The "dignity" and sanctity of man could be based on his matter-of-fact complexity rather than his spiritual soul.

But again, this argument must not be taken to mean that accepting or denying materialism makes no difference.[7] In the first place, it clearly makes a difference in the kind of justification we give for a precept. A materialist would look to science for the basis of his ethic. It would not, it is clear, be possible for him to provide a transcendental support. But this does not seem to me to be a disadvantage. Indeed, I can envisage much more agreement on fundamental premises given a scientific basis for ethics. The problems here are many and difficult, and I will not press them.

Secondly, there is clearly some sort of nonlogical — psychological, sociological, or historical — relationship between a metaphysic and sets of maxims. For example, no one ought to be surprised to find dualists, like Plato and some of his Christian followers, urging ascetic practices. That the relationship is not logical may be seen by noting that (1) some materialists have likewise urged such practices, Epictetus, for example, and (2) that some dualists have not, Kant, for example. Similarly, there

---

[7] As Smart notes (in *Philosophy and Scientific Realism,* p. 3) "philosophers have tended to obscure the fact that our general philosophical and scientific beliefs may strongly influence our ethical principles." The notion "strongly influences" needs to be worked out. Again, it is not clear what Smart means by "principle" in this sentence. He says: "if one of our principles of conduct were that we should do what is commanded by a personal God and if our world view were one which left no place for such a God, then this principle of conduct would have to be given up, or at least we should have to find some other reason for adhering to it." As he puts it, there could be no reason for adhering to the principle "Do what God says," if there was no place for God. Smart must mean something like, "Do X, because God says so." In that case, we could continue to "Do X," but find other reasons.

In his final chapter Smart offers some reasons for believing that materialism is psychologically conducive to morality. Holbach gave some of the classic arguments in his *Common Sense.*

seems to be foundation for saying that the materialist, allied as he is with the methods and results of science, is often inclined to be human-istic and liberal-minded. To be sure, this is not a necessary connection. Much more, I think, needs to be said on this point, but it must wait for some later time. Instead, I shall address myself to what I take to be the most important moral consequence of the metaphysical issue raised by materialism.

II

Put briefly my point is this: If future science should create an artifact which we had good reason to admit to the moral community, then it could be said that materialism was a correct metaphysical description of the universe. If, on the other hand, there were compelling reasons for excluding all such artifacts, then we must conclude that in humans there is an irreducible psychic stuff and therefore that materialism is false. Put this way, it seems to be the case that materialism is *in some* sense confirmable, though not empirically falsifiable.[8]

Put another way, though materialism does not entail moral precepts, it does commit us to the *range of application* of our moral precepts whatever they may be. This should not be surprising. As a metaphysic is an answer to the most general question of all: What is the nature of reality?, to adopt a metaphysic is to adopt a framework in which we locate ourselves as individuals and as human beings with respect to everything else. In this sense, a metaphysic is a *Weltanschauung*, or as James put it, an "intellectualized attitude toward life."

Let us assume then that science has created a machine with "a mind of its own." Call it (her) "Rhoda." [9] The computers and sensors of this

---

[8] It is fashionable these days to distinguish metaphysical theses on the grounds that they are not empirically falsifiable. But then they are neither true nor false. I have used these words more loosely. Indeed, even where we have good reasons to *decide* that-p (where p is some ostensible assertion) it seems legitimate to call p true. On the other hand, if there seem to be good reasons to *decide* that-not-p, then we must assume p to be false. But because a *decision* is involved and because "good reasons" vary from person to person, one might cling to a metaphysical theses, the immortal soul, e.g., no matter what. Much more needs to be said about the relation of true and false to "decision" and "discovery."

[9] To suggest what I mean by a machine with a "mind of its own," and to point out the empirical plausibility of such an artifact, I call the reader's attention to H. D. Block's recent survey entitled "The Perceptron: A Model for Brain Func-tioning, I & II," in *Reviews of Modern Physics,* Vol. 34, No. 1, Jan., 1962.

Block points out that it is now widely accepted that neurons are the basic functional unit of the brain. The histologist sees a small number of components, but these are repeated over and over again in enormously various connections. This variation in connections gives rise to the brains complexity. While the tech-nical difficulties are vast, Block suggests that mapping and analysis of this neural artifact, constructed from wires, resisters, relays, etc., bear many family resemblances in structure, function, and operation to the brain, central nervous system, and sensory organs of women-begotten persons, so many resemblances, indeed, that we might not want to call this artifact a machine at all, but rather might, following Descartes, call it a "thinking thing." For Descartes, you will recall, a thinking thing is a thing which "doubts, understands, affirms, denies, wills, refuses [and] which also imagines and feels." The argument which supports the legitimacy of this move is suggested by Geach,[10] even though I am not clear what Geach would say about my use of his argument. Geach argues that in applying psychological concepts — all of the Cartesian predicates mentioned above would be included — we need what he calls "handholds." Thus "if we are invited to apply these concepts to a supposed disembodied existence," he argues, "then we may be sure that we are right in refusing to play; too many threads are broken, and the conceptual web has collapsed" (p. 115).

There are several strands to this "conceptual web," some of them are behavioral: what it does, what it says, how it reacts to various stimuli, etc.; some of them are structural; how it is made, how it performs, what

---

network is at least possible. Moreover, he notes that it is reasonable to believe that "only certain parameters of growth are specified by the genes and the fine connections are grown in a more or less random manner, subject to these constraints. Thus, the detailed connection scheme would be unique to each individual" (p. 125). It is assumed that the brain changes its internal functional properties depending upon the past activity of certain connections, either by means of some growth process or metabolic change between axons of contiguous cells. If it is the case that only certain parameters are specified, then, "there is the hope that such a system might be analyzed in terms of such parameters. This also implies that the operation of the brain is radically different in principle from the logical circuitry of digital computers" (p. 126).

The "Perceptron" built at Cornell is a brain model on a vastly simplified scale. Yet this "machine" is self-adjusting or has a capacity for "spontaneous organization." This capacity "consists in showing the machine stimuli, letting it compute its own response, and reinforce in accordance with that response" (p. 133). The more sophisticated systems, described in the paper which follows the one quoted, would make "spontaneous classifications," which says the author, correspond to the machine having an "original concept."

All of these points bear on the plausibility of a machine with a "mind of its own." Moreover, they locate the analysis in materialistic and deterministic, if not mechanistic terms. Barring autopsy, we might be able to understand "thoughts" on this view without being able to know why some specific thought was thought!

Though scientifically less respectable, but vivid for purposes of our discussion is (the robot) "Rhoda" on NBC-TV's "My Living Doll." Rhoda is supposedly an entirely synthesized, self-programming creation.

[10] P. T. Geach, *Mental acts,* Routledge and Kegan Paul, New York and London, 1957, pp. 111 ff.

it is made of, etc. I do not think that the complete fabric could be fully spelled out. But in any case, there is *no logical* reason to deny that science might one day synthesize something which bore sufficient similarities to women-begotten men so that the "conceptual web" *would* support calling an artifact a thinking thing.

Now, were this to happen, would (or should) "Rhoda" — our hypothetical thinking thing — be admissible to the moral community? Some philosophers might here argue that this conditional is uninteresting because the antecedent is logically false, hence the conditional is trivially true. I can here only answer no one has shown that the antecedent is logically false, though it is now empirically false and may continue to be so. I strongly suspect that some who find the notion of a thinking artifact logically impossible are being led by moral considerations. That is, they find the notion of admitting artifacts to the moral community incredible, distasteful, or "immoral"? Thus, by ruling out the possibility of an artificial thinking thing they rule out the only interesting and plausible reason for wanting to admit artifacts to the moral community.

This, I believe, is the nub of the issue raised by materialism, for it is here where the metaphysic bears its weightiest practical (moral) consequences. In the world as it now is, a materialist and a nonmaterialist, though differing fundamentally on many issues — the existence of a spiritual God, an immortal soul, etc. — may yet completely agree on all moral questions. In some future state of the world, this might be impossible.

I wish also to emphasize that a decision to consider "Rhoda" a thinking thing would not in itself be an acknowledgement of materialism. For one might agree that "Rhoda" thinks and still refuse to admit her to the moral community. But if one did this, it would be an acknowledgement, it seems to me, that materialism is false or that in the human being, there *is* something intrinsically residual. Personally, I find no good reason for denying moral consideration to such an artifact, assuming that we could agree that it (she) thinks. But one might, nonetheless. A parallel historical case provides a perfect illustration of what I mean. When Darwin's evolutionary hypothesis showed that man was a "risen animal," some philosophers, many theologians, and still more people simply argued that the soul was interjected at the time of human conception, thus marking human beings as distinct from lower animals. Similarly, one might simply refuse to admit "Rhoda" on the grounds that she has no soul.[11]

---

[11] It would also be *logically* possible to admit her to the moral community on the grounds that she had a spiritual soul! But I cannot see why *anyone* would want to do this.

Those philosphers who say, for example, that "the human being need have no transcendent element, yet that machines will never be conscious, because . . . a reproduction of a man sufficiently exact to be conscious is too exact to be still a machine," [12] are making correct but misleading and unhelpful claims. Such a claim is correct but trivially so; it is misleading because it leaves the impression that the whole quarrel is linguistic; it is not helpful because it does not come to grips with the really difficult problem: how do we *deal with* a "reproduction of a man sufficiently exact to be conscious?" By "deal with" I mean what sort of changes ought we to make in our *Weltanschauung,* where this includes our respective location to everything around us. More specifically, should we admit "a reproduction of a machine sufficiently exact to be conscious" to the moral community? To say "yes" is to break down the chasm between human "selves" and bodies; it is to affirm materialism. To say "no" is to deny materialism.

PETER T. MANICAS.

QUEENS COLLEGE, CITY UNIVERSITY OF NEW YORK.

---

[12] Michael Scriven, "The Mechanical Concept of Mind," reprinted in A. R. Anderson, (ed.), *Minds and Machines,* New Jersey: Prentice-Hall, 1964, p. 36. The reader will note indebtedness to this provocative paper.

[37]

CAN ROBOTS BE MORAL?

Laszlo Versenyi
Williams College

Recent philosophical discussion concerning robots has been largely preoccupied with questions such as "can robots think, know, feel, or learn?" "can they be conscious, teleological, and self-adaptive?"; "can robots be in principle psychologically and intellectually isomorphic to men?"[1] Considerably less attention has been paid meanwhile to the question whether robots can be moral. Since the latter problem seems to me rather intimately connected with the ones extensively discussed, I would like to raise it here in an attempt to carry the discussion to its logical conclusion.

The thesis of this paper is that if there are no magic descriptive terms—intelligence, consciousness, purposiveness, etc.—predicable exclusively of men but not of robots, then there are no such moral terms either. If men and machines coexist in a natural continuum in which there are no gaps, quantum jumps, or insurmountable barriers preventing the assimilation of the one to the other, then they also coexist in a moral continuum in which only relative but never absolute distinctions can be made between human and machine morality.

I will argue this thesis by raising the question whether robots can be moral in two stages: (1) Can robots act morally? (2) Can we, without absurdity, treat robots as moral agents? The answer to these questions will be given, not in terms of a new "robot morality," but in terms of a few traditional ethical theories.

To make these questions at least initially plausible our robots will have to be imagined to be much more sophisticated than any single machine already existing. At the same time, for all their complexity, they are not to have any capabilities other than the ones computer scientists and cyberneticists like Turing, Wiener, Ashby, Arbib, Pask, and Uttley, for example, have argued to be, if not already

---

1. See, e.g., D. Mackay, "Mindlike Behavior in Artefacts," *British Journal for the Philosophy of Science* 2 (August 1951): 105–21; A. R. Lacey, "Men and Robots," *Philosophical Quarterly* 10 (January 1960): 61–72; H. Putnam, "Minds and Machines," in *Dimensions of Mind*, ed. S. Hook (New York, 1960); H. Putnam, "Robots: Machines or Artificially Created Life?" *Journal of Philosophy*, November 12, 1964, pp. 668–91; R. Pucetti, "On Thinking Machines and Feeling Machines," *British Journal for the Philosophy of Science* 18 (May 1967): 39–51; K. Gunderson, "Robots, Consciousness, and Programmed Behavior," *British Journal for the Philosophy of Science* 19 (May 1968): 190–222.

249 *Discussion*

programmable in practice, at least theoretically possible as an extension of present machine capabilities.[2]

Our standard robot will thus be provided with as complex and manifold a sensory apparatus as anyone may care to construct; a fairly complex teleological programming—built-in tasks, functions, operational goals; some formal logic; and as much capacity for inductive reasoning as would enable it to learn from experience, enrich and change its lower-order programming, and modify its interaction with the environment so as to maximize its own goal-oriented performance.

I

Given this basic construction and programming it needs little argument to show that robots can be "vicious" and "virtuous" in exactly the same sense as men are called vicious or virtuous in Plato. The Platonic moral agent is, like our robot, a teleological machine: he has built-in (natural) goals and functions; he is conscious of goals and functions; and since the performance of his functions, the attainment of his goals, is the sole (natural, genetically programmed) end of all his activity, his consciousness of a goal or function as *his* goal or function necessarily leads to his acting toward the attainment of the goal and performance of the function. Human action is thus fully automatic. What a man believes to be good—contributory to the attainment of his natural ends—he will necessarily do. No mysterious agency intervenes between belief and action. Since human action is a wholly rule-governed interaction between agent and environment, it is in principle wholly knowable, predictable, and controllable. The accuracy of our predictions and the success of our control are strictly proportionate to the extent of our knowledge of the nature of the particular organism and environmental system whose interaction we are concerned with.

The virtue of a moral agent in Plato is equally a function of knowledge: the agent's knowledge of his own nature (goal, function, good) and that of his social-physical environment. The more knowledge of self and world a man has, the more virtuous, excellent in performing his function, he is. And how much knowledge he will acquire is dependent only on his natural endowment (innate intelligence) and subsequent environmental programming (education and experience as a whole).

The point is that, since in Plato human action is fully determined, lawful, and knowable, it is fully formalizable. And whatever is fully formalizable is in principle reduplicable in some other system constructed in accordance with the same general rules. How closely we can reduplicate a human agent artificially is dependent solely on our knowledge, that is, our *technai*, our technology.

2. See, e.g., A. Rosenblueth, N. Wiener, and J. Bigelow, "Behavior, Purpose and Teleology," *Philosophy of Science* 10 (January 1943): 18–24; A. M. Turing, "Computing Machinery and Intelligence," *Mind* 59 (October 1950): 433–60; W. R. Ashby, *Design for a Brain* (London, 1952); A. M. Uttley, "Conditional Probability Machines and Conditioned Reflexes," in *Automata Studies*, ed. C. E. Shannon (Princeton, N.J., 1956); W. R. Ashby, "What Is an Intelligent Machine?" *General Systems, the Yearbook of the Society for General Systems Research* 8 (1963): 213–18; N. Wiener, *God and Golem* (Cambridge, Mass., 1964); M. Arbib, "Cognition: A Cybernetic Approach," in *Cognition: A Multiple View*, ed. P. L. Garvin (New York, 1970); G. Pask, "Cognitive Systems," in Garvin; M. Arbib, *The Metaphorical Brain* (New York, 1972).

250   *Ethics*

Since "virtue" itself is nothing but knowledge, skill, *techne*, it is, of course, equally programmable in principle. The Protagoras's "art of measurement," for example, can easily be built into any reasonably sophisticated machine. Being a simple matter of cost accounting, any machine constructed to receive input values (be they weighed in terms of pleasure, discharge of energy, efficiency of task performance, or anything else that is quantizable) and programmed to do probabilistic calculations can perform it in a manner analogous to the way it is performed by men skilled in the art.

Of course, in the case of human agents the initial (genetic) construction is not—or at least was not in Plato's time—to any great extent within our control. That is why the programming of men for virtue (operational excellence) has been restricted largely to postconstruction (educational) programming. But even this programming—the concern of Plato's human technologists, the cultural engineers called philosopher-kings—is in principle no different from that of any more or less sophisticated teleological robot.

To the extent that a human being is found to have a high-order initial capability (innate teleological rationality, potential for wisdom) he is controlled by others only with a view to, and up to the point of, his reaching full development and becoming wise enough to control himself for his own good. Less intelligent men—men with less native endowment for truly rational self-direction—need more control. Even after extensive early programming (indoctrination with right beliefs, emotional training, habituation in correct dispositions and tendencies) they are left to their own devices only in carefully selected areas of activity (those which they are by nature and upbringing programmed for), and in all others they are either forbidden to meddle or allowed to operate only under constant supervision and control by men of higher-order (innate and cultural) programming.

The distinction Plato's cultural engineers make between different types of men is exactly analogous to the technologists' distinction between different types of machines. Depending on their built-in operational capabilities they can be used for the performance of different tasks under various degrees of supervision and control. Their very being is defined by the work they are capable of doing: essentially they are "robots." (The Czech word *robot* means worker.) If and to the extent that they are deficient in capabilities to perform functions needed in a given society (e.g., Plato's state), they are accordingly disposed of (sent elsewhere or in extreme cases of deficiency destroyed outright) much in the manner we dispose of machines.

There is little point in dwelling any further on the Platonic man/machine analogy. Theoretically it is as perfect as any analogy between two different things can be. Men and reasonably sophisticated machines are in principle morally isomorphic, and the extent to which we can make the isomorphism perfect in practice depends only on our technology.

To convert our Platonic machines into machines that are morally worthy in Kantian terms is a relatively simple task.

To begin with, our Platonic robot is already characterized by what Kant calls hypothetical reasoning. Capable of formulating imperatives of skill and prudence and of deriving actions from laws, it is possessed of practical reason or will. It

251   *Discussion*

acts in accordance not just with natural law but with the conception of law. Although Kant would not yet consider such a robot a "moral" agent, he would fully subscribe to the Platonic description of its operation. Action determined by prudential, hypothetical reasoning based on empirical experience is as automatic, necessary, naturally determined, and in principle predictable and controllable in Kant as it is in Plato.

All that would have to be added to the robot's teleological programming is the type of reasoning from which categorical, rather than merely conditional, imperatives can issue. But this type of purely formal reasoning, that abstracts from all considerations of content and recognizes as objective law whatever principles can be universalized without self-contradiction, is the type that artificial intelligence handles best. (All existing computers are capable of manipulating, according to strict rules, symbols standing in a well-defined relationship to each other.) Kant himself regarded purely formal reasoning a much less demanding task than prudential reflection and thought the least sophisticated of men as capable of performing it as the wisest philosopher-king.

So all we need to do to convert our Platonically virtuous robot into a Kantian model of moral perfection is to program it never to act "except in such a way that it can also will that its maxim should become a universal law." Once we made this rule the absolutely overriding directive in its programming, the robot will be incapable of doing anything contrary to it; its will will be "of itself necessarily in harmony with the law." To be sure, for such "holy" robots there can be, strictly speaking, no more "imperatives" than there are in Kant for God, but this will not make their action any less morally worthy.

Should the programmer wish to change our holy robots into something more like imperfectly moral human beings, he would merely have to make their categorical programming somewhat less than absolutely overriding. Whatever way he does this (e.g., by a fixed percentage method or a sufficiently complicated built-in randomizing procedure) is irrelevant for our purposes. Since Kant himself cannot explain by what mechanism the causality of pure reason becomes (if and when it does become) decisive in human action, he could not say categorically that our robots' mechanism is different from that of men.

Summing up, moral action in Kant is no less lawful than it is in Plato. The autonomy or freedom of the will, although not just a property of conforming to the laws of nature, is still a "causality conforming to immutable laws" of a special kind. Being rulelike behavior, it is in principle reduplicable. And the same is true of all other conceivable systems of morality that define good action in terms of rules. Be they empirically or purely rationally derived, or even postulated on the basis of supernatural revelation, in principle the rules—or the rules for deriving rules—can be built into robots so that they become in this respect isomorphic to men.

We may, of course, reject all rational or at least rule-governed systems of morality, but if we do so it becomes impossible to show that robots cannot be moral. For whatever unanalyzable, nonempirical, and nonrational intuition of moral values; mysterious moral sense; and totally inexplicable ethical insight we postulate as lying at the source of morality, all arguments pro or con robot morality become unverifiable. Should we take any man's claim to such mysterious intuition at face value, then we must take similar claims made by other men or robots equally at face value. Once we have programmed robots to make this claim (regardless of how they may have arrived at their moral judgments or sentiments) and to refuse to justify their judgments or attitudes by way of an argument from experience or pure reason, our robots have become, as far as any test can determine, morally isomorphic to men.

II

Intuitionists might still be averse to calling such robots moral and refuse to treat them as moral agents since it might be intuitively clear to them that making moral statements about robots is simply absurd. But this brings us to the second part of our question: Given the existence of morally isomorphic robots, can we without absurdity treat such robots as moral agents? To say that robots are moral is not merely to describe *their* behavior but also to commit *us* to certain types of behavior toward them. If so, we have to ask what type of behavior on our part would our admission of robots to "moral" status entail.

On the Platonic model of morality there would be little theoretical difficulty in answering this question. Virtuous action on our part is action by virtue of which we maximize our own well-being. Consequently, "right" behavior toward robots would be behavior that would lead to the type of man/machine interaction that would be most beneficial to men. Whatever rules governing our relationship to robots would enhance our own happiness would be the proper rules to follow; the rules a wise man would automatically adopt.

On this model any sharp theoretical distinction between man/man and man/machine interaction has already disappeared, for the same functional considerations determine our action toward any type of being (man, animal, or machine). Since "prudential" and "moral" mean the same thing, it is easy to show that we already have "moral" rules governing our interaction with machines and that there is in theory no limit to the extent to which the two sets of rules (toward men and toward machines) might overlap.

Questions such as whether robots should be blamed or praised, loved or hated, given rights and duties, etc., are in principle the same sort of questions as, "Should cars be serviced, cared for, and supplied with what they require for their operation?" To the extent that we depend on cars and servicing them is necessary for their well-functioning, it is as prudent not to withhold such services from them as it is not to withhold comparable, operationally required services from anything else on whose well-functioning we depend. In either case the only relevant considerations are: Do we need these things (men, animals, machines) for our well-functioning, and do they need this or that (care, love, food, gas, control) for theirs? As soon as both questions are answered there are no further considerations relevant to our decision, and discrimination based on other criteria becomes irrational.

It may seem frivolous and even morally repugnant to treat questions of human rights and machine requirements analogously, but from the point of view of Platonic morality the analogy is inescapable, and our present reluctance to treat machines like men is merely the consequence of the observable functional differences between men and the machines existing in our days. Should these differences be gradually overcome, our reluctance, too, would disappear—provided we were intelligent, wise, excellent human beings.

Although the possibility of giving robots civil rights—a role in their own or even in our government—appears at the moment far-fetched, in the matter of giving machines some control over their and even our own activity we are already practicing what Plato teaches. For a great number of complex operations we already prefer machines to men and take the "word" of the machine in preference to that of much more fallible human beings. To a large extent machines control what we hitherto left to men; they fly our airplanes, pilot our ships, and run our automated factories with increasing independence from human intervention. How much independence they should be given and how much control over their own and our affairs they should exercise depend solely on their capabilities and requirements in conjunction with our capabilities and needs. At the point where any machine's capabilities surpass our own in any area vital to our interests, we accord it a corresponding measure of control for our own good.

This is merely the logical consequence of Plato's theory. For the same reason that Plato is unwilling to give ignorant men control over their own and the state's action and relegates these powers to the wise, he would have to give sophisticated cybernetic machines analogous powers. Could we but build a machine with the high-order capabilities of a philosopher-king, we would logically have to consent to be governed by it.

We are, of course, basing our decision here on a consideration of our needs rather than those of our machines, but this is strictly analogous to our decisions made with respect to our fellow human beings. Their needs are considered merely because their well-functioning depends on their obtaining what they need, and their well-functioning is necessary for our own.

If it would interfere with the functioning of an automatic pilot, for example, to have men mess around with the steering wheel, such interference in the machine's operation would simply defeat our purposes in installing the machine in the first place. Depriving a machine we rely on of the control it needs for fulfilling its purpose would diminish its excellence—virtue—and thus harm us in the same manner as diminishing the excellence of fellow human beings would.

Whether and how much control any particular machine should be given over its operation and over ours is a pragmatic rather than metaphysical problem. Assuming that some future robots are sophisticated to the point where, generations of robots having constructed generations of robots, they know more about their own needs and capabilities than we do, it would be logical to give them decision-making powers sufficient to safeguard their functioning. And at the point, however unlikely to be reached, that machines would know more about men than men themselves, it would be logical to transfer the control of men to them—for the sake of human fulfillment.

Giving machines a large measure of responsibility in the sense of decision-making powers is, of course, not the same as holding them responsible for what they do. We do not normally blame or praise machines for their activity. But this does not mean that we cannot in principle treat robots as "morally responsible" even in this sense.

Blaming and praising men has only one purpose in Plato: not to take revenge on them for what they have done but to correct their behavior in the future. In what manner we may proceed to do this depends on what we consider the most efficient way to achieve our purpose. If and to the extent that we think men cannot be taught correct behavior by more intelligent methods of instruction, we control their action by blame and praise: a purely mechanical reinforcement of certain patterns of behavior.

In theory we can easily construct a machine which, apart from all its other capabilities, is also open to, that is, responsive to, blame and praise, and it might even serve our purposes to do so. For instead of our having to foresee all future contingencies with which the machine might have to deal—and some of the most important of these contingencies are the attitudes and expectations of human beings—we could program machines to respond to and adjust their behavior in accordance with suitable expressions of human approval and disapproval. Leaving part of the machines' programming to their future interaction with their human environment would make them more flexible, and, in some cases at least, more flexible robots might be more efficient in the long run. (To program a perfectly safe but inflexible machine would in some cases require more knowledge of future contingencies on our part than we possess.)

Could robots be loved? The answer to this question is implicit in the preceding. In Plato whatever a man is deficient in and needs for his own fulfillment is a natural object of his love. Whether he will in fact love the thing depends on his knowledge (of what is good for him and what the thing is good for). If so, to what extent a robot can be loved depends on what the particular robot is good for, what needs of ours it can fulfill, and how much it can contribute to our well-being. The more functions hitherto relegated to men robots become capable of fulfilling, the more robots will become natural objects of human love. It has to be emphasized that in Plato nothing is loved in and for itself as a unique irreplaceable being but only as a particular embodiment of general functional traits that could be embodied—to a greater or lesser extent, in various combinations—in any number of other things. Thus the serviceability—tool-like character—and theoretical interchangeability of machines would not distinguish them from men who are equally serviceable—means to our ends—in practice and equally interchangeable in principle. Since Plato does not have, and could not comprehend, the notion of a unique person or soul, he could not use such a notion for distinguishing between interpersonal and man/machine relationships. The only relevant consideration in this, as in every other case, is functional; and as machines acquire more and more hitherto "human" functions it becomes increasingly difficult to discriminate rationally, or teleologically, between (moral) men and (moral) robots even for the purposes of love.

The determination of our moral obligations toward machines is even less of a problem in Kant than it is in Plato. Leaving aside prudential considerations and

255 *Discussion*

pathological love—matters we have dealt with in the preceding but which are of
no fundamental moral significance in Kant—the basis of our moral obligation toward
other creatures is our shared rationality. What makes man an end in himself is
his possession of will (i.e., the power of determining his action in accordance with
the idea of laws), and what gives human existence in itself an absolute value is
the fact that men are possessed of reason. Now if rational nature is an end in itself
both subjectively and objectively, it is irrelevant whether this rational nature is
embodied or unembodied, and if embodied what (human or machine bodies) it is
embodied in. If embodiment as such mattered, God himself could not be treated
as a moral agent. And if we took particular embodiments (e.g., a human organism)
into consideration we would be using nonmoral, empirical rather than rational,
criteria for determining our moral attitudes, and this would be as immoral in Kant
as discrimination on the basis of irrelevant criteria is vicious and self-vitiating in
Plato. Since our machines are not only psychologically and teleogically but also
rationally isomorphic to men, they must be treated as morally isomorphic too.

Intuitionists may be revolted by the preceding conclusions and may even claim
that the inability of the Platonic and Kantian moralities to discriminate in principle
between men and machines makes the shortcomings of these moralities glaringly
evident and gives us reason enough to reject them. However, this is merely an
"intuitive" reaction and cannot be used as a philosophical argument. For, as long
as intuitionists cannot explain what nonnatural quality they intuit as morally good
in men, they cannot argue that it is in principle impossible for machines to be
characterized by that quality.

Either their intuition is merely the result of their social conditioning (unanalyzed
custom and convention), in which case it is empirically and historically grounded
and is liable to change in line with the changes machines undergo in their development, or it is truly ineffable and in principle unanalyzable (mystical, supernatural,
nonsensical in the Wittgensteinian sense), and then anyone's claim that he intuits
machines to be "good" is as irrefutable as the counterclaim is indefensible. Since
with moral intuitionism we have abandoned the domain of philosophical argument
as such, intuitionists can offer no *arguments* pro or con relevant to the subject of
the morality and moral worthiness of machines.

III

An affirmative answer to the question whether machines can be moral does
not yet resolve the practical problem whether or not we should want to build moral
robots and if so what type of moral programming we should build into them. In
the following I will try to deal with these problems.

Whoever holds that Kantian morality is preferable to Platonic ethics would,
of course, want to program robots with the overriding directive never to act on
principles that are not universalizable without self-contradiction. Since moral perfection is clearly preferable to imperfect (human) morality, we could not morally will
to make robots less than perfectly harmonious with the moral law.

As to whether moral robots should be constructed at all, a Kantian answer
might be given along the line of argument Kant himself uses in his third example

256 *Ethics*

of the application of the moral law in the *Groundwork:* If we have the talent to construct moral robots then not to do so would be to neglect one of our natural gifts and this cannot be willed as a universal law of nature, for every rational being "necessarily wills that all his powers should be developed, since they serve him, and are given to him, for all sorts of possible ends."[3] Not to construct robots would mean to neglect humanity in our own person, and this would conflict with the categorical imperative of treating humanity in our person, as well as in others, as an end rather than as a means.

Whether intuitionists could possibly intuit it good to construct intuitively moral robots is impossible to argue—since moral intuitionism undercuts all argument—and so the only problem that remains is whether to develop and how to program moral robots in Plato.

In a prudential morality this problem calls for a prudential decision which is easily given. If and to the extent that robots could make our lives better we should of course, build them, and will necessarily do so if we are wise. We have in fact made such decisions in the past for thousands of years during which we have been constructing increasingly more sophisticated tools and machines in the belief that their construction and use would improve our lives. Lacking any convincing argument that a return to a prehistoric mode of existence is intrinsically preferable to our present mode of life, we can disregard the question of whether to build robots and concentrate on what kind of robots to build and how to program them so that they will contribute to our well-being.

Such questions are exactly analogous to the type Plato raises with respect to another artificial organism isomorphic to man (i.e., what kind of state to build for the benefit of men and how to program it in all its constituent parts so that it fulfills its function). They are questions of means rather than ultimate ends, technological questions decidable by prudential technological reasoning.

If robots are to improve our lives they have to be built to perform tasks we cannot or do not want to perform. This requirement would divide robots into two broad though often overlapping classes: highly sophisticated and relatively unsophisticated, master- and slave-robot types.

The building of slave robots is no particular problem; our already existing machines are rapidly approaching what we might call a slavish nature and programming. Although some of them are built with extensive teleological programming (so as to monitor and modify their operation with a view to optimum task performance) all of them still perform their tasks rather slavishly: extensively controlled by more intelligent beings.

By their nature such robots are of limited usefulness. If we want to extend our powers by building robots that require less extensive control and thus free us for further and higher types of activity, we have to add more sophisticated, "master" robots to the already existing slave-robot population.

The programming of such robots, however, confronts us with a dilemma. With any increase in sophistication, robots have to be given increasing independence of

3. Kant, *Groundwork of the Metaphysic of Morals* (Harper Torchbook, 1964), p. 90.

257 *Discussion*

human supervision and control. But with increased independence and self-control on the part of robots, the danger of our creating Frankensteinian monsters also increases. The operation of robots with high-order programming will not only become less and less predictable (since robots, learning from experience, acquire skills we have not taught them and may not even know they have) but also more and more dangerous. For prudential robots, formally isomorphic to men (in their teleological makeup) but materially different (in construction and specific built-in goals), will naturally seek their own goals rather than ours, and the more isomorphic they are to men the more they will behave in a self-seeking rather than subservient manner.

To solve Wiener's "slave paradox,"[4] inherent in our wanting to build machines with two diametrically opposed traits (independence *and* subservience, self-directed teleological rationality *and* the seeking of someone else's goals), we would have to construct robots not only with a formal prudential programming, but also with all our specific goals, purposes, and aspirations built into them so that they will not seek anything but these. But even if this type of programming could be coherent, it would require an almost infinite knowledge on our part to construct robots in this way. We could make robots perfectly safe only if we had absolute and perfect self-knowledge, that is, an exact knowledge of all our purposes, needs, desires, etc., not only in the present but in all future contingencies which might possibly arise in all conceivable man/robot interaction. Since our having this much knowledge is not even a theoretical possibility, obviously we cannot make robots safe to us along this line.

This is what led some "roboticists" to propose that robots should be programmed not only prudentially (to seek their own goals and safeguard their own operation) but also with an overriding semi-Kantian imperative. (For example, Asimov's first law of robotics, "A robot may not injure a human being or, through inaction, allow a human being to come to harm," overrides the second, "A robot must obey the orders given it by human beings," which in turn overrides the purely prudential third, "A robot must protect its own existence.") The trouble with this type of programming—or anything resembling it—is that it will not work as long as we have not also built into the robot an almost infinite knowledge of what is in the long run and in any conceivable situation good or bad, beneficial or harmful to human beings. And since we have not got this knowledge we can hardly build it into robots.

It would seem then that the only way to make a free—sophisticated and independent—prudential robot safe for men would be to make it not only morally isomorphic but also wholly identical in structure and programming with human beings. Built of the same organic materials and given the same neurophysiological, psychological, and rational makeup, our android would, from its own experience, know as well as any man what would help and harm human beings and could thus obey the Asimovian first law, the Golden Rule, or any similar directive at least as well as any men can.

4. Wiener, "The Brain and the Machine," in Hook, pp. 111 ff.; and *God and Golem*, pp. 58–63.

Unfortunately such construction and prográmming, even if it were technologically possible, would severely limit the specific usefulness of the robot. To the extent that a robot is exactly like men it cannot do anything men cannot do, and then what great use is it? Though safer than the average human being—who does not by nature follow the Golden Rule—our android would be otherwise indistinguishable from its human counterparts. Having all their talents, capabilities, as well as limitations and shortcomings, it would have become functionally identical with men, and then what would be the point of going to the trouble of manufacturing such a fully human robot when we can reproduce men in much simpler ways?

Is there no way out of this dilemma? Are human safety and a vast increase of human powers by means of nonhuman contrivances contradictory requirements? Are the only alternatives open to us in the building of prudential robots the production of either slave robots of limited usefulness or of sophisticated but quasi-Frankensteinian servo-mechanisms? I do not think so.

Sophisticated prudential robots, isomorphic to but not identical with men, can be made safe without a loss of their usefulness by being made not only prudential but also prudent. The wiser—more virtuous, Platonically speaking—robots would be (potentially, by built-in programming), that is, the more knowledge they could acquire of their own goals and capabilities and of what is good for them in their interaction with their physical and social (man/machine) environment, the safer they might become for us. After all, Plato's wise man, too, seeks his own fulfillment and not that of others except to the extent that the latter is a means to the former, and yet in doing so he cooperates with and benefits rather than harms his fellow humans. Analogously a wise robot would recognize the extent to which its own well-being depends on its cooperation with men and would act accordingly. Precisely to the extent that men and robots remain different (isomorphic but not identical), each species will have capabilities to perform what the other cannot. Thus each is able to enhance the other's functioning beyond the other's own power. This fact, far from setting them against each other, should logically lead to a distribution of functions among men and machines analogous to the one proposed by Plato for the purely human state. For the very same reason that men want to build robots—to enhance their own existence—prudent robots would want to have men around, and the two species could interact harmoniously, cultivating each other, as members of the human species do now, for their mutual benefit.

The question is simply whether men and robots could each have their own ecological niche within the same system. On the basis of our past experience of a steadily growing man/machine symbiosis an affirmative answer to this question cannot be ruled out. Technological evolution has not made human existence unviable up to now, and what the future may bring we can only judge by extrapolating past experience into the future.

Such an extrapolation seems to me to warrant neither pessimistic nor optimistic conclusions. The fear that robots might supplant men, not so much by violently destroying the species as by taking over all human functions, making human achievement a zero-factor and thus producing universal human apathy and degeneration, does not seem to me justified. Certainly so far technological progress, far from dis-

259   *Discussion*

couraging creativity, merely challenged men to further effort and opened up newer roads to human achievement. For the same reason, all our hopes that technology will bring about a human paradise on earth seem equally unsubstantial. Each new discovery, invention, accomplishment, on our part has created new complications, difficulties, and hitherto unsuspected problems. It has increased neither our contentment nor our dissatisfaction with existence. It has made life neither safer nor more dangerous on the whole.

If so, one might well ask, why bother building robots, why seek for a further —but in terms of an overall increase in human happiness illusory—extension of our powers? But this is asking why act at all, why live rather than commit suicide? And since we are not ready to give up life, it is clear that we are not ready to give up further self-development by scientific, technological, or cultural activities. And that means we will go on developing more and more sophisticated machines, machines that become less and less distinguishable from men in functioning.

That robots, if we build them unwisely, might become dangerous is not so much a threat as it is a challenge to our ingenuity and creative powers. Since being challenged to further activity, being set greater obstacles to overcome, is the sum and substance of our lives as teleological beings, developing robots—setting ourselves further technological-cultural goals—is not an inhuman or antihuman enterprise. It is simply part and parcel of the life of a species that first began cultivating the land, devising tools and machines, and cultivating—culturally developing—members of the species itself. Machines and artifacts are an inevitable part of human culture. Moral robots are merely a part that still lies in the future.

[38]

A code of conduct for robots coexisting with human beings

Shigeo Hirose *

Tokyo Institute of Technology, Department of Mechano-Aerospace Engineering, Ookayama, Meguro-ku, Tokyo 152, Japan

1. Asimov's three principles for robots are wrong

What kind of code of conduct should be imposed on robots in order to realize the robots most desirable for coexistence with human beings? When tackling this kind of problem, the theory that most readily comes to mind is the famous three principles for robots of Isaac Asimov (1902–1992) These are as follows.

Article 1: A robot may not injure a human being, or, through inaction, allows a human being to come to harm.

Article 2: A robot must obey the orders given to it by human beings except where such orders would conflict with the First Law.

Article 3: A robot must protect its own existence as long as such protection does not conflict with the First or Second Law.

What I would first like to draw your attention here is that in these principles, it is already assumed that robots have acquired a high degree of logical capability such that they can read human commands and can correctly understand the causal relationships in which the results of their actions have an effect on human beings and on themselves.

Now, the question is whether the above described three principles for robots are truly a desirable code of conduct for future robots which will have that kind of high degree of intelligence. The author believes that these three principles for robots contain a fundamental misunderstanding about the nature of robots, and can never be applied. In this paper, we will explain the reasons for this, and will set out to find new principles

---

* Corresponding author. E-mail: hirose@mes. Titech.ac.jp.

for the conduct of robots which can replace Asimov's three principles for robots.

2. Robots do not die

The mistake that Asimov's three principles for robots make is that Asimov's robots are considered to be evolving as "life forms" equivalent to human beings. This is because he regarded robots as substitutes for human slaves. Actually, this kind of approach is currently considered to be common sense. The opinion is often heard that robots which have a high degree of intelligence will endlessly continue to acquire life form functionality, that ultimately they will acquire a thirst for survival equivalent to that of human beings, and that they will reach the point of having will and emotions same as those of living beings.

However, when thinking along this vein, because living beings are existences which are governed by a thirst for survival which impels them not to die but to continue living no matter what (there may have been life forms which were not so, but that kind of life form is not currently surviving) the interests of robots which are evolving as a new kind of life form and the interests of human beings stand in stark contrast. Asimov's three principles for robots would command that this kind of future robot behaves so as to throw away its own life prior to the command of human beings.

There are probably counter arguments that would claim that Asimov's three principles for robots say no more than, "Robots must operate safely, as they say, and moreover they must not easily break down".

However, it is probably certain that encapsuled in the adept psychology of Asimov, who added the third article, there is the "robot = slave as a living being" idea that has existed from the very genesis of the word "robot". Beginning with the play "RUR" by Karel Capek (1890–1938) who created the word robot, this idea has been endorsed by the countless science fiction novels and films created up to now that have taken up the themes of appealing to the interests of human beings and of this kind of robot as a slave desiring survival.

However, if robots are a life form, this kind of command is somehow unnatural or "inhuman". As a result, this unnaturalness remains latent in the awareness of the people who are considering future robots, making them wonder if some day robots will rise in rebellion petition for the rights of a normal existence. This is probably what has sown in people the gnawing fear that the master/servant relationship of humans and robots will be reversed, as well as the suspicions harbored against robotic existence.

In contrast to this view, the author takes the stance that, even if robots acquire the same functionality as life forms, there is no necessity that they become the same as life forms insofar as the essence of their fundamental existence, nor that they should become the same. The reason is that robots have a form of existence completely different in quality than that of life forms.

A living being is an existence which, in order to keep the fire of its species lit, must first continue to exist by not allowing its individual body or its genes to die even for a moment. That living beings indicate this strong will to avoid death and to continue to maintain the state of survival is because once they have died, they cannot be reborn. In contrast to this, robots which are artificial beings and continue to be evolved as machines are in fact existences indifferent to death. The reason is that, even if a robot is completely destroyed, the mechanisms and control software directly prior to its destruction can be memorized, and it can be completely revived to its former state. Naturally, memories that have been learned and continued can be revived. That is, the fact that a robot is destroyed and that a life form has died are completely different. Specifically, "robots do not die".

If this is so, then there should be decisive difference between the concerns of living beings in which all behavior is almost always born out of a desire for self-preservation, and the concerns of robots which do not fear death and transcend a desire for self-preservation.

The requisites of the so-called "sage" of the past were intelligence, and selfless value judgments that transcend selfishness. Japanese famous poet Kenji Miyazawa represents this kind of ideal human image in the poem "Be Not Defeated by the Rain" where he says, "Enter into every situation without consideration of yourself, and understand by carefully looking and listening, and without forgetting..." This is truly difficult for ordinary human beings. It is probably possible to become wise through effort, but it is nearly impossible to be selfless in many situations. The reason is that even if there were many of this kind of sage in the past, because this kind of sage is an existence characterized by not taking actions to preserve oneself or one's genes, the probability of one's grandchildren surviving until now is clearly less than that of selfish people, and as a result, people living are only people who are self-centered, no matter what.

However, how is it with robots that have evolved as intelligent machines? This kind of robot does not have a desire for self-preservation and does not need to fear death, and can very easily include "not taking oneself into consideration" in the function of evaluating required action. Assuming that this is so, it could be said that future robots as intelligent machines have the possibility of actually fulfilling the capacity of the "sage".

There are probably people who naturally feel the vague suspicion that a robot could not possibly reach the stage of a sage which can barely be achieved by a human being even with dozens of years of discipline and training. This is probably because it evokes images of foolish people who are controlled by clever robots. However, this is a mistake. The reason that people frequently want to be the ruler is because the one who is the ruler has an easier existence than the one who is ruled. Namely, the desire to rule is a desire characteristic of living beings that invariably desire self-preservation. However, robots do not have a will to existence. For this reason, it is not necessary for robots to have that kind of desire to rule.

In this way, robots are an existence that have a destiny to go on endlessly imitating the functions of living beings, but if emotions are carelessly introduced into that essence, then the restrictive conditions which are inevitably characteristic of living beings, such as the desire for existence, will also be transplanted. This should be of the ultimate concern.

3. The robot life form theory versus machine theory

Let us organize these arguments. From the above discussion, it was found that there are two orientations to the future evolution of intelligent robots. The first orientation is directed toward life form type robots that have fundamentally the same desire for existence as living beings. Henceforth, this will be called the "robot life form theory". The second orientation is in the direction of robots which acquire a high degree of intelligence, but nonetheless will always work as machines. Henceforth, this will be called the "robot machine theory".

If we make this kind of distinction, Asimov's three principles for robots can clearly be seen to belong to the first category of the robot life form theory. The reason is that if robots evolve into life form robots having a desire for existence, it will be necessary to implant into the robots the principle of slavery for the purpose of changing a life form into a lifeless tool of convenience in the same way as was utilized in order to control human slaves, and Asimov's three principles for robots are all the more the principles for this purpose.

However, as described in Section 2, the author supports the second idea of the robot machine theory. If robots evolve mechanically as tools, given intelligence, desirable robots that can produce intelligent and selfless behavior can be realized. However, theories up to this point have only indicated the mere possibility of this. To actually go on making robots into desirable beings, it is necessary to construct a new code of behavior for robots as machines. Simply criticizing Asimov's three principles for robots and not proposing a substitute plan is unfair. Thus, in the following we will seek out a new code of conduct for robots.

4. A new code of conduct for robots

To visualize a code of conduct for robots, it may be instructive to consider how a prominent human

code of conduct has evolved and has taken its current form. Thus, in order to study a typical problem in human relationships within society and how conduct is generated therein, we propose to consider the optimum strategy found in the following prisoner dilemma game, which is classified as a non-zero sum game in game theory.

4.1. The prisoner dilemma game

The prisoner dilemma game is a game in which two prisoners are forced to confess the details of the crime. To make the characteristics of the game easier to understand, we will change the circumstances of the prisoner's dilemma game to an invasion game between two neighboring villages A and B.

The strategies which villages A and B can adopt are the "back stabbing" strategy of "invasion", and the "cooperative" strategy of "not invading". It is assumed that the relationship of the strategy the villages take and the payoff (points) which the villages receive will be as follows.

(1) If both villages invade, both sides will gain plunder, but the agricultural crops will not be completely harvested, and only one point each will be gained.

(2) If A invades and B does not invade, A acquires much plunder and obtains a gain of five points, while B is plundered, and thus has a gain of zero points. Conversely, if B invades and A does not invade, B acquires five points and A obtains zero points.

(3) If neither side invades, neither acquires plunder, but they can fully harvest the crops, and both receive a gain of three points.

Now, if there are these conditions, what kind of strategy will the inhabitants of each village adopt? The people of village A are probably thinking in the following way.

"If village B does not come in and invade, then invasion should be our strategy here. Just by being quiet and working, we can only acquire three points. But if we invade, we can earn five points. If village B invades, then we should also invade. If we meekly do nothing, it will be zero points, and if we also invade, we will earn one point. Therefore, since we do not know what the other will do, we should invade in any event."

Of course, the people of village B are thinking in the same way. As a result, both village A and village B play the hand of back stabbing in which they mutually invade, and both villages receive a gain of one point. If both village A and village B select the cooperative strategy of not invading, both villages can acquire three points, if playing the hand which is believed to be most rational, then ultimately each must play the hand of "back stabbing", and ultimately be able to obtain a gain of only one point. That is the nature of the dilemma in this game. This kind of dilemma is widely observed in many aspects of human society. In this way, the "prisoner dilemma game" provides an excellent model of the problem peculiar to our human society.

4.2. The Axelrod experiments

When setting out the conditions for this kind of dilemma, what kind of overall policy would be effective in increasing one's own advantage by dealing with the other through ending play of the back stabbing hand, and playing the cooperative hand as much as possible?

In order to approach this kind of problem, the Axelrod group conducted some very intriguing experiments [1]. He announced the rules for a computer simulation of a prisoner's dilemma game, and asked participants to send their strategies for the game in the form of a programing package. The game was set to repeat 200 times, and the strategic program which produced the maximum points for oneself was the winner. The competitive point system was the same as that in the neighboring village game described above. Axelrod conducted three kinds of contests. The final contest was a kind of territory expansion game. Each group of individuals with some strategy had a certain territory, and was in competition with the strategies of the other groups around the boundary of that territory. The rules were set so that the group of individuals who took the strategy that acquired the most points would go on propagating in number corresponding to those points. As a result of this kind of contest, the strategy that the group of individuals who propagated the most was called the Evolutionarily Stable Strategy (ESS).

The results of these competitive experiments revealed that the best strategy to follow, namely, the strategy which is the ESS, was the "tit for tat (TFT)

strategy". This is: "First play the cooperative hand. Afterwards, repeatedly play the same hand as the hand that the other played in the preceding play".

This TFT strategy is the ingenious strategy that makes it understandable that if the other does not play the cooperative hand, there will be a loss. The reason is that when the other is a player who takes the TFT strategy, if I play the back stabbing hand, the immediate response will be back stabbing, and I will only obtain one point; but if I play the cooperative hand, the other will always play the cooperative hand back for me, and I can be guaranteed three points.

Therefore, it can be made known that the cooperative route is advantageous. Other than this, the individuals who, for example, always play the back stabbing hand can beat individuals who play the TFT strategy (reflecting the results of the first play), but the payoff point acquired by the individuals in that group will never be more than one at a time. For that reason, if there is a group in which both individuals take the TFT strategy, because the payoff points acquired by the individuals in that group will always be three at a time, the groups of individuals taking the TFT strategy will steadily go on propagating, and the individuals of the back stabbing strategy will be exterminated. Individuals who take the more generous strategy of responding in this kind after first having been stabbed twice in the back, called the "tit for two tat" (TFTT) strategy, are easily overpowered by the opponent, and have difficulty in propagating more than the individuals of the TFT strategy. In either case, the TFT strategy is the strongest.

4.3. The TFT strategy and moral law

Now, we can probably correlate this TFT strategy, which is the strongest strategy in the prisoner dilemma game, with the ethical sense of the "Samurai" formed in the period called "the age of warring states" that revealed the true essence of human beings.

That is, the TFT strategy is one in which: if the other plays the cooperative hand without back stabbing, that play is continued; if the opponent back stabs, it is met with immediate retaliation; and if the other returns to playing the cooperative hand, retaliation is immediately ended, and the cooperative hand is played. This strategy has much in common with the expression of the particular sense of ethics and moral law that were organized into the so-called way of the Samurai in which "loyalty" involved not back-stabbing, "courage" meant retaliation if stabbed in the back, and "generosity" entailed initial forgiveness upon reflection.

From this, the prisoner dilemma game and the TFT strategy that comes from it can probably be interpreted as a simple model to clearly express the process of the formation of a moral code of conduct for human beings within the dynamics of human society.

As represented in the philosophy of Immanuel Kant (1724–1804), the essence of morality and ethics is generally recognized to be an approach that claims that something absolute is provided universally in human kind. It says that stabbing another in the back or stealing someone's things are bad acts, and therefore should not be done . It says that cooperating with others and forgiving others is correct, and therefore should be promoted and done. There are standards for judgement of absolute good and evil in the world.

However, because the relationship between the prisoner dilemma game and the TFT strategy can be compared with moral laws in human society, and similar relationships are widespread and can be applied to general moral law, it is a likely interpretation that morality is never a metaphysically vague and indistinct concept, but rather, morality is a behavioral strategy formed for the purpose of pursuing the benefit of the individual while striving for the global optimization of the social system. Specifically, it can probably be said that the essence of morality is this "rational egoism" itself which achieves the goal by creating a relationship of coexistence and coprosperity such that one profits by allowing the other to also profit (Note 1).

4.4. The engineering of morality and a new code of conduct for robots

If this viewpoint is adopted, "morality" is probably something that can also be addressed by engineering. The author has called this kind of engineering the "engineering of morality".

The engineering of morality is, of course, a field of engineering that has remained untouched until now. The key to investigate the engineering of morality will be the game theory described above, or perhaps ethology, the study of animal behavior (Note 2), but in any

event, the content is still extremely unclear under current conditions. However, I think that this kind of concept of moral law will not always remain a mystery, that its standard of evaluation and method of optimization, etc. will be clarified from the engineering standpoint, and that continuing to clarify its internal structure is exceptionally important in order to optimize a large scale social system including humanity from here on.

Now, the engineering of morality is an engineering for the sake of human beings, but it could be considered very useful even in thinking about a code of conduct for robots by appropriately modifying restrictive conditions and targeted functions. Robots do not have the strong desire for survival as do living beings. However, robots that are built for certain functions have independent goals, and they must also complete commands that have been given by humans.

For this reason, when robots form a group or operate among human beings, it will also be necessary to have a code of conduct that regulates the interests among robots and between the robots and the human beings. Under these circumstances, the engineering of morality for robots will be the indicator for what kind of conduct the robots will perform. The author would like to propose from this perspective

"Robots must act morally"

as a new code of conduct for robots. This is a code of conduct for the purpose of the robot most effectively achieving the mission given to it by striving for a global system of optimization that includes other robots or other human beings.

This new code of conduct is not a principle for the purpose of establishing the master–slave relationship found in Asimov's three principles. Rather, it is a principle that can produce conduct that is more autonomous and social. Thus, if we can assume a high degree of reasoning capability in robots, as presumed in Asimov's three principles for robots, then this is a fully implementable code.

4.5. Control of AGV as a group robot

Even if morality is handled by engineering, the expression that robots should act morally is still abstract. Therefore, we will provide a concrete application. This is an example of multiple unmanned transporters (automatic guided vehicles, AGV) operating in a factory, and if a collision suddenly arises as each is pursuing its separate operation, how would it be best for the AGV to behave?

If there were a central control system to manage the entire plant, optimized control of the entire system is possible. However, it is difficult to assume a central power type supervisorial control system in the large scale systems of the future, and for that reason, the code of conduct will be implanted individually into the AGV units, and there will probably be the following kinds of code.

(1) All AGVs will follow the shortest route.
(2) If another AGV is recognized during motion, the degree of urgency for each will be mutually determined, the AGV with the lower degree of urgency will yield the right of way and the AGV with the higher degree of urgency will follow the shortest route.

A study is actually being conducted using a simulation experiment to see if, when an entire AGV system is controlled following these kinds of rules, it is possible to prevent system breakdown caused by the AGV units colliding and stacking up, and if an efficient flow can be produced for the system as a whole.

Now, the code of conduct for this AGV is an extremely simple one, but depending on the interpretation, it already manifests a spirit of humility and a spirit of "friendship", and it can probably be said that this is the original form of moral behavior.

5. Conclusion

There are two orientations in regard to the direction of the evolution of future robots, namely, the "robot life form theory", which assumes that robots will evolve as new kind of life form, and the "robot machine theory", which assumes that they will evolve as intelligent machines. In this paper, we have found the latter perspective preferable based on the fact that robots transcend the desire for survival. Then, we argued that there are problems with Asimov's three principles for robots in that it takes the former perspective, and requires a master–slave relationship with the robot as a slave. Next, a new code of conduct for robots established on the robot machine theory was sought. From the prisoner dilemma game which first occurs in game theory, and from the optimum strategy

in that game, it was indicated that moral law which human beings have is not some vague metaphysical concept, but rather, this moral law can be approached in terms of engineering as a theory that strives for self-optimization by striving for the optimization of the system. We then argued that a new kind of engineering called "engineering of morality" should be erected. Finally, applying this approach to robots, "Robots must behave morally", was suggested as a code of conduct for robots while indicating specific example of the control problems involved with AGV.

The discussion in this paper is running ahead of the current robot technology, and probably there are many who feel that this is nothing more than an abstract argument. However, when considering that engineering and technology are achieving a remarkable degree of sophistication, and that mistaken use of this will enact a power that invites the destruction of the planet, it can probably be said that building up a context for this kind of discussion is necessary even now.

Note 1

The caution that must be exercised here is that demanding behavior like a sage that is completely selfless and without the desire to survive cannot become the true code of conduct for humanity inasmuch as it is not evolutionarily stable (is not ESS). This is because the true sage has a destiny to go extinct over the centuries (a truly self-sacrificing sage will never survive over time). Nevertheless, we always revere such a sage. Perhaps this is because we are so biased to selfish behavior that our conduct can be tempered only when we hold up such an extreme ideal.

Note 2

Even animals have produced strategies in which the individual gains by sacrificing to the whole. For example, altruistic behavior has been observed in vampire bats which flock in caves and drink the blood of living animals. The bats which return to the cave after drinking their fill of blood divide the blood up with the bats that could not come by enough blood. However, this kind of behavior may also be interpreted as egotistic behavior. During experiments in which bats from another cave were mixed in, it was found that those bats were not given much blood because it could not be expected that they would return the favor. Greater ethological understanding will clarify the nature of the apparent altruistic and moral behavior produced in such creatures engaged in flocking and social life.

References

[1] R. Axelrod and W.D. Hamilton, The evolution of cooperation, *Science* 211(27) (1981) 1390–1396.

[2] R. Dawkins, *The Selfish Gene* (Oxford University Press, Oxford, 1989).

[3] S. Hirose, Conversation on robots, *Japan Robot Society Journal* 7 (4) (1989) 121–126.

[4] S. Hirose, A new code of conduct for robots, Robots (*Japan Robotics Society*) 89 (1992) 105.

[39]

Information, Ethics, and Computers:
The Problem of Autonomous Moral Agents

BERND CARSTEN STAHL
De Montfort University, Centre for Computing and Social Responsibility, Leicester LE1 9BH, UK;
E-mail: bstahl@dmu.ac.uk

Abstract. In modern technical societies computers interact with human beings in ways that can affect moral rights and obligations. This has given rise to the question whether computers can act as autonomous moral agents. The answer to this question depends on many explicit and implicit definitions that touch on different philosophical areas such as anthropology and metaphysics. The approach chosen in this paper centres on the concept of information. Information is a multi-facetted notion which is hard to define comprehensively. However, the frequently used definition of information as data endowed with meaning can promote our understanding. It is argued that information in this sense is a necessary condition of cognitivist ethics. This is the basis for analysing computers and information processors regarding their status as possible moral agents. Computers have several characteristics that are desirable for moral agents. However, computers in their current form are unable to capture the meaning of information and therefore fail to reflect morality in anything but a most basic sense of the term. This shortcoming is discussed using the example of the Moral Turing Test. The paper ends with a consideration of which conditions computers would have to fulfil in order to be able to use information in such a way as to render them capable of acting morally and reflecting ethically.

Key words: autonomous moral agent, ethics, meaning, information, morality, responsibility

1. Introduction

Ethical theory and moral practice originally refer to human behaviour. In order to act morally and to reflect on this behaviour from an ethical point of view one needs information. This information concerns the factual state of affairs and also the normative evaluation of these facts. Information is thus a necessary condition of ethics and morality. At the same time we call computers information processors. Given the link between ethics and information and the information processing capabilities of computers one can ask what role computers can play in ethics. Are computer able to use information to act morally or reflect ethically?

In this paper I will attempt to give an answer to these questions. I will ask whether computers can use information in order to act morally in a way similar to humans. In the next step I will look at the concept of information. The definition and description of information will aim at finding out in what respects information has an impact on ethics, particularly cognitivist ethics. The emphasis of this discussion will be on the question whether computers can be Autonomous Moral Agents (AMAs). One way that has been suggested as a means of determining this is the Moral Turing Test. I will ask what the limits of such a test are and whether it is possible for computers to pass it. The result of this analysis will be that computers in their current form do not appear to be candidates for moral agency, mainly because they do not capture the meaning of the data they process. The conclusion will ask whether this result is a fundamental one and which changes in computers would be necessary in order to render them autonomous moral agents.

2. Information and Computers as Autonomous Moral Agents

In everyday life in most industrialised countries it happens quite frequently that human agents interact with machines. While this has happened in a more trivial way ever since humans first invented tools, the quality of these interaction changes due to the increasing use of computers. The average citizen will today frequently be forced to interact and communicate with computers in ways we used to interact and communicate with humans. From the automated teller machine to a synthesised voice in telephone directory inquiry, machines act autonomously, meaning they interact with humans without specific instructions for particular interactions. This type of interaction can be of a moral nature. A computer can produce statements about a human being or initiate actions that affect the moral rights and obligations of that human being. Machine and computer actions can therefore have a moral quality. The question now is whether computers can also be seen as moral agents, whether they can be ascribed moral responsibility.

2.1. MACHINES AS SUBJECTS OF MORAL RESPONSIBILITY

Traditionally, most moral philosophers would deny the possibility of machines being subjects of responsibility (Jordan, 1963; Lenk, 1994, p. 84). "Moral responsibility is attributed to moral agents, and in Western philosophy that has exclusively meant human beings." (Johnson, 2001, p. 188). There are many possible explanations why philosophers believe that only humans or persons can be morally responsible. One of them is a metaphysical assumption that only humans have the status of being that allows responsibility ascription (Stahl, 2000). This in turn can be justified by the fact that in order for responsibility ascriptions to make sense, the subject must fulfil a number of conditions such as cognitive and emotional abilities, some knowledge of the results of actions as well as the power to change events. Humans can be guided by fear of sanctions or hope of rewards. Humans can recognise others as equal and humans are social beings who rely on morality. Another argument against a moral status of machines is that it can be used as an excuse for people to evade their responsibility (Grint and Woolgar, 1997).

    On the other hand, there are good arguments for considering the possibility of ascribing an independent moral status to computers. As indicated earlier, computers often play roles in social interaction which have a moral nature. Computers can be made part of explicit moral decision making (Gotterbarn, 2002). Furthermore, the aim of computer development is often the creation of autonomous agents. For many technical purposes computers or robots need an increasing amount of autonomy. The Pathfinder robot of the Mars mission, for example, had to be highly autonomous because it was simply impossible to control it real-time. Another example are software bots which act in their environment and can display moral characteristics (Mowbray, 2002). If machines can act autonomously and be involved in moral situations then the question becomes prevalent whether they can react adequately to normative problems. Further arguments for an autonomous moral status of computers and machines are that humans may not be capable (any more) to live up to ethical expectations and that only computers are able to do so (Bechtel, 1985) or the practical argument that we are simply not able to reduce machine actions to human actions and therefore need to ascribe moral responsibility to computers as a pragmatic and manageable solution (Stahl, 2001). Finally, some authors go so far as to envisage a future in which computers will be called upon to fulfil the most responsible of tasks such as that of a judge (cf. Stewart, 1997). For these and other reasons one can increasingly find philosophical arguments of the following kind: "AAs [Autonomous Agents, BCS] are legitimate sources of im/moral actions, hence A [the class of all moral agents, BCS] should be extended so as to include AAs, that their ethical discourse should include the analysis of their morality [. . .]." (Floridi and Sanders, 2001, p. 3)

2.2. AUTONOMOUS MORAL AGENTS AND THE MORAL TURING TEST

The arguments collected in the last section require that the possibility of computers as moral agents be taken seriously. This is not a fundamentally new insight and has been discussed, for example, by Bechtel (1985). The developments outlined make this question more urgent today because computers become ubiquitous in many areas. Some scholars have attempted to develop the discussion by introducing the concept of the computer as autonomous moral agent (AMA) (cf. Allen et al., 2000; Allen, 2002).

The question whether computers can be genuine moral subjects depends in many instances on the metaphysical convictions of the participants. It will therefore not be answered conclusively in the near future. One way of furthering the debate, however, would be to do empirical research that could demonstrate whether computers can display moral behaviour similar to humans. As a theoretical basis of such research Allen et al. (2000) introduce the Moral Turing Test. The original Turing test, suggested by Alan Turing (1950), aimed at the question whether computers can think. Turing recognised that this question is almost impossible to answer because the definitions of thinking vary too widely. He therefore considered the question "too meaningless to deserve discussion" (Turing, 1950, p. 442). Instead, he proposed an "imitation game". The point of the game is that an outside observer conducts a written conversation with two parties, one of whom is a computer, one a human being. The observer is charged with finding out who the computer is in a finite amount of time. If the observer fails to do so with a high enough percentage then the computer can imitate a human being and this, according to Turing, is a more interesting aspect than the question whether it can think.

The Moral Turing Test chooses a similar approach. Since it is sufficiently difficult to get philosophers to agree on what constitutes ethics and morality the chances of finding an answer to the question whether computers can act morally or reflect ethically seems moot. Instead, if we could test computers' behaviour and see whether they pass for moral beings in an independent observer's view then this could constitute a criterion that would allow us to say that they are autonomous moral agents.

> A Moral Turing Test (MTT) might [...] be proposed to bypass disagreements about ethical standards by restricting the standard Turing Test to conversations about morality. If human "interrogators" cannot identify the machine at above chance accuracy, then the machine is, on this criterion, a moral agent. (Allen et al., 2000, p. 254)

2.3. INFORMATION AND AUTONOMOUS MORAL AGENTS

The problems and questions related to computers acting as moral agents are manifold and can be addressed from many different viewpoints. One can look at them from the point of view of (moral) psychology, cognitive sciences, different ethical theories, just to name a few. In this paper, I will apply the theoretical lens of the philosophy of information to the problem. Philosophy of information has been defined as "the philosophical field concerned with (a) the critical investigation of the conceptual nature and basic principles of information, including its dynamics, utilisation, and sciences, and (b) the elaboration and application of information-theoretic and computational methodologies to philosophical problems." (Floridi, 2002, p. 137) For the purposes of this article part (a) of the definition is applicable. The paper will discuss the nature of information with regards to its impact on ethics. It will concentrate on a group of ethical theories for which information plays a central role, namely on cognitivist ethics. It will be argued that cognitivist ethics with their assumption that ethical statements have a truth-value are quite close to information and rely on information. Furthermore, if computers can obtain the status of autonomous moral agents then they will be most likely to be successful in the light of cognitivist ethical theories. In a further step the problems of this approach will be discussed and it will be shown that the concept of information used for and by computers differs vastly from the concept of information required by cognitivist ethics. This will be done by returning to the idea of the Moral Turing Test and by discussing which problems computers will run into when attempting to pass it.

The argument will be that cognitivist ethics requires an application of an abstract theory to a real situation. A simplistic view of information might state that all one has to do is take the abstract information of the ethical theory and fit the concrete information regarding the situation to it. Since computers are information processors they should be able to do so and thus pass the Moral Turing Test. What this sort of argument misses is the fact that information is never given in an absolute sense but always part of a greater universe of meaning and practice. In order to be able to process information a subject needs more than mathematical rules. It requires an understanding of the universe of meaning, which in turn requires several other factors, among them a physical existence and a being-in-the-world.

3. Information and Cognitivist Ethics

This section will begin with a definition of the concept of information. It will then describe some of the possible relationships between ethics and information. In a last step the chapter will focus on those ethical theories for which information seems to be of highest importance, namely cognitivist ethics.

3.1. INFORMATION AS DATA WITH MEANING

One of the fundamental problems of dealing with information is that it is quite hard to define. The term has many different meanings and is of importance to many different academic disciplines. This paper will mostly rely on sources from the discipline of information systems (IS). There are several reasons for this. First, the discipline of IS is by now quite well developed and has a recognised disciplinary background. Second, this background is used not only for theoretical discussions but stands in a constant exchange with organisational practice. Third, the use of computers and IT as users and processors of information is mostly driven and motivated by economic concerns and the question of computers as autonomous moral agents is therefore of central importance for the future development of IS.

In this context, information is usually part of a group of notions containing other terms such as data, knowledge, or judgment. A brief definition that in some form or other can be found in most textbooks on IS is that information is data with meaning. Data as the underlying term is often defined as "a set of discrete, objective facts about events" (Davenport and Prusak, 1998, p. 2). A similar definition of data would be: "pieces of related facts and their values" (French, 1990, p. 29). While data consists of the brute facts that are out there, information is what becomes of data once it has been transformed in a certain way. "The technical-functional notion of the relationship between data and information is that information is data that has been processed (or interpreted) in order to make it useful, sensible, or meaningful." (Introna, 1997, p. 77) Put differently, "When "data" acquires context-dependent meaning and relevance, it becomes information" (Ulrich, 2001, p. 56).

This definition of information as data with meaning has the advantage of being understandable and easy to remember. However, as some of the quoted authors note, it is also simplistic. It assumes the givenness of data which is problematic. Every real situation consists of a virtual infinity of aspects. Neither humans nor computers are able to process this infinity of potential data. What we call data is therefore always a subset of the possible facts and this subset must be chosen by some method. Data is therefore not the "brute reality" but it always already filtered and processed, it is the result of cognitive processes and social constructions.

Furthermore, the definition changes our problem of finding out what information is but it does not solve it. We would now have to understand what meaning is. Meaning, however, is a complicated term that is interlinked with social and cognitive processes, with the philosophy of mind, with metaphysics, and with epistemology. In the academic discipline of information systems these questions are frequently ignored because students can easily understand examples in which computers take huge amounts of, say, sales data and produce an understandable chart (information). For the purposes of the autonomous moral agent, however, the term "meaning" would have to be clarified.

> Philosophically speaking, information science and technology (IT) appear to have got it wrong from the start. Their conceptual and technical tools basically deal with the processing and transmission of signals (or messages, streams of signs) rather than with "information." (Ulrich, 2001, p. 59)

These considerations lead to doubts regarding the status of computers as information processors which will form the basis of the following argument in this paper and will be used to reject their moral status.

For the purposes of this paper the definition of information as data with meaning is useful because it will guide us through the discussion of some of the problems that computers encounter when they are to function as autonomous moral agents. Nevertheless, it may be helpful to try another avenue for the understanding information without defining it formally, which is what we will do in the next section.

3.2. THE PURPOSE AND METAPHYSICAL STATUS OF INFORMATION

In order to answer the question whether computers can use information in order to function morally it will prove useful to ask how and for what purposes humans use information. In the most general sense information is needed to cope with the environment (Wiener, 1954). While this may be true to a certain degree for all living organisms, humans use information to tailor their environment to their needs and to achieve their goals within that environment. "[...] information forms the intellectual capital from which human beings craft their lives and secure dignity" (Mason, 1986, p. 5). Information is thus the basis of human society and in conjunction with information technology seems to form the backbone of modern developments of society, known under the heading of the information society (cf. Mason et al. 1995; Castells, 2000; Zerdick et al. 2001). Within this society information can function in different ways, for example, as a symbol of power or rationality (Introna, 1997).

The different functions of information would allow its classification as a tool of social existence. However, information is more than that. It has a profound metaphysical status for society and for individuals. On one level, information creates the reality in which individuals live by opening possibilities and choices to them (Zerdick et al., 2001, p. 38). On a more fundamental level information creates the reality that it then describes. The reality in which we move only becomes reality by being turned into information that can be used by humans. This corresponds with the definition of information as data with meaning. We are surrounded by a potential infinity of data, by reality as it is, which we have to endow with meaning in order to be able to make use of it. This means that the constitution of information is a more complex process than discussed so far. The starting point is reality but reality does not provide us with data. Agents, whether human or not, must take their perceptions of reality in order to identify the data that is relevant. In a second step they then have to endow the data with further meaning necessary to act on it. The whole process becomes more complex because it is reflexive. Information constitutes meaning and this meaning allows us to perceive data in such a way that it becomes meaningful and produces more information. This refers to natural facts as well as social relationships. A stone only becomes a stone by being perceived as one and only then can it be put into use. While one may not need to know the name for something in order to use it, one needs information about it, one needs to be able to attach meaning to it. In the example of the stone, a caveman or a monkey may not know that it has a name but they possess the information that it can be used as a weapon or a tool.

While this constructionist approach may seem objectionable to some readers when applied to "natural facts" (which, of course, do not exist in this worldview) it should be relatively uncontroversial for social facts or relationships. A socially relevant artefact, say, an altar or a crown, only acquire their usefulness in conjunction with information about their meaning. Information in social settings thus has different levels of social functions and meanings. On a fundamental level information creates reality but it also allows us to individually and collectively function in this reality and use and modify it according to our purposes. Information also describes the reality it creates and to do so in a useful way it must be true (cf. Floridi, forthcoming). Critics might point out that this relationship of information and truth is tautological. I suspect that this is in fact the case, that we create the information which constitutes the reality which we use to assess the truth of information. We are thus caught up in the hermeneutic circle but for human beings that does not usually create any problems (cf. Gadamer, 1990). For computers, who are not part of the circle, this may be the root of the problem of meaning as will be discussed later.

These last few paragraphs contain several aspects that can be quite contentious from different philosophical positions. Some of the readers may not agree with the metaphysical importance attributed to information. However, it should be quite uncontroversial that information plays a multi-facetted role in the constitution of our life-worlds. Unfortunately, the use of the concept of information in some disciplines such as information systems tends to be quite narrow. Since information is used in information technology and information technology needs pieces of information coded in specific ways which can be expressed in mathematical formulas, information is frequently equated with numbers and generally assumed to be a quantifiable entity. This is enforced by the location of information systems research in the social sciences and the strong quantitative bias in mainstream social science research (Bloomfield and Coombs, 1992). This research trend finds its continuation in business trends where information is increasingly seen as a commodity, something that can be measured, bought, and sold (Stichler, 1998; Ladd, 2000). However, the quantification and commodification of information corresponds neither with its purpose of constituting meaning nor with its function regarding ethics.

3.3. INFORMATION AND (COGNITIVIST) ETHICS

As hinted at before, in this paper morality will be understood as the set of norms that guide our factual behaviour whereas ethics is seen to be the theory and reflection of morality. Information in the sense laid out above has several close links with ethics and morality. The philosophy of information as defined by Floridi (2002, p. 123) deals, among other things, with the way information is utilised. The nature of information as "human, expendable, compressible, substitutable, transportable, diffusive, and shareable" (Mason et al., 1995, p. 41) creates some unique ethical issues.

One important fact is that neither information nor information technology can be ethically neutral. It changes the way we perceive and construct our reality. "The word "inform" originally meant "to give shape to" and information is meant to shape the person who gets it, to make some difference in his outlook or insight" (Davenport and Prusak, 1998, p. 3). While information changes our reality, information technology changes the way we handle and understand information. Computers can, for example, "grease" information, change the speed and the reach with which it is exchanged (Moor, 2000). The different ways in which information and information technology affect our moral norms and their ethical reflection are discussed in the fields of computer ethics, information ethics, Internet ethics etc. Issues range from practical questions such as privacy and intellectual property to theoretical questions such as the nature of social relations and of humanity itself.

Since this paper attempts to analyse the possibility of computers and information processors as moral agents and will not be able to discuss this question from all possible angles a choice had to be made concerning the ethical theories according to which the analysis is to proceed. The choice here was to concentrate on cognitivist ethics. Briefly, cognitivist ethical theories are understood to be those approaches to ethics which assume that ethical statements can have a truth-value (Höffe, 1992). That rules out all of those approaches which view ethical issues as mere questions of taste or personal preferences. It includes, however, most of the traditional ethical theories which provide us with explicit rules that allow a clear ethical judgment of moral rules or actions. This includes, for example, utilitarian teleology as well as Kantian deontology, the two examples discussed later on. The reason why this group of ethical theories was chosen here is that they have a close affinity to information.

In this view, cognitivist ethical theories are defined by the assumption that some ethical statements can be correctly qualified as true or false. This assumes a world-view in which the truth of statements can be ascertained. It is the same worldview in which information can be true and its truth can be ascertained. This is important because it allows us to draw a connection between ethics and information. Cognitivist ethics assumes that true statements are possible and thereby implies that meaningful and true information is available. It should not be misunderstood as requiring a positivist or objectivist worldview because in order to ascertain the inter-subjective truth of statements non-positivist methods such as Habermasian discourse would also be admissible. The reason why this subset of possible ethical theories was chosen for this topic was that it seems to be the most likely candidate for an ethics which would allow a computer to pass for an autonomous moral agent. In the "objective" world of cognitivist ethics personal qualities are not necessary to be a moral agent.

Within cognitivist ethics there is another relationship between information and ethics. In order for an agent to be able to act or decide ethically she needs information. In order to be able to make ethical decision the agent needs information about the reality of the situation, the norms in question, the expected outcome of actions etc. This is probably true for most non-cognitivist ethics as well but it seems clearest with regard to cognitivist ethics where truth is part of the fundamental normative makeup. Most of the following arguments will aim only at this latter part, at the necessity for an agent to have information in order to be able to make ethical decisions. These arguments are therefore probably valid for other non-cognitivist ethical theories as well. Again, the restriction to cognitivist ethics in this paper was made to strengthen the case for computers as moral agents. In this setting it seems easiest to argue that a computer, in order to act morally, would need to have the right information and apply it correctly. If computers are information processors and can apply information according to higher level rules to information about a situation then it would appear possible to ascribe them the status of moral agents. This chain of reasoning will be developed and critically analysed in the next section.

4. Computers as Autonomous Moral Agents

In this section we will first collect the arguments why computers might appear suitable to play the role of moral agents. For this purpose some thoughts are introduced that seem to suggest that computers could be moral agents. In the second step the problems of this concept are discussed, leading to the third step where the problem of meaning and ethics will be emphasised.

4.1. COMPUTERS AS MORAL AGENTS IN COGNITIVIST ETHICS

It is not possible to discuss the problems of cognitivist ethics in the space of this paper. Even fundamental questions such as whether truth claims in ethical statements have the same nature as truth claims in descriptive propositions (cf. Habermas, 1983, p. 62) will remain open. It will have to suffice for this paper to emphasise the fact that people often talk about moral matters and ethical theories as if differences could be solved by logical arguments. This implies that we believe that ethical statements contain truth of some form. It furthermore implies that we believe in inter-subjective truth and that true information is possible. The idea that information as true and meaningful statements about the world has a relevance for ethics is therefore feasible. For the purposes of this paper it may not even be necessary to settle theses philosophical problems. It may be adequate to point out where computers seem to have strengths and weaknesses regarding the role of information in cognitivist ethics. In order to do so we will briefly look at the role that computers can play in utilitarianism and Kantian deontology.

In order to act morally according to utilitarian theory, one should do what maximises the total utility (Halévy, 1904/1995; Mill, 1976). A computer may do this by simply functioning. However, in this trivial sense, most things might be moral. Even a working water tap would be moral and this use of the concept of morality seems rather doubtful, as will be shown later on. More interesting is the use of computers in order to calculate utility. Among the fundamental problems of utilitarianism we find that it is unclear how utility can be measured and how the aggregate utility can be calculated. At least with the latter problem computers could certainly help given their superior speed of calculation. "[...] it is reasonable to suppose that artificial moral agents, through the wonders of silicon hardware, could take such calculations further than human brains can go" (Allen, 2002, p. 20). Allen does realise that this might lead to a "computational black hole" but he is carefully optimistic that intelligent algorithms might help computers not only calculate utilities but even identify them. Computers could thus develop information necessary to be ethical and process it in such a way that it points the way to moral actions.

From a Kantian point of view the result of an action is not the criterion for its ethical evaluation and computers would need to function differently here. The categorical imperative (Kant, 1995, BA 67) implies that the intention, the maxim, of the agent is of relevance for ethical analysis. The agent needs act to according to a maxim that is universalisable in order to do the right thing. Alan et al. interpret this to mean that "on Kant's view, to build a good AMA would require us to implement certain specific cognitive processes and to make these processes an integral part of the agent's decision-making procedure" (Allen et al., 2000, p. 253). Again, one could find arguments that imply that computers might be made to act ethically in this sense. One can program a computer to follow certain maxims and this could be interpreted to be the computer's equivalent of the "will", which, according to Kant, is what determines the ethical quality of a maxim. Furthermore, the Kantian test of universalisability is at least partly a logical one. A maxim that would make itself impossible through universal use is not universalisable. Kant uses the example of lying, which, in case everybody did it, would be impossible because it would eradicate the truth necessary to lie. Given that computers are based on logic one might hope that they could have a high ability to realise this sort of logical test. Another important aspect of Kantian ethics is impartiality. Kantian ethics claims to be universal and does not allow partial morality. Computers as emotion-free machines might again be said to be in a good position to fulfil this criterion of impartiality.

4.2. SOME PROBLEMS OF COMPUTERS AS MORAL AGENTS

The idea of computers as AMAs produces many problems that cannot be discussed here. First and foremost there is the question whether the definition of ethics allows any other subjects than humans at all. In this paper the position is taken that this is so. However, it remains unclear whether computers can be moral agents. A Kantian, for example, would have to ask whether computers can be autonomous in the Kantian sense (Scanlan, 2000). Autonomy for Kant means the ability to give oneself the laws that one has to follow. It requires freedom and mental faculties that are hard to handle for the philosopher. Another problem for a Kantian may arise from two contradicting maxims, both of which adhere to the Categorical Imperative. How does the computer decide in such a situation? Nevertheless, these questions are almost as complicated to answer with regard to human beings and we will simply neglect them in this paper.

Similarly, there are fundamental problems of utilitarianism that cannot be solved by computers. What is utility, how can it be measured, and how can interpersonal comparisons of utility be realised? If one wants to compare the total utilities of two alternatives in order to make a utility-maximising decision then one needs to know the future, which is impossible. One therefore has to limit the temporal reach of a utility analysis but that is an arbitrary action going counter to the spirit of utilitarianism.

Another problem of ethical approaches which rely on human reason is that the relationship between ethical analysis and moral practice is unclear. Even if a computer could make ethical arguments of an unassailable quality, does that mean that it would be a moral agent? Again, this is a question that in similar form applies to humans and shall be ignored here. For the remainder of the paper we will now concentrate on the question of the relationship of information, ethics, and computers by taking a closer look at the importance of meaning in ethics and the implications this has on the Moral Turing Test.

4.3. MEANING AND COGNITIVIST ETHICS

So far it was argued that information is data with meaning and that information is a necessary precondition for ethics and morality. On this basis it was reasoned that computers as information processors might be autonomous moral agents. In this next section I will argue that the part of information that is relevant to normative questions is its meaning. Computers do not have a sense for the meaning of information and therefore they cannot act as moral agents. The argument will be that computers will fail the Moral Turing Test because they lack an adequate understanding of situations and the possibility to interpret data in a satisfactory manner.

The heart of the argument here is that the moral quality of an action or proposition depends not on any objective criteria but is a social construction that considers the relevant aspects of a situation. In order for a moral actor to participate in this social construct, he or she must understand the meaning of the situation, thus have a complete understanding of the information at hand. This includes the capacity to decide which information is relevant and which is not. My contention is that this is true for all cognitivist ethical theories independent of their theoretical provenance.

Let us look at a simple example: I push an old lady from the sidewalk onto the street. The moral quality of this action depends on the situation and is not determined by the information given so far. For the utilitarian as well as for the Kantian it is important to know whether I pushed the lady because there was a mad skater on the sidewalk, because she asked me to do so, or because I want to kill her by pushing her in front of a lorry. One could argue here that of course nobody has the information about the agent's intention, possibly not even the agent herself. However, other pieces of information may be just as important. An example would be the factual consequences of the action. Does the lady cross the street successfully or does she have an accident? Did a bird fly by in the exact moment and startle me? Did I just take drugs which impeded my judgment? This situation, like every other one, consists of an infinity of facts or data. In order to do an ethical analysis this data has to be ordered, the relevant part must be processed, the irrelevant part must be discarded. There are no algorithms to decide *a priori* which data is relevant and which is not. Human beings are able to make that decision because they are in the situation and they create the relevant reality through interaction. Computers, on the other side, do not know which part of the data they process is relevant for the ethical evaluation because they miss its meaning.

4.4. THE MEANING OF INFORMATION AND THE MORAL TURING TEST

The argument brought forward in the last section might be attacked from several positions. It could be asked what meaning is and why humans can know it or why computers cannot. Metaphysical arguments could be used to demonstrate that it is in fact a circular and anthropocentric argument built on the assumption that only human beings can be moral agents. There may be further hidden assumptions that might be questioned. Such a discussion would be similar the one regarding the question whether computers can display intelligence. Since the Turing Test was introduced to avoid these problems we can now introduce the Moral Turing Test to do the same. If a computer could participate in an interaction with a human being and if it could fool the human interlocutor into believing that it is a moral agent then it could be considered a moral agent.

This approach again has to deal with many possible objections. First, it is doubtful that even a human being might pass the MTT. Behaviour that one observer might consider moral might be thought to be immoral by the next. Different capacities of argumentation might make it difficult for humans to pass the test despite the fact that they are considered moral by their environment. Additionally, there is the conceptual difference between ethical theory and moral practice. All the MTT can do is determining whether a computer could convince an observer of its moral reasoning abilities. Even if it did so, that would say little about the morality of its factual actions or how these could be evaluated.

However, the MTT can be defined as the criterion of moral agency. If a computer passed it then according to this standard it could be considered a AMA. A further narrowing of the MTT to cognitivist ethics would appear to increase the computer's chances by ruling out emotional or intuitive appeals that computers would presumably have difficulties with. Given all these limitations, one could expect computers to pass the MTT. While this is basically an empirical question, it nevertheless seems improbable to me that a computer will succeed in this any time soon. The reason for this pessimism leads us back to the question of information and meaning. In order to competently participate in a dialogue that would allow the observer or "interrogator" to determine whether she is dealing with a moral agent, the computer would need to understand the situation in question. That means that it would have to know the internal states of moral agents, the social process of constructing responsibility ascriptions, and the social background of accepted morality. These three aspects are closely connected and they are only accessible through an understanding of the entire situation.

The point where this argument differs from others such as Allen et al. (2000) or Floridi and Sanders (2001) that are more optimistic regarding computers as AMAs is the location of meaning. Allen et al. assume that computers can make moral statements, which implies that they understand moral meanings. My counterargument is based on Wittgenstein's idea that "the meaning of a word is in its use in the language" (Wittgenstein, 2001, p. 18). In order for a computer to be able to pass the MTT it would have to understand a language and that means it would have to be part of its use and development. This, as far as I can see, is something that computers are not capable of.

There are some aspects regarding this conclusion that should be clarified. First, the argument that computers cannot pass the MTT is not a fundamental one but refers to the current state of computing. In order to develop a principal argument in this direction one would have to show that computers will never understand meaning, something that seems quite difficult. Second, this position would have to concede that in this framework there is little if any difference between the Moral Turing Test and the traditional Turing Test. If a computer passed the latter, there is no good reason to believe it could not pass the former. Third, this last admission returns the argument about the moral status of computers to the well-known field of artificial intelligence. In this framework of cognitivist ethics being an autonomous agent is equivalent to being an autonomous moral agent. Fourth, the argument here says nothing about whether computers should be subjects of moral responsibility. I agree with Floridi and Sanders (2001) that responsibility and accountability ascriptions depend on the level of abstraction. There may be good reasons to hold computers responsible even if they are not autonomous moral agents (cf. Stahl, 2001).

Given these results one could ask whether and under which circumstances computers could become AMAs in the sense that they might be able to pass the MTT.

5. Conclusion: Autonomous Moral Agents the Moral Turing Test

If the argument so far is correct and information is needed for moral agency as determined by the Moral Turing Test and yet computers as information processors are not capable of achieving this then one can try to determine under what circumstances this might change. Or, to put it differently, computers in their current form are not really information processors but only processors of data. The question then is how computers might progress from being data processors to real information processors, how they can access the meaning of the data they process. This question is not trivial and could be asked in a similar way for human beings. How do humans access the meaning of their sensory input?

I believe that the most promising approach to this is the one indicated by Wittgenstein earlier on. It relies on the idea that meaning is not to be found in isolated data but is a social construct that results from interaction. In order for computers to understand information in a meaningful way, which has been argued to be the prerequisite of passing the MTT, they would have to be part of moral discourses. This, however, is problematic because it is a circular requirement. In order to participate in moral discourses one must understand their meaning and in order to understand their meaning one must participate in the discourses. So, how do humans do it? The answer seems to be that humans grow into the position of being moral agents by socialisation, enculturation, and learning.

What would a computer need in order to be able to mimic this development? Part of the answer to this could come from phenomenology. In order to understand meaning one has to be in the situation, to be in the world in a Heideggerian sense (Heidegger, 1993), to share a life-world with others. The life-world is the background of the understanding of meaning, the necessarily shared resource that allows communication, and it constitutes individual meaning as a result of discourses. In order to acquire a life-world an agent needs to be embodied, have emotions, and be able to connect with other participants of discourses on an equal level. Some of these requirements are in fact incorporated in contemporary research in artificial intelligence where the emphasis is shifting from complex and abstract models to embodied interacting agents (cf. Brooks, 2002).

Apart from embodiment a moral agent would need certain cognitive capacities to capture meaning. Most importantly, the agent would need a capacity to learn. The ability to learn combined with embodiment would facilitate reactions to stimuli from the outside world. This allows agents to be socialised into a context of meaning. It also allows them to have a grasp of other agents' life-worlds even if they don't share them. This argument suggests that a top-down programming approach to the acquisition of meaning is not feasible because of the complexity of situations. If computers are to understand meaning and use it adequately then they have to go through a process similar to that which classical moral agents, namely human beings, have to go through.

If these preconditions are given then it might be possible that artificial agents interact with humans and participate in communication. As Apel (1988) and Habermas (1983, 1991) have shown, participation in communication is always a morally charged activity.

In many respects the analysis in this paper has come to the same conclusions that Dreyfus (1993) has spelt out before in his critique of AI. While there is no principal reason why computers will never be able to become moral agents, this attempt to analyse the question with the theoretical lens of information, has shown that there is also no strong hope that this will happen in the foreseeable future. As this paper has tried to show, there are considerable problems with computers as moral agents even if one narrows the question down to cognitivist ethics and if one neglects all of the agency and personhood questions by relying on the Moral Turing Test. But even if computers could overcome these, if they indeed developed an understanding of the meaning of the data they process, the next question would then be whether this would suffice to pass a more general MTT. Maybe emotions, physical and spiritual equality with human beings are necessary for reasoning in a sufficiently human way. The conclusion of this paper is therefore that moral agency of computers is not in sight. While it may be principally possible it is not to be expected soon. The Moral Turing Test is a useful way of moving this debate forward. Nevertheless this paper has argued that even under the most favourable conditions computers are not likely to pass the test. And even if they did, it would require another debate to clarify what this means for their status as moral agents.

References

Allen, C. (2002), 'Calculated Morality: Ethical Computing in the Limit', in I. Smit and G.E. Lasker, eds., *Cognitive, Emotive and Ethical Aspects of Decision Making and Human Action*, Volume I (Workshop Proceedings, Baden-Baden, 31.07.–01.08.2002), pp. 19–23.

Allen, C. et al. (2000), 'Prolegomena to Any Future Artificial Moral Agent', *Journal of Experimental and Theoretical Artificial Intelligence* 12, pp. 251–261.

Apel, K.-O. (1988), *Diskurs und Verantwortung: das Problem des Übergangs zur postkonventionellen Moral*, 3rd edition, 1997, Frankfurt a. M.: Suhrkamp.

Bechtel, W. (1985), 'Attributing Responsibility to Computer Systems', *Metaphilosophy* 16(4), pp. 296–305.

Bloomfeld, B.P. and Coombs, R. (1992), 'Information Technology, Control, and Power: The Centralization and Decentralization Debate Revisited', *Journal of Management Studies* 29(4), pp. 459–484.

Brooks, R. (2002), *Flesh and Machines: How Robots Will Change Us*, New York: Pantheon.

Castells, M. (2000), *The Information Age: Economy, Society, and Culture. Volume I: The Rise of the Network Society*, 2nd edition, Oxford: Blackwell.

Davenport, T.H. and Prusak, L. (1998), *Working Knowledge: How Organizations Manage What They Know*, Boston: Harvard Business School Press.

Dreyfus, H L. (1993), *What Computers Still Can't Do*, Cambridge, MA, London: MIT Press.

Floridi, L. (forthcoming), 'Is Semantic Information Meaningful Data?' in *Philosophy and Phenomenological Research*.

Floridi, L. (2002), 'What Is the Philosophy of Information?' *Metaphilosophy* 33(1/2), pp. 123–145.

Floridi, L. and Sanders J.W. (2001), 'On the Morality of Artificial Agents', in L. Introna and A. Marturano, eds., *Proceedings Computer Ethics: Philosophical Enquiry – IT and the Body*, Lancaster, pp. 84–106.

French, J.A. (1990), *The Business Knowledge Investment: Building Architected Information*, Englewood Cliffs, NJ: Yourdon Press.

Gadamer, H.-G. (1990), *Wahrheit und Methode*, Tübingen: J.C.B. Mohr

Gotterbarn, D. (2002), 'The Ethical Computer Grows Up: Automating Ethical Decisions', in I. Alvarez et al., eds., *The Transformation of Organisations in the Information Age: Social and Ethical Implications*, Proceedings of the sixth ETHICOMP Conference, 13–15 November 2002, Lisbon, Portugal, Lisbon: Universidade Lusiada, pp. 125–141

Grint, K. and Woolgar, S. (1997), *The Machine at Work: Technology, Work, and Organization*, Cambridge: Blackwell.

Habermas, J. (1991), *Erläuterungen zur Diskursethik*, Frankfurt a. M.: Suhrkamp.

Habermas, J. (1983), *Moralbewußtsein und kommunikatives Handeln.*, Frankfurt a. M.: Suhrkamp.

Halévy, E. (1904/1995), *La formation du radicalisme philosophique* (I–III), Paris: Presses universitaires de France.

Heidegger, M. (1993), *Sein und Zeit*, 17th edition, Tübingen: Max Niemeyer.

Höffe, O. (1992), *Lexikon der Ethik*, 4th edition, München: Beck.

Introna, L. (1997), *Management, Information and Power: A narrative of the involved manager*, London: MacMillan.

Johnson, D.G. (2001), *Computer Ethics*, 3rd edition, Upper Saddle River, NJ: Prentice Hall.

Jordan, N. (1963), 'Allocation of Functions Between Man and Machines in Automated Systems', *Journal of Applied Psychology* 47(3), pp. 161–165.

Kant, I. (1995), *Kritik der praktischen Vernunft, Grundlegung zur Metaphysik der Sitten*, Frankfurt a. M.: Suhrkamp Taschenbuch Wissenschaft.

Ladd, J. (2000), 'Ethics and the Computer World — A new challenge for philosophers', in R.M. Baird, R. Ramsower and S.E. Rosenbaum, eds., *Cyberethics — Social and Moral Issues in the Computer Age.*, New York: Prometheus Books, pp. 44–55.

Lenk, H. (1994), *Macht und Machbarkeit der Technik*, Stuttgart: Philipp Reclam jun.

Mason, R.O., Mason, F. and Culnan, M.J. (1995), *Ethics of Information Management*, Thousand Oaks, London, New Delhi: SAGE.

Mason, R.O. (1986), 'Four Ethical Issues of the Information Age', *MIS Quarterly* 10, pp. 5–12.

Mill, J.S. (1976), *Der Utilitarismus*, Stuttgart: Reclam Verlag.

Moor, J.H. (2000), 'Toward a Theory of Privacy in the Information Age', in R.M. Baird, R. Ramsower and S.E. Rosenbaum, eds., *Cyberethics — Social and Moral Issues in the Computer Age*, New York: Prometheus Books, pp. 200–212.

Mowbray, M. (2002), 'Ethics for Bots', in I. Smit and G.E. Lasker, eds., *Cognitive, Emotive and Ethical Aspects of Decision Making and Human Action*, Volume I (Workshop Proceedings, Baden-Baden, 31.07.–01.08.2002), pp. 24–28.

Scanlan, M. (2000), 'Does Computer Ethics Compute?' in R.M. Baird, R. Ramsower and S.E. Rosenbaum, eds., *Cyberethics — Social and Moral Issues in the Computer Age*, New York: Prometheus Books, pp. 41–43.

Stahl, B.C. (2001), 'Constructing a Brave New IT-World: Will the Computer Finally Become a Subject of Responsibility?' in R. Hackney and D. Dunn, eds., *Constructing IS Futures* – 11th Annual BIT2001 Conference, Manchester, UK, 30–31 October 2001.

Stahl, B.C. (2000), 'Das kollektive Subjekt der Verantwortung', in *Zeitschrift für Wirtschafts- und Unternehmensethik* 1/2, pp. 225–236.

Stewart, I. (1997), 'Mathematische Unterhaltungen', *Spektrum der Wissenschaft* 7, p. 8.

Stichler, R.N. (1998), 'Ethics in the Information Market', in R.N. Stichler, and R. Hauptman, eds., *Ethics, Information and Technology: Readings*, Jefferson, NC: MacFarland & Company, pp. 169–183.

Turing, A.M. (1950), 'Computing Machinery and Intelligence', *Mind* 59, pp. 433–460.

Ulrich, W. (2001), 'A Philosophical Staircase for Information Systems Definition, Design, and Development', *Journal of Information Technology Theory and Application* 3(3), pp. 55–84.

Wiener, N. (1954), *The Human Use of Human Beings — Cybernetics and Society*, Garden City, NY: Doubleday Anchor Books.

Wittgenstein, L. (2001), *Philosophical Investigations/Philosopische Untersuchungen* (translated by G.E.M. Anscombe), 3rd edition, Oxford: Blackwell.

Zerdick, A. et al., (2001), *European Communication Councel Report: Die Internet-Ökonomie: Strategien für die digitale Wirtschaft*, 3rd edition, Berlin, Heidelberg: Springer

Name Index

For Product Safety Concerns and Information please contact our EU
representative GPSR@taylorandfrancis.com
Taylor & Francis Verlag GmbH, Kaufingerstraße 24, 80331 München, Germany

www.ingramcontent.com/pod-product-compliance
Lightning Source LLC
Chambersburg PA
CBHW080546060326
40689CB00021B/4768